FREGE
Philosophy of Language

MICHAEL DUMMETT

FREGE
Philosophy of Language

Second Edition

Harvard University Press
Cambridge, Massachusetts

Library of Congress Cataloging in Publication Data

Dummett, Michael A E
  Frege: philosophy of language.
  Bibliography: p.
  Includes index.
  1. Frege, Gottlob, 1848–1925—Linguistics.
2. Languages—Philosophy.
P85.F7D78 1981   401   80-29692
ISBN 0–674–31930–3 (cloth)
ISBN 0–674–31931–1 (paper)

for Ann

Contents

Preface to the first edition

I AM ALWAYS disappointed when a book lacks a preface: it is like arriving at someone's house for dinner, and being conducted straight into the dining-room. A preface is personal, the body of the book impersonal: the preface tells you the author's feelings about his book, or some of them. A reader who wishes to remain aloof can skip the preface without loss; but one who wants to be personally introduced has, I feel, the right to be.

This book is the first volume of two about Frege: it deals with his philosophy of language, and the second will treat of his philosophy of mathematics. Like all distinctions, this distinction has in practice required some arbitrary decisions. I have left until the second volume a full consideration of Frege's definition of analyticity, since this notion plays little role in his philosophy of language, but an important one in his philosophy of mathematics; what mention there is of it in this volume is chiefly to point out the former fact. For the same reason, I have said comparatively little here about Frege's doctrine of classes. It is an essential thesis of Frege's logicism that the notion of class belongs unequivocally to logic; but he does not attempt to demonstrate its logical status by making much use of it in non-mathematical connections. In discussing a writer whose work was as unified as that of Frege, there has inevitably been some overlap; the philosophy of mathematics is not totally eschewed in this volume. The chief reason for splitting the book into two volumes has been its length, and the desire to see some of it in print.

This book has been a very long time in the writing. Partly this has been due to my own unorganized methods of work, partly to the fact that to write about Frege is to write, from a particular perspective, about the problems that most engage contemporaries in two very active branches of philosophy. If, to take an extreme case, one were to write a book on Plotinus, there would, or at least could, be a clear stage at which all but the actual writing was finished; at which the material had been first mastered and then evaluated, and only the actual arrangement remained to be done. With Frege, it cannot be like that for anyone actively interested in the subjects about which he wrote: almost every thought one has, or encounters in the work of another, about logic, the philosophy of language or the philosophy of mathematics, is apt to change what one is disposed to say in expounding or commenting on Frege's ideas. For this reason, the book underwent for years a continuous process of revision; at no stage did my ideas remain sufficiently static for all parts of the manuscript to appear satisfactory. I was repeatedly told that I should call a halt to the process: but how can anyone publish what he knows he can improve?

There is also a quite different reason why I have taken so long. In the autumn of 1964, most of the book, which was then to have been in one volume, was in a finished state, and it needed only a few months' work to complete it. That I did not finish it in early 1965 was due to a conscious choice. I conceived it my duty to involve myself actively in opposition to the racism which was becoming more and more manifest in English life. For four full years, this work occupied virtually the whole of my spare time. As a result, I had to abandon hope, for the time that this involvement lasted, of completing my book. I make no apology for this decision, nor do I regret it. Bertrand Russell, in a television interview given shortly before his death, was asked whether he thought that the political work on which he was engaged at the end of his life was of more importance than the philosophical and mathematical work he had done earlier. He replied, 'It depends how successful the political work is: if it succeeds, it is of much more importance than the other; but, if it does not, it is just silly.' One may, all the same, have to undertake something knowing there is only a small chance of success: if someone is faced by a great and manifest evil to the elimination of which he has some chance of making a contribution, the countervailing reasons must be strong to justify his refusing to make it. What has made it possible for me largely to disengage myself from work for anti-racialist organizations, and so find time belatedly to complete this book, has been that, in the first phase of that struggle, we were decisively defeated. In collaboration with my wife, to whom this book is dedicated, and whose involvement in the struggle was even more intense than my own, I have indicated elsewhere (*Justice First*, edited by Lewis Donnelly) my reasons for thinking that, by 1968, Britain had become irretrievably identified by the black people living here as a racist society, and that those primarily responsible for this disaster were our politicians, of the Labour and Conservative Parties alike. This tragic termination of the first phase of the struggle has two consequences: first, that the defeat of racism in Britain will now take several generations, where, if our leaders had shown any sense of responsibility to anything but their own short-term political advantage, it might have been over in a decade; and, secondly, that the alienation of the racial minorities is now so great that a white ally in the struggle can, except in special circumstances, play only the most minor ancillary part. It was only at the stage at which, outwitted by those who could, after all, draw on a long tradition of the tactics of handling subjugated populations, I felt that I no longer had any very significant contribution to make, that I thought myself justified in returning to writing about more abstract matters of much less importance to anyone's happiness or future.

I am well aware that most people will take the statement that Britain has been transformed into a racist society, that this was avoidable but has been effected chiefly by the irresponsible behaviour of politicians, that it is by far the most important development in this country since the War, and that it will be the source of great suffering for all our children, white and black, as the expression of a hysterical fanaticism. I am also quite certain that, in fifty years' time, it will be accepted by all as the merest platitude. I should like to take this inappropriate opportunity to express my thanks to and admiration of all those with whom I have worked in these years, particularly Vishnu Sharma, Rev. Wilfred Wood and Mary Dines.

Returning to a book one had almost completed some years before is a frustrating experience. Some chapters I physically could not find; some seemed badly expressed, or, at least, not how I wanted any longer to express them. But I realized at last that, if I set myself to continue until it was the best possible book on the subject that I thought I could write, I should have embarked on an infinite process. I know the arrangement is far from ideal, and that this is due in part to preserving large sections written years ago, while wholly rewriting others: I hope the principal defect lies in the arrangement. Roughly speaking, the case stands thus: the Introduction and Chapters 17–19 are entirely new additions to the book; Chapters 11–15 have been very extensively rewritten; Chapters 1–4 have been redrafted, with little change of content; and Chapters 5–10 and 16 are substantially in the form in which I found them when I came back to the book. The result, I fear, is that there is some repetition, and, possibly, although I have tried to avoid this, some clash in the opinions expressed. I hope, nevertheless, that the book as a whole expresses a fairly coherent analysis and assessment of Frege's views. I should like to take this opportunity to thank my publisher, Colin Haycraft, without whose encouragement I do not think I should have completed the task, but whose tact relieved me of embarrassment whenever I failed to get as much done as I had promised.

The book attempts, not only an exposition, but also an evaluation. This again has required arbitrary decisions. It is impossible adequately to evaluate Frege's doctrines without forming opinions about topics of which he did not treat, or considering views on which he had no opportunity to comment. Some sections of the book are therefore hardly about Frege at all, but about matters which must be considered if one is to judge whether Frege spoke the truth. On the other hand, it was impossible to deal with all such matters; so sometimes I have simply indicated what the necessary enquiry would be, without attempting to pursue it.

Like most philosophers, I am much indebted to conversations I have had with others over the years: in particular, I should like to express my gratitude to Elizabeth Anscombe, Peter Geach and Donald Davidson. I will not indulge in the conventional fatuity of remarking that they are not responsible for the errors this book may contain. Obviously, only I can be *held* responsible for these: but, if I could recognize the errors, I should have removed them, and, since I cannot, I am not in a position to know whether any of them can be traced back to the opinions of those who have influenced me.

There is some irony for me in the fact that the man about whose philosophical views I have devoted, over years, a great deal of time to thinking, was, at least at the end of his life, a virulent racist, specifically an anti-semite. This fact is revealed by a fragment of a diary which survives among Frege's Nachlass, but which was not published with the rest by Professor Hans Hermes in *Freges nachgelassene Schriften*. The diary shows Frege to have been a man of extreme right-wing political opinions, bitterly opposed to the parliamentary system, democrats, liberals, Catholics, the French and, above all, Jews, who he thought ought to be deprived of political rights and, preferably, expelled from Germany. When I first read that diary, many years ago, I was deeply shocked, because I had revered Frege as an absolutely rational man, if, perhaps, not a very likeable one. I regret that the editors of Frege's Nachlass chose to suppress that particular item. From it I learned something about human beings which I should be sorry not to know; perhaps something about Europe, also.

All Souls College, Oxford, 1972   M.D.

Preface to the second edition

THE PRINCIPAL DIFFERENCES between this edition and the original one consist in the provision of a full index and of textual references in the margins. The compilation of the index has been a very great labour, even though I have had assiduous help from Dr Mark Helme, formerly of Oxford University, now at the Technische Hochschule, Hanover, and Mr Charles Donahue, of Amherst College. Both of them took a great deal of trouble to compose draft versions of the index, Dr Helme at my request, and Mr Donahue quite unsolicited, and I owe both of them my warmest thanks. Without their help, I do not think I could have completed the task; even with it, I have found it both laborious and difficult. I hope very much that it will, collectively, save readers as much time as it has, collectively, taken to compile. I confess to feeling some continued scepticism about this. It was of set purpose that, in the first edition, I made only a brief subject index. One reviewer remarked that the selection of entries was bizarre: but they were those which I, who after all knew the book quite well, felt would be the ones whose context it would be difficult to guess or to remember. I thought that, with the help of the index of names, other topics would be easy to locate, or else were dealt with in so many different passages as to make an index entry virtually worthless. Reviewers, however, unanimously condemned my decision as a misjudgment; I doubt if there was a single one who did not complain of the lack of a full index. The defect has now at last been remedied by the combined efforts of three people; any reviewer or reader who still finds the index inadequate is cordially invited to help improve it in case there is ever a third edition.

In the case of the index, my decision, if erroneous, was deliberate; but the paucity of textual references in the first edition, about which, again, almost every reviewer protested, was due to an oversight. My apologies are due to those readers who were left in uncertainty where to look to verify that Frege, or any other of the writers mentioned, said what I attributed to him. I had not intended the book to suffer from such an omission; but, while writing the book, I found that it gravely impeded the flow of composition for me to stop to locate a particular remark I was citing from Frege or from some other philosopher, and, to avoid this, I adopted the policy of writing from memory, seldom pausing to look up a passage. My intention was eventually to do just what I have now done, namely to insert textual references in the margins; unfortunately, overwhelmed by the unexpected amount of work it was necessary for me to do on the book after delivering the typescript, I forgot to carry out this plan. I have been relieved to find that only in two cases had my memory for what Frege or others had said in any serious way betrayed me. At the same time, it has been borne in on me that it would often have been illuminating to quote the exact wording: but to do so would have entailed more extensive changes in the text than I wanted to make.

In locating the references to Frege's works, I have again had the assistance of Dr Helme, for which I am once more extremely grateful. I hope that they will be found helpful and easy to follow. Lists of the abbreviations used are appended to this preface; to understand the page numbers in brackets which follow some of the references, the reader should read the explanatory matter preceding the lists.

Frege is probably the clearest of all philosophical writers; at any rate, I do not believe that any surpasses him in clarity, though some may be claimed as his equal in this respect. I therefore did not think, when I wrote the book, that I needed to expend time in defending the interpretation I had adopted of his ideas. I knew, indeed, that some commentators had advanced conflicting interpretations, and alluded to a few of these; but they seemed to me largely perverse and based on an insufficient familiarity with Frege's works. I was confirmed in this impression by discovering that one of these deviant interpretations, which I had happened to controvert in print in my article 'Frege on Functions: a Reply', was decisively refuted by explicit statements in the unpublished writings Frege left behind. It therefore appeared to me superfluous to engage in argument for the correctness of the interpretation put forward in the book: I thought it necessary to do no more than to state what I took Frege to mean, supposing that it would then be apparent, to anyone who looked carefully at his writings, that that was indeed what he did mean. This assumption admittedly made my omission of the references even more heinous; but, though it was no doubt naïve, it was not, I hope, presumptuous. I did not conceive of the interpretation of Frege as a matter for serious controversy; I assumed that a careful reading of him was enough to make his meaning plain. I therefore had no idea of claiming any originality for my interpretation: the merit that I strove to give to my book was that of a thorough reflection upon the grounds and consequences, and hence upon the truth, of Frege's ideas.

Since 1973, when the book was first published, a great deal has been written about Frege; and it would now be impossible to make the same assumption. The greater part of what has appeared concerning Frege since that time has not been aimed at doing what I had tried to do in this book, namely to think through more deeply the problems which Frege's theories were intended to solve, and those which were generated by his solutions. Before one can profitably treat the work of a philosopher in that way, one has first to make sure of having understood him aright, and persuade others that he should be so understood; and it is precisely with the correct under-standing of Frege that most recent writing about him has been concerned. A whole range of rival interpretations, not just of the details of Frege's theories, but of their fundamental import, has been advanced; it has been in the domain of exegesis, rather than of commentary, that originality has been sought. It would be wrong to blame those who are convinced that they alone have grasped Frege's intended meaning for putting forward their interpretations and criticising those of others: provided that they also believe that Frege, when so understood, is a philosopher of interest and importance, they cannot do otherwise. It is nevertheless possible to regret the situation that now obtains. Until agreement is reached concerning the basic content of Frege's doctrines, fruitful discussion of those doctrines must be postponed. In view of the exceptional clarity of Frege's writing, it ought not to be as difficult to arrive at such agreement as, at the moment, it appears to be. It is therefore much to be hoped that the present phase of dispute over the principles of the interpretation of Frege will soon come to an end, to be succeeded by a period when a more profitable style of dis-cussion can be resumed. To my mind, the principal reason for being in-terested in Frege is the very direct bearing that his ideas have upon the problems of most pressing concern in philosophy as it is practised within the analytic tradition. Obviously, their bearing on these problems cannot be assessed until we are clear what his ideas were. But, as with any other philosopher, exegesis is not an end in itself, but only an essential preliminary to evaluation. A philosopher whose work proves to have been so obscure that exegesis never terminates in consensus has worked almost wholly in vain; but, on the face of it, were that to be the case with Frege, there could hardly be any philosopher for whom it was not so.

For these reasons, if I were setting out to write this book now, I should be unable to proceed as in fact I did. I should have to devote much space to defending the interpretation of Frege that I adopt, and to refuting alternative interpretations, before proceeding to any critical discussion of his ideas. The book does indeed contain some rebuttals of what seem to me wholly or partially mistaken interpretations, for instance those of Marshall and Grossmann and of Tugendhat; but most of the alternative interpretations have been advanced since the book was first published, and so were not available to me for discussion. I originally attempted to write, as an extended preface to this second edition, a defence of the interpretation of Frege set out in the book, with a critical examination of rival interpretations. But I found it impossible to do this adequately within even the very generous space allowed me for it by my publisher; I therefore converted what had originally been written as a preface to this edition into a separate book, *The Interpretation of Frege's Philosophy*, which is appearing as a kind of companion volume to this second edition of my original book. Obviously, this is to do things in an unnatural order. The ideal course would have been to write a wholly new book about Frege, interspersing justification of the interpretation offered amongst the exposition of it. But that would also have had many disadvantages. For one, I should have been forced to repeat much of what is in the present book; this might have discouraged readers of the first edition from looking at the new material, and would have been tedious for those whom it did not so discourage. For another, it would have meant forgoing the advantage, from the standpoint of cost, of being able to use the existing plates; and, in any case, I simply did not have the time. This book was always meant to be the first of two volumes, to be followed by a second on Frege's philosophy of mathematics. That second volume I have had, in a nearly complete state, ever since the publication of the first edition of this one: but a series of commitments to which I have had to give priority has prevented me from completing it. For this, I apologise to those who have been hoping to see it, and hope soon to be able to finish the work. One of the things that has impeded my bringing it to completion was the composition of *The Interpretation of Frege's Philosophy*, originally begun as a means of bringing out the present edition of this book; even if it had never been so conceived, I should have felt the need to comment upon the plethora of what seem to me deviant and erroneous interpretations of Frege's fundamental doctrines more pressing than the completion of my second volume. Anyone reading the book for the first time in the present edition who also wishes to look at *The Interpretation of Frege's Philosophy* will find it easier to read them in the order in which they were written, since in the latter book I was compelled to assume some awareness of what my interpretation was in order to avoid lengthening the book by repeating what is contained in this one. This book presents an interpretation of Frege, and discusses his views as so interpreted; the companion volume says very little about whether or not Frege's views are sound, but defends the interpretation here given and aims to demonstrate the incorrectness of other interpretations.

In preparing this edition, I have made a few changes in the text itself. These I have kept to the barest minimum, in order to save cost. Apart from the corrections of misprints and a few stylistic improvements, I have altered only what appeared to me to be definitely untrue or at least badly misleading. There are many other passages which I should have liked to rewrite; but to do so would have involved a complete resetting, which would have greatly increased the cost. Moreover, once embarked on such an extensive revision, I should have found it difficult to stop short of writing a complete new book, which, for the reasons already given, I did not wish to do. All the changes of any substance are mentioned and explained in full in *The Interpretation of Frege's Philosophy*; here I shall only indicate them briefly.

The textual alterations of more than a completely trivial character are as follows:

P. xiv, lines 12–10 from the bottom: the remark, now more exactly quoted, about mathematicians and philosophers was from an unpublished article, not a letter.

P. xv, line 15: 'few' replaces 'no'; Frege did make some overt pronouncements on the subject, indicated in the margin.

P. 26, lines 2–10: Frege's views on unanalysability are more exactly stated than before; a full discussion of the subject is given in *The Interpretation of Frege's Philosophy*.

P. 55 line 18: 'detachable' replaces 'supervenient', which did not express the sense I intended.

P. 72, lines 9 and 10: I was wrong, originally, to say that Frege never says that colours are objects; he does so, by an obvious implication, in *Grundlagen*, § 65 and § 106n.

Pp. 93–4, last two lines of p. 93 and lines 1–9 of p. 94: I have been criticised for my original remarks on Frege's use of the word '*Bedeutung*' on the ground that he *always* uses it to mean what I mean by 'referent'. This is not actually true: the most striking counter-example is on pp. 55–6 of his letter to the editor (Peano) of the *Rivista di Matematica*. However, it is sufficiently nearly true for me to have thought it better to soften my original remarks.

P. 97, lines 12–14: I have restated the Afla/Ateb example slightly more accurately.

P. 98: in line 7, I have suppressed an unjustified reference to Quine, and, in lines 14–16, made a more accurate comment on the Afla/Ateb example.

P. 127, lines 4–16 and lines 21–2, p. 132, lines 4–2 from the bottom, and p. 133, lines 4, 7 and 8: in the original version, I stated, wrongly, though I think understandably, that Kripke understood 'meaning' as what I have, in this edition, called 'connotation'; I have now corrected this misattribution, and have discussed the matter in *The Interpretation of Frege's Philosophy*.

P. 127, lines 24–38, p. 128, lines 2–4, 17–18 and 20–33: I have made fairly substantial changes to these passages. There was some inaccuracy in their original formulation, providing some foundation for Kripke's criticism of it in the Preface to the book version of *Naming and Necessity* (Oxford 1980). I wished to maintain three principal theses: that an explanation of the truth-conditions of modalised sentences by appeal to rigid designation can always be replaced by one in terms of scope; that the notion of rigidity can itself be explained only by a prior understanding of the use of a term as having wide scope; and that the only phenomenon to be explained by a theory of either kind is the behaviour of modalised sentences, there being no legitimate relevant distinction between kinds of modal status independently perceived as attaching to non-modal sentences. There were also two subordinate theses: that the ambiguity of modalised sentences containing definite descriptions could be explained by regarding the latter as sometimes rigid (though scope, in general, is an indispensable notion); and that parallel ambiguities sometimes arise for modalised sentences containing proper names like 'St. Anne', there being no ground to rule out of order the reading not favoured by Kripke but according with his assignment of epistemic necessity. In FPL_1 I clumsily epitomised the principal theses by equating an ascription of rigidity with a wide-scope reading, an equation justified at the level of the effects of the two mechanisms and of what is involved in understanding them, but not at that of the mechanisms themselves. I went on, yet more misleadingly, to equate flexibility with narrow scope. I did not intend by this to convey that Kripke believed that definite descriptions always have narrow scope in modal contexts, pointing out in that very passage that he did not. My point was, rather, that to assign them wide scope in certain cases was to undo, for those cases, the effect of representing them as intrinsically flexible, a procedure that struck me not only as pointless but as serving artificially to magnify whatever genuine dissimilarity could be claimed between the behaviour of proper names and definite descriptions. My remarks were thus all intended to be understood at the level of the effects and grounds of the rival semantic theories, not at that of the working of those theories; but they were misleadingly expressed, since they were untrue when taken at the level not intended. I have discussed this matter at length in

Appendix 3 to *The Interpretation of Frege's Philosophy*.

P. 182, lines 20 and 29: I originally stated, with a carelessness for which I cannot account, that the distinction between sense and reference first appeared in 'Über Sinn und Bedeutung', whereas of course it did so in *Function und Begriff*; this is now corrected.

P. 194, lines 12–11 from the bottom: 'This fact may be expressed' replaces 'This is just what Frege means'. This is, I think, one of only two cases, though an important one, in which I ascribed to Frege a statement that he nowhere explicitly makes. I still believe that the doctrine follows inescapably from principles that are certainly Frege's, but it was quite wrong to claim his authority for it. The matter is discussed at length in *The Interpretation of Frege's Philosophy*.

P. 214, last line: there was originally a reference here to the supposed unpublished article mentioned at the bottom of p. 212. Actually, the symbolic notation mentioned towards the top of p. 215 occurs in a letter to Russell, indicated in the margin. It will have been obvious that the footnote on pp. 212–13, referring to the *Nachgelassene Schriften* published in 1969, was added after the composition of the passage to which it is attached, the whole chapter having in fact been written before that volume appeared. I now think that my memory very probably had misled me, and that I had conflated in my mind various different passages in Frege's unpublished writings; references to these are given in the margins of pp. 213–15.

P. 228, line 6 from the bottom: 'express' replaces 'repeated'; the observation is not in fact a common one in Frege's writings.

P. 241, line 15: 'concept' replaces 'predicate', which was simply a slip.

P. 242, line 22: 'recognition statement' replaces 'statement of identification', and similarly in lines 2–3 of p. 243; this was a careless misuse of my own technical terminology.

P. 253, line 10 from the bottom: the three points now said to be 'essentially Frege's' were originally attributed explicitly to him. I think that they are very much in his spirit, and are close to what he says, but they cannot, as they stand, be claimed as his. This is a case in which, if I had looked carefully at his words before writing the passage, I should have made a cleaner separation between exposition and commentary.

P. 267, line 5 from the bottom: I originally said that my emendation was in full accord with Frege's other views. This is not true: he held explicitly that the reference of an expression must depend solely upon its sense. He also held that, in a properly constructed language, the same expression would in all contexts have the same sense, so that even his own theory of indirect senses has to be regarded as the best account possible for the intrinsically defective means of expression employed in natural language. This whole matter is discussed in great detail in *The Interpretation of Frege's Philosophy*, in tandem with a discussion of Frege's views on indexical expressions.

P. 308, line 7: ' "Der Gedanke" ' replaces ' "Die Verneinung" '; not only did I leave out most of the references, but here gave an incorrect one.

P. 367, lines 16–14 from the bottom: originally I mentioned only 'Der Gedanke', and not the unpublished 'Logik'. In lines 11–7 from the bottom, I have replaced an example indeed given by Frege by another, more tendentious one, also given by him (not, of course, using *my* name).

P. 383, line 14: I originally ascribed the introduction of the term 'token-reflexive' to Peirce rather than Reichenbach; I owe the correction to Professor David Kaplan.

P. 384, lines 7–9: here the example of Frege's used on p. 367 of the first edition replaces another example of my own.

P. 450, line 8: '10' replaces '11'; likewise, in line 11 of p. 453, '10' replaces '12'; in both cases, I had given an incorrect reference to my own book.

P. 471, line 7: 'as it is now commonly' replaces 'that is, the notion as'. I have been criticised for this remark, on the ground that Kant uses *Gegenstand* very extensively. But in *Grundlagen*, § 89, Frege ventures the opinion that Kant's use of *Gegenstand* was in a somewhat different sense. I believe him to have been perfectly right in this suspicion; and I think that the contemporary philosophical use of the term 'object' is much closer to Frege's than to Kant's. I have therefore left my remark substantially unaltered, but have softened the wording to lessen the risk of misunderstanding.

Pp. 539–40, last line of p. 539 and lines 1–4 of p. 540: in the first edition, I again wrongly ascribed to Frege the doctrine, for functions and concepts, that, on p. 194, I had ascribed to him concerning relations; the rewording avoids the false ascription. As remarked apropos p. 194, there is a full discussion of the question in *The Interpretation of Frege's Philosophy*.

P. 543, lines 5–7: there was here again an incorrect reference, to *Function und Begriff* instead of to the review of Husserl.

P. 551, lines 5–7: I have changed the wording here to avoid the suggestion, which, as is apparent from the next paragraph, I did not intend, that Geach believes that the meaning of a substantival term 'X' can be explained independently of the phrase 'the same X' but in such a way as to determine the sense of that phrase. On the contrary, the thesis, cited on p. 564, which appears on the very last page of *Reference and Generality*, that we have first to understand or to explain the expression 'is the same X as', and can then explain 'is an X' as meaning 'is the same X as something', has subsequently come to play an increasingly dominant role in his thinking about these

matters. I did not foresee that; but I had no intention of making the suggestion mentioned above, which, however, could have been read into these three
lines as I originally wrote them. I have devoted a chapter of *The Interpretation of Frege's Philosophy* to a more up-to-date discussion of Geach's views
on relative identity.

P. 553, lines 5–8: the original version of these lines stated that, for Geach,
unrestricted quantification is itself meaningless, a statement later corrected,
on p. 557; I have modified the sentence so as to avoid a suggestion I was in
any case going to withdraw.

P. 554, lines 10–8 from the bottom: there is a minor change here, to avoid
the same false suggestion as on p. 553.

P. 557, lines 17–18: the first half of the sentence originally read, 'Earlier
I described Geach as rejecting unrestricted quantification as meaningless,
but this was misleading'; in view of the changes on pp. 553 and 554, this
would now be out of place.

P. 560, lines 15–17: I have made another change here, for the same purpose as the changes on pp. 553 and 554.

P. 560, lines 10–13 from the bottom: the paragraph beginning on line 8
from the bottom has been completely changed, in order to take account of
Geach's later writings, particularly his article 'Existential or Particular Quantifier?', in which he has elaborated his doctrines. As explained in the
paragraph as it now stands, the distinction between 'Some A is F' and 'For
some x, x is an A and x is F' is clear; provided, indeed, that we have accepted
Geach's view that there can be proper names 'b' and 'c' such that the
criterion of identity associated with 'b' is not that expressed by 'is the same
A as', but yet 'b is the same A as c', and hence 'b is an A', are true. It then
follows that restricted quantification, expressed as 'Some A is F', or, in the
notation I employ, 'For some $\boldsymbol{v}$ in A, $F(\boldsymbol{v})$', is *not* to be explained in terms
of unrestricted quantification, at least not as simply equivalent to 'For some
$\boldsymbol{\mathscr{A}}$, is an A and $F(\boldsymbol{\mathscr{A}})$', just as Geach had argued. For this reason, I have
also softened the ending of the preceding paragraph, which originally said
that Geach's polemic against the 'orthodox' conception of unrestricted
quantification ends by completely evaporating, and now says only that it
appears to do so. But it appears to me to be in doubt whether the later
explanation, cited in the present version of the paragraph ending on line 3
from the bottom of p. 560, is in line with what Geach originally wrote in
Reference and Generality; everyone sees much greater continuity in his own
work than others see, and this may be a case in point. The whole theme of
Chapter 16 is the connection between quantification and identity. On p. 562,
I quote Quine as asserting a direct connection between them, but without

explaining it; and, as remarked on p. 553, Geach too appears to perceive such a connection. One way to explain that connection is suggested in the paragraph running from the bottom of p. 554 to the top of p. 555. Geach could not accept that, since it involves an absolute relation of identity; but he could have accepted the analogous connection between restricted quantification 'for some $\mathcal{N}$ in A' and the relative identity-relation expressed by 'is the same A as' stated in the parenthetical sentence towards the top of p. 555. Indeed, it is precisely this proposal that Geach has now adopted and made the ground for his distinction between restricted and unrestricted quantification, as stated in my revised paragraph on p. 560. On this explanation, the notion of a criterion of identity is essential to the explanation of restricted quantification: 'Some A is F' is true just in case, for some proper name 'a' with which is associated the criterion of identity expressed by 'is the same A as', 'a is F' is true. But, as remarked on p. 555, Geach appeared, on p. 190 of *Reference and Generality*, expressly to repudiate that view. In that book, a substantival term 'A' is said to be capable of subject-uses, and then to function as a common name; but I have found no trace of any thesis that it can then be used to name only an individual the criterion of whose identity is expressed by 'is the same A as', rather than other individuals of which 'is an A' is true. If Geach had not appeared to reject the view suggested on p. 555, the ground of his distinction between restricted and unrestricted quantification would have been quite clear, as it became when, eventually, he did adopt it.

P. 564, lines 16–24: I have altered these lines, which, though not, I think, incorrect as I intended them, could, as originally written, have been interpreted to yield a false account of Geach's view.

P. 565, lines 2–6: the same applies here as for p. 564.

P. 567, line 6 from the bottom: 'hardly any' replaces 'that no', because it seems probable that Quine does believe in unrestricted quantification.

P. 568, lines 11–14: these lines have been made a little more precise.

P. 630, line 14 from the bottom: I originally wrote that Cantor's review was the only one that *Grundlagen* received; there were in fact two others. In the last line of the page, 'four' replaces 'three'.

P. 642, line 9: I have corrected a misquotation from Wittgenstein.

P. 642, last two lines: I previously had the third period end in 1904. For reasons explained in *The Interpretation of Frege's Philosophy*, it now seems to me better to take it to run until 1906, the year in which, I believe, Frege discovered that his solution to Russell's paradox would not work, and therefore lost faith in his entire logicist programme.

P. 657, lines 11–5 from the bottom: for the reason given above, I have taken the fourth period to start in 1907 (strictly, in August 1906).

P. 659, lines 1-2: I have cited 'Der Gedanke' where, before, I wrongly cited 'Die Verneinung'.

P. 663, line 15: 'only once uses' replaces the incorrect 'does not use'. Likewise, in line 16 'mainly' replaces 'only'.

P. 683, lines 17-7 from the bottom: I have rewritten these lines, which, in their original form, were heavily criticised by Hans Sluga as suggesting that Frege contributed to the overthrow of Hegelianism in Germany, on the ground that it had long ceased to have any influence there. This criticism is probably correct. What is not correct is the idea, canvassed by Sluga, that my representation of Frege as playing a part in the overthrow of Hegelianism was a major theme of the book: this is in fact the only mention of Hegel or of Hegelianism that occurs in it. Still less correct is the suggestion that this was a ground, even the principal ground, for my construing Frege as a realist. I have devoted a chapter of *The Interpretation of Frege's Philosophy* to the relation between idealism and the thought of Frege, and a further chapter to Frege's realism.

In the Preface to the first edition, I alluded to my involvement in the effort to combat racialism as the reason why completion of the book had been so long delayed. I am often asked whether I take a more optimistic view of the situation than I did then. It would be wrong to allow my remarks on the subject in the original Preface to stand without a brief answer to this question. Unhappily, the situation has worsened to just the degree that could have been predicted. Black people and white now inhabit two different Britains. Most white people are completely unaware of what is common experience for black people; they are oblivious of the conditions we as a nation have created. They know little or nothing of the racial murders and the assaults on black people's property occurring with ever-increasing frequency; of the cynical dilatoriness of the police when telephoned for help, or their indifference when attacks are reported to them; of the brutality practised by the police themselves against black people, to the extent that it is now hazardous for any black youngster to visit the West End of London; of the imprisonment, without trial, of hundreds of people every year on suspicion of having given false information when lawfully admitted to the country, or even only of having failed to volunteer information for which they were not asked; of the fact that many of those thus imprisoned are subsequently 'removed', still without recourse to a court of law, and that the rest, when released after weeks or months, have no redress for wrongful imprisonment; of the insecurity that this creates in people whose lawful admission, perhaps many years ago, gives them no safeguard against being at any moment arrested, imprisoned and 'removed'; of the effect on young people born in this country of being asked, at hospitals or employment exchanges, to produce their passports to prove their 'immigration status'; of the savage effects of racial discrimination in housing and employment; of the way in which this has grossly intensified the incidence of unemployment among young black people, and significantly so for older ones as well; of the farcical ineffectiveness of our anti-discrimination laws; of the conscious and unconscious prejudice manifested by many teachers; of the sense of alienation and of hopelessness that now afflicts most black people. The catalogue sounds grim enough in itself. It is far grimmer stated in terms of individual experiences: a teenage boy being arrested and held where his father could not find him, within a few days of his undergoing the shattering experience of coming home to find his mother murdered, her blood spattering the walls, on suspicion, not of any complicity in the murder, but of being of different parentage and so not entitled to remain in the country; a woman who, after being settled in Britain for many years, spent a year in New York nursing her dying sister, to find herself refused re-admission on the pretext that she had abandoned her ordinary residence. Such things are due to eighteen years of indoctrination in the belief that no calamity could be greater than that one black person who can be got rid of should be allowed to remain. Those, numerous among civil servants, magistrate's and the police, who have succumbed to this indoctrination are now, by any objective standards, literally mad; but madness of this sort is very usual amongst us, and so it is not noticed.

That white people are for the most part unaware of these things is partly due to their being very little reported in the national press, but also to a conditioned blindness. If, for instance, I refer to the national outbreak of racial hysteria in the summer of 1976, which ended in several deaths, all black people will know what I am talking about; but most white people will miss the allusion, even though those events were blazoned across the front pages of every newspaper. The feelings of black people do not count; they have to be dealt with, but they are not cared about. Politicians assure us of their concern for good race relations. Their only recipe is to try to appease the hostility of white people to black ones by tightening still further the already harsh restrictions upon the entry and conditions of stay of the latter, a recipe which, over nearly two decades, has brought about constant deterioration in race relations. Their inability to think of any other remedy is due to its simply not occurring to them to pay any attention to the feelings of black people, to wonder whether their feelings may have any bearing on the state of race relations. This state of affairs cannot indefinitely continue.

Black people feel deprived both of respect and of any ground for hope. They have been very patient. In a society indifferent to and oblivious of their sufferings, they have suffered much injustice and much violence, and they have remained almost wholly law-abiding. No one can be expected to endure for ever, without hope of improvement. If their endurance snaps, things will then either very quickly get much worse, or at last begin to get better. That will depend on whether we listen to the voices demanding stern suppression of disorder, or belatedly ask ourselves what we have been doing wrong. Let us hope that it does not come to that, but that we and our leaders begin to look with clear eyes at the state of affairs we have so wantonly brought about by our inability to react without quite needless panic to the presence of a small number of black people among us.

New College, Oxford, 1980   M.D.

Textual references

Textual references given in the margins of this edition each begin with an abbreviation for the name of the work cited: this is in Roman letters when the work is one by Frege or an edition of works by him, and in italics when it is by another writer. The two sorts of abbreviation are here listed, separately, in alphabetical order. An asterisk to the left of any entry in either of the following lists indicates that the work in question is cited in the Bibliography, pp. 685–93. The publication details of unasterisked items are here given in full. For asterisked items, only the author, title and date are given; reference should be made to the Bibliography for full publication details. At the end of each asterisked entry there is given, in brackets, a reference to the Bibliography, by number of entry for items in sections A to D, and otherwise by page number. For works by Frege, a dagger to the right of the abbreviation indicates that the work in question is included in G. Frege, *Kleine Schriften*, ed. I. Angelelli, 1967 (B(2) of the Bibliography). Except where otherwise stated, the references in the margin are by page number of the edition here cited (or here first cited), or, for asterisked items, cited in the Bibliography. The principal exceptions, noted below, are references to books by Frege and by Wittgenstein, which are by section number. Frege's articles are thus cited by page number of the original publication. This is the most convenient method, since, until recently, it was the usual practice, in later editions and translations such as *Kleine Schriften* and *Translations from the Philosophical Writings of Gottlob Frege* by P. T. Geach and M. Black, 2nd edn., 1960 (C(2) of the Bibliography), to give the original pagination. More recently this practice has, most regrettably, been abandoned, for instance in G. Frege, *Conceptual Notation and related articles*, trans. and ed. T. W. Bynum, 1972 (C(11) of the Bibliography) and in G. Frege, *Logical Investigations*, trans. and ed. P. T. Geach, Oxford, 1977. The former contains, besides an English version of *Begriffsschrift*, translations of the articles listed as A(2) to A(4) in the Bibliography; the few marginal references to these articles have been given by page number of *Conceptual Notation*. *Logical Investigations* consists of English versions of the three last articles, 'Der Gedanke', 'Die Verneinung' and 'Gedankengefüge' (A(21) to (23) of the Bibliography): references to these are by page number of the original publication, followed, in brackets, by the page number of *Logical Investigations*. Most annoyingly, the volume of *Posthumous Writings* by G. Frege, trans. P. Long and R. White, Oxford, 1979, which is a translation of *Nachgelassene Schriften* (D(1) of the Bibliography), neither follows nor indicates the pagination of the German edition; references to *Nachgelassene Schriften* are therefore by page number of that book, followed, in brackets, by the corresponding page number of *Posthumous Writings*. In the same way, G. Frege, *Philosophical and Mathematical Correspondence*, trans. H. Kaal, ed. B. McGuinness, Oxford, 1980, which is a translation of part of *Wissenschaftlicher Briefwechsel*, fails to give the page numbers of the German edition, though it does give the numbers of the items of correspondence: references to *Wissenschaftlicher Briefwechsel* are therefore by page number of the German version, followed, in brackets, by the page number of *Philosophical and Mathematical Correspondence* whenever the letter in question is included in the latter.

Works by Frege

*BG† 'Über Begriff und Gegenstand', 1892 (A(10)).
*Bs *Begriffsschrift*, 1879; references by section number (A(1)).
BW *Wissenschaftlicher Briefwechsel*, ed. G. Gabriel, H. Hermes, F. Kambartel, C. Thiel and A. Veraart, Hamburg, 1976.
*CN *Conceptual Notation*, trans. and ed. T. W. Bynum, 1972 (C(11)).
Coh† Frege's review of H. Cohen, *Das Prinzip der Infinitesimal-Methode und seine Geschichte* (Berlin, 1883), *Zeitschrift für Philosophie und philosophische Kritik*, LXXXVII, 1885, pp. 324–9.
*FB† *Function und Begriff*, 1891 (A(7)).
FT† 'Über formale Theorien der Arithmetik', *Sitzungsberichte der Jenaischen Gesellschaft für Medizin und Naturwissenschaft für das Jahr 1885*, Supplement to *Jenaische Zeitschrift für Naturwissenschaft*, XIX, 1886, pp. 94–104.
*Ged† 'Der Gedanke', 1918 (A(21)).
*Gg *Die Grundgesetze der Arithmetik*, 1893 and 1903; references by volume number and section number (or page number for Preface and Appendix) (A(11) and (16)).

*GG1† 'Über die Grundlagen der Geometrie', 1903 (A(17)).
*GG2† 'Über die Grundlagen der Geometrie', 1906 (A(19)).
*Ggf† 'Gedankengefüge', 1923 (A(23)).
*Gl *Die Grundlagen der Arithmetik*, 1884; references by section number (and page number of Introduction) (A(5)).
*Huss† Frege's review of E. Husserl, *Philosophie der Arithmetik* (Leipzig, 1891), 1894 (A(12)).
*LF† Letter by Frege to the Editor (Peano) (Letter del sig. G. Frege all'Editore), 1896 (A(14)).
Ne† 'Le Nombre entier', *Revue de Métaphysique et de Morale*, III, 1895, pp. 73–8.
*NJ† Frege's notes to Jourdain's article about him, 1912 (A(20)).
*NS *Nachgelassene Schriften*, ed. H. Hermes, F. Kambartel and F. Kaulbach, 1969 (D(1)).
Re† *Rechnungsmethoden, die sich auf eine Erweiterung des Grössenbegriffes gründen*, Jena, 1874.
*SB† 'Über Sinn und Bedeutung', 1892 (A(9)).
*Schr† 'Kritische Beleuchtung einiger Punkte in E. Schröders *Vorlesungen über die Algebra der Logik*', 1895 (A(13)).
*Ver† 'Die Verneinung', 1918 (A(22)).
*WF† 'Was ist eine Funktion?', 1904 (A(18)).
ZS† *Über die Zahlen des Herrn H. Schubert*, Jena, 1899.

Works by other writers

*CAB A. Church, 'On Carnap's Analysis of Statements of Assertion and Belief', 1950 (Bibl. p. 689).
Cat Aristotle, *Categories*; standard references by page, column and line.
CI H. S. Leonard and N. Goodman, 'The Calculus of Individuals and its Uses', *Journal of Symbolic Logic*, V, 1940, pp. 56–68.
CPG The Collected Papers of Gerhard Gentzen, ed. M. E. Szabo, Amsterdam, 1969.
CPP The Collected Papers of C. S. Peirce, ed. C. Hartshorne and P. Weiss, Cambridge, Mass., 1931–58; references by volume and page number.
EA B. Russell, *Essays in Analysis*, ed. D. Lackey, London, 1973.
ESL H. Reichenbach, *Elements of Symbolic Logic*, New York, 1947.
*FLPV W. V. O. Quine, *From a Logical Point of View*, 1953 (Bibl. p. 685).
*FM F. P. Ramsey, *The Foundations of Mathematics and other logical essays*, 1931 (Bibl. p. 685).
*HTW J. L. Austin, *How to Do Things with Words*, 2nd edn., Oxford 1971

(Bibl. p. 688).

ILT P. F. Strawson, *Introduction to Logical Theory*, London and New York, 1952.

*IMT F. Waismann, *Introduction to Mathematical Thinking*, trans. T. J. Benac, 1959 (Bibl. p. 692).

*Ind P. F. Strawson, *Individuals*, 1959 (Bibl. p. 692).

*IWT G. E. M. Anscombe, *An Introduction to Wittgenstein's Tractatus*, 1959 (Bibl. p. 688).

LC H. P. Grice, 'Logic and Conversation', in *The Logic of Grammar*, ed. D. Davidson and G. Harman, Encino and Belmont, 1975, pp. 64–75.

LE B. Russell, 'The Limits of Empiricism', *Proceedings of the Aristotelian Society*, new series XXXVI, 1935–6, pp. 131–50.

LFM Wittgenstein's Lectures on the Foundations of Mathematics, Cambridge, 1939, ed. C. Diamond, Hassocks and Ithaca, N. Y., 1976.

*LK B. Russell, *Logic and Knowledge, Essays 1901–1950*, 1956 (Bibl. p. 658).

LLP P. F. Strawson, *Logico-Linguistic Papers*, London, 1971.

LM P. T. Geach, *Logic Matters*, Oxford, 1972.

*MA P. T. Geach, *Mental Acts*, 1957 (Bibl. p. 689).

*MBF E. Tugendhat, 'The Meaning of "Bedeutung" in Frege', 1970 (Bibl. p. 692).

Meth W. V. O. Quine, *Methods of Logic*, New York, 1950.

*Mg H. P. Grice, 'Meaning', 1957 (Bibl. p. 690).

*MM J. E. Littlewood, *A Mathematician's Miscellany*, 1953 (Bibl. p. 691).

MN R. Carnap, *Meaning and Necessity*, Chicago, 1956.

*NB L. Wittgenstein, *Notebooks, 1914–1916*, 1961 (Bibl. p. 693).

*NN S. Kripke, 'Naming and Necessity', 1972 (Bibl. p. 690).

*OR W. V. O. Quine, *Ontological Relativity and other essays*, 1969 (Bibl. p. 691).

OST D. Davidson, 'On Saying That', *Synthese*, XIX, 1968, pp. 130–46.

PB L. Wittgenstein, *Philosophische Bemerkungen*, ed. R. Rhees, Oxford, 1964; English translation, *Philosophical Remarks*, trans. by R. Hargreaves and R. White, Oxford, 1975; references by section number.

PG L. Wittgenstein, *Philosophische Grammatik*, ed. R. Rhees, New York and Oxford, 1969; English translation, *Philosophical Grammar*, trans. A. Kenny, Oxford, 1974, with same pagination as German edition.

*PI L. Wittgenstein, *Philosophical Investigations*, 1953, 1958; references by section number (Bibl. p. 693).

*PK A. J. Ayer, *The Problem of Knowledge*, 1956 (Bibl. p. 688).

*PL W. V. O. Quine, *Philosophy of Logic*, 1970 (Bibl. p. 691).

*PM B. Russell and A. N. Whitehead, *Principia Mathematica*, 1910–1913;

references by volume and page number (Bibl. p. 692).

*<i>PoM</i> B. Russell, *Principles of Mathematics*, 1903 (Bibl. p. 692).

PP B. Russell, *The Problems of Philosophy*, Oxford, 1946.

*<i>QME</i> G. Harman, 'Quine on Meaning and Existence', 1967–8 (Bibl. p. 690).

*<i>RG</i> P. T. Geach, *Reference and Generality*, 1962 (Bibl. p. 690).

*<i>RIT</i> W. V. O. Quine, 'On the Reasons for Indeterminacy of Translation', 1970 (Bibl. p. 691).

*<i>RML</i> K. Gödel, 'Russell's Mathematical Logic', 1944 (Bibl. p. 690).

*<i>SCN</i> N. Goodman and W. V. Quine, 'Steps towards a Constructive Nominalism', 1947 (Bibl. p. 690).

SF M. Schirn (ed.), *Studien zu Frege/Studies on Frege*, Stuttgart and Bad Canstatt, 1976; references by volume and page number.

*<i>Sob</i> B. Sobociński, 'L'Analyse de l'antinomie russellienne par Leśniewski. IV: La correction de Frege', 1949 (Bibl. p. 692).

*<i>SPM</i> P. Bernays, 'Sur le platonisme dans les mathématiques', 1935 (Bibl. p. 688).

ST St. Thomas Aquinas, *Summa Theologica*; references by part, question, article.

*<i>STT</i> A. Church, 'A Formulation of the Simple Theory of Types', 1940 (Bibl. p. 689).

*<i>TLP</i> L. Wittgenstein, *Tractatus Logico-Philosophicus*, latest edn. 1961; references by section number (Bibl. p. 692).

*<i>TM</i> A. N. Prior, *Time and Modality*, 1957 (Bibl. p. 691).

*<i>TP</i> G. E. M. Anscombe and P. T. Geach, *Three Philosophers*, 1961 (Bibl. p. 688).

*<i>Tr</i> P. F. Strawson, 'Truth', 1949 (Bibl. p. 692).

*<i>WO</i> W. V. O. Quine, *Word and Object*, 1960 (Bibl. p. 691).

*<i>WT</i> E. Stenius, *Wittgenstein's Tractatus*, 1960 (Bibl. p. 692).

WVC F. Waismann, *Wittgenstein and the Vienna Circle*, trans. J. Schulte and B. McGuinness, Oxford, 1979, with the same pagination, from F. Waismann, *Wittgenstein und der Wiener Kreis*, ed. B. F. McGuinness, Oxford, 1967.

Introduction

GOTTLOB FREGE (1848–1925) was a mathematician who had, as a student, some training in physics and in philosophy. His mathematical work was Re 27 almost wholly confined to the field of mathematical logic and the foundations of mathematics. The investigation of these areas led him into work of a philosophical rather than a mathematical character; but here again, his work was restricted in scope, scarcely ever trespassing outside philosophical logic and the philosophy of mathematics. His life was one of disillusionment and frustration. It was spent almost entirely, until his retirement, at the University of Jena, and his energies were absorbed completely by his academic work: he was not one of those academics who write on subjects of general interest, or take a part in public affairs or controversies—and this is just as well, given his political views, as noted in the Preface. He believed his work to have found no Gg I xi response, and felt as isolated and unlistened to as much at Jena as in the general philosophical and mathematical communities. Yet, despite the apparently narrow scope of his work, and his own belief that it met with almost total misunderstanding or neglect, he would now be generally acknowledged, by philosophers and mathematicians at least, as one of the great figures of the past hundred years.

His title to this position is threefold. First, he was the initiator of the modern period in the study of logic. Logic had always, and rightly, been regarded as a part of philosophy. Rightly, because the concept of *logical consequence* is one of which a successful philosophy is bound to give an analysis; but also because the analysis of many other concepts, and the understanding of the fundamental structure of language and therefore of thought, depend upon possessing, in a correct form, that explanation of the construction of and interrelationship between sentences which it is the business of logic to give. Modern logic stands in contrast to all the great logical systems of the past—

of classical antiquity, of medieval Europe and of India—in being able to give an account of sentences involving multiple generality, an account which depends upon the mechanism of quantifiers and bound variables: for all the subtlety of the earlier systems, the analysis of the structure of the sentences of human language which is afforded by modern logic is, by its capacity to handle multiple generality, shown to be far deeper than they were able to attain. The discovery of the mechanism which enabled this analysis to be given, and the realization of its significance, are due to Frege: if he had accomplished only this, he would have rendered a profound service to human knowledge.

Already when Frege started working, mathematicians such as Boole had for some little time been taking an interest in logic. But it was the discoveries due to Frege which made the subject rich enough to come to be considered a significant branch of mathematics. There is, of course, no discrepancy in assigning a single subject to the two different fields of mathematics and philosophy simultaneously. A subject belongs to mathematics if it is possible to handle it by means of mathematical techniques, and Frege developed logic to the point where precisely that became possible: a subject belongs to philosophy, on the other hand, in virtue of the kind of interest which it has; and, however successful the application of mathematical techniques to logic may be, nothing can deprive it of the interest it must have for philosophers.

After these remarks, it may seem paradoxical to list Frege's achievements as a philosophical logician as his second title to fame after his discoveries in mathematical logic. But this would be only a superficial paradox. Both in logic itself and in the philosophy of mathematics, there necessarily remain questions which the philosopher asks which cannot be resolved by the application of mathematical techniques alone, but require a combination of these techniques with properly philosophical argumentation. Frege's practice shows that he was very well aware of this, and a remark in an unpub-
NS 293 (273) lished article, that a philosopher innocent of mathematics is only half a philosopher, and a mathematician innocent of philosophy only half a mathematician, makes the idea explicit—however untrue the remark may be when applied to other parts of philosophy or of mathematics. Frege's work in philosophical logic is a true foundation: despite all the work that has been done in the subject during this century, Frege's theories of philosophical logic undoubtedly have to serve as the starting-point for anyone working in this area even today; in large part, he provides the terms in which the basic problems can still most fruitfully be posed.

This is of all the greater importance, since the centre of gravity of philosophy has altered (at least among those who follow the 'analytical' Anglo-American tradition). At any time there are certain parts of philosophy which appear more basic than others, in the sense that a correct solution of problems in one branch depends on the prior correct solution of problems in the more basic branch, but not conversely: thus evidently political philosophy is posterior to ethics, and ethics to philosophical psychology. The most far-reaching part of Descartes's revolution was to make epistemology the most basic sector of the whole of philosophy: the whole subject had to start from the question, 'What do we know, and how?' It is this orientation which makes post-Cartesian philosophy so different from that of the scholastics, for whom epistemology, in so far as they considered it at all, was no more than a sidestream. Descartes's perspective continued to be that which dominated philosophy until this century, when it was overthrown by Wittgenstein, who in the *Tractatus* reinstated philosophical logic as the foundation of philosophy, and relegated epistemology to a peripheral position. Frege, unlike Wittgenstein, made few overt pronouncements about the relative positions of philosophical logic and of epistemology in the architecture of the subject as a whole: but by his practice he demonstrated his opinion that logic could be approached independently of any prior philosophical substructure; and he was vehement in his insistence that psychological considerations are irrelevant to logic—that is, that the mental processes which we experience in the course of acquiring or employing concepts ought not to figure in an analysis of those concepts. Frege's philosophical logic, while rooted in his discovery of quantification, the deepest single technical advance ever made in logic, came at just the time when logic was to replace epistemology as the starting-point of philosophy. Although recognition came too late for Frege to be aware of it, it is thus not surprising that his work should by now have come to be seen as of central importance to contemporary philosophy.

NS 3 (3); Coh 392

Frege's third title to fame lies in his work in the philosophy of mathematics. As in logic, this work was twofold—that which employed mathematical techniques and that which employed philosophical ones; and, as in his logical work, they were closely interlocked. Logic was, indeed, for Frege principally a tool for and a prolegomenon to the study of the philosophy of mathematics, as is shown by his general inattention to those features of language, such as tense and modality, which play little or no part in mathematical reasoning. To the study of the foundations of mathematics, considered as itself a branch of mathematics, Frege made profound contributions. Of the more properly philosophical part of his work on foundations of mathematics, it is impossible to say the same as I did about his philosophical

B

logic, namely that it may still serve as a starting-point for anyone now working in the area: his philosophy of mathematics is a starting-point only in a historical sense. It is not true that Frege's formulation of the problems of the philosophy of mathematics any longer strikes us as the most fruitful way to pose the questions that arise in the subject: on the contrary, certain questions which subsequent writers have caused to appear as constituting the central issues passed Frege by as if quite unproblematic. Nevertheless, it remains that Frege's work in this field could not be ignored or treated merely as representing an outmoded approach by anyone now; and, historically speaking, it was Frege who, in modern times, made the philosophy of mathematics again a live subject, and one which, since his work, has made as impressive progress as any part of philosophy. Indeed, the fact that Frege's work in philosophical logic remains fresh and relevant to the problems as we now see them, whereas his work in the philosophy of mathematics appears to a certain extent archaic, is presumably a measure of the more rapid rate of advance that the philosophy of mathematics has made in comparison with philosophical logic.

Frege's first important undertaking, embodied in the *Begriffsschrift* of 1879, was to devise a formal system within which mathematical proofs could be carried out. This involved framing a formal language adequate for the expression of any mathematical statement, together with formal rules of inference adequate for the expression of any train of mathematical reasoning. Although for some decades mathematicians, beginning with Boole, had been subjecting logic to a mathematical treatment, Frege's project was of a completely new kind. The novelty did not lie so much in the fact that Frege's calculus was a formal system in the modern sense: for, though Boole himself had made no attempt to state, for his calculus, which transitions were to be considered permissible, or to circumscribe the class of properly formed formulas, in both of which respects even his practice does not enable us to determine his intentions with certainty, his successors had approached modern standards more nearly. But none of these earlier systems had even given the appearance of constituting languages within which mathematical reasoning could be directly carried out, because, being incapable of the representation of sentences involving multiple generality, they did not embody a deep enough representation of the structure of mathematical statements on which the validity of such reasoning depends.

Frege's purpose in constructing such a formal system was not the modern one whereby, when formal systems themselves are made the objects of mathematical investigation, light is thrown on the nature of mathematical proofs and definitions, but simply to attain the ideal of that rigour to which the whole of nineteenth-century mathematics had been striving. One of the tasks of nineteenth-century mathematics was to replace the fallacious or incomplete proofs which had been accepted in the seventeenth and eighteenth centuries by correct ones, and to supply proper definitions for what had been left undefined or explained only in a mystical and illegitimate manner. In the course of this work, the extent of the logical deficiencies of earlier mathematics was revealed: even Euclid, previously regarded as the model of rigour, was shown to have given proofs defective in that they made tacit appeal to assumptions which had not been explicitly stated. Now, so long as we rely on mere intuition to satisfy ourselves that a proof is correct and complete, or that a definition is properly framed, we cannot be certain, however closely we scrutinize our work, that an error or omission will not be subsequently revealed. It does occasionally happen that a theorem is generally accepted for a number of years, and later an oversight is discovered in its proof, and sometimes it is found to hold only under additional assumptions or not at all. Frege's idea was that, by formulating proofs within a formal system, such errors could be with certainty excluded. We should have an effective method for judging, merely by the form of a purported proof, whether or not it conformed to the requirements for a proof in the system. Complete rigour, and with it genuine certainty, would thus for the first time be attained.

Frege should not be criticized because this was not in fact the use to which formal systems were put. The gain in accuracy and certainty obtained by formalization of all mathematical proofs would not compensate for the length and tedium of the labour required: moreover, the risk of error in checking formal proofs, though different in kind from the risk of error in assessing the intuitive validity of informal ones, is no less great. What proved of importance was not the actual execution of a totally rigorous formulation of mathematical proofs, but the precise delineation of what such a formulation would consist in: this Frege was the first to provide, and the fact that it proved to have a different and much greater significance than he had at first envisaged should hardly be reckoned against him.

The publication of *Begriffsschrift* marked, as Quine says, the beginning of modern logic. This astonishing work was to constitute the logical framework within which the formalization of different mathematical theories was to be effected. It is the first formulation of the functional calculus of second order. It is astonishing because it has no predecessors: it appears to have been born from Frege's brain unfertilized by external influences. In it the modern notation of quantifiers and variables appears for the first time, as also for the first time a modern treatment of sentential operators (quite different from

WO 163; *Meth* vii

Boole's). Negation, implication, the universal quantifier and the sign of identity are taken as primitive: in virtue of the device of quantification, Frege is able for the first time in the history of logic to give an adequate account of the logic of statements involving multiple generality, and to introduce variables for relations and functions. What are in effect truth-tables for the sentential operators are given as informal explanations of them. The first-order fragment of the system constitutes a complete axiomatization of first-order functional calculus with identity; and even if there is no precise statement of the formation rules, and the formulation of the rules of inference is not quite up to modern standards of rigour (because of a vagueness about the operation of substitution), the book is superior in these respects to anything (including *Principia*) before Hilbert and Ackermann's *Grundzüge* forty-nine years later. Besides all this, the book also contains Frege's famous, and fundamental, method of defining the ancestral of a given relation, which permits the conversion of inductive definitions into explicit ones.

Bs 26

After this achievement, Frege turned to the actual formalization of a particular mathematical theory, and naturally chose arithmetic as his first subject. His original conception was to introduce appropriate primitives, and to formulate axioms governing them, and then to derive the theorems of number theory—including statements at that time ordinarily taken for granted instead of being proved—from the axioms in accordance with the rules of the formal system of *Begriffsschrift*. Here we must remember that Dedekind had not yet formulated the axioms for number theory with which we are now so familiar under the name 'Peano axioms', so the work of selecting suitable primitives and axioms remained for Frege to do. However, in the process Frege hit on the famous conception, which has been used to characterize the so-called 'logicist' school of philosophers of mathematics, that arithmetic could, and, to give a correct interpretation of it, should, be so analysed as to employ for it no primitive notions or axioms peculiar to it. (Frege assumed that rules of inference always belong to the logical framework, and are never peculiar to any particular mathematical theory.) Thus all arithmetical statements are expressible, when properly analysed, by using only notions belonging to logic, and, when provable, can be proved from purely logical principles. (It should be noted that Frege never held this to be true of the whole of mathematics: he consistently held the truths of

Re 1; Gl 14, 89; NS 298 (279)

geometry to be synthetic a priori, and therefore not reducible to truths of pure logic. On the other hand, there was for him a purely 'logical' transition from the theory of the natural numbers to analysis, the theory of real numbers.)

In order to render plausible this claim, Frege published in 1884 the

Grundlagen der Arithmetik, in which his method of constructing arithmetic is sketched, without the use of symbols. This book marks the transformation of Frege from a mathematician into a philosopher. He was not presenting a mere axiomatization of arithmetic, which would have required as commentary only enough to make the adequacy of the system for the proof of known theorems appear probable: he was offering an analysis of the concepts of number theory, and this analysis had to be defended as philosophically sound. Moreover, the reducibility of arithmetic to logic must shed light on the philosophical question of the status of arithmetical truths: it showed Mill wrong in thinking them empirical, and Kant wrong in thinking them synthetic. Besides developing his construction of arithmetic far enough to make it probable that it could be continued, Frege had therefore to lay the philosophical foundations of his enterprise, point its philosophical significance and intertwine his exposition with philosophical elucidations.

Almost the whole of the first half of the book is taken up by a brilliant and total annihilation of rival current accounts of the nature of numbers and the status of truths of arithmetic: the rest is devoted to exposition of his own views. His explanation and justification of his own account lead him into a great deal of profound philosophical discussion of issues of general philosophical interest, not especially concerned with the philosophy of mathematics, in particular of the notions of identity, of the meaning of an expression and of analytic truth. Moreover, he makes other assertions about the philosophy of mathematics than those which relate to his analysis of arithmetical concepts and the reduction of arithmetic to logic: the book contains in particular a classic statement of the view that has subsequently been called 'platonism'—'The mathematician can no more create anything than the geographer can: he too can only discover what is there and give it a name.' Gl 96

The destruction of the rival views which he attacks—at least as they had been expressed up to that time, and in the forms in which he was therefore considering them—is definitive. So also are large parts of the construction of arithmetic, of which the most valuable is the definition of the notion 'just as many as' (numerical equivalence) which was later given independently by Cantor. (It is this definition which displays the link between number theory and its application, and gives us a clear insight into the meaning of the question 'How many?', as well as supplying a clear sense for the extension of the notion of numerical equivalence to infinite totalities.) As will be seen in the second volume, other parts of the construction are dubious. The discussions of general philosophical questions contain ideas which deeply influenced Wittgenstein, as also writers like Quine and Church, and which, though still under dispute, are highly germane to contemporary treatments of these questions.

As has already been noted, Frege, as a philosopher of mathematics, is indisputably archaic in a sense in which Hilbert and Brouwer are not. His two main theses are those of logicism and of platonism. An essential step in his construction of arithmetic involved using the notion of a class. This notion is completely unanalysed in *Grundlagen*: Frege remarks only that he assumes that it is known what a class (which he calls the 'extension of a concept') is. When later the paradoxes of set theory were discovered—and in Frege's own formal system of *Grundgesetze*—and the notion of a class was recognized not to be straightforward at all, logicism lost most of its interest. Even the general problem, whether true mathematical statements are necessarily true, and, if so, whence their necessity derives, went out of fashion: the interest focused instead on the kind of meaning—and the meaningfulness—of various kinds of mathematical statement, and it was tacitly assumed that, once the meaning of a statement is given, the nature of its truth (if true) would look after itself. (The problem of the nature of mathematical necessity was revived by Wittgenstein.)

The other thesis, that of platonism, concerned by contrast just the topic which was to dominate debate in the philosophy of mathematics: but here too Frege's archaism is evident. Such assertions as Frege's platonist slogan quoted above sound straightforward. Frege holds that there are mathematical objects which are not created by us (either in the mind or on paper), have not come into being nor will cease to be, but exist independently of us; and that it is in virtue of the properties of and relations between these objects that our mathematical statements are true or false, independently of whether we do or can prove them. The natural first line of attack on such a conception is to criticize the notion of abstract objects; but here we get a surprise. There is a great deal, both in *Grundlagen* and in later writings, about what is meant by the word 'object': and we find that, whereas we had wanted to attack Frege for putting forward a naïve picture, his use of the word 'object' is highly sophisticated, and it is in fact our objections to the notion of abstract objects which he convicts of naïvety. (Though there indeed remain a few writers, such as Goodman, who persist in just this kind of naïvety, and who therefore regard platonism as opposed, not, as is usually and rightly thought, to constructivism, but to 'nominalism'—the rejection of all abstract objects.) On Frege's understanding of the word 'object', the thesis that there are mathematical objects becomes barely disputable at all. But for just that very reason, the essence of platonism—which remains a highly questionable doctrine—cannot reside in the thesis that there are mathematical objects. As Kreisel remarked apropos of Wittgenstein, the question is not whether there are mathematical objects, but whether mathematical statements are objective. Now, that Frege thinks that they are, is clear: but he says very little to support his view beyond what he has to say about objects. Therefore, although Frege is the prototype of a platonist, we cannot look to his writings for much in the way of a justification of platonism as against what we now regard as the serious rival views.

Frege is not, of course, to be held to blame for this: that a doubt could be raised about the objectivity of mathematical truth other than the doubt about the existence of mathematical objects was not, at the time when he was writing, clear even to his opponents. But, just because his was the first coherent formulation of a philosophy of mathematics, and because he so successfully demolished the other formulations currently existing, we find that those parts of his work which have not been accepted as part of the common and no longer disputable stock of knowledge seem interesting, but disconcertingly beside what we have come to regard as the point.

After the publication of *Grundlagen*, Frege undertook a dual task: the rigorous formalization of the construction sketched in *Grundlagen*, and the elaboration of the philosophical logic which forms in *Grundlagen* the framework within which the justification of the construction is set out. The former task was accomplished in his magnum opus, *Grundgesetze der Arithmetik*, of which Volume I appeared in 1893. The latter task was accomplished in a series of articles, published mainly before that date. In these he built up an elaborate and subtle doctrine of philosophical logic. But as the structure became more complex as the number of interlocking pieces multiplied, he fell victim to a certain scholasticism, of which there is no trace in *Grundlagen*. Many of his statements in that book are challenging, but non-paradoxical: they do not affront common sense, because he makes no statement which he does not have a direct reason for considering true. Once he had constructed for himself a philosophical *system*, however, he takes to making assertions, prima facie absurd, whose only ground is that they follow from the system: their intrinsic implausibility does not for him cast any doubt upon the system; it is sufficient if they cannot actually be disproved.

The first volume of *Grundgesetze* carries out within a formal system the construction of arithmetic sketched in *Grundlagen*. The system resembles that of *Begriffsschrift*, though the axiomatization of logic is different, using fewer axioms and more rules of inference: the formulas are treated in a way to some degree anticipatory of Gentzen's 'sequents' in his system NK. The handling of the formation rules and of substitution are more satisfactory. The major difference is the introduction of classes, and, more generally, of 'value-ranges'. (A class is a special case of a value-range, just as a concept is a special case of a function of one argument: value-ranges are the 'extensions' of functions as classes are the 'extensions' of concepts.) The notion of classes was employed once only in *Grundlagen*, but its employment there was crucial. Their theory must be treated as part of logic, if the claim to have reduced arithmetic to logic was to be supported. Since they do not appear in *Begriffsschrift*, and, in *Grundlagen*, no indication is given of what assumptions are made concerning them, Frege had to devise a notation for them, and an axiom to govern them. This was the famous Axiom V, which led to the Russell paradox.

Frege was always, with reason, disappointed with the reception accorded his books: that of Volume I of *Grundgesetze* he found especially discouraging, and he consequently delayed publication of Volume II for ten years. That volume completes the formal derivation of arithmetic, and proceeds to a new subject, the foundations of analysis (theory of real numbers). As in *Grundlagen*, he prefaces the formal construction with a long destructive discussion of rival theories. This is not nearly so successful as the corresponding part of *Grundlagen*. He does not in fact go to the essence of the theories set forth by Cantor, Dedekind, etc.: he criticizes— justly, indeed—the lack of rigour in their presentation. Regarded as a polemic against formalism and various formalistic tendencies in mathematics, it is powerful, if sometimes heavy-handed; as a critique of particular methods of introducing the real numbers, it is valueless. As the book was in the press,

BW 211–12 (130–1)

Frege received Russell's letter announcing his discovery of a contradiction in Frege's theory of classes. As a great deal that is inaccurate has been written on this subject, it is worth while to set the matter straight.

Frege's immediate reaction, as shown in his first reply to Russell, which has

BW 213 (132)

been widely quoted, was consternation. By his second letter, he had recovered his composure. Even while he does not yet see how to avoid the paradox, he remains firmly convinced of the truth of his principal

BW 217–29 (135–47)

doctrines, and on the basis of them dismisses a number of tentative suggestions by Russell (who is casting around among a great many disparate ideas). Halfway through the correspondence, Frege hits on the modification

BW 232–3 (150)

of Axiom V which seems to him satisfactory. (Russell agrees that Frege's solution is probably correct, but by this time has formulated the vicious-circle principle, which of course continues to attract him, despite Frege's objections.)

Frege included an account of Russell's paradox, of his modification (Axiom V′) of the original Axiom V and of the way it avoids the paradox, together with some general objections to other lines of solution, as a hastily written appendix to Volume II. In 1930, five years after Frege's death, the Polish logician Leśniewski proved that Axiom V', though it does not actually lead to a contradiction, yields the conclusion that there are no two distinct *Sob* objects, and is thus manifestly absurd as a basis for the theory of classes, or for arithmetic in particular. In fact, in Frege's own system, though not in one based on standard predicate logic, it does yield a contradiction; for, since truth-values are objects, from the provable distinctness of the True and the False (symbolically $\vdash\!\!\lnot\ (\!\!-\!\!-\ a = \lnot\lnot\ a)$) it follows that there are at least two objects. There is no evidence that Frege ever discovered that Axiom V' had this consequence: but the common assumption, that he remained satisfied with his solution, is almost certainly false. The second step, which anyone would take after weakening an axiom of a theory, is to check that the proofs he has given on the old basis still go through. The most cursory inspection shows that the proof of the basic theorem that every natural number has a successor breaks down when Axiom V is weakened to V': since, as we shall see, it was essentially for the sake of being able to prove this theorem that classes were originally introduced into *Grundlagen*, this would be likely to be the first theorem the validity of whose proof under the weakened axiom Frege would have checked. It is thus probable that Frege very quickly came to realize the uselessness of his solution: since the terms in which he had posed the problem happened not to be those which would point towards a workable solution, he would be apt to conclude that no solution was to be found, and that his whole enterprise of reducing arithmetic to logic had collapsed.

This conjecture tallies very well with the known facts of Frege's subsequent career. In 1903, the year in which Volume II of *Grundgesetze* was published, Frege published two brief articles criticizing Hilbert's *Grundlagen der Geometrie*. After that, he published nothing of interest until 1918: he produced no constructive work at all, while even the polemical articles he wrote added nothing—save bitterness—to what he had done previously. In particular, *Grundgesetze*—still incomplete—was not continued. As a result, Frege did not participate in the second phase of the development of the subject which he himself had founded—mathematical logic and the study by its means of the foundations of mathematics. (The following selection indicates how much occurred between 1903 and Frege's death in 1925: Zermelo's proof from Axiom of Choice of the well-ordering theorem, 1904; his axiomatization of set theory, 1908; Löwenheim's theorem on first-order functional calculus, 1915; Skolem's generalization of it, 1920; Hilbert's 'Axiomatisches Denken' 1918; Brouwer's first attack on classical logic, 1908.) It is known from a letter to Russell in 1912, refusing an invitation to address a

B*

congress of mathematicians in Cambridge, that he was at that time in a state of complete discouragement. In 1918 he began his last attempt to write a comprehensive book on philosophical logic (not dealing with foundations of mathematics); there had been three previous attempts, the first immediately after the publication of *Begriffsschrift*. The last three articles which he published—two in 1918, one in 1923—constitute the first three chapters of this uncompleted book. In 1923–5, the last three years of his life, he wrote several articles, none of them published, setting out his final views on mathematics. The only thing which—he now believed—had been correct in his earlier writings on mathematics was the analysis he had given of the logical form of sentences involving number-words used adjectivally—in his terminology, the principle that the content of a statement of number is an assertion about a concept. The idea of reducing arithmetic to logic had been wholly erroneous, the fundamental mistake lying in introducing the notion of classes, without which the reduction was impossible. The notion of classes, he now held, is a wholly spurious one, generated by a linguistic illusion. The discovery of the contradiction thus overthrew for Frege what he had regarded as his principal achievement, the derivation of arithmetic from logic. The probability that he discovered the inadequacy of his solution combines with the known facts—his abandonment of work in formal logic for good, of work in philosophical logic for fifteen years, and of work in foundations of mathematics for twenty years, his rejection of the theory of classes and of logicism when he did resume work on foundations, and his total discouragement in 1912—to make this hypothesis virtually certain.

Frege was not celebrated in his day. Among philosophers, his work was known only to Russell, Wittgenstein and Husserl. Russell was, of course, considerably influenced by him, Wittgenstein profoundly so. (Russell devoted an appendix to him in *Principles of Mathematics* and criticized at length one thesis of his in 'On Denoting' (1905); and in the preface to Volume I of *Principia* (1910), he and Whitehead wrote, 'In all questions of logical analysis, our chief debt is to Frege.' Wittgenstein spoke in the preface to the *Tractatus* (1921) of 'the great works of Frege', and referred to him repeatedly in the text.) He had some effect on Husserl through his hostile review of Husserl's early work *Die Philosophie der Arithmetik* (1891). Frege trounced the book, seeing it as a classic example of 'psychologism'—the importation of psychological considerations into logic—and of abstractionism (the faulty theory of concept-formation due to the British empiricists). Husserl, to his credit, accepted Frege's criticisms, and in his *Logische Untersuchungen* (1900), which contains a generous reference to Frege, made anti-psychologism one of the principal planks of his platform. (He appears later to have gone back on this, however.) On the other hand, no other member of the phenomenological school appears to have had any knowledge of Frege: and Meinong seems to have had no awareness that Frege had anticipated his doctrine of 'assumptions' and his 'theory of objects', the latter in a vastly preferable form. Among mathematicians, Frege had the respect of Dedekind and of Zermelo. Cantor, however, was hostile. In *Grundlagen* Frege made complimentary references to Cantor, which Cantor repaid by writing a savage and quite uncomprehending review of the book which is reprinted in the collected writings of Cantor with regretful remarks by Zermelo, the editor, about the misunderstanding between these two great men. Frege wrote a brief reply, and retaliated by scoring points off Cantor in Volume II of *Grundgesetze*. Hilbert paid occasional tributes to Frege, for instance in his lecture in 1904 'Über die Grundlagen der Logik und der Arithmetik' to the International Congress of Mathematicians at Heidelberg; but he was content to dismiss his work as vitiated by the paradoxes. Brouwer appears to have been totally unaware of Frege's existence, although Frege, as an arch-platonist, would have been the perfect object of his attack on classical mathematics, and indeed, some of his polemics would have been much more appropriately directed against Frege than against Hilbert. Peano had some correspondence with Frege, but foolishly did not take him very seriously or make much attempt to understand him. (Löwenheim also had a long correspondence with Frege, which, unfortunately, was destroyed by bombing during the war.) With the exceptions I have mentioned, mathematicians and philosophers alike ignored him. This is far from the case now, of course: but in 1925 Frege died an embittered man, convinced both that he had been unjustly neglected, and that his life's work had been for the most part failure.

CHAPTER I

Sense and Tone

THE ORIGINAL TASK which Frege set himself to accomplish, at the outset of his career, was to bring to mathematics the means to achieve absolute rigour in the process of proof. This, of course, has nothing to do with the sequence of thought by means of which a proof is sought for and discovered: it concerns the presentation of the proof once found. What Frege wanted was a framework within which all mathematical proofs might be presented and which would offer a guarantee against incorrect argumentation: of a proof so set out, it would be possible to be certain that it was not erroneous, or valid only within certain restrictions not made explicit, or dependent upon unstated assumptions. To achieve this purpose, it was necessary to devise a symbolic language within which any statement of any given mathematical theory might be framed, as soon as the required additional vocabulary for that theory was specified. This would be, in modern terminology, a formalized language: that is, there would be an effective method of recognizing, for any given collocation of symbols, whether or not it was a formula of that symbolic language. Furthermore, in reference to this language, it was necessary to stipulate formal rules of proof, rules, that is, which would specify in a manner which provided a procedure for effective recognition which sequences of formulas of the language constituted a valid proof. This would have to be done in sufficiently generous a manner for it to be at least plausible that any intuitively valid argument for the truth of any statement of the mathematical theory in question could be replaced by a formal proof, conforming to the stipulated rules, in the symbolic language.

Frege was, thus, proposing to take the step from the axiomatization of mathematical theories, with which nineteenth-century mathematics had been deeply concerned, to their actual formalization. While the axiomatic method strove to isolate the basic notions of each mathematical theory, in terms of which the other notions of the theory could be defined, and the underlying assumptions, from which all the theorems could be made ultimately to derive, what Frege wanted to do was to subject the process of proof itself to an equally exact analysis.

Before an analysis of proof is possible, an analysis has first to be given of the structure of the statements which make up the proof. The validity of a proof depends upon the meanings of the statements which form the premises, conclusion and intermediate steps of that proof, and their interrelation. The meaning of a statement is determined by the meanings of the words or individual symbols of which it is composed, and by the way in which these are put together to form the statement. Notoriously, the linear arrangement of the words in a sentence of natural language conceals the very different roles which words of different kinds play in determining the meaning of the sentence as a whole, and the complexity of the rules which govern the way a sentence may be formed out of its constituent words or other subordinate expressions. Frege's first task was, thus, to give an analysis of the structure of the sentences of our language, adequate at least for such sentences as occur in a train of mathematical reasoning. This analysis could not stop short at the specification of which sentences were well-formed: it must explain also how the meaning of each sentence was determined from its internal structure. In modern terminology, it must be a semantic, and not merely a syntactic, analysis. Frege had, in other words, to provide the foundation of a theory of meaning.

Bs 3, 7
Frege distinguished two elements in the meaning of a sentence or expression, for one of which he reserved the word 'sense' ('*Sinn*'), and for the
SB 31; Ged
63 (9); NS
209 (193);
NS 214 (198);
BW 102 (67)
other of which we might use the word 'tone' ('illumination' ['*Beleuchtung*'] and 'colouring' ['*Färbung*'] being the words Frege himself used for this latter). He explained the difference in this way: to the sense of a sentence belongs only that which is relevant to determining its truth or falsity; any feature of its meaning which cannot affect its truth or falsity belongs to its tone. Likewise, to the sense of an expression belongs only that which may be relevant to the truth or falsity of a sentence in which it might occur; any element of its meaning not so relevant is part of its tone.

The distinction is exceedingly familiar to contemporary philosophers: the
Bs 7
substitution of the word 'but' for 'and' will alter the meaning of a sentence, but it cannot convert it from a true to a false sentence or vice versa; and the
NS 152 (140)
same is true when we replace 'dog' by 'cur'. The difference in meaning between 'but' and 'and' or between 'dog' and 'cur' therefore belongs to their tone and not to their sense. Here it is not the notion of sense, but that of tone, which is problematic. That language permits the construction of sentences with determinate truth-conditions, and that these sentences can

be uttered assertorically, i.e. understood as governed by the convention that the speaker is aiming at uttering only those the condition for whose truth is fulfilled, appears to belong to the essence of language. Even when sentences are uttered in a different mode, e.g. imperatively, it is evidently a requirement of this linguistic practice that the sentence should contain a description of a state of affairs, that namely which will obtain if the command is obeyed, for which we know the conditions under which that state of affairs obtains. What is not immediately clear is how it may come about that an assertion may be incorrect in any other way than by being untrue; how we may convey by what we say more than we are actually stating to be the case. It is, further, unclear whether tone is a single feature of the meaning of a sentence or expression in addition to its sense, or whether, say, a different feature distinguishes 'but' from 'and' from that which distinguishes 'cur' from 'dog'. We shall explore this question later: for the time being we will confine our considerations to the sense of sentences and words.

Quine has ascribed to Frege the doctrine that the unit of significance is   *FLPV* 39
not the word but the sentence. This doctrine is either truistic or nonsensical: in either case it does not represent any thesis stressed by Frege. In a word, the individual letters carry no meaning: the words 'mean' and 'lean', for example, carry no common meaning-component represented by the three letters 'ean'. If the doctrine stated by Quine were taken as involving that the words in a sentence no more carry a meaning of their own than the letters in a word, the doctrine would be absurd, and fly in face of the obvious and crucial fact that we understand new sentences which we have never heard or thought of before, so long as they are composed of words which we know, put together in ways with which we are familiar. If the doctrine is taken as consisting merely in the observation that we cannot say anything by means of a sequence of words that stops short of being a sentence—cannot make an assertion, express a wish, ask a question, give a command, etc., in short do what Wittgenstein called 'make a move in the language-game'—except where the context supplies a supplementation of the words spoken that amounts to a sentence embodying them, then it is truistic: for (in a logical rather than a typographical sense) an expression with which we can make a move in the language-game (or 'perform a linguistic act') is precisely what a sentence is.

It must be conceded that no philosopher before Frege had succeeded in presenting an account of meaning which displayed the reason for the truth of the slogan, 'The sentence is the unit of meaning', in that sense of that slogan in which it is a truism. A continuous tradition, from Aristotle to Locke and beyond, had assigned to individual words the power of expressing

'ideas', and to combinations of words that of expressing complex 'ideas'; and
this style of talk had blurred, or at least failed to account for, the crucial
distinction between those combinations of words which constitute a sentence
and those which form mere phrases which could be part of a sentence.
Indeed, there had been a constant tendency to assimilate the truth of a
sentence to the possession by a complex general description of an application,
as both expressing ideas which are realized in actuality. In insisting on the
crucial nature of the distinction between sentences and well-formed combinations of words that fall short of being sentences, and in giving a theory
of meaning which offered an account of this distinction, Frege thus took a
great stride forward, and contributed something that has become part of the
foundation for any philosophical account of meaning. That, however, is no
defence for ascribing to Frege a crude slogan in place of the careful formulation of the matter which he in fact provided.

Frege's account, if it is to be reduced to a slogan, could be expressed in this
way: that in the order of *explanation* the sense of a sentence is primary, but
in the order of *recognition* the sense of a word is primary. Frege was un-
waveringly insistent that the sense of a sentence—or of any complex expression—is made up out of the senses of its constituent words. This means that
we understand the sentence—grasp its sense—by knowing the senses of the
constituents, and, as it were, compounding them in a way that is determined
by the manner in which the words themselves are put together to form the
sentence. We thus derive our knowledge of the sense of any given sentence
from our previous knowledge of the senses of the words that compose it,
together with our observation of the way in which they are combined in that
sentence. It is this which I intended to express by saying that, for Frege, the
sense of the word is primary, and that of the sentence secondary, in the order
of recognition: any theory of meaning which is unable to incorporate this
point will be impotent to account for the obvious and essential fact that we
can understand new sentences. But, when we come to give any general
explanation of what it is for sentences and words to have a sense, that is, of
what it is for us to grasp their sense, then the order of priority is reversed.
For Frege, the sense of a word or of any expression not a sentence can be
understood only as consisting in the contribution which it makes to determining the sense of any sentence in which it may occur. Since it is only by
means of a sentence that we may perform a linguistic act—that we can *say*
anything—the possession of a sense by a word or complex expression short
of a sentence cannot consist in anything else but its being governed by a
general rule which partially specifies the sense of sentences containing it.
If this is so, then, on pain of circularity, the general notion of the sense

possessed by a sentence must be capable of being explained without reference to the notion of the senses of constituent words or expressions. This is possible via the conception of truth-conditions: to grasp the sense of a sentence is, in general, to know the conditions under which that sentence is true and the conditions under which it is false.

Here we are concerned with the form which a *general* account must take of what it is for a sentence to have a sense (or: what it is to know the sense of a sentence), and of what it is for a word to have a sense (or, likewise, of what it is to know the sense of a word). For the purposes of such a general account, the notion of the sense of a sentence has the priority: for this can be explained by reference to the notion of truth-conditions, whereas the general notion of the sense of a word can be explained only in terms of that of the sense of a sentence in which the word may occur. Of course, this highly generalized notion of the contribution made by a word to determining the sense of a sentence in which it occurs is merely programmatic: to give it any substance, we have first to categorize words and expressions according to the different kinds of contribution they can make to the sense of sentences containing them, and then give, for each such category, a general account of the form taken by the semantic rule which governs them.

Thus, on Frege's account of the matter, we cannot grasp the sense of a word otherwise than by reference to the way in which it can be used to form sentences; but we understand the word independently of any particular sentence containing it. Our understanding of any such particular sentence is derived from our understanding of its constituent words, which understanding determines for us the truth-conditions of that sentence; but our understanding of those words consists in our grasp of the way in which they may figure in sentences in general, and how, in general, they combine to determine the truth-conditions of those sentences.

Consider, as a crude analogy, a very simple code: each code-word consists of a numeral followed by a string of letters. The numeral determines the displacement of the letters in the alphabet: thus the word 'can' can be written as '1dbo' or as '5hfs' or as '26can', etc. In each code-word, each letter and numeral has a uniform significance, in the sense that the determination of the encoded word proceeds by means of general rules: one determines what the encoded word is only by applying these rules to the numerals and letters making up the code-word. On the other hand, one could not explain the significance in the code of any numeral or letter save by reference to the general notion of the representation of a normal word by means of a code-word: unless this conception is first present, there is nothing that can be said about what the code numerals and letters 'mean'.

In the context of this account, it is senseless to ask whether a sentence or a word is to be considered as the 'unit of meaning'.

It is not to be thought that the doctrine that the sense of a word consists only in the contribution that it makes to the sense of a sentence in which it occurs requires that every explanation of a particular word must make an explicit allusion to its occurrence in sentences. The word may be one belonging to a category for which there is a general form of explanation of the senses of words of that category which makes no such explicit allusion. Precisely this is held by Frege to be the case with the category of 'proper names': we give the sense of a word of this category by specifying what it stands for. But this is possible only on the assumption that we have, or can construct, a general account of the cont-ibution which a proper name makes to the truth-conditions of a sentence in which it occurs in terms of the relation between the proper name and the object it stands for: the very notion of the existence of such a relation has a content only in the context of such a general account.

Gl x, 60, 62, 106 The ascription of this doctrine to Frege rests on the thesis, so heavily underlined in *Grundlagen*, that 'it is only in the context of a sentence that a word has a meaning'. What has been said so far does not exhaust the content of this thesis, but it is certainly part of what is intended by it. Thus, to take the example already mentioned, the sense of a proper name is to be explained in terms of a relation which the name has to a unique object, a relation we express by saying that the name stands for the object. Such a sense can be specified without overt allusion to the occurrence of the name in sentences; but to invoke the relation which a name has to the object which it stands for is already to make a covert allusion to such occurrences. Compare the situation in which one is being told the rules of a card game; one's informant says, 'The Ace ranks above all other cards, the 10 below the Ace but above all the rest.' The assignment of an order to the cards is here effected without reference to the mode of play: but it is empty and without significance unless it is later connected with the procedure of play, i.e. unless some rule of the game is expressed in terms of the ranking which has been assigned. In the same way, any explanation of the sense of a word of any kind which is stated without explicit allusion to the determination of the truth-values of sentences in which the word occurs achieves its purpose only if, and in so far as, the terms in which the explanation is given are subsequently used in stipulating the truth-conditions of those sentences. We know what it is for a name to stand for an object only by knowing how to determine the truth-values of sentences containing the name, a piece of knowledge which can be expressed in terms of that relation between name and object. Sentences thus play a unique role in language. It is no great discovery that they do so: Frege's achievement was to give an account which acknowledged and explained this unique role.

In Frege's writings subsequent to *Grundlagen*, the uniqueness of sentences is no longer acknowledged. On the contrary, Frege now assimilated sentences to complex singular terms, regarding them as standing for truth-values in the same way that complex terms stand for objects of other kinds. This was a retrograde step on Frege's part, which obscured the crucial fact that the utterance of a sentence, unlike that of a complex term in general (except in special contexts, such as answering a question), can be used to effect a linguistic act, to make an assertion, give a command, etc. Frege's account of the sense of a proper name will now have to be that it consists in the contribution, for any complex term containing the name, to the way in which it is determined which object that term stands for. Likewise, the general notion of the sense of a word will now have to be taken to consist in the contribution which that word makes to determining what a complex singular term, in which it may occur, stands for, rather than what are the truth-conditions of a sentence in which it may occur. It was Frege's adoption of this new doctrine which, presumably, was responsible for the failure of the thesis, so heavily emphasized in *Grundlagen*, that a word has meaning only in the context of a sentence, to make a single re-appearance in his subsequent writings. We shall observe a certain awkwardness, almost embarrassment, about what he says in his later writing whenever he comes near to this point.

FB 18

CHAPTER 2

Quantifiers

Bs 11   THE DISCOVERY BY Frege, at the outset of his career, of the notation of quantifiers and variables for the expression of generality dominated his entire subsequent outlook upon logic. By means of it, he resolved, for the first time in the whole history of logic, the problem which had foiled the most penetrating minds that had given their attention to the subject. It is not surprising that Frege's approach was ever afterwards governed by the lessons which he regarded as being taught by this discovery.

Aristotle and the Stoics had investigated only those inferences involving essentially sentences containing not more than one expression of generality. Scholastic logic had wrestled with the problems posed by inferences depending on sentences involving multiple generality—the occurrence of more than one expression of generality. In order to handle such inferences, they developed ever more complex theories of different types of '*suppositio*' (different manners in which an expression could stand for or apply to an object): but these theories, while subtle and complex, never succeeded in giving a universally applicable account, either from the standpoint of syntax (the characterization of valid inferences in formal terms) or from that of semantics (the explanation of the truth-conditions of sentences involving multiple generality). As a result of this increasing and never finally successful subtlety, the whole subject of logic fell into disrepute at the Renaissance, as part of the general rejection of the achievements of the scholastic era. Apart from Leibniz—whose work likewise failed to tackle the problem of multiple generality—no more serious work was done in logic by European mathematicians or philosophers until the nineteenth century. Indeed, what would otherwise have been the scandal of the failure, over centuries, to resolve the problem of inferences involving multiple generality was for long concealed by doctrines entailing the non-existence of the problem. Any sentence expressed within first-order predicate logic and containing only one-place predicates is equivalent to some sentence in which no quantifier stands within the scope of any other quantifier. Hence the widely held opinion that relations are merely 'ideal', i.e. that any sentence involving predicates of more than one place can in principle be reduced to one involving only one-place predicates, implied that the study of multiple generality (nested expressions of generality) is unnecessary. That, blatantly, the logic which dealt only with simple generality was impotent to give any account of the simplest mathematical reasoning was a fact to which, almost universally, philosophers, who believed that essentially all the problems of logic had been solved by Aristotle, were simply blind.

It is necessary, if Frege is to be understood, to grasp the magnitude of the discovery of the quantifier-variable notation, as thus resolving an age-old problem the failure to solve which had blocked the progress of logic for centuries. Moore called Russell's theory of descriptions a 'paradigm of philosophy'. The title would be better given to the theory of quantification as discovered by Frege: for this resolved a deep problem, on the resolution of which a vast area of further progress depended, and definitively, so that today we are no longer conscious of the problem of which it was the solution as a philosophical problem at all. But, for the understanding of Frege, it is necessary to do more than apprehend the magnitude of the discovery: it is necessary to be able to understand its nature as it appeared to him. Much that seems too obvious to us to need saying, now that the quantifier-variable notation is simply a basic part of the received apparatus of logic, struck him forcefully as a penetrating insight; until we can think ourselves into the context in which he was writing, we shall often be baffled to comprehend why he argued as he did.

A sentence, or, in most symbolisms, a mathematical formula, is merely a linear ordering of words or signs. The most natural account of the structure of sentences or formulas would therefore consist of taking them as built by arranging the component words or signs in a linear order. Of course, in giving such an account, certain restrictions would have to be imposed on what sequences of words or signs were to be allowed as meaningful; and these restrictions would derive their rationale from the different roles which different words or signs played. For instance, in the expression '2 + 3', the sign '+' obviously functions in a quite different way from the signs '2' and '3': where they are numerals, '+' is an operator which serves to combine two numerals into a complex expression which is again a numerical term (i.e. one which functions just like a numeral, for example in being able to stand on either side of the '=' sign). But in the expression '(2 + 3) × 6', the parenthesis, though again forming part of the linear ordering of the signs, evidently function in quite a different way again: they serve to show that, in relation to the operator '×', the whole expression '2 + 3' is to be treated as unitary. In making any attempt to give an account of the rules governing which expressions of this simple kind are well-formed, or what they mean, it is necessary to jettison the original natural idea that the linear ordering of symbols is a true guide to the process of formation of complex expressions. That is, although of course the final product is precisely a sequence of linearly ordered signs, the process by which it was constructed has to be conceived of, not as consisting of a simultaneous assembling of all the constituent signs, followed by a linear arrangement of them according to determinate rules, but rather as a process of construction which takes place in several stages. Thus the first stage in the construction of the above expression consists in joining '2' and '3' together by '+' to form '2 + 3', and the second stage in joining the expression formed by the first stage to the sign '6' by means of the operator '×'. In the resulting linear expression, the order of construction may be indicated by the use of parentheses, as in '(2 + 3) × 6'; or it may be determined by convention, as in '2 + 3 × 6'; or, as frequently in natural language, the expression may be simply ambiguous as to the order of construction, the ambiguity being left to be resolved by the probabilities conferred by the context.

One of the insights underlying Frege's discovery of the quantifier notation was precisely that this idea, that sentences are constructed in a series of stages, should be applied to the means whereby expressions of generality are incorporated into sentences. In the sentence, 'Everybody envies somebody', multiple generality is involved: it would be represented in quantificational symbolism in such a way that the existential quantifier would lie within the scope of the universal quantifier. It is easy enough to give an account of the truth-conditions of a statement containing a sign of existential generality when that is the only sign of generality occurring in the sentence: the complexities of the medieval theory of *suppositio* arose precisely when the theory attempted to account for an expression of generality governed by another. The difficulty arose out of trying to consider a sentence such as the above as being constructed simultaneously out of its three components, the relational expression here represented by the verb, and the two signs of generality.

Frege's insight consisted in considering the sentence as being constructed in stages, corresponding to the different signs of generality occurring in it. A sentence may be formed by combining a sign of generality with a one-place predicate. The one-place predicate is itself to be thought of as having been formed from a sentence by removing one or more occurrences of some one singular term (proper name). Thus we begin with a sentence such as

Gg I 26, 30

'Peter envies John'. From this we form the one-place predicate 'Peter envies ξ' by removing the proper name 'John'—the Greek letter 'ξ' here serving merely to indicate where the gap occurs that is left by the removal of the proper name. This predicate can then be combined with the sign of generality 'somebody' to yield the sentence 'Peter envies somebody'. The resulting sentence may now be subjected to the same process: by removing the proper name 'Peter', we obtain the predicate 'ξ envies somebody', and this may then be combined with the sign of generality 'everybody' to yield the sentence 'Everybody envies somebody'.

Why is this conception, under which the sentence was constructed in stages, more illuminating than the more natural idea according to which it was formed simultaneously out of its three constituents, 'everybody', 'envies' and 'somebody', in exactly the same way that 'Peter envies John' is constructed out of its three components? The reason does not lie in syntax—at least, so far as this concerns only the determination of which sentences are well-formed—but in semantics. It allows the use only of the simple account of the truth-conditions of sentences containing signs of generality that is adequate for those involving only simple generality, as a general account applicable to all signs of generality, provided that the application is made only to the stage of construction at which the sign of generality in question is introduced. We may here evade questions relating to the range of generality, which, though extremely important, are not to the immediate point, by concerning ourselves only with generalization with respect to human beings. A one-place predicate is, then, true of a given individual just in case the sentence which results from inserting a name of that individual in the argument-place (gap) of the predicate is true. A sentence formed by means of this predicate and the sign of generality 'everybody' is true just in case the predicate is true of every individual, and one formed by means of the predicate and the sign of generality 'somebody' is true if the predicate is true of at least one individual. Once we know the constructional history of a sentence involving multiple generality, we can from these simple rules determine the truth-conditions of that sentence, provided only that we already know the truth-conditions of every sentence containing proper names in the places where the signs of generality stand. Thus, 'Everybody envies somebody' is true just in case each of the sentences, 'Peter envies somebody', 'James envies somebody', . . . , is true; and 'Peter envies somebody' is, in turn, true just in case at least one of the sentences, 'Peter envies John', 'Peter envies James', . . . , is true. We are blocked, however, from making the false assertion that 'Everybody envies somebody' is true just in case one of the sentences, 'Everybody envies John', 'Everybody envies James', . . . , is true, by the fact that the final sentence was not constructed by combining the sign of generality 'somebody' with the predicate 'Everybody envies ξ', but by combining the sign of generality 'everybody' and the predicate 'ξ envies somebody'.

In natural language, the form of the sentence does not reveal the order of construction: just as an ad hoc convention leads us to interpret '2 + 3 × 6' as '2 + (3 × 6)' and not as '(2 + 3) × 6', so an ad hoc convention determines that we interpret the sentence 'Everybody envies somebody' as having been constructed in the order in which the sign of generality 'everybody' comes in at the second stage rather than as having been constructed in the alternative order. If we want to express the proposition which would result from taking it in the alternative order, we have to use the passive and say, 'Somebody is envied by everybody', or a form with a relative clause, 'There is somebody whom everybody envies'. This is because the ad hoc convention which we tacitly employ is that the order of construction corresponds to the inverse order of occurrence of the signs of generality in the sentence: when 'everybody' precedes 'somebody', it is taken as having been introduced later in the step-by-step construction, and conversely. Thus the expressive power of natural language depends upon a certain redundancy at a lower level: it is just because the active form 'Peter envies John' is fully equivalent to the passive form 'John is envied by Peter', and to the form with the relative clause, 'John is someone whom Peter envies', that it is possible to use the ad hoc convention to confer distinct and determinate senses on the corresponding forms when signs of generality are present.

Having gained this insight, Frege proceeded to replace the notation used to express generality in natural language with a new notation—that of quantifiers and variables. The point of this new notation was to enable the constructional history of any sentence to be determined unambiguously without the need for any ad hoc convention and therefore also without the need for any underlying redundancy at lower level. Aside from the convention which rules out this possibility, the sentence 'Everybody envies someone' might have been constructed by adjoining the sign of generality 'someone' to the predicate 'Everyone envies ξ'; but the form 'For every x, for some y, x envies y' could not have been constructed by attaching the quantifier 'for some y' to the predicate 'For every x, x envies ξ'. Whereas in natural language, the sign of generality is inserted in the argument-place of the predicate, so that, when two signs of generality occur, one cannot tell save by reference to a special convention which sign of generality was introduced last in the step-by-step construction of the sentence, and which therefore was the predicate to which it was attached, in Frege's notation the sign of generality was to precede the predicate, carrying with it a bound variable which should also occur in the argument-place of the predicate, thus displaying unambiguously how the sentence was formed.

We have seen that, for the convention according to which the signs of generality occurring in a sentence of natural language are to be regarded as having been introduced in the inverse order of their occurrence to be able to work, it is necessary that, for every sentence containing two proper names, there must be an equivalent sentence in which those two names occur in the opposite order. One way in which this is managed is by the use of the passive voice. Clearly this may be generalized: if natural language is to be able to express whatever may be expressed by means of any finite number of quantifiers occurring in any order, and ambiguity is to be avoided by appeal to the convention cited, then it is necessary that, for any sentence of natural language containing any number of distinct proper names, there be an equivalent sentence containing the same names in any permutation of the original order of occurrence. The redundancy that this demands within natural language at the level of sentences not containing signs of generality is very great indeed: but it does not exhaust the redundancy that is required for the means of expression of generality which natural language employs to be workable.

When the notation of quantifiers and variables is used, there is of course no difficulty about predicates which are formed by removing two or more occurrences of the same proper name from some sentence: the two or more gaps—which together constitute a single argument-place—will be filled by the same bound variable. There is no such simple solution when the notation of natural language is used, according to which the sign of generality has to occupy the argument-place of the predicate. Inserting the same sign of generality in each of the several gaps will not have the required effect: if the sentence 'Someone killed someone' were taken to have the sense of 'For some x, x killed x', then there would be no way of expressing 'For some x, for some y, x killed y'. The difficulty is overcome in natural language by a further redundancy at lower level: for any sentence containing two or more occurrences of some one proper name, there must be an equivalent sentence containing only one occurrence of that name; from this sentence the predicate can then be formed, and a sign of generality inserted into the single gap representing its argument-place. A well-known device for accomplishing this result is the use of pronouns, of the reflexive pronoun in particular. Here it is essential, for the recognition of valid inferences, that the equivalence between the different forms be understood: for instance, the validity of the syllogistic argument:

> Anyone who killed Brutus was a traitor;
> Brutus killed himself:
> Therefore, Brutus was a traitor.

depends upon the equivalence between 'Brutus killed himself' and 'Brutus killed Brutus'.

We can thus say that the ability of natural language to express all that can be said by means of the notation of quantifiers and variables depends upon the possibility of finding, for any sentence containing any number of occurrences of each of any number of proper names, an equivalent sentence containing only one occurrence of each of those names, in any arbitrary specified order. Whether natural language actually has this power is not wholly clear: certainly it often cannot be accomplished without considerable clumsiness.

The quantifier-variable notation thus permitted a single uniform explanation for each universal quantifier and each existential quantifier. (Frege, observing the well-known equivalence of 'for some $x, \ldots x \ldots$' with 'it is not the case that, for every x, not $\ldots x \ldots$', did not in fact employ in his logical symbolism any special sign for the existential quantifier—not even a defined one; but this point is of little importance in the present context.) The scholastic logicians had felt compelled, precisely because they had not hit on the idea of regarding sentences as built up in a series of stages, to attribute a different kind of *suppositio* to signs of generality according (as we should say) to the number of other signs of generality in whose scope they occurred: but Frege's notation enabled this complexity to be avoided. An 'explanation' may here be taken either semantically, as a stipulation of the truth-conditions of sentences containing expressions of generality, or proof-theoretically, as a stipulation of the rules of inference governing such sentences. Such explanations would apply primarily to sentences formed directly by combining a quantifier with a predicate—sentences in which, in modern terminology, the quantifier in question constitutes the principal logical constant. But it is of the essence of the conception of the step-by-step construction of sentences that such an explanation is adequate to account for all other occurrences of quantifiers. The rule which gives the truth-conditions of a sentence of the form '$\exists y\ A(y)$' does not directly apply to the sentence '$\forall x\ \exists y\ x$ envies y', because it is not of that form; but, as we have seen, provided that we know the truth-conditions of every sentence of the form 'a envies b', we can, using that rule, determine the truth-conditions of the doubly quantified sentence, since, in the process of its formation, a sentence such as '$\exists y$ Peter envies y' occurred, which was of that form.

The idea of the step-by-step construction of sentences of course applies more generally than just to the process whereby signs of generality are introduced into sentences: the combination of sentences by means of sentential operators has also to be regarded as part of the step-by-step construction, since evidently it makes a difference to the truth-conditions of a sentence whether a quantifier is regarded as occurring within, e.g., the antecedent of a conditional, or as governing the whole conditional sentence. In just the same way that a single explanation of each kind of quantifier was made possible, so it became possible, as a result of applying the idea of the step-by-step construction to sentential operators, to dispense with the idea of corresponding operators connecting expressions smaller than sentences. In 'Some people are charming and sincere', the connective 'and' does not join sentences together, nor is the sentence as a whole equivalent to any in which 'and' stands between two sentences; but the predicate 'ξ is charming and sincere', to which the sign of generality 'some people' has been attached to form the sentence in question, was derived from a sentence such as 'Peter is charming and sincere', which is equivalent to a sentence, 'Peter is charming and Peter is sincere', in which 'and' stands between two sentences. Thus the use of 'and' to conjoin adjectives can be regarded as another of the devices employed by natural language to convert a sentence containing two occurrences of a proper name into an equivalent one containing only one occurrence of it. Although it is not true that connectives such as 'and' stand only between whole sentences, still the truth-conditions of any sentence containing such a connective are determined once it is known what the truth-conditions are of a sentence in which it does conjoin subordinate sentences; since, in the step-by-step construction of the final sentence, the step at which the connective was originally introduced yielded precisely a sentence of this kind.

In the course of this account, a second fundamental idea, besides that of the step-by-step construction of sentences, has been introduced: that, namely, of the formation of complex predicates out of sentences by the omission of one or more occurrences of a single proper name. Here it is of great importance that the predicate itself is not thought of as having been built up out of its component parts: we do not need to invoke the conception of the conjunction of two predicates, 'ξ is charming' and 'ξ is sincere', to explain the formation of the predicate 'ξ is charming and sincere'; nor do we need to invoke the idea of the application of a quantifier to a two-place predicate, with respect to a specific argument-place, to explain the formation of the predicate '$\exists y \; \xi$ killed y'; nor, again, do we need the operation of identifying the argument-places of a two-place predicate to explain the

NS 204 (187);
NS 273 (253)

formation of 'ξ killed ξ'. We do not, for present purposes, need to invoke the notion of a two-place predicate at all. Given a basic fund of atomic sentences, all other sentences can be regarded as being formed by means of a sequence of operations, which are of three kinds: the application of sentential operators to sentences to form new sentences; the omission from a sentence of one or more occurrences of a proper name to form a one-place predicate; and the application of a quantifier to a one-place predicate to form a sentence.

This account is not precisely the same as that given in a modern textbook of predicate logic: but it is essentially so. Modern symbolism usually differs from Frege's in allowing as well-formed expressions containing variables, known as 'free variables', not bound by any quantifier. Nothing exactly corresponding to a free variable appears in Frege's symbolism. A Greek letter, such as the 'ξ' we have been using, is not properly part of the symbolic language: it is merely a device for indicating where the argument-place of a predicate occurs. It is usual, in modern symbolism, to use the very same letters as 'free variables' as may be used as bound variables. In this case, the statement of the formation rules (rules for the construction of sentences) can be stated very simply, by describing first the formation of 'open sentences' (expressions like sentences save for possibly containing free variables): no separate operation of forming a predicate has to be stipulated, but only the operation of prefixing a quantifier to an open sentence, thus converting into a bound variable the free variable identical in form to the variable attached to the new quantifier. A sentence can then be specified as being an open sentence which contains no free variables. (In the present context the presence of schematic letters is being disregarded: for simplicity, we are considering only the case of a language for which there is a fixed interpretation for the individual constants and predicate- and function-symbols.) This simplification is, however, more or less illusory. When the truth-conditions of sentences are explained, this has to be done inductively, and, since sentences have to be constructed not only out of other sentences but out of open sentences, what in fact has to be defined is the truth or falsity of an open sentence relative to some assignment to the free variables of individuals from the domain of the bound variables. In regard to any given open sentence, such an assignment confers upon the free variables occurring in it the effective status of individual constants or proper names. Moreover, those clauses in the inductive stipulation of the truth-conditions of open sentences which relate to the quantifiers are stated in terms of the truth-conditions of the open sentence to which the quantifier is prefixed which result from holding fixed the assignments to the free variables other than the one which becomes bound by the new quantifier, and allowing the assignment to the latter free variable to run through all the individuals in the domain. This stipulation essentially corresponds to considering the predicate which results from removing every occurrence of the 'free variable' due to be bound by the new quantifier, and asking of which individuals it is true; the notion of a one-place predicate's being *true of* a given individual being explained in the same way as with Frege. Thus we can say that, in the standard form of explanation, a free variable is treated exactly as if it were a proper name at every stage in the step-by-step construction of a given sentence up to that at which a quantifier is to be prefixed which will bind that variable: at that stage, however, it is treated exactly as if it were one of the Greek letters Frege uses to indicate the argument-place in a predicate. Hence we have no real contrast with Frege's explanation of the matter at all, but essentially the very same explanation.

For Frege, the sentence resulting from attaching a universal quantifier to a predicate is true just in case the predicate is true of everything; and we understand, in turn, the notion of the predicate's being true of a given individual because we know this to be equivalent to the truth of a sentence formed by putting a name of that individual in the argument-place of the predicate. Frege did not take this form of explanation as presupposing that we have already a language which actually contains a name for every object: that would make it possible to quantify only over a finite or denumerable domain. Rather, he is making the assumption that, whenever we understand the truth-conditions for any sentence containing (one or more occurrences of) a proper name, we likewise understand what it is for any arbitrary object to satisfy the predicate which results from removing (those occurrences of) that proper name from the sentence, irrespective of whether we actually have, or can form, in our language a name of that object. Thus, where the predicate in question is 'A(ξ)', and 'c' is any proper name, then of course the predicate 'A(ξ)' could have been formed from the sentence 'A(c)' by removing (certain, perhaps all, occurrences of) the name 'c' from 'A(c)': and Frege's assumption is that, if we understand 'A(c)', then we likewise understand, for any object whatever, what the truth-conditions would be of a sentence formed by putting a name of that object, rather than the name 'c', in the argument-place of 'A(ξ)'. And this, again, is precisely the assumption which underlies the explanation of the truth-conditions of quantified sentences which is framed in terms of 'free variables'. Under this explanation, we are supposed to be considering an open sentence 'A(x)' as having certain determinate truth-conditions relative to some particular assignment of an object in the domain of the variables to the free variable 'x': and now, in order to take the step necessary to grasp the truth-conditions of the quantified sentence '$\forall x$ A(x)', we have to consider the truth-conditions for 'A(x)' which result from assigning each object in the domain to the free variable 'x' in turn. Thus it is assumed that, simultaneously with our grasp of the truth-conditions of 'A(x)' under the assignment to 'x' with which we started out, we also understand its truth-conditions under every other assignment to that free variable which could be made. And this assumption is precisely the same as Frege's. Once again, if the domain of the individual variables is non-denumerable, then it is impossible that we should actually have in our language a name for every object in the domain, so that we cannot in such a case actually equate the truth of '$\forall x$ A(x)' with the conjoint truth of all the sentences 'A(a)', 'A(b)', 'A(c)', . . . , formed by putting each name that exists in the language in the argument-place of 'A(ξ)': nevertheless, the assumption which I have stated is made for this case also, just as Frege made the same assumption.

It would thus be quite wrong to oppose Frege's account of the formation of sentences containing signs of generality (quantifiers), and of the truth-conditions of such sentences, to that which is now standard: the difference is purely superficial. But, in order to understand Frege, and, indeed, to gain a correct understanding of the matter in general, it is preferable to consider the explanation as given in Frege's terms. 'Free variables' are merely a convenient notational device which simplifies the statement of the formation rules: they correspond to no type of expression for which there is any need in a language actually in functional use, but exist merely, as required, to serve the alternating roles of individual constant and indicator of the whereabouts of the argument-place in the predicate.

How plausible, then, is the assumption which underlies both Frege's and the now standard explanations of the quantifiers? It is very easy to express that assumption in a manner which makes it appear more plausible than it in fact is. We do this if we state the assumption by saying that, if we understand the truth-conditions of a sentence 'A(c)', then we likewise understand the conditions under which the predicate 'A(ξ)', formed from that sentence, is true of any given object. Such an assumption is indeed plausible: but that is precisely because we have smuggled in, by means of the word 'given', the presupposition that we have some quite determinate object in mind. For an object to be 'given' to us, we must have some means of referring to it or of indicating which object it is that is in question. Perhaps these means of referring to the object lie outside the circumscribed language which we happen currently to be treating of: but, in that case, it would be easy to imagine that language as being extended in such a way as to include a means of referring to the object in question.

It is, indeed, extremely plausible to say that, if 'c' and 'd' are two proper names within a language, and we understand a sentence 'A(c)', then we must also understand the sentence 'A(d)'—provided, of course, that we understand the name 'd'. It is true that the plausibility vanishes if we choose names of objects of quite different categories, e.g. a river and a political party; since, in such a case, the result of the substitution may be to convert a quite straightforward sentence into one about whose meaning, if there is one, we are in the dark: but that is not the sort of case with which we are at present concerned. We are, on the contrary, tacitly assuming that all the primitive predicates and functional expressions of the language are defined for all the objects in the domain of the variables: and, if this is so, then the same must be true for all the complex predicates as well. The assumption is plausible just because we understand the sentence by understanding the senses of its constituent expressions: since we understand the conditions under which 'A(c)' is true by understanding not only what object the name 'c' stands for but also by understanding the expressions which compose the predicate 'A(ξ)', we must in exactly the same way be able to determine the truth-conditions of 'A(d)', once we know for what object the name 'd' stands.

But, of course, this is not the nub of the question: the difficulty arose only because we may not assume that our language contains a name for every object, since, in particular, there may be too many objects for us to have names to go round. To imagine a situation in which we are considering whether or not the predicate is true of some 'given' object is to treat a case in which it is merely accidental that the language we have in mind lacks a name of the object in question. In such a case, the plausibility of the assumption that, from our understanding of 'A(c)', we can derive the conditions under which the predicate 'A(ξ)' is true of the given object, is virtually the same as that of the assumption that we can derive the truth-conditions of another sentence 'A(d)', given the sense of 'd'. But what is in question is not a case of this kind at all: what is in question is, rather, whether we can assume that, from a knowledge of the truth-conditions of 'A(c)', we can derive a knowledge of the conditions under which the predicate 'A(ξ)' will be true of all the objects in a domain, when we do not and could not have the means of referring to each of those objects.

This is evidently a difficult question, and, for the present, we shall not pursue it: for the time being it is enough to have isolated it. What we are at present concerned to understand is the perspective on the philosophical problems of logic and the analysis of language which Frege's discovery of quantification imposed upon him.

The most general lesson which Frege derived from his discovery was a certain disrespect for natural language. The intricate medieval theories of *suppositio* had failed to provide a solution, adequate for every case, of the problem of multiple generality with which the scholastic logicians wrestled for so long. As soon as Frege had hit upon his solution, the reason for the failure of the scholastics became at once apparent: they had followed too closely the leads provided by the forms of expression employed in natural language. As far as the sentence-structure of natural language is concerned, signs of generality such as 'someone' and 'anyone' behave exactly like proper names—they occupy the same positions in sentences and are governed by the same grammatical rules: it is only when the truth-conditions or the implicational powers of sentences containing them are considered that the difference appears. Likewise, as we have seen, the final form of the sentence gives no clue to the step-by-step construction of it in terms of which its sense has to be explained. Misled by these two superficial features of natural language, the scholastic logicians had attempted to explain signs of generality by theories which attributed to them the power of standing for objects, in a manner similar to, though more complicated than, that in which a proper name stands for its bearer, theories which, moreover, ignored the step-by-step construction of the sentences in which the signs of generality occurred, and depended merely on the varying kinds of *suppositio* attributed to those signs of generality. Frege, on the other hand, had solved the problem which had baffled logicians for millennia by ignoring natural language. He had made no attempt to give any systematic account of the truth-conditions or implicational powers of those sentences of natural language which involve multiple generality: instead, he had devised a wholly new means for the expression of generality, for which a sharp and straightforward explanation could be given. If the sentences of natural language had a precise and unambiguous sense, then anyone who understood such a sentence would be able to render it by means of the notation for generality which Frege had devised; if not, then so much the worse for natural language. In neither case was there any need either for a direct account of the means for expressing generality in natural language, or for a set of rules for translating sentences of natural language into Frege's improved language.

NS 6–7 (6–7)   This state of affairs induced in Frege the attitude that natural language is a very imperfect instrument for the expression of thought. At best, it works by NS 74–5 (67) means of principles which are buried deep beneath the surface, and are complex and to a large extent arbitrary; at worst, it allows the construction of sentences allowing of different interpretations, or possessing only an NS 289 (270) indeterminate sense. For reasons not connected with the expression of generality, Frege indeed came later to the conclusion that natural language is in principle incoherent: that is, it would be impossible to devise a set of rules determining the truth-conditions of sentences of natural language which would both agree with the way those sentences are used and avoid the assignment, under certain conditions, of different truth-values to the same sentence. This, of course, should not in itself be taken as a very paradoxical accusation against natural language: it must necessarily hold good if it be true—as it evidently is—that there are intrinsically ambiguous sentences of natural language, sentences, that is, for which no general rule, but only a common-sense appeal to probabilities, can remove the ambiguity. All that can be at issue is how deep this incoherence of natural language lies, that is, how fundamental are the principles governing its structure which would need to be modified if the incoherence were to be removed. Frege believed it to be very deep indeed. Undoubtedly, his predisposition to adopt such a belief was formed by the experience which the discovery of the quantifier-variable notation had given him.

BW 102-3 (68)

Ged 66n (13n)

Secondly, the conception of the step-by-step construction of sentences was deeply impressed upon Frege as a key to the analysis of language. Here it is perhaps worth while to interpose an observation which Frege did not make. There has been much inconclusive discussion by philosophers during the past few decades about where the boundary lies between logic and other branches of philosophy. Much of this discussion has resulted in the conclusion that the boundary is more or less arbitrary. Any branch of philosophy is, on this view, concerned with the analysis of the meanings of some range of words or forms of expression, with determining the truth-conditions and inferential powers of sentences containing those words or employing those forms of expression: since this is precisely what logicians do with respect to the so-called logical constants, no difference of principle appears, and the suggestion is made that the term 'logical constant' cannot be defined save by listing the expressions to which it is to apply. It is this view which forms the background to the vogue for phrases like 'the logic of achievement-verbs', 'the logic of colour-words' and even (God save us) 'the logic of God-talk'.

But, in fact, ever since Frege inaugurated the era of modern logic, there has been to hand a simple and precise principle of distinction. The basic idea of the step-by-step construction of sentences involves a distinction between two classes of sentences and, correspondingly, two types of expression. Sentences can be divided into atomic and complex ones: atomic sentences are formed out of basic constituents none of which are, or have been formed from, sentences, while complex sentences arise, through a step-by-step construction, from the application of certain sentence-forming devices to other sentences, or to 'incomplete' expressions such as predicates themselves formed from sentences, the whole construction of course

c

beginning with operations on atomic sentences. The expressions which go
to make up atomic sentences—proper names (individual constants), primitive
predicates and relational expressions—form one type: sentence-forming
operators, such as sentential operators and quantifiers, which induce the
reiterable transformations which lead from atomic to complex sentences,
form the other. (With the latter should also be grouped any term-forming
operators, such as the description operator, which form singular terms from
incomplete expressions such as predicates.) Logic properly so called may be
thought of as concerned only with words and expressions of the second type,
to which it is apparent that not only do quantifiers and sentential operators
belong, but equally modal expressions such as 'possibly', 'necessarily',
'may', 'must', etc. With words and expressions of the first type, logic is, on
this view, concerned only schematically: that is, it is concerned with the
general rules governing the subdivision of words of the first type into different
logical categories—proper names, one-place predicates, relational expressions, and so forth—and with the ways in which words of these various
different types can be put together to form atomic sentences; but not with
the senses of any particular words or expressions of these different categories.
Thus, for instance, the question whether the sense of the word 'prefer' is
such as to determine the relation for which 'John prefers ξ to ζ' stands as
transitive is of no concern to the logician as such: by contrast, the phrase
'modal logic' is well taken. This principle of distinction has, indeed, the
status only of a proposal: but it agrees so well with practice, and provides so
clear a rationale for differentiating between logical constants and words of
other kinds, that there can be little motive for rejecting it.*

We saw that, in applying the conception of the step-by-step construction of
sentences to the expression of generality, it became necessary for Frege to

* The one expression normally treated as a logical constant which, on this principle,
would be ruled out as belonging to the first type, is the sign of identity. The justification
for this exception is quite different, and might be expressed as follows. Let us call a
second-level condition any condition which, for some domain of objects, is defined, as being
satisfied or otherwise, by every predicate which is in turn defined over that domain of
objects. Among such second-level conditions, we may call a *quantifier condition* any which
is invariant under each permutation of the domain of objects: i.e. for any predicate '$F(\xi)$'
and any permutation φ, it satisfies '$F(\xi)$' just in case it satisfies that predicate which
applies to just those objects $\varphi(a)$, where '$F(\xi)$' is true of a. Then we allow as also being a
logical constant any expression which, with the help of the universal and existential
quantifiers and the sentential operators, allows us to express a quantifier condition which
could not be expressed by means of those two quantifiers and the sentential operators
alone. Thus, the sign of identity is recognized, on this criterion, as a logical constant, since
it allows us to express the condition that a predicate applies to at most one object, which
cannot be expressed without it.

invoke the general notion of a one-place predicate, thought of, not as synthesized from its components, but as formed by omission of a proper name from a sentence. Since this notion of a predicate is so crucial to Frege's whole understanding of philosophical logic, it is worth while to dwell a little more explicitly upon its character than Frege himself did. In order to give a complete account of the structure of the sentences of a language, it is necessary to describe the process whereby an atomic sentence is put together out of its parts as well as the various operations by means of which complex sentences may be constructed step by step from atomic ones. We have seen that, for Frege, these latter operations are of three kinds: first, the use of sentential operators, that is, either the attachment of the sign of negation to a sentence or the joining of two sentences by means of a connective such as 'or' or 'and'; secondly, the formation of a one-place predicate from a sentence; and, thirdly, the attachment of a quantifier to a one-place predicate to form a sentence. If we were considering natural language, we should certainly have to add other operations to this list, for instance, the introduction of modal expressions; but Frege was, as we have noted, primarily concerned with the structure of a language adequate for the expression of mathematical proposi- tions, to which many of such additional devices are irrelevant. As for atomic sentences, Frege considered them as constructed out of expressions of four kinds: logically simple proper names; functional expressions; predicates; and relational expressions. These categories of expression are, of course, precisely those which are treated of in ordinary first-order predicate logic, which is unsurprising, since the languages of which contemporary logic treats have been very little extended beyond Frege's symbolic language (save for the introduction of languages with infinitely long formulas): but, again, for an adequate treatment of the sentences which natural language permits us to form, further ingredients would have to be added—none of Frege's categories could comprise either adverbs or tense-inflections, for example. But, once more, these defects are not relevant to the analysis of the language of mathematics.

To characterize the general form of an atomic sentence, we have first to specify how a *singular term* is, in general, constructed. This specification is recursive, namely: a simple proper name constitutes a singular term; and a singular term can be formed by inserting singular terms into the argument- places of functional expressions. A one-place functional expression is here con- sidered as an expression with a gap in it, indicating where a singular term is to be placed in order to form from it a more complex singular term. Normally, this gap will occur at the end of the expression, as in such instances as 'the capital of ξ' and 'the father of ξ': but there is no reason in principle why it should not occur at the beginning, as in 'ξ 's father', or, for that matter, in the middle; all that is necessary is that it should be determinate where the term that represents the argument is to be inserted. On the other hand, there is no room, in this connection, for the admission of functional expressions containing two or more gaps, considered as having each to be filled by the same proper name or other term. Functional expressions with two gaps will have, indeed, to be considered, but these will be two-place ones, like 'the eldest child of ξ and ζ' or 'the mid-point between ξ and ζ' or 'the greatest common divisor of ξ and ζ': here the two gaps will be considered as being, in general, filled by two different terms. Since the specification of what constitutes a singular term is recursive—that is, certain expressions are recognized as singular terms outright, and instructions are then given for forming new singular terms out of already given ones—it could with reason be said that even the process of forming so-called atomic sentences is in fact a step-by-step one: but the important fact is that we are not here forming new sentences out of previously formed *sentences*, as is the case with the quantifiers and the sentential operators.

One-place predicates and two- or more-placed relational expressions are then conceived in the same general way as one-, two- or more-placed functional expressions: namely simply as collocations of words or symbols with one or more gaps. The difference is, of course, that the process of filling the gaps cannot be reiterated: what results from inserting singular terms in the gap of a predicate or the gaps of a relational expression is an (atomic) sentence, out of which further sentences can be formed only by the different processes we have already reviewed. But the same observation holds good for predicates and relational expressions as for functional expressions: there is no place here for admitting, say, predicates with more than one gap representing distinct occurrences of the same singular term.

At this point some remarks become necessary about Frege's terminology. The distinction was made above between logically simple proper names and the complex singular terms that can be constructed out of them by means of functional expressions. Frege was perfectly well aware of this distinction: indeed, he was very insistent on the difference between a logically simple and a logically complex expression. A logically simple expression may be phonemically or typographically exceedingly complex: but what makes it logically simple is that there do not exist any general rules, the knowledge of which belongs to a speaker of the language, whereby its sense can be determined from the way it is made up out of its constituents. In the case of a predicate or relational expression, a logically simple expression may even be discontinuous, as, for example, 'ξ took ζ to task'. There is in fact complexity

Gg II 66;
App 255;
NS 224-6
(207-9)

here, because of the tense-inflection, but we are here overlooking this factor: it is plain that an understanding of the words 'took', 'to' and 'task' will not suffice, or even help, to determine the meaning of 'took . . . to task'. But Frege made an eccentric use of the phrase 'proper name' to cover everything normally meant by (and everything defined above as) a 'singular term': 'proper name' did not for him imply 'logically simple', as it normally does. In what follows I shall frequently employ the expression 'singular term' or just the word 'term' where Frege would have written 'proper name': but I shall never use the expression 'proper name' specifically in its strict sense, to imply 'logically simple', without signalling the fact.

    BG 197n

    It would be an error to take the notion of logical simplicity, as conceived by Frege, as involving anything more than is implied by the definition given above. Many philosophical writers, for instance Russell, have taken it as a mark of a proper name—at least of what has a truly genuine claim to the title of 'proper name'—that it has an irreducible simplicity: it is not merely itself devoid of logical complexity, but no expression having the same meaning as it could be logically complex. There is no trace of this idea in Frege. A logically simple expression is, for him, merely one which is not composed of subordinate expressions each possessing its own sense and so contributing to determining the sense of the whole: there is no requirement that the sense which is borne by that expression *could* not be carried by one which was in this way logically complex. If a name or other expression is introduced by definition as a brief equivalent of some complex expression, then the expression so defined will itself be logically simple, even though its sense has been stipulated to be the same as that of the complex expression. Of course, we may distinguish between those expressions which are introduced by definition and those which are not; but, since Frege says very little about the senses of words not introduced by definition, this will help us little with the exegesis of Frege. Frege several times emphasized that it is impossible that every word of a language should be introduced by definition, because a definition presupposes a prior understanding of the words used in the defining expression, and the resulting circularity would make it impossible that anything should be learned from this system of explanations. He also clearly stated that the sense of a complex expression is to be regarded as made up out of the senses of the constituent words: it follows that a simple word, introduced by definition as the equivalent of a complex expression, has a complex sense. By contrast, however, Frege nowhere discussed under what conditions the sense of a word should be recognized as simple. While he stressed that it is impossible that every word should be defined, it is only very seldom that he stated, of any particular

    Ver 150 (42)

    NS 275 (255)

Huss 320;
Ged 60 (6);
BG 193

word, that it was impossible that it should be defined; examples for which he did hold this are the sign of identity, the word 'true' and the terms 'object' and 'function'. Frege appears to have acknowledged that the sense of such an indefinable expression is simple in some more ultimate way than that of words which merely happen to have been introduced otherwise than by definition, but which might have been defined if a different choice of starting-point had been made. But the notion of unanalysability played no great part in his thought, and is in no way associated by him with proper names; in particular, he advanced no thesis to the effect that every sentence is analysable into one composed wholly of indefinable expressions.

A further feature of Frege's terminological usage needs mention. He normally used the word 'relation' to mean 'binary relation' only, and similarly in talking about expressions for relations. When he wanted to refer to ternary

NS 269 (249)

relations, or to expressions for them, he expressly mentioned the number of arguments: he never referred to relations of higher degree at all, nor used the word 'relation' independently of how many arguments there were. He seldom used the word 'predicate', preferring his own neologism 'concept-word': but I shall rarely follow this example.

Properly speaking, in discussing the formation of atomic sentences, another kind of functional expression ought to have been mentioned, namely a functional expression of second level, which carries a bound variable with it, and which, in order to form a singular term, is attached to a predicate (the argument-place of which is filled with a bound variable corresponding to that carried by the functional expression or operator). This kind of expression in fact plays a role of the utmost importance in Frege's construction of the foundations of arithmetic: the most familiar example is the definite description operator (whose role in natural language is effected by the definite article). Many accounts of the foundations of logic in fact assume that the only candidates in natural language for the position of complex singular terms are what Russell called 'definite descriptions', i.e. expressions formed by prefixing the definite article to a (grammatically singular) predicative expression. Whether such accounts do or do not accord to such expressions the status of complex singular terms depends upon whether they reject or accept Russell's Theory of Descriptions. If they reject it, then such expressions are to be represented in symbolic notation as singular terms formed exactly in the way described above: that is, 'the founder of Rome' is to be construed as having the form 'the x such that x founded Rome'. On such accounts, first-level functional expressions such as those described above do not occur in natural language. Of course, it would be possible to employ a language which possessed a description operator but no first-level functional expressions: but it would become exceedingly cumbersome to do this in mathematics, as a little experimentation with a formalization of arithmetic in such a language—involving the replacement of the symbols for addition, multiplication and exponentiation by symbols for the corresponding ternary relations—will readily show. That is why neither Frege nor modern accounts of predicate logic dispense with such first-level operators. As to whether natural language contains such operators, or gets on, by means of the description operator, without them, the question has no sharp sense. The means for forming definite descriptions in natural language are certainly far more complex and varied than the simple type of construction carried out by means of first-level functional expressions as described above; at the same time, they are far from identical with the use of the device of a description operator, which involves the employment of bound variables, which do not occur in natural language. Most of the complex singular terms of natural language, therefore, are, properly speaking, neither terms formed by functional expressions nor ones formed with the description operator. Still, if it is a matter of convenience of representation, it is surely more cumbersome and unnatural to take 'the capital of France' as a concealed form for 'the x such that x is a capital of France' than to take it, as Frege does, as analogous to (say)   FB 18 '4!'.

Nevertheless, Frege did admit, and make essential use of, second-level operators of the same category as the description operator, and, to that extent, the characterization of atomic sentences given above is incomplete. Of course, once such operators are included, then the processes of forming singular terms, preparatory to forming atomic sentences, cannot be cleanly severed from the processes of forming complex sentences: for the sentence from which the predicate was formed, to which the term-forming operator is to be attached, may itself have been highly complex, involving quantifiers and sentential operators. The omission of such second-level operators in the above account was intended to avoid this complication, the better to focus attention on the important point.

This point is the necessity for distinguishing clearly—as Frege himself was at no great pains to do—between the notion of a predicate as it is required for Frege's account of the expression of generality, and the notion of a predicate as required in explaining the structure of atomic sentences. These two notions are, in fact, needed to fulfil roles of quite different kinds. The only kind of predicate or relational expression we need consider when we are concerned with the structure of atomic sentences is one which is logically   NS 19 (17) simple. In order to explain how we grasp the sense of such a sentence as

'Brutus killed Caesar', for example, we need only consider it as composed of
its three constituent expressions, the two (simple) proper names 'Brutus' and
'Caesar' and the (simple) relational expression 'killed' (here I am, as in all
cases, once more prescinding from the actual complexity of root and tense-
inflection within the word 'killed'). The relational expression may here be
regarded as a simple unitary expression, as much a linguistic entity capable
of standing on its own as are the two proper names. Like them, it cannot
form a sentence standing on its own (unless the rest of the sentence is
understood from the context); but, like them, it constitutes a word that is
physically capable of being detached from the sentence. If we represent it by
means of Greek letters to show its argument-places, namely as 'ξ killed ζ',
this is only in order to show where the proper names (or other singular terms)
have to be put in relation to it in order to form a sentence: contrast, for
example, 'ξ is married to ζ' with 'ξ and ζ are man and wife'. These indications
how the link between relational expression and proper names is to be made
have to be attached to the relational expression, and not to the proper
names, since how the link is made depends upon it and not upon the proper
names: there is no general rule determining that, e.g., 'Brutus' has to come
at the beginning, or at the end, or in the middle, of an atomic sentence. But
there is no sense whatever in which 'ξ killed ζ' is to be thought of as
formed from the sentence 'Brutus killed Caesar', or any other like it: on the
contrary, that sentence was formed from it, together with the two proper
names.

The notion of a complex predicate, thought of as formed from a sentence
by omission of one or more occurrences of a proper name, is required, by
contrast, only in order to explain sentences formed by attaching a quantifier
to it (or, more generally, expressions formed by attaching to it some variable-
binding operator, for instance the description operator). This notion is
needed at this stage because it is required to give an account of the sense of
the quantifier, and this involves an account of the truth-conditions of the
most general form of sentence that can be constructed by applying that
quantifier: the only correct characterization of this general form of sentence is
'A sentence formed by attaching the quantifier to a complex predicate'.
Once the notion of a complex predicate has had to be introduced for this
purpose, then it also becomes necessary to recognize the complex predicate
as occurring in the sort of sentence from which it was formed: it is this
which gives rise to what people have in mind when they speak about different,
equally legitimate, logical analyses of one and the same sentence. But it
is important to notice for what purpose this sort of 'analysis' is needed.
The representation of 'Brutus killed Caesar' as composed of a (complex)

one-place predicate 'ξ killed Caesar' and, in its argument-place, the name 'Brutus', is required only in order to state the general principle to which we are appealing when we recognize an inference from this sentence, together with, say, 'Anyone who killed Caesar is an honourable man', to the conclusion, 'Brutus is an honourable man'. We need this representation of the sentence, that is to say, in giving an account of inferences in which it and also some sentence involving the attachment of a sign of generality to the complex predicate in question both figure. The representation of the sentence as consisting of 'Brutus' and 'ξ killed Caesar' is quite irrelevant to any explanation of the way in which the sense of the atomic sentence is determined from that of its constituents. An inference may easily arise in which it is necessary, in order to explain the general scheme of inference appealed to, to consider the sentence, 'If Brutus killed Caesar, then Brutus's wife hated Brutus', as composed of the name 'Brutus' and the predicate, 'If ξ killed Caesar, then Brutus's wife hated ξ'. But the possibility of giving such an 'analysis' of the sentence has no bearing on the process by which we form the sentence, or on that by which we come to grasp its sense. We understand the sentence by reference to the process by which it was formed, namely as being put together out of two atomic sentences joined by the connective 'if', those atomic sentences having in turn been constructed by linking singular terms and relational expressions; the thought that one might recognize the complex predicate cited above as occurring within that sentence could be utterly remote from the mind of someone who had the firmest grasp upon its meaning.

In the same way, the notion of a complex relational expression, considered as formed from a sentence by the omission of one or more occurrences of each of two proper names, is strictly needed only when it is desired to introduce, or required to explain, some operator carrying with it two bound variables: for instance, if one wanted to introduce an operator 'Tx,y:' which, attached to a relational expression '$A(\xi,\zeta)$', yielded a sentence 'Tx,y: $A(x,y)$' having the sense of 'For all x and y, if $A(x,y)$, then not $A(y,x)$'. It is true that, although not strictly needed, the notion of a complex relational expression may be very useful in connection with what are known within formalized logical systems as 'derived rules of inference'. Thus, for instance, from any particular sentence of the form '$\exists x \; \forall y \; A(x,y)$' it is possible to infer—if desired, by a series of very simple steps—the conclusion '$\forall y \; \exists x \; A(x,y)$'. In any particular instance, there would be no occasion to invoke the notion of a complex relational expression. But once someone has carried out this chain of reasoning in several particular instances, he may notice the general pattern, and wish to record it mentally (or

c·

otherwise) to be appealed to in the course of subsequent chains of reasoning, without having on each occasion to go through all the individual steps. To express the general form of the inference, it is necessary to employ a schematic representation—such as the 'A(ξ, ζ)' used above—for an arbitrary complex relational expression; and the recognition of the general pattern thus constitutes an implicit appeal to the general notion of a complex relational expression.

Thus a simple predicate or relational expression must be recognized as occurring in any sentence in which it does occur, if we are to understand the sense of that sentence, or even recognize it as well-formed; whereas the notion of a complex predicate has to be invoked only when we have to deal with quantifiers or other expressions of generality; and, when the argument-place of a complex predicate is filled, not by a bound variable, but by a singular term, then it is unnecessary, in order to understand the sentence in which that predicate occurs, to recognize the predicate as occurring in it. Indeed, so much is implicit in saying that the complex predicate is formed, not directly out of its constituent expressions, but from a sentence in which it occurs. When the argument-place of the predicate is filled by a term, then it is only for a different purpose and in special circumstances that it becomes necessary to recognize the predicate as occurring in a sentence: namely in order to recognize the validity of certain arguments of which that sentence may form premiss or conclusion.

Unless this radical difference between the roles of the notions of simple and complex predicates is clearly apprehended, it will be easy to become confused about Frege's notion of an incomplete expression. Frege himself did not draw attention to this difference of role: having demonstrated the need for appealing to the notion of a complex predicate, if expressions of generality are to be explained, he tacitly assimilated simple predicates to complex ones. And, indeed, in one sense such an assimilation represents an economy. Once we have acquired the notion of a complex predicate, we cannot refuse to allow, as a degenerate case, the 'complex' predicate 'ξ snores', considered as formed from such a sentence as 'Herbert snores' by omission of the name 'Herbert'; it would then seem quite redundant to insist on considering, as a separate linguistic entity, the simple predicate '. . . snores'. Nevertheless, it remains the case that, strictly speaking, if 'ξ snores' is treated as a complex predicate, on all fours with, say, 'If anyone snores, then ξ snores', we do need to recognize the separate existence of the simple predicate '. . . snores' as well: for, precisely because the 'complex' predicate 'ξ snores' has to be regarded as formed from such a sentence as 'Herbert snores', it cannot itself be one of the ingredients from which

'Herbert snores' was formed, and thus cannot be that whose sense, on Frege's own account, contributes to composing the sense of 'Herbert snores'. Rather, if there is to be economy, it is the degenerate 'complex' predicate that should be dispensed with, with the sign of generality, in 'Everyone snores', being regarded as in this special case attached directly to the simple predicate.

Now complex predicates form the prototype for Frege's general notion of an 'incomplete' expression. Such expressions are said by him to contain gaps, and, further, to be *unselbständig*: they cannot subsist—they cannot stand up, one might say—on their own. If one considers complex predicates formed by the omission of more than one occurrence of the same proper name from a sentence, the purport of this is immediately clear. The complex predicate 'ξ killed ξ' cannot be regarded as literally *part* of the sentences in which it occurs: it is not a word or a string of words, not even a discontinuous string. There is no part in common to the sentences 'Brutus killed Brutus' and 'Cassius killed Cassius' which is not also part of the sentence 'Brutus killed Caesar': yet the predicate 'ξ killed ξ' is said to occur in the first two and not in the third. Such a complex predicate is, rather, to be regarded as a *feature* in common to the two sentences, the feature, namely, that in both the simple relational expression '. . . killed . . .' occurs with the same name in both of its argument-places. (Not all sentences in which the complex predicate is said to occur will be of that simple structure: but all will have such a sentence as one of their ancestors in their constructional history.) It is precisely in this sense that an expression is said by Frege to be 'incomplete': it does not consist merely of some sequence of words or symbols, but in the occurrence within sentences of such a sequence standing in a certain uniform relation to terms occurring in those sentences. It is for this reason that it cannot liberally be removed from a sentence in which it occurs and displayed on its own: we can only indicate the common feature of various sentences which we have in mind by the use, together with words or symbols belonging to the language, of the Greek letters which represent argument-places. And it is, in turn, just because the complex predicate is thus not really an expression—a bit of language—in its own right, that we are compelled to regard it as formed from a sentence rather than as built up of its components.

When we consider this doctrine in terms of complex predicates, as we have seen these are needed to explain the formation of quantified sentences, the notion of incomplete expressions appears quite unperplexing. The reason why people have found it difficult to understand Frege's doctrine of incomplete expressions is largely that they have concentrated on the degenerate

NS 246 (228)
262 (243)

Gl 60; NS
192 (177);
NS 217 (201)

Gg I 1

case in which there is a simple predicate corresponding to the complex one: or rather, failing to observe the difference in kind between simple and complex predicates, they apply Frege's doctrine to simple ones, and then, not unnaturally, find themselves unable to see its point. This is precisely one of the cases in which Frege, by looking at things from the perspective induced by his discovery of quantification, obtained a very different view of them from the familiar one. Philosophers tackling the notions of subject and predicate naturally incline to scrutinize very simple examples—atomic sentences, proper names (strictly so called) and simple predicates. But for Frege, *the* important notion of a predicate was just that notion of a complex predicate which his discovery of quantification had shown to be required. It is therefore unsurprising that he finds quite different things to say about predicates in general from those which philosophers adopting a more conventional approach find it natural to say. In contrasting Frege's approach with the traditional one, I am not merely opposing what Frege did to what used to happen in earlier times: on the contrary, even so recent a work as Strawson's *Individuals* resolutely holds to what I have described as the traditional approach to the topic of subject and predicate.

If one applies Frege's doctrine that predicates are incomplete in a sense in which proper names and other singular terms are not to simple predicates, and considers only them, then one will, rightly, be at a loss to understand Frege's thesis. Simple predicates are *selbständig* in the way that complex ones are not: they are merely words or strings of words which can quite straightforwardly be written down. In one sense, of course, they are incomplete—they do not constitute a sentence, a 'complete utterance': but, in *that* sense, proper names are equally incomplete. It is true that, in order to give an account of the rules governing the formation of atomic sentences, we must explain the 'valencies' belonging to different words—which expressions can, and which cannot, be juxtaposed, and when we have a whole sentence and when only a fragment of one. It is also true, as we have seen, that, in stating these rules, it is to the simple predicates and relational expressions that we must assign slots into which singular terms have to be fitted, rather than ascribing to the singular terms slots into which the predicates and relational expressions have to be fitted. But this does not make the simple predicates incomplete in the sense that Frege intended when he spoke of incomplete expressions. We might say that, in the case of simple predicates, the slots are external to them, whereas in the case of complex predicates, they are internal. That is, we can know what linguistic entity, considered just as a sequence of phonemes or of printed letters, a simple predicate is, without knowing anything about the slot it carries with it: the slot consists merely in the predicate's being subject to a certain rule about how it can be put together with a term to form a sentence. But the complex predicate cannot be so much as recognized unless we know what slots it carries: they are integral to its very being.

CHAPTER 3

The Hierarchy of Levels

A SENTENCE IS a linguistic unit: it is the smallest bit of language which one can use to *say* anything—to 'make a move in the language-game', in Wittgenstein's terminology. A word, regarded from a different viewpoint, is another kind of linguistic unit: it is the smallest bit of language to which one can attribute a sense.* It is also possible to ascribe a sense to a collocation of several words which does not yet form a whole sentence, but only part of one. It is obvious, however, that not every continuous sequence of words which may occur within a sentence forms a whole to which a sense can properly be ascribed: for instance, the three successive words 'shillings more on' do not form such a whole in the sentence 'The trip costs two pounds five shillings more on Sundays'. Each of the three words in that sequence has a sense, and is used in that sense in the sentence quoted: but the phrase as a whole does not have a sense. Even when a sequence of words has a sense, taken as a whole, and the words composing it occur in succession in a sentence, they may not, in that sentence, compose that or any other phrase having a sense as a whole; for instance, the sequences 'killed a man' and 'my coat tore' in the sentences 'Was what Henry killed a man?' and 'The man wearing my coat tore up the letter'.

So far we have appealed only to a vague intuitive feeling that it is meaningful

* The analysis of a sentence into words, understood in this way, will not always coincide with that which the printer makes: a verb-ending, or the superlative termination of an adjective, would on this criterion constitute a word, while certain sequences of typographically distinct words—for instance, 'New York', 'give up' and 'partial ordering'—would count only as single words by this criterion. Note that, of course, the sense, if any, which an expression carries depends upon the context in which it occurs, and, in cases of ambiguity, on the intention of the speaker. Note also that 'sense' is here being used strictly, so that an expression has, in a given context, a sense only if it is, at least in principle, unnecessary for the understanding of a complex of which it forms part to be supplied with a special explanation of that complex taken as a whole.

34

to ascribe sense not only to words and sentences, but to phrases within sentences, and to an intuitive awareness that not every sequence of words within a sentence constitutes such a phrase, not even when the same sequence might constitute one in another sentence. In order to arrive at some criterion for judging when a given sequence of words, as it occurs within some given sentence, constitutes a phrase to which sense may be ascribed, taken as a whole, and when it does not, we have first to enquire more closely what it means to ascribe sense to a composite phrase. We have seen what we are doing when we ascribe sense to an entire sentence: to do so is to say that we associate with that sentence certain conditions which have to obtain for it to be true. We have seen also what is the ground for ascribing senses to individual words: consideration of the way in which we can use and respond to new sentences that we have never encountered before compels us to recognize that the truth-conditions of each sentence are determined, in a manner implicitly grasped by the speakers of the language, by the words that compose it and the way they are put together within it. We now have to find some rationale for the ascription of sense to complex expressions which are not complete sentences.

This rationale evidently lies in the fact that a sentence is constructed in stages. Grammar already gives some indication of this. We understand implicitly, or, in studying grammar, analyse explicitly, certain rules of sentence-formation: for instance, the rule that a sentence may be constructed out of a subject, the copula and a complement, or out of a subject, a transitive verb and an object; and we likewise understand, or analyse, the various ways in which a phrase may be built up that can constitute a subject, a complement or an object. Each such phrase will be a phrase to which a sense may be ascribed as a whole, but a sequence composed of a proper part of, say, the subject-phrase together with some other part of the sentence will not, in that sentence, constitute such a phrase. Both the examples given above were of this kind: in the interrogative sentence, the subject-phrase was 'what Henry killed', and hence the sequence 'killed a man' cannot be taken as a whole in that sentence; in the second sentence, the subject-phrase was 'the man wearing my coat', and so 'my coat tore' likewise cannot be taken as a constituent phrase. But Frege did not stop short at refusing to recognize as logical wholes expressions which grammar can teach us to detect as illegitimate sequences: he rejected also certain sequences which grammar would acknowledge as units. For instance, in *Grundlagen* he explains that, in the sentence, 'The Emperor's carriage is drawn by four horses', the phrase 'four   Gl 46 horses' is not a genuine logical unit of the sentence: yet grammatically it is as good a unit as, say, 'black horses'.

In giving this ruling, Frege is not really engaged in attempting to understand how our language works, but, rather, directing attention away from the language that we have towards the reconstructed language which, in symbolic form, he wants to use for setting out and analysing mathematical proofs, and on the structure of which he wants to found his philosophical logic. It is plain that the grammatical structure of our everyday language can justly be charged with being misleading in so far as it buries the difference, which logical analysis uncovers, between a phrase of the form 'black horses' and one of the form 'four horses'; the adjective and the noun are quite differently related in the two cases. But to go further and say that the phrase 'four horses' is only a grammatical unit and not a logical unit at all is not justified: all that Frege can really claim is that, in the sentence which in his reconstructed language replaces 'The Emperor's carriage is drawn by four horses', no unit corresponding to 'four horses' appears.

The point involved in this instance is one that we have so far skated round: it would remain the same if we replaced 'four horses' by 'some horses'. We have talked of expressions of generality, and have used as examples of such expressions in natural language words like 'everyone' and 'someone'. These words of course restrict the range of the generalization to persons; and it is comparatively rarely in natural language that we use completely unrestricted generalization, as expressed by words like 'something' and 'everything'. Much more often, we employ 'some', 'every', and similar words, as adjectives, and use them together with a substantive or substantival phrase having a definite content to form a phrase, the substantive serving to delimit the range of the generalization. It was rather natural for Frege, having replaced the means for expressing generality employed in natural language by the notation of quantifiers and variables, to propose that the association of the sign of generality with a restriction of its range be abandoned, claiming, as he very explicitly did, that the same effect could always be achieved by including the content of the restriction in the predicate to which the sign of generality was to be attached. Thus instead of saying, 'There is some animal in the garden', one could say, 'There is something which is an animal and is in the garden': or, using a quantifier, one could say, 'For some x, x is an animal and x is in the garden' in place of 'For some animal x, x is in the garden'. Likewise, instead of 'Every dog barks', one could say, 'Everything barks if it is a dog': with a quantifier, 'For every x, if x is a dog, x barks' in place of 'For every dog x, x barks'. The replacement of the forms of natural language by the quantifier-variable notation does not in any way demand this further step of using unrestricted generalization. The second step is, on the contrary, quite independent of the first: and we shall see later that, harmless as it appeared, it proved in fact to be an utterly fatal step. Nevertheless, the change in the form of expression made this new step quite natural, because, given the use of quantifiers, unrestricted generalization is no more cumbersome than restricted generalization, and there is a great economy and simplification in presenting the rules of inference.

If Frege had employed restricted generalization, he would have expressed 'The Emperor's carriage is drawn by some horses' by 'For some horses x, the Emperor's carriage is drawn by x'. Here the restricted quantifier 'for some horses x' plainly corresponds to 'some horses' in just the same way that 'for some x' would correspond to 'something' in the pair 'For some x, I have trodden on x' and 'I have trodden on something'. The difference is just that already considered, namely that what, in natural language, does the work of the quantifier is a substantival expression standing in the argument-place of the predicate. But with unrestricted generalization, the quantified sentence becomes 'For some x, x is a horse and the Emperor's carriage is drawn by x': and it is now true that there is no unit of this sentence which can be taken as corresponding to 'some horses'. (We are neglecting the irrelevant point that the plural noun implies 'more than one'.)

Frege's doctrine concerning which subordinate expressions within sentences may be considered as wholes possessing a sense which is a constituent of the sense of the entire sentence thus relates to the functioning of his own reconstructed language rather than to that of the language we normally employ. Now, in order to describe in detail the various categories of expression which are recognized under this doctrine, we have to make use of the Fregean distinction between complete and incomplete expressions. Complete expressions are of two kinds (assimilated to one another in Frege's later doctrine): 'proper names' and sentences. By 'proper names' are meant, as usual, all singular terms, including complex ones; as for sentences, the sentential connectives of course provide a means whereby a sentence can be constructed having other sentences as its proper parts. These two categories of expression now form the basis of a hierarchy, the upper ranks in which are occupied by incomplete expressions of various kinds. First we have the two categories of one-place and two-place sentential operators: that is, expressions which form a complex sentence when combined with one or two sentences respectively. Next we have one-place predicates of first level: that is to say, incomplete expressions which result from a sentence by the removal of one or more occurrences of a single 'proper name'. Alongside these is the category of (two-place) relational expressions of first level: that is, incomplete expressions resulting from a sentence by the removal of one or more occurrences of each of two 'proper names'. (Frege very occasionally considered also three-place relational expressions: for the sake of simplicity, however, we can ignore these.)

We have seen that, strictly speaking, Frege ought to have treated separately of simple (one-place) predicates and simple relational expressions, and that these have really no claim to be considered as incomplete expressions; but we have seen also that, with a certain inaccuracy, Frege preferred to subsume these under the general categories of first-level predicates and relational expressions respectively. We have seen also that, so long as the language lacks any sentence-forming operators, whether primitive or introduced by definition, which are to be applied to relational expressions, the category of relational expressions does not strictly speaking need to be recognized at all: but this would be possible only if a special category of simple relational expressions were introduced, instead of subsuming these under the general category of first-level relational expressions. Moreover, we have also seen that, for the representation of frequently recurring patterns of inference ('derived rules of inference'), a recognition of relational expressions in general is essential.

At that stage in the development of his logical theory before he had assimilated sentences to 'proper names', there would have been for Frege no objection in principle to creating categories of incomplete expression related to sentences as first-level predicates and relational expressions are related to 'proper names': corresponding to predicates would be the category of one-place sentential operators, considered as consisting of all those expressions which result from a complex sentence by the removal of one or more occurrences of a single constituent sentence. Such a notion would be required if, for example, one wished, like some logicians, to employ quantifiers binding sentence-variables. Frege did not introduce such categories only because he felt no need for introducing the kind of operator whose use would demand their recognition. The hierarchy does not in fact continue on the sentence side, only on the 'proper name' side.

Still on the first level of incomplete expressions, there are, alongside predicates and relational expressions, functional expressions of one and two places. A one-place functional expression is like a predicate save that it is formed, not from a sentence, but from a complex 'proper name', by the removal of one or more occurrences of a constituent 'proper name': similarly for two-place functional expressions. So far as everyday language is concerned, the recognition of simple functional expressions would seem quite adequate: the considerations which governed relational expressions do not apply here. But in mathematical contexts, the general notion of a complex functional expression is as necessary as the general notion of a function, if a correct analysis is to be given of operators such as that denoting the derivative which can be applied to any functional expression.

Having thus arrived at the various categories of incomplete expressions of first level, the next step is to introduce those of second level. Thus we can consider predicates of second level, having a single argument-place to be filled by a predicate of first level. A quantifier is precisely such an expression: just as the simplest way of forming a sentence from a first-level predicate is to insert a proper name into its argument-place, so the simplest way of forming a sentence from a quantifier is to attach it to a first-level predicate. More generally, a second-level predicate of this kind is to be taken to be any incomplete expression formed from a sentence by omitting one or more occurrences of the same first-level predicate.

This idea may be generalized in various ways. For instance, we may consider second-level relational expressions whose argument-places are to be filled by first-level predicates: an example would be 'There are just as many Φ's as Ψ's', or, using bound variables, 'There are just as many x's such that $\Phi(x)$ as y's such that $\Psi(y)$'. (Here the capital Greek letters indicate the argument-places, just as the small Greek letters did in the case of first-level relational expressions.) A different category is composed of second-level predicates having a single argument-place to be filled by a first-level relational expression. Natural language does not possess any simple expressions belonging to this category; but a complex expression of this kind would be 'for every x, y and z, if $\Phi(x,y)$ and $\Phi(x,z)$, then y is the same as z', which expresses that a relation is many-one.

Obviously there are further categories: for instance, second-level relational expressions having one argument-place to be filled by a first-level predicate and another to be filled by a first-level relational expression. More important are predicates and relational expressions whose argument-places are to be filled by first-level functional expressions of one or two arguments. We should obtain an expression of this kind by removing each occurrence of an expression for a given function from a sentence which expressed that that function was everywhere continuous. Besides these various types of second-level predicates and relational expressions, Frege also considered second-level functional expressions. These differ from the former in the same way that first-level functional expressions differed from first-level predicates and relational expressions, namely by being formed, not from sentences, but from complex 'proper names'. These second-level functional expressions are to be subdivided according to the number and type of their argument-places. The most familiar example, outside mathematical language, of such a

functional expression of second level is the description operator already
discussed: using bound variables, this has the form 'the x such that $\Phi(x)$',
and forms a singular term ('proper name') when its argument-place is filled
by a first-level predicate.

It is important to observe that Frege does not allow for second-level
functional expressions which yield, when their argument-places are filled,
first-level functional expressions. In other words, to abandon for a moment
the practice we have so far adhered to, of speaking wholly in terms
of different types of expression, rather than the kinds of entity for
which they stand, Frege did not recognize the existence of functionals
(second-level functions) whose values were themselves functions. There
would thus be for him no such operation as differentiation: that is, the
expression 'd $\varphi(x)$/d x' would not constitute for him a genuinely unitary
expression which could be considered as having a sense. Rather, we should

WF 665   have to consider instead the expression:

$$\left(\frac{\mathrm{d}\ \varphi(x)}{\mathrm{d}\ x} \right)_{x\ =\ \xi}$$

Gg I 22   This is a second-level functional expression with *two* argument-places, one,
represented by the Greek letter 'φ', for a functional expression of first level,
and the other, represented by the letter 'ξ', for a singular term (here a
numerical term): when both argument-places are filled, the whole will
become a numerical term, standing for the value of the derived function for
the number cited as argument. The general principle here is that an incomplete expression may never be considered as derived from another
incomplete expression by the removal of some constituent expression: we
have always to start with a complete expression, and form whatever incomplete expressions we want to consider from that. This of course places
certain restrictions upon what simple expressions may be introduced by
definition: an operator for differentiation, for example, could not be introduced, but only one for the corresponding second-level function of two
arguments mentioned above. It is plain that this restriction does not in fact
hamper in any way the expressive power of a language that is subject to it:
it is also plain that it may damage its conciseness considerably. It will, in
fact, involve the use of a great many more bound variables than would
otherwise be needed. Thus, even eschewing the usual abbreviation
'$\dfrac{\mathrm{d}^2\ \varphi(x)}{\mathrm{d}\ x^2}$' for the second derivative, we could, by reiteration of the usual
notation, express that the second derivative of x^3 is $6x$ by writing:

$$\forall x \ \frac{d\left(\dfrac{d\,x^3}{d\,x}\right)}{d\,x} = 6x.$$

But, using the notation suggested above, it would become necessary to write:

$$\forall z \ \left(\frac{d\left(\dfrac{d\,x^3}{d\,x}\right) x = y}{d\,y}\right) y = z = 6z.$$

Of course, there would in fact be no reason why, in order to adhere to his principle, Frege would have had to employ so cumbersome a notation: a form such as '$(D_x[\varphi(x)]) (\xi)$' would be perfectly adequate for the expression of the second-level function with two arguments which we are considering, and then the above formula could be written:

$$\forall z \ \left(D_y \left[(D_x [x^3]) (y) \right]\right) (z) = 6z.$$

It remains that adherence to Frege's principle renders illegitimate a considerable number of convenient notations which otherwise appear natural to employ.

Viewed from the standpoint of the functions expressed, the restriction imposed by Frege's principle seems arbitrary: within mathematics, we have occasion to consider mappings of functions of numbers on to functions of numbers just as often as mappings of functions of numbers on to numbers. But from the linguistic standpoint, Frege's restriction is entirely logical. There are two ways in which the restriction can be violated. One is illustrated by the notation $\dfrac{\text{'d}\ \varphi(x)\text{'}}{d\,x}$. When a functional expression, taking the letter 'x' in its argument-place, is inserted into the argument-place indicated by the letter 'φ', we have an expression purportedly representing a function: yet it does not possess an argument-place, as a functional expression ought to do, since all occurrences within it of the letter 'x' have to be taken to be bound variables. This circumstance creates a number of awkwardnesses, when the expression for the derived function is put into an equation. When the other side of the equation is constructed out of the variable 'x', taken as governed by an implicit universal quantifier, as in

$$\frac{d\,x^3}{d\,x} = 3x^2,$$

the awkwardness remains at a theoretical level. It comes out if we write explicitly:

$$\forall x \left(\frac{d\,x^3}{d\,x} = 3x^2 \right),$$

and then enquire which occurrences of 'x' are bound by the universal quantifier '$\forall x$'. Plainly the occurrence of 'x' on the right-hand side is bound by the quantifier: but neither of the occurrences in the expression for the derivative can be considered to be bound by the quantifier, because they are already bound by the expression for the derivative; if they were not so bound, it would be possible to substitute numerals for them, which it is not, on pain of producing nonsense like

$$\frac{d\,4^3}{d\,x} = 3 \cdot 4^2 \,.$$

But when the equation is such that we desire to put something other than the variable 'x' for the argument of the derived function, the awkwardness makes itself practically felt. In the case that we want to put a numerical term for the argument, we have to supply an argument-place that was previously lacking, and write:

$$\left(\frac{d\,x^3}{d\,x} \right)_{x\,=\,4} = 3 \cdot 4^2 \,.$$

In the case that we wish to use for the argument of the derived function a term containing some other variable, we are forced to abandon the purely equational form, and resort to a complex sentence, such as:

$$\text{If } x = 5y + 7, \text{ then } \frac{d\,x^3}{d\,x} = 3x^2 = 75y^2 + 210y + 147 \,.$$

All these awkwardnesses disappear as soon as Frege's principle is adhered to, and we employ a notation such as '$(D_x\,[\varphi(x)])\,(\xi)$': we can then write, in the first case:

$$\forall y \,(D_x[x^3])\,(y) = 3y^2 \,,$$

or even, if we like:

$$\forall x \,(D_x[x^3])\,(x) = 3x^2 \,.$$

(In the latter case, the bracketed occurrence of 'x' is bound by the quantifier, the occurrence in 'x^3' by the differential operator.) In the other two cases, we can write, respectively:

$$(D_x[x^3])\,(4) = 3 \cdot 4^2$$

and:

$$\forall y\,(D_x[x^3])\,(5y + 7) = 75y^2 + 210y + 147 .$$

The other way in which it is usual to violate Frege's restriction is illustrated by the notation '$f'(x)$'. This is an enormously convenient notation, and has the great advantage of allowing the simplest possible representation of the effect of reiterating the operation of differentiating, viz. '$f''(x)$'; nor does it have the awkwardness of the other notation, for here the variable 'x' indisputably stands in the argument-place of a functional expression, so that, provided we know which function the letter 'f' represents, we may freely write '$f'(4)$' and '$f'(5y + 7)$'. But its applicability is confined to those cases in which we have to hand a single letter or sign to represent the function we are differentiating; in other cases we are forced to introduce such a letter as a temporary code, thus producing such forms as:

$$\text{If } f(x) = x^3, \text{ then } f'(x) = 3x^2 .$$

It is thus plain that, if we desire to have a notation which is both universally applicable and does justice to the logical complexity of what is being expressed, we can achieve this only by observing Frege's principle that a functional expression (or other incomplete expression) always yields, when its argument-places are filled, a complete expression.

Because Frege's ontology is so closely tied to his analysis of language, his rejection of incomplete expressions yielding, when their argument-places are filled, expressions that remain incomplete led him also to refuse to countenance functions whose values are functions. What singular terms ('proper names') stand for, in general, are, in Frege's terminology, objects: so, while for Frege there is no restriction on the type of argument which a function may have, it can only have objects as values. It may be thought that this was unreasonable of Frege, since the arguments which had such force at the level of notation do not apply at the ontological level: Frege's reply would be that we can grasp the idea of a function of a given type only via that of an expression for a function of that type; a type of function for which there is no corresponding form of expression is a chimera. These are matters which we shall have to consider when we enter upon the whole topic of Frege's ontology, that is, of the types of entity there are and for which the various types of expression stand. In the meantime, it is sufficient to observe that, on the ontological level as on the linguistic one, the loss of functions with functions as values is retrievable at the cost of a certain increase in complexity. For instance, in place of considering a mapping F which carries a one-place function f of numbers into another one-place function g of numbers, we have to consider a binary operation K_F carrying the function f and a number n into a number m = g(n): the function g can then be characterized as that function such that, for each n, g(n) = K_F(f,n).

The general principles underlying Frege's hierarchy are now apparent, and we can give a more systematic characterization of the hierarchy by *STT* adapting the notation for the theory of types devised by Church. We start with two types of complete expressions: 'proper names' and sentences. These two types are both to be considered as of level o. Given a type of expression, of some level n, we can introduce, as an (n + 1)th-level type of incomplete expression, all those expressions which can be derived from a complete expression, of one or other of the two types of complete expression, by the omission of one or more occurrences of some one expression of the given n-th level type. Furthermore, given two types of expression (not necessarily distinct), of levels n and m, we can introduce as a further type of incomplete expression all those expressions which can be derived from a complete expression, of one or other of the two types of such expression, by the omission of one or more occurrences of each of two expressions, belonging respectively to the given n-th and m-th level types: the resulting type will be of level k + 1, where k = max(n,m). To make this general formulation perspicuous, we introduce a notation for the various types, defined recursively. Let 'o' denote the type of expression which consists of all sentences, and 'i' that which consists of all 'proper names'. Then, if α is a type of level n, [α] is to be the type consisting of all expressions formed from a sentence by omission of one or more occurrences of a single expression of type α, and (α) is to be the type consisting of all expressions formed from a 'proper name' by the omission of one or more occurrences of a single expression of type α; [α] and (α) will both be of level n + 1. Further, if β is another type of level m, then [α,β] is to be the type consisting of all expressions formed from a sentence by the omission of one or more occurrences of some expression of type α, and the simultaneous omission of one or more occurrences of an expression of type β; while (α,β) is to be the type consisting of all expressions formed from a 'proper name' by the same means: the level of both [α,β] and (α,β) will be k + 1, where k = max(n,m). Thus first-level predicates are of type [i], first-level relational expressions of type [i,i], unary and binary sentential operators of types [o] and [o,o] respectively, and one- and two-place first-level functional expressions of types (i) and (i,i). There will be second-level predicates of types [[i]], [[i,i]] and [(i)], being predicates whose argument-places have, respectively, to be filled by first-level predicates, relational expressions and functional expressions. 'There are just as many x's such that $\Phi(x)$ as y's such that $\Psi(y)$' is of type [[i],[i]], while the description operator is of type ([i]): the expression '$(D_x[\varphi(x)]) (\xi)$' is of type ((i),i).

The general principles underlying the construction of this hierarchy of types of expression are thus as follows. First, the principle that we have discussed, namely that each type of incomplete expression has to be taken as derived from one or other of the two types of complete expression, sentences and 'proper names'. Secondly, each expression and each type must be determinate as to the number and types of its argument-places, and the type of expression formed by filling them. That is to say, there can be no such thing as an incomplete expression which will, on different occasions, allow a different number of arguments; nor one which will, on different occasions, allow expressions of different types to fill any one of its argument-places; nor, again, expressions which, according to context, now yield a sentence, now a singular term. (Natural language does apparently contain expressions for relations with a variable number of arguments, called by Nelson Goodman 'multigrade relations': for instance, such expressions as *CI* 50 '. . . are collinear', '. . . are fellow-countrymen', and the like. Such expressions would have, on Frege's principles, to be treated either as ambiguous or as predicates applying to sets.) Further, two incomplete expressions which differ either as to the number or the types of their argument-places, or as to the kind of expression they yield when their argument-places are filled, belong, on this principle, to different types. And thirdly, these three factors—the number and types of the argument-places, and the type of complete expression from which it is formed—completely determine the type of an incomplete expression. That is, each type has to be regarded as comprising *all* the expressions that can be formed by starting either with a sentence or with a 'proper name', and omitting one or two expressions of a given type or types, at one or more occurrences of each.

In order to interpret the notion of an incomplete expression of level higher than the first, we have to know precisely what is meant by saying that an incomplete expression occurs in a sentence or 'proper name', and by speaking of omitting it from that sentence or proper name and subsequently filling the gap so created by another incomplete expression of the same type. Let us take the case of a first-level predicate's occurring within a sentence—the case we have to consider in explaining second-level predicates of type [[i]]. The first-level predicate is an expression

$$.\ .\ .\ .\ \xi\ .\ .\ .\ .\ \xi\ .\ .\ .\ .$$

which has been formed from some sentence

$$.\ .\ .\ .\ a\ .\ .\ .\ .\ a\ .\ .\ .\ .$$

by removing one or more occurrences (here two) of some proper name 'a', and leaving gaps indicated by the Greek letter 'ξ'. If in some longer sentence there is a part of the form

$$.\ .\ .\ .\ t\ .\ .\ .\ .\ t\ .\ .\ .\ .$$

formed by filling those gaps with some (simple or complex) singular term 't', then we shall regard this part as constituting, within that larger sentence, an occurrence of the given first-level predicate. This we have already seen, when we previously discussed the notion of a (complex) predicate. But we have in fact to give a slightly more general characterization of when a first-level predicate may be said to occur within a sentence, because it may occur with its argument-place filled with a bound variable, or with some expression containing a bound variable. What we require, in fact, is the notion of a *pseudo-term*, that is, an expression which is built up in the same way as a singular term save that bound variables as well as simple proper names (individual constants) have been used as the basis of the construction; if we are considering a language containing function-quantifiers, then we must also allow that bound function-variables may have been used in the process of construction, as well as function-symbols. Then, where 's' is a term or pseudo-term, any part of the main sentence that is of the form

$$.\ .\ .\ .\ s\ .\ .\ .\ .\ s\ .\ .\ .\ .$$

will constitute an occurrence of the predicate. (Naturally, where 's' and 't' are different,

$$.\ .\ .\ .\ s\ .\ .\ .\ .\ t\ .\ .\ .\ .$$

will not constitute such an occurrence.)

Let us suppose that 's' is a pseudo-term and 't' a term, and that the main sentence has a part

$$.\ .\ .\ .\ s\ .\ .\ .\ .\ s\ .\ .\ .\ .$$

and another part

$$.\ .\ .\ .\ t\ .\ .\ .\ .\ t\ .\ .\ .\ .\ .$$

If, for instance, we take 's' and 't' to be numerical (pseudo-) terms, then 's' might be '$x + 5$' and 't', say, '$4!$': the expression

$$.\ .\ .\ .\ x + 5\ .\ .\ .\ .\ x + 5\ .\ .\ .\ .$$

must, of course, occur within the scope of some quantifier binding the variable 'x' within the main sentence, and does not compose a logically unitary expression having a sense on its own; it is related to a sentence as a pseudo-term is related to a term. The main sentence

$$----- \ .... \ x + 5 \ .... \ x + 5 \ .... \ ----- \ .... \ 4! \ .... \ 4! \ .... \ -----$$

thus contains two occurrences of the given predicate. We may form a second-level predicate of type [[i]] by removing both of these occurrences and leaving a gap. Since the expression which has to be omitted is itself an incomplete expression, however, this process of removing the incomplete expression from the sentence cannot involve the removal also of the terms or pseudo-terms that, in the main sentence, occupy the argument-place of the expression being removed: so the resultant second-level predicate takes the form

$$----- \ \Phi \ (x + 5) \ ----- \ \Phi \ (4!) \ ----- \ ,$$

where the letter 'Φ' shows the gaps left by the removal of the first-level predicate, and the expressions in brackets show by what its argument-place was filled in its two occurrences in the original sentence. As in the case of first-level predicates, so here even more so: the expression displayed, containing the letter 'Φ', is not to be identified with the second-level predicate, but is only a representation of it; the second-level predicate is not an isolable bit of the sentence, but only a pattern discernible within it. What this pattern consists in is determined only by the explanations, taken jointly, of how the second-level predicate is formed, and what constitutes a result of filling its argument-place. This we now have to explain. Suppose that we now want to specify the sentence that will result from filling the argument-place of this second-level predicate with a new first-level predicate

$$. \, _ \, . \, _ \, . \ \xi \ . \, _ \, . \, _ \, . \ \xi \ . \, _ \, . \, _ \, . \ \xi \ . \, _ \, . \, _ \, .$$

formed from a sentence

$$. \, _ \, . \, _ \, . \ b \ . \, _ \, . \, _ \, . \ b \ . \, _ \, . \, _ \, . \ b \ . \, _ \, . \, _ \, .$$

by the removal of three occurrences of a proper name 'b'. This sentence will be the result of replacing, in the above representation of the second-level predicate, the occurrence of '$\Phi(x + 5)$' by the result of inserting '$x + 5$' in the argument-place of the new first-level predicate, and the occurrence of '$\Phi(4!)$' by the result of inserting '$4!$' in the argument-place of that same predicate. In other words, at all the occurrences of the original first-level predicate which were omitted to form the second-level predicate, there now stand the results of inserting in the new first-level predicate the same terms or pseudo-terms which stood, at those occurrences, in the argument-place of the original predicate.

The way in which the hierarchy of types was specified presented it as a potentially infinite one: it allowed for the possibility of considering third-level predicates, for instance of type [[(i)]], third-level functional expressions, for instance of type (((i))), and, consequently, incomplete expressions of fourth, fifth, or any higher, level. At each stage, it would be necessary to specify what is meant by an occurrence in a sentence or singular term of an expression of the next lower level, what is to be considered as the result of removing one or more such occurrences, and what the result of inserting other expressions of the same type in the argument-place or places of the resultant incomplete expression: but, once this has been explicitly stated for the case of second-level predicates, the principles according to which it is to be done should be clear for all other cases. What, rather, we need to consider at this stage is the sense in which the hierarchy is to be considered as potentially infinite, and the extent to which its higher levels are needed at all.

Given a very simple language consisting of proper names, primitive predicates and relational expressions, and sentential operators, it would be possible to define with respect to it the entire hierarchy of predicates and relational expressions of first, second, third levels, and so on. It would, however, be pointless. There are two primary reasons for recognizing a given type of incomplete expression. First, that there are in the language simple signs belonging to this type, either primitive or ones introduced by definition. The universal quantifier (binding individual variables) is a simple sign of type [[i]], i.e. a second-level predicate with first-level predicates as arguments: so, since Frege wishes to employ this quantifier, he has to recognize the existence of the type [[i]]. We have already seen that, if he had chosen to draw the distinction between simple and complex expressions in a different way, he need not, on this score alone, have concerned himself with the entire type of, in general, complex second-level predicates of type [[i]]: but this would become necessary if one wanted to give a general characterization of the kind of definition one might use to introduce other simple expressions of the same logical type as the universal quantifier. The second kind of reason makes it mandatory to recognize the existence of the entire type, simple and complex: namely, that the type in question constitutes the kind of expression to which a given simple expression can be attached to form a sentence or complex singular term. From this point of view, the use of the universal quantifier makes it necessary to recognize the type of expression, considered strictly as an incomplete expression, to which it can be attached, namely first-level predicates (type [i]). These two kinds of consideration should be kept separately in mind, because they are compelling in a different degree.

Frege in fact freely employs higher-level quantification—quantifiers binding variables of the type of first-level predicates, relational or functional expressions. These quantifiers are themselves expressions of third level, but in the second way their use provides a more compelling reason for recognizing the existence of the various types, viz. [[i]], [[i,i]], [(i)] and [(i,i)], of second-level predicates. Bs 26; Gl 72; Gg I 19–25

The situation is different with functional expressions. If the language contains only simple proper names and first-level functional expressions, it is again possible, though pointless, to generate the hierarchy of functional expressions whose arguments are themselves functional expressions: but it would be impossible to introduce second-level functional expressions whose argument-places were to be filled by predicates, because there would not be in the language any complex singular terms which contained any predicate within them. For this type—([i])—of incomplete expression to be introduced, there has to be at least one primitive operator, such as the description operator, of this type. If, however, we want a compelling reason for considering the general type of expressions of this form, including complex ones, we should have to have some reason for using or introducing an operator which was to be attached to such expressions.

It is now clear in what sense the hierarchy is infinite, but only potentially so. Incomplete expressions being features, not ingredients, of sentences, there is no sense in discussing whether a language contains incomplete expressions of any given type, unless one is asking the restricted question whether it contains any *simple* expressions of that type. With the exception noted in the case of functional expressions, for any type one could always discern that pattern in sentences which constitutes the occurrence of an expression of that type. But unless there are in the language simple expressions which take expressions of the given type in their argument-places, or, at any rate, simple expressions of the given type, it will in general be pointless to single out within sentences expressions of that kind. Frege does not envisage a language which contains primitive expressions of every level, nor, indeed, a language which contains more than finitely many primitive expressions; and therefore, in discussing any particular language, it will probably be necessary to consider only some quite small finite number of types of expression. On the other hand, there is no type in the potentially infinite hierarchy which he would have any objection to considering if some point could be shown for doing so: it would be possible to introduce expressions of any type in the hierarchy by definition if one so desired, and, indeed, to introduce a corresponding kind of variable capable of being bound by quantifiers.

In his later doctrine, Frege regarded sentences as just a special kind of complex singular term. If this is done, then predicates become just a particular kind of functional expression with one argument-place, relational expressions a particular kind of functional expression with two argument-places. The hierarchy then becomes subject to a great simplification, there being only one type of complete expression, which we may call 'g'; only one type, (α), of incomplete expression with a single argument of type α; and only one type, (α,β), of incomplete expression with two arguments, of types α and β respectively. There are then only two types of first-level expression, (g) and (g,g); while, disregarding order, there are just five types of second-level expression—((g),g), ((g),(g)), ((g), (g,g)), ((g,g),g) and ((g,g),(g,g)). This simplification provided a powerful motive for the assimilation, implausible at least at first sight, of sentences to complex 'proper names': but the other grounds for, and the consequences of, this assimilation remain to be explored later.

The systematic exposition of Frege's hierarchy of types reveals it as essentially the same doctrine as Russell's simple theory of types, formulated in terms of Frege's notion of incomplete expressions. Russell's theory of types is a theory of what expressions can be accepted as significant: only certain functions—those of the appropriate type—can 'occur significantly' as arguments of other functions; expressions which violate the theory of types are simply meaningless. Frege's hierarchy of types also provides a theory of significance. It is a fundamental principle of Frege's theory, and one which he reiterates repeatedly, that a symbol for an incomplete expression can never occur without its argument-place, or argument-places, with the sole exception of a bound variable in that of its occurrences in which it occurs next to the quantifier or other operator that binds it. This principle is at once evident from Frege's whole way of regarding the language which he constructed for the purpose of logical analysis: for if an attempt at rendering some incomplete expression of given type had the wrong number or types of argument-place, it simply could not be recognized as a rendering of that incomplete expression. The result of adherence to this principle is that, in Frege's symbolic language, it is not merely forbidden, but actually impossible, to violate the distinctions of type. If, for example, we attempt to insert a first-level predicate '$F(\xi)$' in the argument-place of another first-level predicate '$G(\xi)$', we do not get a sentence at all, for '$F(\xi)$' still contains a gap, represented by the 'ξ', which remains to be filled. If, on the other hand,

Gg II 147n;
BW 243

we attempt to insert a proper name '*a*' in the argument-place of a second-level predicate 'M*x* $\Phi(x)$', we are equally unable to do this, because '*a*' contains no gap into which we can insert the bound variable '*x*'. Thus, so far as Frege's own symbolic language is concerned, his doctrine of levels does not so much prescribe the meaninglessness of certain expressions, as draw attention to their non-existence. It earns the right, however, to be called a theory of significance by the light which it throws, indirectly, upon natural language. Natural language constantly violates the principle that an expression which is by its sense incomplete cannot occur without its argument-place. Most adjectives, for example, are either first-level predicates or first-level relational expressions with their argument-places suppressed. When it is needed, the argument-place can be restored by prefacing the adjective with the copula; and it is evident that we cannot come to understand what such an adjective means save by learning the sense of the predicate formed by attaching it to the copula—for instance, we can learn what 'slimy' means only by learning what it is for something to be slimy. Lacking the device of bound variables, however, natural language provides numerous contexts in which the adjective occurs without the copula, and thus without its argument-place: if such contexts are represented in Frege's symbolic language, the corresponding predicate will contain a bound variable (or complex pseudo-term) in its argument-place. Frege would say that we can only gain an explicit understanding of the tacit workings of natural language—the way in which the sense of this context is related to the use of the adjective in its primary position, after the copula—by observing how such uses of the adjective do duty for what is achieved in the symbolic language by means of bound variables. But, precisely because natural language violates the principle that each expression incomplete in sense must carry with it its argument-place(s), it does become possible within natural language to form meaningless but grammatically correct sentences which violate the distinctions of type and in the symbolic language could not be constructed at all. For instance, the sentence 'Chairman Mao is rare', while perfectly grammatical, is meaningless because 'rare', though in appearance just like a first-level predicative adjective, has the sense of a second-level predicate. The diagnosis and explanation of such failures of significance in natural language can be easily accomplished by reference to the impossibility of constructing a corresponding sentence in the symbolic language.

Russell's reasons for advancing the simple theory of types are in fact exactly the same as Frege's reasons for observing his distinctions of level: though Russell's notation does not register it, he has just the same theoretical notion of incompleteness, which he calls 'ambiguity'. When the theory of types was first presented, the ramified hierarchy and the simple hierarchy were inter-twined: but, as is well known, Russell gave quite different reasons for them, and rightly so, because quite different principles are involved. His reasons for accepting the simple hierarchy are given in Part IV of Chapter II of the Introduction to the first edition of *Principia Mathematica*. Here he says that a propositional function 'is essentially an ambiguity, and . . . , if it is to occur in a definite proposition, it must occur in such a way that the ambiguity has disappeared, and a wholly unambiguous statement has resulted'. This is exactly Frege's notion of an incomplete expression, whose argument-place must be filled in any sentence in which it occurs. He continues, ' "(x). φx" . . . is a function of φx̂; as soon as φx̂ is assigned, we have a definite proposition, wholly free from ambiguity'. In other words, in our Fregean terminology, '∀x Φ(x)' is an incomplete expression in which ' Φ' represents the argument-place: when the argument-place is filled, we shall obtain a complete sentence. 'But', he goes on, 'it is obvious that we cannot substitute for the function something which is not a function: "(x). φx" means "φx in all cases", and depends for its significance upon the fact that there are "cases" of φx, i.e. upon the ambiguity which is characteristic of a function. This instance illustrates the fact that, when a function can occur significantly as argument, something which is not a function cannot occur significantly as argument. But conversely, when something which is not a function can occur signifi-cantly as argument, a function cannot occur significantly. Take, e.g. "x is a man", and consider "φx̂ is a man". Here there is nothing to eliminate the ambiguity which constitutes φx̂; there is thus nothing definite which is said to be a man. A function, in fact, is not a definite object, which could be or not be a man; it is a mere ambiguity awaiting determination, and in order that it may occur significantly it must receive the necessary determination, which it obviously does not receive if it is merely substituted for something determinate in a proposition.' It is evident that what Russell is here labori-ously arguing for is just what Frege achieved, without the necessity for argument, by the rules concerning the distinctions of level, and the presence of argument-places, which govern the structure of his symbolic language.

We have a definite rule, given any type α of expressions, of level n, say, for specifying the type [α] of expressions of level n + 1, if we see any reason so to proceed to the next level. All the types of Frege's hierarchy are thus determinate provided that the basic ones—types o and i—are determinate. The type o of sentences we may take as relatively unproblematic. The same cannot at all be said of the type i of 'proper names'. It might be thought that it is a matter of little importance if uncertainty should arise within natural language about which expressions are to be recognized as 'proper names' and which not, since Frege's hierarchy is, properly speaking, only defined for a language constructed according to the principles of his symbolic language, and natural language deviates from that structure in numerous ways. But this would be a mistake. Frege's symbolic language is a reconstruction of natural language, not something built up entirely from scratch. Once we know which expressions we are to take as proper names, we can proceed with the reconstruction; but, until we know that, we cannot even begin. To this question we now turn.

CHAPTER 4

Proper Names

FB 1-7

BG 195-6,
Gl 51, 57,
66n, 68n

IF WE DO not know precisely what constitutes a 'proper name' in Frege's sense, that is, a singular term, then we likewise do not know precisely what constitutes any one of the various categories of incomplete expression save the sentential operators: for, as we have seen, these categories are defined inductively, starting with 'proper names' as a basis, with respect to their level. Yet it is notorious that Frege never troubled to give any precise characterization of the category of 'proper names'. He usually contented himself with using as a criterion the fact that an expression constituted a substantival phrase in the singular, governed by the definite article. He remained indifferent to the fact that this criterion would be inapplicable to those languages which lack a distinction of form between singular and plural, or to those even more numerous languages which lack a definite article: and equally indifferent to the fact that, even in those languages to which the criterion is applicable, it is inexact in both directions. Frege was perfectly well aware that there are expressions satisfying this criterion which he would not wish to admit as proper names, and others which fail the criterion which he would wish to admit: but he was content to allow the whole distinction between proper names and expressions of other kinds to depend upon intuitive recognition, guided only by the most rough and ready of tests.

Such an attitude is not acceptable. It is true enough that it is often necessary to invoke a human capacity for direct recognition of the possession by something of a certain quality, and sometimes impossible to characterize that quality without reference to our capacity for recognizing it. For instance, none of the several attempts to analyse the notion of something's being funny even looks like providing an individual who lacked all sense of humour with a means for picking out what other people would find amusing: no analysis is available to us of the concept *funny* save as that which is apt to provoke the characteristic reaction of amusement. But an analysis of this kind is tolerable only if we can give a clear description of the response in terms of which we are characterizing the quality: and, in the case of proper names, no such description is to hand. It might be objected that, in some cases, the only description of the response that can be given is the production, when suitably elicited, of a particular verbal description: a man's capacity to recognize colours, for instance, is principally manifested by his capacity to say, e.g., 'Red', when asked, 'What colour is that?', unlike his capacity to recognize something as funny or as painful, which is manifested by non-verbal behaviour. So, the objection runs, it is likewise sufficient to suppose that our capacity to recognize expressions as being proper names is primarily manifested by our ability to apply to them the description 'proper name'.

In this case, however, to be satisfied with such an account would be pitifully inadequate. It is not merely that there would be a great many borderline cases which some would be inclined to accept as proper names and others to reject, with no principle on which either could defend his judgment. It is, rather, that such an account would be unable to display the connection between the classification of some expressions as proper names and the use of those expressions. Being funny and being red are detachable qualities: someone with no sense of humour or someone totally colour-blind misses a lot, but there is nothing else which we can infer that he misses just in virtue of his missing these things. By contrast, someone who cannot recognize an expression as a proper name must either fail to understand the expression, or else must simply fail to grasp the concept 'proper name' but yet be capable of coming to grasp it. Of someone totally colour-blind we may well say that he is never capable of acquiring the concept *red*: but someone who understands language must already have that by means of which he could come to learn which expressions are proper names and which are not, if we could but find the correct means to explain this concept to him.

An expression's belonging to the category of proper names is a feature of its sense: and we ought to be able to say with what aspect of its sense this feature is connected. Frege's use of the expression 'proper name' for all singular terms, including highly complex ones, of course reflects his con- SB 41-2 viction that the primary use of such terms within a sentence is to pick out determinate objects for which the term stands in the same way as a proper name, in the strict sense of 'proper name', stands for its bearer. Now Frege's use of the ontological term 'object' is strictly correlative to his use of the linguistic term 'proper name': whatever a proper name stands for is an object, and to speak of something as an object is to say that there is, or at least could be, a proper name which stands for it. The question therefore naturally arises in which realm, the linguistic or the ontological, the primary

Frege

principle of classification is to be applied. Frege applies the term 'proper name' to some expressions about which we might feel dubious concerning the correctness of its application to them, on grounds other than their complexity: to numerical terms, for instance; and, correlatively, he applies the term 'object' to the entities for which they stand—thus, for example, to numbers. If we leave the application of the term 'proper name' to be determined by intuition, then it remains uncertain at which level, the linguistic or the ontological, this intuition operates: are we forced to count numerical terms as proper names, in Frege's sense, because our intuition compels us to recognize numbers as objects; or is it, rather, the other way round, namely that we are forced to count numbers as objects because our intuition compels us to recognize numerical terms as proper names?

p. 136   Peter Geach, in *Three Philosophers*, opts for the former alternative. According to him, Frege's use of 'proper name' is completely straightforward and unproblematic (save for his extending it to complex terms as well as logically simple ones): it is because he held the questionable philosophical view that numbers are objects that he classified numerical terms as proper names, in accordance with the principle that whatever stands for an object is a proper name. If this account were correct, we should be left wholly in the dark how it is to be decided whether numbers, or entities of any other sort, are objects or not: or what, indeed, making a decision on this issue amounted to. We should, admittedly, be aware that a decision that numbers were or were not objects had consequences for our categorization of certain linguistic expressions; and, if we follow further what Frege says about the structure of sentences in a well-constructed language, we should see that the decision in which linguistic category numerical terms were to go would in turn have consequences for the form that such terms were to take and the way in which they were to be used within sentences. But it would remain totally obscure what principle we were deferring to in allowing these consequences to follow. We should be bound to conceive the matter as being one of recognizing that a certain form of expression was more appropriate to the character of what was being spoken of than an alternative form: but what it was in the character of the entities concerned—in this case, numbers—that we were thus responding to, and which we signalized by saying of them that they were, or that they were not, objects, would remain quite opaque.

Geach's account of the matter is, however, false to Frege's whole attitude to the relation between linguistic and ontological categories. The picture which Geach is using is that of first apprehending a linguistic expression as standing for a certain entity, e.g. a number, then recognizing, by the character of that entity, to which ontological category it belongs, and finally assigning the linguistic expression to an appropriate category in accordance with the categorization of the entity it stands for. Such a picture is remote from Frege's thought. For him it would be impossible to know what it was that some expression stands for in advance of knowing what sort of thing it was (where 'sort' means 'logical category'). More precisely, the only way in which this would be possible would be by a failure to grasp the general concept of something's belonging to the logical category in question. Someone might very well be able to employ proper names, and know what objects they stood for, without having the general notion of 'an object', and in this sense it could be said of such a person that he knew what it was that some proper name stood for, without knowing that that thing was an object: but it would not be possible for someone to have the general notion of 'an object', and know, of some proper name, what thing it stood for, in advance of recognizing that the thing in question was an object. The logical categories into which the things we talk about are divided reflect, for Frege, the different categories of expression which occur in our language; and the division of these expressions into categories depends, in turn, upon the different ways in which they are used in sentences. Someone may well not have formed explicitly the conception of a general kind of expression of which he is well able to use particular instances. But to say that someone had the general conception of a certain ontological category, but was uncertain whether what a given expression stood for belonged to that category or not, would be to say likewise that he was uncertain whether or not the expression in question belonged to the corresponding linguistic category; and that would mean that he was uncertain about the way in which the expression functioned in our language. If, however, he was uncertain about the way in which an expression functioned—where this was not a superficial question of idiom or of stylistic nuance, but of a fundamental feature of its use, such as determines the distinctions of category—then he could not possibly be said to know what it was that the expression stood for.

Thus it is essential for Frege to be able to maintain that each expression may be recognized as belonging to its logical category or type from a knowledge of the way in which it is employed in the language. The distinction between proper names and expressions of other types must be one that can be drawn in wholly linguistic terms, without the necessity for any scrutiny of the things for which the respective expressions stand. Proper names form, indeed, a linguistic category of the most general possible kind: they constitute the only complete expressions that fall short of being sentences. In *Grundlagen*, Frege does recognize the possibility of sub-dividing the category

Gl 26, 60-2,
85; Ne 74;
Gg I xviii;
Gg II 74
of objects, and therefore, presumably, the category of proper names correlatively, into concrete and abstract objects, though he does not attempt a
formulation of the principle of this distinction. The assignment of an
expression to the category of proper names must accordingly depend only
upon the most general features of its use.

It is therefore essential, if Frege's whole philosophy of language and the
ontology that depends upon it are to be even viable, that it should be
possible to give clear and exact criteria, relating to their functioning within
language, for discriminating proper names from expressions of other kinds;
and, if we are to obtain a clear grasp of the way in which natural language
could be reconstructed so as to take on the logically perspicuous form of
Frege's symbolic language, it must be possible to give such criteria as they
apply to the proper names of natural language. If we were unable to be sure
which expressions of natural language were to count as proper names, we
should be unable to carry out the reconstruction. It is thus all the more
surprising that Frege gave so little attention to this problem. It is to be
presumed, not that he thought it unnecessary, but that he thought it unlikely
that anyone would seriously challenge the claim that it could be accomplished.

In giving such criteria, we must presuppose some knowledge of the
language to which they are to be applied. The classification of an expression
as a proper name relates to its use in the language, and therefore it is proper
to suppose that the criteria of the classification are to be used by someone
familiar with that use. It is therefore legitimate to leave at an intuitive level
the recognition of sentences as well-formed or as ill-formed. Mere appeal to
what does and what does not constitute a well-formed sentence will not,
however, suffice to enable us to distinguish proper names from all other
expressions: it is, for instance, implicit in the form of expression for generality
employed in natural language that the word 'nobody' can meaningfully
stand wherever a personal proper name can meaningfully stand (except in
vocative position), and so we must apply other tests to establish that 'nobody'
is not a proper name. These further tests can only relate to the correctness or
incorrectness of certain simple patterns of inference, recognition of which
may again be left at the intuitive level.

What we are devising is a set of criteria for natural language as we know it.
Certainly, if Frege's philosophy of language is sound, the category of proper
names is to be recognized within every conceivable language. But the
principle on which they were to be distinguished, if formulated in such a
completely general way, could only relate to the kind of sense which they
had, that is, to the general form of the semantic rules governing them. What
these are to be taken to be, i.e. what in general the sense of a proper name

consists in, is something which we shall have to enquire into; but that is not the topic of our present enquiry, which is merely to establish that, within the languages we normally use, we can distinguish proper names by reference to certain very simple and evident features of their use.

The inference-patterns to which appeal has to be made necessarily involve expressions of generality. Our language has the feature that the same verbal expression is used for first-order and for higher-order generalization: the word 'something' may represent generalization over objects, or over properties or relations. We shall therefore assume that the word 'something', or the corresponding word in whatever language we are concerned with, can be picked out and is understood, but we shall not assume a knowledge of the distinction between first-order and higher-order generalization. Many natural languages have the feature, tiresome for our purpose, that there is a difference in expression between generalization over persons and over things: so the expression we really to need consider is not the word 'something' but the phrase 'someone or something': to save prolixity, however, I shall write merely 'something', or, when a particular example calls for it, 'someone' (and correspondingly 'it', or on occasion 'he', for 'he or it').

The fundamental form of inference with which we are concerned is existential generalization: roughly speaking, it is a necessary condition for an expression 'a' to be a proper name that it should be possible to infer from a sentence containing it the result of replacing in that sentence the expression 'a' by the word 'something'. This condition is already enough to exclude the word 'nothing' from the category of proper names. But even this condition needs emendation. Since the same word may function in different ways in different contexts, the criteria we are seeking should determine whether or not an expression is a proper name in a particular context: they therefore should apply exactly to every context. But from 'If Peter is still alive, we shall be rescued' it is not possible to infer 'If someone is still alive, we shall be rescued'. We must accordingly reframe the requirement to demand that, from any sentence containing 'a', it shall be possible to infer the result of replacing 'a' by 'it' and prefixing the whole by 'There is something such that . . .'. In a familiar way, we represent this as the demand that, from any sentence '$A(a)$', it shall be possible to infer 'There is something such that $A(it)$'.

This test does not exclude the word 'something' itself: so we make the further requirement that, from two sentences '$A(a)$' and '$B(a)$', it shall be possible to infer 'There is something such that $A(it)$ and $B(it)$'. Of course, in simple cases, e.g. when '$A(a)$' and '$B(a)$' are both of the form 'a is w', where 'w' is some adjective, the conclusion could be expressed in a simpler and more everyday form: but we are concerned with formulations which cover all possible contexts, and it is instructive to note how much we have to approximate to the quantifier-variable notation in order to achieve such formulations. This second requirement excludes not only the word 'something' itself, but also many occurrences of indefinite substantival phrases, such as the phrase 'a sheep': this phrase fails the test as applied to the sentences 'Jones owns a sheep' and 'Henry ran over a sheep'. On the other hand, it does not rule out all occurrences of such phrases: for instance, the phrase 'a poet' passes this test, as it occurs in the two sentences 'Richard was born a poet' and 'Henry has become a poet'. This is, of course, because, in the (slightly unnatural but clearly intelligible) sentence 'There is something such that Richard was born it and Henry has become it', the word 'something' serves to express higher-order generality: we have yet to devise criteria to exclude this possibility.

Our criteria do not as yet rule out the word 'everything': so we may lay down as a third requirement that a disjunction 'A(a) or B(a)' of two sentences may be inferred from 'It is true of a that A(it) or B(it)'. This criterion can also be regarded as excluding plural noun-phrases. It is true that it would be easy to rule them out explicitly, and, indeed, they have already been implicitly ruled out by the requirement that the singular pronoun 'it' be substitutable for 'a' without destruction of the well-formed character of the sentence: but we allowed as a valid criticism of Frege's own crude criterion that it could not be applied to a language lacking a plural inflection of nouns or verbs, and so we may note, as a principle that could be invoked for such languages, the failure, for a plural noun-phrase 'b's', of the inference from 'It is true of b's either that A(they) or that B(they)' to 'Either it is true that A(b's) or it is true that B(b's)'. This failure does not, however, does not always occur: e.g. from 'It is true of undetected murders either that they are very rare or that they do not take place at all' one can infer 'Either it is true that undetected murders are very rare or it is true that undetected murders never take place at all'. This is, of course, because '. . . are very rare' and '. . . do not take place at all' are not first-level predicates: but we cannot invoke the notion of a first-level predicate, which, as we have seen, is defined in terms of that of a proper name.

The criteria we have given so far serve to separate proper names (i.e. singular terms) from other substantival phrases, plural or indefinite, involving in one way or another the expression of generality. That is, they distinguish proper names from substantival phrases of other kinds when such phrases stand in contexts in which proper names could meaningfully stand. They do not, however, rule out expressions which are not proper names, when these stand in positions in which a proper name could not meaningfully be placed. To handle such cases, we have to proceed along different lines.

The difficulty arises at the most basic level. An indefinite noun-phrase is ruled out by our criteria when it occurs as grammatical subject or object: e.g. from 'A policeman struck him' and 'A policeman charged him with assault' it is impossible to infer 'Someone both struck him and charged him with assault' ('There is someone such that he struck him and he charged him with assault'), so 'a policeman' in this context does not qualify as a proper name. But our criteria do not suffice to exclude the same phrase when it occurs as predicate: from 'Henry is a policeman' and 'Peter is not a policeman' it is possible to infer 'There is something such that Henry is it and Peter is not it'. Thus we are not yet able, even in the prototypical case of a singular subject-predicate statement, to distinguish the subject as a proper name and the predicate as not being a proper name. We are in no better position in cases in which the predicate is grammatically an adjective.

The rationale of the distinction was called in question by F. P. Ramsey. *FM* 116-17 Acknowledging that not all pairs of expressions, even with the help of the copula, can be combined to form meaningful sentences, he still questioned why, in a singular subject-predicate statement, we should be disposed to assign a certain priority to the subject, why, that is, we are inclined to regard the subject-term as fixing what the statement is *about*, and the predicate as supplying what is said about that thing. 'Socrates is wise', on this way of looking at it, says something about Socrates: what it says about him is that he is wise. But may we not, with equal right, view it as saying something about being wise, namely that that is one of the things which Socrates is?

Ramsey is, indeed, perfectly right in supposing that, in providing a rationale for distinguishing singular terms from predicates, we can gain nothing by an appeal to the intuitive, and very indeterminate, notion of what is being talked *about*: the second of the two above means of answering the question what someone who asserts that Socrates is wise is talking about is certainly not wrong, and may, according to the context in which the assertion is made, on occasion be the more natural of the two answers to give. If we want to use the notion of 'talking *about* something' in some precise sense, to mark logical distinctions, then we must first provide ourselves with the means of drawing these distinctions, and then define our sense of 'about' in terms of them: it is useless to attempt to draw precise distinctions by the help of the notion 'about' left to be applied in a purely intuitive way. But Ramsey was saying more than this: he is attacking the view of language which makes it natural to take singular terms as being of level o in the hierarchy, but the predicates which may be attached to them to form

D*

singular statements as being of level 1—the same tendency as that which
led Frege to classify proper names as complete expressions, but predicates
as incomplete expressions of first level. If Ramsey were right, there would be
no possibility of giving formal criteria for distinguishing proper names from
all other expressions. We should, at best, be able to devise criteria for distinguishing two large classes of expression, one consisting of singular terms
and the other of predicates: but there would be no general characterization
by means of which we could specify which class was which—we could
identify them only by means of sample members of each class.

Now it is perfectly true that, on Frege's own principles, there exist two
alternative analyses of an atomic sentence such as 'Socrates is wise'. We may
indeed regard it as composed of the proper name 'Socrates' and the incomplete first-level predicate 'ξ is wise': but we may alternatively regard
it as composed of the same first-level predicate inserted into the argument-
place of another incomplete expression 'Φ (Socrates)'. Ramsey's question
is why the former of these analyses should be regarded as in any way more
basic than the latter. Or rather, Ramsey is really attacking the whole conception of a hierarchy of expressions of different level, and thus denying the
distinction between the two analyses: and with this denial goes a denial that
proper names such as 'Socrates' can properly be regarded as 'complete'
expressions in contrast to predicates such as '. . . is wise'. On such a view, the
only complete expression is a complete sentence, which is complete in
virtue of its forming a linguistic expression by means of which it is possible
to say something—to perform a linguistic act, or 'make a move in the
language-game'. Proper names and predicates, as neither of them yet
forming complete sentences, are, on this view, equally incomplete. They do
not, indeed, have the same kind of incompleteness; otherwise two names,
or two predicates, would serve just as well to form a sentence as a name and a
predicate. We have, therefore, to have some conception of logical valency, of
different categories of expression, governed by rules determining that
expressions of certain categories will fit together to form a sentence, while
expressions of certain other categories will not. But this does not, on a view
such as Ramsey's, justify us either in thinking of any expression which
falls short of being a sentence as in any sense complete, nor in taking the
different *kinds* of incompleteness—the different valencies—as being different
levels, so that, having taken '. . . is wise' to be of first level, we find ourselves
having to construe 'Socrates' as being either a complete expression of level 0
or an incomplete expression of level 2.

We have seen already that Frege's general notion of an incomplete
expression relates to something much deeper than this conception of logical

valency—the laws governing which expressions may be combined to form sentences. Rather, the notion of an incomplete expression was required for a satisfactory explanation of the way in which expressions of generality function: an incomplete expression (predicate), as we need to employ the notion for this purpose, is not merely metaphorically but literally incomplete; it is something formed from a sentence by omission, rather than something that was assembled on its own in the course of constructing the sentence from which it can be so formed. This, however, is not what we are now concerned with. This general notion of a complex predicate, considered as an incomplete expression in the full sense, is something that can be defined only in terms of the notion of a proper name, that is, as what results from a sentence by the omission of one or more occurrences of a proper name; we therefore have no problem of distinguishing between a proper name and a predicate in this general sense. But we also saw that, in order to explain the construction of atomic sentences, e.g. singular statements compounded out of a proper name and a simple predicate, we do not need to invoke the notion of expressions which are incomplete in this full-blooded sense. It is only for the sake of economy that Frege assimilates simple predicates to complex ones. Considered as among the basic ingredients out of which we construct sentences, simple predicates are not literally incomplete: we must regard the singular statement as put together out of the proper name and the predicate, rather than regarding the predicate as being formed from the sentence by omission of the proper name. If incompleteness is ascribed to simple predicates, this can only be as a means of expressing the conception of logical valency. And, indeed, in this connection the ascription of incompleteness to the predicates rather than to the proper names is almost irresistible. The predicate has, as it were, a hook in one particular place (usually in the front) to which something must be attached if it is to occur in a sentence: whereas, although admittedly the proper name does not by itself constitute a sentence, we cannot visualize it as having a hook in any particular place which must be attached to something if a sentence is to be formed; the proper name may occur at the beginning, at the end, or in the middle of the sentence.

However, although, no doubt, this fact has some influence on us in making the distinction between proper names as complete and predicates as incomplete seem natural to us, it is a quite superficial feature, and does not constitute an answer to Ramsey's doubts. The error in Ramsey's argument emerges, rather, from a consideration of Aristotle's dictum that a quality has a contrary but a substance does not: the peculiarities of Aristotle's notion of substance are not, of course, in question here, and we may replace 'substance' by 'object'. To say that a quality has a contrary is to say that, for any predicate, there is another predicate which is true of just those objects of which the original predicate is false, and false of just those objects of which the original predicate is true. This is therefore the simplest case of the formation of a complex predicate: if 'F(ξ)' is a predicate (which may be a simple predicate, but is in general to be regarded as having been formed from a sentence 'F(a)' by omission of the proper name 'a'), then 'It is not the case that F(ξ)' is likewise a predicate, formed from 'It is not the case that F(a)' by the omission of 'a'. To say that an object does not have a contrary is to say that, in general, we cannot assume that, given any object, there is another object of which just those predicates are true which were false of the original object, and conversely. We may put this in terms of the legitimacy or otherwise of certain forms of definition, rather than of the formation of complex expressions. Given the predicate 'wise', we may introduce a new predicate, say 'foolish', by stipulating that, for every proper name 'a', 'a is foolish' is to have the same truth-value as 'It is not the case that a is wise': but we cannot, given the name 'Socrates', legitimately introduce a new name, say 'Nonsocrates', by the stipulation that, for every predicate 'F(ξ)', 'F(Non-socrates)' is to have the same truth-value as 'It is not the case that F(Socrates)' —however severely we restrict the range of predicates to which this stipulation is to be applied.

   In order to frame this idea as a definite criterion, we have to consider sentences involving double generality, and this involves some awkwardness in relation to natural language. Making allowance for such awkwardness, however, the following embodies the idea. Suppose that we have a sentence 'S(t,u)' involving two expressions 't' and 'u' both of which pass the tests for proper names which we have already laid down. We now enquire, with respect to 't', whether we may assert 'There is something such that S(it, any-thing) if and only if it is not the case that S(t, that thing)': if we may, then 't' is not a proper name. Likewise, with respect to 'u', we enquire whether we may assert 'There is something such that S(anything, it) if and only if it is not the case that S(that thing, u)': if we may, then 'u' is not a proper name. (In these schematic sentences, the 'it' relates to the 'something', and the 'that thing' to the 'anything'.) Thus, for example, if 't' is 'Socrates' and 'u' is 'wise', 'S(t,u)' being 'Socrates is wise', then we may assert 'There is something such that anyone is it if and only if it is not the case that that person is wise', and hence 'wise' is not a proper name; but we cannot assert 'There is someone such that he is anything if and only if it is not the case that Socrates is that thing', and so 'Socrates' passes this test for being a proper name.

   We recall the distinction we have drawn between two kinds of analysis of a sentence into its constituents. A sentence is constructed out of component words, and we have to assume on the part of a speaker of the language an implicit understanding of the way in which the truth-conditions of the sentence are determined from the words of which it is composed and the manner in which they are put together. This kind of analysis relates to the sense of the sentence, and the constituents of the sentence, with respect to an analysis of this kind, are just the primitive component words together with any subordinate complex expression which is formed at some stage in the process of building up the sentence. Of course a metaphor is involved here—there is no actual procedure of building up the sentence by stages out of its components: but we have seen that we must presume a tacit understanding of the sentence as resulting from such a process of construction in order to account for the way in which a speaker of the language can derive from his knowledge of the senses of the words the truth-conditions of the sentence. Unless a sentence is ambiguous, there is only one correct analysis of any sentence, when we are concerned with an analysis which relates to sense. The other kind of analysis is needed in order to determine the validity of inferences in which the sentence may be involved, and it is unnecessary, for someone to understand the sentence, that he be aware of the possibility of an analysis of this kind: in this sort of analysis, the 'constituents' into which the sentence may be analysed may be complex incomplete expressions which we form from the sentence itself by omitting some other expression or expressions from it, and do not need to have occurred in the process of building up the sentence to which the first sort of analysis relates. Thus, to take a basic type of example, it is essential for recognizing the validity of certain inferences in which it may occur that we be able to construe 'Brutus killed Caesar' as divisible into the name 'Brutus' and the predicate 'ξ killed Caesar', or, again, into the name 'Caesar' and the predicate 'Brutus killed ξ'; but neither of these analyses is relevant to the mechanism by which we grasp the truth-conditions of the sentence—an analysis with respect to sense has to take it as compounded out of the two names 'Brutus' and 'Caesar' and the relational expression 'killed'.

Now, with respect to an analysis of the second type, it is indeed true that, on Frege's own principles, we must admit not only the analysis of 'Socrates is wise' as resulting from putting the proper name 'Socrates' in the argument-place of the first-level predicate 'ξ is wise', but also the analysis of it as resulting from putting the first-level predicate 'ξ is wise' in the argument-place of the second-level predicate 'Φ (Socrates)'. This latter is admittedly a degenerate case of a second-level predicate: but it cannot be dismissed as spurious; if we had no other types of example of second-level predicates, we should have no use for the notion; but, once having it, we have to admit it as applying to this case. Where, then, lies the difference—in effect, denied by Ramsey—between these two analyses?

Analyses of the second kind relate to inferences, and, in particular, to inferences in which generality is involved in premisses or conclusion. Which analysis is relevant depends upon the range of generality involved. If 'Socrates is wise' occurs as one premiss of an inference the other premiss of which is 'Anyone who is wise disregards fashion', then only first-level generality is involved, and the first analysis is the appropriate one. I shall not attempt to construct an example demanding the second analysis, for this would look intolerably cumbersome in natural language, which employs abstract nouns and other periphrastic devices to avoid generality of higher than second level: but what would be needed would be third-level generality, i.e. generalization which, when expressed by means of the quantifier-variable notation, would use bound variables for second-level predicates, of which 'Φ(Socrates)' could be taken as an instantiation. The second-level predicate 'Φ(Socrates)' does have a contrary, just as any first-level predicate does. A second-level predicate represents a quality of a quality, and, given any such second-level quality, there is another possessed by just the first-level qualities which lacked the original second-level quality.

On Ramsey's conception, there would be no genuine distinction between objects and second-level qualities: the supposed difference would correspond merely to the shift in perspective involved in passing from taking, e.g., 'Socrates is wise' to be saying something about Socrates to taking it as saying something about being wise. But, unless the distinction is maintained, it is impossible to recognize the correctness of the Aristotelian thesis that an object has no contrary: we should be unable to understand generalization over objects, as opposed to generalization over all the things that might be true of a first-level quality. A little reflection on such a state of affairs shows it to be impossible: we should be unable to explain, not merely generality, but the truth-conditions even of the most basic atomic statements. For these, the conception of a proper name as standing for an object about which we are asserting that the predicate is true of it is inescapable, whatever may be the case for the extension of this notion to other contexts. It is true that, when our language reaches a certain degree of complexity, we may want to admit the notion of such a second-level predicate as 'Φ (Socrates)': but we could not explain the conditions under which a sentence which resulted from putting a first-level predicate in the argument-place of this second-level predicate was true or false unless we already understood those conditions via the construal of that same sentence as resulting from putting the name 'Socrates', viewed as standing for an object, in the argument-place of the first-level predicate.

This criterion, based on Aristotle's observation that a substance has no contrary, was of value in showing the rationale of regarding the distinction between proper name and predicate in a singular statement as constituting a distinction between *levels* of expression—precisely the view assailed by Ramsey. As an instrument for identifying expressions as proper names it is, however, clumsy, involving as it does double generality. We needed, as we saw, some further criterion, because those we had devised up to that point served to exclude substantival expressions not proper names, and therefore involving generality, standing in grammatical positions accessible also to proper names, but not to exclude predicative expressions functioning merely as predicates. They did not exclude these latter because the tests related to the use of the word 'something', which in natural language can indifferently serve to express first-level and second-level generality. The tests also failed to rule out indefinite or plural substantival phrases standing in grammatical subject-position, but followed by a grammatical predicate which in fact is not of first level, as in 'Undetected murders are rare'. The reason for this failure is the same as in the former case. Counter-examples of this second kind require particular attention. The 'Aristotelian' criterion will, despite its cumbrousness, rule out any predicate functioning merely as a predicate, e.g. 'a man' in 'Plato is a man': but, so far as it can be applied at all without intolerable linguistic awkwardness, it will not rule out 'undetected murders' in 'Undetected murders are rare'. There is nothing of which just those things are true which are false of undetected murders, i.e. something which is frequent just in case undetected murders are rare, on the decrease just in case undetected murders are increasing or constant, etc. The application of the criterion would depend on our tacitly restricting the range of the universal quantifier to second-level predicates like 'is rare': the failure of the criterion, when so applied, results just from the fact that there is a distinction of level between 'undetected murders' and 'rare' analogous to that between 'Socrates' and 'wise'.

What we need, therefore, is some guide to distinguishing directly between a use of an expression of generality, for instance 'something', to indicate first-level generality and one involving second-level generality. This is not in itself too difficult to supply, because, our language being as it is, an actual ambiguity sometimes arises, and we have means for resolving it. Suppose that someone says, 'George dropped something on his toe'; I can always ask, 'What was it that George dropped on his toe?', and I might be given the answer, 'A hammer'. If I now ask further, 'Which hammer?', my informant does not have to be able to tell me; but my question was legitimate—it

Cat 5.3ᵇ. 24

has an answer, whether known or not. Contrast this with 'There is something which George has never learned how to use'. If I ask, as usual, 'What is it that George has never learned how to use?', I may be given the answer, 'A motor mower'. If I now press further, and ask 'Which motor mower has George never learned how to use?', it is just possible that I might be told, 'The one he keeps borrowing from his neighbour—he can manage others all right'—in which case the speaker was using 'something' in the original sentence to express first-level generality: but the probability is that my question will be rejected as displaying a misunderstanding. The speaker did not mean that there is some particular motor mower of which it is true that George has never learned how to use it, but, rather, that what George has never learned how to do is: to use a motor mower. If the speaker had intended by the word 'something' to express first-level generality, then his answer, 'A motor mower', would have been an incomplete answer to my question what George had not learned to use: but, as it was, the answer was a complete one, not admitting of further specification.

It is just by this criterion that we can in practice resolve ambiguities arising from uncertainty whether an expression of generality is meant to be taken as being of first or second level. As we thus employ it, the criterion is that the expression of generality is to be taken as having been of second level if the answer to a request for specification is treated as complete (as shown by the rejection of requests for further specification), although the answer was not a proper name but an indefinite or predicative expression. To use it in this form for our purposes would obviously involve circularity, since we wish to distinguish first-level from second-level generality in order to help in determining when an expression constitutes a proper name. We may, however, avoid circularity by saying: The generality was of second level if a point may be reached where a demand for specification is still grammatically well constructed, but is nevertheless rejected as illegitimate.

Note that we have not laid down that, whenever a demand for further specification is grammatically in order, we have still not attained a proper name. The question, 'Which Cambridge?' (expecting an answer such as 'Cambridge, Mass.') is grammatically licit and may be perfectly sensible: but this does not impugn the status of 'Cambridge' as a proper name. The name 'Cambridge', as used of a city in the United States and of one in England, is in fact equivocal, in just the same way that 'bat' is equivocal as used of a mammal and of what a cricketer or baseball player uses, or that 'prime' is equivocal when used of natural numbers and of beef. The question 'Which Cambridge?' has the same sort of force as 'What kind of bat?' or 'Which sense of "prime"?'; we are able to borrow the idiom which is employed in 'Which bat?' to convey this force, just because that idiom does not have, in connection with a proper name, the kind of use which it does when we ask, 'Which bat?' or 'Which batsman?' To appeal to this fact, however, would involve us in giving an account of when a word was used in two distinct senses, so we do well to eschew it here: our criterion, as stated, involves no such appeal.

From 'Ten years ago undetected murders were very common' and 'Now undetected murders are rare', one may legitimately infer 'There is something which ten years ago was very common and now is rare', so that 'undetected murders' passes that particular test for being a proper name. However, by our criterion, the 'something' in the conclusion of this inference expresses generality of second level: for, if someone asks, 'What is it that ten years ago was very common and now is rare?', and is told, 'Undetected murders', he cannot acceptably ask further, 'Which undetected murders?'. Likewise, if someone says, 'There is something which Wittgenstein was and Frege never was', and, on being asked, 'What?', replies, 'A hospital porter', he cannot further be asked, 'Which hospital porter was it that Wittgenstein once was, but Frege was not?' Since, therefore, we now have a criterion for distinguishing between first-level and second-level generality, we may now require, in all the criteria for proper names relating to inferences involving generality, that the generality involved be of first level.

It would be foolish to claim that the criteria so far laid down would provide a method admitting of no exceptions for distinguishing proper names from descriptions of other sorts. Moreover, in application to any one language, they could without doubt be simplified by exploiting features of that language not held in common with all other natural languages. The purpose of the enterprise has not been a practical one, to enable anyone who did not know how to apply Frege's categorization of expressions into proper names and others to acquire the means of doing so: so far as I am aware, with some exceptions of a kind not yet discussed, no one who has read Frege finds the slightest difficulty in discerning which expressions would count for him as being proper names. Rather, the purpose has been to make it plausible that sharp criteria could be given, which were not ad hoc in the sense of relying on highly contingent features of the languages to which they were applicable, and were of the general kind that Frege's theory requires.

As we saw earlier, for Frege the application of the ontological category-term 'object' is dependent upon the application of the linguistic category-term 'proper name', and not conversely. We can find criteria for an expression's being a proper name—Frege gave crude criteria for this, and we have been attempting to state more precise ones—but it would be senseless to FB 18 lay down criteria for something's being an object: we could not know what a thing was at all unless we knew whether it was an object or not, for we should not even know what form of expression we might use to refer to it; and we could not know what it was even meaningful to say about it, for it is part of Frege's doctrine that whatever can meaningfully be said of an object cannot be meaningfully said of something that is not an object, and conversely. Thus it is not because Frege has first decided that classes are objects that he calls class-terms proper names; it is because class-terms— e.g. 'the class of odd perfect numbers', 'the class of people who are both painters and poets', etc.—fulfil his criteria for being proper names that he calls classes objects. For this reason it is essential that the criteria for the application of 'proper name', as Frege uses it, should relate to the linguistic behaviour of the expressions to which it applies or of which it is refused, rather than to the character of the entities for which they stand.

But it is natural to suspect that, if such highly general 'grammatical' criteria are used, all sorts of expressions will have to be admitted as proper names which it would be, not merely philosophically tendentious, but downright absurd to speak of as standing for objects. We use a wide variety of substantival expressions of all kinds—gerundives, infinitives, abstract nouns—derived from other parts of speech, and these often constitute, or can be used to form phrases constituting, singular terms: that is, words or phrases which function like singular terms in respect of their immediate grammatical role. It would seem absurd, however, to think of all these as standing for objects: to suppose, for instance, that there is such an object as the identity of the murderer (which must be distinct from the murderer himself, since the murderer may be known to many people, while the identity of the murderer is known to him alone) or the whereabouts of the garden hose. The platoon commander's lack of a map of the area was fatal to the operation: are there then such objects as lacks (some of which certain people have, but others of which simply are)? Almost any adjective permits the formation from it of an abstract noun: are there then such objects as sliminess, shininess, reciprocity and incomparability?

The immediate reaction which such examples prompt is, in part, the right one: namely that the use of such abstract nouns and noun-phrases is only an easily dispensable turn of speech. In some instances, this does not take us very much further. To say that the police do not know the identity of the murderer is only an idiomatic way of saying that the police do not know who the murderer is: unfortunately, the clause 'who the murderer is', grammatically a substantival clause, satisfies those of the tests we have so far devised for being a proper name. Thus, if Holmes knows who the murderer is and the police do not, then there is something which Holmes knows and which the police do not know: and this use of 'something', while we should not ordinarily regard it as expressing generality of first level, does not satisfy our condition for an expression of second-level generality. But in other cases, a transformation—just the transformation that would come most readily to hand if one had to explain the use of such abstract nouns— eliminates any occurrence of a substantival expression. To say that the Axiom of Choice is equivalent to the comparability of cardinal numbers is just to say that the Axiom of Choice holds if and only if all cardinal numbers are comparable; to say that cleanliness is next to godliness is to say that a cleanly man is better than any man who is neither cleanly nor godly; and the remark about the platoon commander's lack of a map simply means that the operation failed because the platoon commander had no map of the area.

It would, however, be contrary to Frege's outlook to make indispensability a criterion for an expression's being a proper name. Indeed, he might well be thought to pay too little attention to it. As we shall see, when, in *Grundlagen*, he is arguing that numbers are objects, it suffices for him to GI 57 observe that, besides the adjectival use of number-words, there occurs, in arithmetical statements, also a substantival one, as in, e.g., 'The number 5 is prime', and that, in this substantival use, number-words satisfy his criteria for being proper names. It does not appear to occur to him to enquire whether this substantival use of number-words is dispensable, whether, that is, we could express e.g. 'The number five is prime' by means of a sentence in which the word 'five' occurred only adjectivally. Indeed, it is impossible to say with any confidence what Frege's reply to the present difficulty would have been, since, while he admits a large range of types of abstract object, he neither cites any of the abstract nouns we are presently considering as standing for objects, nor displays any awareness of the danger of being engulfed by a proliferation of abstract objects of this kind.

Probably it is fair, at this stage, to set aside, for special subsequent consideration, those substantival phrases which provide what Quine has called opaque contexts—contexts in which the substitutivity of identity fails—partly because this is such a special feature which in any case throws doubt upon their status as proper names, and partly because Frege had a special doctrine concerning such contexts, although he primarily considered only those which grammatically constitute clauses. Thus, if Rome is the capital of Italy and Italy is the most beautiful country in Europe, then Rome is the capital of the most beautiful country in Europe: but from the fact that the murderer is the secretary of the Club, and everybody knows the identity of the secretary of the Club, it does not at all follow that everybody knows the identity of the murderer. Together with such phrases, we may set aside clauses such as 'who the murderer is' and, equally, 'that Redmayne is the murderer' as it occurs in 'The police know (believe, suspect, etc.) that Redmayne is the murderer'. As for subordinate clauses not constituting opaque contexts, Frege, in his later period, did indeed admit these as standing for objects. We shall have to give this doctrine special consideration: but it is not part of our present problem.

SB 42; Gl 64 Frege expressly considered points, lines, moments, weights, shapes, directions and the like to be objects. He implicitly also so categorises Gl 65; Gl 106n colours: and it is impossible to see any consideration which would compel the recognition of 'the number seven', but not of 'the colour red', as standing for an object, or of 'the direction of the Earth's axis', but not of 'the colour of the Emperor's state robe'. Colour-words, like number-words, have both an adjectival and a substantival use: the substantival uses seem strictly parallel, although the adjectival uses are not. But the colour-words, used as nouns, should not be equated with the abstract nouns formed in the usual manner from the adjectives: it is red, not redness, which is a primary colour or which is complementary to green.

Abstract nouns derivative from adjectives or verbs have a fairly well-defined and uniform set of uses: they are much used as objects of verbs expressing mental attitudes ('I dislike unpunctuality', 'He always notices untidiness'), and, alone or in phrases, as replacing substantival clauses governed by 'that' or 'how' ('He misjudged the importance of the religious disagreements' = 'He misjudged how important it was that people disagreed on religion'): they are also used in conjunction with a large number of what may be called expressions for general structure ('depends on', 'involves', 'is a special case of' and the like). This brief characterization certainly does not exhaust their uses, and there are other forms of expression apt to those large ranges of abstract nouns, particularly ones formed from verbs, which denote states ('He gained his freedom', 'The building is no longer in occupation'). Nevertheless, it is by and large true that learning to handle such abstract nouns is a single process, like learning to use comparative adjectives, and that there is a fairly direct and uniform means of transforming sentences containing them into ones employing the corresponding adjectives or verbs. Colour-words, used as nouns—as opposed to the correlative words ending in '-ness'—stand in sharp contrast to this: their use is linked with that of a special vocabulary of predicates and relational expressions ('primary', 'chromatic', 'warm', 'complementary to', 'deeper than', 'darker than', 'tones with', 'lies between', etc.) which are used either only in this connection or else in special senses which have to be learned. Doubtless anything that can be said by means of this vocabulary, with colour-words used as nouns, could be re-expressed by sentences in which the corresponding colour-words appeared only as adjectives; in some cases, the transformation would be easy, in others it would depend upon a thorough understanding of the principles of application of these predicates: but it would in no case consist merely in a conversion of one general idiom into another. We might say that, by equipping our language with this special vocabulary for talking about colours—comparable to the vocabulary we have for talking about numbers— we are taking colours seriously as objects, in a way in which we do not take consistency, discouragement, partisanship and the rest of the motley host of abstractions seriously as objects.

To put the matter in this way may suggest that there is no firm boundary: whether an expression which satisfies our formal criteria is to be taken as a genuine proper name, albeit of an abstract object, depends, not indeed on the impossibility of extruding it from the language without loss of expressive power, but on the extent to which it is embedded in a special vocabulary; this will, of course, be a matter of degree, and we are therefore free to draw the line according to taste. But there is more of a general principle under-lying the contrast that has just been drawn than this, and it is a principle which has been much explored in recent philosophical work, and one first introduced into philosophy by Frege, and much exploited by Wittgenstein: that with a name must be associated a criterion of identity (the term 'criterion of identity' is itself Frege's). If we are to understand an expression   Gl 62 as standing for an object, then we must be able, in Frege's vivid phrase, 'to recognize the object as the same again': we must, that is, know under what conditions some other term will stand for the same object. If, for instance, I am told, 'This is the River Windrush', and I have no idea how to determine whether it would be right, at some other place or other time or both, to say once more, 'This is the River Windrush', then I know nothing about the expression 'the River Windrush' save the bare fact that it was right to say, 'This is the River Windrush', at that very place and time: I thus do not know what object was being named, or, indeed, that the expression used was being employed as a *name* of an *object* at all. It could have meant, 'This is beautiful', or anything: and even if I know what proper names in general are, and have gathered, from some clue or other, that the expression I was being given was intended as a proper name, I still know nothing about the object named save that it was there then; I therefore know nothing about the use of the name. To the extent that I am uncertain how to 'recognize the object as the same again', not only can I not be said to know what object it is, but I also do not know what is true of it. If, for instance, I know that a river flooded last winter, but do not know what would establish that it was or was not the same river as that of which I am now being given the name, I shall not know, either, what would establish that it was true of the River Windrush that it flooded last winter. In this example, I can know how to recognize the object whose name I am being told as the same again only by being aware (what in this instance the form of the name betrays) that the name is being used as the name of a river, and by knowing how to apply the expression 'same river'. Certainly, the expression ' . . . is the same river as . . . ' cannot in all cases be analysed as meaning ' . . . is a river and is the same as . . . ', though we shall see later that this fact has been misconstrued by some writers. That is, the expression ' . . . is the same as . . . ' does not have a sense that could be applied independently of knowing whether what it was being applied to was a river: to know the sense of 'river' requires learning, specially for this case, the sense of 'same river'. This is most easily seen from the fact that there exist words with distinct senses, where the difference in sense lies wholly in the different way in which 'the same' may be used as attached to those words. If, for instance, it is asked how many books a library contains, the question is ambiguous: we have to know whether 'book' is being used in the sense in which a writer may be said to have written sixteen books, or that in which someone may be said to be able to balance sixteen books on his head. Just the same ambiguity arises if I am asked, 'Is that the book I saw you reading yesterday?': I might reply, 'Well, it is the same *work*, but not the same *copy* of it'. In both cases the ambiguity arises solely because we have two different senses for the expression 'same book' (counting of course involves identity, because it is part of the criterion of counting correctly that the same object is not counted twice). The difference of sense concerns only the criterion of identity associated with the word 'book', not the criterion of application associated with it, where the criterion of application is that which determines when it is correct to say, 'That is a book': with sentences of this latter form there is no room for the ambiguity to arise—the criterion of identity is irrelevant to the truth or falsity of the statement. Such examples are enough to show that the criterion of identity is to be taken as part of the sense of the general term: if I say, 'It is the same book', meaning, 'It is the same work (not necessarily the same copy)', I am not using the phrase 'the same' in any weaker or less strict sense than if I had meant, 'It is the same copy'—it may well be *exactly*, *literally*, the same work; it is the word 'book' which I am using in a sense different from that in which the same sentence might have carried the other meaning. These examples also show that the criterion of identity is not derivable from the criterion of application: however thoroughly I have mastered the criterion for determining when it is right to say, 'That is a book', I can never derive from it the criterion which determines when statements of the form, 'That is the same book as the one which . . . ', are true.

Some common nouns (nouns that admit plurals) possess a sense which associates with them both a criterion of application and a criterion of identity, while others, together with most adjectives, are connected only with a criterion of application. Thus, in ordinary speech (however it may be with geographers and meteorologists), the word 'wind' should be assigned to the latter group: it makes little sense to ask, 'Is it the same wind blowing, or a different one?' Almost all adjectives belong in the second group also: no particular criterion of identity is associated with 'blue' or 'smooth', but that will be invoked which is appropriate to the kind of object being said to be blue or smooth. For this reason, as has often been pointed out, again in the first place by Frege, it makes no sense to ask after the number of blue things Gl 54 or of smooth things in a room. For some adjectives, indeed, we could say that derivatively a criterion of identity was attached to them, in so far as they may be meaningfully applied only to objects belonging to some range having a common criterion of identity: for instance, only a human being may be said to be penurious, and so one could ask after the number of things in a room to which the adjective 'penurious' applied, for then, of course, it would be the penurious *people* in the room who would be counted. But the distinction between the two kinds of general term cleaves pretty closely to the grammatical distinction between noun and adjective: though there are many common nouns to which only the vaguest criterion of identity is associated (e.g. 'noise', 'idea', 'trouble'), still with almost all there will be contexts in which the use in connection with them of the word 'same' or 'different' will not be wholly empty.

Now among nouns with which a criterion of identity is associated, there will be many to which the same such criterion is attached: e.g. 'man', 'woman', 'tailor', 'coward'. 'A is the same man (woman, tailor, coward) as B' really can be analysed as 'A is a man (woman, tailor, coward) and A is the same person as B'. And among any such class of nouns, associated with the same criterion of identity, there will always be one which is most general, i.e. which applies to all those objects to which any general term in the class applies, that is, to all those objects for which that is the appropriate criterion of identity. It may require discussion to identify these most general terms: one might at first be uncertain, for example, whether or not the criterion for 'same person' was always the same as that for 'same animal', or, again, whether or not there exists a general criterion for 'same organism' to which 'same animal' is subordinate (in the sense that 'is the same animal as' could be equated with 'is an animal and is the same organism as'). But that it must be possible to identify such most general terms, one for each criterion of identity that is employed, it seems impossible to doubt. Let us call such terms 'categorial predicates' and the classes of objects to which they apply 'categories'. (On this use, then, categories are large classes of *objects*: henceforth, to avoid confusion, we shall not refer to Frege's yet more general totalities of objects, concepts, relations, functions, etc., as 'categories' but as 'types'.) Among the common nouns having some associated criterion of identity, but not as general in application as the categorial predicates, are some which have the feature that they cannot cease to apply to any object to which they apply: i.e. the criterion of identity is such that they could not apply to some object at one time and not at another. 'Tailor', for instance, is emphatically not such a noun: the same man may at one time have been a tailor and now be one no longer. But 'horse', though not a categorial predicate, is of this kind. 'Horse' is not a categorial predicate because the very same criterion of identity that is used for horses is also used for, e.g., cows, and, if not for quite all animals, at any rate for all vertebrates. But it belongs to this criterion of identity that the same animal could not formerly have been a horse and now be a cow. Admittedly, stranger metamorphoses take place: but if a visitor from another planet were uncertain whether or not horses and cows were different phases in the life-cycle of a single species, he would not have our concepts of *horses* and *cows*. Common nouns exhibiting this feature have in recent literature been given the technical designation 'sortal predicates', and we may conveniently call a class of those objects to which such a sortal predicate applies a 'sort'.

A wide variety of common nouns, then, have as part of their sense a criterion of identity, and this we may express by saying that involved in grasping their sense is knowing to what sort, or at least category, of objects they apply. But, at the same time, there must always be associated a criterion of identity with every genuine proper name; that is, in order to understand a proper name, we must know what sort or category of object it is to be used as the name of. It follows that every proper name must belong to some range of names, with all of which is associated the same criterion of identity: they are names of objects belonging to one category.

Once this is clearly seen, the distinction between colour-words, or names of chemical substances, and the general run of abstract nouns becomes much sharper. Colours, chemical substances and animal species (as opposed to individual animals) can be *identified*. They can be picked out by means of a pointing gesture and a demonstrative 'this' or 'that', and their identity enquired after ('What is that?'); in response they can be identified ('That is beige'). This possibility results from there being well-understood particular uses of demonstratives to indicate (point to) colours, species or chemical substances. This in turn hangs together with our possession of the general nouns 'colour', 'species' and 'substance': colours, species, chemical substances and (cardinal) numbers each form a category, comprising all the objects for which there is a certain common criterion of identity; understanding the particular use of demonstratives associated with each category consists just in knowing the relevant criterion of identity. Colour-words, used as nouns, thus form just such a range as we saw that all genuine proper names are required to belong to. Because we have general nouns, such as 'colour', 'substance' and so on, applying to all the objects in any one of these categories, we can also form complex singular terms by means of which we can refer to objects in these categories and which do not involve any understanding of the corresponding predicates. These are of three main kinds: those simply involving a simple functional expression like 'the colour of ξ', e.g. 'the colour of the sky'; definite descriptions which involve reference to objects of the type which form the arguments of such functions, e.g. 'the colour which both the carpet and the curtains have'; and definite descriptions which involve reference only to other objects of the same range, and the use of the predicates and relational expressions which are applied only to such objects, e.g. 'the colour which lies between red and yellow'. For special reasons, there is no use of demonstratives to refer to numbers: but there are complex singular numerical terms of all three types—e.g. 'the number of men who have climbed Everest' is analogous to 'the colour of Smith's favourite tie', and 'the largest prime factor of 28' to 'the colour complementary to red'.

By contrast, there is no definite range of objects to which, say, sliminess, shininess or resemblance belongs. Sliminess is indeed a tactile quality, shininess a visual quality and resemblance a relation; but one would be at a loss to answer such a question as 'What is *this* tactile quality?' or 'What is the relation between these two things?'—there is no one answer to these questions. This is because there is not associated with a noun such as 'tactile (visual) quality' or 'relation' any definite criterion of identity. For this reason also it is impossible to refer to such entities by means of a definite description which does not explicitly involve the use of the associated predicate or some equivalent one: the only sort of complex expression substitutable for 'sliminess' would be one of the form 'the quality of being . . . ' or of the form 'the quality which a thing has when it is . . . ', where the gap is to be filled either by the adjective 'slimy' or by some longer adjectival phrase with the same content. (An unimportant exception would be definite descriptions involving mention of mental attitudes, such as 'the quality which Jones most dislikes'.) Hence there *could* not be a language which had a word meaning 'sliminess' without also having a word meaning 'slimy', and in which the former was explained in terms of the latter; unless indeed 'ξ is slimy' were rendered by means of an expression like 'ξ possesses the property of sliminess'; and in this case this expression would be logically simple—one could not explain the meaning of 'sliminess' independently of its use in this predicate.

It is true that wisdom and brotherhood, for example, do belong to more definite ranges: wisdom is a virtue (more generally, a character-trait), and brotherhood is a consanguinity-relationship: such a phrase as 'the (consanguinity-)relationship which John bears to James' therefore has a unique reference. We might, accordingly, admit wisdom and brotherhood as genuine objects. What deprives us of any compelling reason to do so is the fact that we have no very extensive vocabulary for talking about virtues or consanguinity-relations that cannot be very directly expressed in terms of people possessing the virtues or standing in the relations: 'Siblinghood is a bar to marriage' obviously means 'People who are siblings are not allowed to marry', and 'Cleanliness is next to godliness' something like 'Anyone who is cleanly is preferable to anyone who is neither cleanly nor godly'. In a primitive language in which every sentence was accompanied by a pointing gesture and could be rendered by a sentence beginning 'This is . . . ', there would be no grounds for any distinction between predicative expressions and singular terms: if 'red' is used only in 'This is red,' there is no sense to the question whether it is a noun or an adjective, and hence there would be no logical difference in such a language between 'This is slimy' and 'This is Socrates'. In order to use 'Socrates', we have to know how to recognize Socrates when we come across him again; but, then, in order to use 'slimy' we have to know how to recognize sliminess when we come across it again. What determines whether a word is to be classified as a singular term or a predicate is whether or not it occurs in other contexts in which predicates are attached to *it*. When its occurrence in such contexts is readily dispensable, as in the case of 'wisdom', it is therefore quite reasonable to regard it as only a spurious singular term, a stylistic variant on the corresponding predicate. In order that such contexts should occur at all (in any not immediately dispensable manner), it is necessary that the term should be recognized as belonging with others to a certain definite range, since a predicate can be understood only by knowing the conditions under which it applies to an arbitrary object of a given range. For 'sliminess' to be a singular term, therefore, it would be necessary not only that we should, as we do, have a means of recognizing sliminess whenever we come across it; but also that the means whereby we do this should exemplify a common procedure for identifying anything within a certain category (the category characterized by the use of that criterion of identity), and this, as we have seen, is not the case. Membership of a definite range is only a necessary, not a sufficient, condition for the non-trivial use of a vocabulary for forming predicates attaching to a term: when this condition is satisfied, but such a vocabulary is lacking, as in the case of 'wisdom' or 'brotherhood', we may leave it a matter of choice whether the word is to be regarded as significantly functioning as a singular term or not. In any case, we have dispelled the first impression that, by the formation of abstract nouns, we can in a trivial fashion mention an object corresponding to every concept.

If we introduce into our language proper names of a new range, standing for objects of a new category, as determined by some criterion of identity, we shall be unable to use these names for anything unless we simultaneously introduce a set of predicates which can be applied to these objects. It was for this reason that the existence of such a vocabulary for talking about colours was of importance in recognizing colour-words, used substantivally, as proper names. The absence of such a vocabulary in the case of the general run of abstract nouns is not, then, a mere matter of degree: it is an inevitable reflection of the fact that, being associated with no criterion of identity, they function in a quite different way, namely in one that may be classified as a mere idiomatic variant of forms of speech which eschew them. It is true that there still may be borderline cases: since in practice we are often content to allow a criterion of identity to remain very much less than sharp, it is not always clear whether one exists at all or not. A borderline case among abstract objects would be character-traits (as possessed by human beings). Nevertheless, the principle is plain: even though an expression passes the more formal tests we devised, it is not to be classified as a proper name, or thought of as standing for an object, unless we can speak of a criterion of identity, determined by the sense of the expression, which applies to the object for which it stands. If this is not the case, and yet we were to persist in using the picture of there being an object of which the abstract noun was the name, it would be an object which could not be referred to in any other way than by the use of that noun. Just because we can say of what sort of object 'green' is the name, viz. a colour, so we can refer to that object in other ways, e.g. as the colour of grass or the colour complementary to red; likewise, the number 7 may also be referred to as the greatest prime divisor of 105, or as the number of days of the week. But because we cannot say what sort of object sliminess is —we cannot supply a sortal predicate applying to it—the possibility of forming any definite descriptions which provide alternative means of referring to it is closed off in advance (except for descriptions which incorporate expressions for mental attitudes, such as 'what nauseates Henry most' and the like). About a supposed object which can only be referred to in one way we can perforce say very few things; and this is what underlay our earlier feeling that we do not take seriously the use of such abstract nouns as names of objects.

The danger that Frege's notion of a proper name, and, with it, his notion of an object, would be reduced to absurdity because serious objects were overwhelmed by frivolous and spurious ones is thus averted. At the same time, we have, I trust, satisfied ourselves at least that the Fregean notion of a proper name is in principle capable of being supplied with precise criteria which are formal and linguistic in the sense which he needs to accord with his outlook, and thus that the reconstructed language of whose semantics Frege is able to give a definite account can be used as a tool in the analysis of the sentences of our actual language.

CHAPTER 5

Sense and Reference

Bs Pref. FREGE'S AVOWED INTENTION in *Begriffsschrift* was to construct a symbolic language adequate for any mathematical theory, and, simultaneously, an effective delineation of rules of inference, with respect to this symbolic language, adequate to embody all proofs within each such theory. This programme entailed an analysis of language, at least of that part of language necessary for the expression of mathematical propositions. The analysis which Frege gave constituted the invention of the language of (higher-order) predicate logic, as we have it now: a language in which the atomic sentences are formed from individual constants (i.e. simple proper names), and primitive functional expressions, predicates and relational expressions, and in which complex sentences are formed by means of the truth-functional sentential operators, and quantifiers of fixed type and level, as required. Frege was aware that extra-mathematical language contains devices not included among these, but attempted no very far-reaching treatment of them.

The analysis of language which Frege undertook involved an analysis of the *working* of language. Frege did not content himself with finding a characterization of the totality of sentences of the symbolic language, nor with a mere stipulation of the rules of inference he thought it adequate to employ. Rather, the description of the structure of sentences of this language was accompanied by an account of the way in which their truth-values were determined, and the rules of inference laid down were then seen to be justified by the rules governing the assignment of truth-values. Frege did not explicitly state the modern distinction between the semantic (model-theoretic) and the syntactic (proof-theoretic) treatments of the notion of logical consequence: but it is implicit in his writing. It is because of the introduction of this dual treatment that it was in Frege's writings that, so late in the history of human thought, logic came of age at last. In Frege's logical theory, there was for the first time offered an account of the determination of the sentences of a considerable fragment of language as true or as false, and therefore, also for the first time, the possibility, not merely of specifying certain rules of inference as valid, but of demonstrating their validity in the sense of yielding true conclusions from true premisses. At the same time, the rules of inference themselves were stated in a manner which obviated any appeal to intuition in the recognition of any transition as an instance of the application of one of these rules: they were, that is, stated as *effective* rules in purely syntactic terms. Although Frege did not expressly define the two notions—semantic and syntactic—of logical consequence, they lie ready to hand in his work: for there, on the one hand, is the formal system, with its precisely stated formation rules, axioms and rules of inference; and there, on the other, are the semantic explanations of the sentences of the formalized language, set out, clearly separated from the formal development, in German in the accompanying text.

Frege would therefore have had within his grasp the concepts necessary to frame the notion of the completeness of a formalization of logic, as well as its soundness. A formalization of some part of logic is sound if, whenever a sentence A is a syntactic consequence of some set Γ of sentences, i.e. can be derived from them by means of a formal deduction, it is also a semantic consequence of them, i.e. is true under every interpretation of its non-logical constants under which all the sentences of Γ are also true. It is complete if the converse holds, i.e. if every semantic consequence is also a syntactic consequence. The sentential fragment of Frege's formalization of logic is complete, and likewise the first-order fragment constitutes the first complete formalization of first-order predicate logic with identity. It was left to Frege's successors to prove this completeness, as also to establish the incompleteness of his, or of any other effective, formalization of higher-order logic. Frege had it to hand to raise these questions: but he did not do so.

In one respect we have progressed very little beyond Frege: the range of language of which we are capable of giving a comparable analysis. We have made some advance in the study of modal operators, expressing necessity and possibility, and some beginning in the study of tenses; Davidson has accomplished much in the application of Frege's logical apparatus to the treatment of verbs of action and to adverbs; Geach has made some start on the study of different ranges of generality; Quine, Hintikka and others have attacked the topic of propositional attitudes. But there is no theory as elegant and as definitive as that of Frege relating to any larger fragment of language than that which his theory was capable of treating: and his theory remains the model for all attempts to extend it to take in a larger segment of our language.

From the standpoint of *logic* as such, we need an account of the working of language only as it relates to truth, since the notion of the validity of a form of inference relates precisely to truth: a form of inference is valid just in case, in each inference of that form in which the premisses are true, the conclusion is also true. Hence, in order to fulfil his original purpose, Frege could have contented himself, as do logicians now, with an account of the structure of the sentences of his symbolic language, and with a specification of their truth-conditions as connected with that structure. The fundamental idea of his symbolic language was, of course, the recursive specification of the totality of sentences: the primitive non-logical constants will serve to construct the atomic sentences, and then the sentential operators and quantifiers provide means to generate further sentences from any given base. All that was needed, therefore, for the purposes of logic, was an account of the way in which the truth-value of an atomic sentence is determined, together with an account of the way in which the truth-value of a complex sentence is determined, given the truth-values of its constituents (the constituents of a quantified sentence being, of course, the instances). For the purposes of logic, we do not need to know what truth is, or how truth is related to meaning: whatever truth may be, and however it may be related to meaning, we know that an inference is valid if we have a guarantee that its conclusion is true, provided that its premisses are; that is enough for the logician.

It was not, therefore, qua logician, but qua philosopher, that Frege pushed his enquiry further; he was not satisfied with giving an analysis of language—or, at least, of a large part of language—adequate for the purposes of the logician: he wanted to give a general account of the workings of language, an account which did not proceed by taking any fundamental concept for granted. An account of the working of language is a theory of meaning, for to know how an expression functions, taken as part of the language, is just to know its meaning. So Frege's philosophy, so far as it is concerned with language generally, rather than specifically with mathematics, is largely constituted by his theory of meaning. It may be labelled 'philosophy of language', rather than 'theory of meaning', if one wishes: but either title is to be preferred to 'philosophy of logic' or 'philosophical logic', for the reason we have just seen; namely, if the term 'logic' is construed in its proper sense, as the study of the relation of *consequence* between statements, then Frege's philosophical concerns go a long way beyond anything that is the proper concern of the logician.

Frege drew, within the intuitive notion of meaning, a distinction between three ingredients: sense, tone and force. That is to say, he distinguished between these three things. He does not use any word to express the general notion of 'meaning', as I have here used the word, and therefore does not claim sense, tone and force as being ingredients in anything more general. Nevertheless, it is plain, from the accounts he gives of these notions, that a difference between two expressions, or two sentences, in respect of any of these three features—a difference in sense, in tone or in force—would ordinarily be accounted a difference in meaning; a mistake about the sense, tone or force intended to be understood as attached to a sentence or expression would ordinarily be accounted a misunderstanding of its meaning. Therefore, we may reasonably say that Frege discerns three ingredients within the intuitive notion of meaning: or, perhaps better, that he proposes to replace the intuitive notion of meaning by the three notions of sense, tone and force.

NS 209 (193);   What I have here called 'tone' Frege refers to as 'lighting' or 'colouring',
NS 214 (198)   but these are less natural metaphors in English, and we may stick to the term 'tone'. Frege also makes a celebrated distinction between the notion of sense and another notion, his term for which has come to be conventionally translated 'reference'. Frege's actual word is, of course, 'Bedeutung', which is simply the German word for 'meaning': but one cannot render 'Bedeutung', as it occurs in Frege, by 'meaning', without a very special warning. The word 'reference' does not, I think, belie Frege's intention, though it gives it much more explicit expression: its principal disadvantage is that it has also become customary to translate the cognate verb 'bedeuten' by the non-cognate verbal phrase 'stand for'. The tradition is unfortunate, but it is established, and I shall therefore for the most part follow it, giving notice when I use some other expression for the noun 'Bedeutung' or the verb 'bedeuten'.

What the customary translation of these words does correctly register is that Frege's distinction between sense and reference could not correctly be called a 'distinction between two ingredients in the intuitive notion of meaning'. Reference, as Frege understands it, is not an ingredient in meaning at all: someone who does not know the reference of an expression does not show thereby that he does not understand, or only partially understands, the expression. Reference, for Frege, is a notion required in the theory of meaning—in the general account of how language functions—just as the notion of truth is so required: but the reference of a term is no more part of what is ordinarily understood as its meaning than the truth-value of a sentence is.

BW 102 (67);   We have already looked at the distinction drawn by Frege between sense
NS 157 (140)   and tone. To the sense of a word or expression belong only those features of its meaning which are relevant to the truth-value of some sentence in which it may occur: differences in meaning which are not so relevant are relegated

to the tone of the word or expression. Thus the words 'dead' and 'deceased' SB 31; Ged 63 (9)
do not differ in sense: the replacement of one by the other could change
neither the meaningfulness nor the truth-value of any sentence; in so far as
they differ in meaning at all, then, the difference lies in their tone. Another
celebrated example—given by Frege in *Begriffsschrift*—is the difference in Bs 7
meaning between the connectives 'and' and 'but'; the replacement of either
by the other could not alter the truth or falsity of what was said. (It could,
in certain cases—e.g. 'all but he', 'husband and wife', 'bacon and eggs'—
destroy its meaningfulness; this is not so, however, when the words connect
whole clauses.) 'Tone' has here been defined in a ragbag way, which will
have to be modified subsequently if we are to leave room for the third
ingredient in meaning, force; moreover, there is no reason to suppose that
all those variations in meaning, between expressions having the same sense
(in Frege's restricted use of 'sense'), which Frege counts as differences in
tone, are uniform in kind. Frege did apparently suppose this. He accounts
for tone as a matter of the association with a word or expression of certain NS 151-2 (139-40)
'ideas' (Vorstellungen), by which he means mental images. This is not a
particularly plausible explanation of the phenomenon: we indeed speak of
words which carry the same sense as having different associations, but we
should be hard put to it to describe the distinct mental images called up by
hearing the words 'dead' and 'deceased', or 'sweat' and 'perspiration', still
less by 'and' and 'but'. Frege makes a poor explanation worse by suggesting
that mental images are incommunicable in principle: no two people can ever SB 30; Huss 317
know that they have the same mental image. It would follow that tone was a
feature of meaning which was, in principle, subjective. This conclusion is a
simple contradiction. Meaning, under any theory whatsoever, cannot be *in
principle* subjective, because meaning is a matter of what is *conveyed* by
language. Someone may, by mistake or design, attach a meaning to some
word different from that which anyone else attaches to that word: but the
meaning must be something that *could* be conveyed to another by the use of
that word, and it must be such that it could be conveyed to another that the
person in question was attaching that meaning to the word; if not, it would
simply not be a meaning at all.

Even were Frege's explanation of tone plausible, namely that it consists in
a propensity which the use of a word has to call up certain mental images, it
would not follow that tone was subjective in principle, since Frege was
mistaken in supposing mental images to be incommunicable in principle.
Tone is not, however, in itself any more subjective than sense: the difference
in meaning between 'and' and 'but' is just as objective a feature, requiring to
be grasped by anyone who wishes to speak English, as is that between 'and'

E

and 'or'. In fact, the difference in tone between 'and' and 'but' is plainly a counter-example to Frege's general account of such differences as having to Bs 7; Ged 64 (9) do with mental images: in *Begriffsschrift* he says that by using the word 'but' a speaker hints that what follows is different from what you might at first suppose. A hint is evidently not the production of a mental image. Because Frege's account of the word 'but' has since become canonical, and because large theoretical claims have been based on such examples, it is worth pausing to note its incorrectness. The claims in question are to the existence of a basic distinction between *asserting* something and merely *suggesting* (or, in a special sense, 'implying') it: if what is merely suggested by a statement does not hold, the statement will not be *false*, but only *inappropriate*. It is difficult a priori to see how there could be a place for such a distinction: how can there be two different ways in which a statement may be factually incorrect, or two different ways of conveying by means of a sentence that something is the case? This initial resistance is overcome by the production of plausible examples: for instance, the use of 'but', explained as in Frege's account, is given as a case of suggesting what is not actually stated. But, of course, Frege's account of 'but' is incorrect: the word is indeed used to hint at the presence of some contrast; but not necessarily one between what the second half of the sentence asserts, and what you would expect, knowing the first half to be true. It has even been claimed that the function of 'but' in 'She was poor, but she was honest' is to suggest that anyone who is poor is unlikely to be honest. But the speaker may have had quite a different contrast in mind, e.g. that poverty is undesirable but honesty desirable. If a club committee is discussing what speakers to invite, and someone says, 'Robinson always draws large audiences', a reply might be, 'He always draws large audiences, but he is in America for a year'; the objector is not suggesting that a popular speaker is unlikely to go to America, but that, while Robinson's popularity as a speaker is a reason for inviting him, his being in America is a strong reason against doing so. The word 'but' is used to hint that there is some contrast, relevant to the context, between the two halves of the sentence: no more can be said, in general, about what kind of contrast is hinted at. It is the indefiniteness of the contrast, and the vagueness of the notion of relevance, that resolve the mystery of the distinction between asserting and suggesting: while we should regard a man's use of 'but' as inappropriate if he was unable to mention a contrast we considered relevant, or genuine, examples of this kind can furnish no foundation for the view that we can assign any *definite* condition as a condition for the appropriateness rather than the truth of a statement.

'But' is a very special kind of example of tone—an example for which

Frege's talk of mental images is totally out of place; is there any ground for thinking that, in more typical cases, tone is subjective in a way that sense is not? It is true, indeed, that an individual may invest a word with a tone which it does not have for most speakers of the language; but, equally well, someone may attach a sense to a word different from the sense attached by others. In either case, if he discovers his divergence from other speakers, he can allow for this in interpreting the words of others; in either case, he will at first, when he has only recently discovered his mistake, have some difficulty in resisting the misinterpretation which was previously habitual with him, and in remembering to understand the word as having its intended and customary meaning. Two circumstances mislead us into thinking of tone as a more subjective feature of a word's meaning than its sense. Let us call the meaning which we are disposed to allot to a word, straight off, without reflection, our 'impression' of its meaning. Someone who has only just started to learn a language probably has no impression of the meaning of several words which he has learned, but whose meaning he can recall only by an effort: for someone who speaks a language fluently and correctly, his impression of the meaning of the words of the language will coincide with their true meaning. If someone has been habitually disposed to misinterpret a word, his impression of its meaning will continue for some time to be the same even after he has found out that he had been understanding it incorrectly; and this applies to sense as well as tone; he has to reflect in order to bring to mind that the word does not have the sense which he is inclined straight off to attach to it. Now, in terms of this notion of an impression of meaning, we can state two differences between sense and tone. First, an incorrect impression of sense is normally gained only by having, at some time, mistakenly supposed that the word was intended to convey that sense which corresponds to the impression; e.g. the word 'incumbency' makes on me the impression of having the sense of applying to the act of lying down in bed, because in childhood I guessed at that sense for it, and for some time took it as having that sense. But an incorrect impression of tone may often be generated by experiences having nothing to do with any mistake about the tone the word is conventionally intended to carry—by, as we say, a particular association which the word has for me, which gives it a special flavour which I cannot dispel, although I have been aware throughout that that has nothing to do with the meaning which the word has for most people. Secondly, in some familiar cases, what is of importance is not a knowledge of the tone which a word or phrase has, in virtue of its commonly accepted meaning, but, precisely, the impression of tone. The most straightforward such case is the evocative—as opposed to the expressive—use of language. If a speaker selects

SB 31

words which serve to convey, along with the content of what he is saying, an attitude of respect on his part to the one he is addressing, his words fulfil an *expressive* function: the hearer can recognize, from the conventions governing the use of the words, that the speaker is intending to convey an attitude of respect towards him. Some languages, e.g. Javanese, possess a whole parallel vocabulary for this purpose. The expressive function is fulfilled as long as the hearer recognizes the attitude which it was the intention of the speaker to convey; it is irrelevant what feelings they evoke in the hearer. The evocative use of language is quite different: here the primary purpose is not necessarily fulfilled by the hearer's recognition of the intention underlying the selection of the words. For instance, words may be used with the intention of arousing in the hearers a sense of pathos: this is, of course, in part a matter of the content of what is said—of their *sense*, in Frege's technical use—but also in part depends on the manner of expression, i.e. on the tone of the words used. In order that the words should have the desired effect through their tone, it is necessary that the hearer's *impression* of the tone should be one of pathos: if, for example, through accident the words used have, for the hearer, comic or obscene associations, the utterance will have misfired. It will not be saved by the mere fact that the hearer is aware that these associations are private to himself, that the words are ordinarily taken as having pathetic overtones, and that it was for this purpose that the speaker used them: for the primary purpose of the evocative use of language does not operate through the hearer's recognition of the speaker's intention, but through their effect in arousing in the hearer a mood or an attitude. Literary effects frequently depend upon skilled attention to the evocative power of words. The evocative use of language does, therefore, depend, in a way in which no other use of language does, upon the dispositions of the individual hearer to react in certain ways. But to conclude lightly from this that tone is always a subjective matter is wrongly to assimilate the expressive to the evocative use, and at the same time to overlook the fact that the two uses between them do not exhaust the function of tone: for instance, the use of the word 'but' rather than 'and' does not serve to convey any attitude on the part of the speaker, in the sense in which a speaker may evince, e.g., a respectful, apologetic or regretful attitude.

The carelessness of Frege's treatment of tone was due to his lack of interest in it: for him it is a very secondary feature of meaning. The things he incorrectly says about tone serve principally to contrast with his view of sense: the sense of a word has nothing to do with any propensity the word may have to call up mental images in the mind of the hearer, and is something wholly objective. It is of much more importance that Frege truly

NS 152 (140)

NS 153 (141)

insisted on these characteristics of sense than that he incorrectly ascribed the opposite characteristics to tone.

The sense of an expression is, to repeat, that part of its meaning which is relevant to the determination of the truth-value of sentences in which the expression occurs. This characterization of the notion of sense serves, indeed, to distinguish sense from other ingredients in meaning: but, for the rest, it is, in itself, purely programmatic. We can get no grasp on the sort of thing which Frege took the sense of a word or expression to consist in without scrutinizing the distinction which he drew between sense and reference. Gg I 32

Frege's notion of reference is best approached via the semantics which he introduced for formulas of the language of predicate logic. An interpretation of such a formula (or set of formulas) is obtained by assigning entities of suitable kinds to the primitive non-logical constants occurring in the formulas. If we assume that these are all of levels 0 and 1, then they are of the following five kinds: individual constants; unary function symbols; binary function symbols; one-place predicates; and (two-place) relational expressions. The interpretation will assign to each individual constant an object; to each unary function symbol a unary function, defined for every object, and having an object as value for each argument; to each binary function symbol, a binary function, defined for every ordered pair of objects, and having, for every pair of arguments, an object as value; to each one-place predicate, a property, defined over every object (i.e. it is in some manner specified, for each object, that that object has, or that it lacks, that property); and, to every two-place relational expression, a binary relation, likewise defined over every ordered pair of objects. Terms are specified as expressions built up, starting with individual constants, by (possibly reiterated) application of the function symbols: each term then has some object as its denotation, under the obvious recursive stipulation that an individual constant denotes the object assigned to it under the interpretation, and that a term formed by applying a function symbol to some term or pair of terms denotes the value of the function assigned by the interpretation to that function symbol for the denotation(s) of the term(s) to which it is being applied as argument(s). Finally, an atomic sentence formed by attaching a one-place predicate to a term is stipulated as true, under the interpretation, if the object denoted by the term has the property assigned by the interpretation to the predicate, false if it lacks the property; likewise, an atomic sentence formed by attaching a two-place relational expression to a pair of terms is true if the objects denoted by the terms stand in the relation assigned by the interpretation to the relational expression, and false if they do not so stand. Complex sentences formed by means of sentential operators

and quantifiers are then assigned truth-values by means of the usual inductive stipulation, starting with the assignment of truth-values to the atomic
sentences as a base.

This procedure is exactly the same as the modern semantic treatment of
the language of predicate logic, save for Frege's avoidance of function
symbols and relational expressions of degree more than 2, and for his assumption that it is unnecessary to stipulate expressly any domain of objects to constitute the range of the individual variables. He made the natural, but, as it
proved, disastrously mistaken, assumption that it was possible always to
take the individual variables as ranging uniformly over all objects whatever:
this is a point which will occupy us later, but is not of importance to the
present discussion.

Such a semantics—such a notion of 'interpretation' as applied to sentences
constructed after the pattern of Frege's symbolic language—provides us
with an account of the truth-conditions of the sentences of the language that
is entirely adequate for the purposes of the logician, and thus enables him to
define the semantic notion of logical consequence and to frame the conceptions of soundness and completeness for a given set of formal rules of
deduction. It is precisely such a notion of interpretation that Frege has in
mind when he speaks of 'reference'. Indeed, this is to put the matter the
wrong way round. Rather, he uses the very same notion of reference in his
philosophical discussions of language—of the theory of meaning—and in his
exposition of the intended interpretation of his formal system in *Grundgesetze der Arithmetik*, that is, in the prose accompaniment to the symbolic
text which sets out the semantics of the system. It is thus plain that his notion
of reference coincides with the notion of an interpretation for formulas of
predicate logic as currently employed in mathematical logic. Why, then, do
we need a notion of sense as well as a notion of reference?

A very bad answer, sometimes given to this question, would be that the
notion of sense is needed by Frege to explain operators which, in Quine's
terminology, create opaque contexts—expressions like 'necessarily' and
' . . . believes that . . . '. It is true enough that Frege does deploy his notion
of sense in treating of such expressions: he says that, within opaque contexts,
a term stands for what, in ordinary contexts, constitutes its sense. But,
obviously, it would be useless to offer any such explanation unless it had first
been established that there is something which, in ordinary contexts, constitutes the sense of a term: so we must be satisfied that there is a prior need
for a notion of sense, as possessed by expressions occurring in ordinary
contexts, before we can invoke this notion to explain opaque contexts.

The question, why there is a need for ascribing sense as well as reference to expressions, may be put in a sharper form, namely: how is there room for any notion of sense, as distinct from reference, given the way in which the notion of sense has been characterized? The notion of sense was characterized by laying down that only those features of the meaning of a word belong to its sense which are relevant to determining the truth-value of sentences containing it. But, once the reference of each word in a sentence has been determined, the truth-value of the sentence is thereby determined. It was just because of this that we were able to assign, non-effectively but determinately, a truth-value to each sentence in the language of predicate logic, relative to some interpretation which fixed the references of the non-logical constants: and in any case Frege himself is explicit, and insistent, that the replacement in any sentence of some word or expression by another having SB 33, 35 the same reference leaves the truth-value of the whole unchanged. It thus appears that the sense of an expression must coincide with its reference, or, at least, that there must be a one-one correspondence between senses and references. Yet, notoriously, Frege held that many senses could correspond to the same reference. How, then, could he find room for such a notion of sense at all?

The solution to the dilemma has already been stated: reference is not an ingredient of meaning. If reference were an ingredient of meaning, then indeed the reference of a word would exhaust—or determine—its sense, since nothing more would need to be known about its meaning in order to fix the truth-value of any sentence in which it occurred (to make allowance for opaque contexts, we ought to say 'in which it occurred as having its ordinary reference'). There would then genuinely be no room for a notion of sense to be squeezed in between reference and tone. But reference is *not* an ingredient of meaning, and so sense can still be explained as constituting that part of the meaning of a word or expression which needs to be grasped in order to decide the truth-values of sentences containing it; and this means: that part of its meaning which determines its reference. Any feature of the meaning of a word which does not affect the reference that it has does not belong to its sense: it in no way follows that two words with the same reference must have the same sense.

What is meant by saying that 'reference is not an ingredient in meaning'? Meaning is an intuitive notion, and a fairly imprecise one: how can we decide the truth of a claim that something does or does not form an ingredient in it, and how can any important philosophical point hang upon the justice of such a claim? In any case, how can such a claim be a representation of Frege's views? We have seen that Frege did not employ any word to cover meaning in the generic sense of that word, in a sense in which it embraces the things which he calls tone, sense and force; moreover, the ordinary German word for 'meaning' he employs in the technical sense which we are conventionally translating 'reference': how, then, can any thesis of Frege's be expressed by the claim that tone, sense and force are ingredients of meaning, but reference is not?

These are very natural objections: but I think that if we seek to understand the claim that reference is not an ingredient of meaning, it will be seen to accord well with Frege's way of looking at the matter, although not with his way of expressing it. Many philosophers, Wittgenstein included, have inveighed against the practice of 'hypostatizing' or 'reifying' meanings—taking meanings to be entities with which words are associated. It is often a little hard to see what conception it is that they find so harmful—what would count as an instance of such illicit hypostatization: but no doubt it is a salutary practice to replace an enquiry into what meaning is by an enquiry into the application or elucidation of certain complex phrases containing the word 'meaning'; thus we may ask under what conditions we wish to say that an expression, in particular a sentence, has a meaning or lacks one; or under what conditions two expressions do or do not have the same meaning. In this way, we may substitute for an enquiry into the nature of meaning one into the nature of significance (meaningfulness) or of synonymy (sameness of meaning). Neither type of enquiry is, however, likely to lead to a satisfactory account of meaning as we intuitively apprehend this notion. Rather, the complex phrase on which attention needs to be concentrated is 'knowing the meaning of . . . ': a theory of meaning is a theory of *understanding*. What we have to give an account of is what a person knows when he knows what a word or expression means, that is, when he understands it. The capacity to use a language is a highly complex ability. Our difficulty lies, not so much in explaining how human beings acquire this ability, as in giving any clear account of what the ability consists in, when acquired—an account, that is, which does not itself employ any concepts which presuppose the notion of understanding, or being able to use, language. An account of understanding language, i.e. of what it is to know the meanings of words and expressions in the language, is thus at the same time an account of how language functions, that is, not only of how it does what it does, but of what it is that it does. No doubt, once we have a workable account of what it is, in general, to know the meaning of a word or expression, we shall derive, as a by-product, an account of what it is for two expressions to have the same meaning, or for an expression to have a meaning at all. Even if we do not, it is no great matter: it is knowing the meaning—understanding—which remains the important concept.

Thus what we are going to understand as a possible ingredient in meaning will be something which it is plausible to say constitutes part of what someone who understands the word or expression implicitly grasps, and in his grasp of which his understanding in part consists. The possession of reference by a word or expression consists in an association between it and something in the world—something of an appropriate logical type, according to the logical category to which the word belongs. To claim that reference is not an ingredient in meaning is, therefore, to claim that our understanding a word or expression never consists, even in part, merely in our associating something in the world with that word or expression.

The claim does not mean any more than this. It does not mean that reference has nothing to do with meaning. On the contrary, on Frege's view, it is precisely via the reference of the words in a sentence that its truth-value is determined. The sense of a word—as opposed to any other ingredient its meaning may have—constitutes the contribution which it makes to determining the truth-conditions of sentences in which it occurs precisely by associating a certain reference with it. The semantic account, formulated entirely in terms of reference, thus quite correctly displays the way in which the truth-value of a sentence is determined from the constituent words of the sentence and the manner in which they are put together. Where the semantic account is lacking is that it does not go far enough back: it postulates an association between each primitive symbol and an appropriate referent, but it does not tell us how this association is established. For the purposes of logic, this is unnecessary: for the purposes of a theory of meaning, it is essential.

The sense of a word thus consists in some means by which a reference of an appropriate kind is determined for that word. To say that reference is not an ingredient in meaning is not to deny that reference is a consequence of meaning, or that the notion of reference has a vital role to play in the general theory of meaning: it is only to say that the understanding which a speaker of a language has of a word in that language—even just that part of his understanding of it which is relevant to his recognition of sentences containing it as true or as false—can never consist merely in his associating a certain thing with it as its referent; there must be some particular *means* by which this association is effected, the knowledge of which constitutes his grasp of its sense. It follows that, upon occasion, the same thing can be associated with two different words or expressions as their referent, the association being effected by different means in the two cases, and the two words or expressions thus having different senses in spite of having the same reference.

A terminological note is needed at this point. Frege almost always uses the noun 'Bedeutung' to apply to the actual thing for which a word stands,

E*

though the verb 'bedeuten' signifies the relation between them. It is nevertheless desirable to be able to draw the distinction between the relation and
the thing to which the word is so related; for the latter we may employ the
word 'referent'. We shall therefore henceforth use the abstract noun 'reference' only as applying to the relation between the word and the thing, or to
the property of standing for something, or, again, to the property of standing
for some particular given thing—context should resolve ambiguities between
these three uses; but we shall use the word 'referent' as applying to the
thing for which the word stands.

It should now be clear that the thesis which we expressed in such un-
Fregean language, that reference is not an ingredient in meaning, not only
has a clear sense, but is in complete consonance with Frege's views. These
views were set out for the first time in the celebrated article 'Über Sinn und
Bedeutung', in which the distinction between the two notions was for the first
time explicitly drawn. In that article, Frege approaches the matter in the first
place in connection with singular terms ('proper names'). The referent of a
proper name is an object: in the standard semantics for the language of
predicate logic, each individual constant (i.e. simple or primitive proper
name) is assigned an object, or, as we should now say, an element of the
domain that has been specified as the range of the individual variables, and
each function-symbol is assigned a function of appropriate degree from
objects to objects (from the domain into the domain); in terms of these
assignments, it is then possible to define inductively a mapping of each term
on to an object (an element of the domain), called its denotation. The notion
of reference, for proper names, thus coincides with that of denotation, as
used in the standard semantics. If the language contains any higher-order
term-forming operators, for instance a class abstraction operator or a description operator, operators, namely, which form a term when attached to a first-
order predicate, thus binding the variable in the argument-place of the
predicate, then to each such operator must be made to correspond a mapping
of first-order properties on to objects, so as to confer a reference (denotation)
on the terms formed by means of it. Thus, for instance, the description
operator 'the x such that . . . x . . .' must be understood as satisfying the
condition that, when a is the one and only object satisfying the predicate
'$A(x)$', then 'the x such that $A(x)$' must stand for the object a.

Frege now argues that the sense of a proper name cannot merely consist
in its having the reference that it has. His argument is set out in terms of the
notion of 'cognitive value', that is, information content. Frege asks how, if
the sense of a proper name consisted just in its having the reference that it
does have, any true statement of identity could be informative. The notion of

'information' being appealed to here does not require any elaborate explication: I acquire information when I learn something which I did not previously know, and Frege is asking how it is possible that I may be in a position to know the sense of an identity-statement, i.e. to understand it, and yet learn something that I did not know before by being told that that statement is true. On the theory that the sense of a proper name consists just in its having the reference that it has, this cannot be explained: for then my understanding of the two names connected by the sign of identity would consist just in my associating with each the object that was its referent, and I can surely not be said to understand the sign of identity if I do not know that an identity-statement is true provided the two names connected by the sign of identity have the same referent. I should thus be unable to understand an identity-statement without immediately recognizing it as true or as false.

In invoking the notion of information to support his contention that the sense of a name cannot consist merely in its having the reference which it does have, Frege is tacitly connecting the notion of sense with that of knowledge; and this is the justification for our representing Frege's views by saying that sense is an ingredient in meaning, where meaning is that which a man knows when he understands a word. For the argument, spelled out in full, runs thus: If the sense of a name consisted just in its having a certain reference, then anyone who understood the name would thereby know what object it stood for, and one who understood two names which had the same reference would know that they stood for the same object, and hence would know the truth of the statement of identity connecting them, which could therefore not be informative for him. The underlying assumption is the compelling principle that, if someone knows the senses of two words, and the two words have the same sense, he must know that they have the same sense: hence, if the sense of a name consists merely in its reference, anyone who understands two names having the same referent must know that they have the same referent.

In grasping the sense of a proper name, we are not merely aware that the name is associated with a particular object as its referent, but we connect the name with a particular way of identifying an object as the referent of the name. Hence two names may have the same referent but different senses: with the two names are associated different methods of identifying some object as the referent of either name, although it happens that it is the same object which satisfies the two pairs of conditions of such identification. Such an account can hardly be doubted when complex 'proper names' (singular terms) are in question; when, for example, one of the two terms presents its referent as the value of a certain function for a certain argument, and the other presents it as the value of a different function for a different argument; or when we have two definite descriptions, formed by attaching the description operator (represented in natural language by the definite article)

to different predicates. Frege uses the metaphor of a route from the name to the referent: names with different senses but the same referent correspond to different routes leading to the same destination. In the case of complex proper names, the difference of route is sign-posted by the structure of the proper names themselves: we could not do justice to their complexity— the way they are compounded out of their constituent expressions—without acknowledging this difference in the way in which we recognize an object as being referent of one name and of the other. Many philosophers have, however, felt drawn to a conception of a category of expressions which are *pure* proper names: names used to refer to objects, for which it would be true that the whole of their meaning consisted in their standing for just those objects which they named. Since complex singular terms obviously do not satisfy this requirement, these philosophers have sought to apply this account to proper names that are logically simple—words which are proper names in the usual, restricted, sense of the expression. Such a view was expressed by Mill; a more sophisticated version of it by Russell. For Mill, the account held good for those words in natural language which we ordinarily call 'proper names'—singular terms which are simple in the sense of not being explicitly compounded out of two or more words, in such a way that their meaning could be determined from the meanings of the constituent words. Russell perceived that such proper names could have been introduced, tacitly or explicitly, as the equivalents of some complex singular terms— definite descriptions, for example—and was therefore prepared to allow that the ordinary proper names of natural language might—in Frege's terminology—have a sense going beyond their mere possession of a certain reference; indeed, he became convinced that they all actually did. But he was still convinced that there must be a category of 'logically simple' names —names which could not even be analysed as the equivalents of complex terms, and which therefore had no more to their sense than just their possession of a particular reference.

The example which Frege gives in 'On Sense and Reference' of a pair of simple proper names having the same reference but manifestly different senses has been endlessly repeated—the example of the terms 'the Morning Star' and 'the Evening Star'. These expressions, though typographically complex, may be claimed as logically simple, for we cannot be expected to determine their sense just from knowing the senses of the constituents:

for one thing, they both refer to a planet, not to a star at all. Granted the principle that whoever knows the senses of two expressions must know that they have the same sense, if they do, it is also evident that the two expressions have different senses, since the truth of the identity-statement 'The Morning Star is the same (heavenly body) as the Evening Star' was an astronomical *discovery*. All the same, the expressions are verbally too close to definite descriptions to have convinced everyone of Frege's thesis that even ordinary simple proper names have a sense to which there is more than their just having a certain referent. It might therefore be helpful to cite another example which Frege gives in correspondence, a hypothetical example very similar to one later used by Quine. Frege imagines a traveller going into an unexplored region, descrying a mountain on the northern horizon and adopting for it the name 'Afla' used by the local people. Another explorer spots a mountain on his southern horizon, and adopts for it the name 'Ateb'. The stories of both travellers receive considerable publicity, and both mountain-names pass into common use: but it is many years until these regions are more systematically explored and mapped, and, when this is done, it is discovered, to the surprise of all, that the two explorers had been viewing the same mountain from different angles; owing to errors on their part in estimating distances, plotting their positions, etc., this had never been envisaged as a possibility. It is thus a geographical discovery that Afla and Ateb are one and the same mountain. Of course, once the discovery is made, either one name will be dropped, or both will be used as in effect synonymous. But, before the discovery was made, they provide an example of two perfectly ordinary proper names used with different senses.

Such an example would have no force against the view subsequently to be taken up by Russell, for whom all ordinary proper names are disguised definite descriptions (i.e. tacitly understood as the equivalents of definite descriptions): Frege could hardly have been expected to foresee the possibility of anyone's combining such a concession with the thesis that there nevertheless exist 'logically proper names' for which sense shrinks down to reference. Examples of this kind are meant by Frege to controvert only the kind of position taken up by Mill. They have led many to suppose that Frege conceives of the sense of an ordinary, that is, a non-compound, proper name as being that of some definite description; e.g. of the sense of 'Afla' as being the sense of some description of the form 'The mountain seen by traveller A on such-and-such a day on the southern horizon'. Of course, in trying to *say* what the senses of different names may be, Frege is naturally driven to citing such definite descriptions: but there is nothing in what he says to warrant the conclusion that the sense of a proper name is

NS 213 (197);
FB 14; BW
196 (127);
BW 234 (152)

BW 128 (80)

NS 242
(224-5)

always the sense of some complex description. All that is necessary, in order that the senses of two names which have the same referent should differ, is that we should have a different way of recognizing an object as the referent of each of the two names: there is no reason to suppose that the means by which we effect such a recognition should be expressible by means of a definite description or any other complex singular term. Other writers may perhaps have maintained this: but there is no ground to impute any such thesis to Frege.

Frege's examples of proper names differing in sense but not in reference—both the Morning Star/Evening Star and the Afla/Ateb one—are carefully chosen. They are chosen, namely, so that we do not have much difficulty in giving an account of the criterion for identifying an object as the referent of the name, as employed before it was discovered that both names had the same referent. In the Afla/Ateb example, the identification of the mountain for which each name stands is clearly tied to the reports given and maps drawn by one of the travellers; in the astronomical example, we are concerned with bodies of which all human beings have the same view (at least before the age of space travel). It is different for names of geographical features familiar to many—e.g. 'the Thames'—and, still more, with personal proper names. In such cases, we know a great deal about the object for which the name stands, and we may appeal to any part of this knowledge in determining whether or not an object presented to us is to be identified with the bearer of the name. If, for example, on a walk I come across a small stream, and I wish to know whether or not it is the Thames that I have encountered, there is not just *one* form that my investigation has to take. It is not merely that there are different ways to find an answer to the question—this is usually true: it is that there are many different questions, the answer to any one of which will settle the identity of the river—for instance, many questions of the kind, 'Is this the river which flows through Clifton Hampden?', or, '. . . through Radcot Bridge?', or, '. . . through Henley?'

Here it is not merely that the sense is over-determined, that it carries far more criteria for identification than are required for the sense of the name to determine an object as referent for it. Rather, it is that we can draw no sharp line between the sense of the name and information that we possess about its bearer. What one person may use in identifying an object as the referent of the name may be, for another whom we should ordinarily take as understanding the name, information about the object: one person may settle that a certain stream is the Thames by tracing it to Radcot Bridge, while another may be informatively told, 'The Thames flows through Radcot

Bridge.' Of course, this is in itself unproblematic: there is no reason why one should not use collateral knowledge in making an identification. Rather, the point is that there is no one condition, sufficient for an identification, which holds good of the Thames just in virtue of the sense of the name, that is, such that ignorance of it would count as showing that a person did not understand the name. One person might be unaware that the Thames flowed through Oxford, and still be said to understand the name 'the Thames'; another might be ignorant that it flowed through Reading, and yet another might even not realize that it flowed through London, and still be capable of using the name correctly. This does not mean, indeed, that there is nothing which is true of the Thames in virtue of the sense of its name—for instance, someone who thought that the Thames was in Russia, or even in Wales, would not be using the name as it is normally used. Moreover, any one person, if he is to be said to understand the name, must be in command of *some* correct means of identifying the river: if he knows only that 'the Thames' is used as the name of a river, and cannot in any way tell which river it is the name of, he is in the same position as one who knows that 'beige' is a colour-word, but does not know which colour it applies to; he has only a partial understanding of its sense. The person who thought that the Thames was in Russia might be in this situation: he knows that the expression 'the Thames' is commonly used as the name of a river, and has the false impression that, when so used, it names a river in Russia; in this case, he also does not profess to know more than part of the sense of the name. If, on the other hand, he uses the name 'the Thames' with a definite criterion of identification in mind, one involving the river's being in Russia, then, whether or not he believes that he is using the name in the same way as others, he attaches a determinate but incorrect sense to the name. It remains, however, that there is no one condition *sufficient for identification* which anybody must know the Thames to satisfy if he is to be said to have a complete and correct understanding of the phrase 'the Thames'.

It is in view of considerations of this kind that philosophers (Ryle, for example) have been disposed to maintain such theses as that proper names 'are not part of the language', or that what fixes their reference is not any part of their meaning: such contentions are frequently backed up by quite false assertions about dictionaries, such as that they do not contain proper names, or that they explain them only by saying flatly 'proper name'. (Dictionaries contain few or no personal proper names, but they frequently contain place-names, adequately defined: and names like 'Florence', 'Germany', etc. require transformation even in translating from one European language to another, let alone when translating into, say, Chinese.)

It is true enough that, in everyday discourse, the term 'meaning' is often applied to proper names as referring to their etymology ('Did you know that "Susanna" means "a lily"?'): but to legislate that everyday idiom has to be slavishly followed in this respect has nothing to do with the thesis of Mill that Frege was controverting. If someone is to be able to employ a proper name in sentences, or to understand its use in the utterances of others so as to be able to judge of their truth and falsity, he must know more about the expression than just that it is a proper name: he must know some correct means for recognizing an object as the bearer of that name. Mill held equally strongly that someone able to use the name in sentences had to be able to pick out the object which it named: his difference from Frege was that he thought that there was no question of any 'means' of recognizing this object, which might differ from one name to another although the object named by both was the same, but that there was, as it were, a direct mental association between the name and the object. Whether or not that which serves to fix for us the reference of a name is to be counted as part of its sense, or its meaning, has nothing whatever to do with the dispute between Mill and Frege: it is a point which could be raised whichever of them one agreed with, and it is a pretty trivial point at that. Since an understanding of that which is necessary to determine the reference of a name is essential to a capacity to use the name within sentences, in which it occurs as a word along with other words, it seems smoother and more natural to allow this understanding as constituting part of the knowledge of the meaning of the name.

There appears even less reason to extrude all but the fact that a word is a proper name from its meaning when we realize that the phenomenon which prompted this response is not confined to proper names, although it is most striking in their case. It has, for instance, frequently been remarked that the identification of chemical substances may resemble that of geographical objects in that a range of distinct criteria may be used in practice without its being possible for us to single out any one of them as that which anyone who understands the sense of the word for that substance must be aware of. The point can equally be made for animal and plant species, for diseases, and the like. It has nothing especially to do with the fact that in all these cases we may speak of names of chemical substances, species or diseases, that we use collective or abstract nouns and a vocabulary for predicating things of what such nouns stand for, as in such sentences as 'Neon is an inert gas', 'The gorilla is rapidly becoming extinct', 'Measles is infectious': the point would remain the same if we used words for substances, species and diseases only as predicates or parts of predicates. It is likely to hold good whenever we have a word for some complex character, condition or process which lends itself to identification by different criteria. In fact, what brings this situation about is precisely the same state of affairs as that which makes it possible for two expressions to have different senses but the same reference. If the same object—or the same state, process or relationship—can be identified by different criteria, corresponding to two expressions with different senses, the two expressions are likely to retain distinct senses only so long as we do not realize that their reference is the same. As soon as we do realize this, we are unlikely to continue to tie the two criteria to the two expressions: we shall almost certainly come to use either criterion indifferently for the application of either expression. And, when we are unconcerned about the possibility that the criteria may diverge, and uninterested in any systematic display of the interrelation between the propositions we hold to be true, that is, in the development of a rigorous theory, we shall frequently be content that different people may come to acquire a mastery of the application of an expression in different ways, so long as they all apply it correctly. For language to function, it is essential that there be agreement among its speakers about the application of the expressions of the language: it is not necessary that there be a uniform foundation for the principles governing this application.

A closely related point is dealt with by Wittgenstein in his discussion of the name 'Moses' in the *Philosophical Investigations*. In a case where *PI* 79 the information which we have about the bearer of the name is uncertain or conjectural, we may be prepared to find ourselves forced to acknowledge the falsity of any single statement about the referent of the name, even when, as things stand at present, we should now regard that statement as an acceptable characterization of the use of the name. Thus, for instance, the question, 'Who was Moses?', or, 'Whom do you mean by "Moses"?', could be answered by saying, 'Moses was the man who led the Israelites out of Egypt', or in a number of other ways, such as 'Moses was the man who gave the Israelites their law in the desert of Sinai', etc. But if it turned out that the man who initiated the Exodus was not the same as the one through whom the law was given, who was in command between the departure from Egypt and the entry into Canaan, who was the brother of the first High Priest, etc., then we might well say that, after all, Moses did not lead the Israelites out of Egypt. We should now restrict the range of acceptable answers to the question, 'Who was Moses?'; but we should not have lost the use of the name 'Moses'. We should lose the use of the name—be forced to say that there was no such person as Moses—only if it ceased to seem probable that there was some one man to whom most of the characterizations which we should now regard as acceptable answers to the question applied: but there is no one such answer which, so long as we retain the use of the name at all, we must regard as a true statement.

Such a situation, as we have seen, does not arise only for proper names, but for other categories of expression as well, although, doubtless, it is more common and more striking in the case of proper names. The occurrence of such situations should not, therefore, be taken as a ground for singling out proper names as functioning in any markedly different way from words of other kinds. Rather, the problem which it raises is of a much more general kind: is sense after all something subjective, and therefore without significance for the theory of meaning as an objective feature of linguistic expressions? The sense of an expression was supposed to consist in the way in which we determined its reference: but now it appears that, often, there is no one favoured way to determine the reference of an expression, but that different people may determine it in different ways, and even that what is taken at one time as an acceptable means of determining it may later be dropped as not agreeing with the others. If so, then what is objective about the employment of an expression, what is shared by all the speakers of the language, is after all its reference. It may be that, for any one speaker at any given time, there are certain means by which he would recognize something as the referent of the expression: but this is a subjective, transitory feature, of no great significance in the general theory of meaning. As we have seen, this conclusion, if it is to be drawn at all, would not be confined to proper names: just as, on this account, the only permanent, objective feature of the use of a proper name would be its reference, so the only permanent, objective feature of the use of a general term would be its application.

This conclusion has been, in effect, embraced by Quine, whose views on this topic will be considered in detail in Chapter 17. Those who would not wish to draw so radical a consequence have for the most part followed the bad example of Frege, by noting, by way of concession, the facts from which it is drawn, and then setting them aside as if they constituted minor irregularities, without facing the threat which they pose to the whole notion of sense, taken as distinct from reference.

It is conceded, by those who raise this objection to Frege's distinction, that, for any one individual at any one time, it makes no sense to suppose that he attaches the reference directly to the expression: there must be some route that he uses for reaching the referent from the expression, for instance, in the case of a proper name, some criterion he has for recognizing an object as being or not being the bearer of the name. The contention is, however, that the sense, taken as the particular manner in which someone associates a reference with an expression, is neither permanent nor common to all speakers of the language, so that what determines the use of the expression, considered merely as an expression of that language to which it belongs, is simply its reference.

This contention is evidently as far removed from actuality as would be the belief that every expression of our language has a single, unalterable and ideally sharp sense. It is difficult to say whether anyone has ever held this latter belief: certainly not Frege, who was perfectly well aware of the variations in sense attached by different individuals or at different times to the same expression, and of the haziness of the senses so attached. Frege can, perhaps, be criticized for tending to view this feature of natural language as one of its many defects, whereas it is probably unavoidable and certainly highly convenient. But the thesis that there is nothing held constant, or shared between the speakers of the language, save the reference is equally far from giving an accurate picture of what in fact happens. Only what is known about the referent of an expression, and is taken by the individual to be reliable information about it, can enter into the sense attached by that individual to the expression; and only what is more or less common knowledge will normally be taken as part of that sense. That by means of which an individual determines the reference of an expression cannot, after all, by the nature of things, rest upon some knowledge possessed by him alone, at least, if the sense he attaches to the expression is to any extent determined by the way in which he first acquired an understanding of its use; for this understanding must have been acquired either by his having been expressly given an explanation of the expression by some other person, or by his having picked up a grasp of its use by hearing examples of that use in the mouths of others. This will, indeed, leave a great deal of play—a wide range of equally acceptable ways of explaining the expression to another who does not know it, or of equally legitimate ways of determining the application of the expression, say in the course of deciding the truth-value of a sentence in which it occurs. It remains, however, that it is very far from being the case that only the commonly agreed reference of the expression fixes the extent of this range. When sentences of natural language are concerned, the notion of a tautology shades into that of a truism: there is often no determinate answer to the question whether a given statement merely conveys the definition (or part of the definition) of a word, or whether it states a truth known to all. But, although of course the notion of a truism is not a completely sharp one, there is a clear difference between a truism and a genuinely informative statement, still more a highly contentious one. Any form of words which can be regarded as a legitimate explanation of one of the words contained in it must express what, for anyone who already understands the word, is at best a truism.

One might acknowledge all this, but still feel that the concessions that have had to be made to this objection against the whole notion of sense rob the notion of its utility, or, at least, of its importance. If we are not, at this stage, to lose the whole point of the introduction of the notion of sense, we must go back to the connection which Frege made at the outset, when first introducing the distinction between sense and reference: the link between sense and informative content ('cognitive value'). In order to determine whether or not a sentence is true, it is enough to know the reference of the various constituent expressions; but, in order to know what information it conveys, we must know their sense. If we simply amassed knowledge in a linear, cumulative manner, no attention to sense would be necessary: a sentence would be informative for a given individual just in case it was not already in the stock of sentences he had already expressly acknowledged as true (or perhaps also of those he was not already disposed at once to recognize as true), and there would be no need to enquire at any later date just what its informative content had been when it was first added to that stock, nor to ascribe any particular such content to it at the later time. But, of course, such a picture of our progress in acquiring information is a travesty. What in fact takes place is a process of continual revision. Sometimes we are led to reject decisively as false what we had previously, tentatively or with equal decision, accepted as true. But just as often we find ourselves in a state of uncertainty, unable to reconcile the claims to truth of new statements inconsistent with some of those we had formerly accepted, and with no clear means before us to achieve a resolution of the conflict. In such circumstances, and in others in which there is no particular opposition to be resolved, but in which a doubt has arisen about whether we may not earlier have accepted certain statements too hastily, we are forced to enquire into the *justification* of statements we had formerly accepted as true. Such an enquiry —which, according to the nature of the statements involved and the character of the doubt that has arisen, may be straightforwardly empirical, or philosophical, or mathematical, or a mixture of these—requires us to determine, wholly or partially, the senses of the statements into whose justification we are enquiring. Precisely because just what it is that we can claim to know has been called into question, we cannot allow that the references of the expressions contained in the statements after whose justification we are asking may be determined by appeal to just anything we may happen to know. What is of interest to us is not, indeed, a historical question—by what means we thought of the references of those expressions as being determined when we originally accepted the disputed statements as true; nor is it a sociological question—how most people would regard the references of those expressions as determined. What we are called on to provide is a reconstruction and systematization of part of our language: we seek to *fix* definite senses for the relevant expressions in order to confer a clear content on the question whether we are justified in accepting the disputed statements as true, and, if so, on what grounds. A familiar, fully-fledged, example of this process occurs whenever a mathematical or scientific theory is subjected to the procedure of axiomatization, or when an enquiry, which may be partly mathematical or scientific, partly philosophical, is made into the foundations of a theory already axiomatized. But the same process, in a less penetrating and more partial manner, occurs in everyday contexts, when no highly articulated theory is involved: it frequently happens, for instance, that we are not disposed either to accept or to reject outright some proposition that has been advanced by another, but wish to enquire into his grounds for holding it, and, in the process, require him to fix more precisely the senses of the expressions he is using in stating it. Of course, while we are aware, in making such stipulations of the senses of expressions, that we are doing more than merely recording generally accepted practice, we are also in part responsible to that practice: we seek to avoid making stipulations which would correspond to statements that would not be generally accepted, or to ones which would be regarded as contentious.

The notion of sense is thus of importance, not so much in giving an account of our linguistic practice, but as a means of systematizing it. The picture of language which Frege employs in discussing sense is that of one in which each logically simple expression of the language is introduced or explained, whether by means of definition or (since it is impossible that every expression be defined) by some other means, in a unique manner, without room for variation, to each person when he first becomes familiar with its use: thereafter, the manner in which it was introduced determines the favoured manner in which he may determine its reference, so that, while of course he may use short-cuts rendered possible by further knowledge he has acquired, he will always bear in mind that sense, that manner of determining its reference, which is proper to the expression, and will appeal to that whenever any question arises as to the justification of or grounds for a statement in which it occurs. The objection we have been considering arises from the fact, as obvious to Frege as to anyone else, that this is a highly idealized picture, which is far from corresponding closely to our actual practice in the use of language. Frege's response to this gap between idealization and reality was a false one: to declare that our actual practice is, so far as it falls short of the idealization, defective, and ought to be purified so as to correspond to the ideal. But the response of the objectors, to repudiate the notion of sense altogether as spurious or at best useless, is in greater error. The ideal picture is of importance, not because we ought to purge our language so as to correspond completely to it, but because, in particular problematic situations, we need to impose a new practice, which approximates to the ideal picture, on the employment of some or other fragment of our language, in order to resolve the problems with which we are faced. It is, however, unreal to maintain a sharp distinction between the practice of speaking a language and the construction of a theory of its working. For theoretical purposes it is often convenient to adopt a picture of one language—the object-language— of whose working we desire to construct a theory, and another language—the metalanguage—in which the theory of meaning or semantics for the object-language is expressed. The theoretical ground for employing such a picture is twofold. First, we are aware, from the studies that have been carried out in the essentially simpler case when the object-language is not a natural language but a formalized one for the expression of some mathematical theory, that it is strictly impossible to construct a complete semantics for a language within that same language, provided we demand a consistent semantic theory. Secondly, by separating object-language and metalanguage in thought, we are able to determine, as seems best suited to the purposes for which the semantics or theory of meaning is being constructed, the application of certain crucial terms—for instance, 'true' and 'false'—without the intrusive necessity of being responsible to the way such terms are commonly applied *within* the language (i.e. the object-language) under consideration. But, when the language in question is our natural language, such a separation of object-language and metalanguage is only a picture. In practice, we cannot effect it, for the simple reason that we do not have any alternative language, richer than natural language, to employ as metalanguage: any new linguistic device, of superior expressive power, or with richer conceptual or ontological content, which we may introduce automatically becomes part of our own language, that is, of the natural language which we happen to speak, and, in view of the intercommunication between speakers of different natural languages, corresponding expressions rapidly become part of every natural language. This means, of course, that we can never succeed in constructing a complete theory of meaning or semantics for any natural language: but that is of no importance. It is of no importance, partly because many of the philosophical problems which most tantalize us, and which would be resolved by the successful construction of a theory of meaning for our language, are resolved when we have shown the general lines along which such a theory of meaning is to be constructed, without the necessity of actually constructing it in detail; and partly because other problems that arise, which may be philosophical or may be quite unphilosophical in character, can be dealt with by the detailed construction of only a fragment of a theory of meaning, since what is in question is the manner of functioning of only a particular fragment of our language. Such problems can be tackled piecemeal, and so the continual growth and enrichment of our language is no obstacle to their solution. But the artificiality of the separation between object-language and metalanguage does not lie only in the impossibility of our constructing any language which could serve as metalanguage: it arises also out of the fact that theorizing about our language and its working, theorizing which is carried out within that language itself, the only language that we have, is not an activity confined to philosophers, linguists and other specialists. It is, rather, an activity in which all speakers of the language constantly engage, however inchoately or inexplicitly, and which consequently affects our actual linguistic practice all the time. We do not merely employ the words of our language according to certain patterns, which a theorist could observe from our practice and encapsulate in his theory: we carry with us pictures, often vague but for all that exceedingly compelling, of the kind of pattern which we are observing in our employment of them, that is, of the kind of meaning which they have. Such impressions of meaning frequently have a decisive influence upon our employment of these words. When, as in the sort of case we have been considering, the justification of certain statements is called in question, we are forced to scrutinize these patterns of use, and perhaps to revise them or make them precise, with the intention of abiding, in our future use, by the new precise patterns. The practice of speaking a language and the theory of meaning which gives an account of that practice can thus not be separated, except in thought: they constantly interact with one another. The notion of sense is, therefore, not a mere theoretical tool to be used in giving an account of a language; it is one which, in an inchoate fashion, we constantly appeal to or make use of in our actual practice (as, for instance, when we challenge someone to make precise the sense in which he is using some expression).

Perhaps one or two disparate examples may help here to make more palatable the thesis I have been maintaining that a great deal of half-explicit theorizing about our use of language influences that use. (This thesis has no resemblance to anything Frege maintained: I have put it forward here solely in defence of Frege's notion of sense against an objection he could perfectly well have formulated, but never concerned himself to develop any explicit answer to.) As a first example, consider the long recognized futility of the positivist objection to scientific and metaphysical paradoxes such as Eddington's statement that physics has discovered that none of the material objects we ordinarily encounter is really solid. The positivist answer is to say that the meaning of the word 'solid' is constituted by the application we learn for it when we first become acquainted with the word, so that it simply is not open to discovery that objects like knives and tables are not solid (the 'paradigm-case' argument). But, of course, the fact is that, in one sense (note the expression, which is one *in use* in ordinary discourse, and not just a technical term of linguistic theory), if physicists have shown such objects to be composed of small particles separated by distances many times their own diameters, then they have shown that these objects are not, after all, solid. (Objections on the score that physicists have not shown that these objects are 'really' any such thing are quite a different matter.) For, as well as following the customary application of the word 'solid', the application according to those criteria we were taught to apply when we first acquired the use of the word, we also have a picture of the content of applying it to some object, namely as involving that the volume of space occupied by the object is continuously filled by matter. Exactly similar remarks apply to the positivist attempt to provide an easy solution of the free-will problem, and many other applications of the paradigm-case argument.

A quite different example concerns our use of the words 'true' and 'false'. These words are likely to figure as important basic notions of a theory of meaning for a language; and, as already noted, the application of them which is made in that theory of meaning has no need to correspond in detail with that application of the corresponding words of the object-language (if it does contain such words). Yet it is impossible to understand the dispositions which we have to apply or refuse to apply the English words 'true' and 'false' to statements made in English if we do not grasp that such dispositions reflect an inchoate theory for the explanation of certain sentential operators in terms of truth and falsity. It is commonly observed that our intuitive application of the term 'false' is largely governed by the principle that a statement is false if and only if its negation is true, supplemented by a general disposition on our part to construe as the negation of a statement the simplest plausible candidate for that role. It is much less commonly remarked that our application of the term 'true' to a statement is almost equally tightly bound up with our use of that statement as the antecedent in indicative conditionals. Because we shall, in Chapters 10, 12 and 13, be much concerned with the notions of truth and falsity, this point will not be further expounded here: all that here concerns us is the fact that our ordinary dispositions concerning the employment of the words 'true' and 'false' are governed in considerable part by a half-formed *theory* about an account of the use of negation and of the indicative conditional to be framed in terms of the truth-conditions of the constituent statements.

As a third example, let us consider the attitude we adopt to philosophical revisionists, such as, for instance, the intuitionists in mathematics. By 'revisionists' I mean those who, on the basis of considerations, sound or unsound, concerning meaning, propose an alteration in the established use of certain expressions or forms of statement: thus the intuitionists propose (among other things) to alter our assessment of the validity of forms of argument employed within mathematical proofs. If we considered any established practice unassailable, just in virtue of being established, such revisionists would have no title to advance their claims: they would be reformists in an area where reform was not to be contemplated. The very test of a theory of meaning would be, on this account, its harmony with observable practice: the revisionists would be self-condemned, because their theory of meaning confessedly entailed consequences inconsistent with that practice. But we do not take such a short way with revisionists of this kind: even when we reject their account, we do not suppose that it is a priori impossible for any account calling for a change of practice to be correct. The revisionist claims that he has arrived at his position by an analysis of the actual meanings of the statements with which he is concerned, as we derive these meanings from the training we receive in employing them. But, according to him, we form, by means of false analogies, a misleading picture of the kind of meanings which we attach to these statements, and, as a result, are seduced into certain particular practices in using them which are abuses precisely because irreconcilable with a correct picture of the meanings which those statements have, and which we have not altered but only misconceived. We do not have to accept any of these revisionist accounts in order to concede the truth of the thesis that our employment of our own language is not merely the phenomenon to be explained by a theory of meaning for that language, but already bears the imprint of our own only half-explicit theorizing about it: it is enough that we treat such accounts as at least conceivably correct.

APPENDIX TO CHAPTER 5

Note on an Attempted Refutation of Frege

Since this book went to press, I have had an opportunity to see Saul Kripke's 'Naming and Necessity', in *Semantics of Natural Language*, ed. Harman and Davidson, pp. 253–355. This essay mounts a strong attack on Frege's theory of proper names, in the strict sense of the term (which, for convenience, will alone be used throughout this note), an attack deserving of extended comment. There are a number of distinguishable issues.

NN 259 (1) Kripke alludes to those, such as Paul Ziff, who hold that proper names have no meaning and are not part of the language, but dissociates himself

NN 255 from them. He attributes to Frege an express declaration that the sense of a proper name is always the same as that of some one definite description, though noting that Frege allowed that a proper name in common use in natural language may have many different such senses associated with it by different speakers. He proceeds to launch an attack on this theory. In fact, Frege made no explicit statement to this effect, and it is extremely dubious that he supposed such a thing. It is true that, in giving examples of possible senses that may be associated with a proper name, Frege expresses these by means of definite descriptions; but this should be considered as merely a device for a brief characterization of a sense, rather than as a means of conveying the thesis which Kripke ascribes to Frege. What is important about Frege's theory is that a proper name, if it is to be considered as having a determinate sense, must have associated with it a specific criterion for recognizing a given object as the referent of the name; the referent of the name, if any, is whatever object satisfies that criterion. Sometimes the criterion may be capable of being conveyed by means of a definite description, in other cases not. It is therefore of importance to note how much of Kripke's criticism depends upon his excessively narrow interpretation of Frege, and how much is unaffected by taking Frege's theory as a 'sense theory' but not necessarily a 'description theory' (in fact, most of it is unaffected by the adoption of the broader interpretation).

Kripke's arguments are quite different from those of Wittgenstein apropos of the name 'Moses'. For Wittgenstein, the sense of a proper name is given, not *PI* 79 by a single specific criterion of identification, but by a cluster of such criteria: for an object to be the referent of the name, it is not necessary that it satisfy all these criteria, but only that it satisfy most of them, or, perhaps, merely a suitable number of them. Thus, for Wittgenstein, the sense of a proper name overdetermines its reference, and is, at the same time, elastic, in that we are prepared in advance to drop some of our criteria of identification if they are discovered not to converge with the others. Kripke regards Wittgenstein's modification as a mere variant of Frege's theory, as much subject to his counter-arguments as the original Fregean form.

(2) Kripke's first argument makes play with a distinction of Geach's I cite on p. 168, viz. that a proper name may be *introduced* by means of a definite description without thereby being stipulated as *equivalent* to it. Kripke describes this situation as one in which the definite description is used to 'fix the reference' of the name, but not to 'give its meaning'. He is prepared to allow that a proper name is frequently introduced in this way; he says further that, by stretching the application of 'definite description', we can force the case of a name introduced by ostension into this mould. Actually, since we do not need to ascribe to Frege the thesis that the sense of a proper name is always that of some definite description, there is no need to go in for any such Procrustean manoeuvre; we may simply say that Kripke agrees with Frege that a proper name is first introduced into the language by associating with it a criterion of identification, but that he differs from him in holding that such a criterion serves merely to fix the reference of the name and not to give its meaning. In fact, Kripke accuses Frege precisely of confusing these two things: he says (p. 277) that Frege uses 'sense' in two senses, both for the way the reference of a term is determined and for its meaning. We shall ask later what Kripke understands by 'meaning'.

Kripke uses various arguments, which will be considered later, to show that the means used to fix the reference of a name on its first introduction does not subsequently remain that which determines its reference. For the time being, however, we are concerned only with that argument of Kripke's which purports to prove that, even where the reference of a name is assumed to be fixed by means of some one definite description, still the description will not give the meaning of th name, i.e. will not be synonymous with it. It is therefore worth while to select an example for which it would generally be agreed that that assumption was true. Among personal proper names (from which, like most writers on proper names, Kripke draws most of his examples), there are very few instances of this; but one is that of the name 'St. Anne'. There are many legends about St. Anne, including an account of her life in one of the apocryphal Gospels; but there is little reason to suppose that any of these stories enshrines a genuine tradition. A due scepticism about these stories is not, however, an obstacle to the acceptance of the existing cult of St. Anne (the celebration of her feast, etc.), although this demands that the object of the cult be taken as having been a genuine historical person. The reference of the name 'St. Anne' can therefore be taken as fixed in essentially only one way, namely by means of the description 'the mother of the Blessed Virgin Mary': but we can claim to know nothing whatever about its referent, save for the obvious facts that she was a married Jewish woman living at the end of the first century B.C., etc. There is not even any presumption that the name she was known by in her lifetime was 'Anne'

NN 285-6   (Kripke makes pointlessly heavy weather of the fact that a proper name may have a translation from one language into another).

In the next chapter (p. 168), the only substance which is given to Geach's distinction between introducing a name by means of a definite description and stipulating it as equivalent to it concerns the case in which the definite description, and therefore the proper name, in fact proves to lack a referent. In such a case, an atomic sentence containing the definite description would, in accordance with Russell's Theory of Descriptions, be false, whereas the corresponding sentence containing the proper name would be neither true nor false: this shows that the proper name and the definite description would not coincide in sense. Kripke, however, claims to discern a far more striking difference than this between proper names and definite descriptions, which would preclude a proper name's ever being equivalent in meaning to a definite description: their behaviour, namely, in modal contexts. It is evidently true, for example, to say, 'The mother of Mary was necessarily a parent', at least where this is understood as meaning, 'It is necessarily true that, if there was such a person as Mary, and there was one and only one woman who was her mother, then that woman was a parent'. But it is not so evident that it would be true to say, 'St. Anne was necessarily a parent', meaning thereby, 'It is necessarily true that, if there was such a woman as St. Anne, then she was a parent'. For surely we can truly say, 'St. Anne might have died in infancy' or 'St. Anne might have remained a virgin all her life'. It appears to follow that 'St. Anne' and 'the mother of Mary' cannot be synonymous.

This part of Kripke's argument has very little force. It bears a certain resemblance to an argument cited by Moore to cast doubt upon the thesis

that 'exists' is not a predicate—more specifically, a thesis of Russell's that
we cannot meaningfully say, 'This exists'—from the fact that one can
usually truly say, 'This might not have existed'. The contrast drawn above
between proper names and definite descriptions in modal contexts is not as
sharp as there made out. After all, even though there is an intuitive sense in
which it is quite correct to say, 'St. Anne might never have become a
parent', there is also an equally clear sense in which we may rightly say, 'St.
Anne cannot but have been a parent', provided always that this is understood as meaning that, if there was such a woman as St. Anne, then she can
only have been a parent. Kripke indeed acknowledges that such a sense
exists, although not in connection with personal proper names. He com-   *NN* 274-5
ments on Wittgenstein's example of the standard metre rod in Paris, and
insists, as against Wittgenstein, that it is perfectly proper to ascribe to that
rod the property of being 1 metre long, on the ground that we can truly say
of it that it might not have been 1 metre long. But, in arguing this, he also
grants that, in another way, it is a priori true that the standard metre is 1
metre long. Of course, this case is not one to do with what is ordinarily called
a proper name: but Kripke wishes to apply his distinction between 'fixing
the reference' and 'giving the meaning' to this case also, holding that taking
the metre rod as the standard is a way of fixing the reference, but not of
giving the meaning, of the word 'metre'. Hence the concession must be
taken to apply to proper names in the more usual sense, at least whenever
there is something specific which may be taken as fixing the reference.

Conversely, however, there is equally a clear sense in which it is true to say,
'The mother of Mary might not have been a parent', and this Kripke also
acknowledges. Thus he says (p. 279) that one might truly say that the man
who taught Alexander might not have taught Alexander, but adds that it
could not have been true that: the man who taught Alexander didn't teach
Alexander. Again, in footnote 25 he says that the teacher of Alexander might
not have taught Alexander, and, in such circumstances, would not have been
the teacher of Alexander. So far, therefore, no difference between proper
names and definite descriptions appears at all. In both cases, there seems to
be an ambiguity in modal statements containing them: the very same
ambiguity in both cases, which accordingly cannot be used to differentiate
the two types of expression.

That the situation as regards proper names appears, so far, exactly like
that with definite descriptions is obscured by the fact that Kripke adopts
completely different explanations of the ambiguity in the two cases. In the   *NN* 279
case of definite descriptions, he says that the ambiguity arises because of
uncertainties of scope (in the sense in which Russell speaks of the scope of a

definite description). If we abbreviate 'x taught Alexander' as 'Tx', the sentence 'The teacher of Alexander might not have taught Alexander' may be written:

$$\Diamond \neg \, T \, (\imath x \colon Tx) \; .$$

If we adopt Russell's Theory of Descriptions, the definite description can be eliminated in more than one way, according to what we take its scope to be. If we take it to be '$\neg \, T(\xi)$', we obtain:

$$\Diamond \; \exists y \, [\forall x \, (Tx \leftrightarrow x = y) \, \& \, \neg \, Ty] \; .$$

This expresses the sense in which the sentence is false, i.e. the sense in which Kripke means to deny it by saying that it could not have been true that: the teacher of Alexander didn't teach Alexander. The definite description is here within the scope of the modal operator. If, however, we take the modal operator to fall, conversely, within the scope of the description operator, so that the scope of the latter is '$\Diamond \neg \, T(\xi)$', we obtain:

$$\exists y \, [\forall x \, (Tx \leftrightarrow x = y) \, \& \, \Diamond \neg \, Ty] \; .$$

This expresses the sense in which the sentence is true, that is, the sense in which Kripke wants to assert that the teacher of Alexander might not have taught Alexander. There is, indeed, nothing special to definite descriptions here; questions of the relative scope of the quantifier and the modal operator arise equally with 'Some teachers might not have been teachers'. It is, admittedly, obvious that anyone who says this must mean

$$\exists x \, (Qx \, \& \, \Diamond \neg \, Qx)$$

(where 'Qx' abbreviates 'x is a teacher'), and not

$$\Diamond \; \exists x \, (Qx \, \& \, \neg \, Qx) \, ,$$

since the latter would be such a stupid thing to say; but with, say, 'Some narcotics might not have been harmful', there is a genuine ambiguity.

Kripke is, of course, vividly aware that to invoke the notion of scope in order to account for the ambiguity is explanatory only when it is supplemented by an account of quantification into a modal context: i.e. when we either can explain when the predicate '$\Diamond \neg \, T(\xi)$' is true of an object, or can give a suitable account of the range of the bound variables as being something other than ordinary objects. We shall in due course consider how Kripke thinks this supplementation is to be carried out.

A theory according to which proper names were merely disguised definite descriptions would have no difficulty with the parallel ambiguity that arises when proper names occur in modal contexts: it can give a uniform account of both kinds of ambiguity, in both cases invoking the notion of scope in the same way. For such an account to work, in the case of proper names, it would be unnecessary either to adopt Russell's Theory of Descriptions or to maintain that proper names are always strictly synonymous with definite descriptions. So long as it is acknowledged, as it must be, that definite descriptions may sometimes lack reference, and that the existence or non-existence of a referent will, in general, affect the truth-value of a sentence in which a description occurs, there will be a need to determine the scope of a description in a complex sentence, whether or not Russell's Theory of Descriptions is taken as the right way of determining the truth-value once the scope has been agreed. One may, indeed, adopt some convention which uniquely determines the scope without the need for any special indication of it; but the question is there to be resolved. Likewise, so long as it is allowed that there may be proper names which are meaningful and yet not guaranteed a reference, and that the possession or lack of a reference by a proper name will in general affect the truth-value of a sentence in which it occurs, the question of scope may arise for a proper name. This is quite independent of whether or not it is held that the question whether a given proper name has reference may always be equated with the question whether some definite description does. It is independent also of whether it is held that an atomic sentence containing a proper name without a reference is false, or, with Frege, that it is neither true nor false. Again, the question may be resolved for all contexts by adopting some uniform convention determining the scope; thus Frege may be represented as having adopted the convention that the scope of a proper name or definite description is always to be taken as the widest possible, i.e. the whole sentence. The question was, nevertheless, there to be resolved.

It is thus plain that, so far as the present point is concerned, any theory which represents proper names and definite descriptions as functioning in essentially similar manners has an advantage over one that widens the difference between them, in that it allows a uniform explanation to be given of what appears to be just the same phenomenon—the occurrence of ambiguity in modal contexts—in the two cases. Kripke, on the other hand, wants to give an entirely different explanation of the phenomenon when it relates to proper names. In this case, he acknowledges no role for the notion of scope: and so he explains the ambiguity by saying that we are concerned, under the two interpretations, with different modal notions, different kinds of possibility. The sense in which we can truly say that the standard metre rod could not but be 1 metre long, or that St. Anne can only have been a parent, is an epistemic one. This does not mean that we are in these cases asserting the kind of epistemic necessity usually considered by philosophers, under which 'It must be . . . ' means 'It follows from what we know . . . ' and 'It may be . . . ' means 'It would be consistent with all we know . . . '. In the present case, our knowledge is genuinely a priori knowledge, given in advance of any particular observations or experience relating to the subject-matter of the sentence. It is knowledge derived solely from a grasp of the way in which the words are used, i.e. from the fact that 'the length of the standard metre rod' is used to fix the reference of '1 metre' and 'the mother of Mary' to fix the reference of 'St. Anne'. By contrast, the kind of necessity that we are concerned to deny when we say that the standard metre rod might have been shorter than 1 metre (e.g. if it had been deformed), or that St. Anne might not have been a parent (e.g. if she had never married), does not depend solely upon our grasp of the use of the words: it is a metaphysical necessity.

NN 261 Kripke reserves the phrase 'a priori' for epistemic necessities of the first kind, and the word 'necessary' for metaphysical necessities.

Kripke's views, thus set out, appear implausible. As remarked, we have one and the same phenomenon occurring both for proper names and definite descriptions. There cannot, therefore, be any argument from this fact alone to the conclusion that a proper name can never be equivalent to a definite description. In the case of definite descriptions, Kripke explains the phenomenon in terms of the notion of scope. For proper names, on the other hand, he considers the notion of scope inapplicable, and therefore invokes a distinction between two kinds of possibility. The argument for saying, in this case, that there are two kinds of possibility seems no stronger than it would be in the case of definite descriptions. When we say that the mother of Mary can only have been a parent, in that sense in which it is true to say this, are we not expressing a priori knowledge, based solely on our understanding of the words, precisely similar to that expressed by saying that the standard metre rod can only be 1 metre long? When, on the other hand, we say that the mother of Mary might not have been a parent, are we not concerned with the very same kind of metaphysical necessity involved in saying that St. Anne might not have been a parent? To explain the ambiguity, in the definite description case, in terms of uncertainty of scope, however, requires that the modal operator be taken as unambiguous: if its sense shifted, we should not need also to suppose that its scope altered, as we pass from one interpretation of the sentence to the other. Quite plainly, these considerations, so far from providing grounds against the assimilation of proper names to definite descriptions, supply substantial evidence in its favour.

This is not to deny that a distinction between the necessary and the a priori is called for. I shall discuss this in detail only in the second volume, when we come to consider Frege's doctrine on analyticity; but for the present we may observe the following. Frege uses both the terms 'analytic' and 'a priori' in an epistemic sense: the status of a sentence, as analytic, synthetic a priori or a posteriori, depends upon the kind of justification that could be given for it (only true sentences are in question): not, indeed, the kind of justification which we in fact possess, if we possess any at all, but that which we should in principle be capable of giving. If, however, we agree with Frege in adopting a realistic interpretation of the sentences of our language, there is room for non-epistemic versions of these notions as well. To adopt a realistic interpretation is to hold that the sense of our sentences is given in such a way as to relate to their determination as true or as false by a reality existing independently of us, and that, in a well-constructed language, every sentence will thus be determined as true or as false, independently of our capacity, even in principle, for recognizing what truth-value it has. Opposed to a realistic interpretation of this kind is any view which holds that the senses of our sentences are always given in terms of the means available to us for recognizing them as true or as false, so that the only notion of truth available to us is one under which a sentence is true only if there is at least some means in principle available to us for recognizing it as true. On any kind of idealistic view of the latter kind, any intelligible notion of necessity must, like the notion of truth, ultimately be of an epistemic character; that is, it must relate to the means by which we could recognize a sentence as true. This is not to say that, from an idealistic standpoint, we might nevertheless not admit several distinguishable kinds of necessity. But, from a realistic standpoint, such as Frege took, the way is open to introduce non-epistemic notions of necessity, although Frege himself did not do so. We may, that is, distinguish sentences as ontically (rather than epistemically) necessary or contingent according to the kind of thing in virtue of which they are true, independently of the means available to us for recognizing them as true; and, within this general notion of ontic necessity, we may be able to distinguish as many varieties as within that of epistemic necessity. A very clear case is precisely one adduced by Kripke. On Frege's view of arithmetic, a provable number-theoretic statement is analytic, in Frege's sense of 'analytic', that is, the epistemic sense. But if we adopt a platonistic view of number theory, i.e. if we interpret it realistically, as Frege did, then the truth of a number-theoretic statement does not depend upon our being able, even in principle, to find a proof of it. Hence it is possible that, say, Fermat's Last Theorem should be true, but not analytic in Frege's sense. It is, however, evident that there would still be an intuitive sense in

F

which it was necessarily, not contingently, true, that is, ontically necessary. In the particular example, this is plain from the consideration that, had it been false, its negation would have been epistemically analytic (since there would be a counterexample which we should be in principle capable of recognizing as such): this is not, of course, to claim that every ontically analytic statement would have this feature.

This distinction should be compared, though perhaps not equated, with that made by Aquinas in rejecting the ontological argument for the existence of God between a statement that is *per se nota* (necessary in itself) and one that is, in addition, *nota quoad nos* (necessary relative to us). The statement that God exists is, he thinks, *per se nota* but not *nota quoad nos*. This means that it is ontically necessary but not epistemically so, and hence there cannot be an a priori proof of it, such as the ontological argument purports to provide. This distinction has been jeered at by those who have argued that, since the language in which the statement 'God exists' is expressed is our language, if it is not analytic relative to us, then it cannot be analytic at all, but must be simply contingent; and they have proceeded to attempt to impale theists on the horns of a dilemma. Either the statement 'God exists', if true at all, is contingently so, i.e. there is a God but might not have been one; or it is analytic, in which case various dire, though dubious, consequences are supposed to flow, such as that one cannot base any expectations on one's belief in its truth. The theist rightly fights shy of allowing that there might not have been a God. He may, indeed, be properly suspicious of the consequences alleged to follow from admitting that 'God exists' is analytic, especially in view of the fact that his opponent's philosophical position usually embraces the thesis that all true mathematical statements are analytic; he may, nevertheless, like Aquinas, feel unwilling to allow that God's existence can be known a priori, by reflection merely on the meanings of the words. What his opponent has overlooked is that, even though the language we speak is our language in the sense that it is we that have given to our words the meanings that they bear, it is nevertheless part of any realist interpretation of language that that meaning is such that we grasp what it is for a given sentence to be true independently of the means we have for knowing it to be true. Until a realist interpretation is shown to be untenable, there remains room for the possibility that a statement may not be capable of being known a priori by us, and yet have a meaning such that its truth-conditions could not but be fulfilled.

These remarks do not purport to give definite substance to the notion of ontic necessity, merely to indicate that there is a fairly compelling intuitive content to the notion, and, on any realistic view of language, room for its

ST I 2 (1)

introduction. A possible way to approach it would be as follows. The simplest statements of our language are those that can be used as reports of observation or of other effective ways of determining their truth or falsity. For such statements, therefore, the realistic and idealistic interpretations coincide: we know what it is for such a statement to be true because we know how to determine it as true. As more complex methods of sentence-formation are introduced into the language, we step outside the range of statements that are even in principle effectively decidable by us. In doing so, however, we retain the capacity for knowing what it is for our statements to be true or false, and our grasp of the fact that they are determinately one or the other. This we do by extending various linguistic devices beyond the range within which we are capable of effectively applying them, by analogy with the more restricted contexts in which we first learned them, and within which we could apply them effectively. The analogy which we implicitly rely on is with a hypothetical observer not subject to the restrictions to which we ourselves are subject. A clear case would be the use of quantification over an infinite domain. We understand the quantifiers in the first place by learning to use them over actually surveyable domains: such a statement as 'Every room in the house has a fireplace' can be checked by inspecting each room in turn, and taking the logical product of the truth-values of the instances so determined. When, now, we use quantification over an infinite totality, say that of the natural numbers, we understand the truth-conditions of a statement involving such quantification by analogy with the primitive case: we tacitly appeal to the notion of an observer who is able to survey the whole infinite domain within a finite time. We ourselves are incapable in principle of doing this, and so, to determine a universally quantified number-theoretic statement as true, we have to have recourse to indirect means, that is, to means which do not directly mirror the way in which the truth-conditions of the statement are given to us. But our understanding of those truth-conditions, and therefore our capacity for conceiving that the statement may be true even though we have no means of recognizing it as such, depend upon the possibility of our transcending in thought the limitations which are, in practice or in principle, imposed upon our intellectual operations.

I do not know whether this is the right account of the matter. I do not even know whether realism can be made plausible, let alone whether, if so, the line just sketched is the right line for the realist to take. But, if it is, then it is clear along what lines the notion of ontic analyticity must be explained. If, for the understanding of a given sentence, it is necessary to invoke the conception of a being whose powers of observation or mental capacities transcended ours in a given respect, then the statement, if true, is ontically analytic if it would be epistemically analytic for such a being, i.e. if it could be known a priori by him. It is not clear that such a notion of ontic necessity would coincide with Aquinas' notion of a statement's being *per se nota*. Some statements are such that, if we can know them to be true at all, we must be capable, at least in principle, of knowing them a priori. Number-theoretic statements are of this kind. Of number-theoretic statements, we can say that, if they are true at all, then they are at least ontically necessary, and, further, that, if we are ever to come to know them, they must be epistemically necessary. Other statements have the character that we may know them to be true without knowing whether they are, epistemically, necessary or contingent. For instance, a statement might in fact be an instance of a provable schema of first-order predicate logic, and yet not recognized by us as such, but known to be true a posteriori, i.e. by ordinary empirical means. In such a case, we should know the statement to be true, but not know it to be epistemically necessary, although it was in fact so. There is no reason to suppose that there may not, equally, be statements which are ontically but not epistemically necessary, which we can know to be true without realizing that, if they are true, they must be ontically necessary. But Aquinas' doctrine concerning the statement 'God exists' fits none of these cases. This is a statement of which we can know that, if true, it is ontically, though not epistemically, necessary, and which we can, further, know a posteriori to be true. I know no reason why, under the account of epistemic and ontic necessity that has been outlined, there should not be statements of this kind; but, in default of other examples, it must remain doubtful whether Aquinas' distinction is the same as the one here drawn.

None of this has, however, very much to do with the topic of the behaviour of proper names and definite descriptions in modal contexts. This can be seen from the fact that both the notions of ontic and of epistemic necessity that have been being discussed concern the status of whole sentences. They therefore can be used, without supplementation, only to explain the occurrence of initial modal operators, whereas Kripke's account of definite descriptions involved treating such operators as capable of standing within the scope of other operators, in particular of quantifiers. In order to provide a sense for modal operators in such contexts, we have to take a step of quite a different kind from that of distinguishing ontic from epistemic necessity: we have, namely, to explain when a predicate containing a modal operator, for instance the predicate '𝜉 might not have been a leader' or '𝜉 might not have been 1 metre long', is true of an object.

Kripke does not draw his distinction between the a priori and the necessary in the way that the distinction between epistemic and ontic necessity has here been drawn. On the account sketched above, epistemic necessity is a stronger notion than ontic necessity: a statement may be ontically but not epistemically necessary, but the converse could not occur. Kripke, however, claims the properties of being a priori and being necessary to be quite independent: not only may a statement be necessary though not a priori; it can also be a priori without being necessary. An example of the latter would *NN 275* be such a statement as 'The standard metre rod is 1 metre long' or 'St. Anne was a parent'. Since the standard metre rod might have been shorter than 1 metre, and since St. Anne might never have become a parent, neither statement can be necessary; but anyone who knows the way in which the reference of the word 'metre' and of the name 'St. Anne' is fixed will know the truth of both statements a priori. According to Kripke, however, a parallel argument will not show that the statement 'The mother of Mary was a parent' is not necessary, since the fact that we may truly say that the mother of Mary might never have become a parent can be explained by invoking the notion of scope.

Kripke expresses some uneasiness about the claim that there are statements *NN 279–80* which are known a priori but are not necessarily true. He thinks that the generally accepted principle that everything a priori is necessary is incorrect as it stands, since, he says, it is undeniably a contingent fact that the standard metre rod is 1 metre long; but he thinks also that there may be a case for reformulating the principle so as to make it correct, although he admits that he does not know how to do this. His reason for suspecting that such reformulation may be desirable is that it is counter-intuitive to suppose that *NN fn. 26* someone who has fixed a system of measurement, say by stipulating that a metre is to be the length of a certain rod, has thereby acquired some information about the world, learned some new fact that he did not know before. Counter-intuitive it undoubtedly is, but it appears to follow from Kripke's arguments: something must, therefore, be amiss with those arguments.

Suppose someone writes out a table showing the purchasing value of the pound each year from 1950 to the present as a percentage of its value in 1950. Is it then necessary that the purchasing power of the pound in 1950 was 100? Obviously, it is both necessary and known a priori. Consider now the statement, 'Jesus Christ was born in 1 A.D.' This statement is certainly *not* necessary, since, according to the scholars, it is not even true. The reference of the dating system now used for most purposes in most parts of the world is no longer fixed by that event by which it was originally intended to fix it. On the other hand, in an earlier era in which the use of this dating system was less widespread, but, where it was used, the Christian religion

was far more dominant, it is to be presumed that, if the discovery had been
made then that the calculation of the year of Christ's birth was in error, the
dating system would have been adjusted accordingly. So at that time—
let us say in 1001 A.D.—it would have been possible, and correct, to assert a
priori that Christ was born in 1 A.D., at least if the speaker was prepared to
admit that he could be mistaken in supposing that Christ's birth took place
1000 years previously. Would someone who made such an assertion a
priori have been expressing a priori knowledge of a contingent fact? Surely
not: it may be a contingent matter that Christ was born in the year in which
he was, but (given the conventions here being assumed about the dating
system) not that he was born *in 1 A.D.* But is it a contingent fact that Christ
was born in the year in which he was? I am not here raising a theological
question, but could equally well ask: Is it a contingent fact that Shakespeare
was born in the year in which he was? Plainly, the answer is 'No', if the
question is taken to be whether the sentence, 'Shakespeare was born in the
year in which he was born', is only contingently true. In the case of
Shakespeare, we may say that this is not the question intended, but rather the
question whether the sentence, 'Shakespeare was born in 1564', is only
contingently true. But, in the case of Christ, the matter cannot be resolved
in this way, or, at least, could not have been in 1001, since the sense, if any,
in which it might be questioned whether 'Christ was born in 1 A.D.' was only
contingently true has yet to be made out. And this is how it is with the metre
rod. If it is a contingent fact that the standard metre rod is 1 metre long, its
contingency is not to be accounted for in terms of the a posteriori character
of our knowledge of the truth either of the sentence, 'The standard metre
rod has the length that it has', or of the sentence, 'The standard metre rod
is 1 metre long.'

In a sense, the sentence, 'I am here', is true a priori: that is, any English
speaker knows that, whenever he consciously utters the sentence, 'I am
here', he will be saying something true. So, if I say, 'I am here', am I
expressing a priori knowledge of some contingent fact? By reasoning as
Kripke does, the fact must surely be taken as contingent, since I may truly
say, 'I might not have been here'. Obviously this is wrong. By saying, 'I
am here', I may succeed in telling someone who hears me where I am: but my
knowledge that I can always truly say, 'I am here', is quite compatible with
my lacking, on a given occasion, the remotest idea where I am. In knowing
that I can truly say, 'I am here', I know nothing at all of my own whereabouts. Equally, if someone has no idea at all what length a metre is, save for
knowing that it is the length of some rod in Paris which he has never seen,
he may still know a priori that the metre rod is 1 metre long, but, in an

intuitive sense, he does not know how long the metre rod is, and hence does not give expression, by his remark, to knowledge of any contingent fact. If someone in 1001 understands the dating system, and hence is able to say a priori, 'Christ was born in 1 A.D.', but has no idea whatever what year it is when he says it, then, again, he does not, by his remark, express any contingent fact. It is, indeed, different if he does know the date, for then there is an at least arguably contingent fact which follows from what he says together with the fact, which he has not stated, that it is then 1001 A.D., the fact, namely, that Christ was born 1,000 years before: but then no one would think that he knew this fact simply in virtue of his grasp of the dating system.

It thus does not appear that the statements which Kripke wants to characterize as both contingent and known a priori can be so described if they are taken unambiguously. In 1001 someone who was ignorant of the principle underlying the dating system but knew what the date was might, if he gave the year of Christ's birth as 1 A.D., be said to know when Christ was born, and to know something substantial thereby; but he would not know the same thing as that known by someone aware of the principle of the dating system but ignorant even what century he was living in. (The improbability of these two extreme cases is beside the point.) We shall note later that it is of crucial importance that two people—these two imaginary individuals, for example—speak the same language and intend to be understood as speaking in that language. (As Quine has in effect pointed out, the situation is not essentially different if they speak different languages, but ones between which there is a generally recognized system of intertranslation.) This fact mitigates the effect of the different ways the two individuals imagined fix the reference of the expression '1 A.D.' Frege would say that they attached different senses to the expression. We are less inclined to describe the situation in this way; and one valid reason for this disinclination is awareness of the relevance of the fact that each intends to be held responsible for using the expression with that reference which is commonly agreed by speakers of the language which they have in common. It is, for this reason, entirely wrong to say that, because they attach different senses to the same expression, they therefore strictly speaking talk different languages. Neverthe- Ged 65 (12) less, it is equally wrong to minimize the truth in the contention that they attach different senses to the expression. We are less ready to admit this than we are to concede that they are different facts which they show knowledge of when they say, 'Christ was born in 1 A.D.' But, as has been emphasized several times, Frege's notion of sense is a cognitive one: difference in cognitive value is precisely what requires difference in sense to explain it.

Kripke wants, indeed, to dissociate the necessary/contingent distinction from epistemic considerations altogether. But this he fails to do. The paradox which we are presently engaged in resolving, and which arose from Kripke's thesis that something can be known a priori and yet be contingent, arises precisely from asking how, by merely stipulating a certain means of fixing the reference of an expression, someone could come to know a contingent fact about the world. If the status of a fact, as necessary or contingent, really had no bearing on the way in which it could come to be known, if at all, then this question would no more be paradoxical than the question how someone, by using field-glasses, could come to know an amusing fact.

What, then, is the fact whose contingency we express by saying that the standard metre rod might have been shorter or longer than 1 metre, but which is not expressed when we say a priori that it is 1 metre long or that it has the length which it has? So long as we pose the question in this way, there does not seem to be any satisfactory answer. Rather, it is not so much that some contingent fact obtains, at least, if we understand a fact as something that can be expressed by means of a sentence understood in some specific sense, but that a certain object, namely the standard metre rod, possesses a contingent property, that of being 1 metre long; or perhaps that a certain length, namely a metre, possesses the contingent property of being the length of the standard metre rod. If we refer to the rod as 'the standard metre rod', then we guarantee that (provided we are referring to anything at all) we are referring to a rod 1 metre in length; if we describe the length of the rod as being 1 metre, then, given that the reference of the word 'metre' is fixed as it is, we guarantee that we are referring to a length which is that of the standard metre rod. But that very rod which we refer to might have been of a different length; that very length which we refer to might not have been that of the standard metre. This sort of contingency cannot be grasped in terms of the notion of a contingent *fact*, but only in terms of that of an accidental *property*. And, indeed, Kripke himself strongly emphasizes the importance for his doctrine of the distinction between essential and accidental properties of an object. But what this means is that we cannot attain to the required notion of contingency by concentrating on the linguistic form 'It is contingent (possible, necessary) that . . .', where the gap is to be filled by an entire sentence; we have, instead, to understand the form 'It is contingently (possibly, necessarily) true of ξ that . . . ξ . . .'. We have to explain, not what it is for the sentence, 'The standard metre rod is 1 metre long', to be contingently true, but what it is for the predicate 'ξ is 1 metre long' to be contingently true of an object; equivalently, we have to

NN 265–6,
279, 288, 314

understand, not the sentence '◇ (the standard metre rod is not 1 metre long)', but the predicate '◇ (ξ is not 1 metre long)'. Just the same will be the case with the contingency which we express by saying that St. Anne might not have been a parent. We cannot understand this as relating directly to the status of the sentence, 'St. Anne was a parent', as this might be used to express something known a priori, but as saying of St. Anne that she possessed the accidental property of being a parent. 'St. Anne might not have been a parent' should not be rendered as 'It is possible that St. Anne was not a parent' but as 'It is true of St. Anne that she was possibly-not-a-parent'. But what this means is that, in order to understand the sort of contingency Kripke alleges to exist in these cases, we are compelled after all to invoke just that notion of scope to which Kripke appealed in the case of definite descriptions. In 'St. Anne might not have been a parent', the name 'St. Anne' must be construed as not being within the scope of the modal operator: precisely this is what is implicit in Kripke's account in terms of accidental and essential properties, as against contingent and necessary facts or statements. It is thus not merely that the uniform explanation, in terms of scope, of the ambiguity that occurs when either definite descriptions or proper names occur in modal contexts is preferable, because more economical, than having, in the latter case, to introduce the a priori/necessary distinction: it is that, in order to understand the notions of necessity and contingency that Kripke uses, we find ourselves forced to appeal to the notion of scope, for proper names as well as definite descriptions.

It is plain that the distinction between the a priori and the necessary, considered as resting on the contrast between that by which we may know a statement to be true and that which makes it true, is not actually involved at all in Kripke's explanation of the sense in which it may be said of St. Anne that she might not have been a parent. We are not, in fact, concerned at all with what it is that makes the *statement*, 'St. Anne was a parent', true: we are concerned with what makes being a parent an accidental property of the woman we refer to either as 'St. Anne' or as 'the mother of Mary'. Indeed, the notion of accidental properties requires, if it is to be viable, a great deal more discussion than Kripke allots to it, for all the use he makes of it; a mere reliance on intuition is not, in such a case, a guarantee that there really is a clear notion here. But, even granted that this notion can be made out, the upshot of our discussion so far is that no shadow of reason has yet emerged for rejecting even the strongest conceivable version of the theory Kripke is attacking, that version, namely, under which every proper name is equivalent to some specific definite description. We are far from committed to upholding any such extreme version of Frege's theory: but, up to this

F*

point, the considerations Kripke adduces, when correctly formulated, serve rather to corroborate the theory than to point to any defect in it.

As we have seen, Kripke does not succeed in disentangling epistemic properties from others as completely as he claims. Properly speaking, Kripke's notions of contingency and necessity do have as little to do with the way a statement is or can be known as that of being amusing; or, better, for him contingency and necessity are not properties of *statements* at all, but of *facts*. His wish to dispense with the notion of sense for proper names leads him to regard a fact as consisting, e.g., in the possession by an object of a certain property, or in two objects' standing to one another in a certain relation. A fact, so conceived, may be taken as forming the content of a particular statement, but it certainly cannot be identified with the thought expressed by the statement, as Frege conceives of it, and hence cannot properly speaking be said to be an object of knowledge at all. The knowledge which someone expresses by means of an assertion (when it is knowledge) is the knowledge that the thought expressed by the sentence used to make the assertion is true; it cannot, properly speaking, be taken to be the knowledge that that fact obtains (in Kripke's sense of 'fact') which is the content of the assertion. Thus, for instance, Kripke's notion of facts leads straight to the conclusion, willingly drawn by Kripke, that the fact which is the content of a

NN 310-11   true statement of identity is always a necessary one: for it is just the fact that a certain object bears to itself that relation which every object bears to itself and to no other. By adopting Russell's Theory of Descriptions, it is possible for Kripke to refrain from applying this doctrine to identity-statements involving definite descriptions. This, however, has no real bearing on the tenability of Kripke's view; it merely serves to make it less evident that the fact conveyed by a statement, as understood by Kripke, cannot be equated with its cognitive content, and thus to prepare the trap which Kripke falls into when he speaks of someone's knowing a contingent fact.

NN 267,   Kripke expresses reservations about the explanatory character of the
fn. 15   treatment of modality in terms of possible worlds very similar to those which will be voiced in Chapter 9: but he nevertheless formulates a great deal of what he has to say in terms of that notion. In these terms, he draws the distinction he sees between proper names and definite descriptions by saying that proper names are rigid designators, while definite descriptions are not.

NN 269   A rigid designator is defined to be a term which stands for the same object in every possible world in which it has a reference at all. Thus the definite description 'the man who led the Jewish people out of Egypt' is not a rigid designator, since there are possible worlds in which it was a different man from Moses who led the Jews out of Egypt; but 'Moses' is a rigid designator, since in every possible world 'Moses' will stand for just that man to whom, in the real world, we refer by means of the name 'Moses', save for those possible worlds in which it has no referent.

Kripke accuses Frege of confusing the meaning of a term with the way *NN* 277 in which its reference is fixed. He fails, however, to explain at all the notion of meaning to which he is appealing; in particular, although he holds that the status of a statement, as a priori or a posteriori, depends on how the references of its terms are fixed, he does *not* say that its status as necessary or contingent is correlative to their meanings. If it were, the meaning of a term would have to be a function defined over some or all possible worlds, whose value for any possible world was an object in that world; the worlds for which it was undefined would be those in which the term had no reference. I shall here borrow the term 'connotation' for the meaning of a term, so understood. The connotation of a proper name, or of any rigid designator, would be a constant partial function.

The thesis that proper names are rigid designators is expressed in terms of the metaphor of possible worlds, and hence, to give it substance, we must remove the metaphor. And, as soon as we try to do this, we see that it concerns nothing other than our old notion of the scope of a term in a modal context. For a definite description, the divergence between its meaning and the way its reference is fixed is not apparent; in other words, the way in which the reference of a definite description is determined in the real world is carried over into each particular possible world. The whole point of saying that, for a proper name, its meaning diverges from the way in which its reference is determined is to make clear that the latter is not taken as carrying over into whatever possible world we are concerned with. This must be understood as meaning that, by using a definite description in speaking of hypothetical circumstances, we intend to say what would, in those circumstances, be true of the object to which the description would then apply, but that, by using a name, we intend to say what would be true of that object which we normally use the name to refer to. This is intelligible only if we already understand what it is to say, of some object, that something would be true of it in given circumstances; and this is just to understand what is meant when the term used to refer to the object is construed as lying outside the scope of the subjunctive conditional. If we do not understand this, the metaphor of the name's having the same referent in a possible world as in the real one cannot be interpreted. To assign to a term a reference varying from one possible world to another is just to take it as having, in each possible world, the reference which it would bear in that world; conversely, to assign it a constant reference is to take it as having, in each world, just that reference which it has in the real world. To take a term in the second way is to explain the truth-condition for a sentence containing it as coinciding with that for the sentence that results from removing the term from the scope of the modal operator. When Kripke says it could not be true that: the teacher of Alexander didn't teach Alexander, he is intending to convey that, within any possible world, it would never be true to say, 'The teacher of Alexander didn't teach Alexander'. Here the definite description is taken to have as referent, within each possible world, the unique object (if any) which in that world satisfies the predicate 'ξ taught Alexander'; and we display our adoption of this interpretation by rendering the sentence with the description taken as falling within the scope of the modal operator, namely as:

$$\neg \Diamond \; \exists y \; \forall x \; [(Tx \leftrightarrow x = y) \; \& \; \neg \; Ty] \; .$$

When, however, we assert that the teacher of Alexander might not have taught Alexander, we are treating the definite description as having, as its constant referent, that referent which it has in the real world, and this is done by taking the description to lie outside the scope of the modal operator.

Kripke's doctrine that proper names are rigid designators and definite descriptions non-rigid ones thus provides a mechanism which both has the same effect as scope distinctions and must be explained in terms of them. We could get the same effect by viewing proper names, in natural language, as subject to a convention that they always have wide scope; Kripke is saved from having to view definite descriptions as non-rigid in some contexts and rigid in others only by explicitly appealing to the mechanism of scope in their case. Such an explanation would not demonstrate the non-equivalence of a proper name with a definite description in any very strong sense: it would simply show that they behaved differently with respect to ad hoc conventions employed by us for determining scope. Kripke's account makes the difference between them seem greater than it is by appealing to different mechanisms to explain comparable phenomena, and by arbitrarily ruling out the use of proper names with narrow scope to yield a sense distinct from the wide-scope reading, save by using a distinct modal operator.

This is not to say that there are no differences between proper names and definite descriptions, of a sort Kripke may be taken as driving at, even in a case of the most favourable kind, such as that of the name 'St. Anne'; and we do not need to look at modal contexts to discern these differences. A large number of definite descriptions are formed from predicates that are significantly present-tensed, and frequently may be true of one object at one time and of another object at another. A consequence of this is that, even when they are so qualified that they could apply to at most one individual, they are still regarded as present-tensed, in such a way as, e.g., to admit the verb 'become' in front of them. Thus we should tend to say that in 1960 Nixon was to be the winner of the 1968 Presidential election, rather than simply that he was the winner; and, in the course of speculating about St. Anne's life, we might say that at a certain age she became the mother of Mary. A definite description will, in general, come to apply to an object at a certain time, even if it is of such a kind that it will continue to apply to it thereafter. (There are, of course, some definite descriptions that apply from the moment the object came into existence.) This is not to deny that a definite description can properly be used to refer to an object at a time before that description became applicable; we can, e.g., quite properly say that the winner of the 1968 Presidential election entered politics in such-and-such a year. By contrast, the condition of being the bearer of a given proper name is not thought of as one that is acquired. This is a point which it is hard to formulate accurately. We may say that, when Miss Smith married Mr. Jones, she became Mrs. Jones, even though the name that she then acquired may be used to refer to her at times before her marriage, e.g. in a sentence like 'Mrs. Jones had a very unhappy childhood'. Here 'Mrs. Jones' appears to function exactly like the definite description 'the wife of Mr. Jones'. But this case should rather be compared to that in which we say that St. Petersburg became Petrograd, and later Leningrad. In this sense, the (tensed) predicate 'ξ became a' is true of an object at the time when the proper name 'a' first came to be used of it, rather than at that at which it first fulfilled the condition by which the reference is fixed. The example of 'Mrs. Jones' confuses us, because in this case the one moment is the same as the other. But we should not say that it was not until St. Anne gave birth to Mary that she became St. Anne. (It may be said that the case of 'Mrs. Jones' is not like that of 'Leningrad', on the ground that, if Miss Smith had married Mr. Jones in secret, so that she continued to be known as 'Miss Smith', it would nevertheless be right to say that, on her marriage, she became Mrs. Jones. What seems to make the difference here is that there is, in our society, a *general* convention regarding the names of married women, whereas what fixes the reference of the name 'St. Anne' is particular to it. On this ground, it might be claimed that appellations like 'Mrs. Jones' are titles rather than proper names.)

These considerations, expressed quite independently of modal contexts or of possible worlds, indeed show that proper names do not function in quite the same way as definite descriptions, even in a case in which there is some one definite description which fixes the reference of a name. If one liked, one might put this by saying that it is not strictly accurate to say that the name 'St. Anne' has the sense of the definite description 'the mother of Mary': rather it has a sense such that it is replaceable either by 'the mother of Mary' or by 'the woman who was to be the mother of Mary', according to context. As already observed, in defending Frege, we are not committed to the thesis that the sense of a name must be expressible as the sense of a definite description, but only to the more general thesis that a proper name has a sense which is that by which its reference is determined, so that there is nothing to trouble us in making the admission that, in the respect des-cribed, proper names behave differently from definite descriptions.

What has this difference in the behaviour of proper names and definite descriptions to do with modality? The point turns on Kripke's use of the notion of accidental and essential properties. We may, from the examples he gives, elicit something like the following, which relates to questions of identity, although not to the identification of an object as the bearer of a particular name. Suppose given an object, of some determinate sort; and consider any predicate which is, at some given moment, true of that object (we need not be supposed to know that it is true). There are now two possibilities. It may be ruled out, by the criteria of identity for objects of that kind, that the predicate, being now true of the object, should later cease to be true of it, or it may not. In the former case, we may say that the predicate stands for a presently essential property of the object, in the latter that it stands for a presently accidental one. A presently essential property is one which the object, having acquired, cannot cease to have: for it is ruled out in principle that we should ever subsequently correctly identify an object recognized as then lacking the property with one, of the given sort, recognized as formerly possessing it. Thus it is a presently essential property of President Nixon that he is not a frog, or indeed that he is a human being: for it is ruled out that we should ever in the future correctly identify a frog, or anything other than a human being, as being the former President Nixon. It is likewise a presently essential property of his that he is over 40, that he is of Caucasian race, or that he is the man who won the 1968 election. It is, on the other hand, an accidental property of President Nixon that he is not a circus clown, that he is male, that he is under 100, or that his complexion is what is called 'white'. This distinction between presently essential and presently accidental properties may be used to elucidate one, very weak, use of the modal auxiliary 'might': at any given time, it may be truly said of an object that it might come to satisfy a certain predicate provided that its present failure to satisfy this predicate does not constitute one of its presently essential properties. (This account is certainly not quite watertight, but it is at least as accurate as Kripke's, and will serve its purpose for the present discussion.) We may now define an (absolutely) essential property of an object as one which, at every time during its existence, was a presently essential property of it, and an (absolutely) accidental property to be one which, at some moment during its existence, was a presently accidental property of it. In terms of this notion, we can elucidate the use of 'might have'. It may be truly said of President Nixon, for instance, that he might never have been a politician, because there was a time in his life at which it would have been true to say that he might never become a politician. It is in just this sense that we can say that St. Anne might never have married, or, again, that the star Polaris might have been nowhere near the celestial North Pole (because, e.g., the Earth's axis might have been differently tilted). It is because the kind of possibility in which Kripke is principally interested is to be explained in some such fashion as this that he finds it difficult to provide an example of an essential property of an object of any given sort which other objects of that sort fail to possess, save for the circumstances of its origin. Of Moses as a new-born baby, for example, almost anything that a man could become could have been truly said to be something that that baby might become; and hence, of any such thing, we may say that Moses might have become it. But we cannot push back the moment in respect of which a property is to be characterized as presently accidental behind the point at which the object came into existence: that is why, in the case of a human being, his parentage and even the moment of his conception seem absolutely necessary to his identity, and are virtually the only examples of essential properties, other than those common to all men, which Kripke is able to cite.

We are now in a position to understand the grain of truth in Kripke's doctrine of proper names as rigid designators. For modal contexts in general, there is no relevant difference between proper names and definite descriptions: but the matter stands otherwise when the name or the description is preceded by the verb 'to be' or 'to become'. We may intelligibly say that the mother of Mary might never have become a parent, or even, at a pinch, that the mother of Mary might not have been the mother of Mary; but we cannot say that St. Anne might not have been St. Anne, and, if we say that the mother of Mary might not have been St. Anne, it is still the definite description, and not the name, which lies within the scope of the modal operator, just as when we say that St. Anne might not have been the mother of Mary (though the two statements are not equivalent). The reason we have already seen: it is not a general feature of the behaviour of proper names in modal contexts, but has to do with the fact that we do not regard such a predicate as 'ξ is St. Anne' as standing for a property that can be *acquired*. The mother of Mary did not become St. Anne when she bore Mary: she always had been St. Anne, because she always had been the one who was to be the mother of Mary. Hence being St. Anne is not a candidate for being an accidental property of anybody. And even this, we have seen, needs qualification. There is a sense in which the mother of Mary may be said to have become St. Anne, not indeed at the time when she gave birth to Mary, but when she was recognized by the Church as a saint and her cult established under the name 'Anne'; and in this sense it could be said that St. Anne might not have become St. Anne, and even that the mother of Mary might not have done so.

Doubtless an account of this type does serve to explain quite a range of modal statements, and, equally, a large number of counterfactuals; though, at least as far as counterfactuals go, Kripke's schema of explanation is insufficiently flexible. It certainly appears that the antecedent of a counterfactual has to represent a possible state of affairs, in some meagre sense of 'possible', if the counterfactual is to be assessed at all as true or false, plausible or implausible: and when we speculate, e.g., what would have have happened if Charlemagne had married the Empress Irene, it is true enough that we tacitly suppose the course of history to have gone exactly the same as in reality up to the occurrence of that imaginary event and its immediate preliminaries. But the antecedents of counterfactuals are not restricted to possibilities of the kind Kripke is interested in: we may quite intelligibly discuss, for example, what Lewis Carroll would have achieved if he had been born fifty years later, or wonder what difference it would have made to Franz Kafka's outlook if he had not been of Jewish descent and upbringing.

The explanation of modal statements and of counterfactuals is not here our direct concern, only their bearing on the meanings of proper names and definite descriptions. It is rather natural to think that, while the actual reference of an expression relates only to the real world, its sense must be determined by what its reference would be in every possible world. For instance, must not the sense of a predicate both determine and be determined by what objects it would be true of in all possible circumstances? It therefore seems very plausible that we may identify the sense of an expression with what I called above its 'connotation'. Kripke has since denied that he meant 'connotation' by his use of 'meaning', though the interpretation is hard to avoid. In any case, the notion of connotation remains a non-epistemic one; that is, it does not give an account of what it is that someone knows when he understands a word, which is precisely what the notion of sense, as introduced by Frege, is required to do. In certain cases, it is at least plausible that there will be a one-one correspondence between Frege's senses and our connotations: but that will be so only for words and expressions of which we can say that there is no gap between their meanings and the way in which their reference is determined, as we saw might, in general, be said of definite descriptions. Even in such a case, the notion of 'connotation' is not a credible representation of the knowledge that someone has when he understands the expression: what someone grasps when he understands a predicate is the principle by which we determine whether or not it applies to any given object, not what its actual extension is in each of the infinitely many possible worlds. Still, if '$F(\xi)$' is a predicate of which we may say that there is no gap between the way its reference (or application) is determined and its meaning, then two things hold good. First, anyone who grasps the principle by which we determine whether it is true of any given object will be able to say, given a sufficient description of some possible world, whether or not it would be true of a given object in that world. And, secondly, someone who does not fully grasp the sense of the predicate may be able to discover this by describing imaginary circumstances, and asking whether the predicate would or would not be true of given objects in those circumstances. But this breaks down precisely in the case in which there is a gap between the meaning and the way in which the reference is determined, that is to say, in the case of rigid designators. The gap shows itself in the divergence between the answers to the questions, 'Would you call a person "St. Anne" if she proved not to have been the mother of Mary?' and 'Would that person (viz. St. Anne) still have been St. Anne if she had not become the mother of Mary?'; and just for that reason the answer to the latter question is of no help in telling us how the reference of the name 'St. Anne' is determined, i.e. how we should recognize someone as the bearer of the name.

Kripke operates, let us recall, with two notions of possibility, an epistemic and a metaphysical one. The epistemic possibilities are, so to speak, the things that could have turned out to be so, so far as we knew; the metaphysical possibilities are those that are *really* possible, irrespective of our knowledge. There are things that could not have turned out to be so, but are real possibilities nonetheless: e.g. that the standard metre rod might not have been 1 metre long, or that St. Anne might not have been the mother of Mary. Conversely, there are things which could have turned out to be so, but are nevertheless not real possibilities. The Morning Star might have turned out to be a different celestial object from the Evening Star, but this is

NN 307, 331-2

not a real possibility, since it is an essential property of the planet Venus (as of everything else) that it is identical with itself. Even if this distinction were the right one to draw, it is plain that it is the notion of epistemic possibility that is required if we want to represent sense as a function from possible states of affairs to reference. Sense is (to repeat yet again) a cognitive notion: it relates to our mastery of language, i.e. to the way in which we set about determining the reference of our words. Hence, if we want to get at the sense of an expression by imagining states of affairs and asking what its application would then be, these states of affairs should be taken as those which might turn out to be so, whether also classifiable as real possibilities or not.

Actually, it has been argued here that, although there is a genuine distinction between epistemic and ontic possibility, Kripke misdraws it. The supposed distinction between types of possibility, between what what could have turned out to be so and what might really have been so, which Kripke uses to characterize most of his examples, is much better explained as a variation in scope. To appeal to the notion of scope requires, as we have seen, that the notion of a *statement's* being necessarily or contingently true must be supplemented by that of an *object's* having an essential or accidental property: but this distinction is misrepresented by Kripke as being one between different types of necessity (between being necessary and being a priori) that may independently apply to the same subject, viz. a statement. The notion of a property's being essential to an object does not *compete* with that of a statement's being necessarily true, since they are not ascribed to the same thing. That is why the former may be taken as supplementing the latter, so that we may use both to interpret a modal operator without conferring any ambiguity on that operator: it is this that makes it possible to appeal to the notion of scope at all. All this has, however, as we saw, very little to do with the difference in behaviour of proper names and of definite descriptions: both, in modal contexts, may have wider or narrower scope. If it were correct to say, tout court, that proper names are rigid designators, this would, in our terms, be a way of saying that their scope always included the modal operator. But, as we have seen, the phenomenon Kripke is alluding to is of much more restricted application than he supposes: it relates only to occurrences of proper names after verbs like 'be' and 'become', not to all occurrences in modal contexts. In Kripke's terminology, this means that proper names do not always function as rigid designators; in ours, that they sometimes occur within the scope of a modal operator. Once this is allowed, and once it is recognized that what is relevant is not the (quite genuine) distinction between epistemic and ontic possibility, but the quite different one between a contingent statement and an accidental property, then the way is open to consider even a proper name as a flexible designator: that is, to consider what object, if any, would, in a given possible world, constitute its referent, if that referent were determined in the same way as is done in the real world. ('Possible' here must mean 'epistemically possible': that is the only relevant notion when we are concerned with the epistemic question what we grasp in grasping the use of a word.) With the doctrine thus revised, there would indeed be a one-one correspondence between Fregean senses and Kripkean meanings. It would remain that it was the former of these two notions that was the genuinely explanatory one.

(3) Kripke does not rely solely upon arguments from modal sentences: he claims that, where some definite description is used to fix the reference of a proper name, not only may we say that the bearer of the name might not have satisfied the description, but, in some cases, we may actually discover that he or it does not. Thus, perhaps the way most people would favour to explain the reference of the name 'Kurt Gödel' is by means of the description 'the man who first proved the incompleteness of arithmetic': but, for all that, it is perfectly intelligible to suppose that it might be discovered that *NN* 294 Gödel was not the first to prove the incompleteness of arithmetic, or even that he was an impostor and never proved it himself at all.

In this particular example, as Kripke grudgingly admits, the explanatory description is easily amended so as to circumvent the difficulty, namely to 'the man under whose signature a proof of the incompleteness of arithmetic was first published'. Nevertheless, it is quite true that the point is one of some general importance. But, unlike the objection to Frege's account which we considered under (2), the present one, and the related one we shall consider under (4), does not demand a rejection of Frege's account, but only a modification of it along Wittgensteinian lines. If the objection treated under (2) could have been sustained, it would have shown definitely that the sense of a proper name can never be identical with that of a definite description. Admittedly, we rejected Kripke's claim that Frege believed such an identity to hold in the case of every proper name; it remains that it is essential to Frege's account that the sense of a proper name can be that of a definite description, and will be so for any proper name that is introduced by means of a definite description: hence, if the argument had worked, it would have been a flat refutation of Frege's account. To this argument, Wittgenstein's modification of Frege's account, by replacing a single sharp criterion for identifying the referent by a cluster of alternative ones, of which we are prepared in advance to abandon any fairly small subset, is quite irrelevant. If the argument had worked, it

would have told just as much against the modified account as against the
original one.

The present objection is entirely different. Not only can it be met by a
modification of a Wittgensteinian type, but consideration shows that only
such a modification will account for those cases in which the objection
fails. For, in so far as a single definite description supplies someone with
the only means he has for determining the reference of a name, he cannot
treat as intelligible the suggestion that the description does not apply to the
bearer of the name. A young child, who has learned of Shakespeare only that
he was the author of *Hamlet*, *King Lear* and other plays, can make nothing of
the information that some people think that it was not Shakespeare who
wrote them: he is bound, on being told this, to ask, 'Who, then, was Shakespeare?' As Kripke himself points out, in a rather different connection, it
would be no use to reply, 'The man generally supposed to have written
those plays', for, in order that it be possible to suppose that a particular
thing is true of a certain man, there must be some means of identifying that
man otherwise than as the man of which that thing is true. If we have all
agreed to use the name 'Q' as the name of a document containing sayings of
Jesus and drawn upon by the writers of the first and third Gospels, then there
is no content whatever to the supposition that there was such a document as
Q, but that it contained no mention of Jesus and was unknown to any of the
Evangelists.

NN 296

What makes it possible to entertain the possibility that Gödel might be
discovered not to have proved, or not to have been the first to prove, the
incompleteness of arithmetic is the fact that there exist other generally
accepted ways of determining the reference of the name 'Gödel'. This is
always the case with any name about whose bearer a good deal is known by
at least some who use the name; and it is never the case with a name about
whose bearer practically nothing is known save that it satisfies the description which fixes the reference of the name. Hence something like Wittgenstein's modification of Frege's account is not merely adequate to meet this
objection, but is actually called for by the facts. Of course, we can imagine a
document being discovered which was identifiable, and identified, as a copy
of Q; and we can also imagine that it was later decided by scholars that,
despite considerable overlap between sayings recorded in this document and
those reported in the Gospels, nevertheless none of the Evangelists had seen
this work. In such circumstances, we should be led to assert, what we now
cannot regard as intelligible, that there was such a work as Q, but that it was
not seen by any Evangelist. But this very fact—that a sentence formerly
devoid of content should have been rendered intelligible and, indeed,

correct—makes it irresistible to say that, in such a case, the sense of the name 'Q' would have undergone an alteration: from having associated with it a single sharp criterion of identification, it had acquired a different criterion or, perhaps, a cluster of them.

Another of Kripke's examples concerns the name 'Newton': he supposes children to be introduced to the name by being told that Newton was the man who discovered that there is a force pulling things to the earth. He thinks that such children have a false belief *about Newton*; and this shows that a description used to introduce a name not only does not give its sense but may not even fix its reference, as was intended. Even if there were several famous historical characters by the name of 'Newton', and even if the misconception were not a common one, it would be clear enough to us what discovery it was of which the child had been given a garbled version, so that we have a straightforward enough reason for saying that it was of Sir Isaac Newton that he had been given misinformation. But the child himself knows nothing of this reason that we have, so that the fact that it is about Newton that the child has that belief has nothing to do with his grasp of the use of the name. When the true state of affairs is explained to the child, he has to abandon the original description as fixing the reference of the name. There seems no reason at all to deny that, in the process, his understanding of, and thus the sense which he attaches to, the name has changed; unless we are prepared to take the heroic course of saying that someone who had no more than heard the name 'Newton', without having any means of fixing its reference, without knowing anything at all about its bearer, would nevertheless understand it and be capable of using it with the reference commonly attached to it.

These considerations shade into those raised by the fourth point made by Kripke, which, again, is one of very general interest.

(4) All of us frequently use proper names of which we can give no very good explanation: not that none exists, but that we do not know it. One kind of example of which Kripke makes much is the name of a theory or part of a theory, such as 'General Theory of Relativity' or 'Gödel's Theorem'. (The latter is certainly a proper name, and not a description: Gödel has proved many other theorems, and, even if he were later to be found not to have proved the incompleteness theorem, it would almost certainly still be called after him.) Kripke points out that many people employ these names without being anywhere near a capacity to state the theory or the theorem which they designate. Actually, this is too strict a demand. Neither Frege nor anyone else would suppose that one did not attach a sense to the name of, say, a city unless one was familiar with its history, or could draw a street-plan

of it or state its population and principal industries. It is sufficient that one have a definite criterion whereby one could correctly identify a city as the bearer of that name. One does not have to be able to state a theory or a theorem in order to attach a sense to its name, just as long as one has adequate means for discovering, of a statement of a theory or theorem, that it is the one denoted by the name; and this identification would not need to go via the person who framed the theory or proved the theorem.

Still, there are certainly cases in which a proper name is used without its user attaching to it anything that Frege would consider a sense. If, when I come home, one of my children says to me, 'Mr. Cunningham telephoned and asked if you would ring him back', the child may no more know the sense or the reference of the name 'Mr. Cunningham', which, let us suppose, he has never heard before, than does a piece of paper on which such a message is written; the child is acting merely as a recording apparatus. But there is no sharp line between such a case and a fully fledged mastery of a name: a whole series of transitional cases stretches from one to the other.

If a person knows of Milan only that it is a city somewhere on the continent of Europe, we should hardly ascribe to him a complete grasp of the name 'Milan'. But how much exactly should he know in order to be said to have such a grasp? If he knows that it is in North Italy, and that Ambrose was once bishop there, even though he could not locate it on a map, is this enough? Are we not all often in a much worse position about the names of less famous places, which we should not hesitate to use, and should be surprised to be told we did not know what they meant?

Suppose that someone, largely ignorant of science, knows of General Relativity that it is that branch of physics in which his nephew specialized at the university. In one respect, he attaches a definite sense to the name 'General Relativity Theory': he has a reasonably precise criterion for identifying some branch of physics as being what the name denotes. Should we say that he has a better grasp of the name than does someone who has no such criterion, but can give a sketchy and inadequate account of the theory?

Of course, this phenomenon is not confined to proper names. Someone may tell, say, a humorous story in which essential use is made of the word 'magenta', although he knows of this word only that it stands for a shade of colour, without any clear idea which: it does not matter to the story.

In a great many such cases, we are exploiting the fact, known to us, that the word we use is part of the common language. We use the name of a town, knowing only that it is a smallish town somewhere in southern Spain, secure in the knowledge that it could be more precisely identified by ourselves or our hearers, when necessary, by means of maps, reference works, road signs or questions addressed to people living in the area. Kripke amuses himself by attributing to his opponents a 'transcendental deduction *NN* 293 of the existence of encyclopedias', but the situation would be essentially the same, though far less convenient, if writing had not yet been invented: what we are relying on is the fact that the name is part of established usage. This does not mean that someone so using a name, say 'Stow-on-the-Wold', can be said to attach to it the sense, 'The town known to its inhabitants as Stow-on-the-Wold' or 'The town generally known in English as Stow-on-the-Wold': the sense of a name must provide a criterion of identification independent of any pre-existent use of the name, and similarly with other kinds of words; it must be a sense with which the name could be newly introduced into the language. What it means is, rather, that one of the ways in which it is essential to language that it is a common instrument of communication is that there is no sharp line between the case in which a speaker makes a fully conscious employment of the sense canonically attached to a word and that in which he acts as a recording apparatus. We are able to exploit the fact that a word has a generally recognized sense, which may be discovered by standard means, even when we have only a partial knowledge of that sense; and we do.

At the opposite extreme lies the private use of names, by which I do not mean names in a private language, as this notion is criticized by Wittgenstein, namely as something in principle incommunicable; but, for example, the use of nicknames, as employed by members of a small circle. A man may even employ a special name, for a person or place, for his own use only, e.g. in writing what is to be seen by himself alone, for brevity or out of facetiousness, or for many other reasons. In such cases, it is evident that, unless the user of the name has a perfectly definite criterion for identifying its bearer, then that name has no determinate sense and hence no determinate reference. An intermediate case is that of the private sense for the public word, where, however, the intention is to determine the same referent as that which the word has in its public use. A child, or an adult, may attach to the name 'Innsbruck' only the sense 'that place where Aunt Rosemarie broke her ankle', while realizing perfectly well that the name is the generally accepted name of a place which others identify by quite different means. It is crucial, for the understanding of what someone says, that we know whether he intends a word he uses to be taken as part of the common language or not. When someone uses a private word, knowing it to be such, it is obvious that he does not; and, sometimes, he may use a public word in a sense, private to himself though known to his hearers, which he intends to be followed in case of conflict. Thus, someone may have fallen into the habit of referring to Westminster Abbey as 'Westminster Cathedral', and, even though informed that that is really the name of a quite different building, persist in using the name that way: every time he uses it, he intends his hearers to understand, 'the building that *I* call "Westminster Cathedral" '. (A similar, though more complex, case would be that of deliberate adherence to a widespread, though erroneous, use, as when someone refers to the short poem beginning, 'And did those feet . . . ', as *Jerusalem*, knowing quite well that Blake gave that title to a different and much longer poem.) More usually, in so far as a question arises, a private sense is subordinated to the intention to conform with the publicly agreed reference of the name. Someone who can pick out Innsbruck from among other cities only by the fact that it was there that his Aunt Rosemarie broke her ankle will nevertheless, in using the name 'Innsbruck', intend to be taken as referring to the city for which that name is ordinarily understood as standing; so that, if he happens to be mistaken in supposing that it was in Innsbruck that Aunt Rosemarie broke her ankle, it will nevertheless have been Innsbruck, and not the city where that accident in fact occurred, that he will have been talking about. Such a case is therefore less like that in which someone uses a private nickname, with a precisely delineated sense, than like that of someone who, in the fashion of a recording apparatus, uses a name to which he attaches no definite sense, but of which he knows that, as a word of the common language, it has such a sense, and intends it to be so understood.

It is not possible that none of those who use a name have any criterion for identifying the bearer of the name, that all of them use it with only a partial criterion in mind, but with the intention of referring to the commonly agreed referent: for there would, in such a case, be no commonly agreed referent. It is conceivable, for example, that a wide circle of people were in the habit of using the word 'Easthampton' as the name of a town in England, say with a vague impression that it was somewhere in the East Midlands. In a sense, the name would be part of the English language; it might even appear in a number of dictionaries, with the entry 'town in the East Midlands of England'. Those who used the name would do so with the intention that it be understood as having its commonly agreed referent. But, if we suppose that there is no single person who knows, and no printed reference-book which supplies, any determinate way of identifying a town as being Easthampton, then the name has no referent and no definite sense.

May it not be possible, however, that there are some speakers who attach to a certain name a purely private sense, although in each case the referent is the same; but that, although the name may be said to belong to the common language, there is no canonical means of identifying its referent, and therefore no public sense attaching to it, as opposed to the many private senses? With a single type of exception, it is hard to fabricate examples: but a case might be that of the name of a wood, seldom visited and in an area which had never been surveyed. Each person would identify the wood as one seen or visited by himself or by some acquaintance on some specific occasion, or as the location of some particular episode; the place is mentioned too rarely and there is too small a common stock of knowledge about it for there to be any commonly agreed method of explaining the reference of the name; but what makes it a word of a common language or dialect is that all, or most, of the divergent explanations of it determine the same referent, and the speakers know that this is so. Such a case is indeed conceivable: what takes the place here of an intended subordination to the commonly accepted sense of the name is an intended subordination to the reference common to all, or to a majority, of those who use the name. In fact, the situation approximates to this whenever the name is one of a person, an animal, a boat, etc., that has not attained any degree of celebrity. In discussing proper names, these tend to be the kinds of names on which philosophers concentrate, so that their special features are too readily generalized: with proper names of other sorts, there is far more often what can be recognized as the sense attached within the language as a whole, one given by a canonical form of explanation of the name. But even in the case where such a public sense does not attach to the name, its reference depends upon there being some speakers who attach a determinate sense to it, that is, a determinate criterion for identifying its bearer, even though none that is uniform from speaker to speaker.

In the use of a proper name which belongs to the language as a whole, and is not the idiosyncratic usage of an individual or group (here of course again the dividing line is blurred), there are two distinguishable features. On the one hand are the senses attached to the name by individual speakers, that is, the particular propensities they have for identifying an object as the bearer of the name. On the other, very often, there is the sense of the name as a word belonging to the common language, that way of determining its reference which constitutes the principle of nomenclature accepted as correct and to which, normally, a speaker intends to subordinate his use of a name even when he does not himself know what its public sense actually is. Dictionaries, encyclopedias, atlases, text-books, etc., do not have to exist; but they do exist, and their existence has its effect on the practice of using language, in that they are recognized as carrying authority though not infallible. In a non-literate culture, the tradition of correct usage, including the correct employment of proper names, will be enshrined in different institutions: in anything properly termed a language, rather than a dialect, there will be such a conception of correct as against incorrect ways of using words. It is a mistake to dismiss that conception as mere snobbery, an attempt by one social class to impose its speech-forms on the others, or to invest them with a spurious cachet (like the drivel about U and non-U terms which was current some years ago). Such an element does, undoubtedly, usually intrude; but it should occasion no surprise that human beings do desire, and strive, to impose upon their language a certain stability, effected by the recognition of standards of correctness, just as they seek to regulate other conventional activities by laws, customs, principles of etiquette, etc. Without agreement, language ceases to function as an instrument of communication; without the recognition of some authority, however imprecise, as to what is and what is not correct, such agreement becomes more difficult to maintain. Compilers of dictionaries who purport to be undertaking a purely descriptive rather than prescriptive task are either the victims of a confusion which denies in principle the possibility of labelling as incorrect anything that anybody says, or else are ignorant of the role which dictionaries do in practice play in literate societies.

Naturally, this is not to deny that language changes, or to pretend that anyone can or hopes to resist all such change. In particular, as already acknowledged, both the public and the private sense attached to a proper name consist, not in a static propensity for identifying something as its bearer, but in one that may be constantly modified by the acquisition of new knowledge about the object named. It is only when problems arise that it becomes desirable to arrest temporarily the process of modification, to fix, for general purposes or for a particular discussion, a precise and determinate sense for a word, proper name or otherwise. Such problems may arise when the existence of a referent comes into doubt, or when criteria of identification appear unexpectedly to diverge; or, as we have noted, they may arise because of a need to systematize knowledge of some topic, or to enquire into the exact justification of what is generally held.

Thus the simple model whereby a proper name possesses a unique and specific sense, common to all users of the name, which determines its reference, requires qualification in many respects before it becomes a realistic picture of our actual employment of names. Frege did not consider it a realistic picture of actual practice: he knew it perfectly well for an idealization, but considered it an idealization that displayed the essential mechanism of language, as well as one to which for scientific purposes we need constantly to try to approximate. In actual practice, senses are blurred, vary from speaker to speaker, fluctuate with time, in all the ways described and doubtless others. In this they are no different from other words: all attacks on the notion of sense, as applied to proper names, may be made with equal justice to extend to very many other classes of words, and, when that extension is made, their force is seen to peter out. What must be resisted is the temptation to think that the need for these multiple qualifications of the simple account in order to do justice to the complexity of actual linguistic practice destroys the utility of the original model, whereby a name has reference in virtue of its sense; for that model displays the only mechanism by which a name could acquire reference, even though the actual working has been simplified for the sake of perspicuity. It is not a choice between Frege's theory and some alternative theory: there is no other theory.

This remark may appear preposterous: has not Kripke supplied just such an alternative theory? Before I attempt to justify the remark, it is worth giving some attention to a part of Kripke's article that lends great force to the rest, because it makes a number of quite just observations which are, however, less closely connected with the other doctrines than he makes it appear.

(5) Kripke applies his notion of a rigid designator to expressions which are not ordinarily thought of as proper names. We have already noted one example of this—a term for a unit of measurement, such as 'metre'. Others are mass terms, such as 'water' and 'gold'; terms for physical phenomena, *NN* 315-38 such as 'heat', 'light' and 'sound'; and words for kinds of organism, such as 'cat' or 'ant'. By Frege's criteria, all of these, in certain of their uses, would CN 84 count as proper names; and, at least in the case of words for kinds of organism, there is a sense in which such uses are primary. Kripke quite rightly observes that a term like 'tiger' is not applied solely on the basis of purely *NN* 317-18 qualitative criteria. Even if there were found to be on Mars creatures resembling men in every respect, they would not be men, unless, indeed, their presence were due to interplanetary travel that occurred millennia ago; to be a man is not merely to be an animal describable in a certain way, but to be a member of a race, i.e. descended from a common stock. ('Species' would be, as it were, too specific a term to use here: there are many species of ants, but it is nevertheless in accordance with the ordinary meaning of 'ant' to say that white ants are not true ants, because they are not genetically connected with other ants, save in being insects.) Thus the use of the predicate ' . . . is a tiger', as applied to individual beasts, is in a sense dependent on the use of 'the tiger' as the proper name of a race of animals (in a sense, that is, which does not require that the latter be actually learned first, or even that it actually exist within the language). Kripke is actually more concerned to insist that we do not determine the application of such terms by purely superficial qualitative criteria, e.g. an animal which to outward appearance

was just like a tiger but which was in fact a reptile would not be a tiger. In most cases when we deny a common genetic origin to superficially similar creatures, we do so on the basis of a divergent internal structure, but it is the (presumed) common origin, and not the structural similarity, which is the decisive factor. Kripke's point can thus actually be strengthened, as it has been here: even if creatures *exactly* like men arose from dragons' teeth, they would not be men, because not children of Adam. A dictionary entry under a word like 'tiger' provides, normally, a definition of the word used as the name of a species or broader genetic group: e.g. an entry under 'whale' beginning 'any of various marine mammals of the order Cetacea, . . . ' is to be understood in the sense in which the blue whale is one such mammal, the sperm whale another, not that in which an individual sea-beast can be said to be a mammal. It is tacitly understood that to call an individual beast a 'whale' is to predicate of it membership of any one of the species characterized by the definition.

Somewhat similar remarks apply to mass terms. These can be used as proper names of substances, as in 'Water is a compound', 'Water has a boiling point of 100° C.', etc., but are rather differently used in 'Give me a glass of water', 'He fell into some water', and the like. There is, of course, in their use no reference to common origin; but Kripke is entirely right in *NN* 316 saying that it is part of their meaning that they are used to refer to distinguishable *kinds* of stuff. In some few cases, origin is important. I suppose that, even if chemists had succeeded in reproducing the exact structure of silk, what they produced would still be artificial silk and not silk, and similarly with wood. In general, however, we should be inclined to say that what mattered was not superficial appearance but chemical composition. Kripke gives the example of fool's gold, and surely the resemblance could be much closer; something might for everyday purposes be indistinguishable from water, and still not be water, because of a different chemical composition; and, as Kripke says, citing the case of 'heavy water', conversely.

What does all this have to do with Kripke's views on proper names of people, places, etc.? Kripke's idea is that the superficial properties by which we originally identify a race of animals or a kind of material constitute the *NN* 325 way in which we 'fix the reference' of the corresponding word. Just as, when we fix the reference of a personal proper name, we do not purport to employ an essential property of the individual named, so these superficial characteristics are not claimed as essential properties of the species or type of substance; just as we may abandon as incorrect the means we first used to fix the reference of a personal name, so we may later allow that these are not really even accidental properties of the species or substance. Gold might not have been yellow: it may not even in fact be yellow (we may all be suffering from an illusion). But it is necessarily an element—no chemically compound substance could be rightly identified as gold, however like gold it appeared—even though, when we first fixed the reference of the term 'gold', we had no idea of its being an element.

All this appears to fit so smoothly into Kripke's technical apparatus that it seems to provide strong reinforcement for his doctrines about proper names, although actually it has very little to do with them. No one supposes that the reference of a proper name is determined solely by qualitative features of the individual either at the time at which the name is used or at the time that is being spoken of, that is, by features whose presence or absence can be determined by examination of the individual at the relevant time. If, to take a crude example, the reference of 'Manhattan Island' is fixed by 'the long narrow island off the Atlantic coast of the United States with all those skyscrapers, just by the Statue of Liberty', that does not preclude the use of the name at, or of, a time when the island did not yet have, or no longer has, all those features. That is precisely why it is essential to the understanding of a proper name that one knows the criterion of identity associated with it; the sense of a personal proper name requires that its bearer be identified as the same man as the one who, at an appropriate period, fitted some description (if that is how the reference of the name has been fixed). For this reason, if the description by which we attempt to fix the reference of a name is later found not to have a unique application, we do not insist that anyone fitting the description is a referent of the name, but feel bound to change the sense of the name. There is, indeed, as Kripke recognizes, a very good analogy here with names of species or of kinds of substance, which is precisely why Frege is right to classify these as proper names, along with names of individual people, places, stars, etc. In order to grasp the sense of the name of a species, or, more generally, a race of animals, we have to know the criterion of identity for a species or a race, namely a common descent. It is certainly no part of the sense of the name that any individual member of a species have all the features by which the species is picked out (the existence of freaks, sports, etc., is always provided for); it is not even excluded that there may prove to be a whole sub-variety lacking some of these features. Just as someone is the referent of a given name provided that he is the same man as the one who at a given time answered to a certain description, so a beast is (say) a tiger provided that it is of the same species as those which satisfy the characteristic description. Again, just as, when we try to fix the reference of a name, we are aware that we might have failed to do so, so, when we try to pick out a kind of animal, we must be prepared to find that we have confused two genetically distinct kinds. Somewhat similar remarks apply to kinds of substance, although the criteria of identity here are less precise.

All that this shows is that Frege was right to classify such words, in certain of their uses, as proper names, to which must be added the observation that other uses are, in a sense, dependent on these ones; it has no tendency to show that there was anything incorrect about Frege's model of the sense of a name. Kripke's efforts to show that that by which we originally identify the species or the substance might not be true of it at all—'might not', that is, in the sense 'could turn out not to be in the real world', rather than his favoured sense 'might not have been in some other possible world'— are bizarre and quite unconvincing; we need not take seriously his suggestions that it may be that no gold is yellow, that all cats have only three legs, or the like. It really is part of the sense of the word 'gold' that its characteristic examples are yellow, or of 'cat' that it applies to the members of a quadrupedal species. But it is not part of the sense of 'gold' that something white cannot be gold, or of 'cat' that a three-legged monstrosity, born of a cat, is not a cat.

In this discussion, it has nowhere been suggested that Kripke's distinction between essential and accidental properties is untenable or useless. I do not know whether or not it is useful to apply it, as Kripke does, to the genetically significant structural features of animal species, or the underlying chemical structures of substances: but it is certainly no part of my thesis to deny this. All that I am denying is that it is in any way helpful to construe the term 'meaning', as applied to words like 'tiger' or 'water', so as to make this meaning relate solely to the actual structural properties of the species or the substance, regardless of the means by which we identify it, or even of whether we are aware what those properties are. The grain of truth in this contention is one which is fully in accord with Frege's doctrine, viz. that it is part of the sense of such a word that it stands for a species or a kind of substance, not for something recognizable by external appearance alone.

(6) Section (4) ended by my saying that there is no alternative theory of proper names that can be opposed to Frege's. This may be thought grossly unfair. True enough, Kripke himself disclaims possession of a theory: but he claims to give a better and quite different picture. But what is it a picture *of*? Is it a picture of what a speaker's grasp of the use—his use, or the correct use—of a name consists in? It can hardly be this, because it alludes to matters quite outside the knowledge of the individual speaker, namely the history of the name from the moment of its original introduction to its use by that speaker. In any case, if it were this, it would not stand in the kind of opposition to Frege's account that Kripke represents it as standing; for to grasp the

NN 280, 300–1

NN 302

use of a word just is to attach a sense to it. Is it, then, a picture of what reference consists in, for names; that is, an account of what it is for a proper name to stand for an object? It may well be so understood: but only as serving as a kind of stipulative definition of the phrase 'The name . . . stands for the object . . . '. It cannot be an account of what endows a proper name with reference, as Frege understands the term 'reference'. For reference, as it figures in Frege's theory of meaning, has an essential connection with sense: the sense—which is what a speaker knows when he understands the word— must be capable of being exhibited as a means of determining the reference. The notion of reference ought not, that is, to be idle within the theory of meaning. When someone knows the sense of a sentence, what he knows is how the truth-value of the sentence is to be recognized, whenever we are in a position to do so: and if a reference is to be significantly attributed to a word, then, for at least some sentences containing the word, the account of the process of recognizing that such sentences have one or other truth-value must involve the recognition of something as the referent of that word. If this is not so, then, however clearly we may be able to explain the attribution of something which we choose to call 'reference' to that word, the notion of reference we are employing has no role to play within the theory of meaning, as far as it relates to that word. Kripke's account, however, does not describe anything which could be involved in anyone's recognition of an object as the referent of a proper name: hence, though it may succeed in stipulating a sense in which we might, for some purpose or other, choose to say that, by using the name, someone had referred to the object, the sense of 'reference' so stipulated can have no part in any theory of meaning, that is, in a theory of what the use of proper names consists in so far as a mastery of a language requires a mastery of that use. In any case, Kripke himself repudiates any claim that he has provided an account (even stipulative) of what it is for an object to be the referent of a name: for, as he points out, his account *NN* 302 itself invokes the notion of reference.

Kripke's account is this. First, there is an initial baptism, i.e. the name is introduction by ostension, or by means of a definite description that fixes its reference, or in some other way. At this initial stage, then, things are just as Frege says (provided that we drop the ascription to Frege of the view that the sense of every proper name must be that of a definite description). Subsequent speakers use the name with the intention of using it with the reference with which it was originally endowed. Later still, yet other speakers pick up the use of the name; and they employ it with the intention that it shall have the same reference as it had in the mouths of those from whom they learned it. This process continues, and so the use of the name is passed from link to link of a chain of communication: what joins each link to the next is its causal connection with it, together with the persistent intention to use the name with the same reference as the previous speaker.

If we ignore the bit about intention, then what we have is something that might be interpreted as an explanation, or stipulation, of what it is for a name to stand for an object: a name stands for an object if the use of the name is causally connected, via a chain of communication, with the original introduction of the name, and, when the name was originally introduced, it was invested for the time being with a sense which determined it as the name of that object. There is, indeed, nothing objectionable in introducing a notion of reference so explained: the question is what use such a notion is. Even if it could be demonstrated that reference, as so explained, coincided extensionally with our intuitive notion of a name's standing for an object, this question is still to be answered; for the proposed explanation in no way serves to give the point of the intuitive notion of reference. Certainly, the notion of reference, as explained in terms of a chain of communication, has no bearing on the way in which we do, as a matter of practice, determine a sentence containing the name as true or as false. We can rarely establish with certainty, and sometimes cannot establish even with probability, the existence of such a chain of communication; we cannot trace the use of the name back in time to its first introduction. And, even when we can, such etymological research plays no part in our ordinary procedure for determining a sentence as true or as false. The notion of reference, explained in this way, bears no relation to our understanding of our language, to our mastery of the practice of using it. Admittedly, one might, by means of a notion of reference as thus explained, give an account of what it is for sentences of our language to be true or false: but this would, again, be a mere stipulation of new notions of truth and falsity, which would have at best an extensional coincidence with the notions of truth and falsity which we employ intuitively or which are needed for a theory of meaning for our language, that is, a systematic account of its actual working.

In any case, there is no reason to suppose that the notion of reference, as explained in terms of a chain of communication, would coincide extensionally with the intuitive notion. As Kripke remarks, if I call my pig 'Napoleon', this may be causally connected with the use of the name for the Emperor, but leads to no identification of the Emperor with the pig. Indeed, the same is true of the use of the name 'Napoleon' for Napoleon III, or of any other dynastic name or any case in which one person or place is called after another. It is for this reason that the qualification is introduced that the use of the name must be made with the intention of effecting the same reference as that from which it was derived; a qualification which of course destroys the possibility of taking the account as an explanation, or even a stipulation, of the notion of reference. This is, however, just the difficulty: we have not been told what the required intention is an intention to do. Each speaker must intend to refer to the same object as the speaker from whom he heard the name: but what is it to refer to an object? We should gain some guidance on this if we were told what it would be to fail in this intention. But apparently the intention is a self-fulfilling one. There are, indeed, self-fulfilling intentions, and ones which occur in connection with reference: if I use the name 'Harold Wilson', and intend thereby not to refer to the leader of the Labour Party but to some other man of that name, then I have not referred to the leader of the Labour Party, although I may be taken as having done so and held accountable for having been so taken. But the existence of such a self-fulfilling intention is intelligible only because it is possible to describe an action which would constitute the fulfilment of that intention independently of the presence of the intention. That is, of course the action could not be correctly described as 'the fulfilment of the intention' unless the intention were present; but it could be described as effecting what the intention was an intention to do. Thus, if I use an expression such as 'Harold Wilson, the archaeologist', or 'Harold Wilson—I don't mean the politician—', then I certainly do bring it about that, if I am referring to anyone, it is not the leader of the Labour Party; and I should do so independently of any intention I might have to achieve such a result—even, if I were in a state of great confusion of mind, if I had the intention thereby to refer to the leader of the Labour Party. It is because we know what it is to refer to something, by the mere use of words (given that the speaker is conscious and in other respects in a normal mental state, etc.), independently of any background intention, that we can allow, in cases of ambiguity, that intention determines reference and is to that extent self-fulfilling. But that is just what we do not know, on Kripke's account. It appears that, if someone uses a name with the intention of referring to the same thing as did the speaker from whom he heard the name, then he cannot but succeed: but we have no idea what it would be to refer to that thing in a way that did not depend upon the presence of such an intention; and so we cannot grasp what intention it is that we are required to have—what it is that we must intend to do—if we are to effect this feat of referring to an object.

In actual practice, it is highly dubious that an intention to effect the same reference as did a previous speaker is always fulfilled: why should it be? We can never trace out in detail a chain of communication of the kind Kripke describes. Often, however, we can, by making a large number of plausible

G

conjectures, render it quite probable that an earlier use is etymologically
connected with a present one, though often we cannot go back all the way to
the original introduction of the name. But, in the same way, we can sometimes establish with reasonable probability that a name has been unwittingly
transferred from one bearer to another. Kripke's account leaves no room for
the occurrence of a misunderstanding: since to speak of a misunderstanding
would presuppose that the name did in fact have a sense which could be
misunderstood. Thus, for instance, there is now a German card game called
'Tarock'. This word is undoubtedly derived etymologically from the same
word as formerly employed in Germany, and still in Austria, as the name of
the game played with the special form of pack generally known in England as
the Tarot pack. A form of this game is still played in part of Germany under
the name 'Cego', while the name 'Tarock' is now exclusively used for a
distantly related game played with a more ordinary form of pack. It is
possible that this change in the reference of the name 'Tarock' is the result of
a deliberate transference. But it is equally possible that it is the result of a
misunderstanding; that, at each step in the etymological chain, each speaker
intended to use the name with the same reference as previous speakers, but
that a confusion occurred about what that reference was. (It is easy to see
how this could have happened. The game now called 'Tarock' was formerly
known as 'bayrischer Tarock', presumably because of its resemblance to the
game formerly called 'Tarock'; in the meantime, of the several variants of the
latter game, only that known as 'Cego' survived in Germany.) Such a supposition is perfectly intelligible to us, because we have a criterion, although
imprecise, for 'the same game', and we have a criterion for determining what
game a name is being used as the name of, independently of the historical
origin of the name. It is the business of a theory of reference to explain what
that criterion is. Kripke's account does not purport to be a theory, in this
sense. Still, it would be fatal to its apparent capacity to act at least as a
surrogate for such a theory to admit that the existence of a chain of communication, even welded link to link by the presence of the necessary intention to preserve reference, might still not guarantee that the reference was
preserved.

   In the case of words of other kinds, we should not have the slightest
inclination to say that an intention to use a word as others use it would be
bound to succeed: a person may quite well be unaware that he is using a
word in a different way from others. In the case of a proper name, if we arm
ourselves with the Fregean distinction between sense and reference, we can
not only explain what determines the reference of a name, but we can admit
the possibility that the sense undergoes alteration while the reference remains

constant; the multiple ways in which it must be conceded that sense may be incompletely determinate, or may vary from speaker to speaker, do not undermine the account. Kripke wants to throw away the sense/reference distinction in favour of a causal connection backed by the intention to preserve reference. He himself acknowledges that the necessity to invoke this intention disqualifies his account as an explanation of what reference consists in; but, if it is to be explanatory at all, it ought at least to be taken as characterizing persistence of reference. Of course, in some few cases, the intention to achieve the same reference as a previous speaker is an essential ingredient, even a nearly exhaustive one, in the use of a name. If there survives a single text, from some ancient historical source, mentioning a certain individual, about whom the text tells us virtually nothing but his name, then, until more information becomes available, any use of that name can be taken only as referring to whatever man the ancient writer was referring to. Such a case is, however, atypical: it is a mistake to think that, in contemplating it, we have uncovered the true mechanism of reference. Kripke expressly wishes to allow that the association with a name of a description which in fact does not apply to the person or thing for which the name was originally introduced does not deprive that name of reference to that person or thing: it merely reveals a false belief about the referent of the name. There is therefore no room in Kripke's account for a shift of reference in the course of a chain of communication: the existence of such a chain, accompanied all the time by the required intention to preserve reference, must be taken as guaranteeing that reference is in fact preserved. Intuitively, however, there is no such guarantee: it is perfectly possible that, in the course of the chain, the reference has been unwittingly transferred. Once this is conceded, the account crumbles away altogether. We are left with this: that a name refers to an object if there exists a chain of communication, stretching back to the introduction of the name as standing for that object, at each stage of which there was a *successful* intention to preserve its reference. This proposition is indisputably true; but hardly illuminating.

CHAPTER 6

Some Theses of Frege's on Sense and Reference

IN THIS CHAPTER, I shall complete the exposition of Frege's doctrine concerning sense and reference; of the points here discussed in preliminary fashion, some will be taken up in greater detail later.

NS 275 (255);
BW 127, 156
(79, 98)
(1) *The sense of a complex is compounded out of the senses of the constituents.* For Frege, we understand the sense of a complex expression by understanding the senses of its constituents. In particular, we grasp the sense of a whole sentence by grasping the senses of the constituent expressions, and, of course, observing how they are put together in the sentence. This does not mean merely that our route to a grasp of the whole complex happens to lie through grasping the senses of the components: it is, rather, that what our understanding of the complex consists in is an apprehension of its structure together with a grasp of the senses of the components. Our grasp of the sense of a proper name, for instance, may be taken as our associating with it a particular way of determining some object as its referent. If the proper name is complex, if, for example, it is formed by filling the argument-places of some binary functional expression with two simple proper names, then our means of determining a reference for the complex proper name will relate to the senses of the two constituent simple proper names, and to the means we associate with the functional expression for determining the value of the function for any given pair of arguments. We thus could not assign that sense to any expression save as determining the referent as being the value of that function (given in that manner) for those two arguments (given in that manner). We might well, of course, associate the same reference with an expression in some other way, but we could not associate the same sense with it without viewing the expression as having a parallel

152

structure. Thus the complexity of the sense of an expression is preserved through definition: if a simple expression is introduced by definition as being equivalent to a complex one, we can grasp the sense of the former only via the definition; that is, it is only by conceiving the defined expression as equivalent to the complex by means of which it was defined that we can assign that sense to it which the definition conferred upon it. The sense of a complex sentence is thus actually composed of the senses of its constituents.

When the complex expression is a complete sentence, Frege calls the sense which it expresses a 'thought'. This notion of a thought fulfils for Frege the role which the notion of a proposition fulfilled in British philosophy, especially in the hands of Russell and Moore, in the first part of the twentieth century. There is, however, a crucial difference. Since Moore and Russell drew no distinction, for what they considered to be genuine proper names, between sense and reference, the meaning of a proper name, that is, the object for which it stood, was for them an actual constituent of the proposition. While the proposition was intended by them not to be a full-blooded denizen of the real world, so to speak, the fact that among its constituents were actual objects belonging to that world gave it a curious hybrid status: and Moore and Russell were constantly perturbed by whether or not to identify true propositions with facts, which they took to be fully part of the real world, or merely to regard the one as corresponding to the other, whether to admit the existence of false propositions, and similar problems, and constantly changing their minds on these points. Frege had no such problems. His 'thoughts' were, like Russell's 'propositions', that to which, primarily, we ascribe truth and falsity: for Russell, the sense in which a belief is true or false is a secondary one, relating to whether the proposition which is the object of the belief is true or false; for Frege, likewise, the sense in which a sentence is true or false is a secondary one, relating to whether the thought it expresses is true or false. Frege felt no impulse to take the notion of facts seriously, to admit facts as a category of entities which we must regard as among the inhabitants of the real world. But, in any case, he is quite clear that a thought does not have as its constituent the referent of any expression in the sentence which expresses it. The thought expressed by 'Everest is the highest mountain in the world' has, as one constituent, the sense of the proper name 'Everest': it does not have the mountain itself as a constituent—a thought is not the sort of thing of which a mountain can be a part.

Frege occasionally speaks (in his unpublished writings) of the 'realm of sense' and the 'realm of reference'. The realm of reference just is reality, that reality of which we speak and in virtue of which the thoughts which

NS 142 (131);
Ged 61 (4–5)

NS 273 (253)

NS 150 (138),
189 [8] (174
[8])

BW 127 (79)

NS 133 (122),
209–10
(192–3), 275
(255); GG1
371

we express are true or false: it is the entire universe, for there is nothing in the universe of which we may not speak and which may not therefore constitute the referent of some expression which we use. But the realm of sense is a very special region of reality: its denizens are, so to speak, things of a very special sort. The exact ontological status of senses Frege found it embarrassing to describe: there is nothing that can be done with a sense save to grasp it, express it and thereby convey it to another, and, in the case of a thought, assert that it is true, or ask whether it is true, or the like. For all

NS 145-6
(134), 214
(198)

that, Frege did not want to say that thoughts, or senses in general, are mental entities: for he was afraid that that would make them too little unlike 'ideas', i.e. mental images, and perhaps share with these the incommunicability he supposed them to possess. In particular, he did not hold, to parody Berkeley, that the being of a sense consisted in its being grasped. Thoughts, and senses in general, were for Frege timeless entities, that neither come into nor pass out of existence. His reason for holding this is that he supposed that, otherwise, he would be unable to hold that anything was true at a time when there was no one to think it: for what is either true or false is a thought, and, if the existence of a thought depends upon its being grasped, there would be nothing to be true at a time when there was

NS 146-7
(135)

no one who grasped it. When dinosaurs roamed the earth, surely it was true that the earth goes round the Sun, or that $2 + 2 = 4$, even though there was no one capable of grasping either thought? One might reply that the ascription of a truth-value to a thought is timeless, i.e. not relative to a date, although the existence of the thought depends at least on there being a language in which it is capable of being expressed or a mind capable of grasping it: but the point is not one of any great moment. (Note that, for Frege, a thought is not something capable of being true at one time and false at another. The thought expressed by 'The Earth goes round the Sun', as uttered now, is not the same thought as that expressed by the same sentence a hundred years ago, because everything that goes to determine the intended reference, and thus the truth-value of the thought, whether contained linguistically in the sentence or not, goes to determine the thought expressed.) In any case, thoughts are *objective* entities. One person or set of people may associate with one and the same word or sentence a different sense from that associated with it by another person or set of people: but a given sense is capable of being grasped by anybody, and it is possible to determine for certain whether or not the sense expressed by some word is the same for any two given people. Similarly, senses are, for Frege, immutable. If it be objected that the sense of a word—for instance, that of 'prevent'—may change, Frege would regard this as being like saying that the number of people in the room has decreased. In the latter case, we do not mean that there is any one number which has grown smaller, but that the number of people formerly in the room is larger than the number now in the room—two different numbers are involved: likewise, the sense which 'prevent' used to have is different from that which it has now; two different senses are involved, but there is no one sense which has altered. It might still be objected that the former sense of 'prevent' has changed from being the sense attached to that word to no longer being attached to it: but Frege would hold that there is no change *in* the sense, any more than there is a change which occurs *in* the number 5 when, of five people in a room, one leaves.

It is clear that insistence on such a way of speaking may be harmless—just a matter of notational convention, as it were: what is less clear is whether Frege meant it in a harmless way. It is, as already remarked, a common complaint for a philosopher to make of another philosopher that he 'hypostatizes' or 'reifies' meanings. This complaint is often made by Quine; and remarks which sound as though they have a similar intention occur quite often in Wittgenstein. We can perhaps illustrate what is the vice in question by means of an example used by Frege for a slightly different purpose, namely the direction of a line. One can easily imagine a philosopher, e.g. the early Moore, saying that directions are entities to which lines stand in a peculiar, indefinable relation which we denote by saying that the line 'has' the direction. What is wrong with this is that it suggests that one could know what a direction was without knowing what it is for a line to have a certain direction: that we could be acquainted with directions and with lines without knowing that there was this peculiar relation holding between some lines and some directions. We do, indeed, have proper names for certain directions (e.g. 'North–South'); but it would be impossible to know what the word 'direction' meant without knowing what 'direction of a line' meant, or to be given a direction save by being given it as the direction of some line or as bearing some relation to the direction of a particular line. It is the same with the notion of sense: we cannot understand the word 'sense' save by understanding 'sense of an expression', and we cannot characterize a sense save as the sense of an (actual or possible) expression. We can, indeed, conceive of senses that are not the senses of any expression which is actually used, namely by imagining a use for an expression which is not the use of any actual expression, and then speaking of the sense which an expression so used would have.

There are three distinct positions which could be adopted about what belongs to the realm of sense. (i) It could be held that we are capable of apprehending senses directly, and that we associate words with them only because we lack the capacity to communicate thoughts from one person to another save via a sensible medium (aural or visual). On this view, the sense of a word does not consist in the use that is made of it, but is something which we grasp, independently of the use of language, by a faculty of intellectual intuition: learning the use of words is merely learning to associate them with senses so grasped. (ii) It might be thought that a sense was something which could only be conceived by us as the sense of an actual or possible expression, and that we possessed no faculty for grasping senses other than the capacity for learning to use words and the sentences built out of them: but that nevertheless a sense is not something which *in principle* could not be apprehended—by some being whose powers we could not describe—otherwise than as the sense of a word or symbol. (iii) Finally, one could hold that the sense of a word was completely analogous to the direction of a line: that to speak of any being whatever as grasping a sense could be understood only as ascribing to him the capacity to use a word or symbol (more properly, in view of the other ingredients in meaning, to grasp a certain central feature of its use). This is the view which Wittgenstein expresses by his comparison between the sense of a word and the powers of a chesspiece: to grasp a sense otherwise than as the sense of an actual or possible symbol would be as impossible as to know the powers of the Rook without having any notion of what a chessboard or a chesspiece is. The word *has* a sense, and is not, as on the first view, a code for it, just as the Rook *has* certain powers of movement, and is not a code for them.

Of these three views, it is clear that the first is mistaken. It is not evident, however, that the second is wrong. For instance, when the knowledge of a fact, or the will that a state of affairs come about, is ascribed to God, or to an angel, it is not obvious that this involves ascribing to God, or to the angel, the use of symbols corresponding to the words by means of which we should state the fact or describe the state of affairs. Admittedly, these examples support the second view only if we assume that knowledge and will involve a relation to what Frege calls a 'thought', and accept Frege's identification of a thought with the sense of a sentence which expresses it: the examples could be held, with equal right, to call in question these assumptions, rather than the correctness of the third view of the character of senses. If those assumptions are not questioned, the thoughts ascribed to God, or to the angels, or to any creature supposed to be capable of grasping a thought without the need for any *vehicle* of thought, would have, in order to be the same thoughts as those we express by means of sentences, to have exactly the same complexity as our thoughts, to be composed in the same way of senses identical with the senses of the words which make up our sentences. It is, admittedly,

NS 154 (142)

NS 288 (269)

Gg II 96

difficult to see what the apprehension of this complexity would consist in on the part of any being capable of grasping a thought without a vehicle.

Presumably it is the first view that is being attacked when philosophers denounce the practice of 'hypostatizing' senses: at least it seems that this is what Wittgenstein has it in mind to reject. It is not so clear that this is all that Quine is opposed to: it may be that he would object—as Nelson Goodman would certainly do—to speaking of the sense of such-and-such a word even on the part of someone who was ready to allow that one could not characterize a sense otherwise than as the sense of a word whose use is known or described, on the ground that this is to admit unnecessary or unintelligible entities into one's ontology. (He certainly tends to recommend giving up speaking of 'the meaning' of a word in favour of speaking—at most —of two words' having-the-same-meaning, i.e. being synonymous: this is certainly inadequate, since it is impossible to explain in general what is meant by 'knowing (or learning) the meaning of a word' in terms only of the relation of synonymity.) In so far as Quine would advance this further objection, he is committing the fallacy attacked by Frege of 'asking after the meaning of an expression in isolation' from the sentences in which it occurs— in this case, the expression 'the meaning (sense) of . . . '.

It is impossible to tell from Frege's words which of the three views of what belongs to the realm of sense he held. It would be natural to conclude, from the terminology he favours, according to which senses are objective, eternal, immutable entities, that he held to the first view: but this terminology certainly *can* be interpreted as a harmless manner of speaking, intended only to emphasize the communicability of sense as against the alleged ultimate incommunicability of tone. Certainly, all the cardinal doctrines of Frege's philosophical logic can be interpreted in accordance with the third (or the second) view. At any rate, if Frege adhered to the first view, it did not lead him into the characteristic errors of method which usually result from such an attitude, that is to say, into the attempt to analyse senses otherwise than via an analysis of language. Admittedly, Frege was impressed—probably excessively—by the defectiveness and lack of perspicuity of natural language, but he responded, not by ignoring language, but by inventing, describing and analysing more perspicuous linguistic devices, such as the quantifier-variable notation. This is not to say that there is nothing essential to Frege's doctrines which is opposed to what Wittgenstein understood by his slogan 'The meaning is the use': for what he understood by this is very far from being exhausted by the third of the three views of sense.

(2) *The sense of a word does not consist of a mental image.* Frege strongly

G*

Gl x, 58–60

SB 29; NS
151 (139);
NS 214 (198)

Gl 64
PI 251

Huss 316–17

NS 78–80
(70–1)

attacked, in *Grundlagen* and elsewhere, the empiricist conception of sense as consisting in the propensity a word may have to call up in the mind of speaker or hearer any associated mental images. As we have seen, for Frege, if any part of the meaning of a word is to be explained in this way, it is its tone, a relatively unimportant ingredient. Part of his argument is based on the false dichotomy between mental images as subjective and incommunicable, sense as objective and communicable: but enough of the argument stands for it to be fully compelling. Of some objects, for instance, the Earth, we can form no image that is not ludicrously inadequate; of others, such as numbers, we can form none at all; of a direction, we can form no image other than that of the line which has the direction. (Compare Wittgenstein's remark in the *Investigations* about an image of the *length* of a line.) All these are images of objects: what image can we have of a property other than of an object which has that property? No image can portray the role of the word in the sentence: in more Wittgensteinian fashion, we might put it by saying that the image cannot show how it is to be applied; and, if it does not show that, then it does not contain within itself the sense of the word. An empiricist attempt to get over this difficulty is the theory of abstraction, by which, through attending to only those features of a number of objects which they have in common, we succeed in framing an image which is indefinite in irrelevant respects, and thus can correspond to the meaning of a general term. Of course, this theory had already been strongly attacked by Berkeley from within the empiricist camp; but it still maintained a vigorous life in Frege's day, pervading, for instance, Husserl's *Die Philosophie der Arithmetik*, of which Frege wrote a devastating review. Of course, the theory landed in its greatest absurdities when attempting to give an account of the genesis by abstraction of the idea of number: given, say, three cats, Husserl thought, we can, by abstracting from what differentiates them, arrive at the general idea of *cat*; by abstracting still further from everything that differentiates them not only from each other but from anything else, we arrive at the pure idea of *three*. Even at the first stage, Frege was able joyously to ask, when we have, by the wonderful faculty of not paying attention, removed everything that differentiates them from each other, do we have anything left which makes them three rather than one? Even if we did, at the final stage we would not have three of anything, because there would be no 'anything' for there to be three of: if nothing distinguishes them from anything else, we cannot ask how many *of them* there are, because we have destroyed the meaning of the phrase 'of them'.

This is one of the points on which Wittgenstein was deeply indebted to Frege, and the exposition in the *Investigations* owes much to him, and is definitive. The point does not need labouring here, because it can be regarded as conclusively established: but to Frege is due the principal credit for the fact. Berkeley was there before Frege, of course. But, while Berkeley appreciated the fact that we needed to know how to *use* the mental image, and acknowledged that the meanings of some words were unconnected with images, but only with what he calls 'notions', which is merely an expression for the meaning of a word, he still clung to the conception that mental images played a crucial role in our understanding of a large range of words. It was left to Frege to perceive that the sense of a word has, intrinsically, nothing to do with mental images whatever.

(3) *The reference of an expression is determined by the references of the components.* This is a crucial thesis of Frege's doctrine. Sense determines reference—for it consists precisely in the particular manner in which we associate its referent with a word or expression; but reference does not determine sense, since we may associate the same referent with different expressions in different ways—this is the whole reason for employing a notion of sense as well as of reference. However, if we are solely interested in the reference of a complex expression, we need take account only of the references of its components: if, in a complex expression, one component is replaced by another having a different sense but the same reference, the sense, but not the reference, of the whole will be altered. For instance, if in the complex proper name 'the capital of Denmark', we replace 'Denmark' by 'the smallest Scandinavian country', we shall obtain a phrase having the same reference as before. The functional expression stands for a certain function, and this function must have the same value for a given argument independently of the way in which we determine what that argument is. In the same way, the truth-value of a sentence is dependent only upon the references of its constituents, not their senses: whatever we say of an object must be true or false of that object independently of the particular way in which we choose to determine which object it is that we are speaking about.

FB 13–14

SB 35; NS 276 (255–6)

SB 32

Sometimes, in his published writings, Frege slips into saying that the referents of the constituents of a complex expression are parts of the referent of the whole, on analogy with the parallel doctrine about their senses. I think that the absurdity of this (which would involve, for instance, that Denmark was part of Copenhagen) was concealed from him by the fact that he uses only the one word 'Bedeutung' for the purposes for which I have been using both 'reference' and 'referent': it would be plausible, although unnecessary, to say that the mechanism of standing for a certain object which a complex expression has contains as a component the mechanism whereby a

SB 35–6; GGI 373

constituent name stands for another object; but it is not in the least plausible
PG 200   to say that the latter *object* is a component of the former; and this was a
NS 275 (255)   doctrine retracted by Frege in some of his unpublished writings.

(4) *An expression can have sense but lack any reference.* This is one of Frege's
best known doctrines; and it is one of the hardest to hold in position in his
philosophical system taken as a whole.

The obvious examples are complex proper names: either definite descrip-
SB 28; NS   tions formed by attaching the description operator (represented in natural
193-6 (178-   language by the definite article attached to a singular substantival phrase)
180)   to a predicate which either applies to nothing at all or else applies to more
than one object; or a term formed by attaching to the name of an object an
expression for a function which is not defined for that object, for instance
'the capital of Antarctica'. But there is no reason why a simple proper name
SB 33-4; NS   may not lack a reference also. We should not, as Frege often does, cite as
208 (191),   examples of names having sense but no reference personal names used in
133-4 (122)   fiction, for these have in fact only a partial sense, since there is no saying
NS 141-2   what would warrant identifying actual people as their bearers; while the
(129-30)   use of a name in literary criticism to refer to a fictional character differs
again from its use *in* fiction, for here, while the sense is quite specific,
the reference does not fail. We need names used with a serious, though
unsuccessful, intention to refer. One example, given by Geach, is that of
TP 137   the name 'Vulcan' once adopted by astronomers for the planet postulated as
having an orbit inside Mercury's; another would be that of the mythical
Stanford student in whose existence the students induced the University ad-
ministration to believe for a whole term; or, again, a spurious joint identity
established by two people, good at disguise, for criminal purposes.

So far, all seems clear and unproblematic. Such an expression has a sense
because we have a criterion, perhaps quite sharp, at any rate at least as sharp
as for most names having a genuine reference, for an object's being recognized as the referent of the name: but it lacks a reference, because as a
matter of fact there is nothing which would identify any object as the
referent of the name; there is no object which satisfies the condition determined by the sense for being its referent. What could be more straightforward?

Early Russell thought in much the same way: only, because he did not have
a distinction between sense and reference to operate with, but only one
undifferentiated notion of 'meaning', it did appear problematic to him. We
cannot say that such a name does not have a meaning: for otherwise sentences
in which it occurred would be merely nonsensical. Hence we must say that

it has a certain object as its meaning; only, this object does not possess the special, and important, property of existing. There must *be* such an object—which Russell rendered by saying that the object must have being—or else we should be talking nonsense when we used the name, and there would be nothing that we were speaking *about*. Thus Russell was led to draw a distinction between being and existence, existence being the narrower concept: any statement of the form 'X has being' could only be either true or non- $PoM\ 71$ sensical, since, if it had a meaning, then there must be an object about which it was being asserted that it had being, an object which was the meaning of the name, and so this object must have being, even if it did not go so far as to exist.

But Frege had the distinction between sense and reference to make use of, and so he had no need to postulate any realm of shadowy non-existent objects which yet had being, and could therefore be talked about and were talked about whenever we used one of these empty proper names. In one straightforward sense, someone who seriously used one of these names was not talking about anything: he thought he had succeeded in singling out some object about which he wished to make some assertion, but he had not succeeded in doing so. But from that the conclusion did not need to follow, for Frege, that what he was saying was senseless: the name he used, and the $NS\ 208\ (191$ whole sentence containing it, had a perfectly good sense; what the name lacked was merely a reference.

For Russell, the Theory of Descriptions was a liberation: it involved explaining sentences containing definite descriptions otherwise than on the model of proper names. A definite description was not really functioning as a singular term at all—it just had the surface appearance of being one: a sentence of the form 'The x such that Fx is G', where 'G' is a simple or primitive predicate, says both that everything that is F is G, and that there is one and only one thing that is F. Hence such a statement is just plain false in the case when Frege, taking 'The x such that Fx' to be a complex proper name, would say that it lacked a reference; and we are liberated from the necessity of positing an object with being but without existence to be the meaning of the definite description.

Such an account could not have the same attractions for Frege: he was never involved in the net in which one may feel forced to say that there *are* objects which do not exist, and hence he did not need to be liberated from it. Still, even if he did not have the same motives for welcoming it, why should Frege not have adopted the Theory of Descriptions when it was proposed?

The theory has certain disadvantages. The most notorious is the necessity for 'scope operators'. I stated the theory above only for the case in which 'G' is a simple or primitive predicate: but, if we allow it to apply when the definite description occurs as the argument of a complex predicate, then we immediately generate an ambiguity when we try to negate the sentence: for we do not know whether to interpret the resulting sentence as the negation of the sentence in which the definite description occurs as the argument of 'G', or as one in which the definite description occurs in the argument-place of the negation of 'G' (i.e. of the predicate 'not $G(\xi)$'). The two interpretations would yield different truth-values precisely in the case in which the definite description lacks, on Frege's account, a reference: on the former interpretation, the sentence would be true in that case, on the latter interpretation it would be false. It is difficult simply to ban the latter interpretation since it is the one that is most frequently intended in natural language. Hence Russell has to resort to cumbersome auxiliary notations to indicate within what predicate, i.e. within how much of the sentence, we are to regard any given definite description as occurring: and this makes for a most unattractive symbolism.

This is actually the least of the difficulties of the theory. It arises only because Russell did not carry his theory to its natural final stage. If definite descriptions are not genuine singular terms at all, but are only masquerading as such, then in a properly devised logical symbolism they ought no longer to appear in masquerade. A sentence containing a definite description is explained by Russell as expressing a relation between two properties—that expressed by the predicate in whose argument-place the definite description occurs, and that expressed by the predicate out of which the definite description is formed—in just the same sense as that in which a sentence of the form 'Most *F*s are *G*s' expresses a relation between two properties. If, therefore, Russell had adopted for such a sentence a symbolic expression which displayed its character as expressing a second-order relation of this kind, he would not have been afflicted by difficulties about ambiguity of scope due to an inappropriate symbolism. Thus, instead of writing 'The *x* such that *Fx* is *G*' as '$G(\imath x [Fx])$', and getting into difficulties about what '$\sim G(\imath x [Fx])$' was to mean, he could have written '$Ix [Fx, Gx]$', where 'I' represents a kind of quantifier, but a binary one, applied to two predicates simultaneously, binding all occurrences of the variable '*x*' within the square brackets. The negation of the whole sentence would then be, unambiguously, '$\sim Ix [Fx, Gx]$', while the result of negating the predicate '*G*' would be '$Ix [Fx, \sim Gx]$'.

The disadvantages of the Theory of Descriptions are, rather, of a different kind. First, if it is to be a complete means of disposing of what are apparently well-formed singular terms without a reference, it forces us to construe all complex proper names, and all simple proper names introduced by explicit definition as equivalent to a complex one, as definite descriptions. The ban on introducing proper names, at least by explicit definition, is troublesome in any context: but it is also entailed that we can recognize no such linguistic category as that of functional expressions. In natural language, this is not particularly irksome: we have no difficulty in reconstruing such a phrase as 'the capital of Denmark' as arising, not by putting the name 'Denmark' into the argument-place of the functional expression 'the capital of ξ', but by attaching the description operator 'the' to the complex predicate 'ξ is a capital of Denmark'. But, within mathematical language, the restriction is very tiresome indeed: in arithmetic, we should have to abandon the symbols '$+$' and '$.$', and all other function-signs, in favour of the corresponding predicates, e.g., in the case of addition, a ternary predicate '$A(\xi, \zeta, \eta)$' interpreted as meaning 'η is a sum of ξ and ζ'. There would then be no such thing as a numerical expression, or indeed as a numeral, save for those finitely many such taken as primitive, and there would be no equations save for those in which a numeral stood on either side.

This difficulty has still been expressed at the level of awkwardness of notation, and could be parried by someone who answered, 'Let us for convenience actually employ a misleading notation, as long as we remember what it ultimately translates into'. But the major defect of the Theory of Descriptions was that it prompted the hunt for the 'logically proper name'. If the Theory of Descriptions was to do what was required of it, then it must rule out as being only a sham proper name any apparent singular term which lacked a reference: so even some expression which is, to surface appearance, not a definite description but a (simple) proper name must, if it lacks a reference, be declared to be a concealed definite description. But, by the same token, the same must be said of any apparent singular term which *might* lack a reference: for the logical category to which an expression belongs cannot depend on what may well be a contingent question of whether there exists anything satisfying certain conditions, but must depend solely upon the kind of meaning that it has. Hence, to be accepted as a genuine proper name, there must be a logical guarantee that it has some object as its meaning (i.e. as its referent). Thus, virtually all the expressions normally taken to be proper names are rejected as not being genuinely so, and the search is undertaken for the terms that can be identified as logically proper names (with notoriously absurd results).

Perhaps it would then be possible to admit some *genuine* functional expressions too, if any could be found which were logically guaranteed to stand for a function having a value for every argument: for the point of rejecting apparent singular terms as disguised definite descriptions did not turn so much on their complexity as on the possibility that they might lack a reference. But the idea of such logically genuine functional expressions did not occur to Russell, and it is unlikely that he would have been willing to identify anything as such.

But, then, why do there need to be any genuine proper names? Why could not Russell have accepted the conclusion which Quine later advanced, that *every* apparent proper name is really a disguised definite description, that there are no proper names at all? (Quine merely says that proper names can be 'eliminated' in favour of definite descriptions, understood in accordance with the Theory of Descriptions.)

We have seen how crucial a role the linguistic category of proper names plays in Frege's philosophy of language. The notion of a first-level predicate, or of every other linguistic category, is explained in terms of the notion of a proper name. But might we not circumvent this difficulty? Might we not first single out that class of expressions which Frege accepts as proper names, and, in terms of it, introduce the conception of predicates and other incomplete expressions, and then, as it were, go back and correct first impressions by showing that the expressions which Frege recognizes as proper names are all to be construed as explicit or disguised definite descriptions, to be construed in accordance with the Theory of Descriptions? That is, with reference to a language which contained only explicit definite descriptions, and no other apparent singular terms, would it not be consistent to combine: (i) Frege's criteria for picking out (pseudo-)singular terms; (ii) Frege's account of incomplete expressions in terms of the omission of one or more occurrences within a sentence of a (pseudo-)singular term; and (iii) Russell's Theory of Descriptions?—It seems that it would be consistent: that the acceptance of the crucial role of proper names in explaining the linguistic categories does not depend on their function in a sentence being explained as Frege explains the function of a proper name. 'Their function in a sentence' here refers to the semantics we give for sentences containing apparent singular terms. But it is just here that the essential difficulty occurs. The classical semantic account of sentences whose main operator is one of the quantifiers—the account given in the first place by Frege, and adopted in principle by every subsequent logician who accepts classical two-valued logic—depends essentially on taking the truth-value of the quantified sentence to be an infinite sum or product of the truth-values of all possible instances, where, of course, an instance is arrived at by putting a proper name (individual constant) into the argument-place of the predicate to which the quantifier has been attached. Of course, we do not require that the language actually contain a proper name (even in Frege's extended sense in which it means 'singular term, simple or complex') for every object in the domain of quantification; we do not even require (when the domain of quantification is non-denumerable) that it be possible that a language could contain a name for every such object. The truth-value of the quantified sentence is an infinite sum or product of the truth-values of all sentences which could be formed by putting a name for an arbitrary member of the domain in the argument-place of the predicate, whether or not the language contains such a name. This is often expressed by contemporary logicians by considering the predicate as containing in its argument-place a free variable, and then taking the infinite sum or product of the truth-values that result from every arbitrary assignment of an object in the domain to that free variable. But this is just a mode of saying the same thing: for to assign an object in the domain to the free variable, and then consider the truth-value of the free-variable sentence under that assignment, is just to consider the free variable as being used as a name of that object. Hence the notion of an expression's functioning as a proper name, that is, of its having some particular object as referent and as occurring in a sentence which is then determined as true or false according as the predicate does or does not apply to the object, is essential to the standard classical explanation of the quantifiers: and, since the Theory of Descriptions explains the meanings of definite descriptions—the semantics of sentences containing them—in terms of quantification, it is useless to propose the elimination of proper names altogether in favour of definite descriptions. That does not mean that a language containing only definite descriptions, and no proper names, is inconceivable. What it means is that, if the standard explanations of the quantifiers give a faithful account of their sense, an understanding of such a language would presuppose and depend on an understanding of the way in which proper names function. The language itself need not contain any—any more than our language needs to contain a name of every object: but the idea of a language containing proper names would have to underlie the mastery of this language. Now, Russell's theory leads him to the conception that an expression can function as a proper name only if it is logically *guaranteed* to have a reference, and he is faced with the problem of making it plausible that there are any such logically proper names, which he sought to resolve by producing putative examples. If he were to have taken refuge in the idea that our language contains no such logically proper names, he would still have had to make it plausible that there *could be* such things in some language, and that we have the conception of how such logically proper names would function: and, deprived of the possibility of finding any examples, he would have found it even harder to make this plausible.

Thus Frege did not have the motivation for abandoning his own theory and adopting the Theory of Descriptions which Russell had for relinquishing his own earlier theories and propounding the new Theory: and Frege's eschewal of the Theory of Descriptions saved him from the fruitless search for the logically proper name which led Russell into such implausibilities. But it led him into other implausibilities, almost equally great. For Frege, any expression, simple or complex, which passed the tests which we have reviewed in Chapter 4 and there attempted to make more explicit, was to be accepted as functioning as a genuine 'proper name' (singular term). What that meant for him was that an atomic sentence in which such a proper name occurred was to be taken as expressing a true thought just in case the predicate did apply to the object which was the referent of the proper name, a false thought if the predicate did not apply to that object (in the case that the atomic statement was formed by putting the proper name into the argument-place of a one-place predicate; likewise the sentence, when formed by putting the proper name into one argument-place, some other proper name into the other argument-place, of a relational expression, expressed a true thought if the relation held between the referents of the two names, a false thought if it did not so hold). Since in natural language it is possible to form

SB 33, 40   proper names having a sense but no reference, it followed that an atomic sentence in which such a proper name occurred expressed a thought, well

NS 211 (194)   enough, but a thought which was neither true nor false. And this property must carry over to any complex sentence formed, in part, from such an atomic sentence, that is to say, any sentence whatever containing such a proper name having a sense but no reference: for the truth-value of a complex sentence is determined as a function of the truth-values of the component sentences; so, if one of the components has no truth-value, the whole can have no truth-value.

It is of the greatest importance, for the understanding of Frege, to grasp that, while this was, for him, the correct account of how matters stand with regard to natural language, it was a totally unsatisfactory state of affairs, revealing a defect of natural language, which must be remedied in any properly constructed language such as Frege's own symbolic language. It is often said that Frege eliminated this feature from his symbolic language— that is, that he so constructed that language that it was impossible for proper names to occur in it which lacked a reference—for the sake of greater convenience in manipulation. That is grossly to understate the case, on Frege's understanding of it. For him, it was not a matter of convenience but of necessity. He thought, that is, that it is impossible to give any coherent account of the functioning of a language in which it is possible to construct well-formed sentences which lack a truth-value; in modern terminology, that no coherent semantics is possible for such a language—no determinate and consistent set of rules determining the truth-conditions of every sentence in the language. We muddle along with natural language because we do not attempt to formulate such rules and do not press our implicit intuitive understanding of them to the point where contradictions would be generated. But this remains, nevertheless, a defect: and for scientific purposes—that is, both for use in scientific investigation and as the object of a scientific study of language—we need a language which lacks this defect. That is the cardinal difference between Frege's account of proper names and the revival of that account associated with the revolt led by Strawson against the Theory of Descriptions. Strawson agreed with Frege that sentences containing a name without a reference might still be meaningful (i.e. express a sense), but that they could not be used to make a statement, true or false: but, unlike Frege, he saw nothing at all amiss with this state of affairs. SB 41; FB 19–20

In a properly constructed language, then, it must be impossible to form a proper name lacking a reference. This would be achieved if three conditions were satisfied. First, all the simple (primitive) proper names (individual constants) must be provided with a reference. Secondly, every first-level functional expression must be defined for every object (or ordered pair of objects) as argument: for instance, there must be nothing corresponding to the binary function denoted by 'ξ/ζ', as ordinarily understood within the theory of rational or real numbers, which is taken as undefined when the second argument is o. And, thirdly, a similar condition must hold for every second- or higher-order primitive functional expression, in particular, that denoted by the description operator, if there is one. (In his only formal system which admits a description operator, that of *Grundgesetze*, Frege actually uses a first-level operator which acts upon a term denoting a class containing a single object to yield a name of that object.) A second-level operator, e.g. a description operator or class-abstraction operator, must be explained in such a way that the term formed by attaching it to any predicate whatever has a determinate reference. If, as with the description operator, we are really only interested in certain cases (in this instance, in predicates which apply to exactly one object), then we may stipulate the reference in the other cases in any way that happens to be convenient: all that is essential is that we should make some definite stipulation. NS 167–9 (154–6); NS 212 (195–6)

Gg I 11

Why Frege thought that it was impossible to give a coherent semantics for a language containing well-formed sentences lacking a truth-value, we shall enquire a little later.

RG 75   In *Reference and Generality*, Geach advances a hybrid theory designed to mitigate the implausibilities of both Russell's and Frege's accounts. A definite description occurring after the verb 'to be' or other verb, such as 'to become', taking a grammatical complement, is to be construed as predicative: that is, the definite article here serves to form one predicate from another, rather than a singular term, so that the verb 'to be' is to be interpreted as the copula and not as the sign of identity: 'x is the F' is to be understood to mean 'x is an F, and, for every y not identical with x, y is not an F.' Russell had been compelled to interpret a definite description in the same way, when it is the grammatical subject of the verb 'exists': Geach's interpretation avoids an implausibility which Frege's account involves, since Geach can regard 'a is the F' as plain false whenever there is no object, or more than one, which is F. In other positions, Geach accepts Russell's Theory of Descriptions as a correct account of definite descriptions. But, since he accepts Frege's sense/reference distinction, he gives a Fregean account of proper names in the strict sense, that is of singular terms which are logically unitary, even when these are introduced by definition: this enables him to eschew the search for the logically proper name. When a proper name is introduced into the language by means of a definite description, Geach holds that it is not being presented as an exact equivalent of the definite description: it is being presented as a name, whose sense is determined by its being introduced as standing for the object to which alone the definite description applies, and which will therefore have that object, if there really is one, as its referent, and which will lack a referent if there is not. If there is no such object a sentence in which that name occurs will therefore be neither true nor false: if the name were to be replaced by the definite description by means of which it was introduced, the sentence would become straightforwardly false.

This eclectic theory contrives to stay close to common sense, and to avoid the worst excesses into which Russell's and Frege's theories respectively drove them. But it does not go very deep: it does not, for instance, expose to scrutiny Frege's reasons for supposing that no coherent semantics could be given for a language whose sentences might lack a truth-value, still less subject to any examination the significance of saying of a sentence that it is neither true nor false.

We should note that Strawson's account takes explicit notice of the use of demonstratives, accompanied by an implicit or explicit pointing gesture, and of token-reflexive expressions like 'I' and 'you', whereas Frege's account is designed for a language which does not possess such devices. Strawson therefore speaks of one and the same sentence being used to make different statements on different occasions, and hence allows no sense to speaking of a sentence's being true or false (the sentence being considered as a type): the sentence may be meaningful or meaningless, whereas only a statement made by uttering it on a particular occasion can be true or false (Strawson does not speak of a statement's being neither true nor false, but only of an utterance of a sentence failing to bring about the making of a true or false statement; but this is a mere terminological idiosyncrasy, of no significance either way). For Frege, on the other hand, the sentence may, in a derivative sense, be called true or false (or neither), according as the thought expressed by it is true or false (or neither), since he is not speaking of sentences which express different thoughts on different occasions of utterance. Frege was, of course, perfectly well aware of the existence of first- and second-person pronouns, of tenses and of demonstratives: and he insists that a sentence containing such devices does not, of itself, express a thought, but only in combination with those features of the surroundings of an utterance of it which determine the reference of the components, and hence pin down a thought which may be regarded as being determinately either true or false (or neither). But he offered no exact account of the workings of these pieces of the machinery of natural language, and preferred to conduct all his discussion in terms of sentences which of themselves express such a determinate thought. NS 146 (134);
Ged 64
(10–11)

Is there any corresponding situation in which an incomplete expression of natural language may lack a reference although having a sense? We may take the case of predicates as typical: those of functional and relational expressions involve absolutely parallel considerations. One obvious case will be that in which a complex predicate itself contains a proper name without a reference, as, for instance, the predicate 'Vulcan orbits ξ' as it occurs in 'Vulcan orbits the Sun'. Frege singles out a different and less trivial case, that in which the predicate is not defined for every argument: for instance, we should normally take the predicate 'ξ is male' as being defined only for animate objects, or character-predicates, such as 'ξ is scrupulous', 'ξ is generous', as being undefined for babies. Of such predicates, Frege says that they do not really have any reference at all. They might be said to stand for properties (what Frege calls 'concepts') whose boundaries are at certain places indeterminate: but Frege, descending to rhetoric, says that a property with indeterminate boundaries, a property such that there is no telling, for certain objects, whether or not they have it, is no property at all. The analogy is, of course, that, by means of such a predicate, a sentence may be formed Gg II 56, 58,
64

NS 133 (122);
NS 168 (155) that has no truth-value, namely by inserting in the argument-place of the predicate a name for an object over which the predicate is undefined: evidently, since the predicate is neither true nor false of such an object, that sentence can be neither true nor false. But, of course, the analogy is imperfect. The presence of a name which lacks a reference deprives any sentence of a truth-value: but the presence of a predicate which in this sense has no reference deprives only certain sentences of truth-value; if what occurs in the argument-place is the name of an object over which the predicate is defined, there is no intuitive reason to say that the sentence lacks a truth-value. The more natural thing to say would be that we have not completely specified the reference of the predicate. But Frege would want to press the question, 'Does it have a referent or doesn't it?'; and he would find the answer, 'It has an incompletely specified referent', distasteful. For Frege, the referents of expressions—whether proper names or incomplete expressions—are things in the real world; they are the extra-linguistic correlates of linguistic expressions: they are what we talk *about*. And the real world contains no incompletely specified thing—that is, it contains no things which are intrinsically incompletely specified. Of course, if I give an incomplete specification, then I have given a specification which will fit more than one thing, and so, if we have incompletely specified the referent of an expression, we might say that it has, as referents, all those things which will fit the incomplete specification (not just one incompletely specified referent). But Frege does not want to think of any expression to which a reference can be attributed at all as having more than one referent: and so he prefers to say, of a predicate that is not everywhere defined, that it has no referent at all. After all, such a predicate may not yield a sentence that is intuitively devoid of truth-value when names of objects over which it is defined occupy its argument-place: but it will certainly in general do so whenever its argument-place is occupied by a variable bound by a quantifier, for no truth-value will be determined for the quantified statement if a truth-value is lacking for certain instances. Again, in a properly constructed language, Frege held, there will be no such predicates: every predicate, and every functional and relational expression, in such a language will be defined for every object. We shall revert to this point later.

As a matter of fact, there is in natural language, though not in Frege's or any other symbolic language, a more exact analogue to the case of a definite description. That is, in natural language, we sometimes construct definite descriptions of higher level. We have already noted that expressions of generality are often used in natural language to give the effect of second-level quantification, without there being any overt distinction to mark off this use from that when they express generality of first level. Relative clauses may thus be used to form second-level definite descriptions, e.g. such a phrase as 'what Frederick has always wanted to be', or 'what five members of the staff have recently become'. Phrases of this kind are used predicatively, that is, form, with the copula, a complex predicate; to take them as intended to stand for an object would be to misunderstand them. Just as with ordinary definite descriptions, they may fail of reference because the existence and uniqueness conditions which they tacitly claim fail to hold: it may be that there is no such thing as what Frederick has always wanted to be, either because Frederick has never had any constant ambition, or because there are several things which he has always wanted to be; likewise, if five members of the staff have recently become members of the Communist Party, and another five have recently been elected Fellows of the Royal Society, then again there is no such thing as what five members of staff have recently become. No logician has ever found it useful to have a description operator of second order, such as this 'what' of natural language represents: which is perhaps why Frege did not take this case as that in which a predicate may fail of reference.

(5) *The reference of an incomplete expression is itself incomplete.* This, again, is one of Frege's most famous doctrines. We shall not attempt a full examination of it here, reserving that for a subsequent chapter. GG1 371-2; FB 31

Some critics of Frege have found the whole conception that reference is to be ascribed to expressions other than proper names something to jib at. In the case of proper names, it is not problematic that, in general, there are objects which we use them to talk about and for which they may be said, therefore, to stand. This—the relation between a name and its bearer—is surely Frege's model for the relation between an expression and its referent. But what reason is there to suppose that the use of this model is justified in other contexts? Why do we need to suppose that expressions in other categories have any extra-linguistic correlates in anything resembling the way in which proper names have? The relation of reference between, for instance, a relational expression and the relation for which it stands is not supposed by Frege to be the *same* relation as that between a name and its bearer, but only an analogous one: how, then, can we be sure that there is any analogy, or that we know how we are supposed to draw it?

In introducing Frege's notion of reference, I tried to forestall this sort of objection by explaining it in terms of the familiar semantics for a quantificational language: reference is that which has to be ascribed to the primitive expressions of such a language—individual constants, predicates, relational and functional expressions—in order to give the truth-definition for sentences of the language. Then it becomes absurd to think of reference as attaching only to the singular terms of the language: a reference of a different kind attaches to the predicates and relational and functional expressions also, and, indeed, also to expressions like the sentential operators and the quantifiers. We are not accustomed to thinking of these latter expressions in the same breath with the individual constants, predicates, etc., because they do not appear in the atomic sentences of the language, and are therefore involved only in the recursive clauses of the truth-definition: but, under the general rubric, they may be ascribed a reference also.

When the matter is put this way, the objection is then made to turn upon the distinction between sense and reference. In the case of proper names, it may be allowed that Frege successfully made out a case for ascribing to them a sense distinct from, and not determined by, their reference. But why do we need such a distinction in the case of incomplete expressions? Perhaps in their case to grasp their sense just is to know their reference, and there is no question of doing so by one means rather than another.

A great deal of ink has been wasted advocating the thesis that Frege intended no distinction between sense and reference for incomplete expressions. Some of Frege's unpublished writings are explicit about the matter. But, in any case, the point could have been derived from his published ones. It is true that we derive from these very little help by enquiring whether Frege thought that incomplete expressions, like proper names, could have a sense but no reference (a possibility that would clinch the existence of a distinction between their sense and their reference): for, although we have seen that he did think this, it is not clear that the kind of example he gives, of a predicate or other incomplete expression not everywhere defined, ought not at the same time to be considered one in which the expression does not have a completely specified or determinate sense; and perhaps Frege, in his severity, might be willing to say of such an expression that it really had no sense at all (he nowhere expressly pronounces on the point). But what is, after all, of more importance is whether two predicates, etc., can have different senses but the same reference: and it is no use discussing this without determining what is a correct view, on Frege's principles, of the notion of two predicates' having the same reference. And, on this point, he is explicit.

If the reference of an expression is truly to be identified with the interpretation of it as understood in standard classical semantics, then the criterion for identity of reference ought to be extensional. And that is what Frege says, subject to a qualification. The qualification is that we cannot, strictly

NS 128 (118);
NS 209-10
(192-3); BW
96 (63)

NS 128 (118),
133-4 (122-3)

speaking, talk of identity in connection with the referents of incomplete expressions: for identity, properly speaking, is a relation between *objects*, a relation of first level. But, Frege says, there is a relation between concepts (which are the referents of predicates) which is the analogue of the relation of identity between objects, and this is the relation of co-extensiveness. The analogue of the statement '$a = b$' is the statement '$\forall x\,(Fx \leftrightarrow Gx)$': and it is plain that this statement can hold good even though the predicates '$F(\xi)$' and '$G(\xi)$' have quite different senses.

NS 130-3
(120-2)

NS 197-8
(181-2), Huss
320

This settles conclusively the question whether there is a distinction, in the case of predicates, between sense and reference. But there is a feature of Frege's notion of reference, as applied to incomplete expressions, which makes no appearance in the standard semantics for a quantificational language, that, namely, which is expressed in the heading of this section. In the standard semantics, an interpretation of a predicate is a set, that of a two-place relation-symbol a set of ordered pairs, and so on. But Frege insists that the referent of any incomplete expression must itself possess a kind of incompleteness analogous to that of the expression itself. The referent of a predicate is a concept; that of a relational expression a relation; that of a functional expression a function: and all these must be conceived of as having a kind of incompleteness exactly agreeing with the incompleteness of the expression. What does this mean?

FB 6-7; Gg I
1-4

First, a note on terminology. The German word 'Begriff', as used by Frege to apply to that for which a predicate stands, is less unnatural in this use than its nearest English equivalent, 'concept'. In English, we should naturally interpret a 'concept' as being that which a person possesses when he grasps the *sense* of a word or range of words: but 'Begriff', for Frege, applies to the *referent* of a predicate, not its sense, and is thus correlative to 'Funktion' ('function'—the referent of a functional expression) and to 'Beziehung' ('relation'—the referent of a relational expression). Any English writer, advancing such a doctrine, would find it natural to employ, in place of the word 'concept', the word 'property', and it is often useful to make this substitution in considering what Frege says about concepts, in order to avoid the misleading suggestions of the English word 'concept'. It remains preferable to retain the word 'concept' when translating Frege or giving an account of his views, because the use of 'property' would involve other corresponding changes: where Frege says that an object 'falls under' a concept, we should have to say that it 'had' a property, and so forth. (Frege also occasionally uses 'Begriff' in a non-technical sense, where only the English word 'concept' would be appropriate, or in a context to which both the technical and non-technical senses are relevant.) It is also important to note

BG 198

BG 201

Gl 19, 21, 29

that, for Frege, it is only a (one-place) predicate that has a concept as its referent—a second-level predicate having a second-level concept as referent, and so on—there being no such restriction on the ordinary English use of 'concept'. If this terminological point is not grasped, serious misunderstanding can result. Of, for instance, an atomic sentence, formed by putting a proper name in the argument-place of a simple (first-level) predicate, Frege says that it is used to make a statement about an object (the referent of the name), saying of it that it falls under a certain concept (the referent of the predicate). If, however, we consider a sentence formed by attaching a quantifier to a first-level predicate, Frege considers the quantifier as a predicate of second level, having a second-level concept as its referent: and he accordingly says that such a sentence is used to make a statement about a first-level concept (the referent of the predicate), saying of it that it falls under the second-level concept for which the quantifier stands. The phrase 'a statement about a concept' would naturally be taken in English to apply to a conceptual observation, in the sense of one which holds true, if at all, in virtue of the sense of some word used or mentioned in the statement. This, of course, is not in the least Frege's intention: concepts, for him, belong to the 'realm of reference', that is, are as much part of the real world as are objects, and so statements about them may be true for purely contingent reasons bearing on the way the world happens to be just as much as may statements about objects; any existential statement is, for instance, an example of what Frege calls a 'statement about a concept'.

Gl 47

Now, what Frege is attempting to avoid, by his doctrine of the incompleteness of concepts, relations and functions, is the problem of 'how universals are related to particulars'. In the traditional approach to the 'problem of universals', predicates and the corresponding abstract proper names are lumped together indifferently as standing for universals of a certain kind; relational expressions and the abstract proper names corresponding to them are likewise indifferently grouped as standing for universals of another sort. It then appears problematic how sentences succeed in actually *saying* anything, true or false, for the sentence has appeared to degenerate into a list: Russell expresses this by saying that the proposition disintegrates under analysis. When we say, 'Iago hates Othello' or 'Neptune is as large as Uranus', we must be doing more than merely listing the referents of our words, two particulars and a universal in each case; we must be doing more than just mentioning in succession Iago, hatred and Othello, or Neptune, equality of magnitude and Uranus, for we are saying, in each case, that the relation in question actually *relates* the objects. But, then, we want to ask, how do the particulars get related in the proposition by that relation? What

BG 205

invisible glue joins the universal with these two particulars? Some philosophers, whom, for want of a better word, we may call logicians, identified that part of the sentence which effected this cohesion as the copula, which in our second sentence is plain to see, but in the first sentence has disguised itself as part of the verb 'hates'; such sentences, when displayed in full explicitness, must, according to such logicians, be rendered after the model of 'Iago is a hater of Othello', where copula and universal term are now disentangled. But, in any case, the real problem was not, what part of the sentence represents the cohesive element, but, rather, what exactly is the job which it succeeds in doing. Moreover, this was a dual problem. In one sense, the relation only succeeds in relating the particulars when the proposition is *true*, e.g. if Iago really does hate Othello. So we have the problem: how does a relation succeed in inhering in certain particulars in such a way as to make a relational proposition true? But this cannot be the only sense in which a relation may relate particulars, for otherwise there could only be true relational propositions: there must be a sense in which the relation relates the particulars *in* the proposition, although it may not *really* relate them, i.e. may not relate them in reality.

Russell, Moore, Bradley and many others grappled with these problems, as among the hardest in philosophy. For Frege, the problems are entirely spurious. They are generated by confusing abstract objects with concepts and relations, or rather, by taking predicates and relational expressions to stand for abstract objects rather than for concepts and relations. A concept and an object, or a relation and two objects, need no glue to fit them together: they fit together naturally, in a way we can think of as analogous to that in which a predicate and a proper name, or a relational expression and two proper names, fit together to form a sentence. And this will seem to us natural and unproblematic as soon as we grasp that we can think of a concept *only* as the referent of a predicate, of a relation *only* as the referent of a relational expression. This means both that, for any given concept or relation, we can think of it only as that which some predicate or relational expression stands for (not necessarily a unique one), and that, to arrive at the general notion of a concept or of a relation, we must first gain the general notion of a predicate or of a relational expression, and then understand a concept as being what, in general, a predicate stands for, a relation as being what, in general, a relational expression stands for. After all, on the traditional approach, it was still necessary to distinguish two kinds of universals—properties like bravery and relations like hatred: and what distinguished them save the fact that one was denoted by a predicate and the other by a relational expression? But, since we can gain an understanding of what a relation is by no other way than by coming to understand the use of a relational expression in sentences, it was a mistake from the outset to imagine that a relation could also be denoted by some abstract proper name. Either the abstract noun does not have to be taken seriously as a name at all, but is a mere periphrastic device for expressing sentences in which the corresponding relational expression occurs; or else it is the name of an abstract object, which presumably has some stateable connection with the corresponding relation (a connection which need not be uniform as between all such abstract objects and the corresponding relations), but is not to be identified with it.

If we construe concepts or properties and relations after the model of abstract objects, then indeed we shall be faced with the problem how a relation relates, how a property inheres in an object. But, if we only ever think of a relation as that for which a relational expression stands, a concept as that for which a one-place predicate stands, then these problems simply vanish. It is, as it were, of the essence of a concept or property to be *of* an object, of a relation to be *between* two objects. This last sentence does not use Frege's terminology: but it expresses precisely what he expresses by saying that a concept and a relation are both incomplete, the concept with a single incompleteness and the relation with a double incompleteness.

Perhaps the clearest case for our intuition is that of a function. Once more, for Frege the only possible route to a grasp of what a function is is via an understanding of the working of functional expressions. When we have grasped the use of simple functional expressions, whereby complex proper names can be formed from simple ones, we have the idea of certain functions. When we gain the more general conception of complex functional expressions, arrived at by discerning a common pattern in a number of different complex proper names, then we have arrived, or nearly so, at the general notion of a function. And, if we have really grasped the working of functional expressions, then we are aware of the entire difference between functions and objects. It is the entire being of a function to have values for various arguments: that is, we can refer to an object as being the value of a certain function for another object as argument (a number, for instance, as the value of a particular function for another number as argument), and to two objects as being the values of the same function for different objects as arguments; and (save that variables bound by quantifiers must be allowed to occur in an argument-place of a functional expression) that is the only way in which we ever refer to a function. We cannot refer to the function 'by itself', just because the only sort of expression by means of which the function can be referred to is a functional expression, an expression, namely, which, being incomplete, cannot occur on its own, or as a separable part of a sentence. It becomes thus wholly natural to say that a function, like the expression which stands for it, is also, and analogously, incomplete.

A functional expression, upon being completed, is no longer a functional expression, but a proper name. Likewise a function, upon being completed by an argument or arguments, is no longer a function but an object. Of course, such language is highly figurative; there is no one entity which suffers a certain kind of operation called 'completion', after which it has been transformed into an entity of a different kind: the function *is* the mapping from objects to objects, this mapping being, again, no kind of actual operation or transformation. We must avoid the trap of saying that it is a 'transformation in thought', for, although in a sense this is quite right, it would miss Frege's conception of the function as belonging to the 'realm of reference', and would suggest that it was something to do with the sense of a functional expression as we grasp it. It may be felt that, if a function is thus to be thought of as incomplete, as being con-stituted by a mapping from objects to objects, there is no need to main-tain that it is any kind of inhabitant of the real universe: the real universe contains the objects, and the functions just represent particular ways in which the objects can be referred to. And it is true enough, in a sense, that, once we know what objects there are, then we also know what functions there are, at least, so long as we are prepared, as Frege was, to admit all 'arbitrary' functions defined over all objects. (A survey of the totality of all objects does not yield a survey of the totality of all possible *senses* of functional expressions defined over them; but that is not what is in question here.) But the fact that the one determines the other is, for Frege, no reason to consider the latter any less real than the former: if the objects are part of the real world, then so are the functions defined on them. After all, among the statements which we make about reality will be statements about functions: and these may depend just as much upon contingent features of reality as do the statements we make about objects.

The doctrine of the incompleteness of concepts, relations and functions is the foundation of Frege's theory of the distinctions of level and of type. If a universal may be referred to equally well by means of a predicate and by an abstract proper name, then, by the use of the latter, it will be possible to say—perhaps only falsely—of the universal what can also be said of a particular. But, if a concept can only be referred to by means of a predicate, it will be literally impossible to say of the concept what can be said of an   BG 200-1
object: for what is said of an object is said by means of a first-level predicate, an incomplete expression having an argument-place for a proper name; and

into that argument-place an expression standing for the concept cannot be
fitted, at least so as to form a complete sentence, for that expression will
itself be a first-level predicate, and there will be nothing to fill *its* argument-
place. Conversely, it will be equally impossible to say of an object what can
be said of a (first-level) concept: for what is said of the concept is said by
means of a predicate of second level, that is, an expression which contains
an argument-place for the first-level predicate, and carries with it a bound
variable for insertion into the argument-place of that predicate; and, if we
put a proper name in the argument-place of the second-level predicate,
there will be nowhere for the bound variable to go—it will just be left
dangling. Thus, for Frege, it is not merely senseless to violate the distinctions
of level: in a properly constructed language, it is literally impossible. (A
very good criterion for a language's being so constructed as to display
explicitly the logical form of its sentences is that in that language it is
impossible to construct sentences corresponding to those in other languages
which would be rated as well-formed but senseless.) Frege insists that an
incomplete expression, in a properly constructed language, such as his own
symbolic language, must always carry with it its argument-places, which
may, of course, be filled either with actual arguments or with bound variables.
(Without this restriction, it would be possible to violate the distinctions of
level and of type.) The restriction applies also to bound variables which
range over the totality of entities of a given type: they too must always
carry with them the appropriate number and type of argument-places, the
only exception being their occurrence with the quantifier (or other variable-
binding operator), showing which subsequent occurrences of some bound
variable are to be regarded as being bound by that quantifier. The reason
for that restriction is evident: in Frege's eyes, if an expression were to
occur without the correct number and types of argument-place, it could not
be recognized as the same expression again: it could not be recognized as an
expression of the sort it was intended to be, that is, as an expression standing
for the sort of thing it was intended to stand for. In the same way, a bound
variable occurring without the right number and types of argument-place
could not be recognized as having the range it was intended to have. If we
can understand an expression as standing for a concept, relation or function
of a given type only in virtue of its being an expression with that type of
incompleteness, then we can recognize an expression as standing for the
same concept, relation or function only if it has the same type of incompleteness. This is why the distinctions of type are needed as well as the distinctions
of level: a relational expression of second level, for example, could not
indifferently accept either a proper name or a first-level predicate in one

Gg I 23

of its argument-places, because it could not be recognized as the same expression in different such occurrences.

(6) *The sense of a proper name fixes the criterion of identity for the object named.*
As we saw in Chapter 4, the notion of a criterion of identity, which has played so prominent a role in recent philosophy, was introduced by Frege, as was the very phrase 'criterion of identity'. In order to grasp what object a   Gl 62
name is being used to stand for, it is necessary to know, in Frege's phrase, 'how to recognize the object as the same again'. Frege was the first to see   Gl 66
clearly that we use quite different criteria of identity for objects of different kinds, and to see that this alone was enough to require that a proper name should have a sense which consisted in more than the bare association of the name with its referent, as Mill conceived of a proper name: one of the ways in which we may learn what it is to refer to an object of that kind at all is by learning the use of proper names of objects of that kind, and thus learning the criterion of identity associated with them. We may also learn such a criterion of identity by learning the sense of a general term—what is nowadays called a 'sortal term'; but this case is not really different, since what distinguishes a sortal term from other kinds of predicative expressions (other general terms) is precisely that we can form by means of them definite descriptions, the criterion of identity associated with which is fixed by the sortal term. Mill wrote as though the world already came to us sliced up into objects, and all we have to learn is which label to tie on to which object. But it is not so: the proper names which we use, and the corresponding sortal terms, determine principles whereby the slicing up is to be effected, principles which are acquired with the acquisition of the uses of these words.

This idea plays a prominent role in the early sections of *Investigations*. There Wittgenstein applies it principally to names of and sortal terms for concrete objects, whereas Frege discussed criteria of identity principally in connection with names of abstract objects, in particular, those names which are formed by means of an operator (functional expression), and whose referents it is natural to think of as capable of being referred to only by a singular term formed by means of such an operator. The sort of operator I mean is one such as 'the direction of ξ', or 'the shape of ξ': it is difficult to see how it would be possible to introduce into the language names of or any means of referring to either directions or shapes save *as* directions or shapes, that is, without the use of some operator of the same kind as 'the direction of ξ' or 'the shape of ξ'; in particular, it is hard to see how one could have a means of referring to directions without first having a means of referring to lines, or of referring to, say, plane shapes without first having a means of referring to plane figures. In the context of such names for abstract objects, Frege is naturally thinking of a criterion of identity as a criterion for the truth of statements of identity in which the sign of identity connects two names formed by means of the operator in question, e.g. a sentence having the form 'The shape of A is the same as the shape of B'. 'Recognizing the object as the same *again*', therefore, is not intended to have any necessary temporal significance: it simply refers to the criterion for judging the truth of a statement of identity purportedly identifying the object as referred to by different means. Wittgenstein's examples in the *Investigations* are much more frequently concerned with ostension, that is, when a concrete object is picked out, on different occasions, by the use of a demonstrative; and here the criterion for identity of an object of a given kind over time is often a crucial, though not the only, consideration. But, although Wittgenstein deals with one sort of case far more thoroughly than Frege, the treatment is entirely in the spirit of Frege: there is scarcely a word with which Frege would have disagreed.

MA 69–71   For some reason, Geach has proposed that the sense of a proper name be considered as constituted wholly by the associated criterion of identity: thus all personal proper names of human beings would have the same sense, as would all names of cities, all names of rivers, all numerals, and so forth. It seems difficult to see the point of this suggestion, which amounts to saying that Mill was only half-wrong. Clearly, in order to be able to use the names 'Jupiter' and 'Mercury', I must know considerably more than that they stand for celestial objects: I must know *which* such celestial objects they, by convention, are used to stand for. If this knowledge is not reckoned to the senses of the names, then it will not be enough to know the sense of any sentence containing them in order to be able to determine its truth-value: we must seek extraneous information, as when a demonstrative is used in a sentence. Since this extraneous information is not provided by the mere circumstances of utterance, but rests on an agreed convention about the use of the names of exactly the same kind as those governing the uses of other words—I am no more free to use 'Mars' to refer to Mercury than I am to use 'elliptical' to mean 'circular'—it seems entirely arbitrary to regard it as extraneous, and deny it the title of forming part of the sense of the name.

FB 14, 18;   (7) *Truth-values are the referents of sentences*. Frege enquires what the referents
SB 34; NS   of sentences can be. This enquiry may strike a reader as wholly unwarranted:
211 (194–5);   why should sentences be ascribed a reference at all? Doubtless it is a matter of
NS 276 (255) the perspective one has on the notion of reference. If we take the relation

between a proper name and its bearer as the prototype—as we are surely justified in doing—then, just as with incomplete expressions, one may be inclined to ask why on earth Frege should assume that there is anything to which a sentence stands in the same or an analogous relation as that in which a name stands to its bearer. But, if we approach it from the angle from which I introduced the notion of reference, that of the standard semantics for a quantificational language, then any fragment of a sentence, or any incomplete ingredient of it (such as a complex predicate), which constitutes a logical unit may have a reference ascribed to it. A fragment or incomplete ingredient of a sentence may be considered a logical unit in two cases: that in which its valuation under a given interpretation of the primitive predicates and other non-logical constants has to be considered in determining the truth-value of the whole sentence under that interpretation; and that in which its recognition as an element of the sentence is required for the apprehension as valid of inferences in which the sentence figures. The latter case has two sub-cases: that in which the fragment or ingredient must be recognized as also occurring in some other sentence; and that in which the original sentence needs to be seen as an instantiation of another sentence involving generality, i.e., in quantificational notation, where the fragment or ingredient must be taken as a permissible substitution for a bound variable. It is just to expressions which in this sense form logical units that Frege does ascribe a reference; for him '(being capable of) having a reference' is just another way of saying 'forming a logical unit'. And sentences, just because they can be constituents of other sentences (including the case in which one sentence is an instance of a quantified sentence), are among such logical units. Looked at from this point of view, truth-values are precisely what we must assign as the referents of sentences: for a referent is, on this understanding of the matter, precisely what has to be taken as the valuation of a given expression within the semantics by which the truth-values of complete sentences are determined with respect to the way they are composed out of their constituent expressions, including constituent sentences.

Gg II App
255

It seems that there is a certain tension between this way of explaining reference and the conception whereby the relation between name and bearer is the prototype for all relations of reference. Given that reference is just what is required for a semantic account of the standard kind (the kind which Frege made standard, though of course later logicians such as Tarski made it a great deal more explicit, and exposed the necessary underlying set-theoretical machinery for a precise formulation), it does not in the least follow that the relation of each type of expression to its referent is even analogous to that of a name to its bearer. Of course, much hangs upon

H

how much is made of the word 'analogous'. To this we shall return later.

Frege—assuming that a sentence must have a reference—argues that the referent of a sentence can only be its truth-value. For the referent must, on general principles, be something that remains invariant under any replacement of a part of a sentence with another expression having the same referent. If we carry out such replacements—substituting for proper names other, perhaps highly complex, proper names with the same referent, and, as Frege does not add but would be entitled to, replacing predicates by other co-extensive predicates—then obviously the sense of the whole changes, so that the thought expressed by the sentence is not a candidate for being its referent: and it is difficult to think of anything else of which we have a guarantee that it will not change, save the truth-value.

It is generally agreed that, if Frege had to ascribe reference to sentences at all, then truth-values were by far the best thing he could have selected as their referents: at least, he did not go down the dreary path which leads to presenting facts, propositions, states of affairs or similar entities as the referents of sentences. Now, the identification of truth-values as the referents of sentences in a certain way marks the watershed between two periods in Frege's development. The distinction between sense and reference, introduced for the first time in the lecture *Function und Begriff*, complements the logical doctrines of *Grundlagen*: it is, really, essential to understanding that work; for, although the distinction had not been formulated when it was written, he makes, in *Grundlagen*, much play with the distinction between objects and concepts, and we cannot grasp what this is supposed to be a distinction between until we understand that objects and concepts are, respectively, the *referents* and not the *senses* of proper names and of predicates. (Nor, without understanding this point, can we easily take his true intention in saying that a statement of number is used to say something about a concept.) But, in the same lecture, the doctrine is also introduced that truth-values are the referents of sentences: and this doctrine is intimately connected with a range of other doctrines characteristic of his later writing, and, indeed, of a whole new doctrinaire *style* which is signally absent from *Grundlagen*.

In order to understand this properly, we need to attend to a point that is often overlooked. The doctrine of levels required Frege to say that no expression could stand for a concept or a relation in just the same sense as that in which a name stands for an object, since it must be senseless to attempt to say the very thing about a concept or relation as that which can be said about an object: the relation of reference, in the case of a concept, can at best be analogous to that which obtains between a name and an

FB 14

BW 96 (63)

Gl 46, 55

object. But, now, how about sentences and truth-values? Is the relation between a sentence and a truth-value the very same as that between a proper name and its bearer, or is it only analogous? Evidently, Frege did not have the same reason for saying that it was only analogous: a sentence is pre-eminently a complete expression, whereas it was the incompleteness of predicates which determined that their referents must likewise be incomplete, and hence of a different logical type, a different level, from objects. But it does not at all follow that all complete expressions have referents belonging to the same logical type. Far from it: proper names and sentences, though both complete expressions in Frege's sense, very obviously function in very different ways. Anyone, unless in the grip of a theory, would be disposed to say that they were linguistic expressions of quite different logical type: all the more should Frege have been ready to acknowledge this fact, when his whole account of sense was based on the unique and central role which sentences play in our language. If, then, proper names and sentences were to have been taken by Frege to have been of different logical type, their referents—objects and truth-values—would have been construed by him to have been of different logical type also; and the relation of a sentence to its truth-value would have appeared as only an analogue to that of a name to its bearer. Only if it is assumed in advance that truth-values are objects, or, equivalently, that sentences are a special kind of complex proper name, can the relation be acknowledged as being actually the same.   FB 18; SB 34; Gg I 2

This point is almost always overlooked in discussions of Frege: it is assumed that, once Frege took the step of holding sentences to have a reference, he was doomed to conclude that truth-values are objects, and that a sentence is just a kind of complicated name for such an object. Those who are not disposed to accept such conclusions therefore identify the fatal step as being the ascription of a reference to sentences at all, thereby concentrating on only one aspect of the notion of reference (the use of the name/bearer relation as the prototype) to the exclusion of the other. But there is absolutely no necessity about it at all: on the contrary, it would have been in line with everything that Frege had said to date if he had held that sentences were of a different logical type from names, and that therefore truth-values were no more objects than concepts are.

The identification of truth-values as the referents of sentences, taken together with the thesis that truth-values are objects, led to a great simplification in Frege's ontology, at the price of a highly implausible analysis of language. Sentences being only a special case of complex proper names, and truth-values only a special case of objects, it follows that predicates and relational expressions are only a special case of functional expressions (unary and binary respectively), and concepts and relations only a special case of functions: concepts and relations are, in fact, just those functions, of one or two arguments, whose values are always truth-values. The doctrine that every function must be defined for every object (to avoid the occurrence of proper names without a reference) now yields the result that, not only must a sense always be provided for inserting any name wherever some name may meaningfully go, but for inserting a sentence in any such place as well. It now becomes a requirement upon a properly constructed language, not merely that if, for example, it contains both numerals and the predicate 'ξ is green', a sense must be provided for '5 is green', but also that a sense must be provided for '$(5=2+4)$ is green' as well. It is tragic that a thinker who achieved the first really penetrating analysis of the structure of our language should have found himself driven into such absurdities. It is not, of course, that there is anything formally wrong with imposing such a requirement upon a language, although, as we shall see, the assimilation of sentences to proper names did have a fatal effect upon Frege's theory of meaning. It is just that Frege's earlier departures from the forms of natural language— in particular, his notation for generality—were founded upon deep insights into the workings of language; whereas this ludicrous deviation is prompted by no necessity, but is a gratuitous blunder.

I do not mean to suggest that, even in this case, all was loss. The new development had one thing to recommend it: namely, if the notion of incompleteness seems more intuitively comprehensible, when applied to functions, than it does when applied to concepts and relations, then a doctrine that enabled one to view a concept or a relation as a special kind of function at least made the notion of incompleteness, as applied to them, more comprehensible. Under the new doctrine, what it means to say that an object falls under a concept (that an object has a certain property) is just that that concept maps the object on to the value *true* rather than the value *false*. To some people, who had found the notion of the incompleteness of concepts and relations difficult to grasp, this is intuitively illuminating. Their difficulty lay in the fact that, while, in the case of functions, the metaphor could be pressed, to give a sense for the 'completion' of a function by an argument to yield a value of that function, in the case of concepts and relations there seems no place for thus extending the metaphor, no meaning to the idea of 'completing' a concept or relation. But, even here, there was no necessity to insist that truth-values actually *were* objects, concepts actually *were* functions. All that was necessary was to admit the existence of an analogy: if a need was felt for a notion of 'completing' a concept, then

Margin notes: FB 15; Gg I 3, 4; NS 129 (119); NS 158 (146)

the upshot would be a truth-value, as, by completing a function, we obtain an object. Too great a price can be paid for making a metaphor palatable.

It now becomes possible to see more clearly why Frege thought that the admission of names without a reference in a language destroys the possibility of a coherent semantics for that language. This has to do only with the recognition of truth-values as the referents of sentences, not with the thesis that truth-values are objects. In accordance with the general principle that, if a part of an expression lacks a reference, then the whole must lack a reference, it must follow that any sentence whatever in which a proper name devoid of reference occurs must itself lack a referent, that is, lack a truth-value. The principle seems clear enough, when we are dealing with proper names: if there is no such country as Ruritania, then there is no such city as the capital of Ruritania. Without the background of the theory of reference, it might seem a trivial terminological matter whether we said that a sentence which, because it contained a name which had no bearer, was neither true nor false lacked a truth-value or had an intermediate one. But Frege, because he takes the truth-value of a sentence to be its referent, is compelled to say that it lacks a truth-value altogether: the choice of saying that it has an intermediate truth-value is not open to him. And, because of all this, it is not possible to him to lay down three-valued truth-tables, ruling only of atomic sentences that they are neither true nor false when a name occurs in them which lacks a reference, but allowing certain complex sentences formed from such atomic sentences to be true, and others false. It is undoubtedly the case that a perfectly coherent semantics can be constructed for a language on such a three-valued basis: we should be apt, for example, to draw up the truth-tables in such a way that every statement of the form 'If A, then A' was true, even when 'A' was itself neither true nor false. Whether such a three-valued logic is an appropriate method for handling the occurrence of names without a reference is not to the point here: it at least shows that the maintenance of Frege's view, for atomic sentences, that the occurrence of names without reference renders them neither true nor false does not require us to set about any hysterical elimination of such names from our language, on pain of being unable to give a systematic account of the workings of that language. But for Frege no such option was open. *Every* sentence in which a name lacking a reference occurred anywhere within it must be devoid of truth-value. I shall not take time to examine whether a workable semantics might not still be constructed in accord with this principle: at least it is clear that it was not altogether absurd of Frege to suppose it could not.

Of course, the difficulty could have been avoided by simply abandoning the principle that the presence in any complex expression of a constituent without a reference must rob the whole of reference. We could, alternatively, take the difficulty as indicating a flaw in the identification of truth-values as the referents of sentences. But the fact of the matter is that here is a point where the two guiding ideas of the theory of reference come into sharp conflict. Looked at purely from the point of view of the notions that need to be employed within a semantics of the standard kind, there is no reason not to take the truth-value of a sentence as being its referent, and, if we wish, to take the state of being neither true nor false as an intermediate truth-value subject to certain three-valued truth-tables. It is, however, the other idea—the appeal to the name/bearer relation as prototype—that makes the principle that lack of a reference by a part must communicate itself to the whole appear so compelling, and so lead to the conclusions about truth-values which we have been studying. The best we can do is to say that the prototype only yields an analogy in the other cases, including that of the relation of a sentence to its truth-value, and that the analogy does not extend to the maintenance of this principle in those other cases, but only where the part and the whole are both proper names. After all, abandonment of this principle does not in the least lead to abandonment of the parallel principle, which is indeed constitutive of the notion of reference, that, while the reference of the parts remains the same, so does the reference of the whole; and we already had some trouble about the principle relating to lack of reference in the case of incomplete expressions.

(8) *Expressions within indirect speech do not have their ordinary reference.* A name which occurs within a substantival clause in which reported speech is conveyed, or following a verb for what has since been called a 'propositional attitude', such as 'believes', cannot, in general, be replaced by another name having the same reference without change of truth-value. It may be true that Henry said that Copenhagen has the world's most bourgeois architecture, or that Henry believes that Copenhagen has the world's most bourgeois architecture; but it by no means follows, in the latter case, that Henry believes that the capital of Denmark has the world's most bourgeois architecture, for he may suffer from the misapprehension that Copenhagen is in Sweden; and in the former case it certainly follows that he did *not*, at the same time, say that the capital of Denmark has the world's most bourgeois architecture, since, however sound his geographical knowledge, to say that about the capital of Denmark is a different thing from saying it about Copenhagen, as shown by the fact that William, believing what Henry said, still does not believe that the capital of Denmark has the world's most

bourgeois architecture. 'That'-clauses of this kind are a particular case of what Quine has called 'opaque contexts'—contexts in which there is no guarantee that a substitution of one name for another, such that the two names, when connected by the sign of identity, yield a true identity-statement, will not convert a true statement into a false one or conversely. Such contexts are not confined to those occurring within substantival or other clauses, as for example in the instance above, 'saying something about Copenhagen', or in 'He is looking for Henry', or, again, in 'Henry will probably live to be 100': but it is natural, and attractive, to hope that it may be possible to find a means of converting every sentence containing an opaque context into one in which that context is wholly included within a clause which is opaque as a whole.

Frege concludes that, in such a context, a name does not have its ordinary reference: it must, within such a context, be being used to talk about something other than its usual referent, and he says that it then has an *oblique* reference. By this device Frege saves the principle that, whenever an expression occurring within a sentence is replaced by some other expression having the same reference, the truth-value of the sentence remains unaltered. When the name occurs within an opaque context, the replacement of it by a name apparently having the same reference is not really a counter-example to this principle, because neither name, in such a context, has its usual reference, and therefore, in that context, their references may well *not* be the same.
SB 28; NS
276 (256)

This is not, however, a mere mechanical device for saving the appearances, for preserving from refutation a principle found to admit of exceptions. It is not so, because, when we construe the referent of an expression as being that which we are talking *about* by the utterance of a sentence containing the expression, then the principle is forced on us as one admitting of no exceptions whatever. That is, if, as it occurs in a given context, a name is genuinely being used to stand for a given object, then the whole statement will be true or false according as the complex predicate formed by omitting that occurrence of the name from the sentence is true or false of that object: and such a predicate must be true or false of the object independently of how the object is referred to; hence a sentence resulting from filling the argument-place of that predicate by any other name also having that object as referent must result in a sentence with the same truth-value as the original one. When we encounter an apparent exception, we are *compelled* to conclude that, in that particular context, the name did not have the object in question as its referent.
SB 28

The notion of a complex predicate's being true or false of an object is, of course, crucial to Frege's semantics, i.e. to his explanations of the quantifiers. Let us take as an example a sentence of the form '$\forall x\,[F(x,x)\rightarrow G(x,b)]$', where '$F(\xi,\zeta)$' and '$G(\xi,\zeta)$' are simple relational expressions and 'b' is a simple proper name. Then this sentence was formed by attaching the quantifier '$\forall x$', construed as a predicate '$\forall x\,\Phi(x)$' of second level, to the complex first-level predicate '$F(\xi,\xi)\rightarrow G(\xi,b)$'. The sentence is then understood as being true just in case this complex predicate is true of every object. The predicate was, in turn, formed from some sentence of the form '$F(a,a)\rightarrow G(a,b)$' by the omission of three occurrences of the proper name 'a'. Such a sentence was originally formed from the atomic sentences '$F(a,a)$' and '$G(a,b)$' by connecting them with the binary sentential connective '$\rightarrow$'.

Now, because '$F(\xi,\zeta)$' and '$G(\xi,\zeta)$' have been taken to be simple relational expressions, there is no difficulty about the way in which the truth-values of '$F(a,a)$' and '$G(a,b)$' are determined: the senses of '$F(\xi,\zeta)$' and '$G(\xi,\zeta)$' are given by some means of determining their reference, that is, between what objects the corresponding relations hold; so, given that we know the referents of 'a' and of 'b', we know the conditions for the two atomic sentences to be true, namely if, respectively, the relation for which '$F(\xi,\zeta)$' stands holds between the referent of 'a' and itself, and the relation for which '$G(\xi,\zeta)$' stands holds between the referent of 'a' and the referent of 'b'. There is also no difficulty about the complex sentence '$F(a,a)\rightarrow G(a,b)$': its truth-value is determined from those of its constituents by the truth-table for the connective '$\rightarrow$'. But the last step, the formation of the quantified sentence, requires that we know what it is for the predicate '$F(\xi,\xi)\rightarrow G(\xi,b)$' to be true of any arbitrary object. In what does this understanding consist?

Well, clearly, in order to grasp the condition for this complex predicate to be true of an arbitrary object, say q, we have to consider the condition for the truth of the sentence which would result from filling the argument-place of the predicate by some proper name, say 'k', for q. It is not necessary, for any particular object, such as q, that we should actually know of a proper name for it: it is enough that we can envisage the introduction of a proper name on which is conferred a sense which would make q its referent. We should then obtain a sentence '$F(k,k)\rightarrow G(k,b)$'. The condition for this sentence to be true coincides with the condition for the predicate '$F(\xi,\xi)\rightarrow G(\xi,b)$' to be true of the object q. But the condition for the foregoing sentence to be true is given in a manner exactly parallel to that in which the condition for the sentence '$F(a,a)\rightarrow G(a,b)$' to be true was given: that is, its truth-value is determined from the truth-values of the atomic sentences '$F(k,k)$' and '$G(k,b)$' by the truth-table for '$\rightarrow$'; while the truth-conditions for the atomic sentences are again determined by the references of the relational expressions '$F(\xi, \zeta)$' and '$G(\xi, \zeta)$', as applied to q and to the referent of 'b'.

It is necessary to Frege's analysis of language that, if we understand—grasp the sense of—any sentence, i.e. know the condition for its truth, then we must also grasp the sense of any predicate that can be formed from it, that is, we must know the condition for that predicate to be true of any arbitrary object. To know the condition for such a predicate to be true of an object is to know the condition for the truth of another sentence, which need not be an actual sentence of the language, but, rather, a sentence which might be formed if a proper name with that object as referent were added to the language. The justification for this assumption, that from an understanding of a sentence can be derived an understanding of any predicate which can be formed from the sentence, is that the sentence the condition for whose truth coincides with the condition for the predicate's being true of a given object is constructed in a manner completely parallel with that in which the original sentence, which we are assumed to understand, was constructed. In other words, if we understand any sentence, then we likewise understand any sentence that can be formed from it by the replacement of some proper name, in one or more of its occurrences, by some other proper name the referent of which we are given.

Now, to return to the question at issue, the simple predicates and relational expressions of the language are by definition extensional, that is, the truth-values of the atomic sentences formed from them depend only on the references of the proper names which are put into their argument-places. for we should not regard an object as being the referent of a name unless the sense of each simple predicate were given in such a way that the truth-value of the atomic sentence formed by putting that name in the argument-place of the predicate was determined by whether or not the predicate was true of that object. This extensionality of the simple predicates and relational expressions will be transmitted to the complex predicates, provided that the means of sentence-formation supplied by the quantifiers and the sentential operators, and any other devices for the formation of complex sentences, are themselves extensional: that is, provided that the truth-value of a complex sentence depends only on the truth-values of the constituents (where, in the case of the quantifiers, by a 'constituent' is meant an instance). In this case, therefore, it will necessarily be true that a sentence containing some occurrence of a proper name will be true just in case the predicate formed from the sentence by omitting that occurrence of the name is true of the object which is the referent of the name. What happens, then, in a case in which a method of sentence-formation is used which is

H*

not extensional, that is, when a sentence is formed which contains an opaque context? In such a case, a name occurring within that context will not contribute to determining the truth-value of the sentence solely in virtue of its (ordinary) reference. Hence it will not be possible to consider the result of omitting that occurrence of the name from the sentence as yielding a predicate which is true or false of the object which is the (ordinary) referent of the name according as the original sentence was true or false: for the supposition that the argument-place of that predicate is to be filled by a name having that object as its (ordinary) referent is insufficient to enable the truth-value of the resulting sentence to be determined. Thus, if the name, in such an occurrence, is to be regarded as having a reference at all, it cannot be to the object which is its ordinary referent, but must, rather, be to another object which is likewise the oblique referent of any other names which *can* be substituted for that name in that context without alteration of truth-value.

By consideration of what substitutes are possible without change of truth-value in opaque contexts, Frege concludes that such substitution is possible just in case the expression substituted has the same (ordinary) sense as that it replaces, and hence proposes that the oblique referent of any expression be taken to be what ordinarily constitutes its sense. This applies quite generally, and not only to proper names: in particular, a whole sentence occurring within an opaque context, for instance as the substantival clause after a verb for a propositional attitude, must be considered to have as its (oblique) referent, not the truth-value which is its ordinary referent, but the thought which it ordinarily expresses and which ordinarily constitutes its sense. For, just because the context is non-extensional, the sentence does not contribute to determining the truth-value of the whole of which it is a constituent solely in virtue of its ordinary reference, i.e. of its truth-value: in order to determine what, in this context, is its reference, that is, is that by which it contributes to determining the truth-value of the whole, we have to go back to the beginning again, to the way the sentence was built up out of its constituent atomic sentences, and that in which these were built up out of their component proper names, predicates and relational expressions, and consider the oblique references of each, and how they jointly determine the oblique reference of the sentence.

In the last section, we discerned two guiding ideas governing Frege's doctrine of reference. One was the use of the name/bearer relation as the prototype of the relation of an expression to its referent. The other was the conception of the reference of an expression as its semantic role, its contribution to the determination of the truth-value of a sentence (not the

SB 37

mechanism whereby this contribution is effected, which would be apter as a characterization of its sense). These two ideas are not necessarily in conflict, for the use of something as a prototype is a vague principle, which does not determine how far the analogy is to be pushed; though we have seen that sometimes Frege was inclined to push it to a point where it did come into conflict with the other guiding idea. The notion of reference as the semantic role of an expression is programmatic: it could be made to fit with a great variety of conceptions of what the reference of various types of expression was, according as we selected one or another form of semantic account. We know, however, what kind of semantics Frege proposed for at least part of our language—that part which is mirrored within his symbolic language—and so, with this background, the notion of reference becomes more specific. In particular, the semantics which Frege favoured fits very well, in the case of proper names, the identification of the referent of a name with what we ordinarily consider as its bearer—what it is the name of. (Whether it fits equally well with the use of the name/bearer relation as the prototype for the notion of reference as applied to expressions of other kinds than names, we shall leave for a later enquiry.) For, since the conception of reference as semantic role is purely programmatic, we cannot, merely on the basis of this conception, tell for sure that the reference of a proper name can be taken to consist of a relation which it has to an object as its referent, still less that that object can be taken as being (what we ordinarily take to be) its bearer. It is only by combining the conception of reference as semantic role with the picture of the reference of a name as consisting in the relation it has to its bearer that we arrive at any specific semantic account of the role of proper names in sentences. If we leave out of account the former conception, of reference as semantic role, then the proposition that the bearer of a proper name is its referent becomes merely a *definition* of the notion of reference as applied to proper names: and we are left completely in the dark what the point of introducing such a notion by definition may be, still more how we are to extend the notion by analogy to other kinds of expression. If, on the other hand, we disregard the identification of the referent of a name with its bearer, then we have an as yet merely programmatic notion: we know that the reference of a name is to be its semantic role in sentences, whatever that may be, but we have no delineation at all of the form which this semantic role takes. Thus the two guiding ideas, far from being in opposition, are complementary: both are needed. (What is not at all so clear is how far the use of the name/bearer relation as prototype in guiding us to the right extensions of the notion for other types of expression gives us the right model of the semantic roles of expressions of such other types: but this, as already said, is to be left for later exploration.)

If we were operating *merely* with the notion of reference as semantic role, without any background of a proposed form of semantics to show how this notion was to be applied to proper names, then the notion of oblique reference would have no justification: all that the existence of opaque contexts would suggest would be that the name/bearer relation was *not* the appropriate model for the reference of proper names, not the correct way of making the notion specific, simply because the model would not work for opaque contexts. If, on the other hand, we were taking the notion of reference, as applied to proper names, as simply being *defined* as the name/bearer relation, without requiring of the notion that it play any particular role in our semantic account of the language, then again there would be no need to attribute an oblique reference to names occurring in opaque contexts; for there would be no particular reason to expect that the substitution of a name with the same reference would leave the truth-value of the sentence unaltered, nor any reason to invoke the notion of a predicate's being true of an object taken as the referent of a name. It is, again, only the combination of the two ideas that motivates the introduction of the notion of oblique reference. The reference of a name is to be its semantic role in sentences: but it is proposed that this role can be explained by taking its bearer to be its referent, and having a notion for simple predicates, which can be extended to complex ones, of their being true or false of each given object. This proposal is threatened by the occurrence of opaque contexts. Instead of abandoning it, Frege proposes to save it by regarding reference as, to this extent, dependent on context, so that the bearer of a name is not in *all* contexts its referent, but it has, in certain special contexts, a different one.

(9) *Only in the context of a sentence does a word stand for anything.* This thesis is not only propounded, but heavily underlined, in *Grundlagen*, where the mistake of ignoring it is cited as the source of many philosophical errors: but it makes no subsequent appearance in Frege's work. It impressed Wittgenstein so deeply that it appears, virtually word for word, in both the *Tractatus* and the *Investigations*.

Gl x, 60, 62, 106

TLP 3.3; PI 49

But what does this gnomic utterance mean? Surely a word has a sense independently of any sentence in which it occurs: it is because this is so that we are able to understand the thought expressed by some sentence we have never heard before. And the sense determines the reference: so the word has a reference in itself, and not as considered as occurring in a particular place in a particular sentence. True enough, in natural language there are ambiguous words, carrying two or more senses, so that we have to tell from the context in which particular sense the word is being used in that context: but this is surely another feature of natural language which Frege would regard as a defect, and so he would hardly construe an assertion of its existence as a profoundly important philosophical principle.

When Frege wrote *Grundlagen*, he had not yet formulated his distinction between sense and reference, and so it is quite possible that the words 'Bedeutung' and 'bedeuten', as they occur in the various statements of the thesis, have the more general senses of 'meaning' and 'mean', so that, in terms of Frege's later vocabulary, we could more accurately render the thesis by saying that it is only in the context of a sentence that a word has a *sense*. But what could it mean to say this? One interpretation of it has been given by Miss Anscombe in her book on the *Tractatus*, as it applies to   *IWT* 66 names. To assign a reference to a name or a set of names, she points out, could only have a significance as a preparation for their use in sentences; analogously the assignment of a reference to physical objects could only be understood as a preparation for the use of those objects within some representative arrangement. If, for example, I take some coloured counters, and say, 'Let this one stand for the Government, this one for the Opposition, this one for the Church, this one for the Universities, this one for the Army, this one for the Trade Unions, . . .', and so on, I shall be understood on the presumption that I am about to make some arrangement of the counters by means of which I intend to represent some relations between these institutions, and assert that they obtain. If I do not go on to make any such arrangement, but simply start talking about something else, my earlier declarations lose their original intelligibility: I cannot, when questioned why I said all that, reply, 'Oh, I just wanted those counters to stand for those things, that's all'; for their standing for those things only amounts to anything if they are to be used to effect some symbolic representation by means of which a thought is expressed. Otherwise, my stipulation of their reference is like my saying, in the course of explaining a card game, 'Ace is high', and it later turns out that the ranking of the cards plays no role in the game; or it is like my saying, 'Suppose there is life on Mars', and then failing to draw any consequences from this hypothesis, and, when challenged, saying, 'Oh, I simply wanted you to suppose that'; or, perhaps, it is most like giving a definition of a word and then not subsequently using that word. Certain utterances have the effect only of saying something of the form, 'Be prepared to . . .'.

More generally, the assignment of a sense to a word, whether a name or an expression of any other logical type, only has significance in relation to the subsequent occurrence of that word in sentences. A sentence is, as we have said, the smallest unit of language with which a linguistic act can be accomplished, with which a 'move can be made in the language-game': so you cannot *do* anything with a word—cannot effect any conventional (linguistic) act by uttering it—save by uttering some sentence containing that word (save for the cases in which, as in the answer to some questions, the remainder of the sentence is understood from the context). And we have seen that, for Frege, the sense of a word or expression always consists in the contribution it makes to determining the thought expressed by a sentence in which it occurs. That is: the sense of the word consists in a rule which, taken together with the rules constitutive of the senses of the other words, determines the condition for the truth of a sentence in which the word occurs. The sense of a word thus consists—wholly consists—in something which has a relation to the truth-value of sentences containing the word. It may be that we can formulate the sense of the word—that is, the manner of stipulating its reference—without explicit allusion to its occurrence within sentences. But, if so, this will be because the formulation involves some notion which is only significant as being preparatory for such a use. I say, 'Ace ranks above King', and, in saying so, I make no direct allusion to the actual play of the card in the game: but my remark is only significant because it can be taken together with some other rule which does so relate, e.g. 'The trick is taken by the highest card of the suit led'. Likewise, if I say ' "$\xi=\zeta$" stands for the relation which every object has to itself and no object has to any other object', I make no explicit allusion to the occurrence of the symbol '=' in sentences; but my remark can only be interpreted in connection with such an occurrence, that is, as taken in conjunction with such a rule as 'If "$R(\xi, \zeta)$" is a simple relational expression, and "j" and "k" are proper names, then "$R(j,k)$" is true just in case the referent of "j" has to the referent of "k" the relation for which "$R(\xi, \zeta)$" stands'. This fact may be expressed by saying that a relation can be understood only as being the referent of some relational expression: to talk of a relation has no significance unless it is part of a set of specifications which together determine the condition for the truth of some sentence containing a relational expression.

In a certain sense, therefore, sentences have a primacy within language over other linguistic expressions: a sentence is determined as true under certain conditions, which conditions are derivable from the way in which the sentence is constructed out of its constituent words; and the senses of the words relate solely to this determination of the truth-conditions of the sentences in which the words may occur. Of course, looked at in one way, the word has a sense independently of any particular sentence in which it occurs: but its sense is something relating entirely to the occurrence of the word in a sentence, just as the rank of a card is something that relates entirely to some convention governing its play, a convention expressible in terms of the notion of rank.

If, then, we know everything that needs to be known about a word in order to determine the condition for the truth of any sentence in which it occurs, we know the reference of the word; if, in particular, this reference is given to us in the way conventionally associated with that word, then we know its sense. There cannot be anything else, not having to do with the interpretation of sentences containing the word, which we need to know in order to determine the reference, or the sense, of the word. If we commit the mistake of doing what Frege calls 'asking after the reference of the word in isolation', that is, of asking what it stands for in neglect of the fact that the answer can only be, and need only be, whatever is required to give, in combination with rules governing other words, a correct means of determining the truth-values of sentences containing the word, then, in problematic cases, we are likely to come up with an entirely inappropriate answer, such as the image which the utterance of the word has the propensity to call up in our minds.

On this doctrine, sentences are true or false, and sentences are those linguistic expressions by means of which it is possible to *do* something, that is, to *say* something. Of course, how we succeed in doing something with a sentence, considered as being determined in a particular way as true or as false, requires further explanation, and Frege attempted to provide such an explanation: this is the part of his theory relating to an ingredient in meaning which we have not yet considered—force. But the senses of the subordinate expressions which make up the sentences of our language are, for Frege, to be connected wholly with the contribution they make to the determination of sentences containing them as true or as false. This was an enormous step forward in the theory of meaning, a step almost as great as Frege's distinction between the two stages of sentence-formation—the formation of atomic sentences and their transformation into complex sentences. Earlier writers had spoken vaguely of words as conveying ideas, and complex expressions as conveying complex ideas compounded out of the ideas conveyed by the constituent words: a sentence then becomes a particular form of complex expression, and the unique and central character of this category of linguistic expression is left entirely unaccounted for; while the question what it is for a word or expression to stand for an 'idea' is likewise left unanalysed. The sentence is thought of as true just in case there is something in reality corresponding to the complex idea which it conveys, and there is no means of distinguishing this from the case in which there is something in reality to which a complex predicate may be truly applied. Frege's clear apprehension of the central role of sentences was the first step, not merely to a workable theory of language, but to one which was even plausible.

Unhappily, the doctrine which we considered earlier, which regards truth-values as objects and hence assimilates sentences to complex proper names, undermined the sharpness of the original perception. If sentences are merely a special case of complex proper names, if the True and the False are merely two particular objects amid a universe of objects, then, after all, there is nothing unique about sentences: whatever was thought to be special about them should be ascribed, rather, to proper names—complete expressions—in general. This was the most disastrous of the effects of the misbegotten doctrine that sentences are a species of complex name, which dominated Frege's later period: to rob him of the insight that sentences play a unique role, and that the role of almost every other linguistic expression (every expression whose contribution to meaning falls within the division of sense) consists in its part in forming sentences. After the adoption of the new doctrine, only the ghost of the original thesis could remain: the sense of a word now had to be thought of as relating, not particularly to the determination of the truth-value of a sentence containing it, but, more generally, to the determination of the referent of a complex proper name containing it. It is true that, in *Grundgesetze*, Frege maintains, as a sort of echo of his original thesis, that, in order to determine the reference of a certain range of proper names (names of classes), it is sufficient to give a rule determining the reference of every complex name that can be formed from them: but, clearly, such a process must stop somewhere, with an outright stipulation of the references of certain complex names; and no rationale is provided for distinguishing those names whose reference must be stipulated outright, and those for which it is sufficient to lay down the references of more complex names containing them.

We shall return later to further consideration of this thesis: we have not yet exhausted its content.

Gg I 10, 29, 30

SB 28; BW 128 (79)

(10) *The referents of our words are what we talk about.* This slogan may sound like a truism, or, at best, a specification of the way in which Frege is going to use the phrase 'talk about . . .'. In fact, it is much more: it is an expression of Frege's realism.

Frege expends considerable rhetoric in insisting that we do actually succeed in speaking about the actual objects, in the real world, which are the referents of the names we use, and not about any intermediate surrogates for or representations of them. There is a natural temptation to construe expressions which lack a reference to anything in the external world as standing for some kind of mental image. The child who uses the name 'Santa Claus', or the astronomer who, believing that there is an intra-Mercurial planet, uses the name 'Vulcan', must surely be speaking of *something*: since absurdities follow from adopting the view of Meinong—and early Russell—that there are objects which do not exist, objects which are not actual, but merely possible, the only solution seems to be to say that what is being spoken of in such cases is a mental conception. Frege himself could resist the temptation to go down this path by applying his distinction between sense and reference: a person who uses such a name really *says something*—i.e. expresses a thought—but there is not anything *about which* he is speaking. But someone who has started down the path is compelled to go further. If, in using expressions to which nothing in the external world corresponds, one is speaking about some mental conception, this must surely apply also to the cases in which there is something in the external world corresponding to the expression: for one cannot in general tell, just by understanding an expression, whether or not anything in the external world corresponds to it, and it would be strange if something other than what one knows by understanding the expression should determine what kind of entity it directly represents, and which, moreover, presumably constitutes its meaning; presumably, that is, for a philosopher innocent of the distinction between sense and reference which would have saved him from starting down this path in the first place. It then appears to follow that we can never talk about anything in the objective world at all, but only about its mental representation. The familiar problems now arise how to describe the relation between the external object and its mental representation, and how to escape scepticism about the existence of the external objects.

This line of thought Frege was, as a realist in revolt against the prevailing idealism of his day, determined to resist. When I say, 'Mont Blanc is the highest mountain in Europe', it is, he says, the actual mountain, with all its snow and ice, that I am speaking of, not any mental representation of the mountain; and, he adds elsewhere, it is whether that very object does or does not fall under the concept 'highest mountain in Europe'—a concept as much part of the real world, of the realm of reference, as is the mountain itself—which determines whether what I say about it is true or false. It cannot be that, when I aim at speaking of the actual object in the real world, I only succeed in speaking of some mental representation of it: for, if necessary, I can specify that I intend to refer to the actual object, by saying,

Gl 27n; NS
141 (130),
155-6 (143-4),
250 (232)

SB 31; Ged
68

e.g., 'I mean the actual mountain, not a representation of it'. Such a specification precludes the name, 'Mont Blanc', from standing for a mental representation: it must do, since, while it is not wholly in my power to determine for certain that I am referring to anything at all, it must be in my power to determine what sort of thing I am *not* referring to; more generally, what has to be true of something for it to be what I am intending to refer to. But, in the normal case, such a specification only makes explicit the implicit intention with which the name was used in the first place: so it cannot be that, in the normal case, that is, the case when I do not explicitly or implicitly intend to refer to a mental representation, I aim at the actual object, and, falling short, hit a mental representation of it instead. If we cannot succeed in referring to actual, non-mental, objects, then the only conclusion can be that most of the time we do not succeed in referring to anything at all: that most of the things we say are neither true nor false, because devoid of reference. And that conclusion is too absurd to be entertained.

For Frege, then, we really do succeed in talking about the real world, a world which exists independently of us, and it is in virtue of how things are in that world that the things we say are true or false: the thoughts that we express are true or false objectively, in virtue of how things stand in the real world—in the realm of reference—and independently of whether we know them to be true or false; such thoughts would have been true or false even if we had been unable to express or to grasp them, independently, indeed, of our being in the world at all (except, of course, in so far as they happen to be thoughts which entail our existence). In taking up this position, Frege was defying the whole idealist tradition which dominated the German philosophy of his day. This realist ingredient in Frege's theory of reference is, of course, linked with the idea of the name/bearer relation as the prototype for the relation of reference, rather than with the conception of reference as semantic role. The referent of an expression is its extra-linguistic correlate in the real world: it is precisely because the expressions we use have such extra-linguistic correlates that we succeed in talking about the real world, and in saying things about it which are true or false in virtue of how things are in that world. This is to be taken just as seriously for incomplete expressions as for names: the referents of incomplete expressions—concepts, relations and functions—are likewise the extra-linguistic correlates of these expressions, and are just as much constituents of objective reality as objects are: that is why statements which can only be construed as being statements about concepts, or about relations or functions, are likewise statements about objective reality, and are true or false according to the character of that reality.

Gg I xix, xxi

The point about the referents of incomplete expressions is not to be pressed too hard: there is a very delicate balance between the role played in the ascription of reference to these expressions by the idea of the name/ bearer relation as prototype and the idea of reference as semantic role. If we concentrate only on the former, then it becomes highly problematic that reference can be ascribed to these expressions at all, even by analogy; if we concentrate on the latter only, then it becomes totally unproblematic. As we shall see, Frege did not treat the possession of reference by incomplete expressions as being highly problematic: indeed, in the whole of his published writings, he never once attempted to argue for it, although he did do NS 209-10 so in a few places in some of his unpublished writings. Nevertheless, as we (192-3) shall see later, if we analyse the notion of reference as applied by Frege to incomplete expressions, we shall find that the thesis that they have reference is not a total triviality, as it would be were the conception of reference as semantic role the sole constituent of the notion: room is left, at an exactly identifiable point, to dispute it.

An attempt has recently been made by Tugendhat to approach Frege's SF III 51-69 notion of reference from a new direction. This involves, in effect, casting off the use of the name/bearer relation as prototype, and presenting reference wholly as semantic role. It is instructive to study the results of this attempt.

Tugendhat proposes that reference should be understood as what he calls 'truth-value potential'. The truth-value potential of an expression is, in SF III 55 effect, its semantic role, its contribution to the determination of the truth-value of a sentence in which it occurs. Tugendhat does not explain this notion so much by appeal to the semantics which are to be given for the language, a semantics which will lay down what the semantic role of each primitive expression is: rather, what he actually defines is the relation between two expressions of having the same truth-value potential, in terms of the truth-values, assumed as already known, of the sentences in which they occur. Two expressions will then be said to have the same truth-value potential just in case, whenever each is supplemented by the same expression to form a sentence, the two resulting sentences have the same truth-value. Tugendhat does not say what truth-value potential itself is: it could, in accordance with a device introduced by Frege, and compatibly with all that Tugendhat says, be identified with an equivalence class of expressions under the equivalence relation of having the same truth-value potential.

Tugendhat claims that, by introducing the notion of truth-value potential in this way, and identifying it with the reference of an expression (Tugendhat, no more than Frege, makes any verbal distinction between 'reference' and 'referent'), he has isolated that strand in Frege's account which was new and revolutionary, disentangling it from an inconsistent strand from which Frege never succeeded in wholly extricating himself, and which was derived from the traditional account which Frege was, in the main, overthrowing. We have seen that this picture of the situation is entirely wrong. First, the two strands are not in essential opposition to one another, but, at least as far as proper names are concerned, complementary: either is useless without the other. Secondly, that ingredient which consists in taking the name/bearer relation as prototype is not a remnant of the 'traditional' account at all, at least if the tradition we are thinking of is that which dominated German universities and had done so for decades: it is the core of Frege's realism, which constituted the most revolutionary feature of his whole philosophical outlook.

Tugendhat has stripped the notion of reference of the character of being a *relation* to something extra-linguistic: it has become, in his hands, essentially an equivalence relation between expressions. What are the consequences?

Tugendhat claims certain advantages for his proposal. First, that it will become quite unproblematic that sentences, or predicates and other incomplete expressions, have a reference. This we may readily grant; but it is doubtful whether it is an unalloyed advantage. Secondly, that it becomes unnecessary to assimilate sentences to proper names. This is not a particular advantage of Tugendhat's account: as we have seen, it always was unnecessary, and was mediated only by Frege's making the wanton assumption that truth-values are objects. Thirdly, that it becomes demonstrable, instead of merely probable, that sentences have the same reference, i.e. the same truth-value potential, when they have the same truth-value. This claim is entirely preposterous. It would be better to say that, on Tugendhat's definition, it becomes demonstrable that the possession of the same truth-value is *not* sufficient for having the same truth-value potential. Tugendhat's 'proof' is obtained by remarking that a sentence does not need supplementation to form a sentence, and hence concluding that two sentences have the same truth-value potential just in case they already have the same truth-value. But Tugendhat's remark amounts to saying, quite truly, that the null supplementation is *one* supplementation that will convert a sentence into a sentence. Under his definition, in order to show that two sentences have the same truth-value potential, it is necessary to show that any supplementation yielding a sentence, when applied to both of them, will yield sentences with the same truth-value. This will, of course, be so in a purely extensional language, provided that the two original sentences had the same truth-value in the first place. In a language, such as ours, which contains some expressions forming opaque contexts for whole constituent sentences, it will not be so. As we have seen, Frege, just because he wants to take the referent of a proper name to be its bearer, has an independent reason for taking himself to be forced to construe opaque contexts as distorting the usual reference of expressions occurring within them; hence he is able to maintain that truth-values are the referents of sentences despite there being opaque contexts. But Tugendhat's notion of reference provides no motivation whatever for treating opaque contexts as in any way special: indeed, it is not immediately apparent that he has any means available for distinguishing opaque contexts from transparent ones.

If we have already laid down that the referent of a proper name is to be taken to be its bearer, then we can identify opaque contexts as being those in which the replacement of a name by another name having the same (ordinary) referent may alter the truth-value of the whole. But the equation of the referent of a name with its bearer is just what Tugendhat has thrown overboard: so this means is unavailable to him. It would, indeed, be possible to identify them by appeal to true identity-statements: if '$b = c$' is a true statement of identity, and the name 'b' occurs in a sentence 'A' although the replacement of 'b' by 'c' yields a sentence with a truth-value different from that of 'A', then 'b' occurs inside an opaque context within 'A'. But this does not seem to be a great deal of help, since the sign of identity can be picked out only syntactically: we can certainly not identify it as that relational expression such that a statement formed by putting two names in its argument-places is true just in case the two names have the same referent.

For all this, Tugendhat claims as the fourth advantage that he can demonstrate, instead of just laying down, that the reference (referent) of a name is its bearer. (Presumably this means that two names have the same truth-value potential just in case they have the same bearer.) For a non-extensional language, obviously no such thing could be established, for similar reasons to those stated above. But, even in an extensional language, it is not quite correct. There would be no reason for saying that a name without a bearer lacked a reference, i.e. a truth-value potential: it would merely share the same truth-value potential as other names without bearers. There would likewise be no ground for denying to sentences containing such names a truth-value: at best, they could be said to have an intermediate truth-value.

But, now, of course, owing to the way in which Tugendhat has explained his notion of truth-value potential, it is implicitly assumed that all the work of determining the truth-values of sentences has already been done, and therefore that the whole semantic account of the language has already been set out. Truth-value potential is not a notion in terms of which the semantics of the language is given, not one that will do any work in constructing such a semantics: rather, it is a notion which can be introduced once the semantics of the language has been given. And if there is to be any possibility that the assignment of truth-values to sentences generated by this semantics will coincide with Frege's, and hence, in particular, that sentences containing names without a bearer should come out as neither true nor false, the notion of the bearer of a name must have been used in framing the semantics. Hence, at least for proper names, Frege's notion of reference, as being a relation between a name and an object in the real world, must have been employed in the semantics of the language. Thus the primary purpose for which the notion of reference was introduced by Frege has been assigned to something else, no longer called 'reference', while the notion of truth-value potential, which has usurped this name, no longer has this function to perform. It is true enough that—if the language is extensional—one will be able to show that two names have the same truth-value potential just in case they have the same bearer, provided that this is understood to include the case in which neither has any bearer, though, of course, both still have a truth-value potential, as defined. But this is not because some stipulation which Frege found it necessary to make has been avoided: that stipulation has been made in laying down the truth-conditions of atomic statements in terms of the notion of the bearer of a name.

A concept, a relation or a function is supposed by Frege to be something which is wholly extra-linguistic, whose existence is independent of our happening to have an expression for it—in short, a part of the real world. The only way we can gain an idea of such a thing is as the referent of a predicate, relational or functional expression. Thus, as it were, we approach it— apprehend it—via language: but this does not make it any different from an object, for the only way in which we can apprehend an object as being a separate, identifiable part of undifferentiated reality is by understanding it as the referent of a proper name with the appropriate criterion of identity associated with it. But, though we conceive of it *through* language, what constitutes our conceiving it as a part of external reality is that we take it as being the *referent* of an expression: and 'the referents of our words are what we talk *about*'. For Tugendhat, replacing the notion of reference by that of truth-value potential, all this is lost. Just as the objects for which proper names stand cannot be identified with truth-value potentials (it would be ludicrous to suggest that Dr. Tugendhat just *is* the truth-value potential of the name 'Tugendhat'), but at best a one-one correspondence claimed to hold between them, so, likewise, the truth-value potential of a predicate is wholly unlike what Frege takes a concept to be. A truth-value potential, as explained by Tugendhat, is ineradicably language-dependent: whether justifiably or not, Frege thought of a concept as something independent of language in the way an object is, and for just that reason standing to a predicate in a relation analogous to that in which an object stands to its name.

The theory of reference is an attempt at a basis for a semantic account of language. To say just that about it, without specifying anything about the form such an account is supposed by Frege to take, is to reduce the notion to something merely programmatic. To attempt to make it into something not used within the semantic account, but definable in terms of semantic notions as specified by that account, is to empty it of all its interest. Properly to understand Frege's notion, we have to bear in mind both ingredients of it simultaneously, and understand the complementary roles they play. In philosophy we must always resist the temptation of hitting on an answer to the question how we can define such-and-such a notion, an answer which supplies a smooth and elegant definition which entirely ignores the purpose which we originally wanted the notion for.

CHAPTER 7

The Reference of Incomplete Expressions

AT FIRST SIGHT, Frege's ascription of reference to incomplete expressions is highly dubious. In the case of proper names, at least for the archetypal examples of proper names, there is nothing problematic about the ascription to them of reference: what was contentious in Frege's doctrine was the distinction between their sense and their reference. For incomplete expressions, it appears at first sight the other way round: only a philosopher who called the whole notion of sense in question would doubt that incomplete expressions such as predicates have a sense; but the ascription of a reference to them has the ring of paradox or metaphysical excess. Whereas for proper names Frege at least made out a case for the thesis that the reference of a proper name does not determine its sense, and for the sister thesis that a name may have a sense but lack a reference, it seems at first incomprehensible that these theses can be held to apply, e.g., to predicates. In face of these *prima facie* difficulties, many exegetes of Frege have abandoned the attempt to make out a distinction between sense and reference for incomplete expressions. In the *Philosophical Review* for 1955 W. Marshall first expounded the view that, although Frege undeniably used the word 'Bedeutung' in connection with incomplete expressions, he did not intend it to be understood in any abnormal manner, as he did when he applied it to proper names; that the Bedeutung of a predicate was simply its meaning, in the ordinary English sense of 'meaning', i.e. that it corresponded to the Sinn, and not to the Bedeutung, of proper names; and that Frege simply did not apply the word 'Sinn' to incomplete expressions. Why Frege should have adopted so confusing a terminology, Marshall did not think to explain. R. Grossmann, writing in the same journal, subsequently declared that if anything is certain in the interpretation of Frege, the correctness of this thesis is. I should say, on the contrary, that acceptance of it makes totally impossible any understanding of what Frege was saying.

Even writers who have a much better understanding of Frege are liable to mistakes of this sort. Miss Anscombe, in her book on the *Tractatus*, rightly attributes to Frege the ascription of both sense and reference— IWT 45 understood in a way analogous to what they mean in the case of proper names—to incomplete expressions, and points out one way in which a *complex* predicate might come to possess a sense while lacking a reference (namely, by containing a proper name with sense but no reference); but even she goes on to say that for *simple* predicates Frege did not make out that reference did not determine sense. (She actually says that he failed to display a distinction between sense and reference: it is more interesting to regard this as a slip of the pen.) Would it not be as trivial to distinguish between sense and reference for incomplete expressions, if for them the thesis did not hold that reference does not determine sense, as I have argued that it would be to distinguish them for proper names, if that thesis did not hold for *them*? No: because of the apparently problematic character of the ascription of reference to incomplete expressions at all. It appears as highly doubtful that there is anything, not belonging to the realm of sense, to which incomplete expressions are related in a manner analogous to that in which a proper name is related to the object which it names: that there are any entities to be the objective correlates of predicates as, e.g., people are the objective correlates of personal proper names. It is because this appears so questionable that Marshall and Grossmann wish to absolve Frege from the charge of having held any such view. Thus even if it could be held for predicates that their reference determined their sense, it would remain significant to ascribe *both* sense and reference to them, in view of the fact that reference would not usually be ascribed to them at all. In that case, the sense of a predicate—unlike the sense of a proper name—could be regarded just as its possessing the reference which it had; this would be tendentious, in that its sense would not normally be thought of as describable in terms of reference at all. This, at least for simple predicates, will be the view which I have attributed to Miss Anscombe.

It is, indeed, surprisingly hard to confute such an account as Marshall's by direct quotation from Frege's published writings. Nowhere in them does he emphasize that he intends 'Bedeutung' to be taken, when applied to incomplete expressions, in a way analogous to that in which he uses it as applied to singular terms. Nowhere does he *argue* that incomplete expressions must have a reference as well as a sense, or that, in their case also, reference is insufficient to determine sense: this seems puzzling to anyone who views these theses as tendentious and disputable; although, if my view is correct, that when properly understood they hardly appear questionable at all, the puzzle disappears. Hardly ever does Frege speak of the *sense* of incomplete expressions, although he had been at such pains to emphasize that proper names possessed a sense distinct from their reference.

Ggf 37, 39, 40, etc. (55–56, 59, 61, etc.) It is true that in 'Gedankengefüge', the third of the three essays published towards the end of his life, he speaks extensively of the senses of incomplete expressions, and stresses that these senses are themselves incomplete. But from the total absence from these essays of any mention of Bedeutung, together with his earlier insistence on the incompleteness of the Bedeutungen of incomplete expressions, one might naturally suspect that at this period of his life he had abandoned the distinction between sense and reference, or, at least, that, if he retained it for singular terms, he had simply decided to substitute the word 'Sinn' for 'Bedeutung' when speaking of incomplete expressions, never having made a significant distinction between them in this case anyway.

A reading of what remain of Frege's posthumously published writings dispels these illusions. A brief exposition of his views which Frege addressed NS 275 (255) to Ludwig Darmstaedter in 1919 shows him holding the distinction between Sinn and Bedeutung as firmly as ever. Moreover, in the 'Ausführungen über NS 128 (118) Sinn und Bedeutung' of about 1893 Frege says expressly that 'the same distinction can be made also for concept-words' as well as for proper names, NS 209-10 (192–3); NS 262 (243) while in the 'Einleitung in die Logik' of 1906 (as also in the 'Logik in der Mathematik' of 1914) he for once *argues* that incomplete expressions must have reference as well as sense; not indeed very convincingly, but his remarks make it clear that for him the reference of incomplete expressions corresponds to the *reference* and not to the *sense* of singular terms. There are two arguments. First, he says that an (atomic) sentence is made up by putting proper names in the argument-places of an incomplete expression—predicate or relational expression. The proper names (in general) have referents, and, if they do, the whole sentence has a referent —its truth-value. Now, he says, it is 'altogether unlikely' that the expression by means of which we join together certain simple parts having a reference to form a complex whole having a reference should itself lack a reference; for if the part lacks a reference, the whole must lack a reference also. (The same argument, for what it is worth, would work equally well for functional expressions; better, indeed, since the ascription of reference to complex singular terms is less dubious than its ascription to sentences.) Secondly, he says that when I say, e.g., 'Jupiter is larger than Mars', I am NS 209-10 (192–3) stating that a certain relation obtains between the referent of the word 'Jupiter' and the referent of the word 'Mars': this relation *must* belong to the realm of reference, and not to the realm of sense, since the things which it relates themselves belong to the realm of reference. His thought here is: how can anything which belongs to the (very special) realm of sense *obtain between* two objects which do not belong to that realm at all? The being-larger-than, which we ascribe to Jupiter in relation to Mars, must belong as much to the real, objective world—to the realm of reference—and to the same region of it—i.e. not to the realm of sense—as Mars and Jupiter do; for is not that external world—and that particular region of it—as much characterized by Jupiter's being larger than Mars as it is by its containing Jupiter and containing Mars?

Granted, then, that Frege recognized a distinction between sense and reference for incomplete expressions as for proper names and sentences, what is problematic about this doctrine and what is not? We have already seen in the last chapter that Frege made some case for saying that predicates (which we may take as representative of incomplete expressions in general) could, like proper names, have a sense but no reference; and we found in natural language another case making a better analogy. What is more important, we saw how Frege could maintain that the analogue could hold, for predicates, to the possession by two names of different senses but the same reference. The relation between concepts which, according to Frege, is the analogue of the relation of identity between objects is: having the same NS 131-3 extension, i.e. having just the same objects falling under them. Likewise, the (120-2); NS analogous relation between relations would be: holding between just the 197-8 (181-2) same objects; and the analogous relation between functions would be: having the same values for the same arguments. A relation between concepts is, of course, a relation of second level, and is accordingly to be denoted by a second-level relational expression both of whose argument-places are to be filled by (first-level) predicates. Thus the second-level relation which Frege expressly states to be analogous to the first-level relation denoted by:

$$\text{`}\xi \text{ is the same as } \eta\text{'}$$

is that denoted by:

$$\text{`For every } \alpha, \, \Phi(\alpha) \text{ if and only if } \Psi(\alpha)\text{'},$$

the argument-places—to be filled by predicates—being indicated by the letters 'Φ' and 'Ψ'. Frege does not say wherein the analogy resides: but it seems quite evident that it can only reside, and that he held it to reside, in the validity of the principle of extensionality both for concepts (and functions) and for objects. It is true that in his formal system, either of *Begriffsschrift* or of *Grundgesetze*, Frege does not adopt the principle of extensionality for concepts (or for functions) as an axiom: but then in neither system did he

need it—in *Grundgesetze*, in particular, because most of the actual development of the theory is in terms of classes, which are of course explicitly
assumed to be extensional; and Frege did not always put into the axiom-
system all that he held as true—for instance, the principle governing the
value of the description-function when its argument was not a unit class.
In any case, there is nothing anywhere in Frege's writings to indicate that
he held the principle of extensionality to be false for concepts: indeed, his
doctrine of indirect reference in effect precluded him from acknowledging
as genuine any apparent counter-example to the principle.

Gg I 11

NS 128 (118)

    The principle of extensionality for objects is simply the law that, where
'*a*' and '*b*' are singular terms, and '$F(\xi)$' is any predicate, then from the
sentence '*a* is the same as *b*' together with the sentence '$F(a)$' can be inferred
the sentence '$F(b)$': the validity of this law Frege, of course, expressly
acknowledges. The principle of extensionality for concepts, similarly, is the
law that, where '$F(\xi)$' and '$G(\xi)$' are predicates, and '$M\alpha: \Phi(\alpha)$' any
second-level predicate taking a first-level predicate as its sole argument,
then from the sentence 'For every α, $F(\alpha)$ if and only if $G(\alpha)$,' together
with the sentence '$M\alpha: F(\alpha)$,' can be inferred the sentence '$M\alpha: G(\alpha)$'.
For instance, from 'The founder of modern genetics was Mendel' and 'The
founder of modern genetics was a monk' follows 'Mendel was a monk';
likewise, from 'A thing is a man if and only if it is a featherless biped' and
'Rover is not a man' follows 'Rover is not a featherless biped,' and from the
first sentence taken together with 'There have not always been men' follows
'There have not always been featherless bipeds'. Admittedly, there are
apparent counter-examples—involving opaque contexts—to the second
law: e.g. from the above sentence taken together with 'John wondered
whether a man was at the door' does not follow 'John wondered whether
a featherless biped was at the door'. But then there are precisely similar
apparent counter-examples to the first law too: e.g. from 'The founder of
genetics was Mendel' and 'The abbot thought Mendel was ignorant of
botany' does not follow 'The abbot thought the founder of genetics was
ignorant of botany'; and Frege's method for saving the first law from such
apparent exceptions imposed on him a similar method for saving the second
law.

    All this is in complete contrast with what is often said about Frege's
distinction between concepts and classes. Alonzo Church, for example, has
said that for Frege concepts were intensional but classes extensional. This is a
correct account of Russell's views, but not of Frege's. Russell was uncertain
that the principle of extensionality held for what he called 'propositional
functions' (= Frege's concepts); he therefore attempted to define classes in

terms of propositional functions in such a way as to make classes extensional even if propositional functions were not. Since classes were ranged in a hierarchy of types mirroring the hierarchy of types for propositional functions, the extensionality of classes constituted for him the *only* difference between them and propositional functions: when he wrote the introduction to the second edition of *Principia Mathematica*, he thought that propositional functions probably were, after all, extensional, and concluded that the introduction of classes as well as propositional functions was probably redundant. For Frege it is quite different. There is, as we have seen, every reason to suppose that Frege took concepts—and everything else—to be completely extensional. What constituted for him the difference between concepts and classes was the fact that classes are *objects*: the difference is a difference of level; there is no hierarchy of types for classes corresponding to the hierarchy of types for concepts and functions.

FB 19; Gg I 2

However this may be, we have seen that at any rate Frege did expressly state that one cannot properly speak of identity between concepts, but that the relation between them which is analogous to identity is the relation of being co-extensive. In the light of this, the answer to the question whether the reference of a predicate determines its sense is immediate. In saying that the reference of a singular term does not determine its sense, we meant that two singular terms may have the same reference but different senses. When we are speaking of predicates, we are not allowed by Frege to ask whether two predicates may have the same reference but different senses: for the referent of a predicate is a concept, and he regards it as senseless to use the word 'same' in connection with concepts. Rather, we must take the thesis that the reference of a predicate determines its sense as meaning the following: that if '$F(\xi)$' and '$G(\xi)$' are predicates, and the concept which '$F(\xi)$' stands for bears to the concept which '$G(\xi)$' stands for the relation which is the analogue of the relation of identity—namely the relation of co-extensiveness—then the predicates '$F(\xi)$' and '$G(\xi)$' must have the same sense. When would these concepts stand in this relation? As we have seen, when just the same objects fall under them, i.e. when the sentence 'For every x, $F(x)$ if and only if $G(x)$' is true. But it is obvious to everyone that the satisfaction of this condition does not guarantee that the two predicates have the same sense: they might be 'ξ is a man' and 'ξ is a featherless biped', for example.

Huss 320; NS 131 (120)

All this, however, establishes comparatively little. It establishes, namely, that Frege had a notion of a relation between incomplete expressions, which he presented as analogous to the relation of having the same reference as between proper names, which could hold between two incomplete expressions having different senses. The analogy between the two relations is made out: assuming the principle of extensionality—or, what is the same thing, assuming either an extensional language or one for which we can explain away non-extensional contexts by means of some such doctrine as that of Frege concerning indirect reference—the relation holds between two predicates just when they are interchangeable without loss of truth-value, just as does the relation which obtains between two proper names when they have the same reference. But is this analogy a sufficient basis for Frege's ascribing to incomplete expressions the possession of a reference? Is it justifiable to go from the indication of a relation having a specifiable analogy to two proper names' having the same reference to speaking of incomplete expressions as having a reference? What are the referents for which incomplete expressions are supposed to stand?

We saw in the last chapter that there are two ingredients to the doctrine of reference as it applies to proper names: the conception of reference as semantic role; and the identification of the referent of a name with its bearer. The conception of reference as semantic role tells us to what purpose the notion of reference is to be put: it is not just an ornament, but fulfils a vital structural function; for the sense of the word will consist of the way we determine the reference. The identification of the referent of a name with its bearer provides the matter of which the conception of reference as semantic role is merely the form: it outlines the shape that is to be given to the account of the meanings of proper names. It does not, indeed, give us a complete model of what it is to grasp the sense of a proper name; but it tells us that this will have to do with the determination of an object as the bearer of the name. It tells us more than this, indeed: for, if the reference of a name is its semantic role, then the senses of predicates and relational and functional expressions must be given relative to the sort of thing which can be the referent of the proper names which occupy their argument-places. The determination of the truth-value of a sentence formed, for instance, by putting a proper name in the argument-place of a simple predicate must be able to proceed once the referent of the proper name has been determined from its sense, irrespectively of how, in particular, that referent was determined, that is, of what the particular sense of the proper name was: and this tells us a great deal about the sense which a simple predicate can have; it tells us, in fact, that simple predicates must be extensional. Or rather, it tells us this only so far as the occurrences of simple predicates in atomic sentences are concerned: the more general conclusion follows only when we know that the various operators transforming atomic into complex sentences are also extensional. All this follows from the identification of the referent of a proper name with its bearer only if this is taken in conjunction with the conception of reference as semantic role: without this, that identification remains, as we saw, a mere definition, for purpose unknown.

Now, as far as the conception of reference as semantic role is concerned, the ascription of reference to predicates and other incomplete expressions is not dubious in the least. Evidently, they must have some semantic role: and, relying on this conception alone, we have said nothing about what it is. Furthermore, if the reference of a predicate is to be its semantic role, then it will necessarily follow that the reference of two predicates is the same just in case they are always interchangeable without alteration of truth-value; moreover, if we assume the principle of extensionality, which, as we have seen, there is every reason to suppose that Frege did, then this interchangeability will obtain between two predicates precisely when they are extensionally equivalent. Thus Frege has selected exactly the right relation between two predicates as the criterion for their having the same reference.

Why people find the ascription of reference to predicates so paradoxical, however, is that they are not concentrating on the notion of reference as semantic role as the guiding notion, but rather on that whereby the name/bearer relation is the prototype: they find it hard to accept that there is anything to which a predicate stands in a relation analogous to that of a name to its bearer. So far, almost all that we have said about the use of the name/bearer relation as prototype has been in application to proper names themselves: we have as yet made no serious investigation whether it is a good model in the case of incomplete expressions.

Before tackling this question head on, it is necessary first to dispose of a notorious tangle in which Frege enwrapped himself in his essay 'Über Begriff und Gegenstand'. Consider any predicate, say 'ξ is a horse'. According to Frege's doctrine, this expression stands for a concept. If we ask *which* concept it stands for, the natural answer would be 'The concept *horse*'. Thus Frege naturally comes to say that the sentence, 'Blue Peter is a horse', says of Blue Peter that he falls under the concept *horse*, that the sentence, 'For some x, x is a horse', says of the concept *horse* that it is not empty, that the sentence, 'For every x, if x is a horse, then x is a mammal', says that the concept *horse* is subordinate to the concept *mammal*, and so on; at least, this is the terminology he uses in *Grundlagen*. But in 'Über Begriff und Gegenstand' Frege scrutinizes this form of expression more closely, and concludes that it does not succeed in saying what was intended. Such a phrase as 'the concept *horse*' is, by Frege's formal criteria, a proper name (singular term); hence he argues that, if it stands for anything, it must   BG 195 stand for an object. We can, therefore, truly say of what the expression 'the concept *horse*' stands for that it is not a concept, but an object; and, since we speak of that for which an expression stands simply by using that expression, this means that we can truly say, 'The concept *horse* is not a concept but an object'.

In 'Über Begriff und Gegenstand' Frege attempts to brush aside this paradox as a merely apparent oddity due to a harmless awkwardness of language, comparable to the fact that the expression, 'the predicate " ξ is a horse" ', is not a predicate. But this latter fact is no more paradoxical than the fact that the *expression* 'the city of Paris' is not a city: the case would be comparable with 'The concept *horse* is not a concept' only if we had any reason for saying that the predicate ' ξ is a horse' is not a predicate. The fact that the Evening Star is not a star is, indeed, only an apparent paradox; but this is because 'the Evening Star' is in the strict sense a proper name, i.e. it is simple and its sense is not determined from the senses of its constituents; this could hardly be maintained for 'the concept *horse*'. In any case, the paradox is intolerable because it leads to the conclusion that it is not possible, by any means whatever, to state, for any predicate, which particular concept it stands for, or to state, for any relational or functional expression, which relation or function it stands for. Any attempt to say this must, it appears, lead to the formation of an expression which, by Frege's criteria, is a singular term, and by means of which we have not therefore succeeded in referring to a concept (or relation or function) at all, but instead to an object. We may be able truly to say that 'There are four horses now in the field' says something about a concept; but as soon as we try to say which concept it says something about— e.g. by saying 'the concept *horse now in the field*'—we shall have lapsed into falsehood, since we shall have falsely said that the sentence says something about a certain particular *object*. Clearly, if there were no escape from this dilemma—brought to light by Frege himself—this would be a reductio ad absurdum of Frege's logical doctrines.

Soon after the publication of 'Über Begriff und Gegenstand', Frege submitted to the same journal another article resolving the paradox; in what must have been the worst editorial misjudgment ever, it was refused publication, and Frege unfortunately never returned to the matter in his published writings.*

---

* I can find no warrant in *Freges nachgelassene Schriften* for what I have asserted here. The essay which the editors have entitled 'Ausführungen über Sinn und Bedeutung' says much of what I here attribute to Frege, though not all; but, while it cites 'Über Sinn und Bedeutung', it does not mention 'Über Begriff und Gegenstand', published in the same year. It seems incredible that the unpublished essay should have been written *before* 'Über Begriff und Gegenstand', pointing as it does to the escape from the trap Frege there fell into; besides, I have a sharp memory of having read a letter of rejection from the editor of

The whole mistake begins, Frege points out, with the use of the words 'concept', 'relation' and 'function'. The predicate 'ξ is an object', he says, has the peculiarity that it is impossible, by filling its argument-place with an expression of the appropriate kind—i.e. a proper name—to form a false sentence. (If we insert a proper name that lacks a reference, we shall of course obtain a sentence which is neither true nor false; and this is the worst that can happen.) The analogous expression, which is true of everything which is the referent of a predicate, ought therefore to be one whose argument-place demands a predicate to fill it, and, when thus filled, will never yield a false sentence. This means, in particular, that it should be a predicate of second level (just as 'ξ is an object' is a predicate of first level). It is evident that the word 'concept' is quite unsuitable for the formation of such an expression. 'Concept' is, grammatically, a common noun, and can therefore be treated only as if it occurred as the content-word in a *first-level* predicate 'ξ is a concept': if we fill the argument-place of this pseudo-predicate with the appropriate type of expression—a proper name—we shall never produce a true sentence, and if we attempt to fill it with a predicate or predicative expression, we shall not produce a grammatically well-formed sentence at all, but only nonsense. The same of course applies to the words 'relation' and 'function'. These words ought therefore simply to be dropped, as being quite unsuitable for the work they were supposed to do.

One reason for the formation of such a pseudo-predicate as 'ξ is a concept' is our liability to misconstrue such an expression as 'what the predicate "ξ is a horse" stands for'. We misinterpret this expression as a singular term (definite description), and hence attach to it such a phrase as '. . . is a concept'. As soon as we consider the analogy of the way in which we speak of the referents of singular terms, we see that this is wrong. The two expressions 'Mount Everest' and 'what "Mount Everest" stands for' are completely interchangeable: the conditions for their having a reference are the same, and, if they have one, it must be the same for each. This is just to say that the expression 'what "Mount Everest" stands for' must, if it stands for anything, stand for what 'Mount Everest' stands for; which, in turn, is just a special case of the general principle according to which, if, e.g., 'President Nixon' stands for anything, it must stand for President Nixon. By analogy, it follows that 'what "ξ is a horse" stands for' ought, if it stands

Margin references:
NS 192 (177–8)
NS 257 (239)

BW 218–19 (136)

NS 210 (193)

NS 275 (255)

---

the *Vierteljahrsschrift für wissenschaftliche Philosophie* when I studied Frege's Nachlass at Münster many years ago. Perhaps my memory misleads me; or perhaps some papers were lost between the time I saw the Nachlass and its publication in 1969. In any case, the correspondence, when it is published, will, I believe, yield some more on the present topic, including the suggestion about 'έΦ(ε)' mentioned on p. 215.

cf. BW 1, 134, 259

I

for anything, to stand for what 'ξ is a horse' stands for. Hence, in particular, it cannot be construed as a proper name (singular term), for then it would stand for an object, and hence could not have the same reference as 'ξ is a horse'. 'What "ξ is a horse" stands for' ought, indeed, to be completely

NS 133 (122)

interchangeable with 'ξ is a horse'; or rather, with the expression 'a horse', used predicatively. (For Frege, the copula is a mere grammatical device, with no content, which serves the purpose of converting a phrase into a verbal

NS 69 (62)

phrase when grammar demands a verb, just as the word 'thing' serves to convert an adjectival phrase into a substantival one, where grammar demands a noun, or the pronoun 'it' supplies a subject when the sense requires none.) The expression 'what "ξ is a horse" stands for' is thus not a proper name but a predicative expression, which, when we supply it with an argument-place and the copula which is needed to make up a grammatical predicate not yet containing a verb, becomes the predicate 'ξ is what "ξ is a horse" stands for'. (The first 'ξ' indicates the argument-place of this predicate; the second 'ξ', being, in this predicate, between quotation marks, does not indicate an argument-place, but is a constant part of the expression.) This predicate will be completely interchangeable with 'ξ is a horse'.

It is, of course, quite in order for us to construe the relative clause 'what "ξ is a horse" stands for' in this way as a predicative expression. We have already noted that there is in natural language a double use of relative pronouns and of words like 'something' and 'everything', corresponding to the distinction between first-level and second-level quantification (quantification over objects and quantification over concepts, relations or functions). If 'what "ξ is a horse" stands for' is to be construed as a predicative expression, then it must be taken in the second way, that is, as involving second-level quantification, and so as analogous to, e.g., 'what I used to be and he has just become', rather than to, say, 'what you gave me yesterday' (in the most natural employment of this latter phrase). On this interpretation, a sentence like 'Blue Peter is what the predicate "ξ is a horse" stands for' would have to be understood as parallel in construction to, say, 'Blue Peter is what Tsarina and Celerity both are' (namely, a racehorse), differing only in being quite specific: it would thus be just a roundabout way of saying, 'Blue Peter is a horse', just as 'What "Everest" stands for is a mountain' is a roundabout way of saying, 'Everest is a mountain'. Similarly, 'James is what "ξ is a brother of ζ" stands for to John' would be a roundabout way of saying, 'James is a brother of John', and 'George and Margaret are what "ξ and ζ are married" stands for' a roundabout way of saying, 'George and Margaret are married'.

In nothing that he wrote about this topic did Frege provide an expression of natural language truly analogous to the predicate 'ξ is an object', that is, a second-level predicate which demands a first-level predicate in its argument-place and which never yields a false sentence when its argument-place is filled: he merely devised a primitive notation for such a second-level predicate in his logical symbolism (namely the second-level predicate '$\xi\Phi(\varepsilon)$': the 'Φ' here represents the argument-place, but the 'ε' is a bound variable—for some reason Frege used small Greek vowels for all variables bound by an operator other than the quantifier). It is not difficult to devise such an expression in natural language. We have noted the use of a relative clause such as 'what I am not' or 'something which I am not' to form by means of the copula a first-level predicate 'ξ is what I am not' or 'ξ is something which I am not' (unmarried, for example), where the argument-place is of course to be filled by a proper name, to produce such a sentence as 'Paul is what I am not'. Such a sentence could be written symbolically as 'For some $\mathcal{f}$, $\mathcal{f}$ (Paul) and not $\mathcal{f}$ (I)'. There is, however, another use of these relative clauses which represent quantification over concepts. In this use, which also employs the verb 'to be', what is formed is a second-level predicate. A first-level predicate is formed from a sentence by omitting one or more occurrences of a proper name. In the linguistically simplest cases, the proper name has only one occurrence, and that at the beginning of the sentence, in the subject-place; and we have noted to what a large extent the means of expressing generality in natural language depends on the existence of devices for transforming a sentence containing a proper name in more than one occurrence, or in an occurrence other than the subject-place, into one in which that term occurs only in the subject-place (there being no clauses co-ordinate to the main clause). In such a sentence, the grammatical predicate—consisting of the whole sentence other than the subject—will of course contain one main verb. What was called above a 'predicative expression' is formed from such a grammatical predicate in the following way: if the grammatical predicate consists of the copula together with an adjectival phrase or one whose main constituent is a common noun preceded by the indefinite article, the predicative expression is formed by simply dropping the copula; if the main verb is anything other than the copula, the predicative expression is formed by converting the main verb into the participial form of the same tense. Evidently, to almost every predicate in Frege's sense which is formed from a sentence of natural language, there corresponds a predicative expression, constructible with greater or less awkwardness.

Given a relative clause of the kind we are discussing, such as 'what I am not' or 'something which I am not', we can form a sentence by prefixing

BW 218 (136)

to it a predicative expression followed by a finite form of the verb 'to be'. The predicative expression is then used in the only way it can be used—to stand for the corresponding concept: so this use of the verb 'to be' followed by such a relative clause in effect represents a predicate of second level. Examples of such sentences are 'A poet is what Blake was but Hayley was not', 'Unhappy is what all Rumanians seem to be', 'Underpaid is what Peter does not want to be', 'Being laughed at is just what Henry most dislikes', etc. The word 'is' in these sentences is not the copula. In the fourth sentence it may be taken to represent just that relation between concepts which Frege says is the analogue of the relation of identity between objects—coincidence of extension: if we write 'He dislikes being laughed at' as 'He dislikes that he is laughed at', we could, accordingly, render the sentence symbolically by 'For every α, α is laughed at if and only if, for some f, $f(\alpha)$ and Henry most dislikes that f (Henry)'. But the other sentences cannot be interpreted in quite the same way: for we do not wish to say that being underpaid is the only thing which Peter does not want to be, or that a poet is the only thing which Blake was that Hayley was not. If we take the word 'is' in the same way in these sentences, then we must take the word 'what' as equivalent, not to '*the* thing which . . .', but to '*a* thing which . . .'. The expressions ' . . . is what Blake was but Hayley was not', ' . . . is what all Rumanians seem to be', ' . . . is what Peter does not want to be', when so used that the gap is to be filled by a predicative expression, can therefore most simply be represented symbolically by 'Φ (Blake) but not Φ (Hayley)', 'For every α, if α is a Rumanian, then it seems that $\Phi(\alpha)$', 'Peter does not want that Φ (Peter)' (the verbs 'seems' and 'wants' being treated in the same way as 'dislikes' earlier). The difference between the form 'A poet is what Blake was and Hayley was not' and the simpler 'Blake was a poet and Hayley was not' is thus simply that the former emphasizes that the sentence is being regarded as the result of filling the second-level predicate 'Φ (Blake) and not Φ (Hayley)' by the first-level predicate 'ξ was a poet'.

Using this form, we can construct an expression of natural language which represents a second-level predicate, by containing a gap intended to be filled by a predicative expression, and which, when the gap is thus filled, will always yield a true sentence. A particularly suitable expression would be ' . . . is something which everything either is or is not': the gap is intended to be filled by a predicative expression, and the resulting sentence will then say that the generalized law of excluded middle holds for the corresponding concept. The expression may thus be symbolically represented as 'For every α, $\Phi(\alpha)$ or not $\Phi(\alpha)$'. We shall thus replace such incorrect formations as '*Horse* is a concept' (or 'The concept *horse* is a concept') by 'A horse is something which everything either is or is not' (i.e. 'For every x, either x is a horse or x is not a horse'). Likewise, such inappropriate forms as ' "ξ is a horse" stands for a concept' or 'What "ξ is a horse" stands for is a concept' will be replaced by 'What "ξ is a horse" stands for is something which everything either is or is not' (i.e. 'For every x, either x is what "ξ is a horse" stands for or x is not'), where here the expression 'what "ξ is a horse" stands for' is understood as predicative in the way already explained. Relational expressions can clearly be handled in a similar way.

Once pseudo-predicates like 'ξ is a concept' and 'ξ is a relation' have been extruded, there is no longer any means of constructing paradoxical sentences like 'The concept *horse* is not a concept'; nor is there any difficulty in saying what in particular any given predicate stands for. We can, for example, say, 'A philosopher is what "ξ is a philosopher" stands for', or, more informatively, 'What "ξ is a philosopher" stands for is what Socrates and Plato both were'. The latter could be more briefly expressed without ambiguity as ' "ξ is a philosopher" stands for what Socrates and Plato both were'; but the former could not be converted into ' "ξ is a philosopher" stands for a philosopher', because this would naturally be understood after the model of ' "Socrates" stands for a philosopher', and prompt the inapposite question, 'Which philosopher does "ξ is a philosopher" stand for?' This may be compared with the fact that, while we may say, 'Aristotle was what Socrates and Plato both were' (namely, a philosopher), this cannot be converted into 'Socrates and Plato both were Aristotle', in the way in which 'This bed is what Elizabeth and Essex both slept in' can be converted into 'Elizabeth and Essex both slept in this bed'. (The form ' "ξ is a philosopher" stands for being a philosopher' is perhaps acceptable.)

The terminology that would be required for speaking, in a logically correct manner, about the referents of predicates and relational expressions is, as can easily be seen from what precedes, cumbrous and verbose; it is therefore best, when there is no danger of misunderstanding or of antinomies, to revert to the logically erroneous vocabulary of 'concept', 'relation' and 'function'. Nevertheless, we have set ourselves to subject to our scrutiny the thesis that incomplete expressions have a reference; and it is essential that we carry on the discussion, if not in a logically correct terminology, at least with one in mind. If we interpret the sentence, 'There is something which the predicate "ξ is a philosopher" stands for' as saying that there is some concept which 'ξ is a philosopher' stands for, and do not realize that the word 'concept' is quite inappropriate for the work it is here being required to do, then, since 'concept' appears to be a predicative expression of first level, we shall be inclined to suppose that what is being asserted is that there is some *object*—of a peculiar kind—which is the referent of the predicate. Such a claim is, properly, meaningless, and at best obviously false; the expression 'ξ is a philosopher' just does not serve to refer to an object in the way in which the name 'Socrates' does. Hence the strong resistance which many feel to the suggestion that incomplete expressions may have a reference. But, as we have noted, the word 'something' in the sentence 'There is something which "ξ is a philosopher" stands for' has to be interpreted as signifying second-level generality. The sentence says that there is such a thing as what 'ξ is a philosopher' stands for; since, as we have seen, the relative clause 'what "ξ is a philosopher" stands for' is to be construed as a predicative expression, not as a definite description, this means simply that there is such a thing as being a philosopher; and this it is quite impossible to deny. It is impossible, that is, for anyone to deny it who admits it as intelligible; the appearance of tendentiousness in the thesis that reference can be ascribed to predicates thus apparently wholly dissolves away. It is non-tendentious to ascribe reference to proper names, because this is just to say that there are true sentences of the kind, 'There is something which "Mount Everest" stands for', and this is to be construed as a roundabout way of saying, 'There is such a thing as Mount Everest'. When understood in the way suggested, it becomes almost equally non-tendentious to ascribe a reference to predicates: for this is just to say that there are true sentences of the kind, 'There is something which "ξ is a philosopher" stands for', and this in turn is to be construed as a roundabout way of saying, 'There is such a thing as being a philosopher'. (We might write 'There is such a thing as Mount Everest' symbolically as 'For some x, x is Mount Everest', where 'is' is the sign of identity; the analogous rendering of 'There is such a thing as being a philosopher' would then be 'For some f, for every x, $f(x)$ if and only if x is a philosopher'. A rendering in natural language which explicitly uses the predicate 'ξ is a philosopher' would be 'There is such a thing as being what anyone is when he is a philosopher'.)

The sentence, 'There is such a thing as being a philosopher', must be admitted as both intelligible and true by anyone who allows as meaningful any form of second-level quantification; as we have noted, the use of higher-level quantification is extremely common in natural language, and would not be regarded as puzzling or odd by its unsophisticated speakers. There is, admittedly, no precision about the truth-conditions for statements involving quantification over concepts or relations, as such statements are ordinarily understood. It is, however, constitutive of the meaning of the existential quantifier, whatever its range or level, that an existential statement is justified if a true answer can be given to a demand for specification, the demand expressed by the question, 'Namely what?': in other words, the rule of existential generalization is always valid. Thus the statement 'There is something which Plato was but Socrates was not' can be justified by establishing the truth of 'Plato was a writer but Socrates was not': this is enough to guarantee the truth of statements like, 'There is such a thing as being a writer'.

There is, indeed, a divergence here between Frege's criterion for the existence of a concept and that which underlies the use of second-level generalization in natural language. For Frege, a predicate which applies to nothing has just as good a reference as any other; even a self-contradictory predicate has a reference. He holds this because of his general doctrine that, if a part lacks reference, the whole lacks reference: so, if a self-contradictory predicate, for instance 'ξ is sometimes in two places at once', lacked a reference, any sentence containing it would also lack a reference; this would, of course, include sentences denying its application to an individual, such as 'Mr. Heath is never in two places at once', or denying it an application at all, such as 'No one is ever in two places at once'. As we have seen, Frege does allow, on other grounds, that there may be, in natural language, predicates lacking a reference: but, regarding this as a defect, he excludes such predicates from his symbolic language, in just the same way as he excludes from that language proper names which lack a reference. We saw that the sentence, 'There is such a thing as being a philosopher', rendered symbolically by '$\exists\, \mathscr{f} \; \forall\, \alpha\, [\mathscr{f}(\alpha) \leftrightarrow \alpha$ is a philosopher]', is tantamount to the statement, 'There is such a thing as what "ξ is a philosopher" stands for', i.e. to the assertion that the predicate 'ξ is a philosopher' has a reference; and, of course, the extrusion from Frege's symbolic language of all predicates which, by Frege's criteria, lack a reference, has the effect that, for any predicate '$G(\xi)$' of that language, the statement '$\exists\, \mathscr{f} \; \forall\, \alpha\, [\mathscr{f}(\alpha) \leftrightarrow G(\alpha)]$' must be true. This will hold good whatever the predicate '$G(\xi)$' may be, even if it is the predicate 'ξ is not the same as ξ'. In an exactly parallel way, we took the sentence, 'There is such a thing as Mount Everest', which is tantamount to the statement, 'There is such a thing as what "Mount Everest" stands for', that asserts that 'Mount Everest' has a reference, to be rendered symbolically by '$\exists\, \alpha \; \alpha = $ Mount Everest'; and the exclusion from Frege's symbolic language of proper names without a reference likewise guarantees that, for every proper name 'b' of that language, whether simple or complex, the sentence '$\exists\, \alpha \; \alpha = b$' will be true.

By contrast, in natural language, the corresponding form of statement, 'There is such a thing as being . . .', asserting the existence of a referent of some predicate, is not in general trivially true, and may be denied: for instance, there might be a dispute as to whether or not there is such a thing as being too unselfish. This dispute might turn on whether or not there is in fact anyone who is too unselfish: more likely it would turn on whether or not there *could* be such a person. This illustrates a general principle, that when we attempt to justify a statement of natural language involving second-level existential generality by answering the question 'Namely what?', there is a restriction on the kind of predicate which can constitute a successful answer: it must always be a predicate which *could* have an application; and in some contexts it would be demanded that it should in fact have an application. The non-triviality of statements of natural language of the form 'There is such a thing as P' ('P' a predicative expression) is of course paralleled by the non-triviality in natural language of statements of the form 'There is such a thing as *a*' ('*a*' a proper name): this form of statement is non-trivial precisely because the language contains proper names without a reference.

We noted already that Frege's choice for a case in which a predicate lacks a reference is that in which it is not defined for every object: that was why it was a particularly suitable choice to take, as replacing the logically ill-formed '. . . is a concept', the phrase '. . . is something which every object either is or is not'. We also saw that Frege was here following a false analogy: for the presence in a sentence of a predicate which is not defined for every object does not, intuitively, automatically deprive that sentence of a truth-value; only some sentences suffer this fate. But the analogy is even more misconceived than we previously noted. If a sentence contains a proper name which lacks a reference, we may agree that the sentence is neither true nor false: but, at least, if we grasp the sense of the name, we shall know what would have to be the case for it to be true. For instance, if there was no such person as King Arthur, then 'King Arthur fought the Saxons' is neither true nor false: but, if the name 'King Arthur' has a determinate sense, then we know exactly what would have had to be the case for the sentence to be true. By contrast, if the predicate 'ξ is sad' is not defined for chairs, and the predicate 'ξ is red' undefined for numbers, then again the sentences 'That chair is sad' and '7 is red' will be neither true nor false: but we have no idea what would have to be the case to make them true. If it is insisted—as Frege, in his later period, does insist—that names of every kind be admitted to the argument-places of all predicates, i.e. that such sentences are well-formed at all, then these would have to be regarded, not as cases of predicates having a sense but no reference, but, rather, as cases of predicates with a partial indeterminacy of sense: it has not been

FB 20

decided what is to count as a chair's being sad or a number's being red. Because the sense of a predicate is intrinsically different from that of a proper name, there is no exact analogue to this in the case of proper names: but the closest we can get is a name whose sense is partially indeterminate in that the criterion for identifying an object as the bearer of the name is only partly fixed—for instance, if we are undecided whether or not it is required, for someone to be the man whom we refer to as 'Moses', that he should have been adopted by the daughter of a Pharaoh.

However, the principal problem is not to find a way of giving substance to the assertion, made of a particular predicate, that it has a reference. We have seen in any case that there were better ways available to Frege to find an analogy with proper names' lacking a reference: thus, we may say that, since there is no such planet as Vulcan, there is no such thing as being a satellite of Vulcan; or, again, that, since the plate is round and the mat is square, there is no such thing as being the shape which the plate and the mat both are. The principal problem is whether it is legitimate to ascribe reference to predicates generally. Miss Anscombe, in her book on the *Tractatus*, compares Frege's posthumously published repudiation of the IWT 122f terms 'concept', 'relation' and 'function' with Wittgenstein's rejection of 'formal concepts', namely all those expressed by highly general categorial terms, including, not only these three, but also 'object' and 'number'. His point is in part that the difference between, e.g., 'every object' and 'every relation' should be represented by a difference in the type of variable bound by the quantifier, and thus is unlike the difference between, say, 'every cat' and 'every dog', which represent different restrictions on the range of variables of the same type. This part of Wittgenstein's argument does indeed coincide with Frege's ground for rejecting terms like 'concept' and 'relation': they suggest that there is some quite general class of entities, over which we can generalize indiscriminately, and which we can subsequently classify as objects, concepts, relations and so on. Here 'entity' would operate in the way 'object' does in Frege's vocabulary; for, since 'ξ is a concept (object, relation)' is in the form of a first-level predicate, the variables which ranged over the supposed domain of all entities would behave as individual variables, i.e. would carry no argument-place with them. In rejecting this conception, we have no reason to condemn the word 'object' along with 'concept' and 'relation': 'ξ is a concept (relation)' is only masquerading as a first-level predicate, but 'ξ is an object' is a perfectly admissible one, although one that cannot be false of anything of which it is asserted. Wittgenstein's reason for rejecting the term 'object' also is something that does not occur in Frege: namely that it does not fit into his picture theory of the sentence, which involves, in particular, that every sentence, to have a sense, must have true/false poles—must be capable of being true and capable of being false. An entity of any logical type can be represented in a picture only by an entity of the same logical type; and hence we cannot make a picture of something's being of a particular logical type (an object, say)—this will be *shown* in the picture, but the picture cannot *say* it. In particular, a picture can only depict a state of affairs which could have been otherwise: so there could not be a genuine predicate which was true of everything to which it could be meaningfully applied. In *Grundlagen*, indeed, Frege says, apropos of various inapposite explanations of the word 'unit', that a predicate can have a sense only if its applying to something is contrasted with its failing to apply to something: a predicate

Gl 29 which necessarily applies to everything is thereby emptied of content. This remark is, of course, in close agreement with Wittgenstein's conception in the *Tractatus* of what it is for a sentence to have sense: and it is in conflict with Frege's allowing such a predicate as 'ξ is an object' and with his introducing, as primitive, the second-level predicate '$\hat{\epsilon}\Phi(\epsilon)$', as being true of all concepts. Frege would certainly later have repudiated the principle stated in *Grundlagen* as applied to complex predicates: to take this line for all predicates leads to that denial to analytic statements of the kind of sense possessed by contingent ones which is quite alien to Frege's thought and, espoused by the logical positivists, was to be the cause of much philosophical confusion. Whether he would also have repudiated the principle for primitive predicates is unclear. Of course, it is perfectly possible to explain 'ξ is an object' as equivalent to a complex predicate, such as our '$\exists \alpha\ \alpha = \xi$'. Perhaps, however, Frege would have preferred to regard 'ξ is an object' as having a quite special, purely philosophical, role, and hence as exempt from the *Grundlagen* principle.

Now, after this long excursus, how much have we established towards the resolution of our main problem, whether the ascription of reference to predicates is justifiable? At first glance, it might seem that we had succeeded in resolving the problem altogether by our painstaking examination of the true logical form of such an ascription: we have reduced the assertion that a given predicate has a reference to a banality exactly parallel to that to which the ascription of a reference to a proper name amounts. While, in some cases, the ascription of a reference to a given proper name may be an assertion of some substance, it is not disputable that proper names, in general, have a reference; similarly, while, on certain interpretations which we have discussed, it may sometimes be an assertion of substance that a given predicate has a reference, we appear to have so construed the thesis that, in general, predicates have reference as to make it no more tendentious than the corresponding thesis for proper names.

A follower of Quine, however, would claim that we had succeeded, by means of this whole elaborate manipulation of forms of expression, in establishing no more than he could have said right from the outset. For our conclusion was that the existence of concepts—that is, of referents for predicates—required, for its proper expression, the use of second-level quantification, and was beyond doubt, provided that the employment of that device is allowed as legitimate and intelligible. But, for Quine, that was just the point at the outset. For him, 'to be is to be the value of a variable': *FLPV* 15 the criterion of anybody's ontological commitment to a certain range of entities—whether he takes seriously the thesis that there are entities belonging to that range—is his willingness to quantify over them, or, at least, his willingness to assert at least one existential statement involving such quantification. So, for Quine, the existence of concepts, or, equivalently, the possession of reference by predicates, stands or falls with the permissibility of second-level quantification binding predicate-variables. It did not need any detailed enquiry into the proper way of expressing '. . . stands for a concept' to tell him that: he knew it already. Moreover, Quine is strongly disinclined to acknowledge the permissibility of such second-level quantification: so for him the thesis that there are concepts, in Frege's sense, that predicates have a reference, remains as tendentious as it ever was.

Where, then, does the truth lie? Have we really accomplished nothing at all towards the solution of our problem? We have, at least, done one small thing: we have established that the paradox which, in 'Über Begriff und Gegenstand', threatened to expose Frege's whole ontological structure as incoherent can be resolved. We have also, perhaps, succeeded in uncovering the reason why Frege so seldom bothered to argue that predicates and other incomplete expressions have a reference, why he treated this thesis, which appears so bizarre to many, as, in effect, unproblematic. For Frege had not the slightest qualm about the legitimacy or intelligibility of higher-level quantification: he used it from the first, in *Begriffsschrift*, freely and without apology, and did not even see first-order logic as constituting a fragment having any special significance.

If we regard reference solely as semantic role, then, as we have seen, the ascription of reference to any expression which has a genuine logical unity is indeed quite unproblematic. The ascription of reference to incomplete expressions appears controversial only because we invoke—and recognize that Frege intended us to invoke—the analogy with the name/ bearer relation: because we are supposed to conceive of the reference of an incomplete expression as consisting in a relation to a referent analogous to that of a name to its bearer. A Quinean would claim that we had already succeeded in identifying what is controversial about it: if we are to regard predicates as having a reference, we must accept quantification over their referents as meaningful, whereas its meaningfulness is highly disputable. The fact is, that, although we have repeatedly referred to Frege's use of the name/bearer relation as the prototype for the relation of an expression to its referent, we have not yet enquired in what the analogy is supposed to consist, in the case of incomplete expressions. Undoubtedly, the matter of quantification is part of the analogy. It is the fact that a proper name has a bearer, and that its semantic role in the sentence can be explained in terms of its having a bearer, that makes it possible for us to form the conception of the predicate which results from the omission of the proper name from the sentence as being true of or false of any given object: and it is the possibility of this conception which, in turn, allows the introduction of quantification over objects, that is, to attach a quantifier to the predicate to form a new sentence, whose truth-conditions are explained in terms of the predicate's being true of or false of each object, i.e. as the logical sum or product of the truth-values resulting from applying the predicate to each object in the domain of quantification. So, if predicates are to be regarded as having a reference that can likewise be construed as a relation to a referent standing to it after the fashion of bearer to name, something similar must be true. We must, that is, be able to conceive of the second-level predicate which results from the omission of the first-level predicate from the sentence as being true of or false of the referent of any arbitrary first-level predicate: we must be able to do this, because the semantic role of the original first-level predicate is being supposed to consist in its relation to a referent. And, since we can do this, it follows that we must be able to introduce quantification over the referents of first-level predicates, to be explained in a manner quite analogous to the explanation of first-level quantification. So at least part of the analogy does consist in a recognition of the admissibility of second-level quantification, and Quine's views are, to that extent, vindicated. Since the notion of reference, as applied to incomplete expressions, is not (contrary to such views as those of Tugendhat) exhausted by the conception of it as their semantic role, but is informed also by the appeal to the name/bearer relation as prototype, we cannot expect that it would be wholly unproblematic: it is problematic at least to the degree that the use of second-level quantification is problematic.

The claim that quantification is a criterion is made very explicitly by Quine; it was certainly never made explicitly by Frege. We have derived it from Frege's formulations by trying to develop his suggested way of correcting the error of using words like 'concept' and 'relation' into a completely worked out terminology. Is it possible that we have made a mistake, or at least drawn a conclusion in conflict with the views which Frege actually expressed?

As we have seen, to any expression, of whatever level, that forms a genuine logical unit, Frege thinks it proper to ascribe a reference. So this already seems to indicate a divergence between Frege and Quine. Suppose that we had a language which contained no quantification or other expression of generality at all, but only atomic sentences and compounds of them by means of the sentential operators. Since such a language involves no quantification, on Quine's doctrine it would entail no ontological commitment—not even to the existence of objects which were the bearers of the proper names in the language. For Frege, on the other hand, the proper names would have referents—the objects spoken of—and the first-level predicates and relational expressions would also have referents—concepts and relations. For Quine, there is no need to ascribe reference to predicates until second-level quantification is introduced: for Frege, it will be proper to attribute it to them even before quantification of any kind is present. So have we not erred in assimilating Frege's doctrine too closely to Quine's?

It is at least evident that, although on Frege's principles it will be perfectly possible to distinguish, as occurring within the sentences of a language, incomplete expressions of arbitrarily high level, it will often be pointless to do so. In the language we have imagined, containing no expressions of generality, it will still be possible to pick out, within sentences, predicates of second level: for instance, the second-level predicate ' Φ (Socrates) and not Φ (Plato)' from the sentence 'Socrates died by poison and Plato did not'. But there is absolutely no point in discerning such a pattern within that sentence: it is needed neither for explaining the formation of any more complex type of sentence, nor for giving an account of any form of inference in which the sentence may occur. Indeed, for such a language, there will be no point in picking out from sentences any *complex* first-level predicates, such as ' ξ was wise and ξ died of poison'; they also play no role in sentence-formation or in inferences. Of course, *simple* first-level predicates and relational expressions must be acknowledged if the formation of atomic sentences is to be explained.

Relative to any given language, then, we shall certainly not want to invoke an ontology containing more than the referents of those expressions which we need to recognize as logical units occurring within sentences for the purpose either of recognizing the validity of inferences in which those sentences occur, as premiss or conclusion, or of explaining the formation of other sentences. Even when this is acknowledged, however, there remains a considerable gap between Frege and Quine. Of course, a Quinean might say that the gap is narrower than I have represented it: a Quinean view of the language without (overt) quantification would not take it to be ontology-free, because of the proposal that all proper names be reconstrued as definite descriptions, whose analysis along Russellian lines will then involve hidden first-level quantification. But the question still remains unanswered whether our reconstruction of the terminology relating to the reference of predicates has involved a misrepresentation of Frege.

We said, in effect, two things about quantification. First, that to *express* the thesis that expressions of a certain type have a reference involves quantification over their referents; to say that proper names have a reference is to quantify over objects, to say that predicates have a reference is to quantify over concepts. And, secondly, that to acknowledge expressions of a given type as having a reference construed after the model of the relation of name to bearer is implicitly to accept the introduction of quantification over their referents as a legitimate possibility. These two theses may be in conflict with Quine's views, but neither of them contradicts anything held by Frege. If a language does not contain quantification over the referents of expressions of a given type, then it will not be possible to express *within that language* the proposition that expressions of that type have reference: but this has no bearing on the possibility that a correct semantic account of the language, given within some other language, may require the ascription to expressions of that type of a semantic role consisting in a relation to those referents, taken as analogous to the relation of name to bearer. It may, furthermore, be that, whenever the account of the semantic role of expressions of a certain type, as used within a given language, has to be patterned after the name/bearer relation as prototype, then the way stands open for the introduction of quantification binding variables of the same type: it does not in the least follow that this possibility will of necessity be taken advantage of.

We shall not pursue further here the discussion of Quine's divergence from Frege, save to remark that a modification of Quine's doctrine, which would bring it closer to Frege's, would be to say that the ontological commitments embodied in a language included, not only those expressed by quantification within the language, but also those expressed by quantification required in any metalanguage within which it was possible to give a correct semantic account of the original language.

All this, however, by no means resolves the matter. To construe the reference of predicates after the model of the name/bearer relation *entails* admitting second-level quantification as legitimate: but this does not tell us what so construing their reference consists in. It has become a standard complaint that Frege talks a great deal about the senses of expressions, but nowhere gives an account of what constitutes such a sense. This complaint is partly unfair: for Frege the sense of an expression is the manner in which we determine its reference, and he tells us a great deal about the kind of reference possessed by expressions of different types, thereby specifying the form that the senses of such expressions must take. It is true enough, however, that he says practically nothing directly about what the senses of expressions of different types consist in; and this is a legitimate ground of complaint. Indeed, even when Frege is purporting to give the sense of a word or symbol, what he actually *states* is what its reference is: SB 27n
and, for anyone who has not clearly grasped the relation between sense and Gg I 27, 32
reference, this fact makes his hold on the notion of sense precarious. The sense of an expression is the mode of presentation of the referent: in saying what the referent is, we have to choose a particular way of saying this, a SB 26
particular means of determining something as the referent. In a case in which we are concerned to convey, or stipulate, the sense of the expression, we shall choose that means of stating what the referent is which displays the sense: we might here borrow a famous pair of terms from the *Tractatus*, and say that, for Frege, we *say* what the referent of a word is, and thereby *show* TLP 4.022
what its sense is. (This is the correct answer to Russell's objection in 'On Denoting' to Frege's theory, considered generally, rather than apropos of oblique reference, that there is 'no backward road' from reference to sense.) LK 50
Thus, in a certain sense, it may be said that we cannot directly state what the sense of an expression is; and it may be that Frege was therefore under the impression that no general account could be given of the senses of expressions of any one logical type, but only of their reference. If so, he was mistaken. It is only in some cases—those where definition is possible—that we can convey the sense of an expression by means of a specification of its reference: in no case can we do so by a direct specification of its sense, i.e. by a pronouncement of the form, 'The sense is . . . ' (except where this is completed by 'the same as the sense of X', X being another expression). But to grasp the sense of a word is to master a certain ability to determine the truth-conditions of sentences containing it; and there is no reason to impute an ineffable character to such an ability. Even if we cannot say what a sense is, there is no obstacle to our saying what it is that someone can do when he grasps that sense; and this is all that we need the notion of sense for. We are

thus fully entitled to enquire how Frege conceived the notion of sense as applied to different types of expression.

The problem is not primarily one that concerns the notion of sameness of sense, about which also Frege says little. Here only a negative point is clear: it is not sufficient, for two expressions to have the same sense, that it be logically necessary that their referents should coincide. If this were taken as sufficient, then analytically true statements of identity, or statements of the extensional equivalence of concepts, relations or functions, could not be informative: or, at least, their informativeness could not be accounted for in terms of the difference in sense of the two names or incomplete expressions occurring on either side of the sign of identity or the biconditional. This would conflict with the motive for which the notion of sense, as distinguished from reference, was introduced by Frege in the first place. Whether or not a statement is analytic depends, for Frege, on the kind of way in which it can be recognized as true: but, for it to be informative—to have 'cognitive value'—it is necessary that a mere knowledge of its sense be insufficient to guarantee a recognition of its truth, and this is a condition in no way inconsistent with its analyticity. (It is true that in some passages in his posthumously published writings Frege toys with the idea that two *contingent* sentences express the same thought just in case it is logically necessary that they have the same truth-value: but this can hardly be reconciled with his other views.)

It is tempting to reduce the whole question to that of the equivalence of *primitive* expressions (those not introduced into the language via definitions), by applying an idea like Carnap's 'intensional isomorphism': when we have successively removed from two expressions all words introduced by definition, replacing them by their defined equivalents, we can test whether they had the same sense by observing whether each of the resulting forms can be obtained from the other by replacing words by their synonyms. The problem would then reduce to explaining when two primitive expressions were to be said to have the same sense. In applying such an idea to any actual language, we should need to treat as primitive any expression which was not in fact introduced into the language by definition, regardless of whether it could be defined with little alteration of sense. Frege's express observation that, of a given circle of interdefinable expressions, it is indifferent which, in constructing an axiomatized theory, we select as primitive, and his contention in 'Die Verneinung' that we cannot say, of two contradictory predicates of natural language, which is affirmative and which negative, show him as sharply aware that fewer expressions are introduced into natural language by definition than night be. There are,

Huss 320

Gl 91

NS 226-7
(210)

BW 105-6
(70-1)

Huss 320;
Bs 7; Ver 150
(40-1); NS
161-2 (149-
150)

however, scattered passages in Frege which contradict the idea of intensional isomorphism, such as the remarks that a sentence 'A' will have the same sense as the sentences 'It is true that A' and 'A and A'.

SB 34; Ged 61 (6); Ggf 39n (59n); NS 271 (251)

The question what is the criterion for sameness of sense is, however, not the crucial one. The central problem is what the model should be for the notion of knowing the sense of an expression: the general form of description, for expressions of each logical type, of what it is that a man knows when he knows the sense of an expression of that type. For, as we have seen, the notion of sense is introduced in connection with that of *knowledge*: it is required in order that we may give an account of *how* we know the references of the expressions of our language, that is, how we are able to recognize the truth-conditions of sentences formed out of them. For present purposes we may concentrate upon the expressions which occur within atomic sentences—proper names, simple and complex, and simple predicates and relational expressions. As a first approximation to the model for the senses of such expressions which Frege had in mind, we may try the following: To know the sense of a proper name is to have a criterion for recognizing, for any given object, whether or not it is the bearer (referent) of that name; to know the sense of a predicate is to have a criterion for deciding, for any given object, whether or not the predicate applies to that object; and to know the sense of a relational expression is to have a criterion for deciding, given any two objects taken in a particular order, whether or not the relation it stands for holds between the first object and the second.

Such an account, which is the first one that comes to mind on reading Frege's views on sense and reference, has at least this merit: that the notion of reference, at least as applied to proper names, is made to do some work in the account of sense, that is, of our understanding of the words of the language in so far as this relates to the determination of the truth-values of sentences. On this account, the determination of the truth-value of any given sentence goes via the identification of an object as the referent of each proper name occurring in the sentence: guided by the senses of these names, we first identify certain objects as their referents, and, after that, we neglect all special features of those senses save the fact that they determined those objects as their referents; all that remains is to decide whether or not the predicate or relational expression applies to that object or those objects. This would contrast with any account whereby the sense of the predicate relates directly to the sense of the name occupying its argument-place, rather than to the object which forms the referent of the name, and likewise for a relational expression. Such an account would in one way be smoother than an account of the kind we have described, for it would leave open the possibility that the sense of a predicate was such as to yield a true sentence when its argument-place was filled by one name, but a false sentence when it was filled by another name with a different sense, even though the same reference. It would therefore require no special treatment for opaque contexts, such as Frege is forced to provide. But it would leave the notion of reference, except for sentences, altogether unemployed: the sense of an expression would not be given in terms of its reference, that is, as the means of determining its referent, and the notion of reference would be without semantic significance. From all that we have seen of what Frege believed about sense and reference, an account of this kind could not be that which he intended: the notion of reference can have the significance he attributed to it only if we can describe what it is to grasp the sense of an expression in a manner which relates to its reference. The notion of reference, on a theory of sense of the second kind, would be a mere embellishment of the theory, having no functional role to play, like the denotation which Russell ascribes to definite descriptions; and it is plain from everything that Frege says about reference that he did not intend it to be reduced to a useless excrescence on the theory of meaning.

The notion of reference should, rather, play a role analogous to that which, in the simple example used in Chapter 1, the notion of a code-word's representing a word of natural language played in the explanation of the significance of a code-symbol. What is known by someone who understands the code does not consist merely in his knowing which code-word represents which word of natural language (which word in clear), but in his grasp of how the one is determined from the other; but we could not begin to explain the significance of a code-symbol within a word except by employing the notion of a code-word's representing a word in clear, and then explaining how the code-symbol contributes to determining that.

The model of sense for proper names and predicates with which we started is, however, objectionable on two distinct grounds. First, it is formulated in a way that would fit only a completely effective language: it ascribes to anyone who understands a proper name a criterion (effective method) for deciding, for any given object, whether or not it is the bearer of the name, and to anyone who understands a predicate a criterion for deciding, for any given object, whether or not the predicate applies to it. But Frege does not at all require that, for an expression to have a sense, it should be effectively decidable in such a way. We might, therefore, modify the formulation, and say that to grasp the sense of a name is to be able to recognize, when one is presented with it, whatever counts as establishing conclusively that a given object is the bearer of the name; and, similarly, that to grasp the sense of a predicate is to be able to recognize, when one is presented with it, anything that counts as establishing conclusively that the predicate applies to some given object. Even this is probably not in full accord with Frege's ideas. If we are satisfied that some predicate applies to one and only one object, then we can introduce a proper name as standing for the object to which that predicate applies: our grasp of what it is for an object to be the bearer of that name extends (on Frege's realistic conception) beyond our capacity to recognize something as establishing that that object is the bearer of the name; for we know *what it is* for the object to be the bearer of the name even though there is nothing which would establish conclusively for us that it was the bearer of the name. This gap could be closed only if we had some general assurance that, for every true statement, there is something which we could know and which, if we knew it, would establish conclusively for us the truth of the statement. What Frege's stance would be on this thesis, there is nothing in his writings to determine. If we do not invoke this thesis, then we should be forced to say something like: To grasp the sense of a name is to understand what has to be the case, for any given object, for it to be the bearer of that name; and to grasp the sense of a predicate is to know what has to be the case, for any given object, for the predicate to apply to it. The trouble with this formulation is that we can give little content to the notion of possessing knowledge of this kind unless it be verbalizable knowledge—the ability to *say* what has to be the case of a given object for it to be the bearer of the name or for the predicate to apply to it. An ability to *recognize* an object as the bearer of a name, or to *recognize* something as conclusively establishing that it is the bearer of the name, does not have to be construed as verbalizable knowledge: it can be displayed by the propensity which a man shows to proceed in a certain way in determining the truth-value of a sentence in which the name occurs, or to treat something as establishing such a sentence as true. But, if there is one thing about which Frege is absolutely clear, it is that a grasp of the senses of our words cannot, in general, consist in verbalizable knowledge: he insists repeatedly that, while many words may be introduced by means of definition or verbal explanation, it is impossible that all the words of the language should be so introduced, on pain of vicious circularity.   BG 193; Gg I p. 4; Ver 150 (42)

The second kind of objection to the simple model of sense we have described can be formulated by asking what is meant by talking of being 'given' an object. We cannot dismiss phrases such as 'for any given object' or 'given any object' as merely one of the clumsy devices used in natural language for indicating what is expressed in symbolism by the position of a quantifier, like the phrase 'for any particular object'. In understanding a proper name or a predicate, I am supposed to be able to recognize something as establishing that a given object is the referent of the name or that the predicate applies to it: but *what* is it that I recognize to be established? That such-and-such a name stands for the object, or that such-and-such a predicate applies to the object—indeed: but *which* object? The given object, of course: but here we have a right to ask, 'How was it given?'

An object cannot be recognized as the referent of a proper name, or as something to which a particular predicate applies, or thought of in any other way whatever, unless it has first been singled out in some definite way. There is no such thing as judging something to be true of an object, apart from some particular method of identifying the object: it is precisely for this reason that there cannot be a proper name whose whole sense consists in its having a certain object as referent, without the sense determining that object as referent in some particular way. Hence a general criterion for recognizing something as established concerning any object in a certain range cannot genuinely relate to the *objects* in that range, but must relate rather to such objects considered as identified in some particular way. In just the same way, when an arithmetical function is spoken of as being computable if there exists an effective procedure for computing, given any number, the value of that function for that number as argument, we have in mind a particular method of being 'given' the number—say by means of a numeral in binary notation or in the stroke notation: the procedure does not have to yield a value for the referent of 'the population of Hawaii' or 'the smallest $n > 2$ which falsifies Fermat's last theorem' as argument. Thus, in order to construe the interpretation of sense which we are considering, we have to suppose that, for each category of objects, there is some favoured method of being 'given' an object in that category to which the criteria of identification or of application relate. In the case of material or visual objects, or, in general, of objects that can be pointed to, it may at first seem plausible that these criteria should relate to an object considered as identified by the use of a demonstrative accompanied by a pointing gesture. Thus the sense of a personal proper name would consist in the criterion for identifying a man pointed to as the bearer of the name, and, in general, the sense of any proper name '*a*' of an ostensible object (an object that can be pointed to) will consist in the criterion for the truth of what we may call 'recognition statements' of the form 'That is *a*'. Likewise the sense of a predicate 'ξ is P' whose range of definition comprised only ostensible objects would consist in the criterion for the truth of what we may call 'crude predications' of the form 'That is P'.

It is to be required of any adequate interpretation of the notion of sense for proper names that a grasp of their sense must involve a grasp of the criterion of identity associated with them. This requirement is satisfied by the conception of a grasp of the sense of a proper name as consisting in the ability to judge the truth or falsity of recognition statements: for the use of a demonstrative in a recognition statement demands, for its understanding, a grasp of the criterion of identity implicitly appealed to as determining the significance of the ostension. 'That is Fido' has to be tacitly understood as 'That animal is Fido', 'That is the Thames' as 'That river is the Thames': the words 'animal' and 'river' do not need to be known, but the concepts must be grasped in knowing what is involved in identifying something pointed to as Fido or as the Thames.

The relation of predicates to criteria of identity is much more complex. With common nouns, such as 'book', we distinguished two ingredients in their sense: the criterion of application, and the criterion of identity. It seems that, in order to be able to judge the truth or falsity of crude predications of the form 'That is a book', we do not need to be aware of either of the two ways in which 'same book' may be used, or, accordingly, of the possible uses of the phrase 'that book' or of definite descriptions beginning 'the book which . . .'. We are therefore tempted to say that, while a full understanding of the *word* 'book' may require a knowledge of the two different criteria of identity, an understanding of the *predicate* 'ξ is a book' involves a knowledge only of the criterion of application. With such a predicate as 'ξ is dusty', on the other hand, it looks as though no distinction is to be drawn between an understanding of it and an understanding of the adjective 'dusty': in neither case does a criterion of identity come into the matter—only a criterion of application is in question.

We can, of course, legislate that by an understanding of the sense of a predicate we shall mean a grasp only of the criterion of application, taken as consisting in an ability to judge the truth or falsity of crude predications made with that predicate: but we shall then find that a grasp of the sense of a predicate is an inadequate basis for a judgment of the truth-values of atomic sentences formed with it. It is true enough that an adjective like 'dusty' is not associated with any specific criterion of identity: but it does not follow from this that we can give an account of a grasp of the sense of such an adjective which in no way invokes the notion of a criterion of identity. When the argument-place of the predicate 'ξ is dusty' is occupied, not by a demonstrative, but by a proper name, that proper name will itself supply a criterion of identity. We might think that we could explain an estimation of the truth-value of a sentence of the form 'a is dusty' as consisting in a determination whether, when a recognition statement of the form 'That is *a*', accompanied by a pointing gesture, would be correct, the crude predication, 'That is dusty', accompanied by the same pointing gesture, and made on the same occasion, would also be correct. That this would be an over-simple account of the matter can, however, easily be seen by taking '*a*' to be the proper name '*War and Peace*'. It may happen that, on some occasion, I could truly say, pointing in a particular direction, both 'That is *War and Peace*' and 'That is dusty'; but only facetiously could I say, '*War and Peace* is dusty', since the name '*War and Peace*', unlike, say, 'Your copy of *War and Peace*', determines the object referred to under a criterion of identity which makes the predicate 'ξ is dusty' inappropriate. Likewise, it is not enough to know that I could truly say both 'That is *War and Peace*' and 'That is a book' in order to conclude that the statement '*War and Peace* is a book' is true: for the recognition statement and the crude predication would remain true even were 'book' used only in the sense in which there may be twelve books on the shelf, among which three are copies of *War and Peace*, in which case it would be incorrect to say that *War and Peace* was a book. It is therefore evident that the sense of a predicate is never given fully by knowing the criterion for the truth of crude predications made by means of it, if these are so understood that no particular criterion of identity is associated with the demonstratives they contain. It is true enough that coming to grasp the truth-conditions of crude predications, so understood, may be an important first stage in learning the sense of a predicate; but, if a knowledge of the sense of a predicate is to be adequate for the understanding of atomic sentences formed by means of it, it will be necessary also to grasp which criteria of identity the demonstratives in those crude predications may be taken as governed by.

With other predicates, a specific criterion of identity has to be associated from the outset. Thus a predicate such as 'ξ is fickle' can be applied only to human beings, and the capacity to recognize the truth or falsity either of an atomic sentence such as 'Celia is fickle' or a crude predication such as 'She is fickle' (accompanied by pointing or its equivalent) presupposes a grasp of the criterion of personal identity over time. Yet other predicates have no specific criterion of identity associated with them, but any use of them, including a use in a crude predication, requires an implicit invocation of some determinate such criterion: an example would be 'ξ is 54 years old', which may be applied to men, books, institutions and many other things, but makes no sense unless we know to what category of object the age is being ascribed.

Even with these elucidations, the model of sense for proper names and

predicates which we are considering may seem, on reflection, to be implausible. After all, it seems quite reasonable to account for my grasp of
the sense of the personal proper name of some close acquaintance as consisting in my ability to judge the truth or falsity of statements identifying him,
under that name, as the object of an ostension: but can it really be maintained that my grasp of the sense of the name 'Abraham', as used to stand for
a man whom I believe to have been dead for nearly four millennia, consists in
my capacity to determine the truth of a claim that someone I might encounter
was the bearer of that name? It is true enough that, if I understand the
name 'Abraham', I must know what would refute, and, for that matter,
what would vindicate, the claim that, astoundingly, Abraham had managed
to survive until now, and that an aged individual before us was actually
he; and anyone who believes in the resurrection of the dead must be prepared for an actual encounter with Abraham, as Lazarus had in the parable.
But it seems to be stretching credulity to propose that it is in my capacity to
accomplish such rarely called for feats of identification that my understanding
of the name 'Abraham' primarily consists.

When we reflect on proper names, either in the strict or in Frege's
extended sense, for objects which are temporally or spatially remote from
us, we may come to find it very dubious that the determination of the truth-
values of statements containing such names proceeds via the identification
of objects as their referents. Consider the sentence 'Frege was a great
philosopher'. I can judge this statement to be true even though I have
no opportunity to put myself in a position to be able to assert a recognition
statement of the form, 'That is Frege', and then go on to establish the
correctness of the crude predication 'That man is a great philosopher'.
Indeed, even if I had an opportunity to do this, it would be of no help in
determining the truth of the statement. Suppose that Frege, instead of
dying in 1925, had surpassed all historical records of longevity and were
alive today, an ancient, senile shell of a man. Some neighbour, to whom the
sense of the name 'Frege' was given as being the name of that antique
individual whom he saw being wheeled in his bath chair would, indeed,
have to determine the truth of 'Frege is a great philosopher' via the man
whom he knew as the bearer of the name: that is, he would have not only
to read Frege's writings, but also to establish that the old man whom he
knew as 'Frege' was the man who formerly wrote those works. But that is
not how the sense of the name is given to me. In effect, the name 'Frege' is
given to me as standing for the man who wrote *Die Grundlagen der Arithmetik*, *Die Grundgesetze der Arithmetik*, 'Über Sinn und Bedeutung' and all
the rest. Whoever wrote those books and essays was a great philosopher, and,

if challenged about the assertion that Frege was a great philosopher, it would be to the defence of *that* proposition that I should turn: the raising of questions about whether some aged man really was to be identified as the author of those works would be a distraction and an irrelevance if I were concerned with whether or not it was true to say, 'Frege was a great philosopher', as I understand that sentence—however much it might be necessary to go into them if I wanted to persuade someone else that the person he knew as 'Frege' was a great philosopher.

Such examples make the model of sense which we have been considering appear misconceived. An objection of this kind, if well taken, could not be dealt with by some carefully contrived modification of the model. Rather, it calls in question the whole notion of reference, as conceived by Frege in terms of the relation of name to bearer. We have seen that the notion of reference is of interest only if it can be made to do some work in the model we give for the senses of the expressions of our language. It is of little interest in itself whether we can or cannot define the notion of reference precisely for expressions of this or that logical type: what matters is whether we can conceive of the senses of our expressions as consisting in the manner in which we determine their referents, so that the contribution which such an expression makes to the determination of the truth-value of a sentence in which it occurs is exhausted by the identification of something as its referent. What the present objection casts doubt on is precisely the centrality of the notion of reference to a correct model of sense: it calls in question the idea that the determination of the truth-value of a sentence containing a proper name (even of a proper name in the strict sense of a simple proper name) goes via the determination of an object as being the bearer of that name. It seems plausible enough that this may be so when we consider a sentence containing the name of an object with which we are familiar, and whose name we originally learned ostensively, that is, as employed in recognition statements when confronted with the object. It seems wholly implausible when we are concerned with names of objects which we have never encountered and are never likely to encounter.

In fact, the objection is not well taken. In order to grasp that it is not, it is necessary to understand correctly the function of a general account of sense. On our present interpretation of the notion of sense, to grasp the sense of an expression is to have an implicit understanding of a general rule which constitutes the contribution made by that expression to what has to be done to determine any sentence in which it occurs as true or as false. Given the way in which a sentence is constructed out of its component expressions, and given the senses of these expressions, we have, then, an understanding of the means whereby that sentence can be recognized as having one or other truth-value. It does not in the least follow that the route so determined to the recognition of the truth-value of a sentence is the only means whereby that sentence can be established as true or as false; that there are no short cuts. The sense of the connective 'or' is given by the truth-table for it: a sentence 'A or B' can be established as true by establishing either constituent as true, and as false by establishing both constituents as false. The sense of the sentence 'It is raining (in the vicinity)' is given by our understanding of what we have to do to observe whether it is true or false by the use of our sense-organs. If, then, we seek to determine the truth-value of the sentence 'Either it is raining or it is not' by following out the means provided for doing so by the structure of the sentence and the senses of its components, we shall put ourselves in a position to observe the weather, determine one or other of the two disjuncts as true accordingly, and finally conclude, by the truth-table for 'or', to the truth of the disjunctive statement. In fact, of course, we are able to establish the truth of the statement by means of a short cut which may leave us in ignorance of the state of the weather, by noticing that whatever we were to do to determine the truth-value of the first disjunct would result in the establishment either of it or of the second disjunct as true. But this possibility does not show that anything was amiss with the original characterization either of the sense of 'or' or of the sense of 'It is raining'. For any given sentence, there will always be something which we may regard as being the most *direct* means of recognizing it as having one or other truth-value; not in the sense of that means which involves the least expenditure of effort, nor the most practicable or the most certain; but that which corresponds, step by step, with the way in which the sense of the sentence is determined from those of its components. Very often we are in a position to apprehend, precisely from a knowledge of the senses of those components, that, as it were, two or more steps in the direct process of determining the truth-value will cancel each other out: then a short cut becomes possible. Sometimes this is immediately evident, as in the case of 'It is raining or it is not raining': in other cases, our recognition of the possibility of such a short cut depends upon our attention being directed along a certain, perhaps quite complicated, path; this is one of the things which is accomplished by means of an extended chain of deductive inferences. As a simple example, consider the arithmetic predicate 'is perfect'. A perfect number is defined to be a number n the sum of whose divisors less than n is equal to n: so the direct method of establishing whether a number n is perfect, obtained by following the sense of the predicate, is to test each number from 1 to n/2 for whether it divides n, add up those that do, and see whether this sum is equal to n. But a simple theorem of Euclid's establishes that, if $n = 2^{k-1}(2^k - 1)$, where $2^k - 1$ is prime, then n is perfect. We need to establish first that, for any m, $1 + 2 + 2^2 + \ldots + 2^{m-1} + 2^m = 2^{m+1} - 1$; this is intuitively evident from the effect of adding 1 to both sides, or may be simply proved by induction. Now, since $2^k - 1$ is prime, the factors of n other than n itself fall into two classes: $1, 2, \ldots, 2^{k-1}$; and $2^k - 1, 2(2^k - 1), \ldots, 2^{k-2}(2^k - 1)$. By the lemma, the sum of those in the first class is $2^k - 1$; and the sum of those in the second class is $(2^{k-1} - 1)(2^k - 1)$. The sum of these two numbers in turn is evidently $2^{k-1}(2^k - 1) = n$, so that n is perfect, as asserted. If, therefore, we are considering the number 496, and notice that it is equal to $16.31 = 2^{5-1}.(2^5 - 1)$, and that 31 is prime, we may conclude that 496 is perfect, without establishing the truth of this statement directly by writing out its 9 factors other than itself and adding them up. The proof of the theorem enables us to short-cut this process, by displaying a pattern in which the direct computation could be arranged.

If one of the ways of recognizing a man as a great philosopher is by the quality of his writing, then we can judge the truth of 'The author of these works was a great philosopher' by inspecting and judging the works in question, without any detour involving an identification of the author. This is a case in which the short cut is immediately evident from the structure of the sentence: for the application of the predicate can be determined by examination of that in relation to which the referent of the subject-term is to be identified, and therefore this identification in this case becomes an unnecessary detour. (Even here, this short cut depends on the presumption that the works in question were written by a man, and not printed by a computer or dictated by an archangel, and that they were written by one man: anything which established this beyond doubt would ultimately rest upon someone's identification of an individual as the author.) But to give an account of the sense expressed by such a phrase as 'the author of these works' must be to give a uniform means by which the contribution of that phrase to the determination of the truth-conditions of a sentence in which it occurs can be construed. This will be, indeed, to fix some route to the determination of the truth-value of any such sentence as in some way preferred—that is, as what we have called the 'direct' route: it will not involve any claim that in particular cases there may not be another, and a shorter, route. The only method by which this could be done is by some means of identifying an object as the bearer of the name. Any such notion of identification must, as we have seen, relate to some preferred method of picking out the object to be so identified. There is, indeed, nothing mandatory about selecting, as this preferred method, the use of ostension, in the case of concrete objects—and there is nothing in Frege to support this selection; I suggested it as being natural, and for want of any other uniform method applicable to objects of a great many different categories. But any method selected for this role would always admit of short cuts in a large number of cases, and would be none the worse for that. The short cut that is possible, in a particular case, depends on the predicate being used: what is required of the model of sense that we have for any one category of proper names is that it be in principle applicable irrespective of the particular context in which the name occurs.

A different objection to the model we have been presenting is that it invokes epistemological considerations where they are irrelevant. What is needed, on Frege's conception of sense, is that a grasp of the senses of the expressions which compose a sentence should enable us to understand the truth-conditions of the sentence—what has to be the case for it to be true. Such an understanding does not relate to our means of recognition of its truth, which is something quite different: all that is involved is our grasp of what it is that that truth consist in. There may be something in this objection, as far as exegesis of Frege is concerned: it may be that Frege would have rejected an account along the lines proposed as involving excessive reference to our means of recognition. If so, there is ground for suspecting that Frege's theory of meaning was in error at this very place. For what can a model of sense be but a model of what it is to grasp a sense? And if what we have to explain is what it is to grasp the senses of expressions of different kinds—that is, what an understanding of their senses consists in—we have to give a model that displays how this understanding is manifested. We may say, if we like, that a grasp of the sense of a proper name consists in a knowledge of what conditions have to obtain for an object, presented by ostension, to be correctly identified as the bearer of the name: but how can this knowledge be manifested save by a recognition of whatever shows those conditions to obtain?

If I am wrong in this, and there is some non-circular account of the notion of knowing what it is for something to be the case, not construed as verbalizable knowledge (on pain of circularity in the course of explaining what it is to understand words), nor appealing to the recognition of its being the case, then the general form of the model of sense we have been considering can be preserved while the whole model is recast in terms of this notion. What we are interested in in the present context is, after all, this general form, the structure of a model of sense, and not the question how far epistemological notions can legitimately be employed within such a model. But, despite the fact that Frege was undoubtedly highly realist in his whole philosophical outlook, that for him sense was related to truth rather than to the recognition of truth, and despite his constant inveighing against the intrusion of psychological notions into logic (more properly, into the theory of meaning), it is far from apparent that he would have rejected an account of the form we have been considering, on the grounds of the present objection. The notion of sense was in fact connected by him from its first introduction with cognitive notions: the notion of sense was required in the first place in order to explain how our sentences come to have the cognitive value which they have for us. When Frege engages in polemic against psychologism, what he is concerned to repudiate is the invasion of the theory of meaning by notions concerned with mental processes, mental images, and

Gl 26 the like, and the confusion between the process by which we come to acquire a grasp of sense and what constitutes such a grasp. The psychological was

Huss 317 for him a realm of incommunicable inner experience: cognitive notions, notions having to do with the recognition of truth, what he calls the advance

SB 35 from a thought to a truth-value, that is, from the sense to the reference of a

NS 157 (145) sentence, do not belong to the domain of the psychological as thus understood. After all, whether a sentence is a priori or a posteriori, analytic or synthetic, are questions universally understood by those admitting the distinctions as relating to the kind of sense which the sentence has: and

Gl 3 Frege expressly makes these distinctions depend upon the ways in which the sentence can be known to be true (not necessarily the way in which it actually is known, if at all). Even in giving an account of the sense of a particular expression, Frege requires that we remain faithful to the order in which the senses of our words can, even in principle, be acquired: thus he says in *Grundlagen* that 'direction of' must be explained in terms of 'parallel to', and objects against those who define the latter in terms of the former by

Gl 64 saying that lines are parallel if they have the same direction that we could not acquire the notion of direction in advance of the notion of the relation of being parallel. I do not pretend that these facts establish that Frege would have regarded an account along present lines as being legitimate. But the general contention that Frege wanted to extrude everything epistemological from logic or from the theory of meaning is quite misconceived: he wanted to extrude everything psychological; but that was for him a quite different matter.

It is indeed a serious defect of the account, as given so far, that it deals only with names of concrete objects, and not with those of abstract ones, whereas of course Frege was extremely insistent that the distinction between concrete and abstract objects does not affect the status of terms for them as constituting proper names having reference. We shall, however, postpone discussion of abstract objects until a later chapter. It is high time to return to the original question which prompted our attempt to describe in greater detail the form which an account of sense should take: the legitimacy of Frege's ascription of reference to predicates and other incomplete expressions. But, now, if the kind of model of sense which we have been describing in any way approximates to that which Frege had in mind, there appears a very great disanalogy between the notion of reference as applied to names and as applied to predicates. Within our model, the notion of reference for predicates did no work at all: the sense of a predicate consisted in the way in which its application to objects is determined, and there is nothing in the way of an identification of a concept as the referent of the predicate to correspond to the identification of an object as the referent of a name. It seems, indeed, virtually impossible to make any sense of the conception of identifying a concept as the referent of a predicate, because we can make no suggestion for what it would be to be 'given' a concept. Of course, there is in general such a thing as determining that two predicates have the same reference, for this is just the same as determining that they have the same extension: but, in order to construe any case of this as constituting an identification of a concept as the referent of a predicate, we should have to be able to select certain particular predicates as playing the same special role as, in the case of expressions referring to concrete objects, we took demonstratives to play. In any case, it hardly seems that any such activity would be required in order to determine the truth-value of an atomic sentence.

It may be retorted that confining ourselves to atomic sentences is precisely the cause of the trouble. In determining the truth-value of an atomic sentence, we had, in general, to identify an object as the referent of the name, and then determine whether the predicate applied to that object. The parallel case, in which we should expect an identification of a concept as referent of a predicate to be required, would be in determining the truth-value of a sentence of the next higher level: that is, a sentence formed by filling the argument-place of a second-level predicate (a quantifier, say) with a first-level one. In that case, we should expect to have to identify a concept as the referent of the first-level predicate, and then determine whether the second-level predicate was true of it. And it is certainly the case that the truth-value of such a sentence depends on the whole extension of the first-level predicate in a way in which that of an atomic sentence does not. We cannot imagine that any way of identifying two predicates as having the same referent, i.e. as being co-extensive, could be relevant to the truth-value of a sentence applying one of the predicates to a single object; but it seems less irrelevant in the case of a quantified sentence. The truth-value of a

sentence 'For every x, $P(x)$' depends upon the whole extension of the predicate '$P(\xi)$', which, since we are talking of quantified sentences, we may
regard as, in general, complex. Thus, in order to recognize the quantified
sentence as true or as false, it is not in all cases enough to understand, or
recognize the truth-value of, all sentences in the language of the form
'$P(a)$': this would be adequate only if we had an assurance that the language
contained a name for every object. In general, what we must know is what
it is for the predicate '$P(\xi)$' to be true of an arbitrary object; it is rather
natural to characterize this as knowing what concept '$P(\xi)$' stands for, as
opposed to knowing how '$P(\xi)$' applies to the objects nameable in the
language. The possibility of so understanding what it is for '$P(\xi)$' to be true
of any object whatever derives from the fact that the semantic roles of the
proper names in the sentence from which '$P(\xi)$' was formed by omitting some
occurrences of one of them are exhausted by their references, that is, that the
primitive predicates and relational expressions can be considered as defined
over *objects* and not over ways in which objects are presented.

Though it is natural enough to describe a grasp of what, in full generality,
it is for '$P(\xi)$' to be true of an object as knowing what concept '$P(\xi)$' stands
for, this is still very unlike the identification of an object as what a name
stands for. Can we press the analogy any closer? What we saw that we
needed was a particular sentence involving '$P(\xi)$' to stand as analogue to the
recognition statement 'That is a' in the case of a proper name. Such a
sentence would be one expressing the coincidence of reference of two
predicates, that is, a universally quantified biconditional 'For all x, $K(x)$ if
and only if $P(x)$'. '$K(\xi)$' has to be a very special predicate, fulfilling a function
analogous to the demonstrative, so that we may plausibly describe a recognition of the truth of the sentence as identifying a concept as the referent
of '$P(\xi)$'. The only suggestion that comes to mind is that '$K(\xi)$' be a disjunction of predicates of the form '$\xi = a$'. In one way, this suggestion fits
very well. Essentially, Frege explains universal quantification as multiple
conjunction: 'For all x, $P(x)$' is to be true just in case '$P(\xi)$' is true of all
objects, i.e. if the conjunction of the results of applying '$P(\xi)$' to each object
in turn yields the value *true*. There are, however, three strong objections to
it. First, precisely the case with which it does not deal is the one that caused
us in the first place to insist that an understanding of the quantified sentence
'For every x, $P(x)$' depended on knowing what concept '$P(\xi)$' stands for, and
not merely the truth-values of less complex sentences of the language containing '$P(\xi)$', namely when the language does not contain names of all
objects in the domain. If we assume that, nevertheless, it is possible to use a
demonstrative to refer to any object in the domain, we might just escape this

objection by replacing the constituents '$\xi = a$' by predicates of the form 'That is ξ', accompanied by pointing gestures, derived from recognition statements. Secondly, it will not deal with the case when the domain of quantification is infinite. And, thirdly, we have Frege's express repudiation of it, when he says that a universal quantification does not involve reference to all the objects in the domain: when I say that all men are mortal, he says, I do not have in mind some African chief of whom I have never heard.

Huss 327; Schr 454; NS 230 (213)

The notion of identifying a concept as the referent of a predicate, and, similarly, a function as the referent of a functional expression or a relation as the referent of a relational one, is thus not wholly devoid of content; but the content seems thin, and the analogy with the case of proper names forced. It just does not appear that the notion of reference can be made to do the same kind of work, in connection with the senses of predicates, as it does in connection with the senses of names. And for just this reason, Frege's attribution of reference to incomplete expressions appears in the end unjustified. We saw in the earlier part of the chapter that this attribution can, if we wish to take the trouble, be expressed in a manner that resolves the paradoxes into which the theory threatened to fall, and is unobjectionable to anyone who admits second-level quantification. But success in thus vindicating the attribution is worthless unless the attribution can be shown to play some significant role within our account of sense, and unless the analogy with the name/bearer relation which formed the prototype for the whole notion of reference can be sustained and shown to have some content. Ultimately, it does not appear that this can be done.

We cannot fully satisfy ourselves of this until we have considered how second-level quantification is to be explained: but this we will postpone until later. But there is one detail which brings the point home very forcefully to us. We discussed earlier the notion of lack of reference as it applies, or can be made to apply, to incomplete expressions; and we saw that a true analogy with the case of proper names could be found only if we considered, what actually occurs in natural language, a description operator of higher level. Since we can form second-level predicates, expressing conditions to be satisfied by a concept which is the referent of a first-level predicate which may be used to fill the argument-place, we can, if we choose, introduce a second-level description operator capable of being attached to such a second-level predicate. Suppose that '$M\alpha : \Phi(\alpha)$' is such a second-level predicate, and '$I\mathscr{f}[M\alpha : \mathscr{f}(\alpha)](\xi)$' the result of applying to it such a description operator: this expression is itself, of course, a first-level predicate. If '$M\alpha : \Phi(\alpha)$' is satisfied (to within co-extensiveness) by only one concept, then '$I\mathscr{f}[M\alpha : \mathscr{f}(\alpha)](\xi)$' is to stand for that concept, i.e. to be true of just those objects of which a predicate satisfying 'Mα: $\Phi(\alpha)$' is true; but if 'Mα: $\Phi(\alpha)$' is true of no concept, or of two extensionally non-coincident ones, then 'I$\mathscr{f}$[Mα: $\mathscr{f}(\alpha)$] (ξ)' is to be devoid of reference. It has already been pointed out that we do have such a device in natural language: in the sentence 'The dish is the shape which the plate and the table-mat both are', the phrase 'the shape which the plate and the table-mat both are' is a predicative expression, not a singular term, both 'is' and 'are' being the copula, and the word 'shape' serving simply to restrict the range of the quantification over properties; the phrase might be rendered by 'what—in respect of shape—the plate and the mat both are'. If there is no shape which the plate and the mat both are, then the whole predicate 'ξ is the shape which the plate and the mat both are' is devoid of reference. But we can easily see how totally useless it is to have such a second-level description operator. It is true that Frege did not want to have a first-level description operator capable of forming terms without a reference either: but it needs special ad hoc stipulations to deprive a description operator of this capacity. Just because it is the role of singular terms to stand for objects which we wish to talk about, it is entirely natural that we should sometimes construct terms which fail in their aim of picking out an object. But the role of predicates is not to pick out a concept—we still have no clear idea what doing that would be—but, rather, to say something determinate about objects, to be defined as true or as false of any given object; and so it is rather unnatural to construct predicates which fail to do this, otherwise than by containing a name which fails to refer to an object. There is no motivation whatever for introducing the second-level description operator (it occurs in natural language because of the use of the same vocabulary for expressing generality of different levels): what can be clumsily expressed by 'I$\mathscr{f}$[Mα: $\mathscr{f}(\alpha)$](a)' can much more naturally be expressed, without fear of failure of truth-value, by '$\forall\mathscr{f}$[Mα: $\mathscr{f}(\alpha) \to \mathscr{f}(a)$]'. Now that we have considered exactly what is involved, reflection on this brings out very clearly the extent to which the notion of reference is needed for proper names, but only applied by force majeure to predicates. Thus the fact, which earlier we dismissed as of minor importance, that Frege fails to provide a faithful analogy, for predicates, to the case of a proper name's failing of reference, proves after all to have a real significance; not in itself, but as suggestive of the true state of affairs.

CHAPTER 8

The Incompleteness of Concepts and Functions

IN THIS CHAPTER we shall scrutinize in more detail Frege's doctrine that the referents of incomplete expressions are themselves incomplete. Someone might feel that it was pointless to do this, on the ground that we had concluded in the preceding chapter that there are no such things as concepts, relations and functions. Such an objection would reveal a complete misunderstanding of what was established in the last chapter. The earlier part of the chapter established, on the contrary, that there can be no reservation whatever about the existence of concepts, relations and functions, provided that we are prepared to admit second-level quantification; for the present, we shall assume that we are. What the later part of the chapter established was not that incomplete expressions do not have reference, but that the notion of reference does not play the same role in regard to them as it does in regard to proper names. The use of the name/bearer relation as prototype cannot be maintained: the sense of a predicate or other incomplete expression, at least as we require to understand it for the interpretation either of atomic sentences or those involving first-level quantification, is not to be explained in terms of the identification of something as the referent of that expression. In one sense, it remains true to say that the semantic role of an incomplete expression is given by its reference, in that 'identity' of reference entails coincidence of semantic role: a predicate contributes to the determination of the truth-value of a sentence in which it occurs via its reference; otherwise put, what the sense of a predicate has to do is to provide a means of determining the extension of a concept. But the way in which reference constitutes the semantic role of an incomplete expression is different from the way this happens either for a proper name or for a sentence. The sense of a proper name cannot be explained without invoking the notion of reference for proper names, and the sense of a sentence cannot be explained without invoking the notion of a sentence's possessing a truth-value: but the crucial notion for the explanation of the sense of a predicate is that of its being true of an object, for a relational expression that of its holding between two objects, for a functional expression that of its yielding, when filled by the name of one object, the name of another; the relation between an incomplete expression and its referent does not have to be invoked. At least, this is so for sentences involving at most first-level quantification: we have yet to see how things come out for those involving quantification over concepts, relations or functions.

We are not here concerned with the application of the notion of reference to incomplete expressions; rather, taking for granted that it can legitimately be applied to them, however small a role this may play in our semantics or however weak the analogy is to the reference of proper names, we wish to look more closely at Frege's thesis that their referents are themselves incomplete.

Frege's idea that certain constituents of sentences are incomplete, i.e. that we cannot properly account for the manner in which a sentence signifies solely in terms of its containing certain separable component parts, but that we must advert also to its displaying certain *features*, is essential for the understanding, not only of Frege's theory of language, but also of that presented in Wittgenstein's *Tractatus*. It is this which leads directly to

TLP 3.14   Wittgenstein's insistence that what the sentence presents is a *fact*—something that cannot be named, but only stated—and that the sentence is itself a fact, that is, that what signifies, what we have to consider as signifying, is not an object of any kind, but rather something's being the case. Just as Frege would say that that which, in the sentence 'Cato killed Cato', signifies the ascription to an object of the property of falling under the concept *committed suicide* is not any constituent part of the sentence, attached to a proper name of the object, but rather that feature of the sentence which consists of its being composed by putting the same proper name on either side of the word 'killed', so Wittgenstein would say that what signifies that Cato killed himself is not the string of words 'Cato killed Cato', but certain facts about these words. (In the case of an 'unanalysed' sentence like this, some of these facts will not be discoverable merely by inspecting the arrangement of the words in the sentence itself.) This theory is very different from

FB 18   Frege's: for Frege a sentence is a complete expression, and thus a particular kind of object, in just the same way that a proper name is; and this no doubt helps to explain how Frege was misled into the false step of taking a sentence to be only a special case of a complex proper name. Indeed, for Frege the sentence expresses a thought only in virtue of certain facts, namely that its constituent expressions have the senses that they have, and that it is constructed in a certain way out of them; but that which expresses the thought is, for him, the sentence considered as an object, and not as a fact; facts indeed do not figure at all in Frege's ontology. Wittgenstein was forced to disagree: thinking, as he did, that the ultimate constituents of a sentence have no sense, but only a reference, he could draw no distinction between *what* signifies and that *in virtue of which* it signifies. Nevertheless, whether we consider Wittgenstein's picture theory of language to be a correction of Frege's theory or an illegitimate development of it, it had its roots in Frege's notion of an incomplete expression.   Ged 74 (25)

From the standpoint of Wittgenstein's picture theory, it is evident that what a feature of a sentence—a predicate, for example—signifies can only be a feature of the situation depicted, since everything that signifies can do so only by belonging to the same logical type as what it signifies: what is signified by an incomplete expression must therefore be itself similarly incomplete. 'Belonging to the same logical type' must here be taken literally: it does not mean merely 'of corresponding logical type', where the logical type of an expression is assigned according to the logical type of the entity it signifies; the expression, that which signifies, must, on Wittgenstein's account, itself be an entity of the same logical type as the one it signifies. A sentence, on this theory, consists of a number of names—which are themselves objects—standing in certain relations to one another. The names stand for certain other objects, and their standing in these relations signifies those objects' standing in certain other relations. The essence of a sentence would thus be seen in the following way of constructing pictures to represent certain arithmetical states of affairs: an initial segment of the numerals, starting with '2', is written down; if a number is prime, or a prime power, its numeral is written in a uniform colour, a different colour for different primes, and the same colour for a prime and all its powers; if a number has more than one prime factor, its numeral is written using all the colours corresponding to its prime factors. Thus two numerals' containing no colour in common would signify that the corresponding numbers are co-prime, a numeral's being monochrome that it was a prime or a prime power, etc. Properties of the numerals signify properties of the numbers, relations between the numerals signify relations between the numbers.

It might be said that, apart from the implausibility of this as a theory of how language actually works, it does not provide any interpretation for the notion of the *absolute* incompleteness of concepts. In the example, we took numbers as objects, but Wittgenstein would certainly not have done, and many people would agree with him in not following Frege on this. Now, it may be said, given any domain of entities which are to be considered as objects for the purpose of constructing a certain language—or devising certain pictures—we can certainly distinguish clearly between the objects and their properties and relations: but this distinction is *relative* to the prior selection of a domain of objects. What Frege was after was an *absolute* sense in which what predicates and relational expressions stand for is distinguished, by being incomplete, from anything that can be considered an object. Perhaps such an absolute distinction was credible to Wittgenstein, believing as he did in the possibility of arriving at the limit of a uniform process of analysis: this would then yield the ultimately

TLP 3.25   simple objects—what could not but be considered as an object—and the absolute logical type of everything else would be its type relative to these. But in this respect Frege's procedure is the exact reverse of Wittgenstein's: in this respect he was prepared to take language completely at its face-value, and to recognize as an object anything which *could* be spoken of as an object. And if everything that can be regarded as an object is to be admitted to be

cf *PB* 115   one, then it is difficult to see what place is left for anything not an object— for concepts and relations—at all. Relative to numbers considered as objects, arithmetical properties and relations are indeed entities of a different type: but, for the purpose of another language or set of pictures, arithmetical properties could be taken as objects; so how can there be any *absolute* sense in which we must recognize a distinction between objects and entities of a radically different—'unsaturated'—character?

Frege's assimilation of sentences to complex proper names enabled him, as already explained, in his later work to treat concepts and relations as

Gg I 3, 4   being a special kind of functions of one and two arguments respectively. Although he never expressly presents it as such, it is conceivable that he regarded the possibility so provided as supplying an argument in favour of the assimilation, on the score that the incompleteness of concepts and relations can be properly understood only on the model of the incompleteness of functions. If there is such an argument underlying Frege's later doctrine, it is not a good one. Consider, to start with, the case of truth-functions— mappings from truth-values or ordered pairs of truth-values which may be taken as the referents of sentential operators. We have seen that Frege does not allow for the existence of functions whose values are not objects. The ground for this is that functions can be understood only as the referents of functional expressions, and functional expressions are obtained from *complete* expressions by deleting one or more occurrences of each of one or more constituents. This principle, which is reasonable, leads to the required conclusion, that functions can take only objects as values, only if it is first *assumed* that complete expressions always stand for objects. If, on the contrary, it is supposed that there are two distinct kinds of complete expressions, proper names and sentences, and that proper names stand for objects while sentences stand for truth-values, truth-values not being objects but entities of a distinct logical type, the conclusion will instead be that some functions will have objects as values and others will have as their values truth-values. Perhaps it is more convenient to understand 'function' as Frege understood it, that is, as capable of having only objects as values. In this case, truth-functions, on the view that truth-values are not objects but entities of a different type, will not be a special kind of function, but, rather, entities of a separate type from functions properly so called, yet having an incompleteness closely analogous to that possessed by functions proper. There is absolutely no reason why truth-functions should not be considered as analogous to ordinary functions, and the analogy exploited in explaining the sense in which truth-functions are said to be incomplete: the appeal to this analogy offers no compulsion to take it as being more than an analogy, that is, as actual subsumption, and therefore in no way supports the thesis that truth-values are objects.

But, if this can be said for truth-functions, it can likewise be said for concepts and relations, which do in a clear sense map objects or ordered pairs of objects on to truth-values (or, in the case of higher-level concepts and relations, map incomplete entities, or ordered pairs of them, on to truth-values). In their case, too, it will be perfectly possible to explain the kind of incompleteness that they have by analogy with the incompleteness of functions, without supposing them actually to be a special case of unary or binary functions. Quite independently, therefore, of Frege's later thesis that all incomplete entities are functions of various kinds, it is best, in order to understand his claim that concepts and relations are incomplete, to start by asking what is meant by calling functions 'incomplete'.

The primitive conception of a function is given by the vocabulary in which we use the word 'function' only in the context 'function of', where this is used as when we say that 16 is that function of 4 which 9 is of 3 and 4 of 2, or when we say that gravitational force is a function of mass and distance. In describing this way of speaking, it seems natural to say that the function itself cannot be isolated: a number may be a certain function of another number, a magnitude a function of another magnitude, but neither the number nor the magnitude is itself a function; there is no way to allude to the function itself, save by talking about objects which it would be senseless to identify with the function, but which are that function *of* other objects. The idea of a function first arises with the recognition of a common pattern in a series of equations, e.g.

$$2 \cdot 0^3 + 0 = 0$$
$$2 \cdot 1^3 + 1 = 3$$
$$2 \cdot 2^3 + 2 = 18$$
$$2 \cdot 3^3 + 3 = 57$$
$$2 \cdot 4^3 + 4 = 132.$$

This leads to the form of expression whereby we say that these equations express that the numbers 0, 3, 18, 57, 132 are a certain function of the numbers 0, 1, 2, 3, 4 respectively. The common pattern of the numerical expressions on the left-hand sides of the equations may indeed be represented by a certain expression, namely

$$`2 \cdot \xi^3 + \xi';$$

but the function of which we speak can be identified neither with this expression nor with the pattern which it represents. In saying that the equations express that various numbers are a certain function of various other numbers, we are stating the *content* of the equations: the content relates not to the numerals '0', '3', '18', and '0', '1', '2', but to the numbers which are the referents of these numerals; and so the function too must belong to the realm of reference—it must be the referent of the functional expression which is the common pattern of the various numerical expressions.

Once we have attained to this conception of the function as something incomplete, as something which cannot be referred to on its own, but only by means of a *part*—or, more properly, a (partial) *feature*—of some expression which as a whole stands for an object (a number), we can then go on to introduce a vocabulary in which functions are apparently spoken of as if they were complete, as when we say that a certain function is continuous, or everywhere differentiable, or analytic. Here the word 'function' is used in contexts other than 'function of'. But three things are to be noted about this terminology.

(1) Everything that can be said in this terminology can also be said in a terminology in which 'function' occurs only in the context 'function of'—provided, of course, that we employ quantifiers and bound variables. To say that a function of real numbers is continuous at a certain point is of course to say something that can be expressed in terms of the *values* of the function for certain arguments. Furthermore, not only *can* statements of the kind 'the function is continuous' be expressed in this way, but in fact they

have to be introduced in this way: we cannot explain in the first place what we mean by saying that a function is continuous save by rendering this statement by one in which the function-symbol occurs only with its argu- Gg II 147n ment-place (filled with a bound variable). This is connected with:

(2) We could not understand what is meant by talking about functions unless we first understood the mode of speaking according to which 'function' occurs only in 'function of'. One might say that this is not the case: we need only have the notion of the application of a function to a number. We could, that is, think of a function as a 'complete' entity, as a particular kind of object, capable, like any other object, of standing on its own, provided that we acknowledged that it had the peculiar property that, when applied to a number (or a series of numbers), it yielded another number: in this case, we could explain properties of a function, such as continuity, in terms of the results of applying the function to various numbers. But the notion of application is not one that could be introduced *after* the conception of this particular kind of objects (functions) had been explained: the notion of such a range of objects would remain completely without content until the notion of application had been introduced, for it is only in terms of the results of applying the function to numbers that the criterion for identity or difference of functions could be explained, or indeed any of the properties of functions stated. And how are we to explain the notion of 'application'? What curious property does an object have to have to render it capable of 'yielding' a number when 'applied to' a number? We know that water will produce steam when poured on to a fire: but obviously we are not meant to think of the application of a function to a number as something that we do to it, nor of its yielding a number as something that it does when brought into contact with an argument. As long as we persist in trying to regard the functions as just another range of objects, the notion of application will appear as something wholly mysterious and indefinable—as mysterious and indefinable as the relation of a line to the direction which it 'has' if we try to think of directions as being capable of being given otherwise than as the directions *of* lines. The closest we can come to understanding the character of application is to regard it as a function in Frege's sense, namely as a function of two arguments whose first argument is a function in our sense and whose second argument is a number. Evidently if we tried to regard it as again an object belonging to yet another range—say that of functionals—we should have to introduce yet another new notion, that of the application of a functional to a function and a number, and we should be started on an infinite regress. Moreover, even if we regarded the result of the application of a function to a number as being the value of a function in Frege's sense

for a function in our sense and a number as arguments, we should be utterly at a loss to explain the character of this function-in-Frege's-sense. Admittedly, to form a conception of functions in general, we have to be able to recognize the functional expression which is the common pattern in a series of numerical expressions, and in order to be able to form such numerical expressions we have to be able already to use certain simple functional expressions, say '$\xi + \eta$' and '$\xi \cdot \eta$': there have to be primitive functional expressions. But the use of these primitive function-symbols is learned in connection with numerical symbols—numerals—which can be understood independently of their use in the argument-places of these primitive functional expressions. We can teach someone what addition is, what '$+$' means, because we can assume that he already knows what is meant by speaking of the numbers which he is to add. But if application is considered as represented by a primitive operator (functional expression in Frege's sense), how is anyone supposed to learn what it means, since before knowing what it means he can have no understanding of what sort of object the operation is meant to be performed on? He can have no conception of the functions which, considered as objects, are here being regarded as one of the arguments of the operation of application until he knows what application is: and he cannot learn the use of an operator (functional expression) unless he already knows the meanings of the expressions which are supposed to be put in its argument-places. And finally, since in the course of trying to explain this conception of functions-as-objects we have been driven, under pain of entering an infinite regress, into admitting the existence of at least one incomplete entity—application—the thesis that there are no incomplete entities, that everything can be regarded as an object, has collapsed under its own weight: there seems, then, nothing to be gained by insisting on regarding functions as complete entities—as objects—in the first place. (Compare Russell's argument that there must be at least one universal—similarity.)

PP 96

(3) Finally, the notation whereby expressions for functions themselves, rather than their values, appear as singular terms is not viable generally, but only in rather restricted contexts. We can form such expressions as '$f \equiv g$' (meaning that $f(x) = g(x)$ for every x) or 'f is continuous' only when we are using function-variables or have introduced simple names for particular functions. But in general we want to be able to talk about any function for which we can form a functional expression, and functional expressions are *incomplete* expressions. We can use the 'f is continuous' notation only if we stop, each time we want to mention a new function, to introduce a new simple —and typographically complete—symbol corresponding to some incomplete expression that we can form; or at least if we have some regular device for

forming names of functions-as-objects from incomplete functional expressions by means of bound variables—such a notation as Frege's own '$\grave{\alpha} (2 . \alpha^3 + \alpha)$' or the modern '$\lambda x(2 . x^3 + x)$'. This notation therefore becomes parasitic upon that in which functions are represented by incomplete expressions: the incompleteness of the function is shown in the incompleteness of the expression by means of which it has to be introduced. Moreover, the notation which uses what appear to be proper names of functions, and therefore represents what are really second-level predicates as if they were predicates of first level, though it is in one respect perspicuous, is in a more important respect unperspicuous and defective. It is perspicuous in that it emphasizes clearly such an (in reality second-level) predicate as 'is continuous', which in a more explicit notation might appear as a complex pattern difficult to recognize as a unit; but it is unperspicuous in respect of logical transitions. (This is indeed to some extent a weakness of all abbreviations introduced by definition.) An equation may contain a great many distinct but interwoven functional expressions: it may be regarded, now one way, as saying one thing about a certain function, now another way, as saying something else about another function. It is precisely this feature of language which makes it possible to give non-mechanical, non-trivial proofs in mathematics (and elsewhere). In order to exploit this feature of language, it is essential to employ the notation in which functional expressions occur only with their argument-places: in the notation in which they appear only as pseudo-proper names, it will not be possible to recognize any new functions in the statements we make; we are able to mention only such functions as we have explicitly introduced at the outset, or as are the result of a handful of simple operations, such as composition, upon those we have.

In the above discussion, I may appear to have begged the question on several occasions: for I repeatedly made use of such expressions as 'regard the function as an object', 'consider functions as something incomplete', 'a function in Frege's sense', and the like, whereas my intention was to make the above three points, essentially Frege's, as a preliminary to explaining what Frege means by saying that a function is something incomplete. I think there was no real circularity. I did indeed assume an understanding of what it is to regard something as an object—namely, to think of it as something that can be introduced as the referent of a proper name; all that it was necessary to understand as well is that we cannot so introduce the notion of a function without simultaneously introducing that of the application of a function to an object, and we cannot in turn regard application as an object without embarking on an infinite regress.

We have now to state just what is meant by saying that functions are

K*

cf. *LK* 205 incomplete. From what has been said this has become quite evident: an entity is incomplete if it can be introduced in the first place *only* as the referent of an incomplete expression. We cannot explain what a function is except by indicating what functional expressions are and then saying that by a 'function' is meant whatever can be the referent of such an expression. It may be objected that, because of the systematic ambiguity of 'bedeuten', we cannot know what is meant by speaking of a functional expression as standing for something. The answer is that the exposition given in the earlier part of the last chapter of the use of 'stand for' in connection with incomplete expressions gives one a complete account of this use, displays its analogy with (and type-difference from) its use in connection with proper names, and leaves us in no doubt that in general there *is* something which an incomplete expression stands for. (We actually discussed, in the last chapter, the use of 'stand for' only in connection with predicates, the basic principle being that, e.g., 'what the predicate "ξ is round" stands for' must be interchangeable with the predicative expression 'round'. Likewise the expression 'what the functional expression "ξ²" stands for' must be interchangeable with 'square' as used in 'square of', so that, e.g., '9 is what "ξ²" stands for of 3' means just '9 is the square of 3'. The considerations in the later part of the last chapter about the role, in the theory of sense, of the notion of reference for incomplete expressions is irrelevant to the introduction of the notion of a function via the notion of reference.) In making this claim to have satisfactorily explained the notion of reference as applied to incomplete expressions, we are, of course, continuing to assume that it will be possible to justify the use of higher-level quantification.

Incomplete entities are those that can be explained in the first place only as the referents of the appropriate type of incomplete expressions. Having introduced them, we may for some purposes wish to speak about them as if they were objects, i.e. by means of a notation in which they are represented by complete expressions (proper names). However, such a notation will always remain essentially defective: functions can never be properly represented save by incomplete expressions. This is why Frege insists that in his Gg II 147n; BW 243–4 (161) notation a function-symbol, whether a constant or a variable, must never appear without its argument-place(s), save for that occurrence of a function-variable directly next to a quantifier. In the language which we described, as employing the word 'function', but only in the context 'function of', a similar exception would have to be made for expressions like 'There is a function which . . . ' and 'For every function, . . . ': to take a trivial example, a sentence like 'There is a function which 4 is of 2 and 9 is of 3' would belong to this language.

As we noted previously, it is literally impossible, in a language in which each incomplete expression can occur only with its argument-place, to break Frege's prohibitions concerning type: the attempt to put an expression of the wrong type into an argument-place will simply not produce a complete expression. I cannot put a singular term, e.g. 'Aristotle', into the argument-place of 'Φ (Socrates) and not Φ (Plato)', for then there would be nowhere for the names 'Socrates' and 'Plato' to go. Nor can I put a predicate, say 'ξ is bald', into the argument-place of 'ξ is wise and ξ is ugly', for I am then still left with an argument-place. Again, if from the sentence 'For every x, either x is odd or x is even' I drop the second-level predicate 'For every x $\Phi(x)$', I obtain the third-level predicate 'Ξx: x is odd or x is even', whose argument-place must be filled by some second-level predicate; and I cannot fill it by the first-level predicate 'ξ is prime', for there would be nowhere to put the first-level predicate 'ξ is odd or ξ is even'. This is what Wittgenstein meant in the *Tractatus* by saying that Frege's symbolism was such as to make it impossible to form nonsensical sentences.

Gg I 21

TLP 3.325;
BW 151 (93)

There is a minor point to note. The notion of the application of a function to an object is not, as is sometimes said, spurious or mythical: for Frege at least it is a perfectly genuine second-level function of two arguments, one of them a first-level function of one argument and the other an object. If we take the singular term '4!' (or 'the capital of Denmark'), and drop from it *both* the proper name '4' ('Denmark') and the functional expression 'ξ!' ('the capital of ξ'), we obtain the second-level functional expression '$\varphi(\xi)$', which stands of course for a second-level function. The point is not that we must reject the conception of such a function, but that we do not have to explain the notion of a first-level function *in terms of* this second-level function, taken as already understood; and that if we try to conceive of first-level functions as complete entities—as objects—we shall find ourselves doing exactly this.

The analogy between concepts and relations, on the one hand, and functions on the other, is not immediately apparent. This is because the expressions 'property of' and 'relation between', as ordinarily interpreted, do not work in the same way as 'function of'. 9 is a certain function of 3, but it is not itself a function: but wisdom is a property of Socrates, and *is* a property, and brotherhood is a relation between John and James, and *is* a relation. From Frege's point of view, 'wisdom', which appears as a proper name, cannot stand for a concept, nor 'brotherhood' for a relation: if we do not take them as standing for abstract objects, we shall have to construe them as forming eliminable idiomatic variants for sentences employing the corresponding predicate and relational expression. But, even without appealing to the analogy with functions, it remains that the same kind of consideration which shows it impossible to regard functions as a particular species of object shows the same thing for concepts and relations. If we try to consider the predicate or the relational expression in an atomic sentence as standing for an object, as do the proper names which occupy its argument-places, we shall be at a loss to account for the unity of the sentence. We shall have to think of the sentence as saying that the object named by the proper name stands in a particular relation to the object referred to by means of the predicate, or that the objects named by the two proper names stand in a particular relation to the object referred to by the relational expression. We shall once more be in a quandary how to explain the character of this peculiar relationship, which all our assertions involve. Once more, to regard this relation as an object will be to embark on an infinite regress, while to admit it as a relation in Frege's sense—as something incomplete—will be to lose all reason for not having regarded relations and concepts as incomplete in the first place. Once again, we are in any case trapped in a circle: we cannot explain what sort of objects concepts are save by referring to this mysterious relation of falling under a concept (possessing a property), since we can say nothing about concepts without speaking of this relation of (ordinary) objects to them; and we cannot explain what this relation is, since in order to convey what is meant by speaking of a relation, we must presuppose a prior understanding of the kinds of object that can be said to stand in that relation. Moreover, if we try to regard concepts and relations as objects, it will be impossible to explain what difference it is between them which constitutes one a *concept* and another a *relation*. What peculiar property is it which makes, e.g., shininess a *concept* (property) but resemblance a *relation*? Obviously just that we learn to speak of shininess in the first place only by learning to use the *predicate* 'ξ is shiny', and to speak of resemblance only by learning to use the *relational* expression 'ξ resembles η'. But to acknowledge this is precisely to acknowledge that we have to recognize concepts and relations as being incomplete in just the sense I have stated: they can be explained in the first place only as being the sorts of thing for which predicates and relational expressions can stand. Admittedly, once we have done so, we *can* for certain purposes introduce such pseudo-singular terms as 'shininess' and 'resemblance': but, as we have seen, these could not be introduced in advance of understanding the use of the corresponding adjective and verb, and are parasitic on it. This way of speaking is, indeed, fundamentally defective in the same way in which the corresponding terminology for functions was: we can introduce new concepts and relations only ad hoc, by reference back to the predicates and relational expressions which stand for them.

It is left for a later chapter to treat of the problems concerning quantification over concepts, relations and functions; here we note only a particular point concerning the existence of universals, as it appears in Frege's philosophy and in some others. Strawson, as we have seen, follows not Frege but earlier models in his categorization of entities. According to the traditional view, the broad classification is into *particulars*, which are those things which can be referred to only by means of a singular term, not by a predicate (or a relational expression); and *universals* which are those which can be referred to (mentioned, 'introduced') by either a predicate (or relational expression) or a singular term. Thus the same entities (universals) are referred to by means of the noun 'red' and 'is red' where 'red' is an adjective, by 'wisdom' and 'is wise', by 'shininess' and 'is shiny', by 're-semblance' and 'resembles'. This is the idea expressed by Aristotle when he says in the *Categories* that a substance is that of which things can be pre-dicated, but which cannot be predicated of anything, whereas a quality, e.g., can both be predicated of something and have things predicated of it. For Frege, the basic classification is on different lines: an *object* is that for which there could be a language in which it was referred to only by a proper name (singular term); or, to express it differently, which can be referred to by a proper name that can be explained independently of the corresponding predicate. A *concept* is something which can be explained in the first place only as the referent of a predicate; even if there are expressions referring to it which at first appearance function as proper names, the sentences in which they occur will be able to be explained only as variants on sentences containing the corresponding predicate in place of the fictitious proper name. On occasion, there will be pairs of related proper names and predicates neither of which is spurious, such as the noun 'red' and the predicate 'ξ is red'. Here the proper name could be introduced into a language which did not contain the predicate. In this case the proper name will stand for a genuine object; but this object must still be distinguished from the concept for which the predicate stands. But, as we have seen, such apparent proper names as 'shininess' and 'resemblance' are spurious, and do not stand for objects at all.

The Aristotelian doctrine is indeed more subtle than it has here been represented as being. It is also demanded of a substance that it not be '*in*' anything else, or, as we might more naturally say in English, '*of*' anything else: this is meant in the sense in which a direction is 'of' a line. As remarked earlier, we cannot understand what a direction is unless we understand it as the value of the function for which 'the direction of ξ' stands, for some line as argument. It might be objected that we could introduce proper names of directions (e.g. 'North' and 'East') ostensively, without having previously introduced the functional expression 'the direction of ξ'; but when we point out a direction, the pointing gesture has to be understood quite differently from when we point at a person, a place or a colour. We point *at* all these, but we point *in*, not *at*, a direction: that is, the pointing arm does not merely direct our attention towards, but *displays* a line whose direction is the one we wish to indicate. In any case, the point is irrelevant for Aristotle's distinction between what is 'in' ('of') something else, and what is not 'in' ('of') anything else; for he says that a colour is 'in' a surface, and it is certain that names of colours could be introduced independently of the functional expression 'the colour of ξ'. We shall see later a possible way in which Aristotle's distinction can be drawn. This distinction too is incorporated in Strawson's doctrine. Another qualification is introduced by Aristotle in *Metaphysics VII*, where he says that there is one thing which substance *can* be predicated of, namely matter. I take him to be alluding to the following kind of case. If my dog Fido dies, I may point at the corpse and say, 'This was Fido.' This cannot be taken as a statement of identification—'This dog was Fido'—because no dog is present; as Aristotle elsewhere remarks, a dead dog is not a dog. The demonstrative must be taken as referring to a certain piece of matter; but again it would be nonsensical to say that a piece of matter used to be *identical* with Fido, for it is the *same* piece of matter and yet the dog is no longer there. A dog is a different sort of thing from a piece of matter—the criteria of identity are different: it is neither necessary nor sufficient, for something to be the same *dog* at different times, for it to consist of the same matter. Hence the 'was' in the quoted sentence is not the sign of identity but the copula: Fido is being predicated of a piece of matter.

I mention these refinements so as not to be guilty of travestying Aristotle. There is indeed no reason why similar refinements should not be introduced into Frege's doctrine: one might be able, *within* the category of objects, to distinguish those which are universals from those which are particulars, and, within the class of particulars, those which are substances from those which are not. Frege does not deny the possibility of such distinctions: indeed, his vague differentiation in *Grundlagen* between 'concrete' and 'abstract' objects reveals that he acknowledged such a possibility. All that is essential to his doctrine is that such distinctions are posterior to the primary distinctions between objects and concepts, relations and functions, and between these and incomplete entities of higher level, drawn in the way he draws them. It is a consequence of this distinction that the colour red, which

Gl 26, 60–2, 85

is an object, is an entity of a different logical level from the concept *red*. (Such a sentence is of course itself an offence against the doctrine of the distinctions of level: it is like saying, 'Socrates is a different sort of thing from being what Socrates and Plato both were—philosophers.') Now Strawson has an idea for a way in which to draw the distinction he wants to make between universals and particulars. It will, in general, depend upon empirical facts that a given definite description intended to refer to a person has a reference; e.g. it is an empirical fact that two people have climbed Everest, and that one of them got to the top first, and it is therefore an empirical fact that 'the man who first climbed Everest' has a reference. The possession of a reference by definite descriptions of 'universals' —e.g. colours—*may* likewise depend on empirical facts, e.g. if the definite description is 'the colour common to the curtain and the carpet'. But Strawson holds that it is peculiar to universals that we *can* frame definite descriptions of them whose possession of a reference does not depend on contingent facts; for particulars this can never be done. (We have to think of definite descriptions here, not of names introduced by ostension: for it has been plausibly maintained (i) that the fact that a word is introduced by ostension is a characteristic of its sense; (ii) that it is not a contingent fact that a name introduced by ostension has a reference. From (i) and (ii) it of course follows that, if 'red' and 'Jones' are introduced by ostension, then it is not a contingent fact that a word with the sense of 'red' or with the sense of 'Jones' has a reference.) Thus, for Strawson, the definite descriptions 'the colour complementary to red', 'the colour which lies between red and yellow', 'the colour which appears the same whatever the colour of the transparent medium through which it is viewed' would all be examples of definite descriptions which are *logically* guaranteed a reference.

Here Strawson is departing a long way from Aristotle. Aristotle held that to speak of the existence of a quality is always to speak of the existence of a substance which possesses that quality, and similarly for all the categories other than substances. Let us not insist too precisely on an object's being a *substance*, and say that the Aristotelian criterion for the existence of a colour would be the existence of a material or visual object (e.g. the sky) having that colour. If we adopt the Aristotelian criterion of existence, Strawson's distinction simply breaks down. Consider, for instance, Hume's example of the gradation of shades of blue. Imagine a series of strips of material, each coloured a different shade of blue, linearly arranged with the most similar shades adjacent, with purplish-blues at one end and greenish-blues at the other. (Or we may imagine a surface with a continuous variation of colour from purplish-blue to greenish-blue.) At a certain point a single shade is missing: i.e. there is a gap such that the transition between the shades on either side of the gap is more abrupt than that between any two adjacent shades. Hume is interested in the fact that, as he claims, we can imagine the shade which would fill the gap, without ever having seen anything of that shade. For the present purpose, the question is whether we can say that that shade *exists*. Suppose we give names to the shades on either side of the gap, say 'imperial blue' and 'royal blue'. Then we can form the definite description 'the shade which comes between imperial blue and royal blue'. According to Strawson, this is just the sort of definite description which ought to be guaranteed a reference independently of any empirical facts. But if we adopt the Aristotelian criterion of existence, whether this definite description has a reference depends on whether there is any material or visual object which has just such a shade of blue, and this is evidently an empirical question. It is clear, moreover, that the possession of a reference by *any* definite description of a colour will, if we accept the Aristotelian criterion for the existence of colours, depend on some empirical fact—indeed, in many cases, on very well-known facts. Thus, with this criterion of existence, Strawson's method for distinguishing between universals and particulars will not work.

What is Strawson's criterion for the existence of a colour? It is for him sufficient, for there to be a colour satisfying a given condition, that we should understand what it would be to ascribe to an object possession of a colour satisfying that condition; or, rather, that it should not be self-contradictory to ascribe such a colour to an object. Someone who subscribed to the Aristotelian criterion of existence might say that Strawson's criterion was a criterion not for whether there *was* a colour satisfying the condition, but only for whether there *could be*: he might add that a criterion the satisfaction of which could be decided just by knowing the senses of certain words, independently of empirical fact, must always be a criterion, not for what is actually the case, but for what is logically possible. On this view, Strawson has not drawn a distinction between the existence of particulars and the existence of universals, but only between the *actual* existence of particulars and the *possible* existence of universals. The possible existence of a man satisfying a given condition could be decided independently of empirical fact just as much as the possible existence of a colour.

For Frege, a distinction must be drawn when it is asked what should be the criterion for the existence of a colour: are we speaking of the existence of an object or of a concept? The predicate 'ξ is midway in colour between imperial blue and royal blue' undoubtedly has a reference independently of any empirical facts: for it is not necessary, for a predicate to have a reference, that there should be any objects to which it applies—any object falling under the concept for which it stands. There is without doubt such a thing as being midway in colour between imperial and royal blue, independently of whether there is any object which is midway between those two shades: and to say this is just to say that there is such a thing as what 'ξ is midway between imperial and royal blue' stands for. We have seen this to be a consequence of Frege's principle that if a sentence contains a part which lacks a reference, then the whole sentence will lack a reference, i.e. a truth-value, taken together with the impossibility of inferring from the the fact that there is nothing which is midway between imperial and royal blue that any sentence containing the predicate 'ξ is midway between imperial and royal blue' will be devoid of truth-value: evidently, on our assumption, 'Nothing is midway between imperial and royal blue' will be true, while 'Mr. Wilson's tie is midway between imperial and royal blue' will be false. Indeed, for the existence of *concepts*, Frege's criterion is much less strict than Strawson's. It is not even necessary that it should be logically possible that the predicate should be true of any object: the predicate may be self-contradictory, and still have a reference. The predicate 'ξ is a rational square root of 2' contains an implicit contradiction, which we draw out in proving the sentence 'Nothing is a rational square root of 2' to be true: but every well-constructed sentence, which contains this predicate and whose other parts possess a reference, will have a truth-value, so the predicate must have a reference too.   Gl 74; NS 194 (179)

It is quite different when we are talking about the existence of objects. A self-contradictory definite description—one of the form 'the α such that $F(\alpha)$' where '$F(\xi)$' is a self-contradictory predicate—cannot have a reference, and one that is logically consistent *may* not stand for anything: it will do so only if there actually is just one thing to which '$F(\xi)$' applies, not merely if it is logically possible that there should be. In particular, if a range of objects is introduced as consisting just of the values of a certain function, then Frege's criterion of existence for objects of this range coincides with Aristotle's. For instance, the range of colours, considered as objects, consists of the values of the function for which 'the colour of ξ' stands, for some material or visual object as argument. Hence the existence of a colour satisfying some condition expressed by a first-level predicate, such as 'ξ lies between imperial blue and royal blue', will depend upon the existence of some material or visual object whose colour satisfies that condition (to which the predicate applies). 'For some w, w is a colour lying between imperial and royal blue' means 'For some x, x is a material or visual object such that the colour of $\mathscr{a}$ lies between imperial and royal blue.' (Proper names of colours, like 'red' as a noun, could be introduced without use of the functional expression 'the colour of ξ', and even without the predicate 'η is a colour'. The predicate could be used in a language which lacked the functional expression, in connection with colours identified as being in certain places or seen from certain places; hence there could be quantification over colours without appeal to the use of the functional expression. But every colour whose existence would be recognized by the speakers of this language would in fact be a value of the function for some argument.)

It does not, indeed, follow that for Frege the existence of an object is always a contingent matter. For Frege there are 'logical objects'—objects the assertion of whose existence is analytically true, i.e. true in virtue of logical laws alone. (More strictly, there are predicates such that it is analytic that they apply to a unique object.) My reason for stressing this point about the criterion of existence is that it is of importance to the philosophy of mathematics, and in particular to Frege's method of constructing arithmetic from logic. Numbers, like colours, may be considered in two ways. On the one hand, there are expressions in which number-words occur as adjectives, in particular the series of expressions 'There are 0 ...', 'There is just one ...', 'There are just two ...', ..., 'There are $\aleph_0$ ...', ... These latter are predicates of second level, since what they have to be attached to in order to form a sentence is a predicative expression, not a singular term. It makes no sense to ask of an object how numerous it is: we ask of a kind of thing how many objects there are of that kind, i.e. we ask of a *concept* how many objects there are falling under it. As Frege says, to the question, 'How many are England and Wales?', we should have to reply, 'How many *what*?' Thus these expressions are, in a language using the notation of bound variables, represented by: 'There are 0 $\mathscr{a}$'s such that $\Phi(\mathscr{a})$', 'There is just one $\mathscr{a}$ such that $\Phi(\mathscr{a})$', etc.; they are expressions standing for concepts of second level.

On the other hand, in most arithmetical contexts number-words occur as nouns, i.e. as proper names: in such contexts as '28 is a perfect number', '5 divides 15', '8 is the sum of 2 and 6', and so on. These occurrences of numerals therefore stand for numbers considered as *objects*. We shall want to introduce the predicate 'ξ is a number' in order to specify the range of numerical bound variables. This we do naturally by stipulating that the range shall consist of all values of the function represented by the expression 'the number of ...'. This is again a functional expression of second level, since what has to fill the gap is a predicative expression: with bound variables it must be written 'the number of $\mathscr{a}$'s such that $\Phi(\mathscr{a})$'. Thus it stands for a

Gg II 74, 146; BW 223 (140-1)

Huss 321

Gl 57

Gl 72

function whose arguments are concepts, and whose values, like those of all functions, are objects. In order that there should be an object belonging to the range of numbers and satisfying a certain predicate '$F(\xi)$', it is necessary, then, that there should be a concept such that the number of objects falling under that concept (or, as Frege says, the number which belongs to that concept) satisfies the predicate; 'For some $\mathscr{n}$, $\mathscr{n}$ is a number such that $F(\mathscr{n})$' means 'For some $\mathscr{G}$, F [the number of $\mathscr{a}$'s such that $\mathscr{G}(\mathscr{a})$]'.

The criterion for the existence of a number considered as an object thus differs from the criterion for the existence of the corresponding second-level concept in just the same way as the criterion for the existence of a colour considered as an object differs from the criterion for the existence of the corresponding first-level concept. Suppose there were only 8 objects in the universe. Then there would still be such a thing as there being nine things of a certain kind (nine objects falling under a given concept). The second-level predicate 'There are just nine $\mathscr{a}$'s such that $\Phi(\mathscr{a})$' would still have a reference: it would be irrelevant that there would be no concept to which it applied. But the symbol '9', when used as a singular term, as the name of an object, would have no reference: for, if '9' is defined, say, as 'the number one greater than 8', there would be no concept such that the number of objects falling under it was one greater than 8.

CHAPTER 9

Indirect Reference

AS WE NOTED in Chapter 6, there are some sentences which appear to falsify the principle of extensionality for objects, the principle, namely, that from '*a* is the same as *b*' and '*F*(*a*)' we can infer '*F*(*b*)'. To take Russell's example, from 'Scott was the author of *Waverley*' and 'George IV wanted to know if Scott wrote *Waverley*' we cannot infer 'George IV wanted to know whether the author of *Waverley* wrote *Waverley*'. Since contexts which are in this way what Quine calls 'opaque' occur very frequently in substantival clauses, clauses governed by 'that' or 'whether', Frege refers to the topic as that of 'indirect speech' (*oratio obliqua*). Such clauses, constituting opaque contexts, occur not only after verbs relating to what is said or what is thought, but also after modal expressions such as 'It is necessary...', 'It is possible...', 'It is permitted...', etc. There are other opaque contexts, such as those involving modal verbs like 'must', 'need', 'may', and those involving verbs like 'want' and 'look for'. At least in some cases it is possible to render sentences involving such words by means of sentences in which the opaque contexts occur only in substantival clauses. The advantage of such a transformation is that it becomes possible to differentiate between different senses, which in natural language are distinguished by means of many ad hoc devices, in a perspicuous manner by means of the placing of quantifiers. Thus the difference between 'You may write on any page' and 'You may write on every page' is naturally represented by expressing these as 'For every x, if x is a page, then it is permitted that you write on x' and 'It is permitted that, for every x, if x is a page, you write on x'; while the ambiguity of 'I am looking for a man who has been to Ireland', which can be resolved by asking, 'Do you mean a particular man?', can be avoided if we write either 'For some x, x is a man who has been to Ireland, and I am trying to bring it about that I meet x' or 'I am trying to bring it about that, for some x, x is a man who has been to Ireland and I meet x'.

As we have seen, Frege holds that a proper name, occurring in an opaque   SB 28
context, cannot have its ordinary reference. In the sentence quoted above,
about George IV and Scott, 'George IV' indeed stands, as it usually does, for
a well-known king; but 'Scott' cannot stand, as it does elsewhere, for the
man Sir Walter Scott. For if it did, we should have to take the sentence
as saying something about that man: 'the referents of our words are what
we talk about'—we use a name to talk about the object for which it stands.
We should then have to take 'George IV wanted to know whether ξ wrote
Waverley' as a predicate which the sentence is used to assert to be true of
the man Scott. But if a predicate applies to an object, it applies to it by
whatever means we refer to that object: it cannot affect the truth or falsity of
what we say about an object how we have chosen to pick out and refer to the
object we are speaking about. In that case, given that 'the author of *Waverley*'
also (normally) stands for Sir Walter Scott, it would have to remain the
case that the sentence obtained by putting this proper name in the argument-
place of 'George IV wanted to know whether ξ wrote *Waverley*' had the
same truth-value as the original assertion.

Given, then, that a proper name occurring in an opaque context does not
have its usual reference, what does it stand for? To answer this, we must
enquire what replacements do leave the truth-value of the whole sentence
unaltered. To see this, let us consider the case of indirect speech properly
so called. If I say, 'Jones said that Scott wrote *Waverley*', I do not purport to
be giving his actual words; he may have said, 'Sir Walter Scott authored
Waverley' or 'Scott hat *Waverley* geschrieben', and my statement will
still be true. I am professing only to give the sense of Jones's words, the
thought which he expressed. Now the same considerations which applied
to singular terms occurring within indirect speech also apply to the whole
sentence which occupies the 'that'-clause. Normally, as we have seen, the
referent of a sentence is its truth-value. If you replace a part of a complex
expression by another part having the same reference as the one replaced,
the sense of the whole expression may be altered, but its reference remains
the same. Given that we know what function 'the capital of ξ' stands for,
the reference of 'the capital of Denmark' depends only on the reference,   NS 276
not the sense, of the name 'Denmark'; for the value of a given function   (255–6)
depends only on its argument, not on how the argument is referred to. So
if 'Denmark' is replaced by another singular term having the same reference,
say 'the country of which Hamlet's father was king', the referent of the
whole—the city of Copenhagen—must remain unaltered. Hence when a
sentence occurs, with its usual reference, as a constituent of a more complex
sentence, the reference of the whole must remain unaltered when the

constituent sentence is replaced by another with the same reference; that is, the truth-value of a complex sentence will remain invariant under replacement of its constituent sentences by others with the same truth-values. This is obviously the case when the complex sentence is formed out of its constituents just by the (truth-functional) sentential operators. The replacement of a sentence in indirect speech by another with the same truth-value will evidently not in general preserve the truth-value of the whole sentence; so a sentence occurring in such a clause cannot have its ordinary reference. If we ask what replacements are possible without change of truth-value, we discover what its reference in such a context is. We can alter the sentence in the *oratio obliqua* clause, without changing the truth-value of the whole, just so long as we do not change (what is ordinarily) the *sense* of the constituent sentence, so long as it continues to express the same thought. Thus what Frege calls the 'indirect' referent of a sentence—its referent when it occurs in indirect speech—must be what ordinarily constitutes its sense. And this seems entirely natural. When we use a sentence in other contexts, we are using it to express a sense (a thought), but we are not *talking about* that thought: but when I say, 'Jones said that Scott wrote *Waverley*', I am talking *about* the sense of his words, about the thought which he expressed; and I use the sentence in the subordinate clause to refer to that thought.

SB 28; NS
276 (256)

When a proper name occurs in indirect speech, therefore, those replacements of it will leave the truth-value of the whole sentence unaltered which leave (what is ordinarily) the sense of the *oratio obliqua* clause unaltered. Clearly this will happen if and only if the proper name is replaced by another which (ordinarily) has the same sense as it. It seems natural therefore to say that the indirect reference of a singular term is what is ordinarily its sense. The same reasoning will apply to all other constituents of an *oratio obliqua* clause—the incomplete expressions occurring in it: they, too, will stand in this context for what is ordinarily their sense. This can be seen both immediately, since a predicate in indirect speech can be replaced, without a change in the truth-value of the whole sentence, only by a predicate which ordinarily has the same sense; and mediately, since the whole *oratio obliqua* clause stands for its ordinary sense, and its constituent singular terms stand for theirs, the sense of a sentence is built up out of the senses of its constituent parts, and the reference of the whole is determined by the reference of the parts.

According to Frege, the sense of an expression determines its reference. He therefore argues that, since expressions occurring in indirect speech do not have their ordinary reference, the sense they have in this context cannot be their ordinary sense, either; he calls the sense which they carry in indirect speech their 'indirect sense'. Now there is in Russell's famous essay 'On Denoting' a criticism of Frege's distinction between sense and reference, which Russell, inappositely, renders by his own terms 'meaning' and 'denotation' (in fact, Russell's 'meaning' is much closer to Frege's 'reference'). This criticism is extremely confused; but at least we can extract from it a valid criticism of Frege's doctrine of indirect sense and reference, as he stated it. Russell points out that, on Frege's own principles, 'there is no   *LK* 50 backward road' from reference to sense: sense determines reference, but reference does not determine sense. What, then, is the indirect sense of an expression? Frege has told us what its indirect referent is, namely its ordinary sense; but that is not enough to determine what its indirect sense is to be. It is clear that there is no way available to state what the *sense* of an expression when it occurs in opaque contexts is to be taken to be. One might try saying that since 'Socrates', when it occurs in opaque contexts, stands for what, in transparent contexts, is its sense, its sense in opaque contexts must be the same as the sense, in transparent contexts, of that expression which, in those contexts, stands for its ordinary sense: i.e. that the indirect sense of 'Socrates' is the same as the ordinary sense of 'the sense of "Socrates"'; but this is rather implausible. Now consider expressions in double *oratio obliqua*, e.g. 'Scott' in 'Russell said that George IV wondered whether Scott wrote *Waverley*'. Since 'Scott' occurs within the clause following 'said that . . .', by Frege's doctrine it must here stand for the sense it would have in that clause taken as a complete sentence, i.e. in the sentence 'George IV wondered whether Scott wrote *Waverley*'. But in this sentence 'Scott' has its indirect sense; so in the longer sentence it must stand for its indirect sense. Thus in the longer sentence 'Scott' will have a doubly indirect reference (and a doubly indirect sense); its doubly indirect referent will be its (simply) indirect sense, which in turn stands for its (simply) indirect referent, i.e. its ordinary sense. Since we cannot say what the simply indirect sense of an expression is, we cannot even say what its *referent* is when it occurs in double *oratio obliqua*; it would seem to follow that we cannot even know how to judge the truth-value of a sentence involving double *oratio obliqua*. This constitutes a reductio ad absurdum of the whole theory.

There is, however, a simple emendation which can be made to the doctrine, which, with only a small perturbation in the system, dispels the objection. The whole difficulty arises from the principle that the reference of an expression must be determined from its sense alone: it is only by means of this principle that it was possible to deduce, from the fact that the reference of an expression differs when it occurs in transparent and when it occurs

in opaque contexts, that it must have different senses in the two contexts
also. What reason is there for holding to this principle? One arrives at it
by asking, 'What else is there about an expression, other than its sense,
which could be relevant to determining its reference?' Obviously not its
physical properties—its length, euphony or spelling—nor again its tone;
nor its grammatical properties, save in so far as these characterize its sense:
since these and related features appear to exhaust its properties, it appears
that we are left only with its sense as what could determine its reference.
Gl x   But this appearance arises only because we have been 'asking after its
reference in isolation' from the contexts of the sentences in which it occurs,
which Frege expressly forbids. According to Frege, a word does not have a
reference *on its own*, 'considered in isolation': it has a reference only in the
context of a sentence. It is fully harmonious with this view to hold that,
while a word or expression *by itself* has a sense, it does not by itself have a
reference at all: only a particular occurrence of a word or expression in a
sentence has a reference, and this reference is determined jointly by the
sense of the word and the kind of context in which it occurs. The sense of a
word may thus be such as to determine it to stand for one thing in one kind
of context, and for a different thing in some other kind of context. We may
therefore regard an expression occurring in an opaque context as having the
same sense as in a transparent context, though a different reference. The
sense of a word cannot vary from context to context, but is a property of
the word itself, apart from any context: for it is by knowing the sense of the
constituent words, independently of their occurrence in *this* sentence, that
we understand the sentence. If the sense of a word varied from context to
context, this would have to be according to some general rule, if we were
to understand the sentences in which it occurs: and then this general rule
would in reality constitute the *one* common sense which the word possessed.
It is true that we do speak of an ambiguous word as varying in sense from
one context to another. But this is just the case in which we cannot be sure
of understanding aright the sense of the sentences in which the word occurs.
The sense of an ambiguous word is not *determined* by the context; rather, the
context provides grounds for guessing which sense is intended.

With this emendation, there is no such thing as the indirect sense of a
word: there is just its sense, which determines it to have in transparent
contexts a reference distinct from this sense, and in opaque contexts a
referent which coincides with its sense. There is therefore no reason to
think that an expression occurring in double *oratio obliqua* has a sense or a
reference different from that which it has in single *oratio obliqua*: its referent
in double *oratio obliqua* will be the sense which it has in single *oratio obliqua*,

which is the same as the sense it has in ordinary contexts, which is the same as its referent in single *oratio obliqua*. This is intuitively reasonable: the replacements of an expression in double *oratio obliqua* which will leave the truth-value of the whole sentence unaltered are—just as in single *oratio obliqua*—those which have the same sense. The view that doubly indirect sense and reference must be distinguished from simply indirect sense and reference was a mechanical deduction from a slightly faulty theory.

Let us use the expression 'modal logic' to refer to a formal logic containing symbols for expressions inducing opaque contexts for whole sentences. These expressions are of two kinds: sentential operators such as 'It is necessary that . . .', 'It is morally permissible that . . .', and so on; and verbs like '. . . believes that . . .', '. . . tries to bring it about that . . .', '. . . wants it to be the case that . . .', etc. These latter expressions are doubly incomplete: the first argument-place is to be filled by a proper name standing for a person, the second by a sentence. (They may, in accordance with a suggestion by Timothy Potts, be called 'relators'.) Let us now ask: What sort of contribution did Frege make to modal logic?

A logician might be inclined to answer: None. The correct answer is: Precisely the opposite contribution to that which he made to the logic of generality. In the case of generality, he solved the problem which had baffled all earlier logicians by recognizing the need to devise a notation of an entirely different kind from that of natural language; having devised such a notation, he formalized the rules of inference governing it, and sketched, though not in rigorous fashion, the semantics of a language employing it. Now once we have observed (what is implicit in Frege's restriction of attention to instances of grammatical *oratio obliqua*) that opaque contexts are best represented as occurring only in whole clauses governed by modal operators or relators, and have adopted Frege's notation for generality, we have already advanced a long way towards a satisfactory notation for modal logic. (Admittedly, it is by no means demonstrable that all sentences containing opaque contexts can be transformed into ones in which these occur only as parts of whole opaque clauses: this is no more than a hope.) In the case of modal logic, unlike that of generality, Frege neither formulated rules of inference, nor took any additional steps to devise a new notation: instead, he provided a semantic model whereby we could understand the notation of natural language, once emended in these two ways, as perfectly in order. If we do not have Frege's conception of direct and indirect reference— that the *same* expression may in different contexts stand for different entities—we are naturally led, in any attempt to formalize modal logic, into paradoxical results. For instance, a great many formal systems of modal logic embody the absurd principle that every true statement of identity is necessarily true. Starting with the evident logical truth:

(1)   Necessarily Scott was Scott

and the true hypothesis:

(2)   Scott was the author of *Waverley*,

they permit the inference to:

(3)   Necessarily Scott was the author of *Waverley*.

This inference is licensed by the principle of extensionality: from the true statement of identity (2), and the fact, expressed in (1), that the predicate 'Necessarily Scott was ξ' applies to the reference of 'Scott', we are permitted to conclude that this predicate applies to the referent of 'the author of *Waverley*'. (The same argument would lead us to infer from (2) and the fact that George IV believed that Scott was Scott, that George IV believed that Scott was the author of *Waverley*.) The principle of extensionality is accepted because it appears evident that, if a predicate is true of the referent of a name, then it must also be true of the referent of any other name which has the same reference. It is true that the above result can be avoided if we treat definite descriptions according to Russell's Theory of Descriptions, and not, in Frege's way, as genuine proper names: but the same result would follow if we put 'Afla' and 'Ateb' for 'Scott' and 'the author of *Waverley*'; and, moreover, these logical systems usually yield as a theorem the general statement:

> For every *a* and every *w*, if *a* is the same as *w*,
> then necessarily *a* is the same as *w*.

These results no longer follow when we adopt Frege's theory of indirect reference: we no longer think it follows from the truth of (2) that the second occurrence of 'Scott' in (1) has the same reference as 'the author of *Waverley*' in (3), and hence that (3) must follow from (1) and (2). We may indeed adopt a principle of extensionality in our logical system, that from '*a* is the same as *b*' and '*F*(*a*)', '*F*(*b*)' can be inferred: but we must restrict its application to the case in which none of those occurrences of '*a*' in '*F*(*a*)' which are to be replaced by '*b*' are in opaque contexts (the latter syntactically defined). Once we adopt Frege's theory, we make such restrictions on the principle of extensionality with a clear conscience: they no longer appear as ad hoc devices imposed only to avoid paradoxical consequences, but as possessing a clear rationale.

From this it is evident that, from Frege's standpoint, there *could* not be any counter-example to the principle of extensionality, either for objects or for functions. Indeed, in view of the existence of opaque contexts, it would be false to say that, if one sentence is formed from another by replacing one or more occurrences of, e.g., some predicate by another predicate with the same (direct) reference, the two sentences must have the same truth-value. But there can be no counter-example to the principle when it is stated in the following way: that if one sentence is formed from another by replacing certain occurrences of a predicate by another predicate which has the same reference as the replaced predicate in each of those occurrences, then the truth-values must be the same. If we have any apparent counter-example we must conclude that in the occurrences in question, the reference of the predicate is *not* after all the same. If the predicates have the same extension, i.e. if the concepts which they (directly) stand for bear to one another the relation analogous to identity, then the fact that some replacement alters the truth-value will show only that the context in question is, contrary to first appearances, opaque. Conversely, if the context is admittedly opaque, the fact that a replacement changes the truth-value will show only that the predicates do not after all have the same sense. It was for this reason that I asserted that Frege *could* not admit an exception to the principle of extensionality for concepts any more than for objects. Indeed, in his formal system there are no opaque contexts; so there would have to be no qualification to the obvious formulation of the principle of extensionality for concepts in that system.

It may be objected that the notion of indirect reference does not yield a coherent account of quantification into opaque contexts. By this is meant the use of quantifiers, themselves in a transparent context, which bind variables occurring in an opaque context. There is a sharp difference in sense—and in truth-conditions—between, e.g., 'It is possible that, for some x, x will never cease to exist' and 'For some x, it is possible that x will never cease to exist'. The former involves only quantification *within* an opaque context, and means that it is logically possible that there should be something which will never pass out of existence; the latter involves quantification *into* an opaque context, and means that, among the objects which there actually are, there is at least one of which it is logically possible that it should never pass out of existence. In 'Reference and Modality' Quine calls sentences involving quantification into opaque contexts *senseless*; but they certainly cannot be senseless, since a number of locutions which occur constantly and are apparently well understood, involve quantification into opaque contexts. The problem is not to decide whether they are meaningful or not, but to find a framework within which to give a satisfactory semantic account of their meaning. An example is 'Marlowe does not know who murdered Tremayne'. This may be rendered 'For every x, Marlowe does not know that x murdered Tremayne': it certainly does not mean, e.g., 'Marlowe does not know that, for some x, x murdered Tremayne', i.e. 'Marlowe does not know that someone murdered Tremayne'. Another example is given by

MA 92-3 Geach, following Russell: 'There are more people here than I expected.' This means 'For some n, there are more than n people here, and I expected that there would be at most n people here', and certainly not, 'I expected that, for some n, there would be more than n people here and there would be at most n people here.'

It is not difficult to explain, within the theory of indirect reference, those sentences in which all the occurrences of the variable, other than the occurrence immediately next to the quantifier, are within an opaque, and not also in a transparent, context. The variable in 'For every x, Marlowe does not know that x murdered Tremayne' must range over the *senses* of personal proper names, not over what are ordinarily their referents, i.e. people: it must range over everything that could be the referent of a personal proper name when inserted in the blank of 'Marlowe does not know that . . . murdered Tremayne'. Here 'proper name' must be understood in its strict sense, not in Frege's extended sense: the variable cannot range over the senses of all definite descriptions of people, or other complex singular terms for people; for it may be that just one person murdered Tremayne, and Marlowe knows this, so that the sentence 'Marlowe knows that the murderer of Tremayne murdered Tremayne' is certainly true, without its being true that Marlowe knows *who* murdered Tremayne; or, again, Marlowe may know that the man with whom Tremayne had an appointment at 11 o'clock murdered Tremayne, but still not know who murdered him.

Even in such cases, however, there are two possible interpretations. Even if we ignore the possible slurring over of the difference between disbelieving something and simply not believing it, there is a treble, and not merely a double, ambiguity in such a sentence as 'He does not believe anyone to be perfect'. It may mean, 'He does not believe that, for some x, x is perfect', or it may mean, 'For every x, he does not believe that x is perfect'. The latter interpretation means that there is no *particular* person whom he believes to be perfect, which is quite compatible with his believing that there is *someone* who is perfect. But this second interpretation can itself be taken in two ways. Suppose he is a child who believes in Santa Claus, and he believes that Santa Claus (but no one else) is perfect: are we to say that 'For every $\varkappa$, he does not believe that $\varkappa$ is perfect' is false or true? That is, given that the variable '$\varkappa$' is to range over the senses of personal proper names, should it range over every sense that a proper name could have, including such a name as 'Santa Claus', or only over those senses to which a genuine referent corresponds, i.e. over the senses of names of *actual* people? If we adopt the first interpretation, then we might say that the second interpretation is properly to be rendered by 'For every $\varkappa$, if $\varkappa$ exists, then he does not believe that $\varkappa$ is perfect'. This obviously affects the previous example concerning possibility. If the variable in 'For some $\varkappa$, it is possible that $\varkappa$ should never cease to exist' is taken as ranging over the senses of all singular terms, including those which have no reference, then the sentence is hardly to be distinguished from 'It is possible that, for some $\varkappa$, $\varkappa$ should never cease to exist'. The contrast we drew between them depended on the tacit assumption that, in the first sentence of the pair, the variable ranged only over the senses of those singular terms which in fact stand for something; and it may be thought that what was intended would be more properly expressed by writing, 'For some $\varkappa$, $\varkappa$ exists and it is possible that $\varkappa$ should never cease to exist'.

We cannot dispense altogether with that interpretation of quantification into opaque contexts in which the variable has to be taken as ranging over the senses of terms which lack a reference, for there are cases in which such an interpretation is clearly required: if a historian attributes the invention of the ancient Egyptian economic system to Joseph, then there is evidently a sense in which he attributes its invention to a particular person, irrespective of whether Joseph is taken to be a genuine historical character. Since, however, we appear to have a means of rendering the stricter interpretation in terms of this wider one, namely by the use of ' . . . exists' as a predicate, it seems natural to take the wider interpretation as the one that is always required. But, apart from any qualms we may have about such a use of 'exists', this would demand that we always understood sentences calling for the stricter interpretation as implicitly involving simultaneous quantification into an opaque and a transparent context. Such quantification also occurs in the example about expecting fewer people: in the sentence, 'For some n, there are more than n people here, and I expected that there would be at most n', the variable 'n' occurs both in an opaque context and in a transparent one other than next to the quantifier itself. This appears to present a difficulty of construal. For, in its occurrence in the transparent context, 'there are more than n people here', 'n' must surely range over numbers, not over the senses of numerals; it must, that is, range over the referents of expressions which could fill the gap in 'There are more than . . . people here'. But in its occurrence in the opaque context, 'I expected that there would be at most *n* people', it must range over the *senses* of numerals (not, of course, over the senses of all numerical expressions), that is, over the referents of numerals as occurring in the gap of 'I expected that there would be at most . . . people here'. How can the same variable range over different domains in distinct occurrences?

Evidently, it cannot. Since, then, sense determines reference but not conversely, it appears that we must say that the variable ranges over the senses of numerals in both occurrences, in the transparent as well as the opaque context. But, in this case, the predicate 'there are more than ν people here' which forms the transparent context must be interpreted as having a special referent, not its ordinary one: namely as standing for a concept under which fall just the senses of those numerals which ordinarily stand for numbers of which the predicate, 'there are more than ν people here', taken as having its ordinary reference, is true. (It is unnecessary, for the present discussion, to determine the logical type of number-words as used adjectivally in such contexts, and hence the level of the predicates whose argument-places they fill.) Moreover, it will become necessary to apply the same analysis to an unquantified sentence like 'There are more than 9 people here and I expected that there would be at most 9 people here': for we are in effect holding that we can apply, to the complex predicate 'There are more than ν people here and I expected that there would be at most ν people here', formed from such a sentence by omission of both occurrences of the numeral, a quantifier binding a variable ranging over senses of numerals; hence, in the unquantified sentence, the numeral must in both occurrences have its indirect reference, i.e. stand for its sense. Therefore in the unquantified sentence also the predicate 'there are more than ν people here' must have its special reference.

It is to be noted that this 'special referent' does not coincide with the 'oblique' referent, as defined by Frege. The oblique referent of the predicate is the sense of the predicate when taken as having its ordinary reference. If, in such a sentence as 'Jones believes that there are more than 9 people here', the expression 'there are more than ν people here' is taken as having its special reference, as explained above, and '9' is taken as having its oblique reference, i.e. as standing for its sense, then the whole phrase, 'there are more than 9 people here', must be taken as standing for one or other truth-value, according as there are or are not more than 9 people present; and then it ought to be possible, by parity of reasoning, to replace, without loss of truth-value for the whole sentence, the clause governed by 'that' by any other sentence with the same truth-value; and this it patently is not. The whole point of introducing the notion of special reference is to nullify the effect of taking the variable which fills the argument-place of the predicate as ranging over the senses of numerals, or of taking the numeral which fills its argument-place in the unquantified sentence as having its indirect reference: that is, to restore to the clause standing in the transparent context the reference—namely, a truth-value—which it would have if all its constituents were taken as having their direct reference. A predicate within an opaque context can therefore not be taken as having its special reference, as here defined, because a clause in indirect speech is required to stand for a thought, and not a truth-value.

Since it would be possible to attach a quantifier to any predicate formed from a sentence part of which constituted an opaque context, we shall end up with the following account: Within any opaque context, all expressions have their indirect reference; within any transparent context occurring in a sentence in which an opaque context also occurs, all names have their indirect reference, and all primitive incomplete expressions have their special reference. Such a theory appears to work out; but it has become cumbrous, and its cumbrousness threatens its credibility, just as that of the medieval theory of *suppositio* eventually destroyed its credibility, more than any defect in its operation. Moreover, the theory calls into question once more the whole notion of the ordinary reference of proper names, when occurring in purely extensional sentences, as being to their bearers. For we have been driven to allow that, in certain transparent contexts, incomplete expressions have to be taken as being defined, not over the (ordinary) referents of the names which fill their argument-places, but over the senses of those names. But, if such an account can be made to work, why can it not be generalized to all occurrences of those incomplete expressions? Would it not be simpler to take every predicate and other incomplete expression as having its special reference in all transparent contexts, so that the notion of the (direct) reference of a name will drop out of account altogether, and all we shall ever be concerned with is the sense of the name?

This suggestion seems tempting; but it is not coherent. The notion of special reference has in fact been explained only by invoking the notion of the ordinary reference, both of the predicate and of the name which fills its argument-place: the special referent of a predicate '$F(\xi)$' is a concept under which the sense of a name 'a' falls just in case the ordinary referent of the name 'a' falls under the concept which is the ordinary referent of the predicate '$F(\xi)$'. Moreover, the notion of the sense of a name is given as consisting in our means of recognizing something as its referent; we cannot retain the notion of sense, while suppressing that of (ordinary) reference; if we lose the notion of reference, we thereby lose that of sense, for sense is just the way in which reference is presented. Even if this is granted, it might be thought an accident that we explained the notion of special reference via that of ordinary reference; there must, it would seem, be some predicates which are understood as defined directly over the senses of names, rather than over their ordinary referents, just because there exist intensional predicates. But even this conclusion fails if it is possible to render all sentences containing intensional contexts by ones in which the intensional context is a whole constituent sentence: and this gives an additional motive for hoping that such transformations are always possible. If the transformation is always possible, then all intensional contexts are to be explained in terms of predicates or relational expressions defined over thoughts: we need an explanation of when someone believes a thought to be true, asserts it to be true, tries to bring it about that it is true, etc., and also of when a thought is necessarily true, in various senses of 'necessary'; but we do not have to consider any primitive predicates or relational expressions as being defined over the senses of expressions smaller than whole sentences. Thus, for instance, we understand the complex predicate 'Charles intended ξ to be present', i.e. 'Charles intended that ξ should be present', as defined over senses of personal proper names, because we understand what it is to intend a thought to be true, and we understand how the sense of a personal proper name, e.g. 'John', contributes to the determination of the thought expressed by the result of putting it in the argument-place of 'ξ is present', e.g. by 'John is present'.

But there is, in any case, a further difficulty, arising from the possibility of higher-level quantification. Consider first the sentence, 'There is someone here I did not expect'. This calls for the analysis, '$\exists x$ (x is here and I did not expect that x would be here)'. Accordingly, we must take 'x' as ranging over the senses of personal proper names, and the predicate 'ξ is here' as having, in the transparent context, its special reference. The quantified sentence is true just in case some unquantified sentence such as 'John is here and I did not expect that John would be here' is true: accordingly, in any such sentence, 'John' must be taken, in both occurrences, as standing for its sense, and the predicate 'ξ is here', in the transparent context, as once more having its special reference. But from the unquantified sentence we can also infer 'John is something that I did not expect he would be' (namely, here), which is to be analysed as '$\exists f$ [f(John) and I did not expect that f(John)]'. Since the predicate, 'ξ would be here', in the opaque context in the unquantified sentence is required to have an indirect reference, i.e. to stand for the sense of the predicate 'ξ is here', it follows that the variable '$\mathscr{f}$' must be taken as ranging over the senses of predicates. But, since it is also required to occupy the argument-place, in a transparent context, of the second-level predicate 'Φ(John)', it follows, by the same reasoning as before, that in the original unquantified sentence the predicate 'ξ is here', in the transparent context, must have its indirect reference. But this is a contradiction, since we have already decided that, in that original sentence, the predicate must have its special reference, and have remarked that special reference and indirect reference cannot be identified.

The upshot of this is that we have to see the entire context, apparently transparent but occurring within a sentence in which an opaque context also occurs, as in reality opaque, with all the expressions contained in it having their indirect reference, the effect of the disguised opacity of the context being undone, not by any special reference possessed by any of its parts, but by the tacit application to the whole of a single operation mapping sense on to reference. Such an operation might be expressed by 'It is true that ...' (without any presumption that this phrase is always to be thought of as inducing an opaque context), construed as converting any expression standing for a thought into one standing for the corresponding truth-value. Thus 'John is here and I did not expect that John would be here' is to be analysed as 'It is true that John is here, and I did not expect that John would be here', where both 'that'-clauses constitute opaque contexts, and the scope of the first 'that' does not extend over the conjunction. The entire clause 'that John is here' then stands for the thought expressed by 'John is here', and the phrase 'It is true ...' is to be construed as a predicate true of true thoughts and false of false ones. The notion of special reference now falls away as unnecessary.

Apart from quantification into opaque contexts which ranges only over the senses of those names which have reference, there are other sentences involving, upon analysis though not superficially, quantification simultaneously into an opaque and a transparent context. Consider, for instance, such a sentence as 'Paul called the Governor of California a racist'. This cannot be interpreted as meaning 'Paul said that the Governor of California was a racist': for Paul may not have referred to the individual of whom he was speaking as the Governor of California, but have mentioned him by name or by some other means. It has, rather, to be analysed as 'Paul said, of the Governor of California, that he was a racist', and this can only be represented as 'For some α, α is the Governor of California and Paul said that α is a racist'.

L

Should we have qualms about treating 'exists' as a predicate in the rendering 'For some x, x exists and John believes that x is perfect' of 'John believes a particular actual individual to be perfect'? There is a prevalent misconception that Kantian arguments have shown that 'exists' cannot be taken as forming a predicate 'ξ exists'. In fact, the arguments, when rehearsed, always prove to assume the point which is really at issue. They assume, that is, that if 'exists' were a predicate, it would be a predicate that was true of everything; and they then have little difficulty in establishing that such a predicate would be very unlike others. But these arguments have little force against those views which they are intended to controvert, for instance a belief in the possibility of a valid presentation of the ontological argument for the existence of God: for these views involve, not merely that 'exists' is a predicate, but that it is a predicate which is true of some things and not of others, that is, that there are things which do not exist. Only if we assume that we can truly ascribe certain predicates to God without having first presupposed or established that he exists, can the ontological argument, at least as classically presented by Descartes and Anselm, get under way without begging the question at the outset.

The crucial question is, then, whether 'everything' (when expressing first-level generality) is synonymous with 'everything that exists' or not. Supposing the question to be resolved in favour of the first alternative, it still does not follow that 'exists' is not a predicate: for instance, if 'ξ exists' is taken to be a predicate true of everything, then, as long as 'Tame tigers

NS 70 (62)

exist' is interpreted as 'Some tame tigers exist', it will convey precisely the information that it is required to convey; 'Tame tigers do not exist' must, of course, be construed as meaning 'No tame tigers exist', as we should ordinarily grant. Even when an apparent proper name stands in the argument-place of the predicate we shall get the right result if we construe it as a disguised definite description and adopt Russell's Theory of Descriptions: if 'Dionysius' is such a disguised definite description, and 'exists' is a predicate true of everything, then 'Dionysius existed' conveys just what is intended by it, under this interpretation, and the same holds true of 'Dionysius did not exist' provided that we take 'Dionysius' as within the scope of the negation sign. Even if we adopt Frege's theory that a sentence is neither true nor false if it contains a name without reference, 'Dionysius existed' will be true just in case 'Dionysius' has a reference, although, unfortunately, 'Dionysius did not exist' can never be true.

It is, of course, the case that, if we take 'exists' as being a predicate which is true of everything, then the informational content of a sentence containing the word 'exists' will never include the fact that the predicate 'exists' is true of any given object or objects: for this will never be news. And just this is what all the arguments which purport to prove that 'exists' is not a predicate amount to. If I say, 'Some tame tigers growl', and you believe me, then you will learn, if you did not know it already, that some, among those objects which share the properties of being tame and of being a tiger, also have the property of growling; but if I say, '(Some) tame tigers exist', you will not learn that, among those objects which you know to share the properties of being tame and of being a tiger, there are some that have the further property of existing; you will learn, if you learn anything at all, that there are objects which share the first two properties; and, if you knew this already, you will learn nothing. But this does not show that 'exists' cannot be interpreted as standing for a property which everything has (a concept under which every object falls): if we suppose that it does show this, we are making too crude an identification of the informational content of a sentence and its truth-conditions. Of course, the informational content of a sentence as a whole is determined by its truth-conditions as a whole: but that does not mean that what we learn from the sentence is just that the grammatical predicate is true of the objects to which the grammatical subject applies. An exact parallel is provided by Frege's account of statements of identity. The sign of identity is taken by Frege as standing for a relation which everything has to itself and nothing has to anything else. The informational content of a statement of identity can therefore never amount to a particular object's having the relation of identity to itself, for this is never news. Rather, it is just in virtue of the truth-conditions for statements of identity that we may learn from them that two names with different senses have the same object as their referent. It does not follow, as Frege originally maintained in *Begriffsschrift*, that the sign of identity has to be taken as standing for a relation between names (or between their senses, as he would later have said): that would be, again, to make too simple a connection between informational content and truth-conditions. Rather, it is just through our grasp of that relation between objects for which the sign of identity stands that we are able to derive, from the truth of a statement of identity, that a certain relation obtains between the senses of two names. In just the same way, it is precisely by taking 'exists' to stand for a property which every object has that we are able to endow sentences containing it with just the informational content that they carry: to derive from the truth of 'Tame tigers exist' that 'ξ is a tame tiger' is a predicate which applies to something, and from 'King Arthur existed' that 'King Arthur' is a name which has a reference.

The most telling objection to the thesis that 'exists' is a predicate which applies to some things but not to others derives from the experience of Meinong in his ill-fated attempt to maintain that thesis. The thesis goes, of course, with taking our expressions of generality as ranging, not only over actual, but also over merely possible (and, in Meinong's case, also over impossible) objects, and with taking names which lack an actual referent as standing for a merely possible (or, again, perhaps an impossible) one. In that case, we are faced with the problem when a predicate is to be held to apply to a non-existent object: and the answer which forces itself on us is that it must apply whenever its doing so follows from the mere sense of the name of the object. It is precisely from making just this move that, as we have seen, the ontological argument starts. But now, if 'exists' is a predicate like any other, there is no reason why the requirement of satisfying this predicate may not be incorporated into the sense of some complex name; indeed, there is nothing to prevent us inserting, at the beginning of any definite description, the word 'existent': and it will then appear that we are committed to the thesis that true sentences result from putting any such complex proper name into the argument-place of 'ξ exists', i.e. that the referents of all these complex proper names exist.

No such trouble arises in our case. We have taken quantifiers which effect quantification into opaque contexts as binding variables which range over the senses of proper names, including those which lack a reference; but, to take care of those cases in which, in effect, the range of the variable is restricted to proper names which have a reference, we proposed construing such cases as having a tacit additional clause using the predicate 'ξ exists'. In such a case—for instance, 'For some α, α exists and John believes that α is perfect'—the variable that occurs in the argument-place of 'ξ exists' is ranging over the senses of names, and so 'ξ exists' must here be interpreted as standing for a concept under which fall the senses of just those names which have a reference; and thus quite differently from the interpretation discussed above, as standing for a concept under which every object falls. But, even where a definite description is an allowable replacement for the variable, we are going to run into no trouble of the kind that Meinong had. If we replace the variable 'α' in the argument-place of 'ξ exists' by 'the existent golden mountain', we do not get a clause which we have any reason to take as true. The 'existent' which occurs in this definite description has to be identified with that predicate which is true of everything, and so its insertion does not alter the content of the definite description 'the golden mountain' at all: the whole definite description continues to have a sense to which no referent corresponds, and so the clause 'the existent golden mountain exists' is straightforwardly false, and no paradox arises.

If it seems troubling to interpret the word 'existent' in a manner divergent from that in which, in such a context, the word 'exists' is being understood, this can be avoided by allowing that the predicate 'ξ exists' always stands for a property that every object has, and regarding the whole clause 'α exists' (or, equally, 'the (existent) golden mountain exists') as governed by our operator 'it is true that . . . ' which induces an opaque context but nullifies its effect. At least, this can be done so long as we agree to count an atomic sentence containing a name without a reference as false, and its negation as true. The sentence, 'The golden mountain exists', is then plain false, and it makes no difference whether 'existent' be inserted after the definite article or not; and the same remains the case when we throw the whole sentence into a technically opaque context by prefacing it with the words 'It is true that . . . '.

The reason why an appeal to such a use of the verb 'exists' would land us in no trouble, such as that which beset Meinong, is precisely that here all is being done in the context of Frege's theory. In Frege's theory, the sense of a name consists of the means we have provided for determining an actual (existent) object as its referent. This sense can, in certain special contexts, become the (indirect) referent of the name, the referent which it has in that context: but this is quite different from holding that a name always has an *object*, of the kind which it purports to name, as its referent, but that this object may not be actual, but may be merely possible or even impossible. For Meinong, the name 'King Arthur' has only one referent in all contexts, and this referent is certainly a man, though he may never have existed, but merely have been possible. For Frege, the name may or may not have a direct referent, according to historical fact; but its indirect referent, when it has it, is nothing like a man, being the sense of a word, and is just as actual as anything else. There is therefore, within Frege's theory, no motivation for supposing that, even when a name has its indirect referent, any predicate contained in it must be true of that referent.

It may be objected that Frege's theory of indirect reference has in fact made no contribution to the development of modal logic; that the idea which proved effective in providing a semantics for modal logic was the totally different one of possible worlds. The essentials of this are as follows. Suppose that we have a (first-order) language which has, in addition to the ordinary logical constants, a single unary modal operator '$\Box$'. To avoid complications, we suppose that quantification into modal contexts is not permitted: any sentence is built up from non-modal sentences by application of '$\Box$' and the sentential operators only. For the sake of example, let us read '$\Box$' as 'Castro knows that . . . ', and let us suppose that we have both a model

W for the true non-modal sentences, and a determinate intended assignment U of truth-values to all sentences of the form '$\Box A$', which we call 'pseudo-atomic' sentences. By use of the standard truth-tables, U determines a valuation of all modal sentences of the language. We shall call any truth-value assignment V to the pseudo-atomic sentences 'admissible' if the set of sentences 'A' such that V assigns to '$\Box A$' the value *true* is both consistent and closed under the relation of *modal consequence*; where a sentence 'B' is a modal consequence of a set Γ if it is derivable from Γ by the standard natural deduction rules for first-order logic together with the rule that, if 'D' is derivable from 'C_1', . . . , 'C_n' (n $\geq$ O), then '$\Box D$' is derivable from '$\Box C_1$', . . . , '$\Box C_n$'. We assume that the 'correct' truth-value assignment U to the pseudo-atomic sentences is admissible. This assumption is, indeed, not at all plausible with respect to the interpretation of '$\Box$' which we took as our example; it involves that Castro knows the truth of every modal consequence of whatever he knows.

We shall call the ordered pair (W,U) 'the real world'. Now let M be any structure for the non-modal part of the language, with the same domain as W, in which all non-modal sentences 'A' such that U assigns to '$\Box A$' the value *true* are true; and let V be any admissible truth-value assignment to the pseudo-atomic sentences such that every modal sentence 'B' for which U assigns the value *true* to '$\Box B$' comes out true under V. Then we shall call the ordered pair (M,V) a 'possible world'. We are concerned with the totality of all such possible worlds. In terms of our example, a possible world is just a structure for the extensional fragment of the language, and a truth-value assignment to its pseudo-atomic sentences, consistent with what Castro knows: i.e., everything that Castro knows must be true in such a world, but truth-values may be distributed among sentences which Castro does not know to be true in any way whatever, provided that the controlling assumption is maintained, that the set of sentences known by Castro to be true (in this possible world) is consistent and closed under modal consequence. It is then easily seen that a sentence '$\Box A$' holds in the real world (W,U) just in case 'A' holds in every possible world (M,V).

We now reiterate the procedure, that is, we extend the absolute notion of a possible world to that of a world (M',V') possible relative to a given world (M,V). (M',V') is such a world if M' is any structure, with the same domain as W, for the non-modal sentences, in which all such sentences 'A' for which V assigns to '$\Box A$' the value *true* are true, and V' is any admissible truth-value assignment to the pseudo-atomic sentences such that every modal sentence 'B' for which V assigns the value *true* to '$\Box B$' comes out true under V'. Then it can in the same way be easily seen that any sentence '$\Box A$'

holds in the world (M,V) just in case 'A' holds in every world (M',V') possible relative to (M,V).

It might be thought that we should need to impose special conditions on possible worlds to reflect the properties of particular modal operators. For instance, it is agreed by all that no one can know something that is false, and it might therefore be thought that, for the interpretation 'Castro knows that . . . ' of '□', we should need to require that, in any world (M,V), if V assigned the value *true* to '□A', then 'A' must come out true under M and V; i.e. that '□A → A' must come out true in every world (M,V). But this is not so. Of course, since everything that Castro knows *is* true, '□A → A' will come out true, for every 'A', in the real world (W,U). If, furthermore, for any given 'A', Castro knows that, if he knows that 'A' is true, then 'A' is true, that is, if '□(□A → A)' is true in the real world, then '□A → A' will be true in every world (M,V) which is possible relative to the real world, and we do not need any special provision to make this the case. If, on the other hand, for some 'A', Castro does not know that, if he knows that 'A' is true, then 'A' *is* true, then, for all Castro knows, it might be the case that he knew that 'A' was true, while in fact, 'A' was false: that is, a world (M,V) in which '□A' was true but 'A' false would be a world consistent with Castro's knowledge. (Of course, on our assumptions, if Castro does not know that, if he knows that 'A' is true, then 'A' is true, then he cannot know that 'A' is true. For '□A → A' is a logical consequence of 'A'—we are interpreting the connective '→' classically—and we have assumed that the set of sentences known by Castro to be true is closed under logical consequence. Thus there can be no objection to a world (M,V), possible relative to the real world, in which 'A' is false.)

Thus, given any modal operator '□' satisfying our condition that the set of sentences 'A' such that '□A' is (really) true is consistent and closed under modal consequence, we can describe a system of ordered pairs (M,V) over which is defined a relation of relative possibility; and, in terms of such a system, we can give a semantics for the operator '□', namely that '□A' is true in any world (M,V) just in case 'A' is true in every world (M',V') possible relative to it. Conversely, we are unable to do this for any modal operator that does not satisfy our condition. Once we have the general idea, then, indeed, certain questions arise about the structure of the system of possible worlds corresponding to each specific interpretation of the modal operator; and other questions arise about the possibility of various restrictions, simplifications or modifications of that system. A question of the first kind is whether, if 'A' is entailed by Γ in the sense of being true in every possible world in which all sentences of Γ are true, 'A' must be a modal consequence of Γ (the converse is evident). This will depend on U: e.g., 'A' is not in general a modal consequence of '$\Box$A'; yet if, for every n$\geq$o and each 'A', '$\Box^n$ ($\Box$A$\rightarrow$A)' is true in the real world ('$\Box^n$' here representing n consecutive occurrences of '$\Box$'), then 'A' will be entailed by '$\Box$A'. This in turn corresponds to a condition on the relation of relative possibility, viz. that it be reflexive. Thus entailment may coincide with a relation wider than modal consequence, specifiable by adding further rules of derivation. Hence we are led to study formalizations of modal logic, embodying such additional rules, in terms of the structures of the corresponding systems of possible worlds. A question of the second kind is whether, relative to some such modal logic, we can restrict the range of possible worlds in some manner, so as no longer to admit, as a world possible relative to a given one, *every* ordered pair (M,V) complying with the conditions laid down, while still preserving the semantic condition for the truth in a possible world of a sentence '$\Box$A'. In particular, it may be asked whether, whenever a finite set Γ does not entail a sentence 'A', a *finite* system of possible worlds for which the entailment fails always exists.

In this manner we obtain a very smooth semantic theory for different formalizations of modal logic, in which '$\Box$' represents various kinds of necessity-operator or other modal operator, by means of algebraic techniques as applied to the structures of the relational systems, consisting of possible worlds under the relation of relative possibility, which correspond to these differing formalized modal logics. But the technical facility in studying alternative principles of modal logic which is conferred on us by the use of the notion of possible worlds ought not to be allowed to obscure the fact that it is only quite rarely that it has any explanatory power at all. In fact, just because, provided that the modal operator '$\Box$' with which we start satisfies the condition that the set of sentences 'A' such that '$\Box$A' is true is consistent and closed under modal consequence, we can always define a suitable notion of possible world in terms of which a semantics for '$\Box$' can then be stated, the notion cannot have any general explanatory power. It is only in those cases in which the conception of a possible world, and of what it is for a modal or non-modal sentence to be true in such a world, can be independently explained, that the conception has any such power. Almost the only case where this is so is that in which the conception of possible worlds is forced on us by the intuitive meaning of the operator at the outset, namely the tense-logical operators, which are not modal operators in the sense of ones inducing opaque contexts, in the ordinary sense, at all. Thus, if '$\Box$' is interpreted to mean 'It will always be the case that . . . ', then it is entirely natural to give a semantics in which the possible 'worlds' are the states of the universe at all future instants of time. In this case, not every ordered pair (M,V) consistent with the truth of every 'A' such that '□A' is now true gives a description of the universe at some future instant. A restriction has been placed upon which possible worlds are admitted, just because it is here independently clear what the 'possible worlds' are: the notion has not been arrived at by invoking the conception of a description of the universe compatible with the truth of each 'A' such that '□A' is true. The only comparable case for which the notion can be independently explained is when it is used to give a semantics for intuitionistic logic, which, again, is not on the face of it a modal logic at all. In no single case, so far as I know, of a modal logic, in the strict sense of the logic of an operator inducing an opaque context, has the notion of possible worlds been used to give anything that could be recognized as an explanation of the sense of the modal operator. In fact, the opacity of modal contexts—the defining characteristic of modal operators proper (as against other non-classical ones)—is merely an embarrassment to the possible worlds conception, which throws no light on quantification into modal contexts.

In any case, the conception can be invoked only for certain operators, those, namely, satisfying the condition relating to modal consequence. The operators obtained by inserting a proper name in the first gap of ' . . . believes that . . . ', ' . . . knows that . . . ', ' . . . tries to bring it about that . . . ', and similar phrases for 'propositional attitudes', do not satisfy that condition. No one believes or knows all the logical consequences of whatever he believes or knows, or else anyone who believes (say) the axioms of Peano arithmetic would also believe all the provable theorems of that theory. We could extend the possible worlds technique even to such cases if we construed a possible world as an assignment of truth-values to all sentences that was not required to yield a classical interpretation of the logical constants; but now the picture of possible *worlds* has become quite inappropriate. But in fact it is easy to see that there cannot be a *logic* of belief or of knowledge in the ordinary sense at all. This does not mean that there cannot be a logical theory which allows the occurrence within sentences of opaque contexts induced by such expressions: it means that we cannot introduce such relators as logical constants governed by determinate axioms such as, e.g.:

$$B(x,p) \ \& \ B(x,p \rightarrow q) \rightarrow B(x,q) \ ,$$

where 'B(x,p)' abbreviates 'x believes that p'. This is because belief and knowledge are ineradicably *vague* notions. Roughly speaking, a person believes something to be the case if an expression of that belief can fairly easily be elicited from him by prompting him appropriately; and similarly

L*

for knowledge. Of course, we have to guard, on the one hand, against the cases in which we should say that the 'prompting' consisted in the presentation of new evidence for the truth of the belief, and, on the other, to allow for the cases in which an expression of the belief cannot easily be elicited because the person is embarrassed, or afraid, to profess it. But here the margin between the case in which the prompting was a mere eliciting of a belief already held, and that in which it led the person prompted to (what he took to be) a realization that the proposition in question was true, is not sharply drawn, and cannot be sharply drawn. The simplest form of prompting is the straightforward question, 'Do you believe that . . . ?'. But the response which such a question will evoke may depend heavily on the context in which it is put. Perhaps, when a certain subject is under discussion, it will elicit one answer, when another subject is the topic, another; perhaps when it is asked in a context in which the person had in the forefront of his mind that he had committed himself to two other propositions from which the one in question follows by an elementary rule of inference, it will elicit an assent, but, asked out of the blue when the person was not recalling his previously framed conclusions on related matters, a dissent. It would be a mistake to attempt a sharp delineation of the circumstances in which the eliciting of an expression of belief was to be taken as demonstrating the presence of a belief already held, because the notion of the beliefs a man holds at a given moment just is not sharp. There are propositions to which I should instantly assent, if I were presented with them and asked to give a judgment. Can I be said to believe all such propositions? We should, rightly, be reluctant to agree to this: we should argue that I can hardly be said to believe some proposition which has never occurred to me. But, certainly, I do not have to have some proposition in mind at any given moment for me to be said to believe that proposition: I may have believed it steadily for years, although only rarely have I been occupied in thinking about relevant matters. Is it, then, the fact that I at one time formulated the proposition that makes the crucial difference? Surely not: even though instantly willing to assent to it the moment I was asked, I might so totally have forgotten my earlier consideration of it that it was just as if I had never thought of it before.

Consider the following case. John and Jane are talking. There is a fact about Jane which John knows; but Jane may not know that John knows this. Or it may be that Jane does know that John knows this fact about her, but John does not realize that Jane knows this. Or, again, John may, after all, realize this, but Jane may be unaware that John realizes that she knows that he is in possession of this fact about her. Apparently, we may continue this series of suppositions indefinitely: in each case, there is a certain amount of knowledge possessed by Jane and by John, respectively, but there is some fact, which does obtain, but which one or other of them does not know. And, now, while any one of this series of descriptions may fit the actual case, it is surely possible that none of them is correct. At least, there is surely a case in which there is nothing of which either of them is unaware, in which everything is open between them: John and Jane look into one another's eyes, in a moment of complete frankness, and both realize that each of them knows just what the other knows; at least, on the score with which we are concerned! Or, after all, they may both have just been discussing, quite explicitly, the fact about Jane in question. What, then, are we to say about John and Jane? Do they both have an infinite amount of knowledge? Namely, John knows this fact about Jane, and Jane knows that John knows this fact about her, and John knows that Jane knows that John knows this fact about her, and Jane knows that John knows that Jane knows that John knows this fact about her, and so on indefinitely. It seems quite absurd to attribute to each of them an infinite amount of knowledge of this kind; and it also seems that we can agree that, in the case imagined, it would be wrong to say, of any one of the conjuncts in this infinite conjunction, that it does *not* hold, e.g. that John does *not* know that Jane knows that John knows the fact in question. To any one of the sentences in this infinite series with 'Jane' as subject, John would surely, as soon as he had succeeded in unravelling it (if he could be bothered to do so), instantly assent ; but, the greater the difficulty of unravelling the sentence, and the less likely John is to have formulated such a sentence mentally, the more reluctant are we to say that it expresses some piece of knowledge which he has, although we should still feel it misleading to say that he did *not* know it.

Can we not, however, attain sharp notions of belief and of knowledge by prescinding from the requirement that something should already have occurred to someone, in order that he may be said to believe or to know it? Could we not, that is, appeal to an idealized sense of 'belief' and of 'knowledge', under which the fact that a person would instantly assent to a proposition is a sufficient condition for his believing it to be true, or, together with other conditions distinguishing knowledge from belief, knowing it to be true, without his having had to have considered it ever before? We could do so; but it would do us little good. For, if we are set on avoiding indeterminacy, there are only two extreme ways in which we can avoid the indeterminacy produced by the dependence of assent upon context. Either we say that we shall count a person as believing something only if he would assent to it, if directly asked, in any context whatsoever, and, then, of course, if the definition is taken seriously, it will have the result that there is hardly anything that anyone believes at all, for there will always be circumstances so distracting as to prevent the amount of attention or consideration, however minimal, being given; or we say that we shall count a person as believing something provided that he would assent to it in some context which did not involve the production of new evidence. If we say the latter, then we shall be led to notions of belief and of knowledge such that a person's beliefs or items of knowledge are closed under logical consequence, at least first-order consequence. For the whole point of proof is that it provides a series of contexts in which, without the production of any new external evidence, the assent to each line of the proof is inevitably elicited from anyone who had followed the proof to that stage; anyone who understands the language will, having assented to earlier lines, and having that assent freshly in mind, assent to the next line: and the completeness theorem for first-order logic assures us that, for any first-order consequence of a set of premisses, there exists a proof of it from them employing only elementary transitions which must be granted by anyone who understands the language.

Moreover, nothing that has been said so far has yet faced the fundamental fact about belief (one which does not concern knowledge), that what we may in some contexts be disposed to assent to we may in others be equally disposed to withdraw. A man may perfectly well hold contradictory beliefs, even ones which are patently contradictory: he tends to give expression to them in different contexts. Faced with a context which has features of both kinds, or simply reminded of what he said on another occasion, he may become aware of the contradiction, and will withdraw one of the propositions; but his disposition to withdraw one of them does not show that he did not formerly really believe both. A definition in terms of readiness to assent in *some* context will thus have most of us believing everything, since anything is a logical consequence of a contradiction; unless, indeed, it counts a propensity under certain conditions to withdraw a belief as a criterion for not ever having had the belief, which it certainly is not.

Another notion which resists axiomatization is that of triviality. This notion cannot be, for Frege, a mere vague intuitive notion; it is one of some theoretical importance. It arises, by contrast, from the notion of 'cognitive value' (informational content), in connection with which the notion of sense was originally introduced by Frege in 'Über Sinn und Bedeutung'. His original question was how a true statement of identity could have cognitive value: and the solution was that '$a = b$' will have cognitive value if the senses of 'a' and 'b' are different. But, if this explanation is correct, then it follows that, when the senses of 'a' and 'b' are the same, then '$a = b$' will have no cognitive value; in particular, '$a = a$' will have none. We may say that 'A' is trivially true when 'A' has no cognitive value. Or rather, since presumably the cognitive value of a sentence is relative to the amount of information an individual already possesses, 'A' is to be called 'trivially true' just in case it cannot have any cognitive value for anyone. Of course, to someone who does not know the sense of 'A', it may always be informative to say that 'A' is true: he will not learn the truth of the thought expressed by 'A', but he will learn that the sentence happens to express a true thought, or, at least, one taken by his informant to be true; so we should take 'anyone', in the above characterization of trivial truth, to mean 'anyone who knows the sense of "A"'. Trivial truth, on Frege's understanding, and, indeed, on anyone's, is a much stronger notion than analyticity: we have already observed that '$a = b$' may be analytically true, even though 'a' and 'b' have different senses. An analytic statement has cognitive value for anyone who had not previously grasped that it was true; and, in mathematics, we are constantly becoming aware of the truth of hitherto unrecognized analytic statements. (This proposition does not depend upon the correctness of any thesis as to the analyticity of mathematical statements: within any axiomatized theory, the proof of a new theorem always involves establishing a new analytic statement —namely, that the theorem holds if the axioms do—even if neither the theorem nor the axioms are themselves analytic.) We may generalize the notion of trivial truth in this way: a sentence 'A' is trivially true if anyone who understands the senses of the expressions occurring in it will recognize it as true; contraposing, if a failure to recognize it as true demonstrates a failure to grasp the sense of the sentence. It seems at first as though this should, for Frege, be a sharp notion: if the expressions of the language have sharp senses, then it should be quite determinate which sentences are trivially true. This does not follow, however; for, however determinate the senses of expressions of the language may be taken to be, this does not involve that the notion of an individual's grasping the sense of any such expression is itself sharp. Protracted failure, in favourable circumstances, to recognize the truth of a sentence which appears to be trivially true will indeed be taken as a criterion for failing to understand the sense of the sentence, even in the absence of any external symptom of a failure to understand any of the expressions contained in it. But, on the one hand, almost anyone can have an inexplicable momentary aberration; and, on the other, if the circumstances are favourable enough, then ability to understand the sentence will often be sufficient to induce assent even when the sentence would not be said to be completely trivial. Such favourable circumstances will be provided, once more, by the display of a deductive proof. We cannot say that the property of being trivially true is transmitted to logical consequents, on pain of making trivial truth coincide with analyticity; yet it seems hard to resist the thesis that, if 'A' is trivially true and 'A → B' is trivially true, then 'B' is trivially true, precisely because the citing of the antecedent (and not just its truth) provides a context in which it would be impossible not to recognize the truth of 'B'.

We have taken it as implicit in Frege's treatment of opaque contexts that all sentences involving them are to be transformed into ones in which only whole clauses are opaque. Certainly Frege did not prove this to be possible, nor can we demonstrate its possibility. But, if it proves to be possible, then we can take it as equally implicit in Frege's treatment that modal operators and relators are to be explained by taking them as admitting, in their (opaque) argument-place, an expression of a *thought*. That is, we do not need to consider any predicate or relational expression as defined over the senses of expressions other than sentences: we need to consider when a *thought* is to be said to be believed, or to have been asserted, by someone, and, likewise, when a *thought* is necessarily true, etc. Such a reduction of the question is made possible only by the admission of quantification into opaque contexts; for, since evidently not all opaque contexts can be taken to be complete sentences, we can hope to render them all as whole clauses only by permitting such clauses to contain variables bound from the outside. That such quantification can be understood depends, again, on the theory of indirect reference: it is precisely in virtue of that theory that it becomes possible to maintain that modal operators and relators can be fully explained by an explanation which relates directly only to the case when an expression for a complete thought, i.e. an actual sentence, occupies their argument-places. Thus Frege's account provides the basis on which any account of modal expressions is to be founded: it determines the direction in which that account is to be sought, and disposes of the objections which have troubled some philosophers and have led them to seek for accounts of belief, etc., of other forms than those which take the objects of belief and other attitudes to be thoughts. Frege's account does not, indeed, provide a semantics in the sense of anything usable for giving a completeness proof for a modal logic; but such a semantics, powerful as it is as a technical tool, is very far removed from an elucidatory account of the senses of modal expressions. In this respect, a semantics for modal logic of the 'possible worlds' type stands in complete contrast to Frege's semantics for an extensional language. The latter operates with just that notion of reference which enables us to take the senses of the words of the language as consisting in the way their reference is given to us; a 'possible worlds' semantics for modal logic does nothing of the kind.

Frege does not himself give any specific explanations of modal expressions, unless his account in *Grundlagen* of the terms 'analytic' and '(synthetic) a priori' be counted as such; and these are treated by him as predicates applying to sentences (or to thoughts), rather than as reiterable modal operators. His theory of assertion, interesting as it is, does not purport to be an analysis of the truth-conditions of sentences of the form 'X asserted that A'.

Gl 3

In his last published article, 'Gedankengefüge', Frege lays great stress on the thesis that the *senses* (and not, this time, the referents) of incomplete expressions are themselves incomplete. We naturally ask: Is the sense of an incomplete expression incomplete in the same way as its referent is, or does its incompleteness consist merely in its being the sort of sense appropriate to an incomplete expression? On the first alternative, the sense of a functional expression would itself be a function: while there would be no need to consider the sense of a predicate to be a *concept*, it would be a function of one argument; the sense of a relational expression would be, not indeed a relation, but a function of two arguments. On the second alternative, the sense of an incomplete expression would be an object, just as much as the sense of a singular term; it would be incomplete only in that it would be necessary, in order to grasp the sense of the incomplete expression, to understand it as an expression containing argument-places which, when these were filled by singular terms, yielded a singular term.

Ggf 37 (59)

When we consider only the way in which the sense of an expression is referred to in transparent contexts, namely by the use of the phrase 'the sense of . . .', the second alternative seems the more reasonable. Such an expression as 'the sense of the predicate "ξ is a dog"' indeed appears to be a singular term, and hence to stand for an *object*. If we take the sense of a predicate to be a function, then this expression is logically as ill-formed as 'the concept which "ξ is a dog" stands for', and for much the same reason. It ought to be replaced by a functional expression, one containing an argument-place: presumably, when this argument-place was filled by an expression standing for the sense of a proper name, we should obtain an expression for the sense of the sentence which resulted from putting that name in the argument-place of the predicate. Thus, where we write the functional expression as, say, 'the sense of "ξ is a dog" of η', we should be able to say such a thing as 'The thought that Fido is a dog is the sense of "ξ is a dog" of the sense of "Fido"'. To say the least, this interpretation is both cumbrous and unnecessary.

When we consider opaque contexts, the matter appears differently. Consider the sentence, 'Plato believed that Socrates was wise'. The name

'Socrates' occurs in an opaque context, and so stands for its sense; likewise the predicate 'ξ was wise' must stand for *its* sense. If the sense of 'ξ was wise' is, like that of 'Socrates', an object, then it is impossible to see how they combine to form a thought. The whole clause, 'Socrates was wise' stands, in the above sentence, for the thought which it expresses, and therefore functions as a complex proper name. A complex proper name cannot be composed merely out of other proper names—expressions standing for objects: it must contain a functional expression also. So it appears that, in this sentence, 'ξ was wise' cannot stand for an object, but must stand for the function whose value for the sense of 'Socrates' as argument is the thought that Socrates was wise (and whose value for the sense of 'Alcibiades' as argument is the thought that Alcibiades was wise, etc.). Since we said that in an opaque context 'ξ was wise' stands for its sense, it will follow that the sense of 'ξ was wise' is this function.

This is the line taken by Church in 'The Logic of Sense and Denotation'. This essay describes a logical system which, Church claims, embodies the essentials of Frege's logical doctrines. Most surprisingly discarded as inessential is the doctrine of incomplete expressions and the incompleteness of their referents: functions are considered as complete entities, designated by complete expressions, though a distinction of types is observed, similar to Frege's but without the justification which he offers for his. This type-theory also differs from Frege's in that there are functions whose values are not objects. Furthermore, contrary to Frege's view, *necessary* identity of reference is taken as the favoured criterion for identity of sense, though alternative criteria are also suggested. Most striking, perhaps, is the fact that the doctrine of indirect reference is abandoned. In place of expressions which in transparent contexts stand for one thing, and in opaque contexts stand for another, we have only expressions which in all contexts have the same reference. For each expression there is another which stands (in all contexts) for its sense. Instead of writing 'Plato believed that Socrates was wise,' we shall write something like 'Plato croyait que Socrates$_1$ was-wise$_1$,' where 'Socrates$_1$' and 'was-wise$_1$' stand for the senses of 'Socrates' and 'was-wise' respectively, and 'croyait que . . .' does not induce an opaque context. There is an infinite hierarchy: there will be an expression 'Socrates$_2$' which stands for the sense of 'Socrates$_1$', and so on. (We can indeed reproduce this hierarchy in Frege's system, by means of the series: Socrates, the sense of the name 'Socrates', the sense of the expression 'the sense of the name "Socrates"', . . . But we have seen that, if we adopt the emendation previously suggested, this infinite hierarchy need not be appealed to in order to explain multiple *oratio obliqua*.) These divergences from Frege's actual ideas, in a logical system purporting to give a faithful representation of them, are, however, not germane to the present question. What is relevant is the fact that, in Church's system (which does accept, from Frege's later doctrine, the equation of concepts and relations with functions), the sense of a functional expression, e.g. 'was wise'—that is, what Church takes to be the denotation of 'was-wise₁'—is identified with the function which maps the sense of a singular term on to the sense of the expression which results from attaching the functional expression to that term.

This identification is reasonable so long as we are considering Frege's notion of sense as something invoked only in order to explain modal operators and relators. It was of course not introduced in this way: had it been, it could hardly have served to *explain* anything. Rather, 'sense' is first introduced as a correlative of 'understand': the sense of an expression is what we know when we understand it. Indeed, the notion remains schematic until we have a theory of sense—an account of what, for each class of expression, has to be known, in order to know its sense; and we have seen that Frege does not provide a complete theory of this kind. But that some notion of sense, correlative to understanding, is required, only philosophical confusion can, I think, lead us to deny. And from this point of view—which is fundamental for the notion of sense—the sense of a predicate can in no way be regarded as a function mapping senses of proper names on to thoughts.

On the model of sense considered in Chapter 7, the sense of a predicate is the criterion for recognizing that the predicate applies to a given object. The thought expressed by the sentence which results from putting a proper name in the argument-place of the predicate is: that the criterion may be recognized to be fulfilled for an object which has been recognized as the bearer of the name. Now the sense of the predicate does indeed determine, for any name whose sense is known, what thought is expressed by the sentence which results from filling the argument-place of the predicate with that name. But the sense of the predicate cannot be thought of as being given by means of the corresponding function, because if we did not already know what the sense of the predicate was, we could not know what was the thought which was the value of the function for the sense of some name as argument. It may be objected that this is precisely how we do learn the sense of predicates: we first learn the senses of particular atomic sentences in which they occur—by learning the criteria for recognizing such sentences as true or false—and then, knowing the senses of the proper names which occur in them, we grasp the general rule for determining the criterion for recognizing as true or as false an arbitrary sentence formed by putting in the argument-place of the predicate a name whose sense is known. It is not necessary to deny that with most sentences—including all sentences we understand without having heard them before—we derive our knowledge of the thought expressed from our understanding of the senses of the constituents; it is necessary only to hold that, in order to perceive what function constitutes the sense of the predicate, we are able to learn what thought *some* sentences containing the predicate express in advance of knowing the sense of the predicate.

To this objection we may give two answers. (i) When we consider what the criterion for recognizing an atomic sentence as true or as false actually consists of, we realize that it must be complex in a way corresponding to the analysis of the sentence into proper name and predicate. On our model, we have, at least when we follow the most direct means for determining the truth-value of the atomic sentence, in the sense of 'direct' explained in Chapter 7, first to identify the object for which the proper name stands, and then to recognize the predicate as applying or not applying. Even if our model of sense requires modification, the procedure of recognizing the truth-value of the sentence must be two-fold in some such way as this. Hence we cannot grasp the sense of *any* atomic sentence in advance of knowing the sense of the predicate. (ii) In any case, the sort of sentence the objector has in mind is really, on Frege's view, an incomplete expression. It is, namely, one which contains a significant present tense, so that it will express different thoughts when uttered at different times. Thus it is really an (in most cases) complex predicate of the time, considered as indicated demonstratively. It is impossible to conceive of any method of grasping the thought expressed by a sentence like 'The Earth is round', which expresses the same thought whenever it is uttered, in advance of a knowledge of the senses of its constituents.

If the sense of a predicate is, then, not a function, how are we to resolve the difficulty about the unity of a clause in *oratio obliqua*? The answer is simply that Frege's doctrine of indirect reference requires one further emendation. The sense of a predicate is indeed to be considered an object—the referent of the expression 'the sense of the predicate'; but its referent in opaque contexts is not this sense, but the associated function, which maps the sense of a name on to the thought expressed by the sentence formed by attaching the predicate to that name. The *referent* of an incomplete expression, whether direct or indirect, must always itself be incomplete.

CHAPTER 10

Assertion

THE NOTIONS OF sense and reference do not suffice for a complete account of language. If we know of a language only what sense the expressions which occur in it have, and thereby their reference, we know nothing which can tell us the significance of uttering an expression of this language: the *point* of doing so. Suppose for instance that some Martians observe human beings (remaining themselves unobserved). Among other human activities is the use of language. We will suppose that these Martians have some method of communicating with one another, but that this method is so unlike human language that they do not recognize this as an instrument of communication. Some human activities—e.g. the use of money—require quite complex descriptions in order to impose some order on the mass of observations which the Martians make of the human actions involved; we may say that they can interpret these activities only in the light of a *theory*. They wish to arrive at a theory of human language by means of which they can interpret our linguistic activities. Now even if, by some extraordinary chance, they hit on an account of human language in terms of the senses of expressions, considered as determining their reference, it is clear that this account would have to be supplemented before it constituted a theory of the kind they were looking for; at least, if we take the word 'sense' here in the way Frege uses it. On his way of regarding the matter, the sense of a word consists of a rule such that the rules governing the words occurring in some complex (complete) expression together give us a means of determining the reference of the complex expression, or, at least, a criterion for recognizing an object (or a truth-value) as its referent. (This is his *later* view, on which a sentence is only a special kind of name.) If the Martians know about our language only what the senses of its expressions are, they know only that, when a certain complete expression is uttered, there is a particular means for recognizing an object (or truth-value) to be associated with that expression as its 'referent';

but, as one might say, they do not know what anyone is *doing* in uttering that expression. Their account does not yet constitute a theory of language, because it only gives a certain complex procedure for associating certain objects with certain expressions; it does not go on to describe any observable regularities to which the use of language conforms in terms of the association which has been set up. For this reason it is powerless either to explain why human beings make certain utterances at certain times, or to assign further events as the consequences of such utterances. In particular, we must remember that the account in terms of sense and reference merely assigns every sentence, all of whose parts possess a reference, to one of two arbitrarily labelled classes, true sentences and false sentences, in accordance with the rules which govern the component words of the sentence and constitute their sense. The referent of a sentence is its truth-value: but there is nothing in the theory of sense and reference, taken by itself, to distinguish one truth-value from the other. We have no way of knowing what objects or other entities the two truth-values are, and hence what is the difference between them, except by considering them as the referents of sample sentences.

In order to see this latter point more clearly, let us make use of an analogy with games. A formal description of chess could be given by describing the initial position of the pieces, and giving rules for what constituted a legitimate move from any given position. Players make moves alternately, and the game ends when there is no legitimate move. The end-positions are classified into three categories: White checkmates Black, Black checkmates White, and stalemate. (For expository purposes, I ignore other kinds of draw, as well as resignations.) This formal description suffices for the mathematical theory of chess, and for the formulation of chess problems. In terms of it one can state and prove such theorems as that it is impossible to force mate with two knights, or describe a position and ask whether it is possible to arrive at it from the initial position by a series of legitimate moves. It will not, however, suffice by itself to provide us with a 'theory' of chess as an activity: it is not enough to tell anyone what it is to play chess. This can be seen from the fact that there could be a large number of variant games each sharing the same formal description: for instance, the game in which each player tries to force his opponent to checkmate him, or again the game in which it is White's object to produce a checkmate (of either side by the other) and Black's to achieve stalemate. The difference between these various games lies not in the initial position or what constitutes a legitimate move, but in what winning consists of. From the formal description it is impossible to tell what, in playing chess, a player is trying to do, namely to produce an end-position which falls into a particular one of the three categories. To have a description of language just in terms of sense and reference is like having only the formal description of chess without this further information about what constitutes winning.

For someone who is already familiar with other games, the formal description needs only to be supplemented by the statement that White wins if he checkmates Black, and Black wins if he checkmates White. Here we are relying on his knowledge of other games to provide him with an understanding of the word 'win'. On the other hand, if he were not previously familiar with the activity of playing games, this statement would not supply what he lacked: it would give him only alternative labels for the three categories of end-position—'White wins', 'Black wins' and 'Neither wins'—without telling him that playing chess consists of making legitimate moves with the intention of arriving at an end-position of a particular one of these three kinds. Clearly, if we are interested in giving an account of playing chess as a human activity, we must give an account which does not, by presupposing an understanding of the word 'win', assume that something is known about the activity of playing games in general. Similarly, if we suppose that the Martians understand the significance of assigning truth-values to sentences otherwise than as the assignment of them to arbitrarily labelled categories in accordance with certain rules, we are crediting them with a prior knowledge of some activity akin to human language. They would have already to know what 'true' and 'false' meant, presumably in connection with something which they used as an instrument in communication. In that case, we should have smuggled into the account of our language in terms of sense and reference an element external to it. Now, just as it is possible to describe to someone what it is to play chess without presupposing that he understands what winning is, and therefore that he already understands some similar activity, so it should be possible to describe the activity of using language without presupposing that it is already known what significance it has to call one class of sentences the class of 'true' sentences and the other the class of 'false' sentences; this feature, to be expressly described, is not contained in the characterization of our language in terms of sense and reference.

One way to put this point, without Martians or analogies, would be as follows. Uttering an expression which refers to an object has in itself no significance, considered in isolation from any context which determines what the person is trying to do by uttering that expression; only a context will give a point to his utterance. If, e.g., I say, out of the blue, 'the highest mountain in the world', I have indeed uttered an expression which is endowed with a certain sense, and thereby with a certain reference; but, until

I have indicated what point I had in mind in doing this, I cannot be considered to have done anything *right* or *wrong*. The natural reaction to my utterance would be, 'What about it?', or, 'Well, go on.' The moment a context of a certain kind is provided for my utterance, it acquires a point, and, in some cases at any rate, becomes a matter of my having succeeded or failed, of having done something correct or incorrect. An example would be a case in which my utterance followed someone else's having asked, 'What is Mount Everest?' Here the question supplies an intention for my utterance: I uttered the expression with the intention of uttering an expression whose referent was Mount Everest; in uttering it, I was not merely giving voice to an expression with a certain reference, but using it to *say that* its referent was Mount Everest. The primary case is, however, the utterance of *sentences*: the utterance of a singular term in response to a question can be considered an abbreviated form of utterance of a sentence, e.g., in the above case, of the sentence, 'Mount Everest is the highest mountain in the world'. Now the utterance of a sentence does not require a particular context to give it point, but is governed by a general convention—at least in certain types of situation—that in uttering them we are understood as saying that their reference is truth. (I render Frege's terms 'the true' and 'the false' by 'truth' and 'falsity', which are more natural in English.) This remark is meant only to indicate what has been omitted from the account of language in terms of sense and reference, not to be explanatory. The utterance of a sentence serves not only to express a thought, and to refer to a truth-value, but also to assert something, namely that the thought expressed is true, or that the truth-value referred to is truth. We of course do not explain what this activity of assertion is by saying that it consists in *saying that* a certain truth-value—the truth-value of the thought expressed by the sentence—is truth; for the expression 'say that' is here used, not to mean 'utter a sentence expressing that', but as a synonym of 'assert that'. The following would escape this objection: there is a general convention whereby the utterance of a sentence, except in special contexts, is understood as being carried out with the intention of uttering a true sentence.

Judgment is to grasping a thought as assertion is to the expression of a thought. Merely to have a thought—in the sense of grasping it and fixing one's attention on it—is different from judging *that* that thought is true—from doing what Frege calls 'advancing from the thought to the truth-value'. This difference is the same difference as that between merely expressing the thought, without intending to be understood as claiming that it is true, and asserting it. In the interior case, indeed, it is difficult to see how we can express the difference without circularity, and it is conceivable that Frege

FB 22n

NS 150 (139);
NS 201 (185)

SB 33, 35
NS 133 (122)

held it to be impossible to do so. In the exterior case a natural first idea is to try to express this difference without circularity by appeal to the notion of intention. The obvious difficulty is that a man's actual intention does not determine whether he is making an assertion or not. A man may say something, knowing or believing it to be false, with all sorts of intentions, perhaps, as in the case of the pathological liar, with the very intention to say something false; or a man may say something about which he has no opinion whether it is true or false, again with varying intentions. In none of these cases does the fact that he does not have the intention to say something true make it false to say that he has made an assertion. To this one might reply that it is necessary, for him to be making an assertion, that he should at least pretend that he is saying what he does with the intention of saying something true: if he makes it quite evident that he is not intending to say something true, then he will not be taken as making an assertion; for instance, if he is telling a story.

Here we need to note the following points. A man may say something with more than one intention: e.g., he might quote a line of poetry both because it struck him as beautiful and because he believed that the thought it expressed was true. He is only asserting that thought, however, if the latter intention is the primary one: this would be shown by whether, if someone convinced him that the thought was not true, he would be prepared to modify the words; if his primary intention was, e.g., to give the poet's words, he would of course not be prepared to do this. It does not in general matter what steps he is prepared to take to ensure the truth of what he says. If a man says, 'I am driving to Cambridge', and then learns that he is going in the opposite direction, his reaction may be not to withdraw what he said, but to make it true by turning round and going the right way: this does not make what he said any less of an assertion. What *is* essential, however, is not only that he should in fact be prepared, by altering either what he says or what happens, to make what he says true, but that his intention in making his original utterance should be such that he regards it as mandatory thus to strive to make what he says agree with what is the case; no further choice remains to be made. I put the qualification in because of the following case. Suppose a schoolmaster, whose authority is flimsy, says to a class, 'You will learn by heart a sonnet every day next week.' He means this not as an assertion—either a prediction or an announcement of his intention—but as a command. The boys deliberately neglect this imposition. At first the master attempts to enforce it, by reiterating it with threats of punishment. When they continue to defy him, he decides he will lose less face if he withdraws the command than if he lets them get away with flagrant disobedience; so, inventing some pretext, he countermands the order. Certainly, when he first said, 'You will learn a sonnet each day', he did so with the intention that what he said should be true; and in a sense this intention was primary, since he was not prepared to go on saying it when it proved that it was certainly not going to be true. But what shows that his original utterance was not, for all that, an assertion is that his decision to withdraw the command was a *new* decision, not implicit in the intention with which he originally said what he did; he could, consistently with that intention, have continued to reiterate the command, even when it was plain that it was going to be disobeyed. As a summary of all this, we might try the following formulation: A man makes an assertion if he says something in such a manner as deliberately to convey the impression of saying it with the overriding intention of saying something true.

We have become involved in making some extremely subtle distinctions. In particular, it is doubtful whether the notion of intention will, by itself, bear the weight of these distinctions. For instance, in discussing the last example, we invoked the notion that an intention for the future might not be 'implicit in' the intention with which something was done: but what does this mean? After all, the schoolmaster might, at the time of giving the command, have had the intention of withdrawing it as soon as its unenforceability became evident: this might have been a settled policy of his, which he was bearing clearly in mind at the time of giving the original command. Our difficulty arises from the fact that we have tried to characterize the activity of assertion without taking into account its being a *conventional* activity: the fact that a sentence expresses an act of assertion is as much a matter of linguistic convention as is its having the sense it has (in Frege's use of 'sense'). This is not to deny that there are sentences which can be used to perform any one of a number of linguistic acts: I may say, 'You will learn a sonnet', as a prediction, as an expression of my intention, or as a command. What constitutes my *meaning* the sentence in any one of these ways is my intention to be understood as performing that one of these linguistic acts. What makes it possible for me to have such an intention is the existence of a general convention endowing the utterance of certain sentences—and this one in particular—with a certain significance.

Convention, which forms the background to, when it does not govern, almost all our actions, can be crudely classified into two types. These correspond roughly to games with stakes (or other rewards or penalties) and games without. In a game with stakes winning and losing are associated with certain definite consequences—e.g., the exchange of money. If one was describing such a game to someone who did not already have the concept of a game (of winning), one would have little inclination to characterize winning by reference to the intentions of a player; one would simply say, 'If the end-position belongs to this class, the first player receives an agreed sum from his opponent'. It is consonant with this that we do not judge whether a person is in fact playing such a game by reference to his real or apparent intentions: even if he declares his intention of losing, the imposition of the penalty serves to distinguish losing from winning, and hence to determine what game he is playing and that he is playing it. While it is true that the mere making of the moves does not in itself constitute playing the game—if, e.g., either the player or his opponent does not know the game, or they have expressly stipulated that they will not play it—the mere intention of a person *in* playing it is irrelevant to whether he is playing it or not.

It is different with a game in which there are no stakes—chess, for example. Someone can play chess with the intention of losing—if, e.g., he is playing with a rich but irascible uncle; but if he makes plain his intention of losing, he would no longer be said to be playing chess. (If he and his opponent had agreed both to try to lose, they would be playing one of the variant games.) The reason for this is that winning at chess does not normally have any consequences: it is one of those things which we do 'for their own sake'. In describing the practice of playing this game, we have no means of explaining the fact that checkmating your opponent constitutes winning otherwise than by saying that people have the custom of making these moves while trying to arrive at such an end-position.

This distinction applies to conventional activities in general. Some actions are performed against a background of conventions whereby certain definite consequences are associated with them. Others rest on a tacit agreement to perform them only with a particular intention. The line between the two types of convention is of course extremely hazy. The consequences of a conventional act most usually follow only because of a consent among the persons involved to bring about, or to accept, such consequences; it is only in exceptional cases that the consequences are imposed by one set of people without regard to the consent of the other set. The consequences of an act are often to be properly stated as consisting of someone's acquiring a right or an obligation; the right or the obligation may be waived, and the notions of right and obligation are applicable only where there is a tacit agreement to observe them.

A command has definite consequences: disobedience to a command given by a person in authority confers on that person a right to punish, or at least reproach, the person commanded. For this reason, the utterance of a sentence of a certain form, unless special circumstances divest this act of its usual significance, in itself constitutes the giving of a command. It is irrelevant what intentions the person speaking may have had: it is, for instance, possible to give a command in the hope that it will be disobeyed, and that one will therefore have an excuse for punishing the person commanded; or again, one may simply be carrying out the duty of transmitting the orders given by a superior. An assertion has no such definite consequences. (It of course has consequences in the wider sense that a difference may be made to the course of events by the making of an assertion: it is essential to the understanding of assertions that we know what it is to act on an assertion. But it does not have consequences of such a kind that its conventional significance consists in a tacit agreement to bring about, and accept, such consequences in given circumstances involving the assertion.) Assertions take place against the background of a custom of uttering them with the intention of saying something true (together with all those conventions which determine the sense of the assertion, i.e. the conditions under which it is true).

Our earlier difficulties, which involved us in the drawing of fine distinctions, thus arose from our having posed the wrong problem. We considered utterances in general, regarded as endowed with a sense but not with a demarcation into types of utterance (assertion, command, etc.), and tried to specify which of them constituted assertions by reference to the intention of the speaker. Rather, the correct approach is to consider utterances as conventionally demarcated into types, by means of the form of linguistic expressions employed, and then to enquire into the conventions governing the use of the various types of utterance.

In order, then, to describe the use of assertoric sentences, we have to add to our stipulation of the rules which determine the sense of such sentences, and thereby the method by which they are classified into true and false, a specification of the convention governing such utterances. Let us for the present state this convention by saying merely that it is that we should utter such sentences with the intention of uttering only true ones: we postpone till later the enquiry how adequate an account this is. Here we encounter a minor difficulty. Besides sense and tone, we have discovered a third element in what would ordinarily be called the meaning of such a sentence: for it would certainly be regarded as part of its meaning that a sentence was conventionally understood to express an assertion, and not, e.g., a command; but this is not any part of what Frege counts as its sense, i.e. that which determines under what conditions it is true or false. It is, however, at first unclear what element of a sentence of natural language it is which carries this constituent of its meaning, which, following Frege, we may call its assertoric *'force'*. Many writers—for instance, Russell in *Principles of Mathematics*—have located it in the indicative mood of the verb, but at first sight this does not seem to be quite right. If I say, 'Either he has gone out or he is asleep', I am not asserting that he has gone out or asserting that he is asleep, and yet both verbs are in the indicative mood. In fact, the suggestion is (roughly) correct, as we see if we consider the case of commands. Just as there is something at least approximately right in saying that we understand a statement when we know the conditions under which it is true and the conditions under which it is false, so we may say that we understand a command when we know the conditions under which it is said to have been obeyed and those under which it is said to have been disobeyed. (Since only a statement is said to be true or false, and only a command to have been obeyed or disobeyed, we are here presupposing that the statement has been recognized as a statement and the command as a command.) Moreover, the explanation of the use of the sentential operators in imperatives is parallel to the explanation of their use in statements. Just as we may draw up a truth-table for 'or', so as to show the conditions under which a complex statement formed by its means is true or false in terms of the conditions under which its constituents are true or false, so we may draw up an 'obedience-table' for disjunctive commands. Thus could say that the command 'Either shut the door or open the window' was said to have been obeyed just in case at least one of the commands 'Shut the door' and 'Open the window' was obeyed, and to have been disobeyed only if both these commands were disobeyed. But there is an oddity about saying this. If I say, 'Either shut the door or open the window', I have not given any command to shut the door, nor have I given a command to open the window. We do not normally speak of commands which have not been given; still less do we speak of obeying or disobeying commands which have not been given.

Regarded just as an awkwardness of formulation, this is easy to get round: we need only speak of doing what would have been obedience to the command 'Shut the door' if I had uttered that as a complete sentence. What this is intended to bring out, however, is that the imperatival force governs the sentence as a whole, and not its constituent clauses taken separately. The conventional sign of this imperatival force is the imperative mood of the verb, and, since each clause contains a verb, both clauses contain verbs in this mood. Logically speaking, however, the disjunctive imperative is not formed by connecting by means of 'or' two sentences each carrying imperatival force, and so each expressing a command: the imperatival force is imposed on the sentence as a whole. This means simply that the convention governing imperatives, whereby the person giving the command acquires the

NS 183 (168);
NS 192 (177);
NS 214 (198);
Ggf 42 (64);
PoM 35; Ver
152 (45); NS
140 (129)

right to punish or reproach someone who disobeys, does not apply to the utterance of all imperative sentences, but only to the utterance of those which do not occur as constituents in a complex sentence. The fact that this holds good for assertions also is slightly obscured by the use of the word 'statement'. 'Statement' differs from 'command' in that we do speak of the truth or falsity of statements that have never been made; but an oddity would appear if instead of 'statement' we used 'assertion', which resembles 'command' rather than 'statement' in this respect. The assertoric force applies only to the complete sentence taken as a whole. Its constituent clauses are not used, or taken to be being used, to make assertions on their own. Thus a logically correct symbolism will possess an assertion sign, used to convey the assertoric force, which is attached to the sentence as a whole, and not, like the indicative mood, to various constituents of it severally.

But do we need an assertion sign at all? In the *Tractatus* Wittgenstein says that it is logically quite superfluous, and in the *Investigations* he says that it merely functions like the full stop—it serves to mark off the beginning and end of the sentence. In *Principles of Mathematics* Russell falls into confusion through a desire to say both that, e.g., 'Peter is a Jew' is the same proposition when it occurs alone and when it occurs in 'If Peter is a Jew, then Andrew is a Jew', and that it is not. It must be the same, because otherwise modus ponens would not be valid; it cannot be the same, because then 'Peter is a Jew; if Peter is a Jew, Andrew is a Jew; therefore, Andrew is a Jew' would be the same as 'If both Peter is a Jew and if Peter is a Jew, then Andrew is a Jew, then Andrew is a Jew', and it was precisely Lewis Carroll's discovery (in 'What the Tortoise said to Achilles') that it was not. Frege provides a solution by saying that the sense of the two occurrences of 'Peter is a Jew' (the thought expressed by them) is the same, but that the assertoric force is present in one and lacking in the other. But are they not simply the same? Consider the following gibe, made by Miss Anscombe in her book on the *Tractatus*: ' . . . the view that "assertion" is an extra feature which somehow gets added to the sense . . . could be compared to arguing: " '7' must mean 7 in 'I had 7–3 apples'; so we must distinguish, even in empirical propositions where numerals occur, between the use of a numeral to designate a number of things, which we will call its positive use, and uses where it has the same sense but does not designate a number of things. Some extra feature therefore attaches to the use of the numeral in 'I had 7 apples', but not in 'I had 7–3 apples' ". By this argument, we might propose to symbolize that "extra feature" by prefixing the sign "P" for "positive" to certain occurrences of numerals, and think it necessary to write: "I had P7 apples" and "I had P(7–3) apples".'

Ver 152 (45);
Ggf 42 (64)
NS 201 (185);
NS 214–15
(198–9); Bs 2;
Gg I 5; LF
58–9

TLP 4.442

PI 22

PoM 35

IWT 121

Our arguments showed that the account of assertoric sentences in terms of their sense and their reference is not enough by itself to characterize their use: the additional element is the convention governing their employment to make assertions. We have not shown that this feature of their use has to be symbolized by any feature of their linguistic expression. This will be so only if the kind of sense which a sentence has is insufficient to determine which linguistic convention governs its utterance.

If we consider what we said about 'obedience-tables' for imperatives, we see that it is very natural to assimilate the description of imperatives to that of assertoric sentences. Instead of using the distinct pairs of notions truth/falsity, obedience/disobedience, we could use a neutral pair of terms, say 'correct' and 'incorrect', for both: thus we may call an utterance 'correct' if it either expresses a true assertion or a command which is obeyed, and 'incorrect' if it either expresses a false assertion or a command which is disobeyed. In order to understand a sentence which is either assertoric or imperative, then, we have to know two things: under what conditions it is correct and under what conditions incorrect; and whether it is used to make an assertion or to give a command. (We are here presupposing that it is understood what an assertion and a command in general are, i.e. that the conventions governing the utterance of assertoric and imperatival sentences are known.) The conditions for the correctness or incorrectness of a sentence could then be considered as endowing it with a certain descriptive content, which is in general independent of whether it is being used to make an assertion or give a command; this descriptive content corresponds precisely to what Frege calls the sense of a sentence, or the thought it expresses. In order to understand the sentence, to know its use, it will be necessary that it should contain another symbolic element, conveying the force with which it is used; something playing the part of an assertion sign or command sign. Here the assertion sign is doing much more than merely marking the beginning and end of the sentence.

An advantage may be claimed for this account, that it reveals as a purely grammatical feature of our language what otherwise appears as a puzzling logical fact about imperatives. In a disjunctive command, both clauses are put into the imperative mood; but in a conditional command, only the consequent is, and the antecedent remains in the indicative. If we do not notice that the imperatival force applies to the sentence as a whole, and that what are joined by means of sentential connectives are merely sentences considered as having a sense—a descriptive content—as yet neutral between being assertoric or imperative, we can easily think that the disjunctive command is formed by joining two commands, and the conditional command by joining a statement and a command; and we may then rack our brains to discover why we cannot join two commands by means of 'if'—why we cannot get an imperative into the antecedent. (At first sight, we *can* join a command and a statement by means of 'or': actually, 'Keep back or you'll get hit' is a warning or a threat—i.e. a prediction or an expression of intention; it is no more a command than 'Do that again and you'll get into trouble'. A different case is 'Shut the window or we'll all freeze to death'. This genuinely contains the command to shut the window, but not disjunctively—it does not leave the person addressed any choice whether to shut the window or not, as does 'Shut the window or open the door': it is an elliptical combination of the command 'Shut the window', and the prediction, 'If you do not shut the window, we shall all freeze to death'.)

In fact, the difference between the mood of the verb in disjunctive and in conditional commands lies in the grammatical distinction, which is logically without significance, between subordinate and co-ordinate clauses. Since the imperatival force is signified in natural language by the mood of the verb, it is necessary to have a rule determining which verbs in a complex sentence are to be put into the imperative mood; and the rule is that only the verb in the main clause, or any co-ordinate main clauses, is affected. Since the clauses in a disjunction are counted as co-ordinate, but the antecedent of a conditional as a subordinate clause, this explains the apparent difference. That there is logically no difference can be seen by adopting a mode of expression in which the imperatival force is conveyed by a prefix to the whole of the sentence, the rest simply carrying what we have called the descriptive content, namely where every command begins 'Bring it about that . . . ' Then the disjunctive command becomes, e.g., 'Bring it about that either you do not go out or you put on your coat', and the conditional command 'Bring it about that if you go out, you put on your coat'; the difference has disappeared.

A parallel analysis could be given of various other types of sentence as well—optatives, for example. In particular, it could be applied to those interrogatives which expect the answer 'Yes' or 'No'—what Frege calls 'sentential questions'. This is slightly obscured by a quirk of Indo-European languages. One would expect that the convention governing the asking of sentential questions would be to answer 'Yes' if the thought expressed by the corresponding assertoric sentence were true, and 'No' if it were false; but in our language negative and disjunctive questions are exceptions to this rule. If I say, 'Isn't he at home?', the answer 'No' conveys that he is not at home, not that he is; and if I ask, 'Is he in England or America?', it is facetious to reply 'Yes,' meaning that he is either in England or America.

Ged 62 (7);
NS 8 (7)

I am told that West African languages follow the more logical convention in these respects.

On this view, assertoric sentences, imperatives, sentential interrogatives and optatives would all express thoughts: they would differ only in the force attaching to them—the linguistic act which was performed by uttering them. We can do various things with an expression of a thought: assert that it is true, ask whether it is true, command that it be made true, wish it were true. Our analogy with board games may be elaborated in order to provide a parallel—not, of course, exact—for this model of language. Let us distinguish a number of board games—chess, draughts, Halma, go, backgammon, Chinese chequers—regarded this time as completely characterized by their formal description: we imagine that in each there is a threefold classification of the end-positions, and that the same arbitrary labels (say 'A', 'B' and 'C') are used for the three classes of end-positions in the formal descriptions of all the games. Now for an arbitrary one of these games we may stipulate a mode of playing this game by characterizing the objectives of the players in terms of the three classes of end-positions: e.g. one mode of play is for the first player to attempt to secure an end-position of class A, while the second player attempts to secure one of class B, and so on. Thus we determine a particular procedure of playing by specifying two things: the game played, and the mode of play. Here the game, understood in this way, corresponds to the sense of a sentence, the thought expressed: the game is characterized solely by the means of determining its outcome. The mode of play corresponds to the force with which the sentence is uttered, i.e. the type of linguistic act which its utterance effects.

This view cannot really be ascribed to Frege; certainly it was not his main motive for his doctrine of assertion. In 'Über Sinn und Bedeutung' he explicitly repudiates the view that any sentences other than assertoric express thoughts; rather, he regards the difference between assertoric, interrogative, imperative and optative sentences as a difference in their *sense* rather than in the force attaching to them. Thus he says that, just as assertoric sentences express thoughts, so interrogatives express questions, imperatives commands and optatives wishes. This view we may regard as definitely wrong: that is, when taken in conjunction with Frege's distinction between sense and force for assertoric sentences. In particular, it leaves Frege open to a charge which, by taking the opposite line, he could have escaped. In *Introduction to Mathematical Thinking*, Waismann criticizes Frege's explanation of number-words on the grounds that he has explained them only for their occurrence in *statements*; he has not explained them as they occur in questions or commands. Now evidently Frege's purpose is to explain the *sense* of

SB 38-9

IMT 114

number-words, their contribution to what we have called the descriptive content of a sentence, and this, on the view expounded above, will be the same whether they occur in statements, commands, questions or other types of utterance. On the view Frege advances in 'Über Sinn und Bedeutung', on the other hand, there would at best be no proof that Waismann's charge was not justified.

Frege makes a certain modification of this view in his 'Der Gedanke', published towards the end of his life (1918). There he still thinks that an imperative expresses a command, considered as something parallel to a thought; but he now thinks that a sentential interrogative expresses the same thought as the corresponding assertoric sentence, and differs from it only in the force attached to it. Of course, to make out that the assertion sign (as opposed to the notion of assertion) is not redundant, only one other type of sentence which has a thought for its sense is needed.

There is indeed one kind of sentence which Frege recognized, from the time of *Begriffsschrift*, as having a force other than that of an assertion, and to which he attaches a sign for that force in his symbolic notation—the only alternative to the assertion sign in his logical symbolism: sentences which are used to give definitions. To these Frege prefixes the sign '⊩'. He says in *Begriffsschrift* that they do not express assertions but serve to *stipulate* the sense of a new symbol. On the other hand, they do not furnish a straightforward example of sentences with which the assertion sign is not to be used, because they contain a new symbol to which a sense has not yet been assigned, and so, when they are used *as* definitions, they do not express a thought at all. As soon as we attach to the new symbol the sense which the definition confers on it, the sentence no longer functions as a definition, but is transformed into an assertion: and indeed Frege employs a rule whereby any formula of the form '⊩A' may subsequently be repeated in the form '⊢A'.

Sentential questions and definitions, however, obviously did not constitute Frege's original reason for thinking the assertion sign necessary; and he emphatically did think it necessary. In the course of a controversy between him and Peano about the respective merits of their logical notations, Peano dismissed the assertion sign as superfluous, since it preceded every theorem; Frege retorted that a correct logical analysis reveals the necessity for such a sign, and it is therefore a mistake to omit it even if no ambiguity results. Its necessity appeared to him to depend, not so much on there being, besides assertoric sentences, sentences of different forms which expressed the same thoughts but carried a distinct kind of force, but on the possibility of using assertoric sentences as complete sentences but stripped of their assertoric

Ged 62 (6–7)
Ver 143–4
(31–2)

Bs 24
Gg I 27

LF 58–9

force. Here we might naturally think of sentences used to state suppositions, what Meinong, who, subsequently to Frege, also had the idea of distinguishing thoughts from judgments, calls 'assumptions'; and it is true that Frege, when he is considering interior mental acts, distinguishes entertaining a thought from judging it to be true. But Frege's account of inference allows no place for a corresponding external act of supposition. Gentzen later had the highly successful idea of formalizing inference so as to leave a place for the introduction of hypotheses in a manner analogous to that in which, in everyday reasoning, we say, 'Suppose . . .': e.g. 'Suppose m/n is a square root of 2'. We require no warrant for introducing any new hypothesis, and we reason from it in accordance with just the same rules as those governing inferences from premisses which we assert outright: the point of the procedure being that, from the fact that certain consequences follow from some hypothesis, we can draw a conclusion which no longer depends on that hypothesis; e.g. if contradictory consequences follow from certain premisses together with a given hypothesis, we can, on the basis of those premisses alone, conclude that that hypothesis is false. As Gentzen observed, a formal logic which employs the procedure of introducing hypotheses is both closer to the modes of inference which occur in informal reasoning, and able to dispense with the necessity of stipulating logical axioms (forms of logically true statements) as well as rules of inference. In supposition, a thought is expressed but not asserted: 'Suppose . . . ' must be taken as a sign of the *force* (in our sense) with which the sentence is uttered. (Certainly it is not logically an imperative: I could, having said, 'Think of a number', ask 'Have you done so yet?', but it would be a joke if I asked that question having said, 'Suppose the witness is telling the truth'.) However, not only does Frege not make use of supposition in formalizing logic, but his general account of inference rules out the possibility of taking supposition as a separate linguistic act at all. According to him, one can make inferences only from *true* premisses, and hence not from a mere hypothesis. When, for example, I reason thus:

NS 201 (185);
NS 214 (198);
Ged 62 (7)

CPG 78

NS 195 (180);
Ver 145 (34);
NJ 240 (BW
118); NS 264
(244)

Suppose $\dfrac{m}{n}$ is a square root of 2.

Then $\dfrac{m^2}{n^2} = 2$.

Hence $m^2 = 2n^2$,

the logically correct analysis of my argument would be:

M

$$\text{If } \frac{m}{n} \text{ is a square root of 2, then } \frac{m^2}{n^2} = 2.$$

$$\text{If } \frac{m^2}{n^2} = 2, \text{ then } m^2 = 2n^2.$$

$$\text{Hence, if } \frac{m}{n} \text{ is a square root of 2, then } m^2 = 2n^2.$$

Here '$\frac{m}{n}$ is a square root of 2' does not appear as a complete sentence at all, but only as a constituent in a more complex sentence. Thus sentences introduced by supposition are not available for Frege as examples of assertoric sentences occurring as complete sentences but without assertoric force.

The sentences which Frege does give as examples of this are those occurring in fiction and drama. The actor shouts, 'There is a bomb in the next room!', but he is not asserting, and is not taken as asserting, that there is a bomb in the next room; the novelist writes, 'My life had become an emotional blank', but he is not asserting that anyone's life had become an emotional blank. All this is indeed true; but not for a reason that justifies the use which Frege makes of it. Of the actions performed by a character in a play, the actor who takes that role for the most part really does those which are not conventional (a few he merely pretends to do); more exactly, he is said really to do such an action under some description whose applicability does not depend upon the existence of some convention governing the action. For instance, the actor *really* shakes hands with someone. But if some action is considered under a description which applies to an action only in virtue of the existence of some convention, we do not say that the actor really does it: for example, in shaking hands with someone, the actor does not really *greet* him. This is not, however, because the actor is like someone from another culture who is not observing the convention: rather, it is because he is performing the conventional action in a context which is governed by a *further* convention—that of dramatic representation. This is indeed a convention—a special language-game: someone who knew our language, but was unfamiliar with the activities of acting plays and telling stories, really would not understand the utterances of actors and story-tellers. But it is not a language-game on the same level as, e.g., those of asking questions and giving commands. It is a convention which governs all the actions, conventional as well as non-conventional, which the actor performs within the context of the play, and endows them with a particular significance: and it does this to the conventional actions in virtue of the conventions which ordinarily govern them. Not any old way of shaking hands will do: the actor must

Ggf 47 (72);
GG2 425

SB 33-4;
NS 252 (234);
NS 142 (130);
Ged 63 (8)

shake hands in the way which, in the absence of any context governed by a special convention, would constitute a greeting.

Thus, if we used an assertion-sign, the actor would have to use it too. The reason he is not making assertions is not that he is doing *less* than that—merely expressing thoughts, say—but that he is doing *more* than that—he is acting the making of assertions. What constitutes his doing this is his uttering the assertoric sentence—with the assertion-sign if we have one—in a context which determines the significance of everything he does in that context—on the stage in a theatre at an announced time. This general context is enough: it is not necessary for him to preface every sentence (and every conventional action) by a sign to show that it has this special significance—a sign for the 'dramatic force'. But even if we were to demand this, such a sign would precede and not replace the assertion sign, if there was one. And for this reason the cases in which such a sign would be used cannot demonstrate the necessity for the assertion sign: for that, we need cases in which the assertion sign would have to be replaced by another sign, or possibly simply omitted. (It might be thought that the sign for the dramatic force and that for assertion ought rather to be combined into a single new sign; but this would be a false economy. The sign for the dramatic force can govern all kinds of act—linguistic and non-linguistic, conventional and non-conventional: we certainly should not want to introduce one new sign for dramatic assertion, another for dramatic command, another for dramatic greeting, another for dramatic standing up, etc., etc.)

We have a natural tendency to think of these various linguistic acts—making an assertion, expressing a thought—as the external expression of an interior act of adopting a particular mental attitude. This tendency is of course reinforced by the fact that to some of them interior acts or events do correspond—an act of judgment, or a thought's suddenly occurring to one, though not as true or as false; though indeed asking oneself a question is somewhat unlike asking someone else a question, and giving oneself a command very unlike giving someone else a command. The analysis of these interior acts and events is a matter of epistemology, not of logic; but the *linguistic* acts should be classified as conventional actions, not as the external expression of interior states. Assertion, for example, is to be explained in terms of the conventions governing the use of those sentences which are understood as having assertoric force, not as the utterance of a sentence with the intention of expressing one's interior act of judgment (or interior state of belief) that it is true. This point—that assertion consists in the (deliberate) utterance of a sentence which, by its form and context, is recognized as being used according to a certain general convention—was not grasped by the

BW 126-7
(78-9); *PoM*
503-4

Russell of *Principles of Mathematics*, nor by the Wittgenstein of the *Tractatus*; nor indeed was it ever clearly grasped by Frege either. Russell tries to distinguish between a logical and a psychological sense of 'assertion'. He is inclined to say that for a proposition to be logically asserted is for it to be true; but then he sees that that cannot be right, since in the proposition 'If the Earth is larger than Mars, Mars is larger than Mercury', the proposition 'The Earth is larger than Mars' is just as true as when it stands alone, but it is not asserted in the complex proposition; he is then at a loss to say just what logical assertion can be. Wittgenstein goes even further, and says that 'assertion is merely psychological' (*Notebooks 1914–16*, p. 96); in this he is

IWT 116

supported by Miss Anscombe in her book on the *Tractatus*. This supposed 'psychological' kind of assertion which appears in Russell and Wittgenstein is a phantasm produced by the mistake of interpreting assertion as the manifestation of an internal mental attitude adopted towards the proposition; in fact, there is nothing any more psychological about assertion than about

PoM 35

the sense expressed by a sentence. Russell wants also a logical kind of assertion, partly in order to distinguish a complete sentence from one which occurs as a constituent in a complex sentence, partly to distinguish a sentence like 'Caesar died', which can be used to make an assertion, from a substantival phrase, like the 'death of Caesar', which cannot. Since it is to be 'logical', Russell wants it to be dependent solely on the sense of the sentence —and what can this be but its being true, or perhaps its truth's being intrinsic and not extrinsic to it? Wittgenstein is of course right in dismissing *this* notion of assertion, but wrong in concluding that assertion is psychological.

Frege never quite rid himself of the idea that assertion is the expression of a mental attitude; this explains some of the curious things he said about it, for instance his selection of an actor's speech as a case in which the assertion sign is not required. If assertion is the expression of a mental attitude, then the actor does not have this mental attitude, and so should not use the assertion sign. If we think of assertion as a mental act, my remark that an actor does not do *less* than assert a thought, but *more*, rings oddly; for if he did more, he should perform some mental act over and above that of assertion—and he does not even perform that; but of course I meant that he is observing the convention for the use of assertoric sentences, and another convention governing everything he does in the context, including that. It is amusing to note that Frege, in giving examples, is always careful never to put the assertion sign in front of a false sentence. This also explains why Frege expresses his view of inference so oddly. There is indeed something right in what he says. Although we may, contrary to Frege's view, regard suppositions as complete sentences, still supposition is different from other linguistic acts in that it is possible only as a preparation for further acts of the same speaker: namely for a series of utterances not themselves assertions (but consequences of the supposition), which culminate in an assertion. I could not just say, 'Suppose 2 has a rational square root', and then stop; I could not even stop at the next stage, say 'Then for some integers m and n, $m^2 = 2n^2$': I must go on to discharge the original supposition. So it is plausible—though not, I think, mandatory—to take Frege's view that these are not complete sentences at all, but that we have merely an abbreviated device for making conditional assertions. But why does he express this by saying, 'We can make inferences only from true premisses', rather than, 'We make inferences only from premisses which we take to be true'? I think the answer is that taking something to be true is a psychological matter, and Frege had set his face against the importation of psychology into logic. If we make the emendation, 'We make inferences only from premisses which we have asserted', and recognize that assertion is not anything psychological, the difficulty is overcome.

NS 195 (180); but cf. Ggf 47 (72); BW 118

This rings oddly, however: for surely it cannot be even plausibly maintained that we make inferences only from premisses that we have *asserted*; I may make a silent inference from something which I have not asserted and do not intend ever to assert. The oddity arises from the fact that the word 'inference', like the word 'judgment', is normally applied to the *interior* act, not, like 'assertion', to an exterior act performed by addressing certain words to somebody. The procedure we have agreed on, however, is to give an account of these exterior linguistic acts directly, by describing the conventions governing the use of the various forms of expression: the alternative procedure, of describing first the nature of the various interior acts, and then explaining the various types of utterance as being conventionally used to express the occurrence of these mental acts, we have rejected as leading to the confusion of psychology with logic. We are therefore not concerned with the character of the interior act of inferring the truth of a thought from the truth of others, but with the correct method of describing the conventions governing the utterance of a sequence of sentences as a deductive argument, and, in particular, the use of the word 'therefore'. Regarded in this way, Frege's point about inference consists just in his opposing, to an account of the linguistic activity of giving a deductive argument which acknowledges the existence of a distinct linguistic act of supposition, his own account which does not. According to an account of the former type, a deductive argument would consist of a sequence of linguistic acts of four distinct kinds: (1) assertions made without indication of the grounds for them; (2) assertions of thoughts as following from thoughts previously asserted, perhaps taken together with the previous carrying out of one or more subordinate deductions; (3) statements of suppositions; and (4) expressions of thoughts as holding under given suppositions, and as following from thoughts previously registered as so holding, or previously asserted outright, perhaps together with one or more previously effected subordinate deductions. The sign for a supposition would of course be the word 'Suppose', and that for an act of kind (2) or (4) a word like 'Therefore', 'Hence', 'So', etc. However, on Frege's account, which dispenses with supposition as a separate linguistic act, an argument consists of a sequence of utterances of two kinds only: plain assertions (the premisses), as in (1) above; and assertions which are expressed *as* following from earlier assertions, words like 'therefore' being used to convey the force of this special kind of assertion. Thus on Frege's account it would be correct to say, 'A thought is asserted as following from other thoughts only when the latter have been *asserted*'. But, for the reasons we have set out, he misstates his point by saying that we make inferences only from what is *true*.

In her book on the *Tractatus*, Miss Anscombe boldly equates Frege's view of assertion with Russell's: '*Being asserted* (in this "logical" sense) is, for both Russell and Frege, something that cannot possibly attach to a proposition unless it is true' (p. 114). There is little enough warrant for this in Frege's published writings: I know no passage where he excludes the possibility of asserting what is in fact false. There is indeed a tendency in Frege's thought which, combined with the principle that psychology must not intrude into logic, could lead to this: the tendency, just described, to think of assertion as the manifestation of a mental act; though, since Miss Anscombe herself takes assertion to be purely psychological, she cannot diagnose this. Perhaps she is relying on a curious remark of Frege's in an unpublished letter to Jourdain (the same one in which he gives the example

BW 127 (79)   of Afla and Ateb), that, strictly speaking, it is logically meaningless to attach the assertion sign to a false sentence.

Bs 2   Frege's assertion sign '⊢' is compounded out of the content-stroke '—' and the judgment-stroke '|', to give them the names he used in *Begriffsschrift*. '—ξ' is simply an ordinary functional expression: it stands for the

Gg I 5   function whose value is truth for truth as argument, and falsity for all other arguments, i.e., for the concept under which only truth falls.* Thus, if '*a*' is a sentence, '—*a*' is a sentence with the same truth-value, and if '*a*' is a singular term which is not a sentence, '—*a*' is a false sentence. Thus the predicate '$\xi = -\xi$' means 'ξ is a truth-value'. '—' is a primitive symbol in

---

* We are here of course assuming Frege's thesis, adopted in *Grundgesetze*, that truth-values are objects.

Frege's system, and appears to be wholly superfluous. In the system of *Grundgesetze*, all functional expressions are defined for all arguments of the appropriate type: in particular, the two sentential operators '$\top \xi$' ('not ξ') and '$\underset{\xi}{\overset{\eta}{\top}}$' ('if ξ, then η') are defined for all objects as arguments of the two corresponding functions, and the quantifier '$\overset{\mathfrak{a}}{\smile}\varphi(\mathfrak{a})$' ('for every $\mathfrak{a}$, $\varphi(\mathfrak{a})$')

Gg I 6, 9, 12

for every first-level singulary function as argument. If we had variables which ranged over all objects, including truth-values, and we wanted to restrict them to truth-values alone, prefixing the sign '$-$' to each would give this effect; but since all the logical constants are defined for every possible argument in any case, there is no need for this. (The only exception to this is the sign of identity '$=$', which, since sentences stand for objects, can also function as the biconditional 'if and only if'. We cannot assert '$a = \top\top a$' quite generally, since '$\top$' is so defined that $\top a$ is always a truth-value; we could assert only '$-a = \top\top a$'.) In *Begriffsschrift* the distinction is drawn between 'judgeable' and 'unjudgeable' contents (the word 'content' being taken in a vague sense as roughly covering both what Frege later called 'sense' and what he later called 'reference'): an expression for a judgeable content being a sentence, one for an unjudgeable content a non-sentence. The content-stroke could be meaningfully prefixed only to an expression for a judgeable content; the same held good of the two sentential operators. Thus in *Begriffsschrift* the content-stroke does not serve the purpose of turning an expression for an unjudgeable content into one for a judgeable content, whereas in *Grundgesetze* it in effect turns any singular term into a sentence. In *Begriffsschrift* Frege says that the content-stroke serves both to combine the symbols following it into a whole, and to relate any sign to the whole formed by the symbols following the stroke. But these two operations are quite redundant: whatever can meaningfully follow the content-stroke must already constitute a unitary whole, and any symbol that can be joined on to the content-stroke must have already been explained as capable of being related to such a whole. In any case, the content-stroke is superfluous, because it is equivalent to the double negative '$\top \top$' (as Frege would write it, '$\top\top$').

Bs 2

Gg I 5

The judgment-stroke is the sign of assertion proper, that which carries the assertoric force. It is therefore not a functional expression, or part of one: we cannot enquire of it what its sense is, or what its reference is; it contributes to the meaning of the complex sentential symbol in quite a different way. Furthermore, it is only the sentence to which the judgment-stroke is prefixed which may be said to express a sense or to stand for a

truth-value: the whole expression with the judgment-stroke neither expresses anything nor stands for anything—it *asserts* something: it asserts,
namely, that the thought expressed by what follows the judgment-stroke is
true. Thus, although the judgment-stroke is used to say that the thought
expressed is true, it operates in a quite different way from the words 'is true'
or 'it is true that'. We do not succeed in asserting anything by adding to a
sentence without the judgment-stroke the words 'is true', or by prefixing the
words 'it is true that': we merely get another sentence which expresses a
thought and has the same truth-value as before; indeed, as Frege believes,
we get a sentence which expresses the very same thought as before. This
sentence may serve as a constituent in a more complex sentence—as the
antecedent of a conditional, for example: this is enough to show that the
phrase 'is true' or 'it is true that' does not function as a sign of assertion, for
it is meaningless, as we have seen, to attempt to put a sign with assertoric,
or any other, *force* inside a constituent clause in a complex sentence. The
fact that, on Frege's view, the phrase 'is true' ('it is true that') does not alter
or add to the sense of the sentence to which it is attached should not make
us say that it is senseless, for a sentence which contains a senseless expression
will itself be senseless; rather, it has a sense of just such a kind that it does
not alter the sense of any sentence it is attached to. (It is thus like an expression for the identity function, whose value for any argument is that argument
itself: save that this expression merely leaves the reference of the whole
unaltered, whereas 'is true' leaves the sense unaltered.)

It is natural at first to take denial as an activity parallel to assertion. Here
denial would be thought of as the opposite language-game to assertion,
characterized by the intention to utter *false* sentences: the convention
governing the utterance of sentences recognizable as used with negatory
force would be to utter only sentences with the value 'false'. The sign of
negation 'not' would thus be interpreted as a sign of denial, parallel to the
sign of assertion, and conveying, not assertoric, but negatory force. Frege
opposes this view with a conclusive argument: namely that, while it would be
possible so to interpret those sentences in which the sign of negation was the
principal operator, it would be impossible to interpret the negation sign in
this way whenever it occurred in a sentence otherwise than as the main
operator. This is the same argument as before: a sentence formed by prefacing another sentence by the sign of negation may itself serve as a
constituent in a complex sentence, as, say, a clause in a disjunctive or conditional sentence. A sign which conveys force must always relate to the
whole complete sentence in which it occurs; it cannot form part of a
subordinate clause. Hence the negation sign which does occur as part of

FB 22n

Ged 63 (8);
NS 140 (129);
NS 211 (194);
NS 251–2 (233);
Ged 61 (6)

NS 271–2
(251–2)

subordinate clauses must be interpreted differently, namely as a functional expression (sentential operator) which contributes to the sense of the clause in which it occurs. We might add to this a point not stated by Frege, namely that it is not only assertoric sentences which can be negated, but also, e.g., imperatives. Hence, if we were to interpret a negation sign which occurs as the main operator in an assertoric sentence as not contributing to the sense, but as a sign of denial, by parity a negation sign which was the main operator in an imperative would have also to be construed as not contributing to the sense, but as a sign of prohibition, marking the performance of yet another distinct kind of linguistic act and conveying a new kind of force. (The quirk of language, referred to earlier, might save us from an analogous conclusion in the case of questions: 'Isn't he there?' is the same question as 'Is he there?' and as 'Is he there or isn't he?'.) Thus we should have to acknowledge at least three distinct roles for the negation sign: as a sign of denial, a sign of prohibition and as a sign contributing to the sense of the sentence it occurs in. Moreover, we should be faced with a multiplicity of rules of inference: for example, the argument from the premisses 'If he is not a philosopher, he won't understand the question' and 'He is not a philosopher' to the conclusion 'He won't understand the question' will not be an instance of modus ponens. The sentence which occurs as a complete sentence in the second premiss will not be the same as the sentence which forms the antecedent of the conditional in the first premiss. In the second premiss, 'not' is the main operator, and hence will be taken as a sign conveying the negatory force, and therefore not as part of the expression of the thought: the thought will be simply the thought that he *is* a philosopher. But in the first premiss, 'not' does not occur as the main operator, and hence must be taken as contributing to the sense of the sentence in which it occurs: so the thought which this sentence expresses will be the thought that he is *not* a philosopher. Evidently, all this complexity will be avoided if we take 'not', in *all* its occurrences, as an operator used to form, from any sentence, another sentence with a different sense: and hence, by Occam's razor, we must so take it. Denying a thought will then be something intrinsically complex, namely asserting the thought which is the negation of that thought; likewise prohibiting something will consist of commanding its negation. There will thus be no need to invoke any special, primitive, linguistic acts of denial and prohibition.

Thus, given that we have the linguistic activity of assertion, we have no need to recognize any separate linguistic activity of denial. It may occur to one, however, that it must be accidental, if Frege's theory is correct, that we have that one of this pair of linguistic activities that we do, that we have assertion but not denial: why should we not instead have had a convention

M*

whereby we were taken as uttering sentences with the intention of uttering *false* ones, not as well as the convention of assertion that we do have, but in place of it? This possibility has only to be stated to be recognized as spurious. But it may appear that on Frege's theory it ought to be a genuine possibility, and this may then appear as a ground for thinking Frege's theory false.

A cognate point is made by Wittgenstein in the *Tractatus* as follows: 'Can we not make ourselves understood by means of false sentences, just as we did previously by means of true ones? Provided only that we know that they are meant as false. No. For a sentence is true if things are as we say they are by means of it; and if by "p" we mean "∼p", and things are as we mean them, then "p" is on the new interpretation true and not false' (4.062). He draws from this the consequence: 'It is, however, important that the signs "p" and "∼p" *can* say the same. For it shows that to the sign "∼" there corresponds nothing in reality' (4.0621).

Now suppose that we come across a group of people who employ signs, which are prefixed to the beginning of their sentences, to convey the force with which the sentence is uttered; they have also a sign of negation, which can occur otherwise than as the main operator. Let us suppose that they use a certain sign 'ʃ' at the beginnings of some sentences, and that for this our linguists propose alternative interpretations: that it is a sign of assertion, and that it is a sign of denial. On which of these interpretations is adopted will depend the interpretations of all the sentences which can follow this sign. For instance, if 'A' is an abbreviation of a sentence of theirs, and it is noticed that they utter the expression 'ʃA' principally when it is raining, then if 'ʃ' is taken as a sign of assertion, 'A' will be guessed to mean 'It is raining'; but if 'ʃ' is taken as a sign of denial, 'A' will be guessed to mean 'It is dry'. But it is clear that there is absolutely no way of deciding, by observing what they say and do, between the two interpretations of 'ʃ'. It might be thought that we could so decide if we could identify words in their language which had the meanings 'true' and 'false': then we could ask them whether 'ʃ' was a sign that the speaker was trying to say what is true or that he was trying to say what is false. Well, let us suppose that by some means we have identified a pair of expressions in their language as corresponding to the pair 'is true' and 'is false'; let us represent this pair by 'is j' and 'is k'. We have first to decide whether 'j' corresponds to 'true' and 'k' to 'false' or conversely. What observations can we make to decide this? We might notice that, on seeing the rain, they say, 'ʃ(A is j)', and, when they see there is no rain, they say 'ʃ(A is k)'. Now on the interpretation of 'ʃ' as a sign of assertion, 'A' means 'It is raining' and their intention in speaking is to say what is true: since 'A' is true when it is raining, and false when it is not, and they say that it is j when it is raining and k when it is not, 'j' must mean 'true' on this interpretation of 'ʃ', and 'k' 'false'. Now suppose we interpret 'ʃ' as a sign of denial. Then 'A' means 'It is dry' and their intention in speaking is to say what is false. Now 'A', on this interpretation, is false when it is raining and true when it is not. When it is raining, they say 'ʃ(A is j)', meaning to say what is false. What they say will be false, however, only if 'j' means 'true', since, on this interpretation, when it is raining 'A' is false. Hence, no matter which interpretation of 'ʃ' we select, we obtain the result that 'j' means 'true' and 'k' means 'false'. For this very reason, nothing that they say involving 'j' and 'k' can decide between the two interpretations.

The two alternative descriptions of their language are completely interchangeable: they do not describe distinct possibilities at all. Since it is indifferent which we choose, it is clear that we shall always choose the one which resembles the account we give of our own language most closely, namely the interpretation under which 'ʃ' is a sign of assertion and their intention in speaking is to say what is true. It might be objected that we could get a clue as to the correct account from their use of sentences with a different force, e.g., with imperatival force. Suppose that they use a sentential complex 'ΣB' in the way that we use the imperative 'Stand up!'. The sentence 'B' will also occur in sentential complexes with a different force, in particular in the complex 'ʃB'. Since 'ΣB' means 'Stand up!', it might be thought that 'B' must mean 'You are standing up' (considered as without assertoric force); hence we can decide whether 'ʃ' is a sign of assertion or of denial by observing whether they say 'ʃB' when the person they are addressing is standing up or not standing up. But suppose that they say to someone 'ʃB' chiefly when he is not standing. We can still take 'ʃ' as a sign of assertion and 'B' as meaning 'You are not standing'; in order to do this we have only to take 'Σ' as a sign of prohibition instead of a sign of command. It is clear that we should always prefer to suppose they had a sign of assertion and one of prohibition rather than one of denial and one of command; and in any case it remains true that there is no difference between the two possibilities.

The fact that these are only spuriously distinct possibilities may appear to cast doubt on Frege's theory: for does not his theory involve that there would be a real difference between the activities of assertion and of denial? On reflection we see that there is no problem for Frege. The conventions governing the sense of the expressions of a language assign every sentence to one of two classes, membership of which is of course in general determined by non-linguistic considerations depending on the sense of the sentence. The assertoric use of sentences is then to be described by saying that it consists in attempting to utter only sentences belonging to a particular one of these classes. Any possibility of asking, 'Which of these two classes is the class of true sentences and which the class of false ones?', naturally depends on presupposing a prior understanding of the terms 'true' and 'false'. Now what does this prior understanding consist of? What is the principle whereby we can decide which class is to be identified as the class of true sentences? Clearly the only principle available is that according to which the use of assertoric sentences consists in trying to utter only true ones: the class of true sentences is the class the utterance of a member of which a speaker of the language is aiming at when he employs what is recognizably the assertoric use. It is just because this is the only possible principle on which to discriminate between the class of true sentences and the class of false ones that there is no genuine possibility of a linguistic activity consisting in the attempt to utter only false sentences. In just the same way, there is no such thing as a game in which the object is to try to lose. Rather than say that two people are playing chess, but that they have both agreed to try to lose, we shall say that they are trying to win, but that what they are playing is not chess but a variant of it: the difference in the game played here corresponds to the difference in the sense of 'A' according as we take '$\int$' as a sign of assertion or denial. I have, of course, no desire to be dictatorial here: if someone prefers to think it legitimate to say of people that their linguistic convention is to try to say what is false, or that they agree to try to lose a game, the point can be put in a different way. If it is legitimate to say these things, then there is no principle at all whereby we can distinguish, for a given language, the class of true sentences from the class of false ones (or, for a given game, the outcomes which constitute winning from those which constitute losing). Hence the apparent difference in the two alternative descriptions of a language consists in nothing more than a difference in the arbitrary *labelling* of the two classes by means of the words 'true' and 'false'.

Here we are considering 'true' and 'false' as words used by someone wanting to give a description of the use of a language, of the linguistic behaviour of its speakers, from *outside* the language; what we have said does not at all concern the meanings of any words *within* the language. As we have seen, words for 'true' and 'false' within the language can be identified and distinguished from one another quite independently of the decision which class is the class of true sentences, and hence of the decision whether the activity the speakers of the language engage in is that of assertion or of denial. We identified 'j' as meaning 'true' and 'k' as meaning 'false', in effect, by observing the rule that 'A is true' is interchangeable with 'A' and

'A is false' with 'Not A'. Since 'A is j' functioned as interchangeable with 'A', 'j' must mean 'true'; since 'A is k' functioned like a negation of 'A', 'k' must mean 'false'. Of course, since we did not yet know whether 'ʃ' was a sign of assertion or of denial, we did not know which was the class of j sentences and which the class of k sentences, although we knew that 'j' meant 'true' and 'k' 'false'. But then we did not need to know this, in order to understand the use within the language of 'j' and 'k': if we interpret 'They say that the sentence "A" is j' as meaning 'They utter the sentential complex "ʃ(A is j)" ', then we know which sentences they say are j, and which k, and that is all we need to know.

There would be a significant distinction between having a primitive linguistic practice of assertion—uttering sentences so as to be taken as trying to utter a true one—and only secondarily the practice of denial (the assertion of the negation), and, on the other hand, having a primitive practice of denial—uttering sentences so as to be taken as trying to utter a false one—and only secondarily that of assertion (the denial of the negation), only if there were any means of distinguishing the class of true sentences of a language from the class of false sentences independently of the practice of using the language. But this there evidently cannot be. Indeed, there is no way of saying what truth-values are save that they are the referents of sentences, and no way of distinguishing one truth-value from the other save by adverting to the use of sentences to make assertions, and to that feature of this practice which makes it possible to ask whether someone is *right* or *wrong* in what he asserts. And this was precisely the premiss from which we concluded that Wittgenstein's point was no objection to Frege's doctrine of assertion. (It is rather difficult to tell from the context in the *Tractatus* whether it is intended to be one or not; I think that the probability is that it was.)

We saw that Wittgenstein uses his observation to conclude that the negation sign does not stand for anything in reality. This might be taken to mean that there is not any contingent feature of the world in virtue of which we need to use the negation sign; this was certainly what Russell had in mind in making a similar point in *The Philosophy of Logical Atomism*, though of course this fact would not be for Frege a reason for denying that the negation sign had a reference. But for Wittgenstein in the *Tractatus*, this could not be the point, since 'the world is the totality of facts, not of things'. Objects, for Wittgenstein as for Frege, are the referents (Bedeutungen) of names; but for Wittgenstein, when we know what objects there are, we know only what are the *possible* facts; we know nothing about what is contingently the case. Rather, the argument seems to be that if the use of the negation

LK 187, 209, 214

TLP 1.1

TLP 3.144, 3.203, 3.3

sign consisted in its being used to stand for some constituent of the state of affairs we depict by means of a sentence containing it, then it would be impossible to depict that state of affairs by means of a sentence which did not contain a symbol for negation: hence, if 'Not A' were a fully analysed sentence, it would be impossible that 'A' by itself should be capable of being used to mean what 'Not A' now means. Let us suppose for simplicity that 'A' is not merely a fully analysed sentence, but what Wittgenstein calls an 'elementary' sentence, i.e. one which, when fully analysed, contains no logical operators. (Of course, we are here presupposing Wittgenstein's thesis that 'there is one and only one complete analysis of a sentence' (3.25).) Elementary sentences are supposed to be such that no one of them can be

TLP 6.3751   logically incompatible with any other: hence, as Wittgenstein points out, statements of the form, '*a* is red', '*a* is green', where '*a*' refers to a point in visual space, say, and as 'red' and 'green' are ordinarily understood, cannot be elementary sentences, since they are incompatible with one another. Suppose, however, we consider the names of the primary colours, 'red', 'yellow' and 'blue', as being used as mutually compatible: '*a* is red' will then be true if *a*'s colour has red as an ingredient, e.g., is orange, red, purple, brown or white, but false if it does not have red as an ingredient, e.g., is pure yellow or pure blue, or green, or black. Then there will not be this objection to considering statements of the form '*a* is red', '*a* is blue' or '*a* is yellow' as elementary sentences. No doubt there will be other objections; but let us ignore these, and suppose that 'A' is of the form '*a* is red', so understood. Then the argument runs as follows: We *could* use '*a* is red' to mean what we now mean by '*a* is not red'; and this shows that we do not use 'not' to stand for a constituent of the state of affairs we depict by means of a negative sentence, because otherwise we should not be able to depict this state of affairs by means of a sentence which not only did not contain the word 'not', but did not contain any other word in its place; for we should have to have a word to stand for that constituent.

This argument seems quite unconvincing. Let us suppose that '*a* is red', used in this hypothetical way, is taken to depict a state of affairs which contains three constituents, *a*, red and negation; (*a* is not red', as correspondingly used, would depict a state of affairs having only the two constituents *a* and red. All that would be implied is that in this hypothetical language the symbol for negation (for the negation of an elementary sentence) was the *absence* of the word 'not' instead of its occurrence. If we adopt a convention that 'silence means consent', so that I have to say something in order to show that I do *not* agree, it would be absurd to argue that because under this convention I can express by saying nothing what I may have to utter a complicated sentence to express without it, the words I should use in that sentence do not stand for anything in reality. This accords well with Wittgenstein's saying that that which effects the negation in '∼p' is not '∼' but 'what is in common to all the signs of this notation which deny p' (5.512).

The argument which really operates in the *Tractatus* to show that the negation sign does not stand for anything is that otherwise we should have to consider both '*a* is red' and '*a* is not red' as elementary sentences, and this would infringe the law that elementary sentences cannot be logically incompatible, or have any other logical relations with one another. It may then be asked why this law has to be assumed to be valid. There is a not very convincing defence of this thesis in Miss Anscombe's book on the *Tractatus*, where she claims that the existence of a class of logically independent propositions is presupposed by the explanation of the sentential operators by means of truth-tables. I should have thought that the most that could be held to be presupposed was that, for each of the four truth-combinations for two propositions, there existed two propositions having the two truth-values in question. The appeal of the thesis lies rather in its reducing all a priori truth to tautological necessity. If '*a* is red' and '*a* is not red' were elementary sentences, then their incompatibility would be an irreducible fact, something literally in the nature of *things*. Similarly, if '*a* is red' and '*a* is green', considered now as ordinarily understood, were fully analysed sentences, then *their* incompatibility would appear irreducible —perhaps even synthetic a priori.

From Frege's viewpoint, sentential operators contribute to the senses of sentences in which they occur in the same general way as do expressions of other kinds. For instance, the two complexes '$(\neg\beta\to\gamma)\to\delta$' and '$\neg[(\beta\to\delta)\to\neg(\gamma\to\delta)]$' are truth-functionally equivalent, and therefore have the same reference; but, in any case in which the argument-places are filled by the same three sentences respectively, our method of recognizing that a given truth-value is the truth-value of the whole—the computation-procedures which we apply—will be different in the two cases, and therefore the senses of the two expressions are different. If a language contained as primitive a ternary sentential connective 'Wenn β oder γ, so δ', whose truth-table coincided with that for the above two complexes, it could be explained either by giving its truth-table, or as equivalent to one or other of the two formulas; these would all be ways of stating its reference, but, since they would be *different* ways, associated with different computation-procedures, they would assign to the connective different senses.

In the *Tractatus*, Wittgenstein's picture theory of meaning prohibited

IWT 33

TLP 4.0621 him from regarding the occurrence of logical operators in a sentence as characterizing its sense, since they cannot be interpreted as elements of the picture: indeed, he regarded it as an important *discovery* that they do not characterize the sense of a sentence, since, if they did, they would have *TLP* 4.441, 5.4 to have a reference, and there would have to be 'logical objects' (or at least functions). (For Wittgenstein, the—genuine—constituents of a sentence have reference—not sense—and thereby confer on the sentence a sense.) He explains his thesis that the logical constants do not characterize the sense *TLP* 5.25–5.251 of a sentence by saying that they represent *operations*, nòt functions. Miss Anscombe, in her book on the *Tractatus*, offers an unsatisfactory account of *IWT* 117-20 the difference between operations and functions.* In fact, there is no general difference between operations and functions; if we insist that the *WVC* 217 range of an operation be included in its domain, then an operation is simply a special case of a function. The difference Wittgenstein had in mind can be illustrated as follows. Suppose there is a language which contains as logical constants just the two binary connectives 'and' and 'or', and the two quantifiers, but no sign of negation (we will suppose for simplicity that there are no modal expressions in the language). For each simple predicate or relational expression in the language, there is a unique complementary predicate or relational expression. Now in talking *about* the language—not in it—we may introduce the operation of forming the negation of a sentence, defined inductively:

(i) if 'A' is an atomic sentence '$F(a_1, \ldots, a_n)$' ($n \geqslant 1$), then 'not-A' is '$\overline{F}(a_1, \ldots, a_n)$', where '$\overline{F}(\xi_1, \ldots, \xi_n)$' is the complement of '$F(\xi_1, \ldots, \xi_n)$';
(ii) if 'A' is 'B and C', then 'not-A' is 'not-B or not-C';
(iii) if 'A' is 'B or C', then 'not-A' is 'not-A and not-B';
(iv) if 'A' is 'For every α, $G(\alpha)$', then 'not-A' is 'For some α, not-$G(\alpha)$';
(v) if 'A' is 'For some α, $G(\alpha)$', then 'not-A' is 'For every α, not-$G(\alpha)$'.

Now obviously that a sentence of this language is the negation of another one is no characteristic of its sense, since *every* sentence of the language is, in the sense defined, the negation of some other sentence. A fortiori, there is no expression whose occurrence in a sentence is either a necessary or a sufficient condition for a sentence to be a negation. The symbol 'not' neither is nor corresponds to any expression or feature of expressions in

---

* She says, e.g., that a function cannot be its own argument, whereas an operation can be iterated—it can take as its base the result of applying the operation to something else. But in this sense a function can be iterated too—it can take as its argument something which is its value for some other argument.

the language: it was introduced as representing a rule for passing from one sentence of the language to another one.

As Stenius points out, Wittgenstein repeatedly toys with the idea, rejected by Frege, that the negation sign should be explained by considering denial as a linguistic activity parallel with assertion. And perhaps his whole theory in the *Tractatus* of the logical operators should be understood in this light, instead of trying to use his fundamentally confused conception of them as signs for 'operations'. On this account, not only the negation sign but all the logical operators would be regarded, not as contributing to what Frege called the sense of the sentence, but as signs for the force attached to what I shall call the 'sentence-collective'. This 'sentence-collective' must be thought of, not as a single sentence, except in the case of the negation sign, but as a (finite or infinite) set of elementary sentences. To regard *all* the logical operators in this way evades Frege's objection to so considering the negation sign on the ground that it could occur within constituent clauses of complex sentences. The logical operators, regarded as signs for the force conveyed, would have the peculiarity among such signs that they could be indefinitely combined and reiterated. If Wittgenstein had had a theory which allowed him to give an account of the difference between assertion, command, etc., it would have been necessary, in order to view the logical operators as signs for the force conveyed, to reproduce the differences between them for each type of utterance: thus there would be distinct linguistic acts of affirming, denying, disjunctively asserting, conditionally asserting, etc., and also of commanding, prohibiting, disjunctively commanding, conditionally commanding, etc. Moreover, for such a theory to be workable, however cumbrous, there would have to be a difference intrinsic to what is expressed, and not just to the mode of expression, between what is affirmative and what is negative: and the postulation of such a difference depends on the postulation of the existence of elementary sentences—the constituents of the '*unique* complete analysis' of any sentence. Frege expressly denies the existence of a distinction between affirmative and negative intrinsic to the thought expressed rather than to its linguistic expression. Which of the sentences, 'Christ is mortal' and 'Christ is immortal', expresses a negative thought? 'Christ is immortal' because it means 'Christ is not mortal'? Or because it means 'Christ does not die'? Or 'Christ is mortal' because it means 'Christ does not live forever'? Or because it means 'At some time Christ is not alive'? Of course, relative to a particular order of introducing the expressions of a language, and a particular method of defining some in terms of others, we could say which sentences were negative, by reducing each to the primitive vocabulary. But if you learn 'crooked' ostensively,

WT 171-2

Ver 150 (41)

and 'straight' by having it defined as 'not crooked', whereas I learned 'straight' ostensively, and 'crooked' by having it explained as 'not straight', the difference in the senses we attach to 'crooked' are negligible, if they exist at all; and in any case, the important point is that, not only can we learn the words in these different ways, and still communicate satisfactorily, but there is no inherent advantage possessed by one method of learning them over the other. (These last remarks do not purport to represent anything explicitly found in Frege.)

In this connection we may note some other points about Wittgenstein's treatment of assertion. It will surprise readers of Frege to find that both in the *Tractatus* and in the *Investigations* Wittgenstein uses Meinong's term 'assumption' (*Annahme*) in speaking of Frege's doctrine. The explanation of this has been uncovered by some detective work of Miss Anscombe's. Frege says in *Function und Begriff* that a formula such as '$5 > 4$' just gives us an expression for a truth-value without making any assertion. If we did not make this distinction, he says, we could not express a mere assumption [supposition—*Annahme*]—'the putting of a case without at the same time judging whether or not it obtains'. As we have seen, in most of his writing Frege is inclined to deny that there is any such act as the stating of an assumption or supposition in this sense—not, at any rate, as a prelude to deductive reasoning. But Russell, in his appendix on Frege in *Principles of Mathematics*, misinterpreted the word 'Annahme' here as being for Frege a technical term, as it was for Meinong: and in this he appears to have been followed by Wittgenstein. On this (mis)interpretation, a *Gedanke* (thought) is not a proposition but a propositional concept. Earlier in the *Principles* (pp. 48, 52) Russell explains that, while 'Caesar died' is a proposition, 'the death of Caesar' is a propositional concept: he suggests accounting for the difference by saying that truth or falsity is internal to the former, but external to the latter, but admits that this fails to discriminate between 'Caesar died' and 'the truth of the death of Caesar'; he goes on to say that the proposition is (in the 'logical' sense) asserted, the propositional concept unasserted—though indeed this fits badly both with his saying that 'Caesar died' is unasserted in 'If Caesar died, Brutus lived', and with his saying that to be ('logically') asserted is to be true. Russell then takes an *Annahme* (assumption) to be for Frege a proposition: the propositional concept, he thinks, is expressed by, e.g., '$5 > 4$', the proposition by '—$(5 > 4)$'.

Wittgenstein says, 'Every sentence must *already* have a sense; affirmation cannot give it one, since what it affirms is, precisely, the sense. And the same holds for denial, etc.' (*Tractatus*, 4.064). His use of 'sense' is brought out in 3.144: 'One can describe, but not *name*, states of affairs. (Names resemble

TLP 4.063;
PI 22, p. 11n
IWT 105–6
FB 21

points, sentences arrows—they have a sense.)' As Stenius points out, Wittgenstein is here punning on 'sense' = 'meaning' and 'sense' = 'direc- *WT* 171 tion'. That a sentence has a 'sense', whereas a name has only a 'meaning' (Bedeutung), seemed to Wittgenstein, in opposition to Frege, the fundamental distinction between them: a sentence has true/false poles, a name has *NB* 94 not; a sentence as it were points towards one state of affairs, and away from another—a name only points down, to the object it stands for. Stenius, however, superimposes on the doctrine of the *Tractatus* a theory of assertion like Frege's, expressly rejected by Wittgenstein. As we have seen, we can regard Wittgenstein's account of the logical constants as in effect attributing to them the function of conveying the force with which the sentence is uttered: but since he does not recognize the need for a special kind of force attaching to imperative or interrogative sentences, he does not think that a sentence which contains no logical constants needs any sign for the assertoric force attached to it—it is *already* adapted to express an act of assertion. This is wrong, as we have seen; and Stenius compounds the confusion by attempting to superimpose a theory of assertion while leaving 4.064 untouched. Stenius insists that the 'sentence-radical' (that part which serves *WT* 167-71 to express the thought, but does not contain a sign for the force which is attached) itself has a '*directed*' sense, independently of the assertion which can be expressed by attaching the assertion sign to it. Admittedly, the 'sentence-radical' has 'true/false poles', in that its sense consists in a distinction between conditions under which it is true and conditions under which it is false: but we can determine the 'direction' of this sense—which set of conditions it points to and which it points away from—only by considering its use when assertoric force is attached to it, because it is only by reference to its role in assertions that we can identify one set of conditions as those in which it is *true* and the other as those in which it is *false*.

We have seen that a sign for the force attached to a sentence, i.e. a sign conventionally used to indicate which linguistic act is being performed by uttering the sentence, cannot significantly occur within a clause which is a constituent of a complex sentence, but can attach only to a complete sentence as a whole. Or, at least, this is Frege's doctrine. If it is correct, it appears to constitute a powerful method for detecting spurious claims to have identified a new kind of force, or form of linguistic act, and has been so used by Geach. For instance, Strawson once proposed, in effect, that *Tr* 89-97 the words 'is true' should be understood, not as contributing to the sense of the sentence in which they occur, but as expressing the force with which it is uttered; that they signify the performance of one of several special linguistic acts, distinct from ordinary assertion—the act of corroboration, or that of concession, for example. But if the thesis that a sign for force cannot occur within the scope of a sentential operator is correct, then there is a simple way with such a proposal: we have only to observe that a sentence containing the words 'is true', e.g. 'what the witness said is true', may occur as a subordinate clause, as the antecedent of a conditional,

LM 250–4

for instance. In his article on 'Ascriptivism', Geach has dealt likewise with claims that such words as 'ought', 'good', 'responsible', and the like, operate as signifying the performance of special linguistic acts—commendation, evaluation, exhortation, ascription and so forth.

If, on the other hand, the thesis is not correct, then the whole distinction between sense and force comes under threat. It is therefore of the greatest importance to examine the thesis with care.

We are concerned only with those types of force which attach to sentences expressing complete thoughts. On any account of the matter, there are other sorts of force: for instance, the expression of unspecific distress or satisfaction, greeting, summoning, and the asking of non-sentential questions (questions governed by 'Who . . . ?' 'When . . . ?', etc., which may be said to ask after the value of a variable satisfying some predicate). At least as candidates for types of force attaching to complete thoughts, we may list, not necessarily exhaustively: asserting that it is the case that A; commanding, requesting, exhorting, advising someone to bring it about that A; asking whether it is the case that A; expressing the wish that it were, or the hope that it is, the case that A; supposing that it were the case that A; and concluding that, under a given supposition, it would be the case that A. Clearly some of these have sub-species: e.g. if the word 'therefore' is to be classed as a sign of force, as indicating that what is being asserted is being said as following from what has gone before, it qualifies and does not replace the sign of assertion. In what follows, capital letters such as 'A' and 'B' will

PI p. 11n

represent sentences considered as having sense but not force—sentence-radicals, in Wittgenstein's terminology; and we shall use '⊢' as a sign of assertion, '?' as a sign of interrogative force, and '!' as a sign of command.

What meaning might, in general, be attached to the inclusion of a sign for force within the scope of a sentential operator? One suggestion might be as follows. If Henry makes an assertion, or asks a question, etc., then, of course, some report of the form 'Henry asserted that A', 'Henry asked whether A', or the like, is correct. It might then be proposed that any sentential operator, having force-indicators within its scope, should be so interpreted that the report involving the same sentential operator, this time unproblematically, should be taken as correct. Thus, if Henry says, '⊢ (A or B)', the only correct report would be, 'Henry asserted that A or B': it would be quite untrue to report, 'Either Henry asserted that A or he asserted that B', for he did neither. But, on this interpretation, the latter would be the correct report to give if Henry had said, '(⊢A) or (⊢B)'.

In the case of disjunction and assertion, this suggestion evidently works pretty badly. But, in other cases, it may not be so absurd. Suppose that someone says to me, '⊢A'. I may agree; or I may not agree, and indicate my disagreement by saying, '⊢B', where 'B' is a contrary of 'A'. But I may be in the position that I am not prepared to assent to 'A', yet do not want to assert 'Not A' either. In this case, instead of saying, '⊢ (not A)', I might say, 'Not (⊢A)'.

On the interpretation proposed, if Henry says, 'Not (⊢A)', it will be correct to report, 'Henry did not assert that A'. But why should we need any such form? Why cannot Henry secure the correctness of such a report, not by any special form of utterance, but by simply not asserting that A? If he is not prepared to make any contrary assertion, he can simply say nothing at all. One situation in which an overt form is needed to express the non-assertion of something is that in which 'silence means consent'. If it has been agreed, tacitly or explicitly, that I am to be taken as assenting to all the assertions of some speaker to which I voice no objection, I must have some means of expressing that I do not assent, since I am not sure of having any counter-assertion to make. There are many social situations which approach this more or less nearly.

In more general situations, however, the report, 'Henry did not assert that A', could not be a complete report of what Henry effected by uttering 'Not (⊢A)', just because, in the ordinary situation, as opposed to that in which silence means consent, that report would have been true if Henry had said nothing at all, whereas he did say something, of however negative a character. But such a form might be taken to be a means of expressing an unwillingness to assert 'A', where, unless a special social convention applies, just keeping silent, or changing the subject, would be compatible with a willingness to assert 'A', a willingness to deny it, or the lack of either. Under such an interpretation, someone who says, 'Not (⊢A)', might actually be prepared, in other company, to deny 'A', but reluctant to manifest this opinion to his present interlocutor; but he is expressing a view that grounds do not exist sufficient to justify the assertion of 'A'. By keeping silent, he may merely be showing that he does not want to tell you what he thinks; but, by saying, 'Not (⊢A)', he is at least telling you what he does not think.

This provides at least a possible interpretation for applying negation to the sign of assertion: do we in fact have, in natural language, any form which has this effect? That we do may be most clearly seen by considering how we might interpret the negation of a conditional in natural language. Suppose I say, 'If it rains, the match will be cancelled', and you reply, 'That is not so', or, 'I don't think that is the case'. I might answer, 'I suppose you mean that they do not intend to cancel it, but I know that: I think all the same that, if it *does* rain, they *will* cancel it'. You say, 'I know nothing about their present intentions; I am talking about the *future*, too. I just think that it is not the case that, if it rains, the match will be cancelled'. I ask, 'What do you mean? You can't mean that it *will* rain and the match will not be cancelled. Perhaps you mean only that, if it rains, the match will not be cancelled'. You may accept this; but, equally, you may answer, 'I don't mean anything as strong as that: I only mean that, if it rains, the match will not *necessarily* be cancelled: that it *may* happen that it rains and yet the match not be cancelled'.

The modal expressions 'necessarily' and 'may', which have here been introduced into the explanation of what was meant by the negation of the conditional, here express what is known as 'epistemic' modality ('for all I know' or 'as far as I am aware'). Expressions of epistemic modality do not ordinarily occur within the scope of sentential operators, and are best understood, not as contributing to the senses of the sentences they govern, i.e. as determining the truth-conditions of those sentences, but as an expression of the force with which those sentences are uttered. When 'may' expresses epistemic modality, 'It may be the case that A' is best understood as meaning 'Not ($\vdash$ (not A))', where negation of assertoric force is explained as above. Thus, on this interpretation, we have no negation of the conditional of natural language, that is, no negation of its *sense*: we have only a form for expressing refusal to assent to its assertion.

We acknowledged, earlier, a rough distinction of types of linguistic act into more and less formalized kinds—those that had definite consequences, and those which did not—which we compared to games with and without stakes. Those of the less formalized variety can usually be correctly described as the expression of some mental attitude—e.g. assertion is rightly called an expression of belief, and the correctness of such a characterization is not impugned by the occurrence of insincere expressions. This is shown by Moore's paradox—the fact, namely, that one frustrates the linguistic act if one makes an assertion, but immediately states, or otherwise indicates, that one does not believe it to be true. Requests may likewise be said to express a desire for what is requested, since one likewise frustrates a request by adding that one does not want what one has asked for. We have noted, on the other hand, that the giving of a command is not, in general, frustrated by expressing a hope that the command be disobeyed; and the view that the asking of a question was the expression of a desire to know the truth on some matter would entail that examination questions, and many questions asked in the law-courts, in the process of teaching, and in quite ordinary discourse, were not questions in the straightforward sense. It is true that one may misunderstand the purpose of someone's question—take him as seeking information when he was merely preparing to give it, or conversely; but this is shown by what one goes on to say after answering the question, and therefore does not show any ambiguity in the question itself: a barrister might say, 'Never mind what I'm driving at, just answer the question'. We held, indeed, that the right approach to an account of even the un-formalized linguistic acts was not through attempting any analysis, in-dependent of language, of the mental attitudes expressed by the corresponding utterances, but, rather, by a study of the conventions governing those utterances, of the language-game played with them: but that does not destroy the distinction between utterances which can, and those which cannot, be said to express inner attitudes.

There is an infrequent class of cases in which assertion belongs to the more formalized type of utterance. In a time of religious persecution, a man may be subjected to or threatened with torture to induce him to offer incense to the Emperor or trample on the crucifix; in the same spirit, what he is forced to do may be to *say*, e.g., 'Jesus Christ is the offspring of the devil'. Just as, with questions and commands, what matters is what is *said* (with due allowance for things said in acting in a play, quoting, giving a grammatical example, and the like), and not what attitude the speaker evinced, so here it is the saying that counts. The victim may know that his persecutors will be quite aware that, even if he says what they want him to, he will not believe it: what is important to both of them is whether he *says* it or not.

With kinds of force used to effect a linguistic act of the more formalized kind, a parallel interpretation of the application of negation to a force-indicator is even easier to comprehend. On such an interpretation, 'Not (!A)' would register the fact that I was not commanding you to bring it about that A, and 'Not (?A)' the fact that I was not asking whether A. Naturally, there can be no avoiding the consequence that saying, 'Not (?A)', would do a little more than would be done by simply not saying, '?A': by means of the former, I should draw attention to the fact that I was not asking whether A, and thereby give you a stronger warrant for sub-sequently claiming that I did not ask whether A. But the case would never-theless be different from that of assertion, or any other of the less formalized linguistic acts, where we could speak of the expression of an attitude.

When I say, 'Not (⊢A)', I am not merely drawing attention to the fact that I am not asserting that A: I am indicating my unwillingness to assert that A. To the extent that 'It may not be the case that A', as used in natural language, performs the function of 'Not (⊢A)', we may say that the convention under which we understand such a form of words is such that definite insincerity would be involved on the part of a speaker who uttered this sentence, although he privately believed that A: but the convention governing 'Not (⊢A)' might not be as strong as this—what was understood as expressed might be, not necessarily non-possession of a belief that A, but merely unwillingness to express that belief. But, since the asking of a question does not express any attitude at all, the negation of interrogative force cannot express an attitude either—not even unwillingness to ask the question: it merely registers the fact that a question is not being asked.

Do we have forms in natural language with these kinds of force? In the case of imperatives, we clearly do: the 'may' of permission is surely best interpreted this way. 'You may do X' is thus to be taken as meaning 'Not (! you do not do X)', and registers the fact that I am not forbidding you to do X. In certain special cases, this is all it does: those cases namely in which it has been laid down, tacitly or explicitly, that any action of a certain kind is forbidden unless expressly sanctioned; e.g. a mother tells a child not to accept invitations to stay without first asking her permission. (Situations in which it is tacitly assumed that permission needs to be sought are more frequent than ones in which 'silence means consent'.) In the general case, however, the permissive form does rather more, and cannot help doing more, than simply omitting to forbid you to do X. If you are under my authority, and I have not forbidden you to do X, and you do it, I naturally cannot rebuke you on that score for disobedience; but I may rebuke you for having done it all the same, on some other ground. But if I expressly permit you to do X, then I in effect announce in advance that I shall not rebuke you just for doing X; although, of course, I am still free to rebuke you for doing it in this or that circumstance or manner.

With questions, we do quite often have occasion to register the fact that we are *not* asking something or other—to avoid ambiguity, to ward off some unwanted revelation not responsive to the actual question, or to indicate the limits of an inquiry or to what we claim a right to ask after. But there seems to be no special form that is employed, save the negation of the performative, that is, the phrase, 'I am not asking whether . . .'.

Here we see an error in the account given in Chapter 9 of Stenius' book on the *Tractatus*, which otherwise in most respects tallies with that given here. Stenius, following von Wright, writes the sign conveying imperatival force as 'O', and rightly states that 'Not O: P' has a different content from 'O: not P'; the former means 'It is permitted that not P', he says, the latter 'It is forbidden that P'. He holds that a similar difference between the internal and external negations obtains for all types of linguistic act other than assertion and that of asking a (sentential) question. But, he says, if we write the assertion sign as 'I', then 'Not I: P' can only be taken as equivalent to 'I: not P' (p. 163). This enables him to claim that assertion *WT* 163-4 and the asking of questions occupy a special place among linguistic acts (p. 164); perhaps this is related to the claim that is sometimes made that assertion is more fundamental to language than other linguistic activities, and perhaps also to Stenius' mistake about the 'directed' character of a thought. His reason for holding 'Not I: P' and 'I: not P' to be equivalent is that 'I' is not properly to be rendered 'It is asserted that'. He concedes that there is indeed a difference between 'It is not asserted that P' and 'It is asserted that not P': but, he says, there is a difference in mood (i.e. in what we have been calling 'force') between asserting a thing and stating that it is asserted; hence he criticizes Wittgenstein in the *Investigations* for suggesting *PI* 22 that all assertions could be expressed by sentences beginning 'It is asserted that—'.

There is indeed a difference between, on the one hand, rendering the assertion sign by 'It is the case that' and the sign of command by 'Bring it about that', and, on the other, rendering the assertion sign by 'I assert that' and the sign of command by 'I command that'. The latter rendering is in one way preferable: it is possible by means of it to bring out the difference between the external and the internal negation, i.e. between negating the force and negating the descriptive content (sense) of the sentential complex. It is impossible to bring this out by means of the former type of rendering. The reason is that the former type of rendering makes use of phrases which themselves form sentences which, in natural language, express, respectively, assertions and commands: therefore negating them produces only a negative assertion and a negative command, not the negation *of* the assertion or *of* the command. In any event, the two cases are strictly parallel. Stenius could have argued with equal right that, while indeed 'It is not commanded that P' has a different content from 'It is commanded that not P', there is a difference between commanding something to be done and stating that it is commanded.

The renderings 'I assert that' and 'I command that' employ phrases which, in natural language, are used to form what Austin called 'performa- *HTW* 6 tives'. We may explain this term by saying that a performative utterance is one which is used to effect (perhaps in conjunction with some accompanying action) what it signifies. As opposed to an ordinary assertion, it does not state something considered as being the case independently of the act of uttering it. Someone who says, 'I promise to return the loan', *is* promising to return the loan *by* uttering that sentence: he is not asserting something to be true which would be true independently of his having said so. It is essential to the notion of a performative, as explained in this way, that related forms of words, with a different tense, a different subject, or perhaps even with only a different inflection of the verb, should be capable of being used as assertions of the ordinary kind; and also that the same form of words, when it occurs as a constituent clause in a complete sentence, should simply express a thought, and not be used to effect what it signifies. Thus, 'I promised to return the loan', 'He promises to return the loan', and perhaps even 'I am promising to return the loan', are all ordinary, non-performative, assertions; and if I begin a sentence with the words, 'If I promise to return the loan, . . .', these words serve only to carry a certain descriptive content (to express a thought), and not to make any promises. The reason that it is essential to the characterization of performatives that there should be these other uses of the same, or related, forms of words is that otherwise the phrase 'what it signifies' would be without content. Any significant utterance of a sentence is used to effect something, to perform some (conventional) act; but we can without triviality specify what it is that it effects by saying that it is 'what it signifies' only if there are other uses of it which are used to signify the performance of the act in the sense of *stating* that it is performed. Of course, to say of a performative that it effects what it signifies serves in the general case only to identify it as a performative, not to explain what it is that it effects: rather, we have (in the general case) first to explain the convention governing the utterance of a performative of that type, which constitutes such an utterance as a linguistic act of a particular kind—a promise, e.g.—before we can assign to the other uses of this form of words the descriptive content which they have, namely that such an act is performed. The order of explanation must, namely, be this way round whenever the linguistic act in question can be carried out *only* by uttering the performative, as with taking an oath or naming something: this is what I called 'the general case'. In some cases, the act may be capable of being performed by means of other, non-performative utterances: e.g., I can congratulate someone by saying, 'Well done!', as well as by saying, 'I congratulate you'; and, of course, I can assert that it will rain by saying, 'It will rain', as well as by saying, 'I assert that it will rain'. (This latter case does not show, as Wittgenstein suggests in *Investigations* §22, that the assertion sign is redundant, but only that the phrase 'I assert that—' is not the assertion-sign of the English language.) In these cases, it is possible to explain what the linguistic act consists in by describing the convention governing the alternative (and more primitive) utterances which can effect it: thus we can explain the significance of, e.g., the performative, 'I congratulate you', simply by saying that it is a means of congratulating someone, since we can explain the sense of 'congratulate' independently of the use of the performative. These are just the cases in which Wittgenstein would say that the use of a performative replaces that of another form of expression. Not all such 'replacing' expressions are performatives, however: the form 'I intend to—' replaces a certain use of 'I am going to—', but saying, 'I intend', is not intending.

The difference, which Stenius emphasizes, between asserting something and stating that it is asserted is precisely the difference between the use of a form of words as a performative and as a non-performative. To say, 'I promise—', is to promise, whereas to say, 'It was promised—', is to make an assertion, not a promise: there is here genuinely a difference in what Stenius calls 'mood' (= force), though this is dubious when the performative effects the making of an *assertion*. It is precisely this which makes 'I assert that—' an unsuitable rendering of the assertion sign: it is the existence of forms like 'He asserts', 'I asserted', 'If I assert', which constitutes sentences beginning 'I assert that—' performatives, whereas the assertion sign can suffer change neither of tense nor of subject, and cannot be put into a subordinate clause: it can be used only to effect, never to describe, the act of assertion. But this difference between 'I assert that—' and '⊢' does not justify Stenius' claim that negation of an assertion coincides with assertion of the negation. It is the very fact that 'I assert that—' forms a performative, that the verb 'assert' can occur within constituent clauses, that makes it possible to represent by means of it the distinction between denying something and expressing one's refusal to assert it, whereas 'It is not the case that' can be construed only as meaning 'It is the case that not'. Indeed, when the negation sign is attached to a sign of assertion or of command properly so called, it must be thought of as being used in a different way from usual, since normally it contributes to the descriptive content of the sentence. But what makes it compellingly natural to regard the giving of permission as the negation of prohibition, or the admission of something as possible as the negation of the denial of it, is that the one act *cancels* the other. By saying, 'It may be so', I undo just what I previously did by saying, 'It is not so'; by saying, 'You may do it', I undo what I did by saying, 'Do not do it'.

Let us now consider whether force-indicators can meaningfully stand within the scope of the binary sentential connectives. The case of 'and' seems the easiest, precisely because we have the practice of making a number of utterances in sequence. The general scheme thus once more yields a comprehensible result: if Henry says, '(⊢A) and (⊢B)', this has the effect of warranting the report 'Henry asserted that A and asserted that B'; likewise, if he says, '(?A) and (?B)', this will warrant the report, 'Henry asked whether A and asked whether B'. The force of saying, '(⊢A) and (⊢B)' is thus just the same as that of first saying '⊢A' and immediately going on to say '⊢B', and similarly for questions, commands, etc. Indeed, there is no need for 'and' to connect sentences governed by the same force-indicator: someone could say, '(⊢A) and (?B)', or, '(?B) and (!C)', and all would remain unproblematic.

There is no doubt that we do often use 'and' in just this way: we use without a qualm such sentences as, 'He opened the bidding on a 3-card suit, and never imitate his example', or, 'He is the greatest viola player of the century, and what recognition has he ever been accorded?'. (Earlier in the chapter, however, we noticed some misleading examples: 'Move a step further and I'll blow your head off' does not have the form '(!A) and (⊢B)'.) Indeed, if 'and' were the only logical constant in the language, we could always take it as operating on sentences having force-indicators attached. The practical effect of saying, '(⊢A) and (⊢B)', is exactly the same as that of saying '⊢ (A and B)', and likewise with '!' in place of '⊢': there is no significant contrast between a conjunction of assertions and an assertion of a conjunction, or between a conjunction of commands and a command to bring about the truth of a conjunction of propositions. For this reason, it is trifling to insist upon the possibility that force-indicators might occur within the scope of 'and': the meaning yielded is always one that is not significantly different from what can be expressed by putting 'and' within the scope of the force-indicators, or, in the case when two different force-indicators are employed, by just saying two things in succession. This is, indeed, so only as long as we look at 'practical effect' in rather broad terms. If I get 30 days confined to barracks for each order I fail to carry out, it will make a difference to me whether the Sergeant gave one conjunctive command or two con-joined ones. Similarly, if I am required to say either 'I agree' or 'I don't agree' in response to every assertion you make, my performance will vary according as I take you to be making two conjoined assertions or one conjunctive one. Equally, which of these you did may bear on the accuracy, as applied to you, of such an allegation as, 'He *never* tells the truth'.

If 'and' were the only logical constant in the language, however, it would be fundamentally redundant, in view of our practice of performing a number of linguistic acts in succession. 'And' is an important word in the language precisely because it can occur in a sentence in which it is not the principal logical operator: and it is in precisely such cases that it has to be interpreted as conjoining sentence-radicals, that is, sentences to which no force-indicator is attached. It is just in this connection that the inference from 'A' and 'B' to 'A and B' is not a trifling step, i.e. where it is a preparation for detaching the antecedent from some sentence 'If A and B, then C', or, where 'A' and 'B' are of the forms 'A'(*a*)' and 'B'(*a*)', for inferring, 'For some *x*, A'(*x*) and B'(*x*)': and it is in just such cases that 'A and B' must be interpreted as '⊢(A and B)'. Thus the point of having the word 'and' in the language resides in its use as conjoining sentence-radicals, and its use as conjoining sentences having assertoric or imperative force is entirely dispensable.

It does not follow that a sentence containing 'and' as the main operator of the sentence-radical could always be equated with one in which the force-indicator stood before the two conjuncts: the case of interrogatives is a counter-example. It makes the most obvious practical difference whether I say, '? (A and B)', or, '(?A) and (?B)', namely in respect of the kind of answer I am seeking. Though in practice we might answer in much the same way in either case, we know what it is to answer just the question '? (A and B)' and no more, and this is different from answering the two questions '?A' and '?B'.

Disjunction, however, does not seem amenable to the same treatment. If I were to say, '(⊢A) or (⊢B)', with the intention of thereby making it correct to report of me that I either asserted that A or asserted that B, it is impossible to see how my utterance could be construed so as to make such a report correct: in saying, '(⊢A) or (⊢B)', I did not assert that A and I did not assert that B, and so it cannot be correct to say of me that I either asserted one or asserted the other. Similar difficulty attends attempts to interpret '(!A) or (!B)': to the utterance, 'Either I command you to shut the door or I command you to open the window', one could only reply, 'Well, *which* do you do?'. With questions, however, the matter is different: '(?A) or (?B)' does have a natural meaning distinct from that of '? (A or B)'. An instance would be the examination question:

13.   What does Frege mean by 'objects'?
OR
What does Russell mean by 'individuals'?

If I am asked, '? (A or B)', then I am required to say 'Yes' if it is the case that either A or B, and 'No' if it is the case that neither A nor B. But if I am asked '(?A) or (?B)', then I am required *either* to answer the question '?A' *or* to answer the question '?B' (or both, if the 'or' is inclusive).

This interpretation, although natural, is not arrived at by following the original schema of interpretation for the use of force-indicators within the scope of sentential operators. If someone says, '(?A) or (?B)', he cannot be reported as having either asked whether A or asked whether B, for he did not do either. The disjunction comes in, not in the report of the linguistic act, but in that of the response to the question: if an addressee is to respond as the speaker prompts him to, then what he has to do is either to answer whether A or to answer whether B. This schema cannot be applied in the case of assertion, since assertion does not call for a response in the same way that question, command and request do. It can be applied in the case of command, but the result is indistinguishable from the case in which the logical operator falls within the scope of the force-indicator. Something to which the response is just whatever would either be obeying the command to bring it about that A or obeying the command to bring it about that B would merely be a command to bring it about that either A or B; and something requiring as a response whatever would ensure that the command '!A' was not obeyed would be the command '! Not A'.

Let us turn, finally, to the conditional. We have, at the outset, a problem of representation: is a conditional question, for example, to be represented as 'If A, then (?B)', 'If (⊢A), then (?B)' or as 'If (?A), then (?B)'? If we follow the original schema, then, by saying, 'If (?A), then (?B)', Henry would effect a linguistic act which would justify the report, 'If Henry asked whether A, then he asked whether B'. Such a type of linguistic act would appear entirely useless, since by performing it Henry would certainly not thereby be asking whether A, and the antecedent would thus in each case be unfulfilled, rendering the whole act nugatory. But, by distorting the literal interpretation slightly, we could conceive of this form as having the effect of telling the addressee that, if the speaker subsequently asked whether A, he was at that point to be taken as also having asked whether B (otherwise, it was to be as if he had said nothing at all). We should then have a sort of suspended question, in the sense in which magistrates pass suspended sentences. It hardly needs spelling out, however, why we feel no need to have within our language an expression for such a special form of linguistic act.

By analogy, the form 'If (⊢A), then (?B)' would have to be taken as conveying that, if at any subsequent time the speaker asserted that A, he was to be understood as thereby also asking whether B, and similarly for the form 'If (⊢A), then (⊢B)'. Evidently, then, the forms which we should most naturally consider as representing conditional questions, conditional commands and conditional assertions are 'If A, then (?B)', 'If A, then (!B)' and 'If A, then ($\vdash$B)'. The content of the first of these, for example, would be that I wanted to be so understood that, if it was the case that A, then I was to be taken as having asked whether B, but, if it was not the case that A, then I was to be taken as having said nothing at all. This is of course quite different from asking outright whether it is the case that, if A, then B; for, in the former case but not the latter, when it is not the case that A, then there is no question to be answered.

In this sense, there are evidently such things as conditional questions, as on a form which asks, 'If the answer to question 8 was "Yes", are you receiving a grant ?'. It should not be taken as a difficulty that in 'If A, then (?B)', 'A' occurs apparently outside the scope of any force-indicator: the whole context 'If A, then (? . . .)' should be taken as constituting a single force-operator, namely one signalizing the asking of a question conditionally upon its being the case that A; or, better, the context 'If . . . , then (? . . .)' should be regarded as a force-indicator with two argument-places, like '$\vdash$' in 'H $\vdash$A', where this indicates the assertion of 'A' as holding on the supposition that H, within a deductive argument allowing introduction and discharge of hypotheses. This interpretation conforms as closely as possible to the original schema: by saying, 'If A, then (?B)', Henry makes it the case that it can be correctly reported that, if A, then Henry asked whether B. This, of course, is not quite exact as it stands: in no case did Henry actually ask whether B. A strictly accurate report would run: Henry said something which, if it is the case that A, was tantamount to his asking whether B, and, if it is not the case that A, was tantamount to his having asked no question at all.

Granted that there are in this sense conditional questions, are there also conditional commands? Imperatives of conditional form may be divided into two classes: those for which the antecedent is in the power of the agent (the addressee), such as, 'If you go out, put on your coat', and those for which it is not, such as, 'If it rains, put on your coat'. We wish to know whether all conditional imperatives are to be interpreted as '! (if A, then B)', or whether there are some which are better interpreted as 'If A, then (!B)'.

In the case of conditional imperatives belonging to the first of our two classes, there seems an overwhelming reason why they should be interpreted as commands to bring it about that, if A, then B, rather than as commands, conditional upon its being the case that A, to bring it about that B. The reason is, namely, that in such a case the person given the command may falsify the antecedent precisely in obedience to the command. E.g., a child, told to put on his coat if he goes out, may very well choose not to go out in order to comply with the command; and he may be commended for his obedience in acting so. Thus a conditional imperative of this class must, it seems, be interpreted as a command to make the material conditional true, rather than as a conditional command in the sense we are here using that phrase.

With the second of the two classes, there cannot be this reason for preferring the one to the other interpretation, because it is the characterization of this class that the agent cannot bring about the truth of the material conditional by falsifying the antecedent. But, just for that reason, no practical difference could in such a case arise between the two interpretations. Hence, it appears, the only kind of conditional imperative which it is possible to interpret as expressing a conditional command in our sense is that which it is quite superfluous so to interpret.

There do, indeed, occur cases in which the antecedent is in the agent's power, but in which his falsification of it would not earn him the commendation of the speaker. Let us take, as an example, an imperative of request rather than of command: someone whose Fellowship at my College is due to expire says to me, 'If I am re-elected, please do not exercise your right to claim my present set of rooms'. If I accede to his request, it is nevertheless plain that he would not thank me for having voted against his re-election solely in order to be able to obtain his set of rooms without flouting his request. This feature of the situation was not, however, explicitly expressed by the conditional form, but is something which anyone could recognize from the situation itself, as can be seen from the fact that a transformation of the imperative sentence into a non-conditional form, e.g. 'Don't let me be re-elected and have to surrender my rooms to you', leaves this feature unaltered.

It has been suggested by von Wright and Rhinelander that the indicative conditionals of natural language are to be interpreted as conditional assertions rather than as assertions of the material or any other conditional: by saying, 'If A, then B', I do not mean to be understood as making any assertion outright, whose truth-conditions in all cases have then to be determined, but, rather, as saying something which, if it is the case that A, is tantamount to asserting that B, and, if it is not the case that A, is tantamount to having made no assertion. And now the possibility of an inference by modus tollendo tollens appears, in a similar way, to rule out this account. That is, if someone says to me, 'If A, then B', and I accept what he says, and then subsequently discover that not B, I shall conclude that not A. It appears, accordingly, that his utterance cannot be interpreted as 'If A, then (⊢B)', because, in this case, the antecedent is unfulfilled, and yet all is not precisely as if nothing had been said: on the contrary, it is just through the man's having said what he did that I was able to learn that the antecedent did not hold. Thus, it seems, a conditional form which allows of inference by modus tollendo tollens cannot be interpreted as a conditional assertion, but only as the assertion of a conditional statement. But could we not introduce a conditional form which permitted inference by modus (ponendo) ponens, but for which modus tollendo tollens was not permissible? No, we evidently cannot, provided that the observation that the assertion of 'A' would lead to a contradiction is sufficient to entitle us to assert 'Not A'; and this is a matter of the meaning of 'not', and not that of 'if'.

It thus appears that the effect which a conditional command, or a conditional assertion, would seek to achieve, could be gained only by sealed orders, or 'sealed statements'. If I hand a child an envelope on which is written 'Open if and only if you have just gone out', and inside is a slip of paper saying, 'Go back and put on your coat', then presumably I have given a command only in the event of the child's going out, and not one which he could obey by not going out. If, likewise, I hand a person an envelope on which is written, 'Open if and only if A', and inside is a piece of paper saying, '⊢B', then, again, presumably I have asserted that B only in the case that the person discovers it to be the case that A, and so I have not said anything from which he could have inferred that not A. In both cases, if the antecedent is not fulfilled, or not known to be fulfilled, things really are just as if I had said nothing at all. But, it seems, there can be no merely linguistic envelope: no form of words can be conditionally self-cancelling.

Reflection shows, however, that this argument, and the one against the notion of conditional command, are, as they stand, fallacious. We can see this by considering the archetypal case of a conditional speech-act, namely that of a conditional bet. A bet that B, conditionally on the truth of 'A', is a quite different thing from a bet on the truth of the conditional statement 'If A, then B'. What makes the notion of a conditional bet unproblematic is that there are two possible outcomes of an (ordinary) bet: the taker pays the bettor, or the bettor pays the taker. In the case of a conditional bet, if the antecedent fails, the bet is off: neither pays the other. And from this we see that the performance of a conditional speech-act does not require that, when the antecedent is unfulfilled, *all* should be precisely as if nothing had been said. In the case of a conditional bet—a bet that B, conditional on its being the case that A—it may be that the antecedent is at least partially in the power of either bettor or taker. After a time, either may come to the conclusion that there is no hope of his winning the bet, and at that point set about trying to bring it about that the antecedent is falsified, so that at least he shall not lose the bet. There is nothing in the notion of a

N

conditional bet which makes this improper—and, obviously, a great many straightforward bets concern what is in the power of bettor or taker to influence. Any impropriety can arise only from conventions about the subject-matter of the bet, like those which exclude the doping of racehorses, and not from the force of a conditional bet in itself.

What makes something a conditional bet is not that, if the antecedent is unfulfilled, it is just as if nothing whatever had been said, but only that, in that case, it is as if no (categorical) bet had been made. No linguistic convention could possibly guarantee that, in certain circumstances, the performance of a certain linguistic act should have no effect whatever upon the subsequent course of events, unless it were one which would have no effect in any circumstances. If it has some effect in some circumstances, then the thought that it will have that effect in those circumstances may influence the behaviour of someone who heard the utterance, and we cannot lay down a general convention that no one is to be so influenced. (This was the ground for saying that no utterance can be fixed up to be conditionally self-cancelling.) Hence the fact that, when a conditional imperative or a conditional assertoric utterance has been made, some difference may be made to the behaviour or knowledge of the hearer, even though the antecedent is false, does not of itself show that the utterance is not to be interpreted as being, in our sense, a conditional command or a conditional assertion.

Something will be a conditional command if we can say that, if the antecedent is false, it is just as if no (categorical) command has been given; something will be a conditional assertion if we can say that, if the antecedent is false, it is just as if no (categorical) assertion has been made. Does this weaker condition allow us to give a sense to the notion of conditional command or to that of conditional assertion?

This would be the case if we could identify two, as it were, independent possible consequences of the giving of a command or the making of an assertion, as we can identify two distinct possible consequences of the making of a bet, or, also, of the asking of a sentential question (the person answers 'Yes' or he answers 'No'): for then we can always imagine a form of linguistic act which allows that, in a certain case (the non-fulfilment of the antecedent), neither consequence shall follow. This would be so, for instance, in a society in which the giving of commands was a strictly formalized affair, and obedience to a command brought reward, disobedience to it punishment, perhaps irrespective of the meritoriousness or culpability of the person receiving the command. In that case, it would be perfectly possible to have conditional commands, the convention governing which was that neither reward nor punishment followed when the antecedent was unfulfilled.

It would here be quite irrelevant whether or not the falsification of the antecedent was due to the action of the person to whom the conditional command was given: it would be entirely natural that, fearing that he might fail to obey the command if the antecedent were realized, he should take steps to prevent its realization; this would have no tendency at all to make us deny the conditional status of the command.

The fact of the matter is that command, for us, is not as described in this imagined society. For us, the command specifies what is to constitute disobedience to it: disobedience automatically confers, on the person who gave the command, if he had the right to give it in the first place, the right to punish or at least rebuke—a right he does not have to exercise. Obedience does not, on the other hand, confer any right to reward or commendation: it is something which a superior authority has a right to *demand*. Thus in our practice punishment/rebuke are differently related to command from reward/commendation. The former are conventionally related, in the sense that the content of the command determines what shall constitute disobedience, and thus what shall be liable to punishment or rebuke (although, of course, a justified plea of actual inability to avoid disobedience serves as a complete excuse); by contrast, no behaviour secures the right to reward or commendation, while they may be given for any voluntary action taken in order to avoid disobeying. The fact that, in the case of a command expressed by a conditional imperative in which the antecedent is not in the agent's power, we should not say that the agent had obeyed just on the ground that the antecedent was false, is thus no ground for construing the imperative as expressing a conditional command: for there is no question of fixing what shall constitute obedience independently of the determination of what shall constitute disobedience. Someone who has not needed to do anything in order to avoid disobedience cannot be said to have obeyed: but we have no use for a form whereby such-and-such a voluntary action, although it successfully avoids disobedience, is nevertheless stipulated not to count as obedience. Thus, given the conventions which surround the linguistic act of commanding, as it exists among us, we have no place for conditional commands; but there would be such a place were we to have a type of linguistic act similar to commanding, but differing from our actual practice in a clear respect.

Now that we have rejected as fallacious our original argument, from the existence of modus tollens, against the possibility of conditional assertion, it becomes hard at first to see how to settle the issue; because we do not know how to apply the notion of 'consequence' to assertions, so as to be able to ask whether the making of an assertion has only one kind of consequence or two. It is, indeed, clear that the distinction between formalized and un-formalized linguistic acts is not a sharp one. Making a request, for example, is in one sense formalized, like asking a question: for with both acts it is, in general, clear enough what response is called for. But, as contrasted with the giving of a command properly so called, requesting is unformalized, because the consequences of someone's responding or failing to respond in the way sought are not so sharp. But, in any case, assertion stands at the unformalized end of the scale. Making an assertion may, of course, have many conse-quences for both speaker and hearer. But we noted that, with a highly formalized type of linguistic act, such as a bet or a command, the possibility of such an act rests upon a conventional recognition that certain precisely specifiable consequences flow from the performance of such an act, while there may be certain further consequences which follow naturally upon the performance of an act governed by such a convention, but are not themselves part of that convention. In the case of assertion, however, there does not appear to be any such distinction to be drawn.

In this situation, the inevitable impulse is to appeal to the notions of truth and falsity. Whatever ought to be the exact form of description which needs to be given of the conventions governing the linguistic act of assertion, they must surely be given in terms of the conditions under which what is asserted is true and those under which it is false. So perhaps we can character-ize a straightforward, or categorical, assertion as one which is false whenever it is not true, and a conditional assertion as one which allows for the pos-sibility of a gap between truth and falsity, a case in which what was said was neither true nor false, or, perhaps better, in which nothing true or false was said.

This overwhelmingly natural suggestion unfortunately leads us nowhere. The reason is not difficult to grasp. If we accept the distinction between sense and force at all, then it is true of all linguistic acts—or, at least, of those which are effected by the utterance of a sentence expressing a complete thought—that the convention governing them has to be explained by reference to the notions of truth and falsity as attaching to the thought expressed. This, after all, was the whole point: the conditions for obedience and disobedience to a command were to be determined by those for the truth and falsity of the thought which constituted the sense of the imperative sentence, and similarly for all the other cases. So if, in the case of any lin-guistic act, there is to be room for the introduction of a related linguistic act which allows for the possibility of a gap in which there is no consequence of either of two kinds, this must be explainable directly in terms of the kind of consequence which that act had. By appealing to the notions of truth and falsity, all that we achieve is an account of the mechanism by which it is determined under what conditions the consequences will be suspended: we do not attain, what we were after, an account of what it is to hold them to be suspended.

If someone were to announce that he was using a certain sentence 'A' in such a way that it was true under certain conditions, false under certain other, contrary, conditions, and neither true nor false whenever either of the first two types of condition failed, that would by no means make clear the content of an assertion made by him by uttering the sentence 'A'. For, if there clearly was a possibility that the intermediate case might obtain, we should want to know whether, by asserting 'A', he intended to exclude this case, or whether he envisaged it as a possibility. If he refused to answer, then he would not have introduced a new kind of linguistic act, an act of conditional assertion, but merely conferred an ambiguity upon his assertoric use of 'A'. If he said that, by asserting 'A', he wished to be understood as ruling out the possibility that it was neither true nor false, then we should, so far, be at a loss to grasp the point of his distinction between the case when 'A' was false and that in which it was neither true nor false. If on the other hand, he said that, in asserting 'A', he was wanting to be taken as leaving open the possibility that it was neither true nor false, then, again, we should have as yet been given no rationale for the distinction between the case in which 'A' was true and that in which it was neither true nor false.

If the suggestion that indicative conditionals of natural language be interpreted as expressing conditional assertions, that is, as saying nothing either true or false in the case when the antecedent is false, is to be taken as an instance of such a case, then clearly someone who makes a conditional assertion is not ruling out the possibility that what he says is neither true nor false; for otherwise his utterance would be correct only in the case that both antecedent and consequent were true. This does not tally, however, with the use of 'neither true nor false' to apply to sentences containing a name which lacks reference: for, clearly, anyone who seriously uses such a sentence to make an assertion does not envisage the possibility that the name lacks reference. However much ground there may be for saying that a sentence such as 'St. Thomas More's eldest son became a Protestant' is neither true nor false, it is clear that anyone who seriously uttered that sentence assertorically would not be allowing for the possibility that More had no sons, and would retract the statement upon discovering that; if he had meant to allow for that possibility, he would have said something like, 'If More had any sons, the eldest one became a Protestant'. It is thus clear that the 'neither true nor false' of which Frege makes use in speaking of sentences containing names without reference is not the same one as that involved in an account of conditionals as being used to make conditional assertions.

So far, however, we have failed to find any rationale, in the case of conditionals, for the distinction between being true and being neither true nor false: no reason why 'If B, then C' should not be taken as simply true, and thus as the material conditional, in the case when 'B' is false. Equally, we have found no rationale, in the case of sentences containing proper names, for the distinction between being false and being neither true nor false, that is, in effect, for their not being interpreted along the lines of Russell's Theory of Descriptions. In the latter case, the considerations we reviewed earlier did provide such a rationale: but it is important to see its character. The reason was that, by classing 'More's eldest son became a Protestant' as neither true nor false, we obtain a simpler account of complex sentences in which that sentence is, or appears to be, a constituent. If we describe the sentence as straightforwardly false, then we cannot regard the sentence, 'More's eldest son did not become a Protestant', as a negation of the original sentence, that is, as formed from it by the application of the negation operator, and we have, as Russell did, to analyse the original sentence as not having been formed, as it appears to have been, by the insertion of a name in the argument-place of a predicate. If we describe it as neither true nor false, then we can see the negative sentence as formed by the application of a negation operator, one, namely, which transforms a true sentence into a false one, and conversely, and a sentence which is neither true nor false into one which is again neither true nor false.

If we had in our language—which we do not—such a thing as a negation of a conditional, construed as yielding unambiguously a new assertoric sentence, then a similar motive might operate in this case. Suppose, for example, that we had a negation operator 'non' which, in most cases, functioned in a straightforward way, but, when applied to an indicative conditional, yielded a sentence with the content of the opposite conditional, i.e. that which resulted from negating the consequent: 'Non (if B, then C)' was equivalent to 'If B, then non C'. Then, in order to construe this negation operator truth-functionally, it would be necessary to regard 'If B, then C' as being neither true nor false in the case in which 'B' was false, and, once more, to take 'non' as converting a true sentence into a false one, and conversely, and one that was neither true nor false into one that was still neither true nor false. Of course, we should not be compelled to do this: we could alternatively merely take 'Non (if B, then C)' as an idiomatic form for 'If B, then non C'. Which was more convenient would depend upon the behaviour of yet more complex sentences; but there would at any rate be a rationale for the application of the description 'neither true nor false' to conditionals with false antecedents.

In both these cases, ' "A" is false' is being taken to mean 'The negation of "A" is true'; this is, of course, a very natural application for the word 'false'. The equation of ' "A" is false' with 'The negation of "A" is true' may, indeed, be taken as constitutive of the meaning of 'false' (it does not have to be): but then the motivation for saying of certain sentences that, under certain conditions, they are neither true nor false is to enable us to continue to construe certain other sentences as being their negations. It is essential here to grasp two things. First, the characterization of a sentence as true in certain cases, false in others, and neither true nor false in yet a third kind of case, is not yet sufficient to determine the content of an assertion effected by the utterance of that sentence: it remains to be discovered whether the speaker does or does not rule out the possibility that the sentence is neither true nor false. This, by itself, should be enough to teach us that the linguistic act of assertion makes, as it were, no intrinsic provision for the introduction of a gap between two kinds of consequence which the making of an assertion might be supposed to have. And, secondly, the rationale, with respect to assertoric sentences, for the introduction of a gap—an intermediate case in which the statement is neither true nor false—always relates, not to the use of the sentence by itself to make an assertion, but to its use as a constituent of complex sentences, in particular, of sentences formed by the application to it of a negation operator. If we are concerned solely with the content of an assertion effected by the utterance of a sentence 'A', then all that we need to know is which states of affairs are understood to be ruled out by the making of such an assertion; if none of those states of affairs obtains, then the assertion is correct. Any finer distinctions between the different ways in which the assertion may be correct, or fail to be, can be needed only for an account of how the sentence contributes to determining the content of some more complex assertoric sentence of which it is a constituent. (Of course, it may also be needed to account for the way in which the sentence functions when used to effect linguistic acts of kinds other than assertion, for instance, forms, such as questions, which readily yield to conditionalization.)

This argument is not, by itself, a defence of the law of bivalence—the law that every statement is either true or false—even where the 'truth' of a statement is equated with the correctness of an assertion effected by uttering it, and its 'falsity' with the incorrectness of such an assertion. The defence of that law requires consideration of much deeper issues than have been raised here. Without going into these, it is sufficient to indicate that the present discussion could not establish that law unless we make the prior assumption that it must be the case either that one of those states of affairs excluded by the assertion of the statement obtains, or else that none of them obtains. All that follows from the present discussion is that, on these senses of 'true' and 'false', it is impossible that a statement should be neither true nor false, that we could characterize a describable state of affairs as being one in which the assertion was neither correct nor incorrect: a further step is needed to establish that every statement must be either true or false.

What, then, is the outcome of our painstaking investigation? Clearly we have established that, in some cases, it is possible to find a natural interpretation for the application of sentential operators to sentences already containing force-indicators. Thus, properly speaking, Frege's contention that force always applies to a complete sentence taken as a whole, and not to some subordinate part of it, is incorrect. For all that, it should be apparent that the exceptions we have discovered to it do not affect its essential soundness. For the possibility of an interpretation of a use of force-indicators within the scope of sentential operators was not a general one, and did not follow a general schema of interpretation: we had to seek in each case for a possible interpretation; sometimes, following the general schema suggested at the outset, we found one; sometimes we had to employ a different schema; and sometimes none could be found at all. Moreover, the crucial point is that none of these interpretations could be reiterated: we found at most an interpretation for a single application of sentential operators to sentences containing force-indicators, which allowed no possibility of subjecting the resultant whole to yet another sentential operator or yet another force-indicator. The schemas which we employed in arriving at an interpretation turned on a use of the sentential operator in question within either a description of the linguistic act effected by an utterance of the kind considered, or a description of the response which such an utterance sought to evoke. It is not particularly surprising that in some cases we should by this means be able to arrive at a new kind of linguistic act, either one of which we in practice already make use, or one which we do not employ but conceivably might, related in an evident way to the basic form of linguistic act. But of this new kind of force, corresponding to the new kind of linguistic act, it remains true that it cannot in turn be buried within the scope of a further sentential operator. Any qualms which we may, with some reason, feel about the validity of Frege's thesis that force cannot attach to a constituent clause within a complete sentence therefore do not justify any suspicion that the whole distinction between sense and force is liable to collapse.

Have we then, in effect, validated Geach's test for whether a form of words is used to express a proposition which can be asserted, or whether it serves to perform some linguistic act distinct from assertion? The test consists in asking whether the form of words in question can be meaningfully used as the antecedent of a conditional: if it can, then it constitutes a sentence-radical, expressing a thought, to which assertoric force can be attached when it stands on its own; if not, then it already contains some force-indicator, signalling the performance of some linguistic act other than assertion.

Geach's test has behind it an important and valid insight. This insight is that the notion of truth for a sentence has as strong an intuitive connection with the use of the sentence as the antecedent of a conditional as has the notion of falsity with the sign of negation. It is evident, indeed, that we cannot in all cases take the result of negating the main verb to be the negation of the whole sentence. At the same time, as we noted, we have a strong tendency to incline towards an application of the notions of truth and falsity which will allow us to construe the syntactically most obvious candidate for being the negation of a sentence as genuinely being its negation, i.e. to describe a sentence as false just in case the result of negating the main verb is true: it is this which makes certain claims that sentences of certain kinds are neither true nor false intuitively appealing. In a similar way, the manner in which we are intuitively inclined to apply the predicate 'true' is often closely guided by the behaviour of the relevant sentence when it occurs as the antecedent of a conditional. Thus, for example, we barely have in natural language any use for conditionals whose antecedents are themselves conditionals: and this is surely connected with our hesitancy in applying the word 'true' to a conditional at all. The reason why it is the antecedents of conditionals, and not their consequents, which are relevant in this respect, is clear from our consideration of conditional speech-acts. If 'K' is a sentence containing a force-indicator, and 'A' is a sentence-radical, then it is at least conceivable that the form 'If A, then K' will have a point; and in this case, whenever the antecedent 'A' is known to be satisfied, the conditional utterance will have exactly the same force as the simple utterance 'K'. But the cases in which we will want, explicitly or tacitly, to appeal to the behaviour of a given sentence within complex sentences in order to determine how the notion of truth should apply to it will be precisely those in which we feel a reason for distinguishing between the conditions under which the sentence is true from those in which it is correct or appropriate to utter it as a complete sentence: and, for the reason just stated, the behaviour of the sentence as the consequent of a conditional will throw no light on this. On the other hand, we have seen that there is, in general, little to be made of a

N*

conditional in which the antecedent contains a force-indicator. Thus, for example, sentences in the future tense represent a clear case in which we want to make a sharp distinction between the notion of truth as applying to them and that of a condition under which they may be reasonably or justifiably asserted. I may assert such a sentence in one of two cases: that in which I have inductive grounds for doing so; and that in which I assert it as an expression of my intention. These two notions are philosophically highly problematic, and require analysis, which is not easy to achieve; hence the conditions under which a future-tense statement may justifiably be asserted require a correspondingly complex analysis. Moreover, we have here two quite different kinds of case in which a future-tense assertion may justifiably be made. Learning the use of sentences in the future tense undoubtedly involves coming to understand these conditions: that is, learning to express one's intentions for the future, and learning also to recognize the existence of inductive grounds for a statement about the future. If, then, sentences in the future tense never appeared as the constituents of complex sentences, we should naturally distinguish here two different types of linguistic act, the making of an inductively based prediction, and the expression of intention: and we should perceive no need whatever for any distinction between the *truth* of a future-tense sentence and, on the one hand, the inductive justification of a prediction or, on the other, the appropriately worded and sincere expression of intention. In the first case, there would be no room in such an analysis for any distinction between the future tense as used to report present tendencies and as used to make a statement genuinely about the future; in the second case, there would be no room for a distinction between the expression of an intention which I presently have, and the correct announcement of what in fact, when the time comes, I shall do. This does not mean that the second notion, in each of these two pairs, would be absent: we could hardly have the concept of inductive grounds for a prediction unless we had the notion of that prediction's coming true or being falsified; we could hardly have the concept of intention unless we had the notion of the intention's being carried out or failing to be carried out. It means only that we should have no ground for saying that the content of the future-tense statement was *that the event should take place*, rather than that there was inductive evidence that it would, or that the speaker intended that it should: in other words, for ascribing truth-conditions to the utterance distinct from the conditions for the utterance to be justified.

It is the occurrence of future-tense statements as constituents in complex sentences that forces us to ascribe to such statements a truth-value independent of the existence of conditions which would justify their assertion on their own, i.e. as predictions or expressions of intention. Just because conjunction and disjunction do on occasion allow force-indicators to appear within their scope, the antecedents of conditionals present the clearest simple case. It does not matter whether the conditional is to be interpreted as a material conditional or not: the notion of truth is tied to the condition which the antecedent expresses. If a man says, 'If nobody will ever understand my work, my life has been in vain', the condition which the antecedent presents, whose obtaining constitutes the truth of 'Nobody will ever understand my work' as uttered by the man in question, is clearly not to be identified with the condition under which he might justifiably assert, 'Nobody will ever understand my work'.

It seems, so far, that Geach's test is valid. In fact, however, it needs to be severely qualified. The possibility of employing a form of sentence as the antecedent of an indicative conditional does not, of itself, show that the sentence, in so far as it has a definite meaning, must be construed as having determinate truth-conditions.

Let us recall the difficulty we encountered in interpreting such forms as 'If (?A), then (?B)' and 'If (!A), then (!B)'. We tried to interpret the first as conveying, 'If at any future time I ask whether A, then I am to be taken as thereby asking also whether B', and similarly for the imperative form; and this, although intelligible, appeared pointless. There is, however, another possibility: namely to take the conditional interrogative as a means of expressing, 'If I were to be brought to ask whether A, then I should also ask whether B'. This suggestion, for questions and commands, seems even more pointless than the original one: but that is because questions and commands are not the sort of utterance which we are, in general, interested in eliciting from another person. Assertions, par excellence, are: questions are precisely the most direct way of eliciting them, and, more to the point, we are frequently anxious to secure the assent of another to an assertion of our own. For this reason, we could have a use for the complex form 'If (⊢A), then (⊢B)', construed this time as meaning, 'If I were to assert (agree) that A, then I should assert (agree) that B'. It would be of interest to say something of this kind in a discussion in which the other person was trying to induce me to assent to his assertion that B: by such a conditional utterance, I should indicate to him that he can achieve this if he can first induce me to assent to the assertion that A. By a conditional assertion, so understood, I do not attempt to bind myself for all future time to be taken as having asserted that B, if at any time I assert that A, any more than by a categorical assertion I bind myself for all future time to continued assent to that assertion: I merely indicate that, as my mind now stands, assent to the one proposition will lead me to assent to the other.

Such a form of conditional assertion would be of very little use to us, because the occasions are rare on which I can recognize that I should be prepared to assert that B, were I prepared to assert that A, but on which I am not prepared to assert that if A, then B: the assertion of the conditional does duty for the conditional assertion. Not that the two necessarily amount to exactly the same thing; but the margin between them is exceedingly narrow.

It is now immediately evident that, if there exist forms of linguistic act other than assertion such that we have an interest, on occasion, in eliciting such acts from others, then there can be a place for conditional forms of such acts, construed along the above lines—conditional forms, that is, in which the antecedent has to be taken as containing a force-indicator. Unfortunately, on the theories which Geach takes his test as refuting, we are concerned with precisely such types of linguistic act. For instance, Geach wishes to oppose the theory that the statement that a person is responsible for such-and-such an act (i.e. that he did it and could have helped doing it, or, at any rate, is liable to praise or blame for having done it) does not have determinate truth-conditions, and that therefore the utterance of such a statement does not constitute the making of an assertion in the full-blown sense, but, rather, the performance of a different kind of linguistic act—the ascription of responsibility. On this theory, someone who makes such a statement can only in part be shown to be wrong by reference to the non-fulfilment of conditions which must be satisfied if his statement is correct: he is in part merely expressing his resolve to treat the person he is talking about as responsible for the action, as liable to praise, reward, blame, rebuke or punishment, and there are no objective conditions which determine in all cases the correctness of such an attitude. Similar accounts have, of course, been very popular for ethical statements, aesthetic statements, etc., etc. Now we may well suspect that such theories represent rather cheap attempts to resolve difficult philosophical problems by ruling them out of order. But it is clear from what has been said that the attempt to have a short way with them by observing that statements of the various forms in question can perfectly well stand as antecedents of conditionals will not work either. For, if the theories in question were correct, it would still be the case that statements of these kinds, although lacking determinate truth-conditions, would be ones which we should be interested in eliciting from others; and so their appearance as antecedents of conditionals would not be in the least mysterious or inconsistent with the theories Geach wishes to controvert. Indeed, such statements, although not having the character of assertions, would still represent linguistic acts of the kind to which the notion of assent would be appropriate. I may ponder long, on some occasions, over whether or not I shall—am prepared to—ask a certain question, give a certain command, make a certain request or undertake a certain bet: but in none of these cases would it be in place to speak of my assenting to the question, the command, the request or the bet. The reason is easy to see. Assent is an interior act, i.e. it need not have any external expression at the time at which it occurs; there is therefore a difference between deciding whether I am prepared to assent to a proposition and deciding whether I am prepared to express that assent. But asking, commanding, requesting and betting are external operations: they are not the expressions of anything. (It is true that a request is, in part, an expression of wanting, but it is not just that: if someone presses me to say what I want, and I give way and tell him, I am not thereby requesting him to satisfy the want.) I cannot make a bet with or a request of myself: and, though I can in a sense give myself a command or ask myself a question (wonder = *se demander*), I cannot wonder whether to give myself a certain command or to ask myself a certain question. Asking a question, giving a command, making a request or laying a bet may make a difference to what happens, and, in particular, to what happens to me: but they do so in virtue of the fact that the utterance whereby the linguistic act was performed took place. My adherence to an assertion, on the other hand, makes a difference to what happens in two separate ways: by the consequences of its expression, if it is expressed and anyone hears and understands what I say; and by its consequences in my actions, which are consequences in virtue of the interior act of adherence, i.e. of my willingness to assent to it. By accepting an assertion as true, I commit myself to modify my behaviour in some appropriate respect. Now the linguistic acts which, on the theories Geach wishes to refute, gain expression by the utterance of these various forms of statement (statements ascribing responsibility, ethical statements, etc.), share, according to those theories, this feature with assertions properly so called. The whole point of such theories is that, although there are no determinate conditions for the correctness of assent to a statement of one of these forms, nevertheless such assent, when expressed, registers a commitment to some course of action or type of conduct, and, when not expressed, consists in the interior undertaking of such a commitment. In the light of this, it is very evident why we should be interested in eliciting such utterances from others, in a way in which we are not interested in eliciting questions or commands.

These considerations might serve to define a class of linguistic acts wider than the already very wide one consisting of assertions properly so called: we might call the members of this wider class 'quasi-assertions' (which will, of course, include assertions proper). The upshot is, then, that Geach's test is a useful and valid one for discriminating between sentences which may be used to make quasi-assertions and sentences which can be used only to perform other types of linguistic act. Unfortunately, this does not make it very useful, since the theories he was seeking to controvert by means of this test would for the most part concede to the statements to which they denied the status of assertions that of quasi-assertions.

We argued at the beginning of the chapter that assertion is not to be explained as the expression of a mental attitude (belief, judgment or assent); nor can it be described simply by appeal to the notion of the intention with which a sentence is uttered. Rather, there has to be some feature of the sentences which signify their being uttered with assertoric force; and an account of the significance of this feature—and thus of the activity of making assertions—is to be given by describing the convention under which sentences possessing this feature are used. We described this convention in a quite summary way, by saying merely that the convention was to utter such sentences with the intention of uttering only true ones: this requires some elucidation.

This convention is of course something of which we are conscious, not merely something which, as a result of training, we are conditioned to observe. As children, we are trained to try to utter assertoric sentences only when they are true; but, at a certain stage in their learning to use language, all children spontaneously discover for themselves the possibility of lying. When they do this, they are made to understand that the use of language rests on an agreement not to misuse language in this way. (Recognition of the possibility of lying appears to be an important feature of possessing a language. A dog can be trained to bark when a stranger approaches the house; but one reason why we should be disinclined to describe the dog's barking as asserting that a stranger is approaching is that he couldn't bark in order to deceive us into thinking that a stranger was approaching.)

How far is this statement of the convention under which assertoric sentences are used an adequate description of the linguistic activity of making assertions? Suppose that we had a convention whereby a different mode of greeting was used when addressed to married and to unmarried women. We could indeed say that the use of one mode of greeting expressed a man's belief that he was addressing a married woman, but not that it functioned as an *assertion* that she was married. An assertion is generally used to convey information: characteristically the speaker is in a better position to judge of the truth of the assertion than the hearer. The description which we gave of the convention which governs the activity of assertion did not make clear the point of this convention, which can be stated in a general way as follows: we learn to react to the statements of others in the same way that we react to various observed features of our environment. (This formulation indeed slurs over the point that learning to recognize certain features of our environment is essentially bound up with learning to use, and to act on, the kind of statement which reports the presence of such a feature.) It is thus essential to the activity of assertion that the making of an assertion will in general modify the behaviour of those to whom it is made. A child's learning of language involves, not only his learning to utter certain sentences in certain situations, e.g. his learning to say, 'The post has arrived', when he sees the postman put the letters through the letter-box, but also his learning to *act on* these statements when made by others, e.g. to react to someone else's saying, 'The post has arrived', in the same way that he reacts to seeing the postman come, for instance by fetching the letters. This fact is in turn connected with the conventions we observe concerning the justifiable assertion of a statement. When we first learn language, we are taught to make assertions only in the most favoured case, namely in that situation in which the speaker can recognize the statement as being true. One way to observe the convention to try to utter only true assertoric sentences would of course be to utter them only in this most favoured situation; but for the great majority of forms of statement that is not at all what we do. Some forms of statement—those in the future tense, for example—are never uttered in the situation which conclusively establishes their truth; and others, which we originally learned to utter only in such situations, we later learn to utter in circumstances in which we may turn out to have been mistaken. On the other hand, we do not of course learn to make statements on no basis whatever, and, if we did, such utterances would not constitute assertions (even though they were made with the intention of uttering only true statements), because there would not be such a thing as acting on such statements. The process of learning to make assertions, and to understand those of others, involves learning what grounds, short of conclusive grounds, are regarded as justifying the making of an assertion, and learning also the procedure of asking for, and giving, the grounds on which an assertion is made. Within the class of assertions, there are distinct types differentiated by the kind of basis on which they are made: e.g., a prediction and an expression of intention may have their truth-conditions in common, but are distinguished by the kind of reason that may exist for making them. All this would have to be described in any satisfactory account of the activity of assertion: the idea, which Stenius has, that the use of assertoric sentences can be explained simply by saying that we try to obey the rule to utter only true ones, is totally inadequate. Moreover, it is evident that, as soon as we tried to supplement such an account in any detail along the lines I have indicated, we should have to distinguish a number of different types of assertion, and say rather different things about each.

This naturally prompts the question whether there is after all any genuine point in grouping together all those utterances which we class as assertions. This question is answered negatively by Wittgenstein in the *Investigations* §23: 'But how many kinds of sentence are there? Say assertion, question and command?—There are *countless* kinds: countless different kinds of use of what we call . . . "sentences" '. It is indeed true, as we have seen, that the use of assertoric sentences of different types is not wholly uniform. There is, nevertheless, a clear principle on which we can distinguish between assertions and utterances of other kinds: there is also a common feature in the use of all those utterances which can be classed as assertions. We have seen that, for a large range of utterances, their content can be considered as given by means of a distinction between those circumstances in which what they express holds good, and those in which it does not hold good: assertions are distinguished from other utterances in all being governed by the convention that we should try to utter only those whose descriptive content holds good. That this is not a complete account of the conventions under which they are used, and that, in supplementing it, different things have to be said for different types of assertion, does not make the concept of 'assertion' useless.

If a formulation of a principle for distinguishing assertions from other utterances is called for, it may be given as follows: assertions are those utterances which can be used to deceive, i.e. to lie, and which also can occur (perhaps deprived of some sign for assertoric force) as constituents of complex sentences. Both points require a little comment. The asking of a question is in a sense the expression of a desire to know the answer: so one may ask a question in order to deceive someone into thinking that one wants to know the answer. That a question may express such a desire is not, however, part of the convention which is learned when one learns to use and answer questions: it merely results from the fact that a desire to know the answer supplies the usual motive for asking a question. This is shown by the fact, which we have noted, that there is nothing self-defeating in asking a question and at the same time letting it be seen that one has no interest in the answer (if, e.g., one is an official whose duty involves the posing of certain questions); whereas the making of an assertion while letting it be seen that one does not believe it to be true is intrinsically self-defeating. The second point serves to exclude an utterance such as 'Ow!' from being an assertion. 'Ow!' is an expression of pain, and hence may be used to deceive someone into thinking that one is in pain. Unlike 'I am in pain', however, it does not qualify as an assertion, since it could not serve as a subordinate clause in a complex sentence. (In Indo-European languages, the 'assertion sign' is the indicative mood of the main verb; since verbs in subordinate clauses are frequently in the indicative, whatever the force of the complex sentence to which they belong, an assertoric sentence will often go quite unchanged into the subordinate clause. The condition stated is not, however, to be taken as depending on this fact.)

The two conditions we have stated in fact characterize the larger class of what we called 'quasi-assertions'. The use of utterances within this class has two principal features. First, the convention governing the making of them involves a classification of such linguistic acts as *correct* and *incorrect*: an assertion or quasi-assertion requires justification. Of course, with other linguistic acts questions of justification arise: we may ask, of a command, whether the person who gave it was authorized to do so; and we may also ask whether he was wise, or morally right, etc., to do so. But the lack of authority nullifies a command, whereas nothing (save its withdrawal by its author) can nullify an assertion; while questions of what we may call 'extraneous' justification arise also for assertions—'You ought not to have said that' may be backed by 'Because it is not true', but also by 'Because it was impolite', 'Because you had no right to reveal what was said to you in confidence', 'Because it was irrelevant', 'Because it was certain to lead to an argument', etc. Such extraneous justification, or lack of it, is highly apposite to the question whether to perform a given linguistic act: but it is no part of the conventions which underlie the institutions of giving commands and making assertions. And, secondly, assertions and quasi-assertions are to be acted on: they do not merely call for a particular response from the person addressed, as does a question, a command or a request, but commit both speaker and hearer, if the latter accepts what is said, to a line of action, linguistic and non-linguistic.

It is not altogether easy to characterize the sub-class of assertions proper within the wider class of quasi-assertions. Though tempting, it would be tendentious to require of them that there be a uniform method for deriving, from the criterion accepted as justifying the making of an assertion, what it was to act upon it, that is, the line of action one committed oneself to by accepting it. (The expression 'line of action' is here too strong: exactly what actions, if any, are undertaken will, of course, depend upon one's ends, the other statements one accepts as true, etc. The acceptance of an assertion as true is only one determinant, of many, of the line of action one adopts, which is why it is so hard to give a clear account of this feature of the use of assertions. It is nevertheless intuitively clear that there is such a thing as acting on a statement, and that this is an important feature of its use.) Consider, for example, assertions involving the concept of personal identity. We have reasonably sharp criteria which we apply in ordinary cases for deciding questions of personal identity: and there are also fairly clear consequences attaching to the settlement of such a question one way or the other, namely those relating to ascription of responsibility, both moral and legal, to the rights and obligations which a person has, and also to motivation (in the sense that it is ordinarily thought that a person has at least a different kind of motive for securing his own future happiness than for securing that of another). What is much harder is to give an account of the connection between the criteria for the truth of a statement of personal identity and the consequences of accepting it. We can easily imagine people who use different criteria from ours—perhaps as a result of a highly literal belief in reincarnation, or, again, by taking a view of some crucial transition (say an initiation ceremony at puberty) as literally constituting a change of identity. Precisely what would make the criteria they used criteria for *personal identity* would lie in their attaching the same consequences, in regard to

PI 404 responsibility, motivation, etc., to their statements of personal identity as we do to ours. If there existed a clear method for deriving, as it were, the consequences of a statement from the criteria for its truth, then the difference between such people and ourselves would have the character of a factual disagreement, and one side would be able to show the other to be wrong. If there were no connection between truth-grounds and consequences, then the disagreement between us would lie merely in a preference for different concepts, and there would be no right or wrong in the matter at all. Because we feel sure that there must be some connection, but we cannot give an account of it or say how tight it is, we are pulled in both directions: we feel that the disagreement is not a straightforward factual one, but that, at the same time, it is not merely a matter of applying different concepts.

To pick out the sub-class of assertions proper, we evidently need to appeal to the objectivity of their truth-conditions. However, for us the notion of truth-conditions has already been absorbed into that of the sense of an utterance, as opposed to its force. Other theories of meaning are possible, for instance that which makes the sense of an utterance—its content, independently of the force attached to it—depend upon the conditions under which it is said to have been verified: but Frege's theory is that

Gg I 32 we know the sense of a sentence when we know what it is for it to be true.

Assertion 359

Hence any subjective element that enters into a decision whether or not to accept a quasi-assertion must be regarded as relating to its force. If, e.g., the ascriptivist theory is correct, a statement imputing to someone responsibility for an action has, as belonging to its sense, only so much as may be invoked as required for the correctness of the quasi-assertion, and is in principle, though not necessarily in the individual instance, capable of being established to the satisfaction of anyone who speaks the language. An assertion in the strict sense may thus, in this framework, be characterized as a quasi-assertion the criterion for whose justification coincides with that for the truth of the thought which constitutes its sense.

The ideas about meaning which are contained in Wittgenstein's later writings in effect oppose the view that the distinction between the sense of a sentence, as given by a stipulation of its truth-conditions, and the force attached to it is fruitful for an account of the use of sentences. In particular, whereas for Frege the notions of truth and falsity play a crucial role in the characterization of the sense of a sentence, for the later Wittgenstein they do not. He expressly avowed what I have elsewhere called the 'redundancy theory' of truth, namely that the principle that 'It is true that A' is equivalent to 'A' and 'It is false that A' to 'Not A' contains the whole meaning of the words 'true' and 'false'. (See *Investigations* §136, and, even more clearly, *Remarks on the Foundations of Mathematics* I, App. I.) If this is *all* that can be said about the meaning of 'true', then learning the sense of a sentence 'A' cannot in general be explained as learning under what conditions 'A' is true: since to know what it meant to say that 'A' was true under certain conditions would involve already knowing the meaning of 'A'. For Wittgenstein 'meaning is use', and this involves among other things, that we must describe the use of each particular form of sentence directly, instead of trying to specify the use of an arbitrary sentence of some large class, such as assertoric or imperative sentences, in terms of its truth-conditions, presupposed known.

This view is independent of other facets of the idea that 'meaning is use'. Frege divides the explanation of the use which a sentence has into two parts: the stipulation of its sense; and the description of the linguistic act which uttering it constitutes. Frege himself does not spend any time giving any particular account of these linguistic acts: it is possible, as we have seen, that he took them as the expressions of interior acts which could not be described without circularity. We have seen, however, that an adequate account of the various types of linguistic act—assertion, command, etc.—would incorporate much that for Wittgenstein belonged to the 'use' of the sentence. In particular, any description of the activity of asserting—to which we have attempted only the crudest prolegomenon—must take into account the fact that there is such a thing as acting on an assertion made by another. Wittgenstein was very concerned to insist that we can understand language only as an activity which is interwoven with, and plays a role in, all our other activities; and to oppose the view that its essence is the communication of *thoughts*, considered as interior states quite independent of their relation to our external actions. He demands that we should 'make a radical break with the idea that language always functions in one way, always serves the same purpose: to convey thoughts—which may be about houses, pains, good and evil, or anything else you please'. 'Misleading parallels: the expression of pain is a cry—the expression of thought, a sentence. As if the purpose of the sentence were to convey to one person how it is with another: only, so to speak, in his thinking part and not in his stomach'. 'You regard it too much as a matter of course that one can tell anything to anyone. That is to say: we are so much accustomed to communication through language, in conversation, that it looks to us as if the whole point of communication lay in this: someone else grasps the sense of my words—which is something mental: he as it were takes it into his own mind. If he then does something further with it as well, that is no part of the immediate purpose of language'. In these passages Wittgenstein is attacking a conception of language which was probably held by Frege; certainly his account is most naturally interpreted in this way. But—except in so far as Frege took assertion as to be explained as the overt expression of an interior mental act—this conception is not involved in the distinction between the sense of a sentence and the linguistic act performed with it.

These passages can, however, be taken as we took that which alleged the existence of countless kinds of use of sentences: namely as impugning the whole concept of assertion as a useful one within the theory of meaning. And of such a repudiation of the notion of assertion it would be possible to propose two interpretations. The first of these would be a denial of the idea, common to most philosophers who have written about meaning, that the theory of meaning has some one key concept. Frege viewed the key concept of the theory of meaning as being the notion of truth: to grasp the sense of a sentence is to grasp its truth-conditions. Others have taken the key concept to be that of verification (recognition of truth): 'the meaning of a statement is the method of its verification'. Other candidates for the role of key concept have been put forward: but it has been common to philosophers to suppose that there is some one feature of a sentence which may be identified as determining its meaning. Such philosophers have not been unaware that there are many other features of a sentence and of its use

PI 304

PI 317

PI 363

NS 150 (139);
NS 214 (198)

WVC 47, 79

which have to be grasped by anyone who is to be said to understand the language to which the sentence belongs, or to understand that sentence: besides knowing, of an assertoric sentence, what constitutes a conclusive verification of it, we must also, for example, know what is taken to be a justification, short of conclusive, for asserting it, or what are the consequences of accepting it. But the implicit assumption underlying the idea that there is some one key concept in terms of which we can give a general characterization of the meaning of a sentence is that there must be some uniform pattern of derivation of all the other features of the use of an arbitrary sentence, given its meaning as characterized in terms of the key concept. It is precisely to subserve such a schema of derivation that the distinction between sense and force was introduced: corresponding to each different kind of force will be a different uniform pattern of derivation of the use of a sentence from its sense, considered as determined by its truth-conditions. It is difficult to see how, on any theory of meaning which takes meaning as to be characterized in terms of some one key concept, whether that of truth or that of verification or some other, some such distinction between sense and force could be dispensed with.

One way in which these passages from Wittgenstein may be taken is as rejecting the whole idea that there is any one key concept in the theory of meaning: the meaning of each sentence is to be explained by a direct characterization of all the different features of its use; there is no uniform means of deriving all the other features from any one of them. Such an account would have no use for any distinction between sense and force: while it could admit some rough classification of sentences, or particular utterances of sentences, according to the kinds of linguistic act effected by means of them, it could cheerfully regard the totality of such types of linguistic act as unsurveyable—as Wittgenstein does—and would not need to invoke the classification of linguistic acts in its accounts of the meanings of particular sentences. The difficulty with such a theory is to see how it could do justice to the way in which the meanings of sentences are determined by the meanings of the words which compose them. The great strength of a theory which admits something as the key concept for the theory of meaning—at least a theory which is as developed as that of Frege —is that it displays a plausible pattern for the determination of the meaning of a sentence by the meanings of the constituent words: thus, in Frege's theory, this is principally a matter of the way in which such words contribute to determining the truth-conditions of the sentence, and at least the theory makes a beginning on giving a model for the senses of words of different types, viewed as determining truth-conditions; only a little has then to be added to cover those words which serve as force-indicators. If nothing is to be taken as being a key concept, then we are once more without any conception of what the meaning of a word, as opposed to that of a sentence, is to be taken to be.

It is, however, also possible to interpret Wittgenstein as advocating a less radical view than that: namely, not as rejecting the idea that there is a key concept, but as taking the key concept not to lie, as it were, on the side of the *grounds* for an utterance, as do the concepts of truth, verification, confirmation, etc., but, rather, on that of its *consequences*. To know the meaning of a sentence, on such a theory, would be to know what the conventional consequences of uttering it are, both in the sense of the appropriate response, linguistic and non-linguistic, to it by the hearers, and in that of what the speaker commits himself to by uttering it. On such a theory, other features of the use of a sentence, such as what counted as a verification of it, would be able to be derived in some uniform manner from a knowledge of its meaning as constituted by its consequences.

Such a theory would fit some, though not all, of the things which Wittgenstein says in other places. It is difficult to evaluate such a suggestion, because it remains so completely programmatic: we have no conception what such a theory of meaning would look like if worked out. One thing is clear, however: such a theory would have no use for the notion of assertion. Viewed in the light of the consequences of utterances, the class of assertions forms an utterly heterogeneous collection, which could not possibly be of any interest to a systematic account of meaning in terms of consequences.

We have opposed throughout the view of assertion as the expression of an interior act of judgment; judgment, rather, is the interiorization of the external act of assertion. The reason for viewing the two this way round is that a conventional act can be described, without circularity, as the expression of a mental state or act only if there exist non-conventional ways of expressing it; for instance, we can describe the convention governing a gesture of greeting by saying that it is used as an expression of pleasure at seeing somebody, only because it is possible to express such pleasure without the use of the conventional gesture. Most judgments, however, it would be senseless to ascribe to someone who had not a language capable of expressing them, because there is no 'natural' behaviour which, taken by itself, is enough to express those judgments. It might seem odd that an interior version of a conventional act should be possible at all: there is not, after all, such a thing as a purely mental chess-move. (On the other hand, there are games which one can play by oneself, and which do not depend on chance factors, such as solitaire; a man with strong powers of visualization could play a wholly 'interior' game of solitaire.) The reason why there can be an interior analogue of the conventional act of assertion is that the use of language is not of purely social significance. It would be of purely social significance if it consisted solely of, say, commands and reports by observers to those not in a position of observation, as when, e.g., a child calls down the hall to his mother, 'The baker is here'. (Even here, we might think, there would be acts of judgment; for assertions are responses to observed features of the environment, and any recognition of such a feature, whether expressed by an assertion or not, would constitute a judgment as to the truth of the assertion. In this sense, animals perform acts of judgment; but in fact, the notion of acts of judgment would be unnecessary for the description of such a state of affairs, at least if there was no interior verbalization.) But of course the possession of a language alters the behaviour of an individual quite apart from his immediate dealings with others. There are two reasons for this. The use of certain expressions involves procedures for detecting features of the environment which do not reveal themselves to mere observation—for instance, the use of number-words involves the procedure of counting, whereas it is notorious that number can be discriminated only in a very crude way by mere inspection. Moreover, almost all our vocabulary for talking about other human beings depends on the fact that they can use language, and our understanding that vocabulary depends on our understanding the language which they speak or one into which it can be translated. Secondly, as we have already observed, any mature use of language involves a process of deciding what to say (whence the term 'judgment'). When a child is a mere beginner in the use of language, he uses assertoric sentences only in situations in which—so long as he is not misusing them—there is no question that he is right to say what he does. But as his mastery of language becomes more sophisticated, he learns the procedures of weighing conflicting and incompletely conclusive evidence; one of these procedures is, of course, that of making inferences from statements derived from different sources. His own actions will, of course, in part be determined by what statements he accepts, and hence deciding which statements to accept becomes of significance for his own life, and not just as a phase in communication with others. This use of language for private, rather than social, purposes can then be interiorized: the result is the activity of judgment.

CHAPTER 11

Thoughts

Ged 60–1 (4)

FREGE HAS THREE principal theses about the notions of truth and falsity. These are: (1) that to which truth and falsity are primarily ascribed is a thought; (2) truth and falsity are related to sentences as their referents; and (3) truth is indefinable. We shall consider these theses separately in successive chapters.

A thought, in Frege's terminology, is the sense expressed by a complete sentence—a sentence which is capable of being used to make an assertion or to ask a sentential question (a question requiring an answer 'Yes' or 'No'), where, of course, Frege takes the ingredient of meaning which differentiates assertoric and interrogative sentences to be force and not sense. We habitually operate, intuitively, with a notion of that which, by means of an assertoric sentence, may be asserted to be true, and of that about which, by means of an interrogative sentence, it may be enquired whether it is true, this object of assertion or of enquiry being taken as invariant under linguistic transformations, within a language or across languages, which leave the sense unchanged: the answer to a question, 'What did he assert (say)?' or 'What did he ask?', characterizes the relevant assertoric or interrogative utterance up to such sense-preserving transformations. Since a sentence must be acknowledged to have, as a whole, a sense, a sense determined by or composed out of the senses of its component expressions, there seemed to Frege

Gg I x, 32;
NS 262 (243)

to be no obstacle to the identification of the object of assertion or of enquiry with the sense of the sentence. He therefore proposed to call the sense of a complete sentence a thought.

A complete utterance is the smallest linguistic unit by means of which a linguistic act—e.g., the making of an assertion or the asking of a question—can be performed, independently of preceding linguistic context. The word 'sentence' is often used to mean 'complete utterance', as thus explained: but complete utterances will include, for example, what Frege calls 'word-questions'—interrogatives formed by means of 'who', 'which', 'where', Ged 62 (6) 'when', etc.—whose sense neither Frege nor anyone else would take as being a thought. It is thus best to characterize a thought as the sense of a complete assertoric sentence, while recognizing that forms of words which NS 142 (131) could not be used to make an assertion, for instance sentential questions, may sometimes have a thought as their sense. This explanation of the notion of a thought thus appeals to that of an assertion, or at least to the possibility of discriminating between assertoric sentences and others. Whether a sentence is assertoric is independent of the force, if any, actually attached to it: it is irrelevant whether, within a particular utterance, it occurs with assertoric, interrogative or other force attached, or as a constituent of a more complex expression to which such force is attached: all that is necessary is that it should be capable of being used, independently of the preceding linguistic context, to make an assertion. The qualification, 'independently of preceding linguistic context', is needed in order to allow for the kind of ellipsis that occurs paradigmatically in answering a word-question. By replying, 'Fidel Castro', to the question, 'Who is the greatest living statesman?', I do indeed assert that Fidel Castro is the greatest living statesman; but that does not render the name 'Fidel Castro' a complete sentence, since the ability to use it to make that, or any other, assertion depends upon its being uttered as a response to a question. We should naturally say that 'Fidel Castro', in that context, was elliptical for a complete sentence determined by the question. Since, in giving that reply, I do make an assertion, we must therefore surely also say that I did, by uttering the name in that context, also express a thought, the very same thought as that expressed by the complete sentence for which my reply was elliptical. That is to say that, in that context, the name 'Fidel Castro' expressed the same sense as 'Fidel Castro is the greatest living statesman', for a thought is the sense of a sentence. It will thus follow that the sense of an utterance is not determined solely by the senses of the component expressions, but also by the linguistic context. We thus arrive at the following characterization of the notion of expressing a thought: a thought is expressed by any utterance which, in the linguistic context in which the utterance is made, has the same sense as some sentence which could, independently of linguistic context, be used to make an assertion.

Another well-known kind of dependence upon linguistic context occurs with one kind of use of third-person pronouns. In some cases, it is possible to replace a third-person pronoun, singular or plural, by a substantival phrase which yields a complete sentence having the same sense as, in the given linguistic context, the original sentence had: the original sentence then expressed a thought, although it was not a complete sentence. Thus, in 'Although the Chinese invented gunpowder, they originally used it only for fireworks', by replacing 'they' and 'it' by 'the Chinese' and 'gunpowder' respectively, we obtain, from the second clause, the complete sentence 'The Chinese originally used gunpowder only for fireworks': the original clause, 'they originally used it only for fireworks', while not a complete sentence, thus expressed a thought. In other cases, this is not possible. In the sentence, 'If two people frequently play chess together, they learn each other's weaknesses', we may indeed replace 'they' by 'those two people', but this does not convert the second clause into a complete sentence. Of course, sometimes the fact that a constituent clause does not express a thought has nothing to do with the presence of pronouns, but results from the mode of connection: in 'When the Saxons first arrived in Britain, they were pagans', the failure of the second clause to express a thought is due to the indeterminacy of temporal reference in the sentence 'The Saxons were pagans'.

The notion of sense that is being employed when it is said that the elliptical sentence has, in the linguistic context, the same sense as the complete sentence for which it is elliptical cannot, of course, be that ordinarily employed by Frege, according to which the sense of a compound is made up out of the senses of the components, but must appeal to determination of sense, in part, by linguistic context. The conventions governing the giving of answers to questions and one use of third-person pronouns require us to understand certain utterances as elliptical for complete sentences, in a manner that is not very difficult to specify; moreover, this use of pronouns has to be understood before the other use, in which they serve to express generality and are comparable with bound variables, can be grasped. The existence of these conventions is displayed, in the use of natural languages, by the recognition of the relevant principles of inference.

Dependence upon linguistic context is a quite different matter from dependence upon non-linguistic context. In order to understand token-reflexive expressions such as tenses, first- and second-person pronouns, and words like 'here', 'yesterday', etc., it is indeed necessary to grasp the conventions according to which their reference depends upon the circumstances of utterance: but these conventions cannot, in general, be expressed by means of any rule for replacing a sentence containing such token-reflexive expressions by one whose content is independent of context of utterance. Sentences containing token-reflexives cannot be said to be elliptical. Thus, if the notion of a thought were to be understood solely as a special case of the notion of sense, there would be no reason why a sentence such as 'It is very cold today' should not be considered a complete sentence, and thus

Gg I 32; NS
209 (192)

as having a thought as its sense. Unlike the elliptical utterances, there is no natural notion of sense under which the sense of such a sentence would change according to the time and place at which it was uttered: rather, it is characteristic of its sense that the time and place referred to must be determined, in a uniform manner, from the time and place of utterance (in this simple case, by the identity mapping). The thought expressed by such a sentence would, therefore, be one to which it was impossible to ascribe truth or falsity absolutely: rather, it would be a thought which was true at certain times and places, and false at others.

Frege does not want to admit such relativized notions of truth and falsity: for him, a thought must always be true or false absolutely. Hence, he does not permit the identification of the sense of any sentence containing a part whose reference needs to be determined from the occasion of utterance with a thought. Frege allows that, by means of a particular utterance of a sentence of this kind, a thought may be expressed; but he says that, in such a case, the accompanying conditions of the utterance serve, together with the utterance itself, to express the thought. This feature of Frege's notion of a thought cannot be arrived at merely from the characterization of a thought as the sense of a complete sentence: it follows only from the decision to treat a thought as that which may be said to be true or to be false, together with the conviction that truth and falsity, at least in their primary employment, are notions which do not admit of relativization to times, places or other external conditions. [NJ 251; Gg I xvi-xvii; NS 146-7 (134-5)]

Frege made no attempt to work out any precise theory of token-reflexive expressions: almost the only places in his writings in which he takes more than passing notice of them are 'Der Gedanke' of 1918 and the unpublished 'Logik' of 1897. In the essay of 1897, Frege goes further than the observation that the same sentence, where it is one which contains an unsupplemented token-reflexive indication of time, place or person, may be used on different occasions to express different thoughts: he says also that the thought one speaker expresses by means of a sentence containing a token-reflexive expression may be expressed by another speaker by one containing a proper name, as when I say, 'I am cold', and B, hearing me, reports to C, 'Dummett is cold'. In most of Frege's writing, however, what he says has tacitly to be understood as applying only to sentences expressing a determinate thought independently of the circumstances of utterance. We shall, therefore, consider first the thesis that it is thoughts, not sentences, which are, in the first instance, said to be true or false under the simplifying assumption that we are dealing with a language containing no token-reflexive expressions, in which, therefore, every complete sentence does, considered [Ged 64-6 (10-13)] [NS 146 (134-135)] as a type, express a thought; only later shall we return to the question whether this thesis is misleading, or wrong, for a language such as ours.

The most natural general means of characterizing the linguistic activity of assertion is that it consists in saying that the thought expressed is true, and, of the linguistic activity of asking a sentential question, that it consists in asking whether the thought expressed is true. We noted before that such characterizations are essentially circular—they employ the notion of asking, or that of saying in the sense of 'asserting'. They are, however, sufficient to indicate the motivation for Frege's saying that it is a thought to which the predicates 'is true' and 'is false' are to be regarded as applying, in the first place. A complete sentence can, he says, be called 'true' or 'false' in a secondary, derivative, sense, according as the thought that it expresses is true or false: but this sense of 'true' and 'false' can be understood only in terms of the primary sense, under which thoughts, rather than sentences, are said to be true or false.

NS 189 (174) -[8]; NS 193n (178n); NS 251 (233)

In so far as intuition provides any guide in the matter, it suggests that what can be described as true or as false is not so much the sequence of words that a man may utter, as what he said by means of the utterance of them; and here the equivocal expression 'what he said' seems best glossed as 'the thought which he expressed'. Even if someone feels disposed to urge that it is the sentence itself which should be considered true or false, it must be allowed that it is true or false by reason of the sense which is attached to it, and by reason of no other feature internal to the sentence or to the language to which it belongs. In saying that it is the thought which, in the primary sense, is true or false, and that the sentence is so only in a derivative sense, Frege is being faithful to what he likewise says about reference:

SB 27; BW 96 (63)

namely that, properly speaking, it is the *sense* of a proper name which bears the relation of reference to some object, and that it is only in a derivative sense of 'reference' that we can speak of the name itself as bearing this relation to the object; and similarly for expressions of other logical types. This seems, indeed, much less natural intuitively than Frege's contention about what it is that is true or false; although, again, we should readily concede that it was by reason of its sense that the name had the reference that it did.

NS 190 (174) -[11]

Frege's choosing to take the thought as the possessor of truth-value and the sense as the possessor of reference is due in part to his conception of senses in general, and thoughts in particular, as existing independently of whether we have words to express them. Indeed, he sometimes argues for the thesis that it is thoughts to which truth and falsity are primarily ascribed by urging that it would still be true that the Earth has only one (natural) satellite even if there were no human being to express the fact or recognize its truth. If what is true would still be true even if we were not able to express or grasp it, or did not even exist, then that which is true cannot be anything whose existence depends on us, as the existence of a sentence depends at least on the existence of the language to which it belongs, but must be something, like a thought, which exists independently of us. Conversely, given that a thought is taken to be what is true or false, and given also that any true thought which does not relate to us would still be true if we did not exist, it follows that the existence of a thought cannot be dependent on our ability to express it or to grasp it. NS 144–6 (132–4) NS 214 (198)

Although Frege's view of senses, and, in particular, thoughts, as timeless entities is, thus, contributory to his thesis that it is a thought which is said to be true or false, the thesis survives the rejection of this conception of senses. Frege's argument that, if we did not exist, the thought that the Earth has only one natural satellite would still be true, begs the question of the independent existence of thoughts. All that he is entitled to say is that, if we were not here to give expression to the thought, that which makes the thought true would still be the case. It might be retorted, on Frege's behalf, that he does not recognize any such category of entities as those which make thoughts true. It is, indeed, a conspicuous feature of Frege's ontology that he invokes no such entities as facts, as other philosophers have done, to serve as that which true thoughts correspond to, or as what make true thoughts true. On the contrary, for Frege a fact is simply a true thought: the relation between a thought and the related fact, if there is one, is not that of correspondence, but that of complete coincidence. Russell, at one time, held the same about propositions and facts: but the difference is that, for Frege, thoughts, and therefore facts, belong to the realm of sense and not that of reference; an ingredient of a fact, i.e. of a true thought, may therefore be the sense of the name 'Mount Everest', but it could never be the mountain itself, whereas for Russell the actual objects which are the denotations of proper names are constituents of propositions, and, when these are true propositions, therefore of facts. Ged 76 (27) Ged 74 (25) EA 75 LK 56

It may seem, therefore, that it is impossible to rebut Frege's argument in the way suggested without invoking a type of entity, facts, which he does not recognize; indeed, it might seem natural to maintain that the price Frege paid for dispensing with facts from his ontology was precisely to have to regard thoughts in the way he does, as timeless or eternal entities whose existence is not dependent upon the existence in any actual language of sentences which express them, or even of beings capable of grasping them.

This does not hold good, however. In saying that, even if we were not there to express the thought that the Earth has only one natural satellite, that which makes that thought true would still be the case, we do not have to be construed as implying that there is any entity which is the referent of the expression 'that which makes the thought true': all that we are aiming to convey by means of this form of words is that it would still be the case that the Earth had only one natural satellite. If, contrary to Frege's conception, a thought were to be regarded as something whose existence depends upon there being some actual language in which it could be expressed, or at least some intelligent being capable of grasping it, it would follow that there were two conditions for the statement, 'The thought that the Earth has only one natural satellite is true', to be true: first, that the Earth should have only one natural satellite; and, secondly, that there should be such a thing as the thought that the Earth has only one natural satellite, i.e. that there be a language in which that thought could be expressed or a being who was capable of grasping it. For an arbitrary, unspecified, thought, the expression, 'In such-and-such circumstances, that which makes the thought true would still be the case', is an attempt to convey that, in the circumstances in question, all the conditions for the truth of the thought should obtain save, perhaps, the condition that there should in fact be any such thought: there need be no implication that there is an entity of any kind whose existence constitutes the fulfilment of those conditions.

Frege's argument to the timeless existence of thoughts thus has no force; nor, equally, has the similar argument from the timelessness of truth to the thesis that it is thoughts, not sentences, which are true or false. But, by the same token, an objection to the supposedly timeless character of thoughts need not be an objection to the thesis that a thought is that which primarily carries truth-value: we could accept that thesis without being committed to the timeless existence of thoughts, and without having to have recourse to an ontology of facts either.

PROPOSITIONAL ATTITUDES

Given that there are such things as thoughts, the issue whether it is they or sentences to which truth and falsity should be primarily ascribed seems a trivial one; at least within the restrictions which we are presently observing, namely of considering only thoughts expressible by a complete sentence independent of context. Thoughts seem intuitively the more natural choice; but, given an application of 'true' and 'false' to either, their application to the other is easily explained. Within our present restriction, if Frege's notion of sense is accepted, the existence of thoughts is not in question, since, for context-independent sentences, a thought may simply be taken as the sense of a complete sentence. Given that sentences have senses, there can hardly be any ground for entities of any other kind, distinct from sentences, to be the possessors of truth-values. The issue has been a contentious one only where it has been thought possible to avoid recognizing the existence of any rival claimants, besides sentences, for the role of arguments for the predicates 'is true' and 'is false'; no one has maintained that there really are two candidates, the thought and the sentence, but that, of these two, the sentence is the successful one.

Some philosophers have held that the recognition of some entity intermediate between the sentence and the reality which renders it true or false, an entity usually known in English-language philosophical writing as a 'proposition', is essential for an account of belief, expectation, etc.; that sentences such as 'Jones believes that Columbus made the first journey across the Atlantic' must be construed by taking the whole substantival clause 'that Columbus made the first journey across the Atlantic' at its face value, as a term standing for a proposition, to which Jones is being stated to have a certain mental attitude. This analysis agrees with Frege's: to say, as he did, that a sentence in indirect speech has as its referent what is normally its sense is, precisely, to say that in such a context it stands for a thought; and a thought is the closest analogue in Frege's ontology to the 'proposition' of British philosophers. Others have opposed this interpretation of sentences involving indirect speech as resting on too naïve an acceptance of superficial grammatical structure, and as invoking unnecessary entities, and have argued that the word 'that' should not be taken as belonging with the sentential clause which follows it, but, rather, that '. . . believes that . . .' should be construed as an instance of a special kind of incomplete expression, neither a relational expression nor a sentential connective, requiring its first argument-place to be filled by a term and its second by a sentence. This, by itself, is purely programmatic, involving no more than a rejection of the view of belief as an attitude to thoughts or to propositions, without offering anything positive in its place. Often, however, it has been accompanied, or replaced, by the proposal that belief be regarded as an attitude towards sentences: on this view, 'Jones believes that Columbus made the first journey across the Atlantic' is to be analysed as saying that Jones has to the sentence 'Columbus made the first journey across the Atlantic' a particular attitude, namely that of believing it to be true. Here '. . . believes the sentence _ _ _ to be true' is not, in turn, to be analysed as '. . . believes that the sentence _ _ _ is true', but is, rather, to be taken as expressing a primitive relation between people and sentences.

Against this proposal a famous objection has been made, originally by

CAB   Church, on the score of translation. If the proposed analysis were right, the objection runs, then the sentence 'Jones believes that Columbus made the first journey across the Atlantic' would involve a reference to an *English* sentence, viz. 'Columbus made the first journey across the Atlantic', while the German sentence which would normally be taken as the translation of the compound sentence, namely 'Jones glaubt, dass Kolumbus die erste Reise über das Atlantik gemacht hat', would likewise contain a reference to the *German* sentence, 'Kolumbus hat die erste Reise über das Atlantik gemacht', and hence would not be a true translation of the English one. Of course, under the interpretation whereby belief is an attitude to thoughts rather than to sentences, no such difficulty arises, since the substantival clauses 'that Columbus made the first journey across the Atlantic' and 'dass Kolumbus die erste Reise über das Atlantik gemacht hat' may be taken as standing for the very same thought.

It is difficult to treat this objection very seriously. There is no ground for presumption that the practical canons of apt translation always require strict synonymy. On the contrary, translations of fiction and, equally, of historical narrative (including the Gospels) always translate even directly quoted dialogue; and, when a remark about a quoted word or phrase does not retain its truth-value under translation of the quoted expression, it is often regarded as allowable to substitute a non-equivalent expression for the one quoted. (An example occurs in Austin's translation of Frege's *Grundlagen*:

Gl 54   Austin translates the sentence, 'Der Begriff "Silbe des Wortes Zahl" hebt das Wort als ein Ganzes . . . heraus', as 'The concept "syllables in the word three" picks out the word as a whole', for the obvious reason that the English word 'number' has two syllables.)

But, while it is difficult to take the argument from translation seriously, it is equally difficult to take the whole issue seriously. If belief is an attitude towards sentences, then the attitude of believing-true is one which has to be so understood that a man is capable of having such an attitude to a sentence which he has never heard or thought of, which he could not understand, and which belongs to a language that he does not know; and similarly for

WO 213   fear, expectation and the like. Indeed, as Quine points out, if we are to allow that a mouse may fear being eaten by the cat, such an interpretation will require us to ascribe to the mouse an attitude, that of fearing-true, to an English sentence. The elimination, by this means, of reference to thoughts has been accomplished at the cost of requiring us to explain such a sense of 'believes-true', etc., an explanation which will necessarily involve an account of the relation between any sentence and its equivalent within the same language, and that between it and its translation into another language. If there is to be any determinate account of the notion of belief at all, then, on whatever model belief is construed, such an account must be supplied. This requirement is independent of any theses that may be held about intra-linguistic synonymy or interlinguistic translation; such theses will simply be reflected in the resultant analysis of belief. If, e.g., interlinguistic equivalence is held to be only a vague relation, then the semantics required for sentences concerning belief will be that needed for other vague expressions, e.g. 'red' or 'mountain'. Again, if it is held that the correctness of a translation can be judged only relative to some framework, then the ascription to a German of the belief that Columbus made the first journey across the Atlantic must be taken as tacitly related to such a framework. The ascription of beliefs and other 'propositional attitudes' to human beings is evidently connected with dispositions on the part of human beings to use, or react to, certain sentences in certain ways: any account of belief must, therefore, explain the relation which must obtain between the sentences actually or potentially used by the person to whom the belief is ascribed and the sentence used in the course of the ascription to express the belief ascribed. This necessity obtains independently of whether belief is construed as an attitude to thoughts, or an attitude to sentences, or in some other way.

Given that such a relation between sentences has to be invoked in any account of belief, whether the relation be taken to be vague or definite, relative or absolute, it must remain open to us to take belief as an attitude to propositions, where 'the proposition expressed by . . .' is understood as an operator whose range consists of abstract objects the criterion of identity between which coincides with that for the relation in question to hold between the sentences which are its arguments. A denial of this possibility can rest on one of only two things: a despair of the feasibility of giving any uniform account of belief at all; or a superstitious fear of abstract objects. Frege's further step of identifying propositions, as thus schematically understood, with thoughts, i.e. with the senses of sentences, amounts to the thesis that the relevant relation between sentences is that of identity of sense. Such a proposal might, indeed, be rejected by someone who did not believe, with Frege, that the notion of sense was independently required: he would still need, if he wanted to give any account of belief, to give an account of some relevant relation between sentences.

Quine takes the former of these two paths. Having first decided that it is better to construe ascriptions of belief as asserting a relation between a man and a sentence, rather than between a man and a proposition or other

o

WO 215-16 intensional object, he next proposes that it be viewed as merely a predication, and not relational in structure at all: on this view, the only object referred to in the sentence 'Jones believes that Columbus made the first journey across the Atlantic' would be Jones, the rest of the sentence containing no reference either to a proposition or to a sentence. This amounts to adopting the proposal to construe '. . . believes that . . .' as an expression intermediate between a relational expression and a sentential connective, while abandoning the conception of belief as a relation between a person and a sentence. It leaves us in utter perplexity over how '. . . believes that . . .' is to be explained; that is, how we come to understand the application of the various one-place predicates obtained by inserting a sentence in the second argument-place. But that is only a preliminary to Quine's declaring that no analysis is possible, and no use of indirect quotation allowable when we are 'limning the true and ultimate structure of reality' (*Word and Object*, p. 221).

WO 220-1 Quine's argument for this pessimistic conclusion is obscured by his irrelevant invocation of his thesis of the indeterminacy of translation. This thesis concerned, originally, what he calls *radical* translation: translation between languages between which there exists no established tradition of translation. Such translation is, he holds, unique only relative to a given framework of 'analytical hypotheses', and there may be many equally serviceable such frameworks. This is not the place to examine this thesis: it is clear enough that, if it be accepted, any ascription of a belief to a speaker of a radically foreign language must be taken as relative to such a framework; but such a conclusion, while important, would not show the impossibility of analysing such ascriptions of belief, only the necessity of taking them to be so relativized. Quine extends his thesis about the indeterminacy of translation also to non-radical translation, and even to the understanding of a person's utterances by a speaker of the same language, in the ordinary sense of 'language'. Here the case is different: since between (say) Italian and English there is an established tradition of translation, there is a canonical framework to which we can refer any ascription in English of a belief to some speaker of Italian. Likewise, within any one language, there is also a canonical framework, namely what Quine calls the 'homophonic' rule of translation.

True enough, I may sometimes be in doubt whether someone can be meaning what he appears to be saying; and I sometimes resolve this doubt negatively, settling for a non-homophonic rule of translation between his version of English and mine. The thesis of the indeterminacy of translation amounts to the claim that there need be no possible evidence which would resolve such a doubt one way or the other. Given what a man believes, we can (assuming him to speak sincerely) determine what he means from what he says; conversely, given the meanings he attaches to his words, we can tell from what he says what he believes. Unfortunately, we are not given either: we have to derive, from what we hear him say, both what he believes and what he means by his words. The thesis of the indeterminacy of translation is the thesis that there is, or need be, no unique way of slicing up the evidence: if we take his words one way, we shall ascribe a certain set of beliefs to him, if we take them another, then we shall ascribe another set. Even though we accept the principle of charity, that we shall ascribe to other people as many beliefs tallying with our own as possible, it may be, according to the indeterminacy thesis, that, however much evidence we acquire, either set of ascriptions fits the evidence just as well.

This brings out extremely well the intimate connection between belief and sense. There is nothing problematic about ascribing to a man the belief that Persia has a larger population than India, and, in expressing this belief, he need not have used the name 'Persia' (he may well have said 'Iran'). But it is obscure what could be meant by ascribing to someone the belief that Persia is longer than the Amazon: one would naturally ask, 'You mean he thinks "Persia" is the name of a river?', and the reply that he did not use the name 'Persia' would lead one to stigmatize the purported account of his belief as quite out of place. The reliance on what someone says as indicating what he believes depends upon attaching, and supposing that he attaches, a certain sense to his words. Even if he and I speak the same language, my choice of a certain form of words to express his belief does not imply that he would accept it as an apt expression: but my characterization of his belief depends, like everything else I say, on the sense which I attach to the words I use to characterize it. There is no belief which I can ascribe to anyone and characterize as the belief that Persia is longer than the Amazon, though there is indeed such a belief as that 'Iran' is the name of a river. The latter belief may or may not underlie an apparently serious utterance of the sentence, 'Iran is longer than the Amazon'; but it is only in the presence of an assumption about the sense which the speaker attaches to the name 'Iran' that we can say what belief it was that he sought to express by his utterance of that sentence.

This much is common to Quine and Frege. Even if someone attaches the very same senses to his words as I do, it is not a necessary condition for my correctly saying of him that he made an assertion expressed by a certain sentence that he should have uttered that very sentence with assertoric force; but the possibility that he may attach different senses to his words shows that it is not a sufficient condition either. Quine's indeterminacy thesis entails that there will be cases in which there is no objective way of determining which, of two or more proposed interpretations of someone's words, is the correct one (not because this is eternally hidden from us, but because the question has no answer). It would be absurd, on the part of even the most enthusiastic adherent of the indeterminacy thesis, to suppose that such situations arise often between contemporaneous speakers of the same natural language; but, for such situations, it will follow from the thesis that an ascription of belief must always be taken relative to a particular interpretation. This, by itself, does not show that an analysis of the notion of belief is impossible, any more than it shows that translation is impossible or that communication between two speakers of the same language is impossible.

Though he presents it as a corollary of the indeterminacy thesis, Quine's final rejection of sentences involving indirect quotation from the language to be used for limning the true and ultimate structure of reality actually depends on the contention that there is not any one standard for the correctness of an ascription of propositional attitude. 'There is nothing approaching a fixed standard of how far indirect quotation may deviate from the direct. Commonly the degree of allowable deviation depends on why we are quoting. It is a question of what traits of the quoted speaker's remarks we want to make something of; those are the traits that must be kept straight if our indirect quotation is to count as true. Similar remarks apply to sentences of belief and other propositional attitudes' (*Word and Object*, p. 218).

The point is well taken, but it is not a deep point. It is true enough that we often allow ourselves a certain licence in reporting indirectly the statements of another; our reports are accurate only modulo obvious implications and background truths well known to all parties; challenged, we may often say, 'Well, he didn't say exactly that, but that was what it amounted to'. The canon of strict preservation of sense is an ideal to which we often do not make the effort to conform, an ideal to which in the context we are not taken to be striving strictly to conform. It does not follow from this fact that there is no such ideal, that there is no standard by which we can judge indirect quotation as true or false *au pied de la lettre*. Ascriptions of belief and other propositional attitudes are, indeed, vague in a way that indirect reports of utterances are not; because, as noted earlier, there is an uncertainty how much prompting is allowable in order to elicit the response which expresses the belief ascribed: but this is quite a different matter.

Quine takes his point about the variable standards employed in assessing indirect reports as having more weight than it does just because he does not believe that there is any unique criterion for the preservation of sense, that is, a unique admissible scheme of translation. This, as we have seen, is, even if accepted, a point of a different kind: since, if there is to be communication between human beings at all, it must be possible for them to adopt some determinate scheme of intertranslation, this does not infect ascriptions of propositional attitudes with vagueness from a new source, but only compels their relativization to a scheme of interpretation. We may, however, take issue with Quine's methodology here. 'Consider', he invites us, 'how I have persisted in my vernacular use of "meaning", "idea", and the like, long after casting doubt on their supposed objects. True, the use of a term can sometimes be reconciled with rejection of its objects; but I go on using the terms without even sketching any such reconciliation. What is involved here is simply a grading of austerity' (*Word and Object*, p. 210). In the same spirit, he proposes to continue the use of indirect quotation and of verbs for propositional attitudes, except when limning the true and ultimate structure of reality or formulating the fundamental laws of a branch of science. Philosophers have often given themselves a licence to employ expressions on which they have cast doubt: but not in a quite arbitrary fashion, as Quine claims for himself the right to do. If an idiom of natural language proves, on close inspection, to have an unsuspected and irremediable vagueness, this is a good reason for banning it from theoretical discourse, but continuing to employ it in more casual contexts, provided that one can indicate the area and the extent of the vagueness. Another case is that in which an idiom is revealed as misleading, suggesting an underlying structure quite different from that which it actually has; a particular species of such idioms is referred to by Quine as that in which the use of a term may be reconciled with rejection of its objects. Here the idiom may be retained, freed as we are from the temptation to misconstrue it. Yet another case is that of the philosopher who advances some sceptical argument or propounds some antinomy: he believes that there is some resolution of the antinomy or rejoinder to the sceptical conclusion, although he cannot himself provide it, and thus continues to use some expression which he believes, but cannot prove, to be coherent. None of these cases is Quine's. If a certain idiom or expression can genuinely be shown to be in principle incapable of analysis, then it must be eschewed, and that is an end of the matter: no one can claim for himself and his allies the right to continue to use, without explanation, forms of expression of which he has purported to prove that no account is possible, and whose appearance in the writings of his opponents serves as a ground for rejecting their contentions. One may quite legitimately use an expression which one is unable to explain. But if someone claims to have shown that, for some expression, no explanation is possible, then he is claiming it as unintelligible, and it remains unintelligible, if he is right, when he uses it just as much as when anyone else does; he cannot offer as an excuse for saying something unintelligible that he is not feeling in a very austere mood at the time. The double standard leads too easily to doublethink.

OST 137-8   Tacitly in Quine, and explicitly in Davidson, there is an argument from indeterminacy of translation to a rejection of thoughts as the objects of propositional attitudes. The argument resembles that against absolute space and time, and is of the form: if there were such a thing as sense, then there would be a unique, objective criterion for the correctness of translation; but there is no such unique, objective criterion; hence there can be no such thing as sense. This argument is cogent only in relation to a very strong form of the indeterminacy thesis—a form in which, indeed, Quine expressly advances it: even then, it does not lead to the conclusion that statements of belief or other propositional attitudes resist analysis, but only that they must be taken relative to a frame of reference. If there is such a thing as sense, translation is determined uniquely, at least up to synonymy within the language into which the translation is being made. If there is no such thing as sense, then we have to impose weaker criteria for correct translation, which do not determine translation uniquely. But it is impossible to argue conversely, that, if translation is found to be non-unique under weaker criteria than that it be sense-preserving, then there can be no such thing as sense in terms of which a stronger criterion could be framed which would impose uniqueness. It will, of course, be replied that the argument for indeterminacy has proceeded by examining all possible criteria for correct translation based upon observable linguistic behaviour, and that therefore, if there be any such thing as sense, it must be something which is not wholly reflected in linguistic behaviour. Fully to evaluate this reply, it would be necessary to scrutinize the argument for indeterminacy, which I am not going to do in this chapter: but the difficulty is that the argument has been conducted wholly in terms of those features of the practice of using a radically foreign language which can be captured by drawing up a scheme of translation; and this leaves it open whether there may not be such features, observable and determinative of sense, which cannot be captured in this way.

Ggf 36 (55-6);
NS 275 (255)
    Frege's notion of sense, as applied to complex expressions, involves a very narrow criterion of identity. Frege says that the sense of a complex expression, including a sentence, is composed out of the senses of its constituents. 'Composed out of' is a metaphor; but it is used deliberately by Frege to convey something stronger than the non-metaphorical 'determined by'. The value of a number-theoretic function is determined by the arguments of that function; but the number which is the value can be conceived otherwise than as the value of that function for those arguments. To say that the sense of a sentence is composed out of the senses of its constituent words

is to say, not merely that, by knowing the senses of the words, we can determine the sense of the sentence, but that we can grasp that sense only as the sense of a complex which is composed out of parts in exactly that way; only a sentence which had exactly that structure, and whose primitive constituents corresponded in sense pointwise with those of the original sentence, could possibly express the very same sense. (Frege's notion of the senses of complex expressions thus tallies closely with Carnap's intensional isomorphism.)

MN 56–9

Now it is true that the structure of a sentence, as here appealed to, must not be understood in a superficial fashion. It may be correct to recognize each of four different languages as containing a sentential operator of negation: but in one this is expressed by prefacing a phrase to the sentence, in another by enclosing the sentence between two words, in the third by inflecting the main verb and in the fourth by omitting a word that would otherwise occur. We are concerned here, not with surface structure, but with what Chomsky and his school call 'deep structure', or, perhaps, with the structure that is required only for semantic purposes. Nevertheless, it is perfectly possible that, by Frege's criterion for the identity of the senses of sentences, strictly applied, there may be no sentence in a given language which exactly matches the sense of some particular sentence in another language, since the internal structure of the two languages differs at some critical point. In this case, we shall have to make do with only approximate translation, which is good enough for practical purposes. Relatively to the loose criteria we are forced to adopt in practice, it may well be true that translation is not unique: but that would not show that there was no such thing as sense to provide a strict criterion, but, rather, that the criterion it supplied was so strict as sometimes to rule out the possibility of translation altogether.

Thus to reduce Quine's revolutionary thesis of the indeterminacy of translation to the platitude that there may be no exact translation from one language into another, it may be said, misses the point of the doctrine: it may be possible to account for some cases of what Quine calls the inscrutability of terms by appealing to non-isomorphic structure, but not for the indeterminacy thesis in its strongest form, which involves that equally acceptable translations may map a foreign sentence on to sentences with different truth-values. This strong claim does entail that there is no such thing as sense, for it involves that there is no uniquely correct truth-definition for the sentences of the foreign language discoverable from the linguistic behaviour of its speakers. We cannot reasonably demand that every sentence of the foreign language commonly taken by its speakers as true should be translated into a sentence of our language which we generally

RIT 182

take as true; such a demand would indeed often result in there being no correct translation scheme at all, but the demand would be unreasonable in that it would rule out the possibility of ascribing to the speakers of the foreign language a common set of beliefs different from our own. Whatever sense may be, it must involve determinate truth-conditions for unambiguous sentences: if there are sentences whose truth-conditions are not fully discoverable from the linguistic practice of the speakers of the language, but which are not demonstrable as ambiguous on internal grounds, that is, are not treated by them as ambiguous, then there is no sense which is discoverable by the observation of that practice.

This argument, as it stands, presupposes that all ambiguity must be recognized. We might retort that, while all ambiguity must be recognizable, there may, at any time, be lurking ambiguities which await detection. The existence of such hidden ambiguity does depend upon the linguistic dispositions of the speakers of the language—those which will render them capable of recognizing the ambiguity when it is pointed out: but these dispositions will be far from manifest, and very long-term. It remains that, if the strongest form of the indeterminacy thesis can be made out, namely that a language may contain sentences which are neither vague nor ambiguous in virtue of any existing dispositions of the speakers, however long-term, and yet are such that the practice of using them does not determine unique truth-conditions for them, then the linguistic dispositions of the speakers cannot be explained in terms of the notion of sense, understood as related to truth-conditions in the way Frege supposed.

Gg I 32

Or is this, on second thoughts, so certain? Is it, after all, so clear that a determinate sense requires determinate truth-conditions? May there not be some latitude in the way the notions of truth and falsity can be taken as applying to sentences, consistently with the facts about how those sentences are used? For instance, may it not be the case that we might with equal faithfulness to the facts of linguistic practice interpret the indicative conditionals of natural language either as material conditionals or as requiring, for their truth, some stronger connection between their constituents?*

---

* The latter possibility has appeared more attractive than it is. A conditional expression of intention can hardly be construed as conveying more than the intention to bring about the truth of the material conditional; yet, if sincere, it affords a ground for the assertion by another of the same conditional. As observed by Grice, the use of a conditional to give a hint cancels any suggestion of a connection stronger than material; and the same is true of its use as a premiss in certain chains of argument, when, say, the proponent of the argument would be prepared to assert the consequent unconditionally, but his hearer will acknowledge only the conditional, on some ground unacceptable to the proponent. The example will still serve to indicate the kind of case envisaged.

cf LC

The answer depends on how the status of an account of sense in terms of truth-conditions is conceived. Although sense can be taken only as a cognitive notion, an account of sense does not aim to uncover an actual psychic mechanism: to think that it did would run counter to Frege's insistence that sense is not something psychological, does not relate to any inner process. NS 6–7 (6–7) An account of sense must, then, be a theoretical model the test of which is its agreement with observable linguistic behaviour. If so, there seems no reason why there should be any unique such model which tallies with actual practice. This question is one about which Frege was never explicit. If it is required that every feature of the model, including the notions of reference and truth-value, should be separately interpretable as representations of distinguishable aspects of linguistic practice, then, under these interpretations, there can be only one model. If, on the other hand, some of the notions employed in the model, in particular, those of truth and falsity, can be considered as theoretical notions, which cannot be correlated directly with linguistic behaviour, the model being judged correct or incorrect, according to its agreement with linguistic practice, only as a whole, then there may be more than one model which will serve equally well. In the latter case, the indeterminacy thesis even in its strongest form is compatible with the Fregean doctrine of sense and reference: different translations will correspond to different, but equally workable, semantic models. There is, admittedly, no sign that Frege ever contemplated the possibility of such indeterminacy or of such a choice between different semantic representations of a given language: but there is nothing which he says which rules it out, either.

However matters may stand in respect of Frege's notion of sense, it will, according to Quine's own doctrine, be possible to represent the linguistic dispositions of the speakers of a language in terms of a notion of sense provided that we invoke some system of analytical hypotheses: it is merely that such a system will not be unique. Perhaps the use of the word 'sense' here is tendentious: but it seems clear, at least, that the analytical hypotheses will determine specific truth-conditions for the sentences of the language; and certainly they will render translation unique relative to them. It follows that, from the indeterminacy of translation, no conclusion can be derived as to the impossibility of an analysis of statements of belief; the conclusion is merely that any such statements must be taken as relative to some set of analytical hypotheses. Relative to such a set, sentences have determinate senses: hence, as long as the relativity of sense is borne in mind, there can be no objection on this score, either, to taking belief as an attitude to thoughts.

O•

ASCRIPTIONS OF TRUTH-VALUE

The analysis of sentences about belief and other propositional attitudes is
not directly relevant to the topic of what it is that possesses truth-value. The
appeal to the notion of a thought has been felt to be more urgent in the
analysis of sentences such as 'Jones believes that Columbus made the first
journey across the Atlantic' than of ones like 'It is false that Columbus made
the first journey across the Atlantic', because, in the former case, the
substantival clause constitutes an opaque context, within which substitution
which preserves (ordinary) reference may alter the truth-value of the whole,
while, in the latter case, the substantival clause is a transparent context. It
would be perfectly possible, therefore, to construe the subordinate sentence
in 'It is false that Columbus made the first journey across the Atlantic' as
having its ordinary reference, namely as standing for a truth-value, and to
take the sentence as a whole as identifying that truth-value with falsity. If
we were to treat 'is false' in the same way when it occurs in a sentence like
'Goldbach's conjecture is false', this would have the slightly grotesque
consequence that expressions like 'Goldbach's conjecture', 'the second law
of thermodynamics', 'what Robinson said', etc., would have to be construed
as names, not of thoughts, but of truth-values; but this is a consequence
which it is possible to swallow if one is resolute. Frege's doctrine that it is
thoughts which are primarily called 'true' or 'false' does not require us to
take the substantival clause in a sentence beginning 'It is true that . . . ' or
'It is false that . . . ' as having its oblique reference, i.e. as standing for its
(ordinary) sense, any more than his thesis that it is the sense of a proper
name which is primarily said to stand for the referent requires us to interpret
that name as having an oblique reference in a statement of identity. Rather,
the point of Frege's first thesis, that it is thoughts which, in the first place, are
true or false, lies wholly in its complementation of the second thesis, that
truth and falsity are the referents of sentences: truth and falsity are related
to sentences in a way which is (at least) analogous to that in which objects
are related to their names; and that means that the relation to the linguistic
expression is in both cases determined by the sense of the expression—a
fact which Frege conveys by saying that the relation between referent and
expression is derivative from the relation between referent and sense.

TOKEN-REFLEXIVE EXPRESSIONS

Frege treats as unimportant that feature of language which enables us, in his
terminology, to express different thoughts by the utterance, on different

occasions, of the same complete sentence: we have so far followed him in this by restricting our attention to thoughts expressed by means of what Quine calls 'eternal sentences', i.e. ones containing no part whose reference is to *WO* 12 be determined solely from the occasion of utterance. A thought is thus for Frege something which is, absolutely, true or false: it cannot be true at one time and false at another. In the same way, a concept is the referent of a predicate whose application does not depend upon the occasion of utterance: an object cannot fall under a concept at one time, but not at another time; either it simply falls under it or else it simply does not. There is, for example, no such concept as *inhabitant of Berlin*, under which different individuals *Gl* 46; NS fall at different times; we can consider only such a concept as *inhabitant of* 147 (135) *Berlin on 1 January 1880*, under which an object either does or does not fall, without further temporal qualification.

In thus largely ignoring that feature of natural language Reichenbach *ESL* 284–7 called 'token-reflexiveness', Frege evidently departs widely from the way our actual language operates. If, when this feature is taken into account, it is to remain the case that a thought is absolutely true or absolutely false, without temporal or other qualification, then a thought can no longer be identified with the sense of a complete assertoric sentence, when that sentence contains a token-reflexive expression: we have, rather, to say that such a sentence may be used on different occasions to express different thoughts.

The desire to construe 'is true' and 'is false' as absolute predicates, requiring no relativization, appears at first sight completely harmless. Token-reflexive expressions—pronouns such as 'I' and 'you', or spatial expressions like 'here' or 'two miles to the North'—bear a sense which provides a means of determining their reference in a systematic manner from the circumstances of utterance. Evidently the truth of what is said will, in general, depend upon the references of the expressions used. When token-reflexive expressions are used, therefore, truth or falsity will depend upon the circumstances of utterance as well as on the sense of the words employed. If truth-value is to be ascribed to the sentence, considered as a type in Peirce's *CPP* 4.537 terminology, or to the sense of the sentence-type, then it must be relativized to the relevant circumstances of utterance: 'It rains six months in the year' may be true in one place, false in another. It is entirely natural, instead, to take the ascription of truth-value as applying to something in the identification of which the relevant circumstances of utterance have already been taken into account. If we are regarding the subject of such ascription as being a sentence, then we shall take this, not as a sentence-type, but as a sentence-token. Here 'sentence-token' must be construed as covering possible utterances, not just actual ones, for instance as a quadruple $\langle S,c,m,t\rangle$, where S is a sentence-type, c a speaker, m a set of individuals addressed and t a time. If, like Frege, we regard the subject of an ascription of truth-value as a thought, then we shall say that the thought expressed may depend in part on the occasion of utterance.

According to Frege, not only may the same complete sentence be used on different occasions to express different thoughts, but different sentences may be used on different occasions to express the same thought: e.g. I may by saying, 'It rained yesterday', express the same thought as that I expressed yesterday by saying, 'It is raining today'. This use of the notion of a thought is paralleled in some later writing (Strawson's, for instance) by a similar use of the word 'statement'. The purpose is to do more than secure the absoluteness of the predicates 'is true' and 'is false': the notion of a thought (statement) is to subserve an account of the connection between ascriptions of truth-value to different utterances; that is, a semantic theory of token-reflexive expressions which will explain how the ascription of a particular truth-value to one utterance will entail the ascription of the same truth-value to another utterance.

Since the way in which the reference of a token-reflexive expression is determined from the occasion of utterance is, in general, very straightforward, there appears no great difficulty in providing an account of it. It then appears natural to stipulate that two sentence-tokens $\langle S,c,m,t \rangle$ and $\langle T,d,n,u \rangle$ express the same thought just in case the sentence-types S and T are of the forms $A(s_1, \ldots, s_k)$ and $B(r_1, \ldots, r_k)$, where $s_1, \ldots, s_k$ and $r_1, \ldots, r_k$ are, respectively, all the simple token-reflexive expressions occurring in S and T, $A(s_1, \ldots, s_k)$ and $B(s_1, \ldots, s_k)$ have the same sense, and, for each i, $1 \leqslant i \leqslant k$, s_i has the same reference when addressed by c to m at t as r_i does when addressed by d to n at u. It is, of course, quite unnecessary to suppose that a thought expressible by the utterance on a particular occasion of a sentence containing token-reflexive expressions can also be expressed by some 'eternal' sentence containing no such expressions.

In taking this step, however, Frege has weakened his claim that thoughts are that to which truth and falsity are primarily ascribed. Truth and falsity are semantic notions, that is, notions which are required for an account of the working of language, i.e. for a theory of meaning. They must therefore be connected up with what we learn when we learn how to use language; and at least part of this connection will consist in those features of our linguistic behaviour which constitute our recognition of truth and falsity. From this point of view, that to which truth and falsity are ascribed in the first place are particular utterances. It is reasonable enough to say that ascriptions of truth-value depend on the sense of what is said, and hence to regard the

NS 288 (269);
NS 146 (134–135); Ged 64 (10)

ILT 4

senses of complete 'eternal' sentences as proper subjects for such ascriptions. It is equally reasonable to say that, when token-reflexive expressions occur, ascriptions of truth-value depend upon relevant circumstances of utterance. In going further, and making thoughts or statements, considered as the subjects of ascriptions of truth-value, identifiable in certain cases in which both the relevant circumstances and the sentence-types differ (in corresponding ways), we are of course trying to be faithful to a certain feature of our linguistic practice, namely the connections which we acknowledge between ascriptions of truth-value to different utterances. Nevertheless, in associating such criteria of identity with thoughts or statements, we are going beyond immediately evident facts, and laying ourselves open to possible charges that we have selected the wrong units, as possessors of truth-value, for a correct semantic account of our language.

Such an objection must take the form of saying that an ascription of truth-value to a particular utterance is not to be regarded as absolute, but as requiring relativization. Such a thesis must concern the ascription of truth-value to sentence-tokens, since, given the existence of token-reflexive expressions, the thesis that an ascription of truth-value to a sentence-type is not absolute is uncontentious. Someone who holds that 'truth is relative' is not merely saying that, when two people utter the sentence, 'I didn't hear anything', one may be speaking the truth and the other not: he means that, even when the reference of every expression is taken as fixed, a statement may still be true for one person and false for another.

Since Protagoras at least, few professional philosophers would regard the thesis that ascriptions of truth and falsity to eternal sentences need always to be relativized to an individual as coherent. Nor does the thesis that an eternal sentence may be true in one place but false in another command any adherents. But many philosophers have held that truth-value varies over time; that is, that ascriptions of truth-value, to eternal sentences or to sentence-tokens (particular utterances), require relativization to time.

To some philosophers such a thesis appears preposterous—a mere confused transference of an obvious feature of sentence-types, when these contain a token-reflexive time-specification, to sentence-tokens or to eternal sentences. Ayer, for example, believes that arguments for variable truth-value can be blocked off by simply observing that a statement cannot, in itself, be about the past or about the future. Here 'statement' is being used like Frege's 'thought': it is the same statement which is made on Wednesday by saying, 'It will be cold tomorrow', on Thursday by saying, 'It is cold today' and on Friday by saying, 'It was cold yesterday'; a statement, so construed, has no tense. From a point of view such as Ayer's, it seems evident

PK 180–1

that, once we have made the temporal reference part of the criterion of identity for the statement (thought), there can be no further need to relativize truth-value to time: anyone who supposes that there is must be making the same crude mistake as someone who thinks that the statement which is made by means of the sentence, 'Oxford is 60 miles away', when uttered in London, might still be true in London but false in Oxford.

Even if the mistake were as crude a one as this, it would still be interesting to enquire why people are prone to make it in connection with time but not in connection with space. Why is it that the conception of truth-value as varying over time exerts so strong a pull? This pull is felt at its strongest *TP 90-1* when we consider the notion of existence. Geach has argued that the verb 'exists' has two distinct senses: one in which it has no significant tense, and one in which it has one. According to him, it is only in the former sense that it is right to say that 'exists' is not a predicate: in this first sense, it is to be rendered by means of the existential quantifier; but, in the second sense, it is a straightforward predicate. When, for example, we say that the League of Nations no longer exists, we are genuinely making a statement about— predicating something of—the League of Nations, as opposed to the case in which we say that phlogiston does not exist.

If this doctrine were correct, the verb 'exists' would be simply equivocal: after all, what difference of sense could be greater than one involving a difference of logical type, that between a quantifier and a first-level predicate? This is enough to show that the doctrine, as stated, cannot be correct: for, even if there are two distinguishable senses of 'exists', these senses are evidently connected. The motivation for Geach's claim lies in what *PI 40* Wittgenstein says, in the *Investigations*, about the connection between the reference of a name and its bearer: when the bearer of a personal proper name dies, the name does not lose its reference. We do not wish to construe 'phlogiston' as a term having reference, but reference to a merely possible, not an actual, substance: for, as Meinong's experience showed, we run into uncomfortable antinomies when we try to lay down the truth-conditions of statements about possible objects. Admittedly, this leads naturally to restricting the range of quantification to actual objects, which creates difficulties for the interpretation of modalized quantifications: but the interpretation of modal statements is obscure in any case, so that this is no decisive objection. If 'phlogiston' is not to be taken at face-value, as a term like 'water', then 'Phlogiston does not exist' cannot be taken at face-value either, as denying that a certain possible substance has the property of existence. But we hardly want to deny that we can make statements about objects that once existed, but have ceased to exist: unless one is committed to reconstruing all apparent singular terms as definite descriptions, one will hardly want to have so to reconstrue all proper names of objects that have passed out of existence; and, even if one did, one would still have to allow quantification to extend over such objects, and not confine it to those presently in existence. Hence both 'Cleopatra loved Antony' and 'Cleopatra no longer exists' can be taken at face-value.

The error in this account may be recognized by asking whether 'Cleopatra no longer exists' says that Cleopatra *no longer* has a certain property. There is as much absurdity in saying that there is such a person as Cleopatra, who no longer has the property of existing, as of saying that there is such a substance as phlogiston, which lacks the (timeless) property of existing. Beauty is a property which Cleopatra had when a woman, and may have lacked as a baby: but existence, even when temporal, is not a property that may be first acquired and later lost. One may say, 'The road is narrow here'. What is the property that one is hereby ascribing to the road? One would naturally say, 'The property of being narrow at that place', rather than simply, 'The property of being narrow'. Of course, a road may have the property of being narrow, without qualification: but that means that it is narrow along its whole length. Obviously, in this sense, a road may be neither narrow nor wide, because it is narrow in some places and wide at others. If, as we proceed, the road peters out, we might say, 'The road no longer exists here', or, more naturally, 'There is no longer a road here': and, in the sense that it is a property of the road to be narrow at a certain point, it may also be said to be a property of the road not to exist after a certain distance, or, more naturally, not to go to a certain place. But if we conceive of narrowness or width, tout court, as properties of the road, properties which the road has at certain places and lacks at others, then existing and not existing are not properties which the road has at various places.

Temporal existence is thus no more a property than atemporal existence: if 'Cleopatra no longer exists' is taken to ascribe a property to Cleopatra, then the property in question is not that of non-existence, which she is being said to have at this time, but rather the property of not existing at this time. If temporal objects are thought of as having properties of this sort, then beauty, proportion, height, etc., are not properties: only things like being beautiful at a certain stage in one's life are properties. Properties, thus understood, are atemporal, that is, things of which it can make no sense to say that one acquires them or loses them.

The mode of expression which, in respect of space, we often slip into when speaking of things like roads and rivers pervades our whole language when we speak of temporal objects—objects which undergo change and which come into and pass out of existence: it is, simply, the phenomenon of tense. What we think of as properties of material objects are, typically, things that can be predicated of them at a given time, and may be false of them at another time. The reason is quite obvious. The basic predicates of our language, those which we first learn to employ, are ones whose application can be determined by observation. An observation can determine only how the object is at some one time. It might be objected that a single observation can, likewise, can tell us only how the object is at one place. But this analogy holds only for objects, such as roads and rivers, which cannot normally be observed in their entirety: the predicates which apply to objects only as relativized to a place are ones of which we may also say that they apply to only part of the object—the river is swift near its source, sluggish near its mouth, or, again, the needle is sharp at one end, blunt at the other. This is the correct spatial analogue of the case in which it is said that an animal was playful as a cub, irascible in old age: saying that the hills look blue in the distance is the analogue, rather, of saying that the house one lived in as a child seems big in retrospect. Most observational predicates apply to an object as a whole, considered as it is at a particular time: although, of course, the object must be at a particular place when observed, the predicate is not to be taken as relativized to its occupancy of that place (the predicate may not apply to the object at other times when it is in that place). Indeed, the location of an object at a given time is itself something that may be determined by observation (providing the circumstances are propitious at the time in question). We can, of course, conversely determine by observation when an object is at a given place; but not, in general, by one observation made from a suitable place, but by means of a series of observations determining, for each time within some interval, whether the object is at that place at that time.*

* These remarks have been framed so as to be independent of the fact that most objects which we observe are close to us, relative to the speed of light and to the rate at which we make observations, so that in practice, and, until recently in our history, in principle, we take observation as revealing the state of the object at the time of observation. They are independent also of the complementary fact that the primary method of determining the application of an observational predicate can often be employed over a wide range of distances at which the object may be placed. Thus for practical purposes, we determine how an object is at a given time by observing it at that time, whereas, if we want to determine how an object is when at a given place, we do not need to observe it from that place. Undoubtedly our conceptual framework would be very different if we lacked sight and hearing, and had only contact senses. It would also be different if the time-lag in the arrival of light-signals were of constant practical significance. But it is wrong to think that, in either of these cases, the asymmetry between space and time as we now habitually think of them would altogether vanish.

Of course, we employ many predicates whose application cannot be determined by a single observation; ones which apply to an object in virtue not of its presently observable state, but of its previous history. But the use of such predicates can be acquired only after the past tense has been grasped, and this must first be done in connection with sentences which, in their present-tense inflection, are observational: crudely put, 'has grown' can only be learned after the use of 'was small' has been acquired.

In consequence of this, temporal reference functions quite differently from spatial reference. A spatial reference, whether token-reflexive or otherwise, is most naturally construed as a predicate which is true of a given object at a given time: thus 'There are snakes in England' is of the form 'There are snakes which are in England', and 'There are no cowards here' of the form 'There are no cowards who are here', or, more explicitly, 'There is no one who is (now) a coward and who is (now) here'. A temporal reference cannot be so construed, but, rather, qualifies the whole sentence adverbially: 'John is ill today' plainly cannot be interpreted as of the form 'John is ill and John is today'. (It is true, indeed, that not all spatial reference may be taken as predicative, i.e. as giving the location of an object (at the time referred to): not, for example, when a verb of motion is involved, as in 'Henry came here'. In such a case, the place referred to is most naturally taken as the term of a relation (object of an action). The only types of spatial reference which appear to demand to be construed as adverbial, however, are those which relate to position on the object as opposed to its location, as in 'He struck me here', said by somebody pointing to a part of his body.)

The structure of our language thus gives a much more central role to the present tense than to non-temporal token-reflexives like 'here' and 'I'. Of course, if a spatial token-reflexive is used, we have to know where the utterance occurred in order to know which place was referred to, and, if a personal pronoun is used, we need to know who spoke or whom he addressed in order to tell who was referred to: but the spatial or personal reference enters only as an argument to a predicate or relational expression, or, in the spatial case, as itself a predicate, not as a qualification of the entire sentence. The representation of temporal indicators as sentential operators, as is done in tense logic, correctly reflects the structure of natural language: it is no accident that in many languages the verb is inflected for tense, but in none is any spatial indicator incorporated into the termination of the verb (what is actually an operator acting upon a whole sentence or clause is, of course, frequently represented by a verb-inflection or by a particle or auxiliary attached to the verb). Such a representation holds as much for a non-token-reflexive time-indicator as for a token-reflexive one: an adverbial phrase like 'on Christmas Day, 800 A.D.' is best construed as an operator 'It was (is) the case on Christmas Day, 800 A.D., that . . . '.

If we so represent temporal indicators, how are we to construe the innermost constituents—those which contain no overt temporal indicators? Should they be taken as tenseless radicals, or as implicitly present-tensed? *TM* 10 Prior, who initiated the systematic study of tense logic, was concerned with this question, but it is a vacuous one. If we are using only non-token-reflexive temporal operators, the former choice will seem the more natural. We shall then obtain a completely tenseless language, and, if we believe in invariable truth-value, we shall think of the sentences of this language as true or false absolutely; the radicals will not, however, be true or false in themselves, but only true at certain times, false at others. If we are using token-reflexive operators, such as 'It was the case two days ago that . . . ', then every sentence (i.e. sentence-type) will have a truth-value which changes with time, and we may therefore just as well think of the radicals as implicitly present-tensed sentences. Whether we regard them as present-tensed sentences or as incomplete sentences awaiting the application of a (non-token-reflexive) temporal operator is unimportant. What matters is that the basic unit employed in the construction of sentences is something which has to be thought of as having different truth-values at different times: this corresponds to the use in natural language of sentences having a significant present tense.

If (as Frege evidently did) we find it more congenial to think in terms of a *NJ* 251 language purged of token-reflexive expressions, and if, like the later Ayer and many other philosophers, we have no qualms about invariability of truth-value, then of course we may assimilate the radicals to one-place predicates whose arguments are times: the application of a temporal operator then simply has the effect of filling the argument-place, and, since it results in a sentence with an absolute truth-value, any reiterated temporal operator will be redundant (as reiterated modalities are redundant in the modal system S5). Such a way of looking at the language obscures the quite special role of temporal indicators in our language as we actually acquire it. From the point of view of natural language, temporal indicators function in a quite different way from expressions carrying personal or spatial reference: and it is only by appreciating this that we can render intelligible the fact that the notion of truth-value as changing from time to time has a much more powerful appeal to us than that of truth-value as changing from place to place or from individual to individual; this phenomenon remains opaque so long as we think of the conception of variable truth-value as arising merely from the occurrence of token-reflexive expressions. Our language requires the possibility of reference to places, which may be effected token-reflexively or otherwise; but it does not demand the conception of something which may be true at one place and false at another, except in the trivial sense in which this may be said to be required for the interpretation of token-reflexive spatial indicators. It does, however, require an underlying conception of that which is true at one time and false at another, independently of whether we employ token-reflexive time-indicators or not: put differently, it requires the conception of the use of present-tensed sentences, even if there is no other token-reflexive time-indicator.

So far as tensed language is concerned, this shows that truth-value is primarily ascribed, not to thoughts, understood in Frege's fashion, but to what is expressed by tensed sentences, i.e. to that which can be true at one time and false at another. This does not, of course, show that it is incorrect to consider thoughts or statements, endowed with a criterion of identity which takes account of the tense or other token-reflexive feature of their expression, as having absolute or invariable truth-value. What is incorrect is to suppose, with Ayer, that the mere introduction of such a notion of thought or statement imposes a recognition of invariability of truth-value. On the contrary, the semantics which will be proposed for a language constructed by means of temporal operators, as described above, will vary according to the metaphysical view concerning time which is accepted. Someone who believes in absolute, invariable truth-value will propose a semantics as follows. He supposes that there is a unique total course of the history of the world, past and future, so that each radical, or present-tensed sentence, may be considered as having, for each time, a determinate value, true or false, at that time. A temporal operator of the form 'It is (timelessly) the case at t that . . . ' then obviously has the effect that 'It is the case at t that A' is (absolutely) true or false according as 'A' is true or false at t. If token-reflexive temporal operators are involved, let us suppose that the unit of time is a day, and, following Prior, let us write 'It will be the case in n days'   *TM* 10 time that . . . ' as 'Fn', and 'It was the case n days ago that . . . ' as 'Pn': then, clearly, 'Fn A' is true at t just in case 'A' is true at $t + n$, and 'Pn A' is true at t just in case 'A' is true at $t - n$.

This straightforward semantics is not the only possibility, however: it rests on the assumption that there is a unique total course of world history, that which actually has happened and actually will happen, an assumption which the believer in variable truth-value will reject. Let us suppose, instead, someone who agrees that there is a unique actual course of world history up to the present, but thinks that the future is open in the sense that there is no one total future course of world history which represents that which is in fact going to happen. For him, therefore, there are many total courses of world history, at present all equally possible, which coincide up to the present but diverge thereafter. We may envisage the whole structure as a tree (in the mathematical sense), the paths in which represent the various total courses of world history which were possible at the moment of creation. Each node represents the state of affairs, under a given total course of world history, on a particular day: each radical (sentence containing no temporal operators) is determinately true or false at each given node. The fact that the structure is a tree corresponds to our assumption that the actual course of the past history of the world is determinate. The fact that two nodes are distinct does not necessarily represent any difference in the existing states of affairs (the truth-values of the radicals at those nodes), even when the nodes are at the same distance from the vertex (are associated with the same date): it may correspond only to the different routes by which those nodes were reached from the vertex, i.e. the different sequences of events from the creation up to that time.

To say that each radical is true or false at each node is to say that, for each time t and each total course C of world history, each radical is either true or false at t under C. Let us abbreviate a non-token-reflexive temporal operator 'It is the case at time t that . . .' as 'Tt'. Then one possibility is as follows. A sentence 'A' is called true (false) under a total course C of world history just in case it is true (false) at every time t under C. 'Tt A' is true (false) under C if and only if 'A' is true (false) at t under C. 'Fn A' is true (false) at t under C if and only if 'A' is true (false) at $t + n$ under C. 'Pn A' is true (false) at t under C if and only if 'A is true (false) at $t-n$ under C. So far, we have followed the previous stipulations exactly, save that, instead of considering just one total course of world history—the actual one—we are considering every possible such course, i.e. all those which were open possibilities at the creation of the world. The ordinary operators of negation, disjunction, etc., are interpreted by truth-tables with respect to each given time t and course C. We thus obtain a purely classical logic: in particular, for each n, t and C, 'Fn A $\vee \neg Fn$ A' is true at t under C. We now introduce the notion of the *coincidence* of two total courses C and C' *up to* a time t. If we are thinking of the tree structure as given at the outset, then this relation holds when the node $\langle t, C \rangle$ is the same as the node $\langle t, C' \rangle$. If not, then we may define 'C coincides with C' up to t' to mean that, for every *radical* 'A' and every $t' \leqslant t$, 'A' is true at t' under C if and only if 'A' is true at t' under C'. We now stipulate that, for any sentence 'A', simple or complex, 'A' is *assertible* at t under C if and only if, for every C' which coincides with C up to t, 'A' is true at t under C'. For each t, C, n and 'A', 'Fn A' is either true or false at t under C: but it may well be that neither 'Fn A' nor '$\neg$ Fn A' is assertible at t under C.

A semantics of this kind tallies with all those features of our linguistic practice which we acquire when we learn the use of sentences containing temporal operators, including, if it be a fact, our acceptance of the laws of classical logic. In the case of significantly tensed sentences, including the radicals, truth is relativized, not only to a time, but to a possible total course of world history; in the case of sentences with non-token-reflexive temporal operators (eternal sentences), it is relativized only to the latter. The assertibility, of an eternal sentence as well as of a tensed one, is relativized both to a time and to a total course of history: however, the assertibility of a sentence 'A' at t under C depends only on the node $\langle t, C \rangle$, and not on the whole extent of C. Hence, if we are supposing intuitively that, at any given time, there is a unique actual course of world history up to that time, then the notion of assertibility at that time requires no further relativization.

Two features of this semantics may be thought of as disadvantages by a believer in the indeterminacy of the future. Since it validates all the laws of classical logic, it is impossible to refute the argument for fatalism by rejecting certain of these laws, as applied to statements about the future. The desire to escape fatalism has been one of the motives for a belief in the indeterminacy of the future, and many have thought the argument for fatalism inescapable if classical logic is not impugned. Secondly, although no one future course of world history is taken to be the actual one, the understanding of the future tense (or of temporal operators relating to times later than the present) depends essentially upon the conception of a possible total future course of history. An alternative might be to use the previous definition of assertibility as a definition of truth. We shall thus stipulate that 'Tt' A' is true at t under C if and only if, for every C' which coincides with C up to t, 'A' is true at t' under C'; 'Fn A' is true at t under C if and only if, for every C' which coincides with C up to t, 'A' is true at $t + n$ under C'; 'Pn A' is true at t under C if and only if, for every C' which coincides with C up to t, 'A' is true at $t - n$ under C'; and, for every 'A', if 'A' is not true at t under C, then 'A' is false at t under C. The standard operators are, again, interpreted truth-functionally. We shall still have, therefore, that, for arbitrary t, C, n and 'A', '$(Fn$ A$) \vee \neg (Fn$ A$)$' is true at t under C. It will no longer be the case, however, that '$Fn \neg$ A' is true at t under C just in case '$\neg$ Fn A' is true at t under C, as it was under the previous semantics; '$(Fn$ A$) \vee (Fn \neg$ A$)$' may now very well not be true at t under C. The truth of a sentence (eternal or tensed) is still formally relativized both to a time t and a total course C of world history, but it actually depends only on the node

$\langle t,C \rangle$, i.e. on the course of history up to t (initial segment of C). This is essentially the semantics which some commentators on Aristotle have attributed to him. In this semantics, 'Pn A' is true at t under C just in case 'A' is true at $t - n$ under C, and, where $t' \leqslant t$, 'Tt' A' is true at t under C just in case 'A' is true at t' under C; but it does not hold that 'Fn A' is true at t under C whenever 'A' is true at $t + n$ under C, nor that, when $t' > t$, 'Tt' A' is true at t under C whenever 'A' is true at t' under C. '$Fn(Pn$ A)' is always equivalent to 'A', but 'A' does not imply '$Pn(Fn$ A)'. There will, of course, be a strong sense of 'false' under which 'Fn A' is false at $\langle t,C \rangle$ just in case '$Fn \neg$ A' is true there.

In the previous system, 'A' might be true at t under C, and 'Fn A' accordingly true at $t - n$ under C, and yet 'Fn A' might not be assertible at $t - n$ under C. Similarly, in the present system, 'A' may be true at t under C, and yet 'Fn A' false (in the weak sense) at $t - n$ under C: this is just the case when 'A' is true at t under C, but '$Pn(Fn$ A)' false, since, for some C' coinciding with C up to $t - n$, but not up to t, 'A' is false at t under C'. This failure of the equivalence between 'A' and '$Pn(Fn$ A)' may be considered a weakness of the system, but it can be mitigated by introducing a further notion, something like that of assertibility in the preceding system. In the present system, a sentence is assertible at a given time just in case it is true at that time. The relativization of truth-value, in the case of a tenseless sentence 'Tt' A', to a time t should not, however, be taken as relating to the time at which the sentence is being uttered, or is being considered as being uttered, but, rather, to the time at which the truth-value of the sentence is being assessed. We have, of course, to take into account the time t' to which the sentence refers: but, when, at the time t, we are assessing the truth or falsity of the sentence, we are not interested in the truth of the tenseless sentence at the time t'' at which it was uttered, or even at the time t' to which it refers, but at the time t at which we are making the assessment. That is to say, if we are now at the node $\langle t,C \rangle$, we are interested only in those C' which coincide with C up to t; if 'Tt' A' was uttered at t'', and $t'' < t$, we are no longer concerned with any C' which coincides with C up to t'' but not up to t; we are therefore concerned with truth at t rather than truth at t''. The sentence was assertible when it was uttered only if it was true when it was uttered; but, even though it was not then assertible, we may later assess it as true.

These considerations call for no new definition, since the relativization to time of truth for tenseless sentences already takes care of this. In the case of a tensed sentence, say 'Fn A', however, the relativization to time plays a double role: it relates both to the time of utterance (needed in order to fix the temporal reference of the token-reflexive '*Fn*') and to the time at which the ascription of truth-value is being made. We may separate out these two roles by introducing the following notion. Let us say that a tensed sentence

$$\left\{ \begin{matrix} \text{'}Fn\ A\text{'} \\ \text{'}A\text{'} \\ \text{'}Pn\ A\text{'} \end{matrix} \right\}, \text{ uttered at } t, \text{ is } endorsed \text{ at } t' \text{ under } C \text{ if and only if, for every } C'$$

coinciding with C up to t', 'A' is true at $\left\{ \begin{matrix} t+n \\ t \\ t-n \end{matrix} \right\}$ under C'. It will then

follow that 'A' is true at t under C if and only if '*Fn* A', uttered at $t - n$, is endorsed at t under C.

This definition suggests a further variation. We might consider the truth of a tensed sentence as relativized to two times, the time of utterance and the time of assessment. We begin, that is, by supposing that each radical has a value, true or false, at each node. We then define: 'A', uttered at t, is true at t' under C if and only if, for every C' which coincides with C up to t', 'A' is true at $\langle t, C' \rangle$, where 'A' is a radical. Further: '*Fn* A' ('*Pn* A') uttered at t, is true at t' under C if and only if, for every C' which coincides with C up to t', 'A', uttered at $t + n$ $(t - n)$ is true at $t + n$ $(t - n)$ under C'. The equivalence of 'A' and '*Pn*(*Fn* A)' is now restored: that is, for every t, t' and C, '*Pn*(*Fn* A)', uttered at t, is true at t' under C if and only if 'A', uttered at t, is true at t' under C.

Obviously, yet further variations are conceivable. For instance, it may be thought counter-intuitive, or at least contrary to the usage we ordinarily employ, that the second and the third systems both make a sharp distinction between 'It will not be the case that A' and 'It will be the case that not A' ('$\neg$ *Fn* A' and '*Fn* $\neg$ A'), and similarly for disjunction and implication. This it would also be possible to avoid by a suitable reinterpretation of the standard operators. If we merely reinterpret negation so that it commutes with '*Fn*', then the law of excluded middle will fail: '(*Fn* A) v $\neg$ (*Fn* A)' will not hold, since it has been reinterpreted to be equivalent to '(*Fn* A) v (*Fn* $\neg$ A)', which is invalid. If, on the other hand, we also reinterpret disjunction so that '*Fn*' is distributive into it, then the law of excluded middle will be restored, since '(*Fn* A) v (*Fn* $\neg$ A)' will now be reinterpreted as equivalent to '*Fn* (A v $\neg$A)', which is plainly valid (provided that the sentential operators as applied to radicals are understood classically). The result, in the latter case, will be a collapse of our system into the first one, in which all classical laws hold.

By taking the underlying structure to be, not a tree, but only a partial ordering, we may obtain a semantics which accords with a belief in the indeterminacy of the past. Here two nodes will be distinct just in case they represent different existing states of affairs, i.e. just in case at least one radical is true at one and false at the other: we have to replace, in the definition of assertibility or that of truth, the relation of coincidence up to a time t by that of coincidence at a time t.

The upshot is thus as follows. Our use of temporal operators, whether token-reflexive or otherwise, does not require the assumption of a fixed total course of world history. We can describe a semantics for such operators which does not appeal to this assumption. This may be done in either of two ways: either so as to yield a logic which coincides with that obtained by assuming a unique total course of history; or so as to violate either or both of two kinds of classical law, namely: (i) the equivalence of 'A' with '$Fn(Pn\ A)$' and with '$Pn(Fn\ A)$', and (ii) the distributivity of the temporal operators into the standard connectives. (If we are dealing with non-token-reflexive temporal operators 'Tt', (i) takes the form of the equivalence of '$Tt'(Tt\ A)$' with '$Tt\ A$'.) It may plausibly be maintained that these two kinds of classical law are embedded in the actual linguistic practice which we acquire in learning to use sentences containing temporal operators: hence the advocacy of any of the semantic systems which involve a violation of these laws entails impugning part of our ordinary linguistic practice, in the same way as the advocacy of an intuitionistic logic for mathematics entails impugning the ordinary practice which we acquire in learning to handle mathematical statements and to follow or give mathematical proofs.

No one now supposes that established linguistic practice is sacrosanct. The supposition that it is, which was the fundamental tenet of 'ordinary language' philosophy, rested on the idea that, since meaning is use, we may adopt whatever linguistic practice we choose, and our choice will simply determine the use, and hence the meanings, of our expressions: any proposal to alter established practice is therefore merely a proposal to attach different senses to our expressions, whereas we have the right to confer on them whatever senses we please. The error underlying this attitude lies, in part, in the failure to appreciate the interplay between the different aspects of 'use', and the requirement of harmony between them. Crudely expressed, there are always two aspects of the use of a given form of sentence: the conditions under which an utterance of that sentence is appropriate, which include, in the case of an assertoric sentence, what counts as an acceptable ground for asserting it; and the consequences of an utterance of it, which comprise both what the speaker commits himself to by the utterance and the appropriate response on the part of the hearer, including, in the case of assertion, what he is entitled to infer from it if he accepts it. The thesis that these are merely two kinds of meaning, which may be attached as we will to any given sentence without any requirement of conformity between them, is the now rightly discredited doctrine of 'descriptive' and 'evaluative' meaning. It is, on the contrary, plain that we may legitimately demand a certain consonance between the two aspects of the use of a given form of expression, and that the perception of the lack of such consonance is a major, and quite correct, ground for proposals to revise the sense of an expression or to reject it altogether. Undoubtedly it is hard to give a general characterization of what such consonance consists in, and, in particular cases (of which statements about personal identity are perhaps the most striking example), very deep philosophical problems are involved. In the simplest cases, however, it is plain that the requirement of consonance may be expressed as the demand that the addition of the given expression to the language yields a conservative extension of it.* If it is part of the established use of a certain form of sentence, *B*, that it may be inferred from a sentence, *A*, and also that a sentence *C* may be inferred from it, the presence of this form of sentence in the language may be validly objected to if, in its absence, we should not be willing to recognize the legitimacy of the inference from *A* to *C*. (A straightforward example is that of any inappropriately pejorative expression.)

More generally, we may say that the belief in the invulnerability of established usage stems from an unwillingness to regard linguistic practice as capable of systematization in terms of underlying principles of which we are partly conscious and which may be rendered fully explicit. To deny the possibility of extracting such underlying principles is to deny that of a systematic theory of meaning, of any articulated model of the senses of our expressions. It is also, therefore, to deny the possibility of a discovery that there are conflicting principles underlying our ordinary practice, or ones which cannot be rendered fully coherent.

From such tendencies Frege was, of course, completely free. We have seen to what an extent he was prepared to criticize natural language as incapable, without being subjected to considerable revision, of being provided with a coherent semantics; and he took for granted that a language should be such as to render a systematic semantics possible. But, if established usage is not sacrosanct, it is in possession. It is legitimate to propose a semantics which involves the rejection of principles of inference customarily recognized as valid only on the basis of a demonstration that no

NS 7 (6-7);
NS 272 (252);
NS 288 (269)

* See Prior, 'The Runabout Inference Ticket', and Belnap, 'Tonk, Plonk and Plink'. both in Strawson (ed.), *Philosophical Logic.*

semantics which would justify them is coherent. A believer in the indeterminacy of the future, or of the past, unless he subscribes to the first of the semantic systems described above, that which involves no change in practice in our employment of temporal operators, will claim to have such a demonstration. It is not our concern here to enquire into the difficult philosophical problems arising out of such a claim.

An exponent of the first of our semantic systems is in a different position; he has no desire to call in question principles of inference generally recognized. As already noted, this means that he cannot appeal to his deviant semantics in order to refute the argument for fatalism, in so far as this claims to employ only such generally recognized forms of inference. This does not mean that it will be possible to entangle him in all the difficulties to escape which he originally subscribed to the indeterminacy of the future: for his semantic system will allow the introduction of operators which have no classical analogue. For instance, consider the theological argument to the determinacy of the future. The omniscience of God may be claimed as consisting in the truth of every instance of the schema

(*)   If p, then God knows that p.

If the schema (*) is accepted, then, in particular, each sentence of the form 'If Fn A, then God knows that Fn A' must be accepted. But if it is held that every present-tensed sentence is such that either it or its negation is assertible, and a sentence of the kind 'God (now) knows that Fn A' is admitted as a bona fide present-tense sentence, then it will follow, by certain obvious principles, that either 'Fn A' or '$Fn \neg$ A' is assertible, which is just what the believer in the indeterminacy of the future wishes to deny. Such a person will not, however, accept the schema (*) as a correct expression of God's omniscience. Rather, he will introduce a new operator, say 'L', such that 'L A' is true at t under C just in case 'A' is assertible at t under C: God's omniscience is then to be expressed by means of the schema

If $L\,p$, then God knows that p.

Thus for particular purposes a proponent even of the first system will be led to introduce a form of sentence 'L A' which functions as 'A' does in the second system.

Our initial concern was to discover whether Frege's conception of thoughts as the possessors of absolute truth-value remained reasonable when the existence of token-reflexive expressions is taken seriously into account. We saw that spatial and personal token-reflexives created no difficulty for this conception: difficulty threatens only in the case of tenses (temporal token-reflexives), because of the philosophical plausibility of the belief in variability of truth-value. We have also seen that it is impossible to appeal to the conception of thoughts or statements, as Ayer proposed to do, in order to rule out the belief in variable truth-value from the outset. Moreover, we saw that, whether one believes in a unique determinate total course of world history or not, it cannot be maintained, in relation to sentences containing temporal operators, that the primary notion of truth is that of absolute truth, as attaching to thoughts. Now that we have taken a cursory look at various semantic systems which might be proposed as embodying a belief in variable truth-value, it remains to enquire after the final verdict on whether such a belief rules out Frege's conception of thoughts altogether or not.

In all the systems, we have taken the basic semantic notion to be, not just truth at a time t, but truth at t under a possible total course C of world history. Since, however, in the second and third systems truth at t under C depends only upon the segment of C up to t, and since the course of past history is being intuitively assumed to be determinate, we may speak of the truth of a particular utterance as assessed at a particular time, without reference to any total course C of history. The notion of truth has, however, to be relativized to a time even for a tenseless sentence 'Tt A': as already remarked, the time to which the truth of an utterance of such a sentence has to be relativized is neither the time of utterance nor the time t referred to, but the time at which the ascription of truth-value is being made. If we want to adopt the terminology of thoughts, we may thus say that a sentence 'Tt A' expresses at t' a true thought just in case 'Tt A' is true at t' under any course C which coincides up to t' with the actual course of events up to then. Even when sentences containing no token-reflexive time-specification are used, therefore, we must see a thought as determined, not by the sense of the sentence alone, but by that together with a time at which that sense is grasped (or at which truth-value is being ascribed to it). When tensed sentences are in question, there must be a double relativization to time: we must consider both the time of utterance (in order to fix the reference of the token-reflexive temporal operator) and the time, possibly different, at which truth-value is being assessed. For instance, 'Fn A', uttered at t, expresses a true thought at t' just in case 'A', uttered at $t + n$, is endorsed at t' (or, in the third system, is true at t'). Variability of truth-value has, in this terminology, been transformed into variability of thought expressed: we can continue to regard thoughts as having absolute truth or falsity, but at the price of regarding a specific utterance, not as expressing a unique thought, but as expressing different thoughts at different times; not, that is, at different times when the utterance is made (if the utterance is specific, it is made at a unique time), but at different times when the utterance is considered. The conception of thoughts does not, in itself, exclude a belief in variable truth-value: what does exclude it is the combination of the thesis that a thought is absolutely true or absolutely false with the thesis that each sentence-token expresses a unique thought.

The first system is more problematic, because truth at t under C does not depend solely on the segment of C up to t. In the context of this system, therefore, there appears no way of interpreting the notion of a thought so as to attribute to thoughts an absolute truth-value: the only natural way to take the notion of a thought here appears to be to allow that each specific utterance expresses a unique thought (where, e.g., 'Fn A', uttered at t, expresses the same thought as 'Pm A', uttered at t', if and only if $t+n=t'-m$), but to deny that a thought always has a truth-value: the thought expressed by 'Fn A', uttered at t, first acquires a truth-value at the time $t + n$.

The grounds which philosophers have had for believing in variable truth-value, or, what is the same thing, for believing in the indeterminacy of the future (or, much more rarely, that of the past) may be sound or they may be confused: it would take us much too far afield to scrutinize them here. These grounds must concern what it is that we learn when we learn to use sentences in the past or future tenses, whether these contain token-reflexive or non-token-reflexive time-specifications, that is, the correct model for the senses of such sentences. What has emerged from this discussion is that such grounds cannot be dismissed in advance: and the fundamental reason why they cannot is that, whether the conception of thoughts as having absolute truth-value can or cannot be maintained, and whether or not specific utterances are considered as expressing unique thoughts, independently of the time at which we consider them, the notion of a thought, as required for sentences containing temporal operators, is not primary but derivative. We have to regard our utterances themselves as the primary bearers of truth-value—in virtue, indeed, of their senses, and, when they contain token-reflexive expressions, also of the circumstances of utterance. Thoughts are a secondary construct; and their presumed properties cannot therefore be appealed to to rule out a proposed interpretation of the sentences whose utterance is taken to express them. Rather, given the correct semantic model for the use of these sentences, thoughts will or will not prove to have the properties attributed to them.

CHAPTER 12

Truth-value and Reference

TRUTH AND FALSITY are not—or, at least, are not merely—properties of
thoughts, on Frege's view: they are related to thoughts as the referent of any   SB 34
expression is to its sense. Because the doctrine of reference is itself complex,   NS 211 (194)
the thesis that truth-values are the referents of sentences has several strands.

If the notion of reference were introduced in the first place simply as that
of the semantic role of expressions of different kinds, without any appeal to
the name/bearer relation as prototype, then, at the outset, we should have no
inclination to distinguish intensional from extensional contexts, or to treat
the former separately; on the contrary, there would be a natural presumption in favour of a uniform semantic treatment for all contexts. Until this
presumption was abandoned, therefore, we should have a strong ground
for denying that the bearer of a proper name determined its reference,
or that the reference of a sentence was determined by its truth-value.

The conception of reference as semantic role is, in itself, purely programmatic: it does not tell us what the semantic roles of expressions of the
various logical types are to be taken to be; it provides no model for a semantic
account of our language. For Frege, the notion of reference is not, of course,
the bare conception of semantic role: his use of the name/bearer relation
as prototype involves the assumption that the semantic role of every expression which is a semantically significant unit can always be construed
as consisting in its relation to something in the real world. As thus formulated,
however, this assumption is empty, since, whatever our conception of the
semantic roles of expressions of different types, we could always express it in
terms of a relation of reference between the expressions and certain non-
linguistic entities. On the basis of any semantic account whatever, there
will exist a relation of semantic equivalence between expressions of the
same logical type: indeed, if we suppose ourselves equipped with a notion
of truth-value for sentences of the language, we could use the fact of

interchangeability in all contexts without change of truth-value as a criterion for semantic equivalence, even in the absence of any specific semantics. Semantic equivalence will, of course, be an equivalence relation, and hence will partition the expressions of any given logical type into equivalence classes. All we now need to do is to take these equivalence classes as corresponding uniquely to abstract entities, which may then be construed as the referents of the expressions in each equivalence class. This is, in effect, Tugendhat's proposed interpretation of Frege's notion of reference.

MBF   The notion of reference, as thus interpreted, is quite different from Frege's, on a number of counts. First, since we have so far no reason to treat intensional contexts any differently from extensional ones, the criterion of identity of reference (semantic equivalence) will be much stricter than Frege's. It may be, of course, that when we try to give some substance to the as yet purely schematic interpretation by devising an actual semantic account of the language, we shall be driven by the difficulty of providing a uniform semantic treatment for all contexts into finding some criterion of distinction between intensional and extensional contexts, and regarding the latter as primary and the former as requiring separate special treatment. Even in this case, however, the notion of a referent under this interpretation is quite different from Frege's. For Frege, it was a defect of natural language
Gg I 28; FB   that it permitted the formation of expressions which have a sense but lack a
19; NS 193   referent. But on an interpretation of Tugendhat's kind, there can be no
(178-9)   question of an expression's lacking a referent, if it is a genuine semantic unit and has been supplied with a sense: it must then belong to some class of semantically equivalent expressions, and to this class will correspond a referent; the conception of a meaningful expression's lacking a referent becomes simply unintelligible. In particular, on such an interpretation, all referents will be abstract entities, which, in the case of names of concrete objects, cannot possibly be identified with the objects which we normally take to be the bearers of those names: there will be no reason whatever for identifying the realm of reference with the whole of reality; rather, the referents of expressions will form as special a realm as do their senses.

It may be said that, in the same way that we may suppose that the attempt actually to construct a semantics for our language will force on us a distinction between extensional and intensional contexts, so such an attempt will compel us to appeal to the ordinary notion of the bearer of a name. This is perfectly true, as we shall see in more detail later; and the fact that it is so is part of the justification for Frege's use of the name/bearer relation as the prototype of reference. But if our conception of the relation of reference is as under Tugendhat's interpretation, it will not follow that we shall be able to identify the referent of a proper name with its bearer. The most that we shall be able to claim is that the reference of a name, or, what amounts to the same, the class of semantically equivalent expressions to which it belongs, is determined by what bearer it has, if any. Two things will still prevent us from identifying the referent of a name, as thus interpreted, with its bearer: first, the fact that the referent of any name is (on this interpretation) a quite special kind of abstract object, while its bearer may be an object of any sort, abstract or concrete; and, secondly, the fact that, while a name may lack a bearer, it cannot possibly lack a referent (on this interpretation of 'referent').

We thus arrive at the following position. If we start with a merely programmatic conception of reference as semantic role, and expect a uniform semantic account for all contexts, we shall take the criterion for semantic equivalence to be unrestricted interchangeability, and hence will leave no room for a distinction between identity of reference and identity of sense. To apply even this criterion implies the possession of some notion of truth-value for complete sentences. It may then be that, in the course of actually devising a semantics for our language, we find ourselves forced to distinguish intensional from extensional contexts, and to treat the former separately. In this case, we shall take as the criterion of semantic equivalence interchangeability within extensional contexts only: under such a criterion, it is plausible that sentences will be semantically equivalent just in case they have the same truth-value. If, as is likely, the exigencies of the construction of an actual semantic account compel us to invoke the notion of the bearer of a proper name, then we shall be able to formulate, and will be disposed to accede to, the thesis that two names are semantically equivalent if and only if they have the same bearer. Acceptance of this thesis is, however, not at all the same thing as identification of the referent of a name with its bearer. From the thesis that the bearer of a name determines its reference it follows that two names both of which lack a bearer have the same reference: it does not follow that a name which lacks a bearer has no reference. If reference is construed simply as semantic role, then to say that an expression lacks a reference is to say that it fails to fulfil its appointed role. That should mean that, by the use of a sentence containing it, we fail to say anything at all, fail, that is, to perform a linguistic act, to make a move in the language-game. But, from the point of view we are presently assuming, we have no reason to suppose that the lack of a bearer on the part of a proper name has any such devastating effect upon a sentence in which that name occurs.

Frege never lapsed so far from plausibility as to maintain that to utter a sentence containing a name lacking a bearer is to fail to say anything in the sense of failing even to express a thought. That would be absurd, since we can understand such an utterance, and, if we wrongly suppose the name to have a bearer, we can also believe it. Frege did hold that to utter such a sentence is to fail to say anything that is either true or false. But, when reference is construed simply as semantic role, the rationale for saying this remains quite obscure. It is evident, indeed, that, at least in many cases, if someone seriously attempts to make a true assertion by means of a sentence containing a name lacking a bearer, he will be unsuccessful. What is not evident is why his failure should be deemed to be greater than, or different in kind from, the failure which consists in making a false assertion. The use of a sentence in which each expression fulfils its intended semantic role does not guarantee that what is said is true: the conception of reference as semantic role gives no clue why the occurrence in a sentence of a name which lacks a bearer should be held to result in a failure even to say anything false.

(NS 211 (194))

What all this shows is, of course, that our formulation of what is involved, for Frege's conception of reference, in the use of the name/bearer relation as prototype was much too weak. The appeal to this prototype is intended to furnish a specification, partial but substantial, of the form which a semantic account of our language ought to take. To say, as we did, that the use of the name/bearer relation as prototype demands that the semantic role of each type of expression should be able to be construed as consisting in its bearing a relation of reference to some non-linguistic entity does not capture this intention: for, as we have seen, it merely provides a mould into which any semantic account whatever can be poured.

If, starting from the bare conception of reference as semantic role, we have reached the stage supposed above, the stage, namely, of reserving intensional contexts for special treatment and of invoking the notion of the bearer of a name, we shall probably be disposed to agree that, when the bearers of two names are the same, their references are the same: what more is then involved in saying that the referent actually *is* the bearer? Equating the relation of reference, in the case of proper names, with the name/bearer relation is intended to specify the semantic role, not only of proper names themselves, but also of first-level predicates: it does this via the thesis that 'the referents of our words are what we speak *about*'. It is not merely that we can express the semantic role of a proper name as consisting in a relation to some object which figures as its referent, but that, when we utter a sentence containing the proper name, this sentence can be construed as saying something about the object which is the referent of the proper name. This means that the predicate which results from the removal of the proper

SB 32–3; NS 109 (100)

name from the sentence must be taken to have a semantic role which consists in its being true or false of, applying or failing to apply to, each given object (each object, at least, which can serve as referent for a name capable of standing in the argument-place of the predicate). Expressed conversely, we do not require merely that there be some object which can serve as referent of a name, that is, which can satisfy the condition that the referent determines the class of semantically equivalent names to which the given name belongs: we require that the object taken to be the referent be one to which any predicate in whose argument-place the name can stand can meaningfully be applied (truly or falsely); and that, among such objects, that one be taken to be the referent which is such that the resulting sentence is true just in case the predicate is true of it.

In the case of a complex predicate, the notion of the predicate's being true or false of an object is derivative from that of the truth or falsity of the sentence which results from filling the argument-place of the predicate with a name of the object. Hence the principle that 'the referents of our words are what we talk about' imposes a condition on what object can be selected as the referent of a name only in relation to simple predicates, i.e. by specifying what we are to take the semantic role of simple predicates to consist in. The object taken as the referent of a given proper name must be that one of which it is plausible to hold that an atomic sentence formed by attaching a simple predicate to the name is true just in case the predicate is true of that object.

All this might be regarded as a relentless spelling out of the obvious; and so, indeed, in a sense it is. Frege's manner of introducing the notion of reference relies heavily on various intuitive notions which we take for granted: it presumes a prior familiarity with the conception of the relation of name to bearer, of that about which we are speaking when we use a proper name, of a predicate's being true or false of a given object. Because these intuitive notions really are already familiar, long before we embark on any project of constructing a systematic semantics for our language, we hardly notice the appeal that is being made to them when the notion of reference is first introduced: it does not occur to us, for example, that there can be any question about what object it is that should be taken as the referent of a given proper name; that is why we are inclined to accept the notion of reference for proper names as unproblematic, and concentrate on questioning the analogy by which it is extended to expressions of other logical types. It is to the credit of Tugendhat that he is aware that the interesting question is not whether the notion of reference can or cannot be defined or justified, but what work it is supposed to do, and that, in

P

posing this question, he has perceived that it serves the purpose, in Frege's theories, of the notion of semantic role, so that the possibility of denying, for any semantically significant type of expression, that the notion of reference can be applied to it simply cannot arise. But, in the process, he has failed to notice the function fulfilled by the use of the name/bearer relation as prototype, the function, namely, of specifying the form of semantic account to be given. The result is a reinterpretation of Frege's notion of reference which entirely misses the point of Frege's appeal, in his introduction of the notion of reference, to various intuitive, pre-systematic conceptions which we have, such as that of the relation of name to bearer. Because we were hardly conscious of this appeal, when the notion of reference was originally introduced, we feel uncertain, when presented with such a reinterpretation, whether anything has been missed out, and, if so, what. What I have here been seeking to do is to make explicit at what points Frege appeals to these intuitive notions which we ordinarily take for granted, and hence those ingredients in Frege's notion of reference which have indeed been missed out in such a reinterpretation as Tugendhat's.

We have the notion of the bearer of a name, and the conception of a predicate's being true or false of an object, in advance of constructing a semantic account of our language in order to analyse its working, because these are embodied in quite primitive linguistic performances; our acquiring them is part of our learning to use our language. Both are born of the practice of ostension, that is, from our possession, in the use of a demonstrative accompanied by a pointing gesture, of another means than the employment of a name for picking out a concrete object. By means of a recognition statement (a statement of the form 'This is a'), we are accustomed to identifying an object as the bearer of a name; by means of ostensive predications (statements of the form 'This is F'), we are accustomed to applying predicates to objects picked out ostensively. To say that the referent of a name is its bearer, and that the referent is what we speak about, is in effect to say that the semantic roles of proper names and of simple predicates should be understood in relation to these fundamental practices: it is precisely because of our thorough familiarity with these basic linguistic practices that the notion of reference supplies us, as soon as it is introduced, with so definite and readily acceptable a picture of the semantic roles of at least the simplest logical types of expressions.

For Frege, the relation of a proper name of a concrete object to that object is the prototype of the relation of reference. Even in this case, the objects which serve as referents cannot be recognized quite independently of language: it is only because we employ a language for the understanding of which we need to grasp various criteria of identity, both for objects identified by means of names and for those identified ostensively by means of demonstratives, that we learn to slice the world up, conceptually, into discrete objects. But we do have, in the case of concrete objects, a means of picking them out otherwise than by unaided use of linguistic expressions; and in consequence we have, in the possibility of finding (at some time) something which can be identified ostensively as the bearer of a given proper name, a conception of the existence of a bearer. The primitive understanding of the existential quantifier, as ranging over some restricted class of concrete objects, is connected with the practical procedure of scanning or search, culminating in an ostensive predication (or a recognition statement). It is this which makes intelligible the possibility that a name may lack a bearer, and therefore, as soon as the referent of a name is equated with its bearer, that it may lack a referent. This contrasts sharply with the situation under Tugendhat's reinterpretation, in which we could find no rationale for supposing that a semantically significant expression, which had been provided with a sense, might still lack a referent. For, there, the notion of a referent was introduced quite abstractly, via the equivalence relation of semantic equivalence, construed as constituting identity of reference: we had no reason for supposing that the referent of an expression could be given to us in any other way than by means of the operator 'the referent of . . .'; it is therefore, under such an interpretation, no more intelligible to us how an expression can lack a referent than that a plane figure can lack a shape or a set a cardinal number.

Our original, excessively weak, characterization of the force of Frege's appeal to the name/bearer relation as prototype required merely that the semantic role of each type of expression should be construed as consisting in a relation of reference between it and some non-linguistic entity. In the light of our discussion, it now seems reasonable to require, further, that the existence of such an entity should be capable of being grasped by other means than simply by considering it as the referent of an expression of that type. It must be admitted, indeed, that the sense in which this principle holds becomes more tenuous the further away we get from the prototype, proper names of concrete objects. When we move one step away from the prototype, namely to proper names of abstract objects, it no longer holds that we can pick out or refer to the referent of such an expression by means other than the unaided use of language, i.e. of that or some other name; abstract objects cannot be the objects of ostension. Names of abstract objects are, however, always either themselves complex or introduced as the equivalents of complex expressions, in such a way that we can always formulate a condition for the existence of an object to be the bearer of the name, without overt mention or use of the name. (This might seem dubious for names of colours: but colours can be objects of ostension, and, just for that reason, are not properly to be considered as abstract objects.) Thus in this case, too, the possibility that a meaningful name should lack a referent is intelligible: it is intelligible precisely because we possess a conception of the existence of objects of the kind which serve as the referents of the names prior to the introduction of the notion of reference as a tool of semantic theory.

When we come to incomplete expressions, the analogy becomes, as we have seen, yet more strained. For abstract objects, at least of certain kinds, there is still such a thing as identifying an object as the bearer of a name: although we cannot pick out abstract objects by ostension, for particular kinds of abstract objects there are terms which constitute their primary designations, as numerals do for natural numbers; and we may therefore regard the use of a term of this privileged kind as constituting the identification of an abstract object in the way that a concrete object is identified by the use of a demonstrative. By contrast, as we have already noted, the notion of identifying a concept (or other incomplete entity) seems quite inappropriate. The principle that the referents of our words are what we talk about requires us to view a knowledge of the semantic role of a predicate as consisting in a knowledge of when it is true, and when it is false, of any given object, rather than a knowledge of how to identify something as its referent. In the same way, we have seen also that there is an awkwardness about applying to predicates, or other incomplete expressions, the conception that they may possess a sense but still lack a reference: Frege's application to them of this conception is not a true analogy with the case of proper names, and, while we can find a genuinely analogous case, it is of minimal importance. It nevertheless remains that the existence of concepts (functions, relations, etc.) is something of which we have a conception in advance of the introduction of the semantic notion of reference: indeed, as we have seen, the ascription of reference to incomplete expressions can be explained only by the use of higher-level quantification, a form of quantification already present in the language before we begin to devise a semantic analysis of its working. The appeal to the name/bearer relation as prototype is an expression of Frege's realism, the belief that all our linguistic expressions relate to constituents of reality, and that it is therefore in virtue of an objective reality, independent of us, that our sentences are true or false. The referent of a relational expression, say 'ξ is larger than ζ', is as much a constituent of reality as the objects, say Jupiter and Mars, between which the relation holds. This is so because the referents of predicates and relational expressions must be taken to be those things over which we quantify when we employ second-level quantification, not things introduced specially to correspond to classes of semantically equivalent expressions.

Frege's manner of introducing the notion of reference thus embodies a specification of what we are to take the semantic roles of proper names and of first-level predicates and relational expressions to be. The semantic role of a name is to consist entirely in determining the object which is being spoken about, that object, namely, which we can identify as the bearer of the name: the semantic role of a predicate consists, correspondingly, in its saying something about an arbitrary object, that is, in being true or false of any given object, and similarly for relational expressions. Such a model for the semantic roles of names and predicates of course compels us to treat oblique contexts as exceptional. An ordinary predicate must apply to an object, or fail to apply to it, independently of how the object is picked out by the particular name used, since the semantic contribution of the name is exhausted once the bearer is determined; its argument-place must, accordingly, constitute a transparent context, in which one name can be substituted for another, without change of truth-value, as long as the bearer remains the same. The removal of a name from an oblique context does not yield a predicate having this character, and we are therefore forced to say that a name in such a context does not have its ordinary reference.

The identification of the referent of a name with its bearer naturally has the consequence that a name which lacks a bearer lacks a referent: but does it also follow that such a name lacks a reference? Frege could not pose this question, since he makes no verbal differentiation between the referent of an expression—the term of the relation of reference—and the relation of reference itself. Obviously, the answer depends upon the way in which the word 'reference' is construed. A name without a bearer lacks a reference in the sense that there is nothing to which it bears the relation of reference: but it does not follow that such a name has no semantic role, in the sense that its use by a speaker deprives him of the power to perform a linguistic act. As we have seen, Frege is cautious about the extent to which the lack of a reference on the part of an expression has this effect. He specifically allows that the utterance of a sentence containing a name without a bearer may nevertheless constitute the expression of a thought: he nowhere   SB 28
pronounces on whether, when such a sentence is uttered assertively, i.e. with the serious intention of making a true assertion, the speaker does or does not succeed in asserting something. He does hold, however, that, in uttering such a sentence, a speaker fails to say anything either true or false. This conclusion certainly does not follow immediately from the thesis

that the semantic role of a proper name consists in its standing in the relation of reference to its bearer. Someone who held that the presence of a name lacking a bearer in a sentence did not deprive that sentence of truth-value might say that such a name had a semantic role, although it lacked a reference; or, using the word 'reference' to mean simply 'semantic role', he might say that, although it lacked a referent, it had a reference, its reference consisting precisely in the fact that it had no referent. Since Frege uses the same noun 'Bedeutung' for the semantic role of an expression, for the relation of reference which, for him, constitutes that semantic role, and for the referent which is the term of that relation, he could not frame any such thesis: he did not need to, since he would not have accepted it. But there is no necessity to be led, by the fact that Frege's terminology is adapted to the expression of his own views, into accepting those views too readily.

If we are operating with a Fregean semantics for proper names and for predicates, then we must have reserved intensional contexts for special treatment; and in that case we are likely to agree that the truth-value of a sentence determines its semantic role. Even to formulate this thesis requires that we have some suitable conception of truth and falsity: so far we have refrained from enquiring what form this must take. According to Frege, it must be such that any sentence containing a part which lacks a reference, in particular a name which lacks a bearer, must be devoid of truth-value, and every other sentence must be determinately true or false. The argument for the former of these two theses runs as follows. The Bedeutung of a name is its bearer; the Bedeutung of a sentence is its truth-value. But, if a part of a complex expression lacks a Bedeutung, then the whole lacks a Bedeutung: hence, if a name occurring in a sentence lacks a bearer, the sentence as a whole lacks a truth-value.

The force of this argument depends, to a large extent, on whether we take 'Bedeutung' to mean 'semantic role' or whether we take it to mean 'referent'. It is difficult to see how one could deny that if, in a complex expression, there occurs a part which fails to fulfil its intended semantic role, the whole expression must likewise fail to fulfil its intended semantic role. But, then, to assume that, when a name lacks a bearer, it has no semantic role, is to beg the question. Certainly, in a Fregean semantics, the role of a name is to determine an object as its bearer: but we have so far found no ground for saying that, when there is no object that can be so identified, the use of the name frustrates the intention of performing a linguistic act, say that of making an assertion, by uttering a sentence containing it. If, on the other hand, we understand 'Bedeutung' to mean 'referent', then the principle that, if a part of an expression lacks a referent, the whole lacks a referent, is far from compelling. It derives its force, as we have seen, from the case of complex names. If there was no such man as King Arthur, then there was no such man as King Arthur's father; if there is no such planet as Vulcan, then there is no such point as Vulcan's centre of mass. It is by no means obvious, however, that the principle extends to complex expressions of other types. We may, for example, choose to say that, if there was no such person as King Arthur, then there is no concept to be the referent of 'ξ was married to King Arthur': but it is not evident that we are bound to say this, rather than that the predicate has as referent a concept under which nothing falls. We must, indeed, choose the former alternative if we are to follow Frege in holding that, if there was no such person as King Arthur, then a sentence of the form '*a* was married to King Arthur' is not even false: but to use this as a premiss in the present context would be to argue in a circle. The only non-circular ground for holding that such a predicate has no referent is the desire to make the analogy between proper names and incomplete expressions as good as possible by maintaining the principle that, if a part lacks a referent, the whole does: it has no intrinsic plausibility.

It is impossible to resist Frege's argument if we accept the thesis of Frege's later doctrine, that a sentence is of the same logical type as a complex name. For Frege, a concept is related to a predicate in a manner that is only analogous with the relation between the bearer of a name and that name; but, in Frege's later doctrine, the relation of a truth-value to a sentence is the very same relation as that of bearer to name. If this is so, then indeed it follows strictly that, if 'King Arthur' lacks a bearer, then 'King Arthur was childless' lacks a truth-value.

To regard sentences as having truth-values as their referents does not, however, entail the assimilation of sentences to complex names. If sentences are expressions of a different logical type from names, then truth-values are not objects, and the relation of a sentence to its truth-value is, like the relation of a predicate to a concept, only an analogue of the relation of a name to its bearer, not the same relation. The view that sentences are of the same logical type as names rests on the unsupported supposition that the only distinction between types of expression is one relating to the degree or kind of incompleteness that they have, where an expression is incomplete only if it carries an argument-place with it. Names, while they do not have incompleteness of this sort, are nevertheless incomplete in another sense, as contrasted with sentences, in that a sentence does, and a name, by itself, does not, serve to 'make a move in the language-game'. The temptation to assimilate sentences to names would hardly arise in a simple language which contained no expressions of generality or functional expressions of higher level. For the analysis of such a language, we should have no need of the notion of a complex predicate: that of a simple predicate, or a simple relational or functional expression, would suffice. We should therefore have no need for the conception of an incomplete expression as being formed from a sentence by omission. We should still, admittedly, need an account of the way in which expressions of different types hooked on to one another to form sentences, and this would provide some ground for distinguishing names as complete in contrast with predicates and relational or functional expressions. But the sense in which the predicates of a simple language of this kind would be called 'incomplete' would not be that in which Frege applies this term to complex predicates, and, by assimilation, to simple ones: they would not be *unselbständig*, mere patterns common to different sentences, but would be literally fragments of sentences. In relation to such a language, therefore, there would be no urge to blur the distinction between the sense in which names can be called 'complete' and the much stronger sense in which this term can be applied to sentences. In *Grundlagen* the unique logical role of sentences was very firmly emphasized by Frege: there was no reason why he should not have maintained the distinction between them and names. The thesis that sentences stand in a relation of reference to truth-values no more requires that they should be regarded as a special kind of complex name than the thesis that predicates stand in a relation of reference to concepts requires that predicates should be so regarded.

If sentences are agreed to have truth-values as their referents, but this is regarded, not as a special case, but merely as an analogue, of names' having objects as their referents, then, as we have seen, there is no cogent argument from first principles to the conclusion that sentences containing a name which lacks a bearer are devoid of truth-value. The tenability of this conclusion therefore becomes a test for the coherence of Frege's later assimilation of sentences to complex names, since this assimilation certainly does entail the conclusion. Alternatively, even if the assimilation is rejected on other grounds, the tenability of the conclusion serves to test the strength of the analogy between the relation of reference over the domain of expressions other than names and the relation between name and bearer.

The appeal to the name/bearer relation as the prototype of the relation of reference embodies Frege's realistic interpretation of language: when the notion of reference is applied to incomplete expressions, the appeal to this prototype enshrines Frege's realistic conception of functions, concepts and relations as objective ingredients of external reality. But the idea that truth-values are constituents of an independent reality does not play any comparable role in Frege's philosophy. Whether a given thought is true or false is, of course, an objective matter: but that the truth-value of the thought is itself an entity which is one of the components of reality is a conception which is held merely in order to complete the analogy according to which the referents of all expressions are extra-linguistic correlates of those expressions, belonging to the real world, and does not appear to be a thesis which has any significance on its own.

In order to elucidate the question, we have first to ask after the role in a theory of meaning of the notions of truth and falsity. The term 'semantics', at least as commonly applied to formalized languages, usually denotes a systematic account of the truth-conditions of sentences of the language: the purpose of thus assigning a value, true or false, to every well-formed sentence of the language is taken as already understood, and receives no explanation within the semantic theory itself. In a similar way, the rules of a game do not themselves explain, but take for granted, the significance of the classification which they impose upon final positions into winning ones and losing ones. The classification of the sentences of a formalized language into true ones and false ones relates to the purpose for which we want to use the language. But, in the case of a natural language, it is already in use: the only point of constructing a semantics for the language can be as an instrument for the systematic description of this use, that is, as part of a whole theory of meaning for the language, which as a whole constitutes an account of its working. If the semantic part of the theory is taken as issuing in an assignment of conditions under which each sentence of the language, as uttered on a particular occasion, has this or that truth-value, the rest of the theory must connect the truth-conditions of the sentences with the use to which they are put, that is, with the actual practice of speakers of the language. The rules which tell us, for a particular game, when the game is won, when it is drawn and when lost provide for us a sufficient account of what playing the game actually consists in, because we are familiar, from other games, with the systematic connection between the procedure of playing them and the notions of win, loss and draw. In the same way, a semantic theory which determines the truth-conditions of the sentences of a language gets its point from a systematic connection between the notions of truth and falsity and the practice of using those sentences.

That there exists such a systematic connection between the applications of the notions of truth and falsity to sentences and the use of those sentences must be taken as a tacit background assumption for many philosophical discussions of what that application should be. Unfortunately, because it has remained tacit, we are not told by such philosophers in what they take the

P*

connection to consist, and hence we are left in the dark about the significance or consequences of the theses they advance about ascriptions of truth-value. Thus there have been extended debates over whether sentences of some whole class—e.g. ethical statements or scientific laws—can properly be described as being true or false, or again, whether certain kinds of sentence should, in particular circumstances, be said to be false or to be neither true nor false (sentences containing names or definite descriptions without bearers, in particular): but those who have engaged in such debates have, for the most part, failed to make explicit what it is, in their view, that hangs upon the decision. Evidently, they take themselves to be discussing something of more importance than the correct usage of the words 'true' and 'false', namely a fundamental question concerning the analysis of the meaning of the sentences in question. If this is what they are doing, then there must indeed be a systematic connection between truth-conditions and meaning: but, since the disputants do not say what they take it to be, it is left unclear on what grounds the dispute is to be settled.

If, in such disputes, different decisions about the applications of 'true' and 'false' will lead to the ascriptions of different meanings to the sentences in question, then such a difference in meaning ought to be revealed by a difference in more than just the way in which 'true' and 'false' are applied to those sentences: it ought to be revealed in some difference in use which would accord with one or other way of applying the notions of truth and falsity. For instance, we might imagine two languages which resembled each other very closely, and within which we succeeded in identifying expressions which in many ways functioned much as do proper names in our language. These languages might both contain a pair of predicates whose application to most sentences of the languages corresponded very well with that of our words 'true' and 'false'. One difference between the two languages, however, might consist in the fact that, in one language, the word corresponding to 'false' was applied to sentences containing a name without a bearer, whereas, in the other language, the expression corresponding to 'neither true nor false' was applied to them. The question now obviously arises whether this difference reflects a divergence in the meanings attached, in the two languages, to sentences containing proper names, or whether it merely reflects a slight divergence in the meanings of the words translated as 'true' and 'false'. The former alternative can be allowed to obtain only if there is some discrepancy, as between the two languages, in the use made of sentences containing proper names, a discrepancy over and above the difference in the truth-value ascribed to them. If those who engaged in such protracted debate about whether sentences of our language containing names or definite descriptions lacking a bearer should be called false or not had made it clear what, in the case of the two imaginary languages, the decisive difference would have been, then it would have been possible to observe whether sentences of our own language are used in a way to accord with one way of applying the predicate 'false' or the other: in the absence of such an account, the dispute was conducted in a void.

According to Frege, when I grasp the way in which the reference, and thus the semantic role, of an expression is to be determined, then I grasp its sense; in particular, when I grasp the way in which the truth-value of a sentence (as uttered on a particular occasion) is to be determined, then I grasp the thought which it expresses. It is impossible to gain any grip on what it is to express a sense, or, more particularly, a thought, if we try to view the activity of expressing thoughts in isolation from the various kinds of linguistic acts which may be performed in relation to them, that is, the various kinds of force which may be attached to the expression of the thought. Until a connection is made between the truth-value of a sentence and the linguistic activities of asserting, questioning, etc., which can be accomplished by its utterance, we are in the dark as to what truth and falsity are, what is the difference between them, or what is the significance of ascribing them to sentences. Although it is not possible to claim Frege's authority for the dictum, it seems clear that sentences only have a sense in virtue of the practices of using them to make assertions, ask questions, etc. In the same way, there are winning or losing positions in a game only because the game is played, or at least is thought of as being played. If chess were never played, but the rules of chess existed solely in order to frame chess problems, there would be no sense in which checkmate was a winning position. True, many problems are of the form 'White to move and mate in three'; but equally good problems could be posed in which White had to force stalemate in three moves, or had to compel Black to checkmate him. In the same way, if a semantics is given for a language in the ordinary way save that the two possible truth-values of sentences are not labelled 'true' and 'false', but merely designated 'A' and 'B', there can be no sense in asking which value is truth and which falsity, except in relation to an actual or possible use of the language.

Frege gave the outlines of a theory of meaning in which the notions of truth and falsity play precisely the central role that we are requiring. The theory of reference constitutes the semantics for the language in the strict sense: by means of a detailed specification of the references of the primitive expressions of the language, together with the rules for determining the reference of a complex expression from that of its components, we obtain in effect an inductive truth-definition for (particular utterances of) sentences of the language. The theory of sense likewise supplies an account of the cognitive aspect of the language, i.e. what an understanding of an expression of the language consists in, the sense of each expression being the manner in which a speaker grasps what its reference is. Granted, Frege himself leaves the theory of sense in a largely programmatic state, partly because, whenever an expression is definable, the manner in which its reference is stated can be chosen in such a way as to display its sense: a complete account of sense would require a description, for primitive names, of how a speaker identifies their referents, and, for primitive incomplete expressions, how a speaker identifies the referent of a completion of such an expression. Both these parts of a total theory of meaning for a language have to deal with each simple expression individually: together they provide a description of the way in which a speaker of the language associates with each sentence conditions for its truth or falsity. The theory of sense and reference is then to be supplemented by an account of the various forms of linguistic force that may be attached to a sentence: the theory of force thus supplies an account of the various uses that are actually made of sentences in actual speech. The separation of sense and force can only be justified if it is possible, for each variety of force, to give a *uniform* description of the linguistic act which is effected by the utterance of an arbitrary sentence, whose truth-conditions are supposed known, to which a force of that kind is attached. There will thus be one general account of the use of sentences to make an assertion, another of their use to ask a sentential question, and so on, each applicable independently of the particular sense and hence the particular truth-conditions of the sentence. (On Frege's own account of the matter, this holds good only for assertions and sentential questions; but, as we have seen, if a theory of meaning of this general structure is possible at all, the procedure should be able to be extended to commands, requests, expressions of desire, etc.) Finally, an account of tone will treat of certain uses of language ancillary to the primary linguistic acts. The distinctions between sense, tone and force thus provide a diagram of the various parts which make up an entire theory of meaning for a language as conceived by Frege.

Within a theory of meaning of this type, the notions of truth and falsity gain their content from their role within the theory. This role is twofold, corresponding to the division between the semantic and cognitive part of the theory on the one hand (the account of reference and of sense) and to the pragmatic part on the other (the account of force). The semantic part of the theory specifies the *application* of the notions of truth and falsity to sentences of the language (while the cognitive part shows how we recognize the application): the pragmatic part provides the *point* of so classifying sentences as true or as false, by describing the use that can be made of any given sentence in terms of its truth-conditions. Only when the two parts of the theory are taken together does it become possible to ask whether it agrees with what can be observed of the practice of using the language: whether, given the way in which the semantic part of the theory has specified the application of 'true' and 'false' to the sentences of the language, the description that is given in the pragmatic part of the use of those sentences accords with what in fact happens.

The semantic part of a theory of meaning of this kind is related entirely to the determination of the truth-values of sentences: the semantic role (reference) of any expression wholly subserves the purpose of fixing the truth-conditions of the sentences in which it may occur. In speaking of sentences themselves, however, there are two different ways in which we may regard them; and these may give rise to two distinct notions of truth-value. On the one hand, we may think of sentences as complete utterances by means of which, when a specific kind of force is attached, a linguistic act may be effected: in this connection, we require that notion of truth-value in terms of which the particular kind of force may be explained. On the other hand, sentences may also occur as constituent parts of other sentences, and, in this connection, may have a semantic role in helping to determine the truth-value of the whole sentence: so here we shall be concerned with whatever notion of truth-value is required in order to explain how the truth-value of a complex sentence is determined from that of its components. There is no a priori reason why the two notions of truth-value should coincide.

The intuitive notions of truth and falsity are connected primarily with the assertoric use of language. Given the distinction between sense and force, we may view a sentential question as expressing a thought which is true if the correct answer is affirmative, false if it is negative; if we extend the distinction to imperatives, we may view a command as expressing a thought which is true if the command is obeyed, false if it is disobeyed. The application of the notions of truth and falsity to questions and commands is, however, counter-intuitive. This is no objection to the extension; but it does justify treating assertion as the primary and representative case. In order to grasp the content of an assertion, we have to know in what circumstances the assertion is to be judged correct and in what incorrect. If the assertoric sentence is neither ambiguous nor vague, then these sets of circumstances must be disjoint and exhaustive. They must be exhaustive, at least, in the sense that there are no circumstances the recognition of which would entitle us to say that no further information would determine the assertion as correct or as incorrect: if there were, the assertoric sentence could have had only an indefinite, i.e. partially specified, sense. It would be a mistake to reject this thesis by adverting to situations in which, for some reason or other, we are inclined to say that a speaker who purported to make an assertion nevertheless said nothing either true or false, although he expressed a definite thought. Even if there exists a possible situation of this kind, there must be, for it or any other situation, an answer to the question whether, in saying what he did, the speaker intended to rule out the possibility that that situation should occur; or, rather, if there is no answer to such a question, that shows only that the speaker did not make a quite definite assertion. In making an assertion, a speaker wishes to be understood as excluding certain possible states of affairs and allowing for the possibility of others: and, if his assertion had a determinate content, it must stand determinately in one or other relation to each possible state of affairs. If some state of affairs obtains which he was ruling out, then his assertion was incorrect: if no such state of affairs obtains, it was correct.

We may, of course, equally well characterize the notions of correct and incorrect assertion by dividing possible states of affairs into those which verify the assertion in the sense of conclusively establishing it as justified, or that of ruling out the possibility of having to withdraw it. In this case we can say that, if any one of those states of affairs which verify the assertion obtains, the assertion is correct, while, if none of them obtains, it is incorrect. However, this way of approaching the matter is intuitively less clear, because the notion of a conclusive justification of an assertion is somewhat less transparent than the notion of that which is excluded by the making of an assertion. This is akin to the fact that disobedience to a command is a more basic notion than that of obedience to it. The command itself specifies what shall count as disobedience; the notion of obedience carries with it more of a suggestion of commendation, and thereby of allusion to the intentions of the person commanded, so that obedience comes to be best explained in terms of disobedience, namely as effective action undertaken to avoid disobedience. In the same way, the notion of the justification of an assertion contains a trace of commendation, a suggestion that the speaker had reasonable grounds to make the assertion. If a state of affairs is excluded by an assertion, and that state of affairs proves to obtain, then the speaker must withdraw the assertion, no matter how reasonable he may have been to make it: the content of the assertion itself determines in what circumstances it is necessary to withdraw it. There is thus a fairly direct criterion in linguistic behaviour for whether a given state of affairs was excluded by a particular assertion. A state of affairs which shows the assertion to have been justified, in the sense which we require, does not necessarily show the speaker to have had good grounds for making it, and there is no such simple linguistic consequence of a recognition that such a state of affairs obtains: it is therefore best characterized as a situation in which the possibility is excluded that any of those states of affairs should obtain which were ruled out by the assertion, and which would thus compel the withdrawal of the assertion.

In order, then, to explain assertoric force, i.e. to explain the use of sentences to make assertions, all that has to be appealed to is a twofold classification of sentences (relative to occasions of utterance) into those that could be used to make a correct assertion and those which would result in an incorrect one. (We are not here attempting to *define* the notions of correct and incorrect assertion, still less to give an account of the linguistic activity of asserting: we are interested merely in what notions of truth and falsity, as specified by a semantic theory, we should need to appeal to in giving such an account.) As evidenced by our reluctance to apply 'true' and 'false' to nonassertoric sentences, our intuitive notions of truth and falsity are strongly connected with the conception of the correctness or incorrectness of an assertion: under one use of 'true' and 'false', a thought may be called true just in case the assertion of it would be correct, and false otherwise. These are the only notions of truth and falsity which would be needed by someone whose sole purpose was to grasp the content of the assertions made by the speakers of a language, without trying to understand the internal structure of the sentences. A phrase-book gives translations of whole sentences of one language into another, without explaining the composition of the sentences. Someone surrounded by the speakers of a language unknown to him might conceivably come to recognize some simple sentences as assertoric, and to grasp their content as a whole, without divining their internal structure (probably, indeed, only for sentences containing some token-reflexive element, such as a significant present tense, rather than for such sentences as 'Elephants are herbivorous'). If he remained concerned only to comprehend the contents of the assertions taken as a whole, all that would matter to him would be the conditions for their correctness or incorrectness, and therefore what he could take a speaker as excluding by means of an assertion. Any grounds that might exist, for instance, for classifying certain incorrect assertions not as false but as neither true nor false would be entirely irrelevant to his purpose.

It is thus not from a consideration of the notions of truth and falsity as they are needed for an account of assertoric force that we can find a justification for Frege's thesis that a sentence containing a name without a bearer has no truth-value. Someone who seriously uses a sentence containing a name or definite description in order to make an assertion is not envisaging, and is not understood as envisaging, the possibility that the name or description lacks a bearer. Someone says to me (pointing to a house), 'The sole occupant of that house died yesterday'; a third person comes up, and he says to him, 'Someone was living alone in that house, and died yesterday'.

LLP 12   According to both Frege and Strawson, these two sentences have different truth-conditions: if there had been no one person formerly living in the house, the second assertion was false, but the first was neither true nor false. But, whatever this difference in truth-conditions relates to, it is not to the content of the assertions made by the two utterances, as determined by the conditions for their correctness or incorrectness, for these conditions coincide: by the utterance of the first sentence, the speaker was no more taken as allowing for the possibility that the house had previously been empty than by the utterance of the second one.

Again, if we revert for a moment to the suggestion that the indicative conditionals of natural language be construed as used to make conditional assertions in a sense parallel to that of conditional bets, it is plain that the fact that the antecedent proves to be false has no tendency to make the speaker withdraw his previous remark: for, by the utterance of the conditional, he did not intend to be, and was not, taken as excluding the possibility that the antecedent was false. Here, then, the case in which, according to the 'conditional assertion' interpretation, what was said was neither true nor false is one in which the assertion is correct: whatever difference there might be between conditional assertions and assertions of the material conditional, it does not appear at the level at which we are considering merely the content of an assertion, and therefore those notions of truth and falsity relevant to determining it. ,

When, however, we seek to characterize the semantic role of sentences as used, not on their own, but as constituents of more complex sentences, we are concerned with them in the same way as with other kinds of sentence-component, which are incapable of being used on their own. Our basic assumption is that the semantic role of any expression consists in the contribution which it makes to determining the conditions for the truth and falsity of any sentence of which it forms part, where the truth of a sentence is equated with the correctness of the corresponding assertion and its falsity to the incorrectness of that assertion. We have, therefore, to enquire after the way in which a subordinate sentence may contribute to determining the condition for the correct assertibility of a complex sentence in which it occurs. There is no a priori ground for assuming that this contribution will be determined solely by the assertibility-condition for the subordinate sentence: in the case of natural language, it plainly is not.

The simplest way in which one sentence can form a constituent of another is by negating the original sentence. In natural language we do not have (or, at least, do not frequently make use of) any phrase serving straightforwardly as a sentential operator expressing negation. When the grammatical subject is or contains a sign of generality, e.g. 'someone', or when the main verb is governed by a modal auxiliary such as 'must', negating the verb does not yield a sentence interpretable as the negation of the original sentence. It is, however, a fairly natural idea to interpret the sign of negation attached to the verb of an atomic sentence as an operator applying to the sentence as a whole. Under this interpretation, however, the result of thus negating an atomic sentence is not simply to reverse the condition for correct assertibility. We have, rather, to distinguish two distinct ways in which an assertion of the original sentence might have been incorrect: and the only way in which the distinction can be made is according to whether or not any of the singular terms occurring in the sentence lacks a bearer. It is precisely for this reason that, even if we began with a wholly aseptic notion of semantic role, not introduced by appeal to the name/bearer relation as prototype, we should nevertheless be forced to invoke the notion of the bearer of a name in order to construct a semantics for natural language. Let us say that, if the original sentence was false, in the sense that an assertion of it would have been incorrect, but all of the terms it contained possessed bearers, then the sentence was false in the first way (false$_1$); but that, if it were false, in the same sense, by reason of a lack of a bearer on the part of one or more of the terms occurring in it, then it was false in the second way (false$_2$). We may then construe the negation operator as acting on a sentence in such a way as to convert a true sentence into one that is false$_1$, a false$_1$ sentence into a true one, and a false$_2$ sentence into one that is still false$_2$. We are now, in effect, describing the use of the negation sign by means of a three-valued truth-table.

The case in which we are calling the sentence 'false$_1$' is, of course, just that in which Frege calls it simply 'false', while that in which we are calling it 'false$_2$' is the one in which Frege says that it is neither true nor false. Frege's use of 'true' and 'false' is thus plainly not that which we have seen to be appropriate for an account of assertoric force: rather, the distinction between the case in which Frege says of a sentence that it is false and that in which he says that it is neither true nor false is required—at least, so far as our considerations have as yet taken us—only for an explanation of the role of sentences as constituents of other sentences (in particular, their behaviour under negation). The necessity, for this purpose, of making a distinction between falsity$_1$ and falsity$_2$ does not yet justify or even explain Frege's saying of false$_2$ sentences that they lack a truth-value altogether: his reservation of the word 'false' for false$_1$ sentences does, however, accord with the intuitive principle, which strongly influences our employment of the word 'false', that a sentence is false if and only if (what we recognize as being) its negation is true. One exemplification of the intuitive strength of this principle is our hesitancy about applying the word 'false' to conditionals: for in natural language we do not ordinarily form sentences which have the appearance of negations of conditionals.

p. 346   We had in Chapter 10 an example of a language for which there would be a corresponding necessity to subdivide truth into distinct sub-cases. The suggestion that indicative conditionals should be construed as being neither true nor false when their antecedents were false would, as we saw, have a similar plausibility in a language which displayed the following features: there was in the language a unary sentential operator 'Non . . .' which for the most part simply reversed the assertibility-condition of a sentence to which it was applied, but which, when applied to a conditional 'If A, then B', yielded a sentence having the same assertibility-condition as 'If A, then non B'. In that case, in order to interpret the negation operator truth-functionally, we should need to distinguish, for conditionals, two modes of truth: a conditional would be true$_1$ when it was true by virtue of the truth of both antecedent and consequent, but true$_2$ when it was true by virtue of the falsity of the antecedent. The negation operator could then be described as taking a true$_1$ sentence into a false one, a false sentence into a true$_1$ one, and a true$_2$ sentence into one which was still true$_2$. In order to preserve the principle that, if a sentence is true, its negation is false, it might then be natural to reserve the word 'true' for true$_1$ sentences, true$_2$ sentences thus being described as being neither true nor false.

As a technical study, many-valued logic has been developed primarily as a mathematical generalization of two-valued logic, with little regard to intuitive interpretation. The truth-values are divided into those which rank as 'designated' and those which rank as 'undesignated': a formula is defined as valid if, under each assignment of truth-values to its sentence-letters, it comes out as having a designated value. An obvious way to secure an intuitive interpretation for such a many-valued logic, that is, to exhibit it as a genuine semantic structure, is to treat the distinction between designated and undesignated values as corresponding to that between truth and falsity when these notions are understood in terms of the correctness and incorrectness of assertions. Thus an assertion made by uttering a given sentence amounts to a claim that that sentence has a designated value: in order, therefore, to grasp the content of any particular assertion, all that is necessary is to know the condition for the sentence uttered to have a designated value. We do not need, for this purpose, to know anything about the distinction between the different designated truth-values or between the different undesignated ones: an understanding of those distinctions is required only in order to be able to derive the assertibility-condition of a complex sentence from the senses of its constituents, since the semantic roles of the sentential operators are given by truth-tables which relate to the individual truth-values and not just to the distinction between a designated and an undesignated value. For particular reasons, such as the desire to preserve the principle that a sentence is false if and only if its negation is true, it may be felt desirable to restrict the label 'true' to a particular one of several designated truth-values, or to restrict the label 'false' to a particular one of several undesignated truth-values, or both. But, in the absence of a distinction between designated and un-designated truth-values, the mere proposal to regard a certain kind of sen-tence as being, in certain kinds of case, neither true nor false does not tell us whether the state of being neither true nor false is to be regarded as a sub-case of correct assertibility or of incorrect assertibility, and hence does not determine the assertoric content of the sentence.

The applicability of a many-valued logic as a semantic structure depends on our knowing when a constituent sentence may take each of the various truth-values. One possibility is that the atomic sentences can take only two possible truth-values, one designated and one undesignated: in this case, for each other truth-value, there must be a complex sentence which has this value when its constituents have a suitable combination of the two basic ones. This case occurred with our second example: atomic sentences can take only the values $true_1$ and false, but a conditional obtains the value $true_2$ when its antecedent has the value false. Another possibility is that an atomic sentence may take any one of the various values, as with the first example: in this case, we must be supplied with a criterion for distinguishing which of different values, both undesignated or both designated, an atomic sentence may have. In our case, this was accomplished by appeal to the notion of the bearer of a name. Frege held it to be a defect of natural language that it permits the formation of names lacking a bearer; in a properly constructed language, every name would be guaranteed a bearer. For such a language, we should still need to appeal to the notion of the bearer of a name in order to state the conditions under which an atomic sentence was true or false. But, in one respect, it would be less easy to recognize that the notion of a bearer was indispensable in providing a semantics for the language, in that the conception of truth and falsity required in order to state the truth-tables for the sentential operators could be explained without invoking it, for it would coincide with that required for the explanation of assertoric force.

It is true enough that, since we are not compelled to take the negation sign of natural language as a sentential operator, we can provide a two-valued semantics for natural language. The negation sign may be taken as attaching logically, as well as syntactically, only to the verbal phrase, understood as a predicate or relational expression, and the singular term then treated as a definite description in accordance with Russell's Theory of Descriptions. Such an account must, of course, rely on the conception of a predicate's being true or false of a given object, and on that of an object's answering to a definite description; the difference in the representation of the operation of negating the verb allows falsity to be treated as a unitary truth-value. It is often said that the necessity for regarding sentences containing names without a bearer as neither true nor false arises from Frege's determination to treat all apparent singular terms as names; but, at least as far as our considerations up to now have taken us, we are not in a position to give any clear content to this remark. Frege certainly does not treat the singular terms of natural language as 'logically proper names' in Russell's sense, for this would be to take them as guaranteed a bearer, and Frege's whole complaint is that they are not. What is meant, rather, is that a name is an expression whose semantic role consists wholly in its having some particular object as bearer. When this is taken as entailing that, if a name lacks a bearer, then, even though it may possess a sense, it fails to fulfil its intended semantic role in such a way as to deprive any sentence containing it of a truth-value, Frege does indeed hold this; but it is precisely the part of his theory for which we have so far found no rationale. We have seen how, under one quite natural use of 'true' and 'false', a justification may be given for saying of such sentences that they are neither true nor false; but we have found no ground for describing this state as being one of possessing no truth-value at all, or for saying of such sentences that no linguistic act can be performed by uttering them. If, on the other hand, the principle that the semantic role of a proper name consists in its having what bearer it has is taken in a weaker sense, as allowing that the semantic role of certain names may consist precisely in the fact that they have no bearers, then the principle does not rule out construing singular terms as Russellian definite descriptions. For them to be so construed, all that is required is that it be determinate whether the term has a bearer (whether there is an object answering to the definite description), and, if so, which: it is entirely unnecessary that the term be viewed as analysable into a description operator and a predicate. From our present point of view, the whole difference between the two accounts lies in the different ways of taking the negation operator.

The use either of a three-valued logic, or of the Theory of Descriptions, in framing a semantics for natural language leads to obvious inconveniences, and it is no part of our present concern to decide which is preferable: our purpose is only to determine what principles underlying the notions of truth and falsity are being invoked by Frege when he maintains that sentences containing names lacking bearers have no truth-value, and the consequences for the thesis that the truth-value of a sentence is its referent.

It must be conceded that, if we had concerned ourselves with interrogative rather than assertoric force, we should have found a reason for distinguishing two undesignated truth-values for atomic sentences, even in accounting only for the use of these sentences on their own. A sentential question admits of two possible answers, 'Yes' and 'No', and we need to distinguish the case in which the correct answer is 'No' from that in which neither answer is correct (the case in which, as Strawson says, 'the question does not arise'—although it can be asked). This does not invalidate our analysis, however, since the answer 'No' is precisely tantamount to, and is best analysed as, an assertion of the negation of the sentence uttered in interrogative form (at least when that sentence was, syntactically, affirmative). *LLP* 12

Given that, e.g., 'King Arthur did not defeat the Saxons' is construed as the negation of 'King Arthur defeated the Saxons', we need a distinction between falsity$_1$ and falsity$_2$, or, in Frege's terminology, between being false and being neither true nor false: but nothing has emerged to give any ground for regarding this latter state as one of having no truth-value at all, rather than as one of having a second undesignated truth-value, which we may call 'the value X'. The very fact that an account of assertoric force requires only the distinction between having a designated truth-value and having an undesignated one, but not that between the two undesignated values, is sufficient to show that, where the semantic role of a sentence is identified with its truth-value, a sentence containing a name which lacks a bearer does not lack a truth-value, precisely because there is no ground for saying that, by the utterance of such a sentence, no linguistic act is performed. It might be thought, however, that to insist on this point is pedantic: that, provided we do not press Frege's claim that such a sentence is devoid of truth-value so hard as to yield the consequence that an assertion cannot be made by uttering it, the difference between saying that it has no truth-value and that it has the value X is a mere indifferent matter of terminology. Such a suspicion is mistaken. Frege's view leads to consequences for the interpretation of complex sentences which cannot be sustained. If Frege's principle is accepted, that, if part of an expression lacks a reference, then the whole lacks a reference, and if a sentence lacks a truth-value and thereby a reference, it follows that this condition infects any complex sentence of which that sentence is a constituent. Not only is an atomic sentence, or the negation of one, which contains a name lacking a bearer, void of truth-value, but any sentence whatever which contains such a name must likewise be void of truth-value: and this is just the conclusion which Frege drew. If, on the other hand, we regard the state of being neither true nor false as constituting the possession of a third truth-value, the value X, we are at liberty to stipulate three-valued truth-tables for the sentential connectives in whatever way seems best to accord with their observed use: we may, for instance, choose a truth-table for 'or' in which, whenever 'A' is true, 'A or B' is also true, even when 'B' has the value X, or one for 'if' which yields the result that 'If A, then A' is always true, even when 'A' has the value X. We may experience some difficulty in devising truth-tables which preserve the maximum number of intuitively valid forms of argument, but there is no obstacle in principle.

It is plain that there is no inherent reason why we should adopt Frege's course rather than the latter. Our original reason for viewing the presence of a name lacking a bearer as not rendering a sentence straightforwardly false, but as preventing it from being true, applied only to *atomic* sentences and their negations. There simply is no comparable ground for saying the same about such a sentence as, say, 'If King Arthur fought the Saxons, the Saxon conquest was delayed', or as, 'Either King Arthur fought the Saxons or the Saxons encountered little opposition', given that we are supposing that 'King Arthur' is without a bearer. Frege's reason for saying that such sentences are neither true nor false derives wholly from his thesis that atomic sentences containing names lacking a bearer have no truth-value, and therefore no reference, together with his principle about the reference of complex expressions. The former thesis is, therefore, a substantial one: but we have been unable to discover any basis for it.

Given Frege's view that any sentence whatever in which a name lacking a bearer occurs somewhere is neither true nor false, it is readily understandable

SB 41

that he should have regarded the possibility of forming such names as a defect which demands a remedy. The construction of a semantics for a language for which it held that, if any constituent sentence in a complex one had the value X, then so did the whole sentence, would be at best tedious. There would be no valid formulas, i.e. formulas every instance of which had the value true, and no valid inference-schemas in which the conclusion contained any part not occurring in the premisses. It seems irrelevant to argue whether it is literally true that no coherent semantics could be devised for such a language, as Frege implicitly held; it is clear that the awkwardness of constructing such a semantics would be so great that much the best course would be that which Frege took, namely that of reconstructing language so that names lacking a bearer could no longer be framed.

From several points of view, such a reconstruction presents in any case the most convenient way of going about things, but that is not what we are here concerned with. Frege represented that feature of natural language which makes it possible to form complex names, and to introduce simple ones, which have no bearer as more than an inconvenience for the formal logician: he represented it as a failure to accomplish an essential purpose of language, that of guaranteeing a semantic role to every expression on which a sense has been conferred. And the plain fact of the matter is that Frege was wrong on this point: there is no obstacle to constructing a semantics for a language containing names lacking a bearer, even if we take what appear to be negations of atomic sentences as genuinely their negations. In this case, we must allow that atomic sentences, and their negations, are neither true nor false when they contain a name without a bearer, and that this is true of certain complex sentences as well, though not of all: but we shall take this condition as constituting possession of a particular truth-value, the value X.

The status of sentences containing names without a bearer is not of great moment in itself: I have concentrated upon it, not for its intrinsic interest, but as a means of disentangling some of the different strands which go to make up the notions of truth and falsity, as Frege uses them, and which go to make up his notion of reference in general. This is one of the points at which a tension most plainly appears between the two ingredients of the notion of reference—the conception of it as semantic role, and the appeal to the name/bearer prototype. Since Frege's principles lead, in this case, to a false conclusion, they require some revision. This revision must be such as to weaken the power of the role as prototype of the relation between name and bearer. The word 'reference' itself ceases to be useful to us, at least in enquiring how far the revision should be carried, because of its ambiguity between 'having a semantic role' and 'having a referent'. The upshot of our discussion has been that there is no useful distinction that can be drawn between an expression's having a (completely specific) sense and its having a semantic role: in particular, if a sentence expresses a thought, then it can be used to make an assertion, ask a question, etc., and therefore has a semantic role, even though it should contain a name without a bearer; and, in the latter case, it still has a truth-value. Since it seems reasonable to allow that, if any part of a complex expression lacks a semantic role, so does the whole, it follows that, when a name possess a determinate sense, it also has a semantic role, even though it may lack a bearer: its semantic role consists in its having what bearer it has, if any, not in its having a bearer. There seems no reason why we should not allow that the truth-value of a sentence is its referent, and, when a name has a bearer, that that bearer is its referent: but, while the principle stands that if, in a complex name, some constituent name lacks a referent, then so does the complex name, this principle cannot be extended to complex expressions in general, and specifically not to sentences. As for whether a name without a bearer has a reference or not, this question is now a verbal one: it has a semantic role, and it lacks a referent. What is not trivial is that we have been forced to loosen the connection, even in the case of names, between semantic role and the name/bearer relation. The semantic role of a name is still intimately connected with possession of a bearer: but we can no longer say that it consists in an object's being related to it as referent. This, in turn, weakens the force of Frege's appeal to the name/bearer relation as prototype in the case of other kinds of expression. The notion of reference being introduced by Frege as exemplified by the relation of name to bearer, it appears absurd at the outset to suppose that an expression might have a reference while lacking a referent—indeed, while we lack a verbal differentiation between the two, the supposition is impossible to express. The work which Frege requires the notion of reference to do, however, is as an explanation of the semantic role of an expression (of names in the first place), and it is for just this reason that he normally treats it as unproblematic that reference should be ascribed to sentences and to incomplete expressions: but the appeal to the name/bearer relation as prototype allows him to make the assumption that the semantic role of any expression will always consist in an association between it and that ingredient of reality which constitutes its referent. If this is not the case even for the primary case of proper names, then the assumption that it must be so in other cases is correspondingly weakened. We have seen that, in fact, Frege's belief in the existence of non-linguistic correlates of incomplete expressions —concepts, relations and functions—can be justified, but that, nevertheless, the semantic role of such expressions cannot be explained in terms of their referents in anything like the same way as can the semantic role of proper names. The palpable incorrectness of Frege's deductions from his general principles concerning sentences may serve to deter even the most dogmatic disciple of Frege from overrating the analogy between the reference of names and that of incomplete expressions.

We said earlier that the tenability of Frege's view that sentences containing names without a bearer had no truth-value formed a good test for his later assimilation of sentences to complex names. At first sight, the outcome of our discussion does not tell conclusively against that assimilation. If the assimilation is accepted, then, indeed, a sentence containing a name without a bearer can have no truth-value: but, since we have divorced possession of a semantic role from possession of a referent, it seems that we might agree that such sentences had no truth-value, and thus no referent, provided that it were conceded that they still had a semantic role. But it is clear that it would be mere formalism to maintain the assimilation of sentences to names in this way. The notion of the bearer of a name is antecedent to that of the semantic role of an expression, and so to say that a name may fulfil such a role even though it lacks a bearer has a clear substance. But, at least once we go beyond those notions of truth and falsity which are connected with the correctness and incorrectness of assertions, the conception of the truth-value of a sentence just is the conception of its semantic role: a distinction such as that between being false and being neither true nor false, as Frege uses these terms, relates solely to a truth-functional account of the behaviour of sentences under negation or other operators. Apart from this, we have no conception of what it is for a sentence to have a truth-value: and so the proposal to say that a sentence may have a semantic role, to be represented by a particular kind of entry in truth-tables, but still have no truth-value, is an empty adjustment of language devised solely in order to preserve an implausible contention. The evident failure of the analogy between such an adjustment and the perfectly clear thesis that a name may have a semantic role even though it lacks a bearer is itself evidence of the erroneous nature of Frege's later doctrine that a sentence is a complex name of a truth-value.

APPENDIX TO CHAPTER 12

Note on Many-valued Logics

Let us assume that we are dealing with sentential logics with the four operators &, v, → and ¬. Then by a *valuational system* we mean a sextuple ⟨*A*, *D*, ∩, ∪, ⇒, −⟩, where *A* is a set with two or more members, *D* a non-empty proper subset of *A*, ∩, ∪ and ⇒ mappings from *A* × *A* to *A*, and − a mapping from *A* to *A*. The elements of *D* are called *designated* elements of *A*. An *assignment* φ is a mapping from the set of sentence-letters into *A*. Any such assignment φ can be extended to a *valuation* φ̄ which maps the set of formulas into *A* by the conditions:

(i) φ̄ (p) = φ (p)
(ii) φ̄ (A & B) = φ̄ (A) ∩ φ̄ (B)
(iii) φ̄ (A v B) = φ̄ (A) ∪ φ̄ (B)
(iv) φ̄ (A → B) = φ̄ (A) ⇒ φ̄ (B)
(v) φ̄ (¬ A) = − φ̄ (A),

where p is any sentence-letter, and A and B any formulas. If $\mathcal{A}$ = ⟨*A*, *D*, ∩, ∪, ⇒, −⟩ is a valuational system, A a formula and Γ a set of formulas, we may naturally define Γ ⊨ A to hold in $\mathcal{A}$ just in case φ̄ (A) ∈ *D* for every assignment φ such that φ̄ (B) for every B ∈ Γ. When ∅ ⊨ A we may write simply ⊨ A, and put $V(\mathcal{A})$ = {A | ⊨ A in $\mathcal{A}$}.

We may now regard any sentential logic $\mathscr{L}$ as characterized by a derivability relation ⊢ defined in the first place between finite sets of formulas and single formulas, and extended to infinite sets Γ by defining Γ ⊢ A to hold just in case Δ ⊢ A for some finite subset Δ of Γ. Certain restrictions must be placed upon ⊢ if $\mathscr{L}$ is to be recognized as a logic, viz.:

(α) if A ∈ Γ, then Γ ⊢ A;
(β) if Γ ⊢ A and Γ ⊆ Δ, then Δ ⊢ A;
(γ) if Γ ⊢ A and Δ ∪ {A} ⊢ B, then
     Γ ∪ Δ ⊢ B; and
(δ) if Γ ⊢ A and * is any substitution, then
     Γ* ⊢ A*.

Here a *substitution* is any homomorphic mapping of the set of formulas into itself, i.e. a mapping that satisfies: (A & B)* = A* & B*; (A v B)* = A* v B*; (A → B)* = A* → B*; and (¬ A)* = ¬ A*. Γ* is {B*| B ∈ Γ}.

Now if a logic is thus regarded as characterized by a derivability relation, the natural relations of correspondence to consider between a valuational system and a logic are those defined as follows:

(a) $\mathcal{A}$ is *faithful to* $\mathscr{L}$ if Γ ⊨ A in $\mathcal{A}$ whenever Γ ⊢ A in $\mathscr{L}$;
(b) $\mathcal{A}$ is *strictly characteristic for* $\mathscr{L}$ if Γ ⊨ A in $\mathcal{A}$ when and only when Γ ⊢ A in $\mathscr{L}$.

Owing to the way the subject developed historically, however, it is not precisely these relations that have traditionally been considered.

The study of valuational systems is one of the oldest branches of modern mathematical logic: great attention was paid to it by Tarski, Łukasiewicz and other members of the Polish school, and, even in recent times, it has been the principal preoccupation of more old-fashioned logicians such as the late Arthur Prior. The subject has a twofold interest. On the one hand, a valuational system is the best known way of providing a semantics for a logic. One way in which this may be done is that indicated in the body of this chapter, of which of course the two-valued semantics for classical logic is a special case. The elements of the valuational system are taken as truth-values, it being assumed that each sentence has determinately exactly one of these truth-values. The content of the assertion of any sentence then amounts to a claim that that sentence has a designated value. If we use the words 'true' and 'false' as corresponding, respectively, to 'has a designated value' and 'has an undesignated value', then the different designated values become different ways in which a sentence may be true, the different undesignated values become different ways in which a sentence may be false. There is then nothing mysterious about a many-valued logic, so understood: the sentential operators simply happen to work in such a way that we cannot determine the truth or falsity of a complex sentence merely by knowing the truth or falsity of the constituents, but have, rather, to know the particular ways in which they are true or false. A valuational system thus provides a rigorous formulation of a semantics for a language whose underlying logic is a many-valued one, in terms of which we may give proofs of soundness and of completeness for a formalization of that logic. More properly, it provides a framework for the construction of such a semantics: to complete the semantic account of the language, we have to specify the conditions under which an atomic sentence has any one of the various specific truth-values.

A variation on this occurs when we wish to relativize the notions of truth and falsity: for a tense logic, we wish to consider a sentence, not as true or false absolutely, but as true or false at each specific time; for a modal logic, we wish to consider a sentence, not merely as being true or false in the actual world, but as being true or false in each possible world. For such cases, the elements of the valuational system will be mappings from the set of times or the set of possible worlds into the two-element set {True, False}. Other uses of valuational systems are also possible, such as the Beth trees and Kripke trees for intuitionist logic, the elements of which are explained intuitively, not in terms of objective truth-values, but in terms of states of knowledge.

The use of valuational systems to provide semantics for non-standard logics will retain its interest so long as non-standard logics retain their interest. But the great attention formerly paid to valuational systems did not arise solely from an interest in questions of semantics. Rather, valuational systems were studied largely because of the technical power of the method. Clearly, someone who accepted classical logic, as characterized proof-theoretically, but rejected the ordinary two-valued semantics, would nevertheless find the two-element valuational system of great utility in establishing results about classical logic: he would use it, not as giving the intended meanings of the logical constants, but as a purely algebraic tool for proving things about classical logic which could be established only with greater difficulty by proof-theoretic methods. Similarly, valuational systems for intuitionist logic were originally investigated, by Jaśkowski, Tarski, McKinsey, Rasiowa and Sikorski, in a purely algebraic spirit, rather than with any hope of finding in this way a formulation or proof of a completeness theorem for intuitionist logic with respect to the intended interpretation: the valuational systems were merely a useful technical device.

The reason why valuational systems had, in former times, this strong technical interest lay in the unsatisfactory state of proof theory at that date. The founders of modern mathematical logic, Frege, and, after him, Russell, had formalized logical systems on the quite misleading analogy of an axiomatized theory: namely, by reducing to a minimum the rules of inference, and axiomatically stipulating the validity of formulas of certain forms. In such a formalization, attention is concentrated on the postulation of logical truths and the derivation of further logical truths from them. This was quite deliberate on Frege's part: in this respect (and in this respect alone) Frege's new approach to logic was retrograde. He characterized logic by saying that, while all sciences have truth as their goal, in logic truth is not merely the goal but the object of study. The traditional answer to the

Gg I 14

question what is the subject-matter of logic is, however, that it is, not truth, but inference, or, more properly, the relation of logical consequence. This was the received opinion all through the doldrums of logic, until the subject was revitalized by Frege; and it is, surely, the correct view.

Even here, the step which Frege took was not unmitigatedly retrograde. His emphasis on truth as the object of logical study is connected with his awareness, for the first time in the history of logic, of the distinction between what we should call a proof-theoretic (syntactic) and a model-theoretic (semantic) approach: that is, of the distinction between a formal characterization of some pattern of inference and a justification of it as transmitting truth from premisses to conclusion, by reference to some formulation of the truth-conditions of sentences of those forms. The conception of logic as concerned with truth rather than with logical consequence is also due in large part to Frege's interest in mathematical truth, and his desire to display the truth of a wide range of mathematical statements as a sub-species of logical truth. NS 139 (128)

NS 3 (3)

FT 94–5

It remains that the representation of logic as concerned with a characteristic of sentences, truth, rather than of transitions from sentences to sentences, had highly deleterious effects both in logic and in philosophy. In philosophy it led to a concentration on logical truth and its generalization, analytic truth, as the problematic notions, rather than on the notion of a statement's being a deductive consequence of other statements, and hence to solutions involving a distinction between two supposedly utterly different kinds of truth, analytic truth and contingent truth, which would have appeared preposterous and irrelevant if the central problem had from the start been taken to be that of the character of the relation of deductive consequence. The distinction between kinds of truth led in turn to a distinction between kinds of meaning, ordinary empirical meaning and the special kind of meaning possessed by analytic statements, under which the empirical meaning or content of any two analytically equivalent expressions was to be identified. Such a conception indeed diverged widely from Frege's own: Frege's notion of sense was connected with a notion of the informativeness (cognitive value) of a statement which allowed an analytic statement to be informative, and hence allowed two expressions for which it is analytic that they have the same reference to have different senses. Nevertheless, the divergent view which subsequently came to dominate analytic philosophy may fairly be viewed as stemming from Frege's characterization of logic as the study of truth, and, more particularly, from the mode of formalization of logical theory which Frege accordingly adopted.

The first to correct this distorted perspective, and to abandon the false

CPG 81-5

analogy between a formalization of logic and an axiomatic theory, was Gentzen. By replacing the axiomatic formalizations of logic by sequent calculi, Gentzen showed how it was possible to formalize logic solely by a specification of rules of inference, without any outright postulation of logical truths; the price is, of course, a complication of the notion of a rule of inference, to include rules involving the discharge of hypotheses. In an axiomatic theory, our concern is to establish true statements, and the derivation of a statement from other statements is only a means to this end. In logic the process of derivation itself forms the object of study: a direct approach can therefore be achieved only when rules of inference are alone taken as primitive, rather than the validity of single formulas or the truth of single sentences. In a sequent calculus or natural deduction formalization of logic, the recognition of statements as logically true does not occupy a central place. It does indeed yield a set of logical truths, i.e. sentences which can be asserted as dependent on the null set of hypotheses: but it yields them only as a by-product of the processes required for the derivation of true sentences from other true sentences; given these processes, there will be certain sentences which can be recognized as true by appeal to them alone, but whose recognition as having this special status plays no part in the characterization of these processes themselves.* The generation of logical truths is thus reduced to its proper, subsidiary, role, as a by-product, not the core, of logic.

It can be said of Gentzen that it was he who first showed how proof theory should be done. By replacing the old axiomatic formalizations of logic by sequent calculi, and, in particular, by the cut-free systems, he not only corrected our conceptual perspective on logic, but also restored the balance of technical power as between proof-theoretic and alegbraic methods. The axiomatic formalizations are extremely clumsy instruments for proving general results about logical systems, and the algebraic techniques were enormously powerful in comparison; but the cut-free systems of Gentzen provided an instrument whose power exceeded that of the algebraic methods by as much as the latter exceeded that of the axiomatic formalizations. (Contrast, for example, the ease with which the fact that, in intuitionistic logic, ⊢A ∨ B only if ⊢A or ⊢B can be inferred from Gentzen's

---

* In classical first-order logic, the derivation of a formula, not itself valid, from hypotheses none of which is valid, does not require us, in a natural deduction system, ever to write down a valid formula. This is no longer the case, however, in intuitionistic logic: in order to derive B from $(A \to A) \to B$, it will be necessary, in the course of the derivation, to cite the formula $A \to A$. We shall not need, however, to appeal to the fact that $A \to A$ can be proved independently of any hypothesis.

cut-elimination theorem with the algebraic proof of the same result given by Tarski and McKinsey.)

The use of the technically and conceptually unsatisfactory axiomatic formalizations of logical theories, introduced by Frege, led not merely to an excessive reliance on valuational systems as an algebraic technique, instead of the more powerful proof-theoretic techiques later devised by Gentzen, but also to a misleading perspective in the study of non-classical logics and of valuational systems considered under their semantic aspect. A logic tended to be characterized, not, as above, by a relation of derivability, but in terms merely of the set $V(\mathscr{L})$ of provable formulas. (In terms of a logic $\mathscr{L}$ as defined above, we write $\vdash A$ when $\varnothing \vdash A$, and put $V(\mathscr{L}) = \{A| \ \vdash A$ in $\mathscr{L}\}$.) In the same way, in place of the notions of a valuational system $\mathcal{C}$ being faithful to or strictly characteristic for a logic $\mathscr{L}$, as defined above, the relations officially considered were those holding when $V(\mathscr{L}) \subseteq V(\mathcal{C})$ and when $V(\mathscr{L}) = V(\mathcal{C})$. In practice, it was usually recognized that these relations were too weak, and so the defect was patched up by restricting the valuational systems considered to those that had certain additional properties: but this was done in an ad hoc manner, by reference to particular rules of inference or of proof; thus a valuational system $\mathcal{C}$ was called *regular* if $\{p, p \to q\} \vDash q$ in $\mathcal{C}$, and a valuational system $\mathcal{M}$ for a modal logic was called *normal* if $\{p\} \vDash \Box p$ in $\mathcal{M}$. (In particular, as the above examples show, the restrictions were imposed without any regard to the difference of status between a rule of inference and a rule of proof, as these expressions are to be explained below.) Although, officially, $\mathcal{C}$ was said to be 'characteristic' for $\mathscr{L}$ just in case $V(\mathcal{C}) = V(\mathscr{L})$, in practice the relation usually considered was the somewhat stronger one which we may define as follows:

(c) $\mathcal{C}$ is *weakly characteristic for* $\mathscr{L}$ if $\mathcal{C}$ is faithful to $\mathscr{L}$ and $V(\mathscr{L}) = V(\mathcal{C})$.

Suppose that $\mathcal{C}$ is, in our terminology, weakly but not strictly characteristic for $\mathscr{L}$. Then there exist Γ and A such that $\Gamma \vDash A$ in $\mathcal{C}$, but not $\Gamma \vdash A$ in $\mathscr{L}$. Suppose, now, that there is a substitution * such that, for every $B \in \Gamma^*$, $\vdash B$ in $\mathscr{L}$. Then, since $V(\mathscr{L}) = V(\mathcal{C})$, $\Gamma^* \subseteq V(\mathcal{C})$, whence, since $\Gamma \vDash A$ in $\mathcal{C}$, $\vDash A^*$ in $\mathcal{C}$ and hence, finally, $\vdash A^*$ in $\mathscr{L}$. (This uses the obvious fact that, for any valuational system $\mathcal{C}$, $\vDash$ has the property corresponding to condition (δ) on $\vdash$.) Thus Γ and A do stand to one another in a relation which may be characterized solely in terms of the logic $\mathscr{L}$. We may define:

$\Gamma \Vdash A$ in $\mathscr{L}$ if and only if, for every substitution * such that $\Gamma^* \subseteq V(\mathscr{L})$, $\vdash A^*$ in $\mathscr{L}$, and say that, whenever $\Gamma \Vdash A$ in $\mathscr{L}$, the transition from Γ to A *holds as a rule of proof in $\mathscr{L}$*. (When $\Gamma \vdash A$ in $\mathscr{L}$, we say correspondingly that the transition from Γ to A *holds as a rule of inference in $\mathscr{L}$*.) On our supposition, therefore, the logic $\mathscr{L}$ must have rules of proof which are not also rules of inference: a simple example occurs when $\mathscr{L}$ is a modal logic of the usual kind, in which we have $\{p\} \Vdash \Box p$ but not $\{p\} \vdash \Box p$. Let us say that a logic $\mathscr{L}$ is *smooth* when every rule of proof is a rule of inference, i.e. when $\Gamma \vdash A$ whenever $\Gamma \Vdash A$, and *rough* otherwise. Then, for any smooth logic, every weakly characteristic valuational system is also strictly characteristic. It is easily shown that classical sentential logic is smooth. On the other hand, intuitionist logic is not smooth: we have, e.g., $\{\neg p \to q \vee r\} \Vdash (\neg p \to q) \vee (\neg p \to r)$, but not $\{\neg p \to q \vee r\} \vdash (\neg p \to q) \vee (\neg p \to r)$.

The distinction between rules of proof and rules of inference is a perfectly familiar one. It is, nevertheless, remarkable how difficult it has been to work free of the misleading perspective originally imposed on the study of valuational systems by the approach to logic via axiomatic formalizations. T. J. Smiley pointed out some years ago that valuational systems ought to be selected to reflect, not merely the provability property, but the derivability relation, proper to a logic: but even a writer like Harrop, in whose work the distinction between a rule of proof and a rule of inference becomes prominent, treats of valuational systems in terms not in genuine accordance with Smiley's maxim. In fact, Harrop, like Lindenbaum before him, attaches an importance which is quite misplaced from a semantic point of view to valuational systems which are related to logics in a quite special way, which we may indicate by a final definition:

(d) $\mathscr{a}$ is *strongly characteristic for $\mathscr{L}$* if $\Gamma \vdash A$ in $\mathscr{a}$ just in case $\Gamma \Vdash A$ in $\mathscr{L}$.

(Of course, if $\mathscr{L}$ is a smooth logic, the notions *weakly characteristic, strongly characteristic* and *strictly characteristic* coincide.) Thus the Lindenbaum algebra, which Lindenbaum showed to exist for every* logic $\mathscr{L}$, is in all cases a strongly characteristic valuational system for $\mathscr{L}$. Again, Harrop proves a theorem which may be stated thus: Let $\mathscr{a}$ be any finite valuational system, and let $\mathscr{L}$ be the logic such that the relation $\vdash$ in $\mathscr{L}$ coincides with the relation $\vDash$ in $\mathscr{a}$; then there exists a finite valuational system which is strongly characteristic for $\mathscr{L}$. But, for a rough logic, that is, for any logic for which the distinction arises at all, a strongly characteristic valuational system cannot supply the required semantics; that can be done only by a

* If the term 'Lindenbaum algebra' is interpreted as requiring that there be only one designated element, then their existence is established only for a large range of logics.

strictly characteristic one. The inappropriate attention paid to the construction of strongly characteristic valuational systems, and the neglect of questions about the existence of strictly characteristic ones, even in such recent work as that of Harrop, reflects the difficulty which people have found in extricating themselves from the misleading picture of the subject originally imposed on it by the use of the axiomatic formalizations of logic.

The use of valuational systems to characterize the derivability relation, rather than merely the set of provable formulas, of a logic, as has been advocated in this Appendix, is actually undertaken in an article, 'Deducibility and Many-valuedness', by D. J. Shoesmith and T. J. Smiley, which appeared in the *Journal of Symbolic Logic* for December 1971 (Vol. 36, pp. 610–22) after the original draft of this Appendix had gone to press. Shoesmith and Smiley consider a much wider class of sentential logics than envisaged here, including ones which are not compact, i.e. for which there is a notion of derivability from an infinite set of formulas which is not equivalent to derivability from some finite subset. Again, they do not require a logic to satisfy the restrictions (α)–(δ) here imposed, but instead define a logic to be *normally constituted* if it satisfies five conditions, three of which are identical with restrictions (α), (β) and (δ), another of which is equivalent to restriction (γ) provided that the logic is compact, and the fifth of which is simply what we took as the definition of provability. Since in practice most of their results relate to logics that are both compact and normally constituted, in expounding them I shall here continue to use the word 'logic' as implying both those properties, ignoring the complications of their more general treatment, and, in general, translate their terminology into my own.

It is plain that it cannot be simply assumed that Lindenbaum's theorem that every sentential logic has an at most denumerable valuational system which is weakly characteristic for it can be strengthened by changing 'weakly characteristic' to 'strictly characteristic', since, as we have observed, the Lindenbaum algebra for a logic will always be strongly characteristic for it; Lindenbaum's proof thus cannot be made to yield a strictly characteristic valuational system for any rough logic. Shoesmith and Smiley approach the matter from a slightly different angle, being interested not so much in when a weakly characteristic valuational system is also strictly characteristic, but in when a strictly characteristic one exists at all. In fact, they do not make the distinction between rough and smooth logics; nor do they introduce the notions 'weakly characteristic' and 'strongly characteristic', but only '(strictly) characteristic', 'finitely characteristic' and 'characteristic for provability'. 'Finitely characteristic' means 'strictly characteristic with

R

respect to finite sets of formulas'. The notion is needed because a valuational system α may fail to be compact, i.e., where Γ is infinite, we may have $\Gamma \vDash A$ in α even though there is no finite subset Δ of Γ such that $\Delta \vDash A$ in α. In such a case, α may be finitely characteristic for a logic even though not strictly characteristic for it.

By a variation on Lindenbaum's argument, involving the expansion of the sentential language by the addition of non-denumerably many new sentence-letters, Shoesmith and Smiley establish an analogue of Lindenbaum's theorem: namely that a logic will have a valuational system strictly characteristic for it if and only if it has what they call the 'cancellation property'; furthermore, this strictly characteristic valuational system may be taken to have a cardinality at most that of the continuum. The cardinality result cannot be improved, since they show that the Łukasiewicz infinitely-many-valued logic does not have any valuational system of smaller cardinality strictly characteristic for it. However, when we are concerned only to find a finitely characteristic valuational system, the cancellation property remains necessary and sufficient, but the valuational system may be taken to be at most denumerable. In particular, Łukasiewicz's own denumerable valuational system, whose elements are the rationals in the closed interval $[0,1]$, is indeed finitely characteristic for his infinitely-many-valued logic, but it follows from Shoesmith and Smiley's results that it is not compact, and therefore not strictly characteristic for it. Although the corresponding valuational system whose elements are the real numbers in the interval $[0,1]$ has the right cardinality, it was shown by Louise Schmir Hay, in her 'Axiomatization of the Infinite-valued Predicate Calculus', in the *Journal of Symbolic Logic*, Vol. 28, 1963, referred to by Shoesmith and Smiley, that, while finitely characteristic for the logic, it too fails to be compact (see her Lemma B, p. 84). However, Hay shows that the system with the real numbers does have the property which we may call being 'characteristic for consistency', viz. that a set Γ, finite or infinite, is consistent in the logic if and only if it is satisfiable in the system (see Lemma A, p. 79), whereas, by an example of C. C. Chang's (p. 80), the denumerable system with the rationals fails to satisfy even that condition for infinite sets.

Where a set of formulas is defined to be consistent just in case at least one formula is not derivable from it, the properties of being strictly characteristic and of being characteristic for consistency are independent of one another. The example just given shows that the latter does not imply the former. On the other hand, Shoesmith and Smiley point out that, while positive logic (intuitionist logic without negation) has a strictly characteristic valuational system, the set of all formulas (or that of all sentence-letters) is inconsistent but is nevertheless satisfiable. However, this set, while inconsistent, is not *formally inconsistent* in the sense that every image of it under some substitution remains inconsistent; and they neatly point out that, for any given logic, either there are no formally inconsistent sets, or else every inconsistent set is also formally inconsistent: hence we may say that inconsistency is formal for a logic if there exist sets which are formally inconsistent with respect to it. We may then say that, for a logic in which inconsistency is formal, every strictly characteristic valuational system is also characteristic for consistency, though not conversely.

A logic $\mathscr{L}$ which has a finitely characteristic but non-compact valuational system $\mathcal{A}$ is, under our definition, rough. For suppose that $\Gamma \vdash A$ in $\mathcal{A}$, where for no finite set $\Delta \subseteq \Gamma$ does $\Delta \vdash A$ hold in $\mathcal{A}$. Since $\mathcal{A}$ is finitely characteristic, we do not have $\Delta \vdash A$ in $\mathscr{L}$ for any finite $\Delta \subseteq \Gamma$, and hence $\Gamma \vdash A$ does not hold in $\mathscr{L}$. If, on the other hand, for some substitution *, $\Gamma^* \subseteq V(\mathscr{L})$, then also $\Gamma^* \subseteq V(\mathcal{A})$, since $V(\mathcal{A}) = V(\mathscr{L})$. Hence, since $\Gamma^* \vDash A^*$ in $\mathcal{A}$, we have $\vDash A^*$ in $\mathcal{A}$, whence $\vdash A^*$ in $\mathscr{L}$. Thus $\Gamma \Vdash A$ in $\mathscr{L}$. However, although there is, under our definition, a rule of proof from Γ to A which is not also a rule of inference, this is a rather forced use of the terminology, since it is natural to use the terms 'rule of proof' and 'rule of inference' only in application to finite sets Γ.

We have still to state the cancellation property: this holds, namely, of a logic $\mathscr{L}$ if, whenever $\Gamma \cup \Delta \vdash A$ in $\mathscr{L}$, where Δ is a consistent set of formulas having no sentence-letter in common with Γ or with A, then $\Gamma \vdash A$ in $\mathscr{L}$. We may observe that a failure of the cancellation property is another, and very special, case of roughness. For suppose that the cancellation property fails for a logic $\mathscr{L}$ in respect of a particular formula A and sets Γ and Δ. It follows that there can be no substitution * such that $\Delta^* \subseteq V(\mathscr{L})$; for, if there were, we should have, by restriction (δ) on sentential logics, that $\Gamma \cup \Delta^* \vdash A$ in $\mathscr{L}$, and hence, by restriction (γ), that $\Gamma \vdash A$. But then it follows that, for every formula B, we trivially have $\Delta \Vdash B$ in $\mathscr{L}$; whereas, since Δ was assumed consistent, for at least one B, $\Delta \vdash B$ does not hold in $\mathscr{L}$. Where Δ is a finite set, $\mathscr{L}$ is a rough logic in a quite unforced sense.

Shoesmith and Smiley show that certain systems lack the cancellation property, and therefore have no strictly characteristic valuational system; specifically, Johansson's minimal calculus and the modal systems S1, S2, S3 and Lukasiewicz's so-called Ł-modal logic. For instance, the minimal calculus lacks it because $\{p, \neg p\} \vdash \neg q$, but $\{p, \neg p\}$ is consistent and, of course, $\neg q$ is not provable. Although $\{p, \neg p\}$ is consistent in the minimal logic, there is no pair A, $\neg$A of provable formulas, and hence, in the Lindenbaum algebra, $\{p, \neg p\} \vDash B$ for every formula B; likewise, of course,

$\{p,\neg p\} \Vdash B$. No valuational system can be strictly, or even finitely, characteristic for the minimal logic. For since $\{p,\neg p\} \vdash q$ does not hold, there must be, in any finitely characteristic system $\mathcal{A}$, an assignment φ such that $\varphi(p) \in D$, $\bar{\varphi}(\neg p) \in D$ and $\varphi(q) \notin D$. Since, however, $\vdash \neg q$ does not hold, there must be an assignment ψ such that $\bar{\varphi}(\neg q) \notin D$. But then we can take an assignment θ for which $\theta(p) = \varphi(p)$, $\theta(q) = \psi(q)$, and we shall have $\theta(p) \in D$, $\bar{\theta}(\neg p) \in D$, $\bar{\theta}(\neg q) \notin D$, so that $\{p,\neg p\} \vDash \neg q$ does not hold in $\mathcal{A}$, contrary to the fact that $\{p,\neg p\} \vdash \neg q$ and the assumption that $\mathcal{A}$ was finitely characteristic.

There are few sentential logics which arise naturally and which lack the cancellation property: here is an artificial example. Consider the logic $\mathscr{L}$ describable in terms of the valuation system $\mathcal{A}$ where $A = \{1,a,b,o\}$, $D = \{1\}$, and A forms a lattice with respect to $\cup$ and $\cap$, o and 1 being the zero and unit elements of the lattice and a and b being incomparable; further, for any x and y, $x \Rightarrow y = 1$ for $x \leqslant y$, $1 \Rightarrow x = x$, $a \Rightarrow b = a \Rightarrow o = b \Rightarrow a = b$, $b \Rightarrow o = a$, and $-x = x \Rightarrow o$. Then, for any Γ and A, $\Gamma \vdash A$ is defined to hold in $\mathscr{L}$ just in case, for some finite $\Delta \subseteq \Gamma$, and some enumeration $D_1, \ldots, D_n$ of Δ, with or without repetitions, $\vDash (D_1 \rightarrow (D_2 \rightarrow \ldots (D_n \rightarrow A) \ldots))$ in $\mathcal{A}$; equivalently, $\Gamma \vdash A$ holds in $\mathscr{L}$ when A is in the closure of $\Gamma \cup V(\mathcal{A})$ under modus ponens. It may be shown that $\mathscr{L}$ is genuinely a logic, in our sense; conditions (α), (β) and (δ) are immediate, and (γ) may be verified. Then $\mathscr{L}$ lacks the cancellation property: for $\{p,q \leftrightarrow \neg q\} \vdash \neg p \rightarrow p$ holds in $\mathscr{L}$, since $q \leftrightarrow \neg q$ can take only the values o and b, and consequently $\vDash p \rightarrow [(q \leftrightarrow \neg q) \rightarrow (\neg p \rightarrow p)]$ in $\mathcal{A}$; but in $\mathscr{L}$ $\{p\} \vdash \neg p \rightarrow p$ does not hold, for if p is given the value a, $p \rightarrow (\neg p \rightarrow p)$ takes the value b, and so does $p \rightarrow (p \rightarrow (\neg p \rightarrow p))$, etc. On the other hand, evidently $\{p\} \vDash \neg p \rightarrow p$ in $\mathcal{A}$. This illustrates the fact that $\mathcal{A}$ is not even finitely characteristic for $\mathscr{L}$, which, since $\mathscr{L}$ lacks the cancellation property, no system can be. For this reason, although $\mathcal{A}$ was used to describe $\mathscr{L}$, it could not be treated as providing a correct semantics for $\mathscr{L}$, at least not where possession of a designated value is equated with assertibility; for, if it were, there would be no explanation for the failure in $\mathscr{L}$ of $\{p\} \vdash \neg p \rightarrow p$.

The example also illustrates the fact that $\mathcal{A}$ lacks the property that, when $\{A\} \vDash B$, then also $\vDash A \rightarrow B$. Another valuational system which lacks this property is Łukasiewicz's three-valued one (as do all of his many-valued systems). This has three elements, 1, $\frac{1}{2}$ and o, with 1 designated: for each x and y, $1 \Rightarrow x = x$, $x \Rightarrow y = 1$ when $x \leqslant y$, $\frac{1}{2} \Rightarrow o = \frac{1}{2}$ and $-x = x \Rightarrow o$. Then, for example, $\{p\} \vDash \neg (p \rightarrow \neg p)$, but $p \rightarrow \neg (p \rightarrow \neg p)$ has the value $\frac{1}{2}$ when p is assigned the value $\frac{1}{2}$. However, in this case, where the three-valued logic is defined in terms of the three-element system as, in the preceding example, $\mathscr{L}$

was defined in terms of $\mathcal{O}$, we do have $\{p\} \vdash \neg(p \rightarrow \neg p)$, since $\vDash p \rightarrow (p \rightarrow \neg (p \rightarrow \neg p))$. The three-element system is in fact, as Shoesmith and Smiley state, strictly characteristic for this logic, which is therefore rightly described as a 'three-valued' one. The failure of the law that $\{A\} \vDash B$ implies $\vDash A \rightarrow B$ is thus also the failure of the deduction theorem for the logic, although it holds in the modified form that, if $\Gamma \cup \{A\} \vdash B$, then $\Gamma \vdash A \rightarrow (A \rightarrow B)$. That is to say, $\rightarrow$ is not in this logic subject to the ordinary introduction rule, that of conditionalization: the fact that we may legitimately infer B from A is not sufficient ground for asserting A$\rightarrow$B. Of course, where the three-element system, being strictly characteristic for the logic, is taken as providing a semantics for it, $\rightarrow$ has a perfectly clear meaning, as determined by $\Rightarrow$; but the conditionalization rule seems so constitutive of the meaning of 'if' that we can hardly read the symbol $\rightarrow$ in this logic as 'if', and it is somewhat obscure what is the point of having in a language a connective with the curious interpretation which the three-element system imposes upon $\rightarrow$.

CHAPTER 13

Can Truth be Defined?

FREGE, ALTHOUGH A realist, did not believe in the correspondence theory of of truth. In 'Der Gedanke', he contrasts a picture with a sentence or a

Ged 59 (3) thought. A picture may be called 'true' in so far as it corresponds closely with what it is intended to represent. Truth of a picture is, therefore, relational: we can judge whether a picture is or is not a true one only if we know the other term of the relation, namely the object depicted. By contrast, the truth of a

Ged 60 (3) (complete) sentence or of the thought which it expresses is not relational: there is no question of our having first to discover the state of affairs which the sentence is intended to describe, and then to compare the sentence with it to see whether or not it corresponds; the sentence is simply true or false without qualification. Facts, in Frege's ontology, are not further constituents of reality, of the realm of reference, alongside objects, truth-values, concepts, relations and functions. They are, rather, to be identified with true

Ged 74 (25) thoughts: 'It is a fact that Hannibal crossed the Alps' is simply another way of saying, 'The thought that Hannibal crossed the Alps is true'. Facts, as true thoughts, thus belong, not to the realm of reference, but to that of sense. We therefore cannot say that a thought is true just in case it corresponds to a fact: if it is true, then it just *is* a fact, and there are no two things between which comparison has to be made in order to find out if they correspond.

The notion of truth as applied to pictures can, Frege says, be reduced to that of truth as applied to sentences or thoughts: for the truth of a picture consists in a correspondence between the picture and the object depicted, say Cologne Cathedral; and, when we enquire whether this correspondence obtains, we are enquiring after the truth of a sentence, namely 'This picture

Ged 60 (3) corresponds with Cologne Cathedral'. But, just for that reason, the truth of a sentence or thought cannot in turn be reduced to anything else. If, for instance, the truth of a sentence consisted in its correspondence with something, say *W*, then, in order to determine whether this correspondence obtained, we should have to enquire into the truth of another sentence, namely 'This sentence corresponds with *W*'. If the truth of this latter sentence consisted in turn in its correspondence with some further thing, *W**, then, in order to determine its truth, we should have to enquire into the truth of the sentence 'The sentence "This sentence corresponds with *W*" corresponds with *W**'; and in this way an infinite regress is generated. The same reasoning shows that truth is absolutely indefinable: for, if the truth of a sentence were to be defined as its possessing such-and-such characteristics, we should have, in order to determine whether the sentence was true, to enquire into the truth of the sentence which ascribed those characteristics to the first sentence; and again we should be launched on an infinite regress.

This argument gives a first impression of sophistry. For, one might say, by this means we could show that the notion of truth had to be rejected altogether, whether defined or not: for the same infinite regress can always be generated. Suppose that I wish to find out whether Goldbach's conjecture is true. Then I must enquire into the truth of the statement, 'Goldbach's conjecture is true', and hence into the truth of the statement, 'The statement "Goldbach's conjecture is true" is true', and so on. The possibility of the regress thus has nothing to do with whether truth is definable or not. Furthermore, the argument might continue, the regress is not vicious. For suppose it truly said that the truth of a statement A consists in its correspondence with some state of affairs *W*. Then, in determining whether A is true I am determining whether A corresponds with *W*; but this does not involve that I have to frame to myself the thought, 'A corresponds with *W*'; and, even if I do, I can merely ask myself, 'Does A correspond with *W*?', without framing my query in the form, 'Is the statement "A corresponds with *W*" true?'. It is true enough that, in determining that some statement A is true, I thereby also determine the truth of infinitely many other statements, namely 'A is true', 'The statement "A is true" is true', ... But there is no harm in this, as long as we recognize that the truth of every statement in this series is determined simultaneously: the regress would be vicious only if it were supposed that, in order to determine the truth of any member of the series, I had first to determine that of the next term in the series.

This objection succeeds in showing that Frege's argument does not sustain the strong conclusion that he draws, namely that truth is absolutely indefinable. It does not, however, invalidate Frege's argument against the kind of definition of truth which is embodied in the correspondence theory. The objection in fact displays the condition which has to be met if the regress is not to be vicious, a condition, therefore, which is imposed on any legitimate definition of truth, and is not met by a definition of truth in terms of correspondence. The condition is that the definition should yield the result that, e.g., to enquire whether the statement 'Frege died in 1925' is NS 153 (141) true is to enquire whether Frege died in 1925, and likewise for every other statement. That is, the infinite regress can be neutralized provided that the result of applying the definition of '. . . is true' to the specific instance ' "Frege died in 1925" is true' is that this sentence is reduced to the sentence 'Frege died in 1925', and likewise for all other specific instances. This condition is not met by the correspondence theory. It is, indeed, the case that the regress can also be blocked if we disallow the transition from saying that we are enquiring whether the statement 'Frege died in 1925' corresponds with W to saying that we are enquiring whether the statement 'The statement "Frege died in 1925" corresponds with W' is true. But, if we disallow this transition, then we must also disallow that from saying that we are enquiring whether Frege died in 1925 to saying that we are enquiring whether the statement 'Frege died in 1925' is true. In fact, we could say that the fundamental error of the correspondence theory is precisely that it deprives this transition, and its converse, of justification. The result is to sever the connection between enquiry, assertion, belief, inference, etc., and truth. We should be able to say, e.g., that someone asserted the truth of a thought or statement only when he made explicit reference to that thought or statement: for instance, by saying 'Goldbach's conjecture is true', and perhaps by saying something of the form 'Goldbach's conjecture corresponds with G', he would assert the truth of Goldbach's conjecture, but not by saying 'Every even number is the sum of two primes'. One could thus accept the truth of a conclusion without accepting the conclusion, or conversely. I might freely grant that a certain form of inference preserved truth, and assert the premisses, but reject the conclusion: for I have been shown no path from the assertion of the premisses to the ascription of truth to them, or from ascription of truth to the conclusion to acceptance of it.

Frege's argument thus does not show that truth is indefinable: but it places constraints on any acceptable definition of truth. The constraints need to be stated with care. Let us first take 'ξ is true' as a predicate of sentences. We suppose that, among simple and complex names of sentences, certain ones are picked out as canonical. These must be such that, given only the canonical name of a sentence, we have an effective method of writing down the sentence, and, conversely, presented with the sentence, we have an effective method of constructing its canonical name: we may suppose that the canonical name of a sentence is given by spelling it, i.e. by connecting names of its minimal constituent signs by an expression for concatenation. Then the constraint is that, where A is any sentence, and S its canonical name, it should be possible to derive, from the definition of 'ξ is true', the equivalence ⌜S is true if and only if A⌝.* If 'ξ is true' is taken as a predicate of thoughts, we may take as a canonical name of a thought a term of the form ⌜the thought that A⌝, i.e. one such that we may effectively write down a sentence expressing the thought: the constraint then is that we should be able to derive, for each sentence A, the equivalence ⌜The thought that A is true if and only if A⌝, which, if we take ⌜that A⌝ as having oblique reference, we may also render ⌜It is true that A if and only if A⌝.

The thesis that ⌜It is true that A⌝ is equivalent to A is enunciated by Frege himself in the same essay, 'Der Gedanke': 'It is true that I smell the scent of violets' has, he says, just the same content as 'I smell the scent of violets'. Let us call this thesis 'the equivalence thesis'. A preliminary reservation must be made as to the correctness of the equivalence thesis, quite apart from its status within a characterization of the notion of truth: this reservation concerns the application of the equivalence thesis to any language for which the law of bivalence does not strictly hold. Suppose that A is a sentence which expresses a thought which may, in certain circumstances, be neither true nor false. Then the sentence ⌜It is true that A⌝ cannot be equivalent to A: for, when the thought expressed by A is neither true nor false, say because A contains a name which has a sense but lacks a bearer, the thought expressed by ⌜It is true that A⌝ will be false, although, by hypothesis, that expressed by A is not false. It is impossible, even on Fregean grounds, to argue that ⌜It is true that A⌝ will itself express a thought that is neither true nor false, on the ground that it contains, within the substantival clause, a name that lacks a bearer (referent): for we are here taking the substantival clause to have an oblique reference, so that the name will therefore stand for its sense, which we assumed that it had. Of course, for the particular form of words ⌜It is true that A⌝, we can escape this consequence by construing A, in that context, to have direct reference: but then the same difficulty will arise for ⌜The thought that A is true⌝. If 'ξ is true' is taken as a predicate of sentences rather than of thoughts, the difficulty will arise for the sentence ⌜S is true⌝, where S is the canonical name of A.

Ged 61 (6)

---

* Quine's device of quasi-quotation has here been used for precision: '⌜S is true if and only if A⌝' means 'the expression formed by appending to the name S the words "is true if and only if" followed by the sentence A'. The point of the constraint might be better conveyed by saying that the result of applying the definition to the sentence ⌜S is true⌝ will be the sentence A itself: but, where the definition is an inductive one, converted into an explicit definition by Frege's method, the immediate result of applying it will be a sentence beginning, '*S* belongs to the smallest class of sentences such that ...'. The condition must be suitably modified in the case that A contains token-reflexive expressions.

R*

Plainly, if there is to be a sense of 'true' and 'false' under which it is some-times right to say, of a certain sentence or the thought which expresses, that it is neither true nor false, then, in that sense of 'true', the ascription of truth to the sentence or thought cannot be equivalent to the sentence itself.

It may be objected that we are here assuming a two-valued logic for the metalanguage (that part of the language in which a definition of truth is given for sentences in some large fragment—the object-language—of our language); if we assume, as we ought to do, that the law of bivalence fails for the metalanguage as well as for the object-language, then there is no reason why ⌈It is true that A⌉ should not behave exactly like A. This objec-tion is mistaken. We have already noted that, if the failure of A to be either true or false is due to the presence of a name which lacks a bearer, we cannot on the same ground claim that ⌈It is true that A⌉ fails to be either true or false: if we have chosen to use the words 'true' and 'false' in such a way that a sentence may be neither true nor false only when it contains a name, having direct reference, which lacks a bearer, then nothing can compel us to admit further reasons for calling other sentences 'neither true nor false'. The argument was not based on the assumption that the law of bivalence holds generally for the metalanguage, but only on the principle that we can pass from saying that ⌈It is not true that A⌉ is true to saying that ⌈It is true that A⌉ is false. The justification for this lies in the fact that, even in the context of a many-valued logic, we expect negation to carry only false statements into true ones. This is not due to any failure to envisage the possibility of other unary sentential operators in a many-valued logic, but, rather, because the sole reason which exists for labelling only one out of two or more undesignated truth-values 'false' is to preserve the principle that a statement is false when and only when its negation is true.

There is, nevertheless, a clear truth underlying the claim that we must use a two-valued logic for the language in which we state the semantics of a language governed by a many-valued logic; a claim which must not, however, be construed, as it is by some of its proponents, as showing that there is anything incoherent in a many-valued logic. Suppose that we have a truth-value system with m designated truth-values, $D_1, \ldots, D_m$, and n undesig-nated ones, $U_1, \ldots, U_n$; here either m or n may be 1, but we assume not both. A semantics based on such a truth-value system rests upon the same general conception of meaning as that espoused by Frege, that to know the meaning of a statement is to know the condition which must obtain for it to be true. In this case, however, we must distinguish, as we have seen, between knowing the meaning of a statement in the sense of grasping the content of an assertion of it, and in the sense of knowing the contribution it makes to determining the content of a complex statement in which it is a constituent: let us refer to the former as simply knowing the *content* of the statement, and to the latter as knowing its *ingredient sense*. Then to know the content of a statement—the conditions under which a correct assertion may be made by means of it—it is necessary only to know the condition for it to have some designated value: we do not need to know the distinction between the different designated truth-values or between the different undesignated ones. To know the ingredient sense of a statement, on the other hand, we have to know the various conditions for it to have each one of the $m + n$ specific truth-values: and this means merely that the content of a complex statement is not determined uniformly by the contents of its constituents. The underlying assumption of such a semantics is still that each statement is endowed with an ingredient sense of such a kind as to guarantee its possession of some determinate one of the $m + n$ truth-values, independently of our capacity to recognize which one it has. Hence, in order to state the semantics for a language to which such a logic is appropriate, we must, for each of the $m + n$ truth-values, have an expression for the condition of having that truth-value. By means of these expressions, we must be able to state the thesis that each statement has one and only one truth-value, and, in the logic of our metalanguage, conjunction must be distributive over disjunction, so that we can infer the different possible combinations of truth-values for any finite number of statements. More strongly, there can be no objection to taking ascriptions of truth-values to statements as themselves obeying a two-valued logic. As observed, the theory of meaning underlying the use of a many-valued logic is the same as that underlying the two-valued one: there can therefore be no objection in principle to the introduction of certain statements understood as capable of taking only one designated value, say D_1, and one undesignated one, say U_1, with sentential operators, including negation, defined on them which do not lead out of the set $\{D_1, U_1\}$. If this, the most natural, way of handling the metalanguage is adopted, then it will be legitimate to infer 'A does not have the value D_1' from, say, 'A has the value D_2' or 'A has the value U_1', and similarly for all the other truth-values.

In such a case, it is clear that the only general condition that can be imposed is that ⌜The thought that A has a designated value⌝ should be true (have the value D_1) just in case A has a designated value, i.e. should have the same content as A: we cannot expect that such a statement should have the same ingredient sense as A. In particular, if A has one of the values $U_2, \ldots,$ U_n, ⌜The thought that A has a designated value⌝ will differ from it in truth-value, namely by having the value U_1; and if we have for some reason chosen to reserve the label 'false' for the condition of having the value U_1, for instance because U_1 is the only undesignated value capable of being taken by the negation of a statement in the object-language having a designated value, then ⌜The thought that A has a designated value⌝ will be false when A is not false. Likewise, if we have chosen to reserve the label 'true' for the condition of having the value D_1, for instance because D_1 is the only designated value capable of being taken by the negation of a statement in the object-language having an undesignated value, then ⌜The thought that A has a designated value⌝ will sometimes be true when A is not true. None of this is in the least mysterious, once we have grasped the legitimate but comparatively superficial character of the rejection of the law of bivalence involved in the use of a many-valued logic.

Given this reservation, the equivalence thesis appears at least plausible: the question is what is its role in the characterization of the notion of truth. It seems at first sight that, at any rate, the equivalence thesis determines uniquely the application of the predicate 'ξ is true': for it appears to supply a definite criterion for the application of the predicate to any given sentence. On second thoughts, however, this is not so clear. Uncertainty may arise over the intuitive application of 'false' in two ways. In a case in which we are certain how we want to apply 'true' to a sentence A, and in which there exists another sentence which we treat as being the negation of A, to which we are again clear how we want to apply the predicate 'true', we are tugged in two directions: in that of saying that A is false whenever it is not true, and in that of saying that it is false only when its negation is true; this is one kind of case in which the inclination arises to say that, under certain conditions, A is neither true nor false. Sentences containing names without a bearer are of just this kind.

A quite different way in which uncertainty may arise about the application of 'false' is the case in which there is no sentence which we are disposed to regard as the negation of A. An example of this is when A is an indicative conditional of natural language: we attach no definite sense to the form of words ⌜It is not the case that, if B, then C⌝, and, in consequence, the principle that a sentence is false just in case its negation is true finds no application here, and we are accordingly uncertain in what circumstances we may say of a conditional that it is false. We can, in some such cases, have recourse to the alternative principle that a sentence is false just in case it is not true: but, in the case of indicative conditionals, this fails us also, because we are equally uncertain how to apply the predicate 'true' to them. In applying the predicate 'true' to sentences, we are guided by their behaviour as antecedents of conditionals in much the same way that we are guided by the behaviour of the negation of a sentence in applying the predicate 'false' to it. This fact serves to explain why we are uncertain about the application, not only of 'false', but also of 'true', to conditionals themselves, since we barely have in natural language any use for conditionals whose antecedents are themselves conditionals.

Because of this, an appeal to the equivalence thesis fails to help us at just the point at which we need it. We are uncertain about the conditions under which we ought to call such a sentence as 'If there is an election within twelve months, Labour will win' 'true'. The equivalence thesis informs us that the sentence is true if and only if, if there is an election within twelve months, Labour will win. But the reason that we had a difficulty about the matter in the first place lay precisely in the fact that we do not attach any clear sense to a sentence of the form ⌈If, if A, then B, then C⌉; if we did, we should be unlikely to have any hesitation about the application to a sentence 'If A, then B' of the predicate 'true'. We therefore obtain no guidance from being told that if, if there is an election within twelve months, Labour will win, then our conditional sentence is true; for the information is couched in just that form which we found unintelligible in the first place.

In the preceding chapter we stressed the contrast between understanding a sentence as used on its own to make an assertion, and understanding it as capable of being a constituent in a more complex sentence. The former appeared the primary notion, because every other feature of meaning must consist in its contribution to what is conveyed by the utterance of some complete sentence. But the notion of truth, as we understand it intuitively, is dependent on the fact that sentences can be constituents of other, more complex, sentences. Indeed, the notion of the correctness of an assertion is itself in part dependent upon this fact. This does not invalidate the distinction which we made between those notions of truth and falsity which are required for the explanation of assertoric force, notions under which the truth of a sentence is equated with the correctness of an assertion made by means of it, and those notions which are required for a truth-functional account of the sentential operators: but it makes the contrast less stark than we represented it. We left the notion of the correctness of an assertion quite vague. It is clear that a criticism of an assertion as incorrect stands opposed to criticisms such as that it is tactless, irrelevant or in breach of a confidence, which relate to the expression of, rather than adherence to, a belief. But the use of the word 'true' normally involves a distinction beyond this: a distinction between the case when what is asserted actually fails to be true from that in which the speaker merely lacks sufficient warrant for his assertion. If the sentence whose utterance effects the assertion were not one that was capable of occurring as a constituent in more complex sentences, no such distinction could be drawn: the use of the sentence would be completely characterized by saying that it was held appropriate to utter it assertively in such-and-such circumstances, and there would be no room for distinguishing, among these circumstances, those which constituted the assertion as true from those which provided the speaker with a ground or other warrant for holding it to be true.

pp. 350-1   We noted this in Chapter 10 for future-tensed sentences. Except for the utterances of the seer and avowals of religious belief, the making of an assertion about the future is unjustified unless it is being made as a sincere expression of intention or on inductive grounds, or, perhaps, a combination of the two. We should ordinarily allow, however, that such an assertion, although unjustified, might be true, or, although justified, false. If future-tense sentences could not come within the scope of sentential operators, there would be no place for such a distinction between justification and truth. We should, for example, have no basis for distinguishing between an expression of intention and a statement of intention, that is, between the forms 'I am going to marry Jane' and 'I intend to marry Jane', which differ, not in respect of the circumstances in which their utterance is justified, but solely in their truth-conditions. This distinction has to do solely with the different behaviour of the two forms as constituents of more complex sentences, and, particularly, as antecedents of conditionals. Again, we should have no need of the distinction between the genuine future tense, yielding a statement true or false according to what later happens, and the future tense expressing present tendencies, as occurring in, e.g., 'The wedding announced between . . . and . . . will not now take place'. The difference between the two uses of the future tense is registered only in compound sentences, such as a conditional whose antecedent is a future-tense sentence, or one involving a compound tense like 'was going to . . .'. (For present purposes, at least, tenses are to be construed as a kind of sentential operator, so that the sentence 'The wedding was going to take place' counts as a complex sentence having 'The wedding is going to take place' as a constituent.)

This point does not destroy the contrast between truth-conditions as these relate to the correctness and incorrectness of assertions, and as they may be required for many-valued truth-tables for negation or other operators. The notion of truth, as opposed to justifiability, that may be induced by the use of a sentence as the antecedent of a conditional, or as modified by a tense-operator, remains one for which the law of bivalence strictly holds: these considerations provide no motivation for regarding a sentence as being, in certain cases, neither true nor false, but merely allow us to distinguish between having a good reason for saying something and being right in saying it. In the absence of such a distinction, however, we become uncertain how to apply the notion of truth at all: it is precisely because indicative conditionals of natural language can neither be negated nor appear as antecedents of more complex conditionals that philosophers have floundered over the application to them of the notions of truth and falsity. It is, in fact, from the distinction between truth and justification that the realistic conception of truth takes its rise. Within a realist theory of meaning, such as that advanced by Frege, sentences are regarded as having objective truth-conditions, which obtain independently of our recognition of their truth-values, and, in general, independently even of the means available to us of recognizing them. One reason why such a conception appears so plausible is that the notion of truth is born in the first place, out of less specific modes of commendation of an assertoric utterance, from the necessity to distinguish between it and the epistemic notion of justifiability: and this necessity is in turn imposed by the requirements for understanding certain kinds of compound sentence.

Let us now return to Frege's regress argument against the correspondence theory: for we have still not arrived at a satisfactory evaluation of what it is that Frege's argument establishes. The argument ran as follows. The correspondence theory informs me that A is true if and only if A corresponds with *W*. Hence, in order to determine whether A is true, I have to determine whether it is true that A corresponds with *W*. We saw that this regress could be blocked only if we denied the legitimacy of equating 'A corresponds with *W*' with 'It is true that A corresponds with *W*'. But, if we deny this, then we equally sever the connection between A and ⌜It is true that A⌝, and, accordingly, that between accepting that A is true and accepting A, asserting that A is true and asserting A, etc. The moral we drew was that any admissible definition of truth must enable us to derive the relevant instance of the equivalence thesis: by applying the definition to 'A is true', we must end up with a sentence which no longer refers to A, and is, in fact, the sentence A itself. But it may be objected that, by this means, we have merely replaced a vicious infinite regress by a vicious circle. For the equivalence thesis informs me that I may equate ⌜S is true⌝ with A, where S is the canonical name of A: that is, it informs me that the sentence ⌜S is true if and only if A⌝ holds. But my understanding of the connective 'if and only if' is by means of its truth-table: so what I know now is that ⌜S is true⌝ is true just in case A is true. But I cannot use this information unless I know when it *is* the case that A is true; and just this was what I was hoping to find out.

A definition of truth which permits derivation of instances of the equivalence thesis must be one which presupposes an understanding of the sentences the application to which of the predicate 'true' is being specified: it is, in other words, a definition couched in a metalanguage which is an expansion of the object-language; if, e.g., the metalanguage is a natural language, then the object-language will be some large fragment of that natural language not containing the words 'true' or 'false' or related expressions. But it is now clear why it would have been preferable to have been able to formulate our constraint on the definition by requiring it to yield A when applied to ⌜It is true that A⌝ or to ⌜S is true⌝. Any definition gives a means of finding, for a sentence B containing the defined expression, another sentence B* which does not contain it, and is taken to be already understood, where the use of B is to be the same as the (already known) use of B*: in order to avail ourselves of the definition, we are not required to give any analysis of the notions of understanding or of use. There is therefore no objectionable circularity in the fact that, in order to apply the definition to the sentence ⌜It is true that A⌝, we are assumed already to understand the sentence A. But the constraint which we imposed upon the truth-definition has two unfortunate features. First, it presupposes that, for any sentence A over which we are defining the predicate 'true', we understand conditionals having A as antecedent—a presupposition which, as we have seen, may well be false. And, secondly, if the first deficiency is to be remedied by an explanation of conditionals by means of truth-tables, a genuine circularity is induced, since appeal to the truth-table requires us already to know the conditions under which A is true.

We began by construing Frege's sophistical-sounding argument as not establishing its purported conclusion, that truth is altogether indefinable, but as imposing certain constraints on any possible definition of truth. We framed these constraints in a way that assumed that the definition was being given for some one language, and being given in the language for which it was given, i.e. in a metalanguage which contained the object-language as a proper part. The circularity which appears to have been generated would not arise if the definition were being given in a metalanguage quite distinct from the object-language; but, equally, in that case, the equivalence thesis could not be formulated. We have, however, failed to ask what purpose such a definition is supposed to serve, or whether that is the kind of definition Frege has in mind in declaring truth to be indefinable. It certainly does not appear so, at first sight: the kind of definition he is criticizing, that embodied in the correspondence theory, is intended to cover the sentences of all possible languages, not just to apply to a single language at a time; and Frege's general argument against the possibility of defining truth seems to be directed against a definition applicable to sentences of any language simultaneously.

When a new expression is introduced into a language, a definition provides a wholly adequate means of fixing the sense which the new expression is to bear. It is easy to pass from this to the idea that, when an analysis of an existing expression is called for, a definition will serve this purpose equally well. This is frequently a serious error. Sentences containing the problematic expression will have connections with other sentences in both directions: they may be inferred as consequences, but they also have consequences. In general, as we noted in Chapter 10, there are two aspects to the learning   p. 355 of language. A child has to be trained to utter assertoric sentences in certain circumstances; but he has also to be trained to react appropriately to assertions made by others. When he is merely at the stage of uttering simple observation sentences like 'Fire', 'Dog', etc., others may use his utterances as an extension of their own perceptual apparatus, but he can no more be said as yet to be making assertions by means of those utterances than a dog who has been trained to bark when the post arrives may be said to be asserting that the post has arrived. Before the child can be said to make assertions, he must learn to respond to the assertions of others. (Indeed, it must be proper to say of him that he says what he does in order to elicit the appropriate response from others. In this sense we might say that the child cannot assert anything until he can lie. It is this insight which underlies Grice's account of meaning.)   *Mg*

Learning to use a statement of a given form involves, then, learning two things: the conditions under which one is justified in making the statement; and what constitutes acceptance of it, i.e. the consequences of accepting it. Here 'consequences' must be taken to include both the inferential powers of the statement and anything that counts as acting on the truth of the statement. Of course, both are highly complex, and the situation of the small child beginning to learn language introduces the distinction only in its crudest form: at first, the child is trained simply to accept whatever is said to it; but, later, as he gains a more subtle grasp of the admissible conditions for assertion, he learns to enquire into the justification for the assertions of others and to criticize them. I am not meaning to suggest that the distinction between the conditions for asserting a statement and the consequences of accepting it can be treated as a sharp one in advance of its applications: on the contrary, what is reckoned to one or the other side of the meaning of a given form of statement may vary greatly with the particular analysis chosen. A good example would be the word 'valid' as applied to forms of argument. We might reckon the syntactic characterization of validity as giving the criterion for applying the predicate 'valid' to an argument, and the semantic characterization of validity as giving the consequences of such an application. We can, thus, imagine a child being taught to discriminate, by syntactic tests, between valid and invalid arguments of some restricted kind (sentential arguments or syllogisms); if he is taught in a very unimaginative way, he may see the classification of arguments into valid and invalid ones as resembling the classification of poems into sonnets and non-sonnets, and so fail to grasp that the fact that an argument is valid provides any ground for accepting the conclusion if one accepts the premisses. We should naturally say that he had missed the *point* of the distinction; and this point resides in the connection between validity and truth. But, while it is evidently true that the syntactic characterization of validity is more closely connected than the semantic one with the means we employ for recognizing validity, there is no principle which in advance requires us to characterize the conditions for the application of the predicate 'valid' syntactically rather than semantically.

The distinction is thus meant as no more than a rough and ready one, whose application, in a given case, will depend in part on how we choose to slice things up. It remains, nevertheless, a distinction of great importance, which is crucial to many forms of linguistic change, of the kind we should characterize as involving the rejection or revision of concepts. Such change is motivated by the desire to attain or preserve a harmony between the two aspects of an expression's meaning. A simple case would be that of a pejorative term, e.g. 'Boche'. The condition for applying the term to someone is that he is of German nationality; the consequences of its application are that he is barbarous and more prone to cruelty than other Europeans. We should envisage the connections in both directions as sufficiently tight as to be involved in the very meaning of the word: neither could be severed without altering its meaning. Someone who rejects the word does so because he does not want to permit a transition from the grounds for applying the term to the consequences of doing so. The addition of the term 'Boche' to a language which did not previously contain it would be to produce a non-conservative extension, i.e. one in which certain statements which did not contain the term were inferrable from other statements not containing

p. 397
it which were not previously inferrable. (This, as noted in Chapter 11, is a generalization of the point made by Belnap in commenting on Prior's example of an inconsistent sentential connective.) In the case of a logical constant, we may regard the introduction rules governing it as giving the conditions for the assertion of a statement of which it is the main

operator, and the elimination rules as giving the consequences of such a statement: the demand for a harmony between them is then expressible as the requirement that the addition of the constant to a language produces a conservative extension of that language.

A naïve view of language regards the assertibility-conditions for a statement as exhausting its meaning: the result is to make it impossible to see how meaning can ever be criticized, revised or rejected; it was just such a naïve view which led to the use of the notorious 'paradigm-case argument'. An almost equally naïve view is that which distinguishes the assertibility-conditions of a statement as its 'descriptive' meaning and its consequences as its 'evaluative' meaning, dispensing with any requirement of harmony between them, but holding that we have the right to attach what evaluative meaning we choose to a form of statement irrespective of its descriptive meaning.*

An account, however accurate, of the conditions under which some predicate is rightly applied may thus miss important intuitive features of its meaning; in particular, it may leave out what we take to be the point of our use of the predicate. A philosophical account of the notion of truth can thus not necessarily be attained by a definition of the predicate 'true', even if one is possible, since such a definition may be correct only in the sense that it specifies correctly the application of the predicate, while leaving the connections between this predicate and other notions quite obscure.

We may now ask: what purpose is served by a definition of truth from which each instance of the equivalence thesis is derivable? In enquiring into the concept of truth, we may have different purposes in mind. The words 'true' and 'false' are words of everyday speech, and the least ambitious aim we might have is to give an account of their use within our language. Such an account would resemble any other philosophical account of a concept, achieved by means of a description of the use made of some word or expression or a small range of such words and expressions. An account of this kind seeks to elucidate a concept by means of a description of the use of certain expressions, those an understanding of which constitutes possession

---

* This is not to say that the character of the harmony demanded is always easy to explain, or that it can always be accounted for in terms of the notion of a conservative extension. As noted in Chapter 10, the most difficult case is probably the vexed problem of personal identity. An assertion of personal identity has consequences both for responsibility for past events and for motives in regard to future ones. We can imagine people who employ different criteria for personal identity, but attach the same consequences to its ascription: what is difficult is to say where their mistake lies.

p. 358

of the concept and of closely related ones, where the use of an expression is to be taken as comprising both aspects, the justification and the consequences of an utterance involving it. The description of its use is one which could in principle serve to convey that use to someone who was completely ignorant of it, but was familiar with all other expressions of the language. In so far as our aim was simply to explain the use of 'true' and 'false' as words of our language, it would therefore be entirely in order to assume, in explaining the sense of a sentence of the form ⌜It is true that A⌝, that the sentence A was itself already understood.

p. 414 Philosophical theories of truth have usually been of a far more ambitious character. As noted in the preceding chapter, it is normally assumed that the notions of truth and falsity have an intimate connection with that of meaning. If there were a language which did not contain any words corresponding with 'true' and 'false', we should nevertheless expect to be able to apply the notions of truth and falsity to the sentences of that language. This expectation could be interpreted as meaning only that we make another language intelligible to ourselves by a scheme for translation into our own language, so that a sentence of the other language will be called 'true' just in case its translation is true. It is far from evident, however, that intelligibility implies translatability. It is a commonplace that there may often be no exact translation from one language into another: there seems no reason in principle why there might not be a case in which even an approximate translation was unattainable, or even a language for which there were so many such cases that systematic translation was generally impossible. It might remain possible to give in our language an accurate description of the way in which words and sentences of the other language were used, even though this description did not take the form of a scheme of translation from that language to ours: and we are disposed to believe that any such description would have to employ the notions of truth and falsity, as applied to sentences of the language described, or at least would provide a fairly direct basis for the extension of the notions to those sentences.

What underlies this conviction is the belief that truth and falsity are central notions for a theory of meaning for any possible language. The practice of speaking a language is so complex and has so many facets that it is surprising that philosophers should have been so optimistic about the prospects of imposing any fairly simple pattern on the meanings of expressions: for, if it be a substantive thesis that a mastery of that practice constitutes a grasp of the meanings of the words of the language, it is, on any view, governed by a grasp of those meanings. Yet most philosophical observations about meaning embody a claim to perceive just such a simple pattern: the meaning of a sentence consists in the conditions for its truth and falsity, or in the method of its verification, or in the practical consequences of accepting it. Such dicta cannot be taken to be so naïve as to involve over-looking the fact that there are many other features of the use of sentences than that one singled out as being that in which its meaning consists: rather, the hope is that we shall be able to give an account of the connection that exists between the different features of meaning. One particular aspect will be taken as central, as constitutive of the meaning of any given sentence, and a detailed account provided of how the meaning of the sentence, as so con-strued, is determined from the way the sentence is built up out of its com-ponent words; all other features of the use of sentences will then be explained by a uniform account of their derivation from that feature taken as central. The most popular candidate for this central role is the notion of truth; and we have seen that Frege's theory of meaning is precisely one of this kind, one, namely, in which the notion of truth is central, and in which the detailed specification of the semantic roles of expressions of the language, yielding truth-conditions for the sentences formed from them, is to be supplemented by a description of the various types of linguistic act associated with the different varieties of force with which a sentence can be uttered. Each aspect of the use of a sentence will be embodied in a specific linguistic practice, whose description will form part of an account of some particular kind of force: the theory of meaning will thus give a uniform connection between the truth-conditions of an arbitrary sentence and any one particular aspect of its use. Of course, for certain features of the use of sentences, we are much further towards having such a uniform account than for others, e.g., we have a fairly detailed account of the connection between the truth-conditions of sentences and their inferential ties, the latter being an essential ingredient in a description of that particular mode of assertoric force, the assertion of something as following from previous assertions.

Philosophical theories of truth have usually been intended as contributions to delineating the outlines of some theory of meaning in which either the notions of truth and falsity themselves, or some closely related notion such as verification (establishing a statement as true) or acceptance (acknowledging a statement as true), have been taken as central. A theory of truth in this sense attempts something much more far-reaching than an account of the use of the words 'true' and 'false' within the language, and is at liberty to diverge from that account, even as regards the application of these notions to sentences of the language. There can be no a priori assumption that the use that is made within the language of the predicates 'true' and 'false' is precisely that which is required when truth and falsity are taken as the central notions in a theory of meaning. At the same time, this theoretical divergence is greatly mitigated by the fact that the use of the predicates 'true' and 'false' within our language itself reflects a rudimentary semantic theory. The notion of meaning is, after all, one which belongs to our language, and is not confined to some higher realm of discourse in which a theory of language is expressed: and inchoate theories of meaning, and of the connection between truth and meaning, themselves underlie our ordinary employment of the words 'truth' and 'meaning', in particular as instruments in stipulating or elucidating the uses of other words. As we have already seen, to make explicit the principles underlying our intuitive applications of 'true' and 'false' is itself to uncover certain fundamental insights into the relation between truth, meaning and use.

A definition of truth which takes the form of an outright stipulation that every instance of the equivalence thesis shall hold cannot be part of an account of truth which takes that notion as central to a theory of meaning: it can, at best, be regarded as elucidatory of the word 'true' as a word of the language. It relies on a prior understanding of those sentences over which the predicate 'true' is being defined, and does so in such a way as to pre-suppose an understanding of conditionals in which those sentences figure as antecedents. Philosophers have sometimes maintained that the sole explanation that can be given of the notion of truth consists precisely in the direct stipulation of the correctness of the equivalence thesis: a very plain example of this occurs in Appendix I of Part I of Wittgenstein's *Remarks on the Foundations of Mathematics*. We may label this claim the 'redundancy theory' of truth. Its primary significance is as an overt rejection of the idea that the notions of truth and falsity are central to the theory of meaning: to accept the redundancy theory is to deny that a grasp of the meaning of a sentence consists in an apprehension of its truth-conditions, in knowing what has to be the case for it to be true. For, if the *whole* explanation of the sense of the word 'true', as applied, e.g., to the sentence 'Frege died in 1925', consisted in saying that ' "Frege died in 1925" is true' is equivalent to 'Frege died in 1925', then my understanding of the sentence 'Frege died in 1925' could not in turn consist in my knowing what has to be the case for the sentence to be true. Given that I knew what it meant to apply the predicate 'true' to that sentence, such knowledge would reduce to knowledge of a mere tautology in the most literal sense: if *all* that it means to say that 'Frege died in 1925' is true is that Frege died in 1925, then the knowledge that 'Frege died in 1925' is true just in case Frege died in 1925 is simply the 'knowledge' that Frege died in 1925 just in case Frege died in 1925. In the same way, if the whole explanation of the sense of the word 'win' consisted in a stipulation, for each game, of the conditions under which one player or side was said to have won, then a knowledge of what a particular game is could not involve knowing what it is to win that game: for the knowledge that, e.g., one wins a game of chess when either one checkmates one's opponent or he resigns would amount to no more than the 'knowledge' that either one checkmates one's opponent or he resigns when either one checkmates him or he resigns, which is no knowledge at all. Here we have the crucial dilemma of the theory of truth. If, on the one hand, we offer an explanation which does not display the connection between Frege's having died in 1925 and its being true that Frege died in 1925, then we have missed an essential feature of the notion of truth. If, on the other, we explain that connection in the most natural way, by stipulating that it is to hold, then we become impotent to explain the link between meaning and truth, and, in particular, to represent a grasp of meaning as a knowledge of truth-conditions.

A definition of truth permitting the derivation of instances of the equivalence thesis may not take the crude form of an outright stipulation of all instances of that thesis: it may be an inductive definition in the manner of Tarski. The framing of such a definition is a far from trivial matter: it requires an analysis of the structure of sentences of the object-language in order to formulate the inductive clauses; there is therefore a good deal of plausibility in the claim that such an inductive definition exhibits the meanings of those sentences as compounded from the meanings of their constituents. Two doubts nevertheless remain about the scope of this claim. First, would it be possible to hold that such an inductive truth-definition constituted the *entire* explanation of the predicate 'true'? Secondly, what is the significance of framing the truth-definition in a metalanguage of which the object-language is part? Only when this is done is it possible to derive instances of the equivalence thesis: yet it seems puzzling that any essential feature of a predicate defined over the sentences of a language should depend upon the language in which the application of that predicate is specified.

To claim that any specification of the application of the word 'true' to the sentences of one or more languages exhausted the meaning of the word would be to place the very same obstacle in the way of an account of meaning in general as a knowledge of truth-conditions as we saw was placed by the redundancy theory. It would, again, resemble the claim that the meaning of the word 'win' could be completely given by stating, for each game, the criterion for saying that one player or side has won. Someone who literally knew only this about the word 'win' would be able to judge the correctness of assertions to the effect that a particular player or side had won a particular match, but, if he was even unaware that games were competitive activities in which each player or side was striving to win, he would rightly be said to have only a partial understanding of the word 'win', and would not even be able to give any reason why the same word 'win' was used in connection with different games. An inductive definition of truth only has a point when viewed as a proper part of a complete theory of meaning for a language, to be supplemented by a description of the practice of speaking the language which itself employs the notions of truth and falsity whose application has been specified by the truth-definition. This supplementary part of a theory of meaning, which connects the central notions, here those of truth and falsity, with the actual use of sentences in speech, will to a large extent be invariant from language to language, and it is this fact which accounts for the independence of these notions from particular languages. The connection between truth and assertion or acceptance, which resides in the fact that the assertion of a sentence is its assertion *as true*, its acceptance is its acceptance *as true*, will consist in the manner in which the linguistic activities of assertion and assent are to be described uniformly in terms of the truth-conditions of the sentence asserted or assented to.

An account of truth which is formulated in a given language presupposes, on the face of it, an understanding of that language. On the other hand, if truth is to be made the central notion of a theory of meaning for a language, that is, if a grasp of the meaning of a sentence of that language is to be taken as consisting in a knowledge of the condition for it to be true, then, in a sense, the notion of truth must be prior to any understanding of that language. Hence, so far from its being essential that a truth-definition be given in a metalanguage which is an expansion of the object-language, in order that instances of the equivalence thesis be derivable, there appears to be a conflict between the invocation of a truth-definition of this kind and the use of the notion of truth as central to the theory of meaning, even when it is not claimed that the truth-definition *exhausts* the meaning of the word 'true'. Rather, it appears that a truth-definition of this sort can serve the purpose only of explaining the use of the word 'true' *within* the language, instead of the more ambitious purpose of giving a theory of meaning of the language.

The sense in which the notion of truth must be prior to an understanding of a language, if that notion can be taken as central to a theory of meaning for the language, is this: if an understanding of a sentence of the language is to consist in a knowledge of what has to be the case for it to be true, then that knowledge cannot in turn consist in an ability to give a verbal formulation of the condition for the sentence to be true (or of the inductive clauses from which that condition can be derived). If the verbal formulation were to be given in the language in question, or an expansion of it, we should have a circularity; if in some quite different language, it would follow that no language could be understood until some other language was understood. Of course, we can often explain the meaning of an expression by giving a verbal formulation of the condition under which a sentence containing that expression is true, since this is in effect simply to give an alternative form of words equivalent to such a sentence: this possibility therefore tells neither for nor against the conception of truth as the central notion of the theory of meaning (although possibly it has predisposed philosophers in favour of that conception). But, although the ability to express a sentence in different words is often a good test of understanding, and a verbal explanation a frequent means of conveying the sense of an expression, the capacity to find an equivalent sentence, in the same or a different language, cannot possibly be identified with what, in general, the understanding of an expression consists in, for instance, with what a child has learned when he has learned some fragment of our language. If a grasp of meaning is to be identified with a knowledge of truth-conditions, such knowledge must be manifested otherwise than by an ability to state those truth-conditions: it must, ultimately, be knowledge the possession of which can be equated with a mastery of certain specifiable aspects of linguistic practice.

There is, indeed, another possibility: namely, that knowledge of the condition which has, in general, to hold for a given sentence to be true is knowledge which cannot be fully manifested at all. In this case, the notions of truth and falsity employed as central to the theory of meaning are theoretical constructs which cannot be fully cashed in terms of any observable features of linguistic practice, but which can nevertheless be used to frame a theory which imposes a coherent pattern on that practice in the same way as a physical theory imposes an order on the diverse welter of physical phenomena. Whether the notion of truth is thus, ultimately, a theoretical one or not, the negative point remains: a knowledge of truth-conditions which is taken to constitute the understanding of a sentence cannot be reduced merely to verbalizable knowledge.

From this point of view, therefore, a truth-definition considered as that part of a theory of meaning for a language which specifies the application of the predicate 'true', while the rest of the theory goes on to employ this predicate for a description of the practice of using sentences of the language, displays part of what has to be known by anyone who understands the language, but does so only in an oblique way: it gives a theoretical model for a practical capacity. Here 'theoretical' is intended, not, as above, as contrasted with 'fully explicable in terms of what is observable', but in the sense of theoretical as opposed to practical knowledge: the truth-definition represents knowledge which must eventually be manifested in the capacity to use and respond, verbally and non-verbally, to sentences as knowledge that something is the case (knowledge-how in terms of knowledge-that). In this respect, it does not matter whether the truth-definition is expressed in a metalanguage which contains the object-language as a proper part or in a quite different language: taken as part of an overall theory of meaning for the object-language, it must be understood in this oblique way.

If this is a correct account of the matter, then the equivalence thesis plays, after all, no essential role. Our original modification of Frege's regress argument against the correspondence theory located the fatal defect of that theory in its failure to display the connection between, e.g., believing or asserting that Frege died in 1925 and believing or asserting that 'Frege died in 1925' is true: and we accordingly imposed as a constraint on any legitimate definition of truth that it should yield each instance of the equivalence thesis. It is now apparent that this constraint is too strong. It is still a requirement that any definition of truth, or, better, any theory of meaning in which the notion of truth is employed, should exhibit the connection between asserting a sentence and asserting that the sentence is true; and, whenever the sentence is itself one belonging to the language in which the definition of truth or the theory of meaning is formulated, this will entail the derivability of the instance of the equivalence thesis which relates to that sentence. But we need no longer view the matter as requiring that the truth-definition be given in a metalanguage which is an expansion of the object-language: nothing essential is lost if a truth-definition for a language is framed in a language which has no overlap with it, because the required connection between asserting a sentence and asserting it as true is established by that part of the theory of meaning for the language which supplements the truth-definition, and does not depend upon the formulation of the equivalence thesis.

Why, then, did the equivalence thesis originally appear to have so much importance? The reason is that 'true' and 'false' are not only theoretical terms employed in the philosophy of language or the science of linguistics to give a theory of meaning, i.e. a theory of the use of language: they are also words of the language in its ordinary employment. The division into object-language and metalanguage is of theoretical significance only. A theory of truth which attempts to display the role of the notion of truth in an overall theory of meaning is not a completely separate enterprise from an account of the word 'true' as used within natural language: it is not just that an account of the latter kind requires the stipulation of the correctness of the equivalence thesis, in a manner quite irrelevant to a theory of truth in the more ambitious sense. Rather, the presence of the words 'true' and 'false' in our language, like that of other words such as 'meaning', 'statement', 'definition', etc., witnesses to the fact that our actual linguistic practice is to a great extent self-reflective. That is to say, that practice incorporates a rudimentary and only partly explicit theory of meaning for the language itself. In something of the same way, the terms of art used in stating the rules or describing the strategy of a game are, for the most part, not mere theoretical devices used by people describing the game from the outside, as the technical terms of anthropology are used to give external descriptions of social behaviour; they are terms used in the course of playing the game or in the process of learning how to play it. The notions of truth and falsity, as employed within the language, are therefore not divorced from those which may be required as central notions for a theory of meaning of that language, although, as already remarked, we cannot assume in advance that the two kinds of notion will coincide completely, even in application: the notions employed within the language are, as it were, preliminary or rough sketches for the notions needed for a systematic theory of meaning. Even the crudest attempt to state, in (an expansion of) a given language, the application of the predicate 'true' to sentences of that language, as it is required within a theory of meaning for the language, must (with the reservation we previously made for the case of a system with more than two truth-values) yield each instance of the equivalence thesis. Furthermore, the enunciation of that thesis can serve as an expression of the recognition of the connection between asserting (believing, etc.) a statement and asserting (believing, etc.) the statement to be true, without the necessity of explicitly exhibiting this connection by means of a description of the linguistic activities of assertion (expression of belief, etc.) wherein the connection resides. Hence it is that the equivalence thesis comes to appear to be of such central importance in an account of the concept of truth.

The correspondence theory fails as an account of truth because it attempts to characterize the application of the predicate 'true' uniformly for all sentences; since the truth-value of a sentence evidently depends upon its sense, this assumes that the sense of a sentence can be given in advance of a specification of its truth-conditions, but in such a manner that its truth-conditions can then be derived from a knowledge of its sense. Such a thesis is not intrinsically absurd: it amounts to maintaining that truth and falsity are not the central notions for a theory of meaning. What makes the correspondence theory absurd is that it is at the same time an attempt to present a realistic account of truth. We may suppose that some other notions, say those of verification and falsification, ought to be taken as central for a theory of meaning, i.e. as being that in terms of which a semantics for the language is to be stated. In such a case, it will still be possible to introduce some notion of truth-value as a secondary notion, explained uniformly in terms of whatever notion (e.g. verification and falsification) has been taken as central: but the resulting conception of truth and falsity will not be a realistic one. Realism is compatible only with the view that a grasp of the meaning of a sentence consists in a knowledge of its truth-conditions: and in this case there can be no uniform account of the conditions under which a sentence is true, the sense of the sentence being taken as already known, any more than there can be a uniform account of what it is to win a game, it being assumed that it is already known what the game is.

While Frege rightly rejected the correspondence theory, his conception of truth is undoubtedly a realist one, and it is worthwhile to try to make explicit in what this realism consists. Frege's own method of giving expression to his realism is entirely in terms of the notion of reference: the referents of our words are what we talk about, and those referents are not mental representations of the ingredients of reality, but these ingredients themselves. But truth-value is essentially connected with reference. While we are concerned only with the senses of our sentences, as in fiction, it is indifferent to us either what truth-value those sentences have, or whether their constituents have reference or not: as soon as our concern is with truth, i.e., as soon as, by making actual assertions, we 'advance from thoughts to truth-values', it becomes crucial that the expressions we employ should have a reference. It ought, therefore, to be possible to express the principles of realism by means of theses formulated directly in terms of truth.

One such realist thesis would be this: that a thought can be true only if there is something in virtue of which it is true. This thesis naturally evokes an intuitive response, but is not easily explained, particularly in the absence of any ontological realm of facts to constitute that in virtue of which thoughts may be true. Let us call a statement A 'barely true' if A is true but there is no stronger true statement B of which A is not a constituent. Then it is part of a realistic interpretation of truth to hold, of certain forms of statement, that they cannot be barely true: for instance, a disjunctive statement can never be barely true, since, if it is true, one or other constituent must be true. (It was just this principle which underlay the contention, on the part of philosophers who dealt in an ontology of facts, that there are no disjunctive

SB 28; NS 189 (174)-[3]

facts.) A good example would be the case of counterfactual conditionals. It is natural to hold that a counterfactual conditional cannot be barely true: if such a statement is true, there must be some true statement, not of conditional form, whose truth provides an adequate ground for the assertion of the conditional.

These examples illustrate the intuitive force of the idea that, if a statement is true, there must be something in virtue of which it is true: we have the feeling that to suppose that a counterfactual conditional, or a disjunctive statement, was barely true would be to suppose a statement true although there was nothing which made it true. They do not, however, lead us to any clear formulation of the thesis, that is, to any specification of what can count as there being something in virtue of which a statement is true. We come closer to finding such a formulation if we consider another intuitively plausible thesis: a statement cannot be true unless it is in principle possible that it be known to be true. This thesis is unacceptable from a realistic viewpoint unless 'in principle' is interpreted generously. There may be statements whose truth, if they are true, it is in principle impossible that *we* should ever know, given the limitations imposed on us by our position in space and time and our particular sensory equipment and intellectual capacities. Nevertheless, it is difficult to resist the idea that any intelligible statement could, if it were true, be known to be so by some creature suitably placed in space and time and endowed with appropriate faculties of perception and thought. The two theses are closely connected. To describe what would make a statement true is to describe what it would be to recognize it as true, even if the means of recognition are not available to us.

The ground of connection between the two theses lies in the fact that our original grasp of there being something that makes a statement true derives from our use of basic forms of statement as reports of observation. On a realistic conception of meaning, an understanding of a sentence consists in a knowledge of what has to be the case for it to be true; and such knowledge must, in turn, consist in a model for what it would be to recognize the sentence as true by the most direct means. In so far as the sentence is one whose truth we are capable of recognizing, if at all, only indirectly, by deductive or inductive inference, that is because it contains expressions whose sense is given in terms of perceptual or mental operations which go beyond our capacities: but the conception of such operations is derived by analogy from those which we can perform. One example is quantification over an infinite domain: we can understand sentences involving such quantification as having truth-conditions determined by infinitely many instances by analogy with the finite case, even though we are subject to the limitation of only being able to carry out finitely many observations or tests within a finite time.

Even when the thesis that truth implies knowability in principle is interpreted in the weak manner necessary for it to be acceptable to a realist, it has some substance; that is, it places some limits on what ranges of statements are susceptible to a realistic interpretation (model of meaning). It imposes these limits by requiring that there actually be some analogy between the perceptual and mental operations which we do perform and those hypothetical ones of which we are incapable but by tacit reference to which we acquire a grasp of the senses of the less primitive expressions of our language, according to the realist conception of their senses; that there be a recognizable resemblance between these hypothetical operations and those we actually perform. If no such requirement were made, the thesis, interpreted in the realist's way, would indeed be empty of content: in order to account for our understanding of the sentences of any particular range, it would be sufficient simply to invoke a hypothetical faculty of direct awareness of the truth-values of such sentences. For instance, the senses of counterfactual conditionals could be explained by appeal to a hypothetical being able to know intuitively, of any counterfactual, whether it was true or false. It is obvious that such a purely schematic characterization of a hypothetical faculty would provide no answer to the claim that counterfactuals cannot be barely true, and hence resist a realist interpretation, and flout the law of bivalence (where a counterfactual 'If it had been the case that A, then it would have been the case that B' is taken as false just in case the opposite counterfactual 'If it had been the case that A, then it would have been the case that not B' is true). The question is not briefly to be answered exactly when a hypothetical faculty for recognizing statements of a certain range as true has been characterized satisfactorily for these purposes, viz. when it has been so characterized as both to bring out a recognizable analogy with faculties we do have and to maintain an intelligible connection with the means we actually employ for recognizing statements of the range in question as true or false; and I shall not attempt to pursue it here.

The fundamental tenet of realism is that any sentence on which a fully specific sense has been conferred has a determinate truth-value independently of our actual capacity to decide what that truth-value is. For this reason, even if our language contains sentential operators not explainable in terms of two-valued truth-tables, the introduction of the classical two-valued operators, and, in particular, classical negation, must always be intelligible. At the most elementary level occur observation-sentences, and our conception of truth as applied to these sentences relates to the kind of observation which such a sentence can be used to report. (More generally, the notion of truth for any decidable sentence—for instance, an arithmetical equation decidable by computation—relates to the means we have for deciding it.) But, for our language in general, containing as it does many sentences whose truth-value we have no effective means of deciding, the possession of a truth-value is, on a realist interpretation, divorced from our actual means of recognizing truth-value; although an ultimate connection still remains as embodied in the principle that any true statement must be capable of being recognized as such by some suitably placed hypothetical being with sufficiently extended powers.

A realistic conception of this kind is open to attack from anyone who holds that the sense which we confer on the sentences of our language can be related only to the means of recognition of truth-value which we actually possess. From this point of view, what we learn when we learn to use those sentences is not what it is for them to be true or false, but, rather, what counts for us as conclusively establishing them as true or as false: the central notions of a theory of meaning must, therefore, be those of verification and falsification rather than those of truth and falsity. In the case of a sentence for which we have no effective means of deciding its truth-value, the state of affairs which has, in general, to obtain for it to be true is, by hypothesis, one which we are not capable of recognizing as obtaining whenever it obtains. Hence a knowledge of what it is for that sentence to be true is a knowledge which cannot be fully manifested by a disposition to accept the sentence as established whenever we are capable of recognizing it as true: it is a knowledge which cannot, in fact, be fully manifested by actual linguistic practice; and therefore it is a knowledge which could not have been acquired by acquiring a mastery of that practice. Rather, when we are concerned with sentences of this kind, we should regard an understanding of them as consisting in an ability to do just what we actually learn to do when we learn to use them, that is, in certain circumstances to recognize them as having been verified and in others as having been falsified. The truth- and falsity-conditions for any sentence hence should instead be taken as ones which we are capable of recognizing effectively whenever they obtain: it is in just this that the difference resides between the realist conception of truth and falsity and the alternative conception of verification and falsification. An undecidable sentence is simply one whose sense is such that, though in certain effectively recognizable situations we acknowledge it as true, in others we acknowledge it as false, and in yet others no decision is possible, we possess no effective means for bringing about a situation which is of one or other of the first two kinds. Instead of appealing to hypothetical faculties, which we do not possess, conceived of by analogy with those we do possess, which would enable us to convert such an undecidable sentence into a decidable one, we should describe things as they actually are. The actual fact of our linguistic practice is that the only notions of truth and falsity which we have for such a sentence are ones which do not entitle us to regard the sentence as determinately true or false independently of our knowledge. The truth of such a sentence can consist only in the occurrence of the sort of situation in which we have learned to recognize it as true, and its falsity in the occurrence of the sort of situation in which we have learned to recognize it as false: since we have no guarantee either that a situation of one or other kind will occur, or that we can bring about such a situation at will, only a misleading picture of what we learned when we learned to use sentences of that form can give us the impression that we possess a notion of truth for that sentence relative to which it is determinately either true or false.

Criticism of this kind is powerful: except in mathematics, where it forms the basis of the intuitionistic reconstruction of the subject, the consequences of such a conception of meaning have never been systematically worked out. But it is not criticism against which the realist is defenceless. For the realist, the fallacious step in the argument consists in the transition from saying that a knowledge of what it is for an undecidable sentence to be true cannot be fully manifested by a disposition to accept it as established whenever a situation occurs in which we count it as having been verified, to saying that this knowledge cannot be fully manifested by actual linguistic practice at all. Replacement of the notions of truth and falsity, as the central notions for the theory of meaning, by those of verification and falsification must result in a different logic, that is, in the rejection of certain forms of argument which are valid on a classical, i.e. two-valued, interpretation of the logical constants. In this respect, the linguistic practice which we actually learn is in conformity with the realist's conception of meaning: repudiation of realism as a philosophical doctrine entails revisionism about certain features of actual use. For the anti-realist, these indefensible features of our actual practice arise from a false picture which we make to ourselves of the meanings we have succeeded in conferring upon our sentences: but the possibility remains to be explored that it is just by acquiring these aspects of that practice that we come by those notions of truth and falsity which a realist theory of meaning requires us to have.

The genesis of the realistic notion of truth, namely of truth as distinguished from justifiability, is, as we have seen, the use of certain sentential operators, and, particularly, the conditional. Learning the use of sentences in the future tense certainly involves learning the kind of basis on which the assertion of such a sentence is warranted: but, equally, it is impossible to explain the use of a conditional whose antecedent is in the future tense, or, for that matter, of a disjunctive sentence at least one constituent of which is about the future, in terms of a notion of truth for future-tense sentences which coincides with the existence of a warrant for their assertion. We may thus say that it is the use that is accorded to sentential operators as applied to future-tense sentences (including the past tense, applied to form the past-future 'was going to') which compels us to adopt that conception of truth for future-tense sentences according to which such a sentence is true or false according to what is the case at the time referred to (rather than at the time of utterance). This particular example raises no especial difficulty for a conception of meaning as founded on verification and falsification rather than on truth and falsity, for there is no reason why the verification of a sentence should not require a lapse of time. But it necessarily raises the question whether, in other cases, we may not acquire a realist conception of truth for sentences of given kinds by learning the use of complex sentences in which they are constituents. A case that does raise considerable difficulty for a verificationist view is that of past-tense sentences. Whereas there is no absurdity in the idea of verifying an assertion after it has been made, a verification cannot precede the making of the assertion verified. A previous observation can serve as conclusively establishing the truth of a past-tense sentence only in so far as it is known to have been made, e.g. remembered; so, from a verificationist point of view, it is not the past observation itself, but the present memory (or other trace) of its having been made which constitutes the verification of the assertion. This does not mean that the memory has to be treated as a datum from which the previous observation is to be inferred: but it does place the past-tense sentence in the position of an undecidable one, one for which we may now have, or later find, a verification or a falsification, but for which we possess no effective method of obtaining one or the other. Yet it is impossible to interpret, e.g., disjunction, as applied to past-tense sentences, in terms of a notion of truth for such sentences which coincides with the existence of a warrant for asserting them. It is possible to remember that either A or B without remembering whether A or not or whether B or not, and likewise to have inferential grounds for a disjunctive statement about the past without having grounds for one rather than the other constituent. Likewise, the use of the future perfect tense cannot be interpreted in terms of the future verifiability of the past-tense statement.

It is not here the place to enquire whether the realist or the anti-realist is the victor in this dispute: whether the anti-realist can accommodate

s

sufficiently many of the features of our linguistic practice to preserve the plausibility of his interpretation, or the realist can make out that to acquire a grasp of these features amounts to a possession of a notion of truth-value that transcends our methods of recognizing truth and falsity. All that I have sought to do is to make apparent in what a realistic conception of truth and falsity, such as that held by Frege, consists, how it could be opposed and how defended. A rejection of the law of bivalence resulting from the displacement of the notions of truth and falsity from a central position in the theory of meaning in favour of the notions of verification and falsification is of a much more radical character than one based on the advocacy of a system of more than two truth-values; for the verificationist account dispenses altogether with the conception of objective truth-values determined, independently of our knowledge or means of knowledge, by a reality external to us. Frege did not develop a critique of such a rejection of realism, perhaps because the idealism of his day was entangled with an irrelevant psychologism. But his views are sufficiently explicit to make it possible to characterize him as a realist in just the sense explained here; and, even if Frege himself did not train his guns in that direction, it is of interest to locate the point at which a serious attack could be mounted.

CHAPTER 14

Abstract Objects

QUESTIONS SUCH AS whether or not there are any abstract objects, what abstract objects there are, what abstract objects are and how we know that they exist, what is the criterion for their existence, where the dividing line comes between concrete and abstract objects—all these are modern questions. At first sight, such a contention appears ludicrous: one might well think such questions to be as old as philosophy. But the fact is that the notion of an 'object' itself, as it is now commonly used in philosophical contexts, is a modern notion, one first introduced by Frege. As we have seen, Frege's approach to questions of ontology involves a clean break with the tradition which had prevailed in philosophy up to his time, and which is still ex-emplified by such works as Strawson's *Individuals*. According to the ancient tradition, entities are to be categorized as particulars and universals. It is characteristic of particulars that we can only refer to them and predicate other things (universals) of them—say things about them: we cannot predicate them of anything else—we cannot, as it were, say them of anything. Universals, by contrast, can both be predicated of particulars, and also referred to in the course of predicating other things (higher universals) of them. Thus, on this tradition, a universal can be alluded to ('introduced', *Ind* 146 in Strawson's terminology) in two different ways: both by a predicative expression, by means of which we predicate the universal of something else; and by a term, by means of which we refer to the universal in the course of predicating something of it.

Of course, we can, in full accordance with this tradition, distinguish between those terms which we use to refer to particulars and those which we use to refer to universals. But we shall be unable to discern what differen-tiates universals from particulars if we concentrate only on such terms; for the difference lies precisely in the fact that we can predicate universals of other things. Hence, if we want to understand what universals are, we have to concentrate on the predicative expressions by means of which we predicate them of other things: it is by a study of the character of predication that we shall come to understand the essential nature of universals.

For Frege, as we have seen, this approach is fundamentally misconceived. Terms (proper names) and predicates are expressions of such radically different kinds, that is, play such radically different roles in the language, that it is senseless to suppose that the same thing could be alluded to both by some predicate and by some term. It is true enough that we can grasp the sort of thing which a predicate stands for—a concept—only by under-standing the linguistic role of a predicate: but just for this very reason we can never conceive of an expression as standing for a thing of that kind if the expression was incapable of playing that linguistic role.

This contention is not, of course, a mere fiat on Frege's part: he is not arbitrarily choosing to lay it down that the referent of a term shall not be recognized as coinciding with the referent of a predicate. Still less is it a question of mere lack of mental agility—that Frege is incapable of grasping a conception to which philosophers with a more flexible imagination can attain. Rather, Frege is denying that it is possible, on the traditional basis, to construct a workable semantics for a language: we can do nothing with the suggestion that a certain term—say, 'wisdom'—should be regarded as standing for the very same thing as that which a certain predicate—in this case, 'ξ is wise'—stands for. In order to make use of that suggestion, we should have to be able to construct from it an account of the truth-conditions of sentences in which the abstract term occurred, e.g. of a sentence like 'Wisdom is not confined to the old' or 'Wisdom depends on experience'. That would mean explaining the predicate in such a sentence ('ξ is not confined to the old' or 'ξ depends on experience') as applying to something itself given as the referent of a predicate. But that would merely mean construing the sentence in which the abstract term occurred as the equivalent of one containing the corresponding predicate: e.g., construing 'Wisdom is not confined to the old' as an idiomatic variant of 'Not only the old are wise'. There is, of course, no absurdity in such a reconstrual: as we have seen, an acceptance of Frege's notion of objects does not require us un-critically to admit every abstract noun as a genuine singular term; more probably, we shall want to regard most of them as merely used to form idiomatic variations on sentences containing the corresponding predicate or relational expression. But to give such an account of an abstract noun is precisely to deny it the status of a genuine term or proper name: and just for that reason there is no such thing as allowing abstract nouns as real singular terms, but at the same time assigning to them the same reference as that possessed by the corresponding predicate. Seen in this light, the traditional conception is simply incoherent.*

It would be possible to accept Frege's notion of an object, characterized as the sort of thing which can be the referent of a proper name, where it is assumed that the referents of proper names and of incomplete expressions are of radically distinct kinds, and yet to disbelieve in the existence of abstract objects. Such a position is, in fact, nominalism in the latter-day sense, that is, in the sense used by Goodman and Quine. (Nominalism in   *SCN* its original sense meant the denial of the existence of universals, that is, the denial of reference either to predicates or to abstract nouns: in Goodman's sense it means the denial of the existence of abstract objects.) But, because the notion of 'objects', in general, only has its home against the background of Frege's radical distinction between objects and concepts, even the question whether there are abstract objects requires this background for its formulation.

The fundamental question of ontology is, 'What is there?', where, of course, since an actual inventory is not required, the intention of the question is, 'What kinds of thing are there?'. How the question is broken down then depends upon the basic principles of categorization. On the traditional conception, the first step towards breaking it down consists of specializing to the two questions, 'What particulars are there?' and 'Are there universals, and, if so, what universals are there?', where, of course, the second question raises the problem of nominalism as traditionally conceived. The question, 'What objects are there?', on the other hand, arises only against the background of a Fregean ontological perspective, and its companions are, 'Are there concepts?', 'Are there relations?', 'Are there functions?' and 'Are there truth-values?'. The question about objects then may be broken down further into ones concerning concrete objects and abstract objects.

The argument given above against the traditional conception under

---

* It might be thought that a further objection could be grounded on the different truth-conditions for existential quantification over concepts and over abstract objects. Frege insisted that a self-contradictory predicate was nevertheless meaningful, and may be used   Schr 453-4 to construct true sentences: so from 'No man is both wise and foolish' we may validly infer 'There is something which no man is'. If, on the other hand, we believe in qualities, conceived of as universals, i.e. as the referents of abstract nouns construed as singular terms, we shall be likely to require a quality to be logically capable of exemplification, and thus to say, e.g., that there is no such quality as simultaneous wisdom and foolishness. This is not, however, an impressive argument. On any view, we want to allow a sense under which the remark, 'There is no such thing as being both wise and foolish', is true; and, if this is understood in terms of second-order quantification, then that quantification must be taken as restricted to concepts which have application. or to concepts which logically could have an application.

which a predicate and the corresponding abstract noun are taken as having the same reference depends upon the acceptance of the outlines of a Fregean semantics. With anyone who assumes that the correct semantics for natural language is of some entirely different kind, the argument will carry no weight. Given that Frege's analysis of language, and the semantics that goes with it, are basically correct, however, the notion of an object, as introduced by Frege, is evidently the fundamental one required for the study of ontological questions. The notion of an object thus stands or falls with the supposition that Frege's analysis of language—that, namely, which is enshrined in standard classical predicate logic—provides the foundations for the semantics of natural language. There are, of course, many features of natural language with which Frege did not deal: but Frege's faith was that these features could all be fitted in to the general framework that predicate logic supplies, and this is also the faith of all philosophers of language, such as Quine and Davidson, working within the Fregean tradition; certainly we have no other general framework available. The notion of an object has been given sense only against the background of an analysis of language of Frege's kind, and the question, 'What objects are there?', like the more specialized question, 'Are there abstract objects?', arises only against this background.

The notion of an object plays within Frege's semantics a twofold role. On the one hand, objects are the referents of proper names: the truth-conditions of sentences containing proper names, in particular, of atomic sentences, are to be explained in terms of the relation of reference between proper names and the objects for which they stand. Equally, of course, objects are what predicates are true or false of. While we are concerned solely with atomic sentences and combinations of these by means of the sentential operators, we need have the conception of a predicate's being true or false of an object, or a relational expression's holding or failing to hold between a pair of objects, only for simple predicates and relational expressions. It must be extended to complex predicates when we come to the second of the roles played by the notion of an object, namely the account of quantification: objects are required to compose the domains of quantifiers, that is, the ranges of the individual variables which can be bound by quantifiers. However much it may be necessary to depart from Frege's ideas in detail, if Frege's analysis of language is correct in principle, the notion of first-order quantification will be an indispensable tool for the analysis of many sentences of the language, and, wherever first-order quantification is involved, it must be possible to specify a suitable totality of objects as the domain of quantification.

When Frege is arguing that things of a certain kind, for instance numbers, must be taken as objects, he tends to concentrate on the form of expressions standing for those things, that is, to concentrate on the first of the two roles of the notion of an object. Thus, at a crucial point in *Grundlagen der Arithmetik*, Frege wishes to establish that (cardinal) numbers are objects: Gl 57 and he does so by concentrating attention on number-words used as nouns and on numerals as occurring in most arithmetical contexts, and urging that these have to be construed as proper names, i.e. singular terms. It is then fairly easy for him to make a highly plausible case for this contention, e.g. that '5' in '5 is a prime number' or in '5 × 2 = 10' functions as a term, or that 'ten million' does the same in 'The population of Tokyo is ten million'. But the importance of the question hinges much less on the construal of '5' or of 'ten million' in such contexts as proper names, than on the fact that, once he has to his satisfaction established that numbers are objects, he then takes it for granted that they may be regarded as falling within the range of his individual variables; and, in particular, that, where numerical terms are taken as formed ultimately by means of the term-forming operator 'the number of x's such that $\Phi(x)$', we may legitimately fill the argument-place of this operator with a predicate defined over numbers.

Frege made the natural assumption that it is possible to take one single maximal domain, the domain of all objects, as being, in all contexts, the domain of the individual variables. This was a natural conclusion for him to draw from the simple observation that the effect of a restriction of a domain may always be achieved by the use of a predicate satisfied by all and only the members of that domain: 'All men are brave' may be rendered by '$\forall x$ x is brave', where the range of the variable is taken as being the set of men, but equally by '$\forall x$ (x is a man → x is brave)', where 'x' is taken as ranging over any set which includes the set of men; equally, 'Some men are honest' may be rendered either by '$\exists x$ x is honest', where 'x' ranges over the set of men, or by '$\exists x$ (x is a man & x is honest)', where 'x' ranges over a more inclusive set. What more obvious than to suppose that individual variables may always be taken uniformly to range over a single most inclusive totality, intended restrictions being effected always by suitable predicates? That is why Frege proceeds without further argument from the thesis that numbers are objects to the consequence that any individual variable may be taken as ranging over, among other things, numbers. Hence for Frege an interpretation of a formalized language requires only a specification of the non-logical constants: there is no need, for him, to specify especially the domain of the individual variables, since this has been taken once for all as the totality of all objects. This of course contrasts with the standard modern notion of an interpretation, which does demand that we first fix a domain.

We neither need nor can follow Frege in supposing that one single all-embracing domain will serve for all uses of individual variables: for the most direct lesson of the set-theoretic paradoxes is that, at least when we are concerned with abstract objects, there is no one domain which includes as a subset every domain over which we can legitimately quantify: we cannot give a coherent interpretation of a language, such that every sentence of the language can be taken as having a determinate truth-value, by taking the individual variables to range over everything that answers to the intuitive notion of a set, or that of a cardinal number or that of an ordinal. We must therefore separate Frege's basic intuition, the use of quantification understood as relative to a determinate domain as a fundamental tool in the analysis of language, from his incorrect further assumption, that this domain, by being stipulated to be all-inclusive, can be taken to be the same in all contexts.

FLPV 8   Quine is celebrated for a thesis, expressed by the slogan 'To be is to be the value of a variable', about what we are to regard as being the ontological commitment of a language. The thesis amounts to this: that, in order to determine what objects the use of some segment of our language commits us to the existence of, we have to enquire how to analyse that language in terms of predicate logic (allowing the possibility that the analysis will require the use of a many-sorted theory, employing several distinct styles of individual variables): the objects to which we are committed will then be those comprising the domains of the different sorts of individual variable under our analysis.

In some of the earlier formulations Quine sometimes writes as if ontological commitment were carried only by existential quantification, even, perhaps, initial existential quantification, i.e. as if we could settle the question to the existence of what objects we are committed by considering which statements we are prepared to assert of the form 'There exists . . .'. Clearly, however, it is evident that we cannot restrict attention merely to initial existential quantification: a statement of the form '$\forall x \exists y\ B(x,y)$' has existential import just as much as does one of the form '$\exists x\ A(x)$'. But, in any case, existential quantification is no more to the point than universal quantification. If we are giving a semantics for our language by analysing it in terms of the language of predicate logic, and then providing a semantics of the classical kind for the analysed language, we need to specify domains for each sort of individual variable in order to determine truth-conditions for sentences involving, under the analysis, first-order quantification of whatever kind: hence, if the analysis is correct, our ontological commitment comprises all the objects of any of these domains.

Quine sometimes states his thesis as if we were already provided with a number of theories formulated within the framework of predicate logic, i.e. as if the question of ontological commitment could arise only once some analysis of informal language was already given. At first sight, this makes ontological questions seem quite unproblematic: if we are considering only formalized languages, then what objects could a theory formulated in such a language commit us to save those within the domain or domains of its individual variables? Quine of course recognizes that ontological questions may be problematic, and views this as a matter of when a theory formulated in one language may be replaced by another theory formulated in another language: the problem now is to explicate the relevant notion of 'replacement'. This is hard to do without reference back to the informal language which we are trying to analyse: the sense in which one theory may be said to replace another that is relevant to ontological questions is that in which it replaces it as a proposed analysis of a segment of informal language. At least, this is so when the question is whether or not certain entities, e.g. propositions, can be 'eliminated'; what is really at issue here is whether or not there are sentences of our language a correct analysis of which demands that we construe certain expressions occurring in them as standing for propositions. (The matter stands rather differently when the question is one of the 'reduction' of one class of objects to another class, e.g., to give the classic instance, of the class of ordered pairs $\langle x,y \rangle$ to the class of sets of the form $\{ \{x\}, \{x,y\} \}$. Here there is no question of a more correct or more workable analysis, but merely of an equally serviceable one which achieves an economy by mapping one domain into another.)

Ontological questions can thus certainly arise in the absence of an accepted analysis of a given fragment of informal language; and, indeed, they may constitute precisely a way of asking what form the desired analysis should take. What is the case, however, is that a question as to what objects some fragment of language commits us to take as existing presupposes a prior assumption that the general framework within which the correct analysis is to be given is that of the language of predicate logic: for it is only in relation to an analysis of that form that we understand the notion of an object. Quine's thesis has been the object of a number of criticisms and attacks, most of which simply miss this point: it is only in the context of a Fregean type of analysis of language that the question what objects we commit ourselves to can arise, and, within this context, there is no room for argument about whether the crucial question is as to the domains of the individual

s•

variables, because it is by reference to the Fregean semantics for first-order quantification that the notion of 'object' which we are using has been given in the first place.

That ontological questions can be problematic follows, of course, from the fact that Frege's analysis of language purports only to reveal its so-called 'deep' structure, not its surface structure. Palpably, the sentences of a natural language are not constructed in such a way as to reveal on their face that they exemplify the pattern of sentence-formation enshrined in predicate logic. Frege's philosophy of language embodies the faith that it is only by representing the various linguistic devices belonging to the natural language as constituting often far from transparent means of expressing sentence-forming operations of predicate logic that we shall attain an adequate semantics for our language. This faith rests on the partial success of Frege and of others working in that tradition in accomplishing such a programme for analysing natural language, and partly on the absence of any alternative general model of analysis. There remain many problem areas: ontological problems about whether there are propositions, events, etc., reflect remaining uncertainties about how to carry out the programme in such areas.

Quine concentrates upon the second role of the Fregean notion of 'object', namely in explaining first-order quantification, because he does not take seriously its first role, in explaining the use of proper names. His reason for not taking this seriously is that he thinks we can get on without proper names altogether, construing all apparent proper names as definite descriptions, and then analysing the latter in terms of quantification in the Russell manner. Such a proposal does not in fact effect any significant economy, because, even if a language were viewed as not really containing any atomic sentences (because it contained no genuine singular terms), it would be necessary, in order to give the semantics of such a language, to specify, for each predicate, when it was true of any given object (such a specification doing the work of a stipulation of truth-conditions for the atomic sentences). Quine has even coupled this thesis with the assertion that, where we have no infinite domains, quantification can be eliminated in favour of finite disjunction and conjunction. It is, of course, true that, if the individual variables of a language range over a finite domain, and the language contains terms for every element of the domain, then every sentence of the language is equivalent to a quantifier-free sentence. But if, after having in this manner eliminated the quantifiers in favour of finite combinations of atomic sentences, we then eliminate the atomic sentences by construing the singular terms occurring in them as Russellian definite descriptions, we have reintroduced quantification: the process thus seems

merely circular, and it is hard to see how Quine can argue on this basis
that such a language is free of ontological commitment altogether.   OR 62

Quine's assumption that the question, 'What objects are there?', exhausts
the content of the general ontological query, 'What is there?', is, on the other
hand, in sharp contrast with Frege's view. Such a reduction depends upon
holding, as Quine does, that all higher-order quantification can be dispensed
with in favour of quantification over abstract objects, namely classes. From
Frege's standpoint, such a claim would be absurd, because for him the
notion of a class was itself a second-order notion: that is, while for Frege
classes are indeed objects, so that quantification over classes requires only
first-order quantification, we cannot explain what a class is, or, specifically,
define the fundamental relation of membership in a class, without quantification over concepts. Frege's formalization of the theory of classes takes as   Gg I 9, 34
primitive the class-abstraction operator, 'the class of x's such that $\Phi(x)$',
by means of which terms for classes are formed, and defines the membership
relation in terms of it; whereas, of course, modern axiomatized set theory
takes the membership relation as primitive, and defines the class-abstraction
operator in terms of that (by means of a description operator or of a convention for the definition of terms). The possibility of employing a formalized
first-order theory of this kind does not, indeed, end the argument: it is
still necessary to enquire to what extent a first-order theory succeeds in
capturing the intuitive notion of 'class'. Quine emphatically holds that it
does, while Frege, presumably, would deny this: but we shall not here
further pursue this question, which belongs more to the philosophy of
mathematics. At least this much is clear: given the correctness in principle
of a Fregean analysis of language, our ontological commitment depends
principally upon the types of quantification which are to be employed in
our languages as so analysed. Quine would make the correlation a very
direct one, namely that, if only various sorts of first-order quantification are
needed, then we shall be committed only to the existence of the corresponding sorts of objects; but that, if higher-order quantification is needed,
then we shall also be committed to the existence of suitable ranges of
concepts, relations and functions. On Frege's view, this assessment of
ontological commitment is excessively parsimonious, and it will be argued in
the next chapter that, in this, Frege is right as against Quine. From Frege's
standpoint, the matter should be expressed thus: that our ontological
commitment depends upon what expressions of our language (including
incomplete expressions) have to be taken as forming logically significant
units and therefore as having reference; and this will in turn depend upon
the analysis we give of the sentences of the language, and, specifically, upon

what kinds of quantifiers and other second- or higher-level operators such analysis involves. The general point, however, is common to Frege and to Quine: the ontological commitment embodied in a language depends upon its quantificational structure, as revealed by logical analysis.

By implication, Frege recognizes the possibility of drawing a distinction between concrete and abstract objects: that is to say, he employs, in *Grundlagen*, the notion of 'concrete' (*wirklich*, literally 'actual') objects, though only in the course of arguing that not every object is concrete. He puts the distinction to no work, however: for him, abstract objects are just as much objects as concrete ones, and may just as legitimately be taken as the referents of proper names or as belonging to the domain of first-order quantification, and that is an end of the matter. In post-Fregean philosophy, however, abstract objects have been very much a bone of contention. As already noted, some philosophers, notably Nelson Goodman, have propounded a new variety of nominalism, according to which reference to or quantification over abstract objects is not properly intelligible, and must always be eliminated or replaced by some other form of locution. Others have felt unable to espouse such total puritanism, but have held, nevertheless, that the 'countenancing' of abstract objects is a grave step, intellectually sinful if undertaken without necessity, and have therefore seen reductionist devices which allow the elimination of reference to or quantification over them as something which it is a major aim of philosophy to construct. Some, again, have felt that the recognition of abstract objects is tolerable only when they are construed as 'posits', or have argued that it is permissible only because concrete objects too are really posits. Controversy in the philosophy of mathematics has frequently turned on whether mathematical objects, such as natural numbers, real numbers and sets, are to be regarded as independently existing abstract objects or as free creations of the human mind, or, again, as dispensable altogether.

If we are to make any progress in assessing Frege's ready admission of abstract objects as harmless, a regrettable necessity or the primal philosophical sin, we must have some means of supplying some rationale for the distinction between concrete objects and abstract ones. The rough, everyday, distinction between them draws the line according as they are or are not accessible to the senses: 'abstract nouns in *-io* call feminina one and all; masculine will only be things that you can touch and see', as the gender rhyme has it. This makes the distinction relative to human sensory faculties, for it is evidently sometimes a contingent matter whether or not something affects human sense-organs: by such a criterion, light-waves would be concrete but radio waves abstract. Moreover, difficulties would arise, in

Gl 26, 85;
Gg I xviii

applying such a definition, as to what counted as, e.g., 'feeling' something: do we feel the gravitational pull of the Earth, for instance, or do we feel only the pressure of the objects which support us, or, again, do we really feel, not the pressure, but only the objects themselves?

The distinction is evidently connected with that which we noted previously, between those objects which can, and those which cannot, be the objects of an ostension: those which can be referred to by means of a demonstrative accompanied by a pointing gesture (as opposed to the use of a grammatical demonstrative merely to pick up a reference from a previous sentence), and those which cannot be referred to by such means. When we use a demonstrative to refer ostensively to an object,* the context must, indeed, supply an appropriate criterion of identity, or else one must be expressly given by means of a general noun: lacking a criterion of identity, we should not know, as it were, along what plane to slice in order to detach the object from its environment. But we have seen that there are objects which do not permit themselves to be pointed to at all, even when an appropriate criterion of identity is provided. Shapes and directions were prime examples of objects of this kind: a shape has to be given as the shape of some two- or three-dimensional region, a direction as the direction of a line or movement. In such cases, the mere use of a demonstrative, accompanied by a pointing gesture, will not be enough to determine the object referred to, even when the associated criterion of identity is supplied: we have, e.g., to know not only that it is a shape that is being referred to, but how to identify that of which it is being specified as being the shape. Thus an expression which stands for a shape will characteristically employ the functional expression 'the shape of ξ': even when the term is not itself complex, it will have been introduced as the equivalent of some term formed by means of that functional expression.

We evidently have here an adumbration of the distinction between concrete and abstract objects; but it needs considerable refinement before it can be regarded as adequate. The class of concrete objects cannot be simply identified with the class of objects which can be the object of an ostension, at least if ostension is taken literally as involving the use of a pointing gesture: such a characterization would include visual objects, such as rainbows, and opaque material objects, but not, for instance, a colourless gas, a sound or a smell. Furthermore, we have no assurance that the positive characterization we have given of abstract objects—those falling within the range of some function like 'the shape of ξ'—covers the entire complement of the class

---

* We shall note in Chapter 16 that by no means every ostensive use of a demonstrative is to refer to an object.

of objects capable of being pointed to, even under a suitably extended sense of 'pointing'.

Let us first make more precise the conception of a functional expression which is like 'the shape of ξ' in the relevant ways. It makes no difference whether the functional expression is of first or second level: for our purposes the expression 'the number of Φ's' ('the number of x's such that $\Phi(x)$') belongs to the type we are interested in. On the other hand, 'the capital of ξ' emphatically does not, since the introduction of this expression into the language does not serve to introduce a new range of objects: that is, it is part of the intuitive meaning of 'the capital of ξ' that an object within its range is one that can be referred to (e.g. as a city with a certain geographical location) without any use, direct or indirect, of the notion of the capital of a country. We laid it down as a necessary condition for a functional expression to be of the type in which we are interested that its intuitive meaning should not require us to identify objects denoted by a completion of that functional expression with objects referred to by a term not involving that expression. For instance, while it is possible to identify cardinal numbers with certain classes, and thus, relative to such an identification, to refer to some cardinal number by means of a term which in no way involves the functional expression 'the number of Φ's', such an identification is not demanded by the intuitive meaning of the expression 'the number of . . . '. But suppose now that someone claims that names of numbers need not be thought of as involving the function 'the number of Φ's', even when no such extraneous identification is made. We cannot avoid allowing that the name '$\aleph_0$' has as its intuitive meaning 'the number of natural numbers'; and, given the close connection in our language between the finite numbers and the procedure of counting, it is highly plausible that the fundamental intuitive meaning of, say, '67', taken as denoting a cardinal number, is 'the number of numerals from "1" to "67" '. But we can easily conceive of a linguistic community who have no definite number-words other than '0', '1', '2', '3' and '4'. Such a supposition does not deny to the members of this community a grasp of the basic notion of cardinality, that of a bijective mapping or one-one correspondence. They may perfectly well know how to establish, for finite sets or even for infinite sets as well, that one set has fewer members than, or just as many members as, another set, by appeal to the notion of one-one correspondence. They might, by the use of tallies, keep a record of how many things of a certain kind there were, so that, e.g., a shepherd could check whether all of his sheep were in the fold by pairing them against the notches in the tally-stick he kept for his flock. (There is a frequently repeated story—I have no idea whether it is true or not—that various primitive peoples have no number-words for numbers greater than four: but it is always assumed by those who reiterate this story that such peoples must be virtually innocent of the notion of cardinality. As we see from the case described, there is no warrant at all for such an assumption.) The only difference between such people and ourselves is that they have not hit upon the idea of having an arbitrary infinite sequence of expressions to use as a common standard or tally, and thus supply definite answers in all finite cases to the question 'How many?'.

The point of imagining such a community is to supply a language within which there are names of cardinal numbers, namely the words for the numbers from 0 to 4, but it may be claimed that these names are not explained in their language, even tacitly, as the equivalents of expressions formed by means of the operator 'the number of Φ's'. They do not count, but can recognize straight off, as we can do without counting, how many things of a given kind there are when there are less than five of them: so there is no prototypical three-membered set such that the word for 'three' in that language may be said to mean 'the number of members of that set'.

Clearly there is no case for saying that, in such a situation, the cardinal numbers would be being thought of as concrete rather than abstract objects. The interest of this objection lies only in its forcing us to make more precise the stipulation that the intuitive meaning of the functional expression should not require the identification of objects referred to by means of it with objects referred to in some other way. There is a close parallel between the names of numbers, as used in a linguistic community of the kind imagined, and our use of colour-words as nouns, i.e. as the names of colours. Blue is the colour of the sky, but it cannot be maintained that the name 'blue', as ordinarily understood, involves implicitly a reference to the sky or to any other visual or material object as being that of which the object it stands for is the colour. But this fact is not, in itself, a reason for denying the status of abstract objects to colours.

Now if we are to take the example seriously, we must suppose that, in the community imagined, there is a serious practice of using certain singular terms as names of cardinal numbers: their language must contain an operator with the meaning 'the number of Φ's', and they must have some form of arithmetic, that is, a vocabulary for properties of, relations between and functions of cardinal numbers (perhaps only the finite ones); if they were to use number-words only in the contexts in which we use number-words as grammatical adjectives, that is, as answers to questions of the form 'How many Φ's are there?', then they could not be said to refer to numbers as objects at all, and the question whether they took them as abstract objects or concrete would not arise. Thus, even if they have no conception of infinite cardinals, they are somewhat in the position which obtains for infinite cardinals in the absence of the Axiom of Choice: we may suppose that with each set is associated an object as its cardinal number, but we have no systematic way, without appeal to the Axiom of Choice, of selecting a representative set of each cardinality; likewise these people might use variables ranging over cardinal numbers, or over finite cardinals, and formulate, or prove, laws such as the commutative law for addition, etc. It is unthinkable that, where the words for numbers up to four were the only determinate number-words in the language, there should be a serious use of these words as names of numbers (as opposed to a use corresponding to our employment of number-adjectives) without a background such as this.

Now the reason for saying that numbers are abstract objects rests on the character of the transition from giving answers to the question 'How many?' to speaking of numbers as objects. It is quite irrelevant that, for speakers of this language, a statement of the form 'There are three F's' is not, even implicitly, based upon a correlation between the F's and some distinguished three-membered set. What matters is that '3', when used as the name of a number, is understood as standing for something within the range of the numerical variables, i.e. for something which is, for some concept F, the number of F's (of objects falling under F). We might express this by saying that '3', understood as a singular term, is for these people explained as meaning 'the n such that, for any F such that there are just three F's, n is the number of F's'. It is quite unimportant what procedure they use for determining, for a given concept F, that there are, or are not, just three F's—that they tell this by immediate inspection rather than by counting. This has as a consequence only that '3' is not explained for them as meaning 'the number of G's' for any specific concept G: but their use of '3' as the name of a number depends upon their recognizing it as standing for something within the range of the functional expression 'the number of Φ's'. We could not say that they did use '3' as the name of a number unless they took it as a possible value of a numerical variable; and the only possible explanation of the intended range of the numerical variables is precisely as the range of that functional expression. Hence it remains the case that, for these people as much as for us, the use of a term as the name of a number can be explained only in terms of the reference of terms formed from the functional expression 'the number of Φ's', even though the meaning of the numerical term is not explained in the simple manner as equivalent to a specific completion of that functional expression.

In exactly the same way, as remarked above, a similar objection would not suffice to show that colours are not abstract objects. The word 'blue', when used as a noun, i.e., as the name of a colour, rather than as an adjective, i.e., as a predicate applying to material or visual objects, does not mean anything as simple as 'the colour of the sky': but, in just the same manner, we might explain it as meaning 'the c such that, for every x, if x is blue, then c is the colour of x'. What is significant is, once again, not that we are capable of assigning material and visual objects to equivalence classes under the relation of matching in colour otherwise than by referring to individual representative members of the equivalence classes, and so of specifying the colour common to the members of such an equivalence class without designating it as the colour of any particular object, but the transition from using colour-predicates and relations of colour between material objects to using colour-names by which to refer to colours as objects.

It is essential to the understanding of '3', used as a singular term, that we recognize that there are kinds of thing such that '3' stands for the number of things of any one of those kinds; and, as we acquire the use of a colour-word like 'blue', used as a noun, that we understand that there are material or visual objects such that 'blue' stands for the colour of those objects. By contrast, it is quite inessential to a grasp of the use of a name like 'Madrid' that we are aware that there is a country of which 'Madrid' stands for the capital. So we may modify our requirement that, for an object to be abstract, there must be a functional expression such that that object cannot be referred to save as the referent of a term formed from that functional expression; instead, we require only that an understanding of any name of that object involves a recognition that the object is in the range of that functional expression.

Nevertheless, as we saw earlier, there is good ground for denying the status of abstract objects to colours. In our language, as it is actually learned, reference to colours as objects comes in at a fairly late stage. A child first learns to use demonstratives, proper names and other terms to refer to material objects and to visual objects like the sky, and to use various predicates and relational expressions applying to such objects, including colour-adjectives and expressions like 'ξ is the same colour as ζ' and 'ξ is darker than ζ'. Only much later does he acquire the use of colour-words as nouns, i.e. as proper names of colours, and of the functional expression 'the colour of ξ', together with predicates and relational expressions applying to colours, like 'ξ is primary' and 'ξ is complementary to ζ'. But this order of acquisition of concepts, though no doubt a psychological necessity, is not epistemologically necessary. There is no logical absurdity in the supposition that colour-words, used as nouns, should be introduced into the language before there was any means of reference to material or visual objects, and that these names of colours were introduced by ostension: the child would learn the procedure of pointing and asking, 'What is that?', and would associate with the answer (e.g. 'Crimson') the criterion of identity for colours. As we have noted, the construal of the colour-word given in answer as a proper name rather than an adjective depends upon the child's acquiring simultaneously a vocabulary of predicates and relational expressions applied to colours; but there is, again, no logical absurdity in supposing him to do so before he learns to make reference to material and visual objects. The reason that this can be conceived for colours, but not for shapes, is, as we have seen, that, in order to establish what colour is being referred to, we need only to determine the direction of the pointing finger, whereas, in order to determine the shape referred to, we need some means of circumscribing the region of which it is being taken to be the shape.

Our criterion for objects of a certain kind being abstract rather than concrete was that there should be some functional expression such that it was essential, for the understanding of any name of an object of that kind, that the referent of the name be recognized as lying within the range of that functional expression. (Under this formulation, it is no longer necessary to make any restriction on the kind of functional expression in question, since the definition itself rules out those like 'the capital of ξ'.) From the case of colours, we see that we should not construe the necessity invoked in the definition as relative to a particular language or a particular order of acquisition of the different parts of the language: it must govern the use of any terms, in any language, for objects of the given kind. It may reasonably be said of an English speaker that making the transition from the use of colour-words only as adjectives to their use as nouns as well involves an acquisition of the use of the functional expression 'the colour of ξ', and that it is therefore essential, for such a speaker to understand the meaning of a colour-word used as a noun, that he takes it as standing for something in the range of that functional expression. But this is not enough to lead us to classify colours as abstract objects, since we can conceive of a language containing colour-words used only as nouns, and containing no expression playing the role of 'the colour of ξ', since containing no terms which could fill its argument-place.

Colours are, indeed, on the borderline between concrete and abstract objects: they would certainly be classified as universals on the traditional view, and a slightly different way of construing the criterion we have been using would put them on the abstract side of the fence. It remains that there is a highly important distinction between colours on the one hand and such things as shapes and directions on the other, a distinction that we may express by saying that a shape has to be taken as the shape of something and a direction as the direction of something, but a colour need not necessarily be understood as the colour of anything: our result, that colours are to be regarded as concrete objects but shapes as abstract ones, agrees with those of Goodman and Quine, and for much the same reason. The sense in which a shape or a direction must be 'of' something is very akin to the conception of logical dependence which Aristotle expresses by the preposition 'in' *Cat* 1ᵃ 24 when he gives as part of his characterization of a substance that it is not 'in' anything else. Of course, it may be objected that there are shapes such that there is nothing of which they are the shape, so that we ought not to claim more than that, for any shape, there *could* be something of which it was the shape: but here we encounter the question as to the criterion of existence for abstract objects, which we shall treat of later, when we have settled the present question, how to classify objects as concrete or abstract.

The condition we have formulated for being an abstract object is certainly sufficient, but it does not appear to be necessary. Frege cites, as a typical example of an abstract object, the centre of mass of the Solar System. The Gl 26 functional expression, 'the centre of mass of ξ', is certainly not one of the kind we have been considering, but resembles 'the capital of ξ': a centre of mass is a point, and there are many ways in which that point might be referred to otherwise than as the centre of mass of anything. Points, on the other hand, seem eminently to be candidates for the status of abstract object: but it is difficult to find a functional expression which is related to points as 'the shape of ξ' is related to shapes.

A moment's thought will yield a multitude of further examples: things to which we give names, names which certainly function in sentences as singular terms, things which have reasonably well-defined criteria of identity and which can be counted, but which do not appear to lie within the range of any functional expression of the kind Frege considers when discussing the construal of numbers as objects. Conventions in Bridge and openings in chess have what are indisputably proper names in the strict sense, such as 'Solid Suit Convention', 'Blackwood', 'Sicilian Defence', 'Giuoco Piano'. Games themselves have proper names, but are hardly concrete objects: an evening's play at Poker might be classified as an event, and thus a concrete object, but the game of Poker itself is as much an abstract object as the letter A. Indeed, as we reflect on the variety of objects that can be named, the dichotomy between concrete and abstract objects comes to seem far too crude: to which of the two categories should we assign the Mistral, for instance? This feeling, of an unsurveyable multiplicity of types of object, naturally reinforces Frege's contention that the distinction between concrete and abstract objects is not of fundamental logical significance: perhaps there are just objects, and no purpose is served by attempting any finer classification.

To reach such a conclusion is, however, to overlook the crucial question of the kind of sense possessed by proper names or other singular terms for different types of object. We sketched a rough model for the sense of a proper name for a concrete object: to grasp the sense of such a name is to have a criterion of identification of an object as the referent of the name. In many cases, the phrase 'criterion of identification' is too ponderous, and it would be preferable to substitute something like 'propensity for recognition': but the general idea was that a grasp of the sense of the name consisted in a capacity to say, of any given object, whether or not it was the referent or bearer of the name. Here, again, qualification is needed: particularly when the name is a complex one, it may be impossible to determine from mere inspection whether some object presented is that for which the name stands; I understand the term 'Lucy's goldfish' by knowing what is needed, for any given object, to establish that the object is the referent of the term, but, of course, I cannot be expected to be able to determine that question at a glance. At least from Frege's standpoint, there cannot even be a requirement of effective decidability: as long as I can recognize something as settling the question, it is unnecessary that I should be able in all cases to employ some procedure which will lead to a settlement of it.

In offering this account, we were faced with the difficulty of explaining the notion of an object's being 'given' or 'presented': in order to be able to tell, of some object, that it is, or that it is not, the referent of a name, I must have some way of picking out the object that I am identifying otherwise than by the use of the name. In the case of concrete objects, we supposed that this would be done by the use of a demonstrative. On this account, therefore, the understanding of the sense of a name amounts to an ability to determine the truth-value—more properly, to know what would determine the truth-value—of a sentence, containing the name in question, of a quite particular kind, viz. one of the kind we called a 'recognition statement': a sentence of the form 'This is X', where 'X' is the name in question and the 'is' occurs as the sign of identity. Such an ability of course presupposes a grasp of the associated criterion of identity, so that the sense of the name is complex. To grasp its sense, a speaker of the language must, as it were, first know of what kind of object it is the name, i.e. must grasp the criterion of identity associated with it, and then further must be able to know how to recognize a particular object of that kind as the referent of the name.

An account along these lines needs to be modified in any case of a name whose referent is not a possible object of ostension, an object which cannot be presented by the use of a demonstrative accompanied by a pointing gesture (against the background of some understood criterion of identity). Whether or not the distinction between concrete and abstract objects be an apt one, we have already noted that certain objects, of a kind most naturally called 'abstract', cannot be considered as possible objects of ostension. For names of such objects, the account of what it is to grasp the sense of such a name must be revised so as to consider the ability to recognize an object as the referent of the name as relative to some other standard method of being given or presented with such an object. In the case of those abstract objects which can be characterized as being within the range of some functional expression of the kind we have considered, such a method lies to hand: an object of the category determined by any one such functional expression is to be thought of as being given by specifying a particular argument for the function. Where the functional expression is of first level, this will mean specifying an object as argument: e.g. specifying a line of which the object we are concerned with is the direction, or, e.g., a material body of which the object we are concerned with is the shape. It may be that the object which is to be taken as the argument of the function can itself be presented ostensively; if not, then the primitive method of specification of such an object will depend upon the kind of sense possessed by a name for an object of that kind. Where the functional expression is of higher level, e.g. 'the number of Φ's', the argument will not be an object, but a concept, relation or function, and will have to be specified by means of some linguistic expression of the appropriate logical type. We have seen, however, that not every abstract object—a fortiori, not every object which is not a possible object of ostension—can be regarded as within the range of a functional expression of this kind: and so we must seek some more general account of the senses of names.

The notion of what can be an object of ostension is, in practice, nothing like so rigid as we have made it out, in principle, to be. Strictly speaking, a shape cannot be the object of an ostension, in the way that a colour can; and this distinction does mark an important difference between the notion of shape and that of colour, a difference we have taken as a ground for regarding shapes but not colours as abstract objects. But the distinction is very much a difference in principle: we are not ordinarily conscious of the necessity for specifying, of a shape which we are indicating, what we are taking it as the shape of, or of the difference in this regard of a colour that we wish to indicate; not only because we often do specify the object which the colour is the colour of, instead of employing raw ostension, but also because the specification of the object, in the case of shape, is frequently tacit. A letter of an alphabet is, after all, merely a shape—a shape with a particular significance (when what is meant by 'a letter' is a type rather than a token, that is, where 'letter' is being used as when we say that there are twenty-six letters in the English alphabet). But it would be perfectly normal to point to a particular place in a piece of writing or printing, in some script one was not fully familiar with, and ask, 'What is that letter?': the context makes it superfluous to specify what it is that one is taking as forming the letter. When taken as a type, not a token, a move in chess, such as Castling King's side or 1. P-K4 . . . , is surely an abstract object: yet we should feel little oddity about the use of a demonstrative, as in 'What is that move called?' or 'Is that move to be recommended?', even where it was quite clear that 'move' was being used in a type and not a token sense. Conversely, many material objects are not in practice possible objects of ostension, because they are too large and too near, or too small or remote, or simply because they do not affect our senses. One cannot point to the Solar System, though perhaps if space travel progresses sufficiently it may become possible to do so: only an astronaut can point to the Earth. Likewise, one cannot point to a colourless gas; and to smells, sounds and events the notion of pointing hardly seems to apply.

The pointing gesture is an adjunct to the use of a demonstrative when the object indicated emits, reflects or refracts light, and is large enough and near enough to be seen, but far enough and small enough to have a determinate direction. There are several other manners of employing a demonstrative which do not require an ancillary gesture, but can still be regarded as modes of ostension: in one of these, the word 'this' can be construed as meaning something like 'the one we are in' or 'the nearest one'. The occasions on which it is possible to point to a city are comparatively rare: but the phrase 'this city', used to refer to the city in which the speaker is, is extremely common. If one may say, 'this city', or, 'this country', and if such a phrase, though involving no pointing, may count as effecting a species of ostension, then with equal justice the phrases 'this planetary system' and 'this galaxy' may also so count. This form of ostension provides another way in which we may, in the context of our account of the senses of proper names, regard certain objects as being given—given as that object of an understood kind in which the speaker is located or which alone is near at hand to him. And something similar may be held as applying to sounds and smells. If someone asks, 'What is that smell?', he will not use a pointing gesture, since the sense of smell is not directional; and if he asks, 'What is that sound?', he is unlikely to do so, the sense of hearing being so weakly directional: but these too may be taken as types of ostension appropriate to the objects in question, 'that' here being interpretable as meaning something like 'the one currently impinging on our senses'.

It is thus a sufficient condition for something to be a concrete object that it should affect our senses, and can, therefore, be referred to in terms of its sensory impact. This is not, however, a necessary condition, as in the case of a colourless and odourless gas. We might, accordingly, propose as a necessary and sufficient condition that the object be perceptible to some conceivable sensory faculty, though not necessarily one that was even an extension of any of the senses we possess. It would be equally good to say that the presence of the object could be detected by some instrument or apparatus; and this amounts to no more than saying that the object is one which can be the cause of change. More generally, a concrete object can take part in causal interactions: an abstract object can neither be the cause nor the subject of change.

To say that an abstract object cannot be the cause of change seems plausible enough, but the thesis that it cannot be the subject of change is problematic. Cannot the shape of an object change? Cannot the number of sheep on a hill increase? Cannot the centre of mass of Jupiter change position? In the case of number, the answer given by Frege is that there is no one number which is, at all times, the number of sheep on the hill but which is now greater, now smaller, and now vanishes: rather, the change consists in the fact that the number which is the number of sheep on the hill at a certain time is smaller than the number which is the number of G1 46; NS sheep on the hill at a later time. (Frege's actual example is the number of $^{147 (135)}$ inhabitants of Berlin.) We could say the same in the other cases: the centre of mass of Jupiter at one time is not the same point as Jupiter's centre of mass at another time. It is true that we are not absolutely obliged to construc such phrases in Frege's way: we could take, e.g., 'the size of the population of London' as the name of a variable number; but this would have the inconvenience that variable numbers, of this kind, cannot be identified with the numbers that belong to mathematical number-systems, and are quite superfluous, since Frege's method of eliminating them is always to hand. It should be noted, however, that whether or not we speak of objects of a given kind as possible subjects of change is to a marked extent dependent on arbitrary features of the structure of our sentences, or of the analysis which we give of them. If shapes cannot change, and what is called a change of shape is a change, on the part of some object, from having one shape to having another, then the same ought to be said about colours, and we lose our former reason for distinguishing colours as concrete objects from shapes as abstract ones. That reason was that colours can be objects of ostension: but, for a colour to be viewed as a possible object of ostension, it must be allowed to have a position, and hence to be the subject of change, for instance when a colour goes from a given position.

Although Frege's argument may rebut the suggested instances of changes of which abstract objects can be the subject, it still does not show why they cannot be the subjects of other changes. Granted that, when the thirty-first sheep strays on to the hill, there is no number that has increased, is it still not the case that the number 30 has suffered a different change, namely from being the number of sheep on the hill to no longer being the number of sheep on the hill? Inspired by the success of the previous rebuttal, we might attempt to argue that no change has occurred: 30 was, and still is, the number of sheep that were on the hill at a certain time, and is not, and never was, the number of sheep that are on the hill at a later time. But this will not work, since, by this means, we could establish that no change ever takes place: when Robinson grows a beard, he still is a man who was clean-shaven at an earlier date, and he always was a man who would have a beard at that date. If change is to be analysed as Russell suggested, namely as the possession of different truth-values by statements which differ internally only as to their time-references, then presumably a change in an object would be analysed similarly, as a difference in truth-value between two statements containing a term referring to the object, and differing internally only as to their time-references; and, in that case, the above example does illustrate the kind of change which a number may undergo. Our intuitive criterion for what constitutes a change *in* an object is much stricter than this; whether it can be made precise, I do not know, but it is certainly hard to characterize. We might describe an internal change as being one such that Russell's two statements contained no reference to or quantification over any other objects. This would be far too strict: there are certainly relational changes which are nevertheless changes in the object. When a man gets married, or becomes a father, these are certainly changes of which he is the subject; and the paradigmatic example is a change of spatial position. It would still be too strict to admit only those relational changes which actually accompanied an internal change, and too weak to demand only that the relational change be liable to result in an internal one. The closest I can get is that it must be a change which involves some causal interaction between the object and something else; and, in the case of abstract objects,

PoM 469

that brings us back to the principle that they cannot take part in causal interactions, which we now see as a ground for speaking in such a way as not to recognize them as possible subjects of change.

Why cannot an abstract object be involved in causal interaction with other objects? It is tempting to go round in a circle, and say that causal interaction always entails some internal change in the objects involved: but this is not always our picture of causal interaction, for instance not in the case of gravitational attraction. It is, rather, a matter of the non-explanatory character of any statement that can be made about the abstract object in itself. If, for the sake of argument, we accept the popular belief that a red rag infuriates a bull, are we to say that the colour causes the bull to charge? There seems no especial reason why we should not: but this is because we are not regarding a colour as an abstract object, and therefore allowing it to have a spatial position, contingently. We can explain the bull's rage by the fact that the colour was there, where he could see it. Contrast the theory that the taste of a substance is determined by the shape of the molecules. Could we say that a certain shape causes a bitter taste? In so far as we regard a shape as a genuine abstract object, and therefore as not having, in itself, a spatial position, but merely as enjoying the property of being the shape of this or that object or configuration, we are reluctant to say this: the taste resulted, not from the presence of the shape, but from the presence of a molecule of that shape. This reflects the fact that shapes are *of* objects in a way that colours are not: it is not merely that we do not choose to say that a shape is in a particular place, whereas we more readily say this of a colour, but that it would make no sense to say that a shape was in a place, without giving some indication of what it was the shape of. A point has, indeed, spatial location, but, in the sense in which a point cannot move, not contingently so. To give a cause of some occurrence, we must cite some contingent fact. (This truistic principle can be accepted without any deep analysis of 'contingent', since all we need is its intuitive sense of 'something that might have been otherwise'; whether or not a precise explanation is possible for this 'might', it is platitudinous that statements of causality yield counterfactual conditionals.) No contingent fact about an abstract object can be cited that cannot more naturally be construed as a fact about concrete ones, for instance, the concrete object which the abstract one is 'of': and hence we do not regard abstract objects as being themselves causally efficacious or the subjects of causal effects.

What is important about abstract objects is not so much the exact line of demarcation between them and concrete ones: it will have become apparent that this line is not clearly marked, and the way we trace it will depend in detail both on the fine structure of our language, in respects easily susceptible to adjustment, and on how we choose to formulate the criterion of distinction. There is, in fact, no reason for wanting a sharp distinction between concrete and abstract objects: the kinds of singular terms which we employ in our language are too variegated for there to be any point in that. The distinction is nevertheless of importance because of the different ways in which the notion of reference applies to names of different kinds. The sense of a proper name is the means by which we recognize an object as its referent. In the case of a name for a concrete object—the case which forms the prototype for the notion of reference— we may equate a grasp of its sense with a capacity to recognize when a recognition statement involving the name has been established, that is, when an object picked out by means of ostension can be identified as the bearer of the name. To the extent that the notion of ostension may be broadened to include reference to an object by its effect on a sense other than sight, its spatial proximity, or some observable causal effect, this model for the sense of a proper name may be extended to names of concrete objects which cannot be seen or are too large or too small to be literally pointed to. An abstract object, on the other hand, can be referred to only by means of a verbal phrase, unaided by any ancillary device for indicating some feature of the environment, save in so far as it is referred to as the value of a function for some concrete object, picked out by ostension, as argument, i.e. by a phrase like 'the shape of *this*'.

It is precisely the fact that we cannot be *shown* an abstract object that prompts the feeling that such objects are spurious, the feeling which under- lies nominalism of Goodman's sort. A situation in which an object can be identified as the bearer of a name is one in which we are in some manner confronted by the object. In many cases, the object which is the bearer of a given name may be too remote for such confrontation to take place, or it may have long ceased to exist: but we know what such confrontation would be, and hence feel we have a grasp on the notion that, by means of the name, we make reference to the object. But no confrontation with an abstract object is possible: it is usually not located in space and time, and is not perceptible to sense, not even to imaginable senses transcending ours; and so it is easy to fall into a frame of mind in which we feel that we cannot understand what such objects are supposed to be, and must construct an ontology which excludes them.

In *Grundlagen* Frege expresses the deepest hostility to such tendencies. The philosophical error that he wishes to guard against is not nominalism— the rejection of abstract objects—but psychologism, that is, the interpretation

Gl 60

of terms for abstract objects as standing for mental images or other results of mental operations. Such psychologism, he says, springs from the mistake of 'asking after the meaning of a name in isolation from the context of a sentence in which it occurs'; and presumably he would make the same diagnosis of nominalism. If we ask after the meaning of a name of an abstract object in isolation, we are bound to fall back on some mental image, in default of anything else which we could be shown as being the bearer of the name: the corresponding modern mistake would be to conclude that the name did not have any reference at all. On the contrary, Frege says, a name, or any other word, has meaning only in the context of a sentence, and it is only in that context that we may ask after its meaning.

The word here translated by 'meaning' is 'Bedeutung', but Frege had not yet formulated his distinction between reference (Bedeutung) and sense (Sinn), and he never repeated this dictum after the distinction had been formulated. It is therefore possible to interpret the dictum as relating to the *senses* of names and other words. Indeed, it is certainly part of the content of the dictum that sentences play a special role in language: that, since it is by means of them alone that anything can be *said*, that is, any linguistic act (of assertion, question, command, etc.) can be performed, the sense of any expression less than a complete sentence must consist only in the contribution it makes to determining the content of a sentence in which it may occur. For this reason, assigning a bearer to a name would be merely an empty ceremony if it did not serve as a preliminary to introducing a means of using that name in sentences whereby something was said about the object assigned as the bearer. It is precisely because, in Frege's later writings, the unique central role of sentences, which is the key insight embodied in the theory of meaning adumbrated in *Grundlagen*, was so unfortunately lost sight of, that Frege never repeated the dictum that a word has meaning only in the context of a sentence.

This interpretation of the dictum, as a thesis about sense, while exhibiting an important part of its content, does not exhaust it. It is plain from the applications which Frege makes of it that he means more by it than that. One of the ways in which he intends it to be understood is as a defence of contextual definitions. It is possible to miss this, not only because of Frege's later great hostility to contextual definitions, but because of what actually happens in the book about the definition of numerical terms. The example to which Frege principally applies the dictum that we must not ask after the meaning of a name in isolation is that of terms like 'the number 1': yet, when he actually comes to give a definition of such terms, after toying with a form of contextual definition and rejecting it, he gives an explicit definition

Gg II 66

Gl 62–7

Gl 68   in terms of classes. It is nevertheless clear that he does not reject the suggested contextual definition simply because it is a contextual definition. He in fact considers three objections to it, the first of which is, in effect, an ob-

Gl 63   jection to contextual definitions as such: he rebuts the first two objections, and sustains only the third. It is possible to suppose that subsequent reflection on this third objection led him to think it could be generalized to cover all contextual definitions, and so led him to his later opposition to them: but, in *Grundlagen* itself, it is not offered as a general objection to contextual definitions, but merely as a defect in this particular one. On the contrary, con-

Gl 60   textual definition is expressly defended in *Grundlagen*, the example being given, with approval, of the definition, in terms of limits, of the standard notation for differentiation.

If the dictum that a word has meaning only in the context of a sentence were intended merely as a thesis about sense, it would tell us nothing about the kind of sense a name can have: it would not follow that there was anything wrong in asking after the sense, or the reference, of a name in isolation, provided that we were aware that the only point of assigning it one was as a preparation for its use in sentences. The use of the dictum as a justification for contextual definition shows, however, that Frege intended more than this: for a name introduced by contextual definition, there simply is no answer to the question what its reference is on its own; all we have is a method of explaining the truth-conditions of any sentence in which it occurs, and Frege is saying that that is all we have a right to demand. We must thus interpret the dictum as expressing, in addition, a thesis about reference: namely that it is illegitimate to suppose that we may always ask to be *shown* the object which is the bearer of a name. Whether or not an expression is a name depends not upon any very precise knowledge of its sense, but merely on its logical role in sentences, namely on those criteria which we attempted to make explicit when originally discussing Frege's notion of a proper name: these criteria may be called 'formal' in a loose sense, relating as they do partly to syntactical questions about the kind of context in which the expression can meaningfully occur, and also to the validity of certain patterns of inference describable in terms of fairly simple transformations of sentences containing the expression. By such criteria, numerical terms, for instance, are readily recognized as proper names, since the structural analogy between, say, '5 is prime' and 'London is noisy', or between '19 is greater than 3' and 'Chicago is west of New York', is easily established. If, then, we have succeeded in determining precise truth-conditions for all possible sentences containing the names in question, we have done everything that is needed in order to give these names a

sense. Any further question about whether any such name has a reference or not can be, at most, a question about the truth of an existential statement: just as the question whether the name 'Vulcan' has a reference is an astronomical question, namely as to whether there is a planet whose orbit lies inside Mercury's, so the question whether, say, 'ω_1' has a reference is a mathematical question, namely as to whether there is a least non-denumerable ordinal. The truth of the relevant existential statement is to be determined by the methods proper to that realm of discourse, i.e. in accordance with the truth-conditions that we are supposing have been stipulated for sentences of that kind. There is no further, philosophical, question about whether there *really* exists an object to be the referent of the name.

The thesis expressed by the dictum that a name has meaning only in the context of a sentence, thus interpreted, involves repudiating the conception of a special philosophical sense of 'existence' which would permit us to assert that, in this special sense, numbers do not really exist, while continuing to affirm existential statements of arithmetic, such as that there is a perfect number between 7 and 30. The only sense we have for 'exists' is that given by the existential quantifier in the sentences we ordinarily use: if we have provided determinate truth-conditions for a certain existential statement, and, under those truth-conditions, the statement proves to be true, then there exists something satisfying the condition given in the statement, and that is an end of the matter. This, of course, would not disturb the nominalist, who is not one of those philosophers who wish to eat their cake and have it: he would sternly reject the use of quantifiers taking abstract objects, such as numbers, as their domain, and hence would be unprepared to assent to arithmetical statements at all. But it is also part of Frege's thesis that the nominalist is the victim of a superstition about what has to be done in order to confer a reference on a name. If an expression satisfies the 'formal' criteria for being a name; if it forms part of a vocabulary in which we can construct sentences containing that name and other ones involving quantification to which it is related in the standard way in which a term is related to a quantifier; if we have supplied truth-conditions for these sentences; and if, finally, that one of those sentences which states the condition for the name to have a reference is true according to the truth-conditions we have specified: then there is no further condition which needs to be satisfied for the expression to be a name having a reference.

The superstition which leads to asking after the meaning of a name in isolation, and thus, when it is the name of an abstract object, to either a mentalistic interpretation of it or a nominalist rejection of it as meaningless, is the belief that the sense of a name must be given, or at least always can in principle be given, by a confrontation with the object to which the name is to be attached. The sense of a name of a concrete object may indeed be taken to consist in a criterion for identifying an object as the bearer of the name: but what the nominalist and the mentalist overlook is that such an identification itself depends upon the mastery of some linguistic means, other than the use of the name, for referring to the object, namely the appropriate use of a demonstrative expression. Only language can pick out the object from the total surrounding environment, and can delineate it as an object by imposing a criterion of identity. In the case of the name of an abstract object, this means of referring to the object is lacking: all that we need to master is the use of statements of identity, in which the name occurs on the one side and some other complex term for an object of that kind on the other. The idea that the lack of any means of ostension is fatal to the status of the expression as a proper name, and therefore to the status of its referent as an object, is due to a false picture of the concrete object as something which can, as it were, be given to us on its own, independently of any use of language. Once we grasp that this is not so, then we are no longer disposed to exaggerate the role of ostension. We recognize that, even among concrete objects, there are many different kinds, corresponding to the very different criteria of identity we may employ, and that the notion of ostension is not a univocal one, but must be subjected to various modifications according to the kind of object in question. Having recognized this, we can now see names of abstract objects, which cannot be objects of ostension in however extended a sense, not as a radical departure but merely as a further, and entirely natural, extension of a mode of expression which already exhibits great heterogeneity.

These are undoubtedly the lines along which Frege intends us to understand his notions of proper name and of object, the distinction between concrete and abstract objects being acknowledged but made little of, there being no essential distinction between the uses of names of either kind of object, and, in particular, nothing questionable about the use of names of abstract objects. And, certainly, it can only be by thus stressing the role of names within the context of sentences that it is possible to defend or explain names for abstract objects. The defence nevertheless leaves a residual uneasiness. If the sense of a name is not to be given, or not always to be given, in the form of a criterion for identifying an object as the bearer of the name, how, then, is it to be given? It is one thing to assume airily that we can specify truth-conditions for sentences containing names of abstract objects, e.g. arithmetical statements: but how are these truth-conditions to be specified, if we do not begin by laying down what the reference of the constituent terms is to be? Above all, what becomes of the realism embodied in the use of the name/bearer relation as the prototype of reference and in the principle that the referents of our words are what we talk about? In what sense are we entitled to suppose that abstract objects are constituents of an external reality, when the possession of reference by their names has been interpreted as a matter wholly internal to the language?

There is, indisputably, a considerable tension between Frege's realism and the doctrine of meaning only in context: the question is whether it is a head-on collision. For incomplete expressions, Frege held that the application to them of the notion of reference could be effected only by analogy: but we saw that, while the application could be defended, the analogy appeared to break down at a crucial point. Names of abstract objects are supposed by Frege to have reference in just the same sense as do names of concrete ones: and here we feel disposed to say that it is actually only an analogy, albeit a closer one than with incomplete expressions, and an analogy which calls in question the realist picture of their meaning. We have seen that, for names of abstract objects of certain kinds, it is possible to preserve the structure of the account of the sense of a name as consisting in a criterion for identifying the bearer. We have to find, for a given category of abstract objects, some preferred range of names for them: e.g., in the case of natural numbers, we might select the numerals from some particular system of notation; or, in the case of abstract objects forming the range of some functional expression, such as 'the shape of ξ', whose arguments are possible objects of ostension, we might choose the use of that functional expression completed by a demonstrative. Thus, on such an account, the sense of an arbitrary numerical term v would consist in the criterion for deciding the truth-value of any sentence of the form $\ulcorner v = \varkappa \urcorner$, where $\varkappa$ is a numeral: the criterion for determining such an identity-statement as true would here play the role which was played, in the case of the name of a concrete object, by the criterion for determining the truth of a recognition statement. It must be admitted that no warrant for any such suggestion is to be found in Frege's own writings, and, as an interpretation of Frege, it can be defended only on the plea that he is generally unspecific about sense, except in so far as it can be displayed by the form of definition adopted, when a definition is possible. But, if we do not adopt this suggestion, it is hard to see how the analogy can be made out between the attribution of reference to names of abstract objects and names of concrete ones. If we take seriously the advocacy of contextual definitions in *Grundlagen*, then truth-conditions for sentences containing names for abstract objects can be specified by giving a rule for transforming those sentences into ones which contain no even apparent reference to or quantification over abstract objects of that kind: we can interpret sentences about directions in terms of sentences only about lines. This may quite reasonably be taken as a sound method of justifying the use of names of directions: but it would naturally be construed, not as a demonstration that such names have reference in the same way as names of concrete objects, but as a way of explaining their use without ascribing a reference to them.

Here the conflict between a realist theory of reference and the 'context' doctrine is at its sharpest: if the 'context' doctrine is taken in the very strong sense in which Frege appears to take it in *Grundlagen*, in those passages in which he is commending the use of contextual definition, then it seems to provide a way of dispensing with reference altogether. This conflict is reflected in Frege's hesitancy about contextual definitions. The particular objection which he sustains to the suggested contextual definition of terms of the form 'the number of F's' (and likewise of terms of the form 'the direction of a') is that it fails to supply us with a means of determining the truth-value of a sentence of the form 'The number of F's is c' (or 'The direction of a is c'), where 'c' is a name not of the form 'the number of G's' ('the direction of b'). One natural reply might be that we do not need to admit such sentences to our language at all; but, although, at this stage of his career, Frege was evidently willing that not every name should be capable of standing in the argument-place of every predicate, he is sufficiently convinced that objects must be regarded as forming a single category to believe that every identity-statement connecting two names must be given a sense. This scruple surely arises from Frege's realization that there would be an implausibility about the claim that, by means of a contextual definition, a reference had been bestowed upon a certain type of names of abstract objects, if the only way of identifying an object as the bearer of such a name were by means of another name of the same type.

But how is this to be accomplished? Have we not seen that it is a characteristic of the kind of functional expression by means of which we introduce reference to a given range of abstract objects, an expression such as 'the number of Φ's' or 'the direction of ξ', that the objects in its range may not be capable of being referred to except by means of that expression—that we cannot refer to a number save as a number, or to a direction save as a direction? Surely the most we can hope for is that we find a means of specifying that an object not referred to as a number is not a number, one not referred to as a direction is not a direction, rather than that we should be able to find some name by means of which a number or a direction can be picked out otherwise than as a number or a direction.

Frege's solution was, of course, to give an explicit definition of the functional expression in terms of classes. This achieves the original purpose, to find a way of construing numbers or directions as objects that can be identified otherwise than as numbers or directions, namely as classes, and thus, in a way, of making it more plausible that names of numbers and of directions can be regarded as having a reference. As we have seen, the reduction of all abstract objects to classes makes no essential change in the situation: it means merely that there is only one kind of abstract object instead of many. Classes remain objects which can be referred to only as classes; or, if, in accordance with the assimilation of sentences to names, we subsume classes under the more general notion of value-ranges, as is done in *Grundgesetze*, value-ranges remain objects which can be referred to only as value-ranges. Indeed, as we have noted, just this gives rise to concern on Frege's part in *Grundgesetze*: how we are to determine the truth-value of a sentence of the form 'The class of *F*'s is *c*' (more strictly, Gg I 10 'The value-range of *f* is *c*'), where '*c*' is a name constructed without the abstraction operator?

Frege's hesitancy about contextual definitions may thus be seen as due to an only partly conscious realization of the tension between his 'context' doctrine and his realistic notion of reference. Only if we import into Frege's theory of meaning the idea that the sense of the name of an abstract object consists in a criterion for the truth of identity-statements connecting that name with a name of a preferred kind, such as numerals, can we explain the attribution of reference to names of abstract objects at all. But do we, even then, succeed? Can we really justify the claim that abstract objects are constituents of reality in the same sense as concrete ones?

To some extent this depends upon the kind of criterion we admit for the existence of abstract objects. We saw in Chapter 8 that there are divergent p. 257 views on this question, as representatives of which we took Strawson and Aristotle. For Strawson, whereas the possession of reference by a definite description of an individual (particular) is always a contingent matter, there are definite descriptions of universals which are guaranteed a reference: for instance, 'the colour intermediate between yellow and red'. By contrast, Aristotle held that the existence of anything in a category other than substance always depended upon the existence of a substance in which that thing was or of which it could be predicated. This means that there is a colour or a shape answering to a given description only if there is some object whose colour or shape answers that description. On Aristotle's criterion of existence, it is a contingent (though well-known) fact that there is a colour intermediate between yellow and red, since this depends upon

T

there being some material or visual object whose colour is intermediate between yellow and red: in just the same way, the existence of a shade which fills the gap in Hume's graded sequence of shades of colour is not guaranteed, but is dependent upon there being something which has that shade. From this point of view, Strawson's guarantee of existence is a guarantee only of *possible* existence: we can say a priori that there could be an object which had a shade which would fill the gap, but not that there actually is such an object, nor, therefore, that there actually is such a shade.

It is consonant with Frege's realism that he always adopts an Aristotelian, not a Strawsonian, criterion for the existence of abstract objects. We are tempted to think that the criterion of existence in mathematics is Strawsonian, or, to put the matter in Aristotelian fashion, that mathematics is concerned with possible existence, not with actual existence: for instance, that it is a sufficient ground for the infinity of the series of natural numbers that we can say that, for any n, there could be $n + 1$ objects. Frege has no sympathy with this conception: for him, mathematics is as much concerned with actual existence (construed in an Aristotelian manner) as any other science: if we are to be able to establish the infinity of the number-series, we must be able to show that, for every n, there is some kind F of objects such that there actually are $n + 1$ F's.

This example reminds us, however, that, for Frege, it is not at all the case that all true existential statements are a posteriori, or even synthetic. Of course, there is no reason why Frege, or we, should endorse Kant's dictum that they are all synthetic: for Kant, this thesis followed immediately from his definition of an analytic statement as one in which the predicate is contained in the subject, together with the doctrine that 'exists' is not a predicate; but Frege defined 'analytic' in a much more extensive sense, and, if we accept the notion of analyticity at all, we must follow Frege rather than Kant. But the price of saying that there are necessarily true existential statements is, surely, an obligation to admit that, among the things that exist or may be said to exist, some are not in the world, are not constituents of reality in the same way as concrete objects: at least, this obligation appears to accrue if we hold that there are analytically true existential statements, whatever may be the case for the various alternative senses of 'necessarily true'. I do not know whether this is a principle which could be established, whether, that is, the obscure notion of something's 'being in the world' could be made sufficiently rigorous that a demonstration could be given of the claim: perhaps we are discussing no more than the intuitive acceptability of a picture. But the picture does seem to require that what may be called a 'constituent of reality' is something which can be encountered; and, if the existence of something is an analytic truth, a recognition of its existence can hardly be held to constitute an encounter.

Those abstract objects whose existence Frege takes to be analytic might be called 'pure abstract objects', in analogy with the notion of a pure set. If we start with some collection of individuals (non-sets), we may consider first the totality of all subsets of that collection; if, now, we form the union of these two collections, the individuals and the sets of individuals, we may again form the totality of all subsets of this union, that is, sets whose members may be either individuals or sets of individuals; by once more taking the union of this totality with the collection of individuals, we form the basis for a reiteration of the operation of taking subsets, and so on. If we now consider the denumerably many collections which we have formed in this way, we may take the union of all of them to form the basis for a further operation of forming subsets, and so proceed into the transfinite as far as we wish. This is exactly the cumulative hierarchy of sets which forms the intuitive model for set theories of the Zermelo–Fraenkel type. In general, what sets occur in the hierarchy will depend upon what individuals we started with. Some sets will, however, occur in the hierarchy whatever individuals we start with: they are, in fact, precisely the sets that are generated if we start with no individuals at all. Among such sets are the empty set $\varnothing$, its unit set $\{\varnothing\}$ the set $\{\varnothing, \{\{\varnothing\}\}\}$ containing the empty set and the unit set of its unit set, the set $\omega = \{\varnothing, \{\varnothing\}, \{\varnothing, \{\varnothing\}\}, \{\varnothing, \{\varnothing\}, \{\varnothing, \{\varnothing\}\}\}, \ldots\}$, and so on. A set can be represented by a tree, with the set itself at the vertex, and each node representing an object (set or individual) whose members, if any, are represented by the nodes immediately below it. Every path in such a tree will be finite, and hence will terminate at some node representing an object which has no members. Such an object must represent either an individual or the empty set. A set is a pure set, that is, one which occurs in the hierarchy whatever collection of individuals we began with, just in case every terminal node in the associated tree represents the empty set.

What objects we recognize the world as containing depends upon the structure of our language. Our ability to discriminate, within reality, objects of any particular kind results from our having learned to use expressions, names or general terms, with which are associated a criterion of identity which yields segments of reality of just that shape: we can, in principle, conceive of a language containing names and general terms with which significantly different criteria of identity were associated, and the speakers of such a language would view the world as falling apart into discrete objects in a different way from ourselves. Thus, in a certain sense, Frege, with his insistence that proper names have sense, and that this sense comprises a criterion of identity, could endorse the second sentence of the *Tractatus*, 'The world is the totality of facts, not things'. Literally taken, this would be wrong for Frege, since, as we have seen, for him facts belong to the realm of sense and not of reference: rather, we should say that, for Frege, the world does not come to us articulated in any way; it is we who, by the use of our language (or by grasping the thoughts expressed in that language), impose a structure on it.

If we use, as Frege does, an Aristotelian criterion for the existence of abstract objects, then the existence of abstract objects of certain kinds will be contingent: there will be no games which are never played, no languages that are never spoken. Of course, set theory provides us with several mechanisms for achieving the effect of quantifying over possible objects without having to invoke modal notions: if, for instance, we want to consider the totality of possible rhyme schemes without restricting ourselves to those that have actually been exemplified, we may first replace rhyme schemes themselves by their representations by sequences of letters such as 'ababb', and then interpret the notion of sequence set-theoretically so that the existence of a sequence does not depend on the physical occurrence of a corresponding string. It nevertheless remains that, in general, the existence of abstract objects depends upon what concrete objects there are: for instance, sets or sequences of concrete objects. But the existence of some abstract objects does not, for Frege, depend on there being any concrete objects at all. The existence of a number satisfying a certain condition does indeed depend upon there being some concept such that the number of objects falling under that concept satisfies the condition in question. But, since it is not only concrete objects but also abstract ones for which we can ask what is the number of those satisfying some given predicate, it is legitimate, in order to establish the existence of a certain number, to cite a concept under which only abstract objects, perhaps only numbers, fall, and in such a way to guarantee the existence of the number quite independently of what concrete objects there are. It is in just this way that Frege proves, to

his own satisfaction, the infinity of the series of natural numbers: for any natural number n, the number of numbers less than or equal to n is one greater than n, and hence the series of natural numbers never terminates; the existence of the number 0, from which the series starts, is of course guaranteed by the citation of a concept under which nothing falls.

Abstract objects of this kind, whose existence may be recognized independently of the existence of any concrete objects, and therefore independently of any observation of the world, may be likened to pure sets. When we apply the conceptual apparatus with which language supplies us to reality, this results in the discernment of a variety of objects, concrete and abstract: but the apparatus is such that certain objects will be recognized however the reality is constituted to which we apply it; these are the pure abstract objects, like the natural numbers, whose existence is analytic. This is incomprehensible if we think of the world as composed of objects, as coming to us already segmented into objects: in that case, how could there be a whole plurality of eternally existing, uncreated objects? But, once we realize that our apprehension of reality as decomposable into discrete objects is the product of our application to an originally unarticulated reality of the conceptual apparatus embodied in our language, it should not be particularly surprising that certain objects should result from this operation no matter what the reality is like to which it is applied.

Perhaps not: yet just for that reason it appears impossible to regard the pure abstract objects as constituents of an external reality. At this point, the realistic conception of reference seems to have broken down irrevocably. Pure abstract objects are no more than the reflections of certain linguistic expressions, expressions which behave, by simple formal criteria, in a manner analogous to proper names of objects, but whose sense cannot be represented as consisting in our capacity to identify objects as their bearers. The procedure of determining the truth of certain special kinds of identity-statements, for instance, in the case of natural numbers, equations on one side of which is a numeral and on the other the term in question, may perhaps be taken as embodying the senses of such abstract terms, here numerical ones. As such, it bears a recognizable analogy to the procedure of identifying a concrete object as the bearer of a name, and hence serves to explain the analogy between the logical role of proper names of concrete objects and abstract terms. But precisely the point at which the analogy fails is in the use of the realist picture: the recognition of the truth of a numerical equation cannot be described as the identification of an object external to us as the referent of a term, precisely because there is no sense in which it requires us to discern numbers as constituents of the external world.

Platonism as a philosophy of mathematics has a number of distinguishable strands: while in practice they are most often found together, in principle it would be possible to be a platonist in one respect but not in others. Platonism carries with it a certain picture of what mathematical statements are about: namely that they relate to, and are rendered true or false by, an objective reality external to us just as do statements about the physical universe; but, in the case of mathematical statements, the reality which we are concerned to describe consists of structures of abstract, changeless objects, while statements about the physical world describe structures of temporal, concrete objects. As Frege said, 'the mathematician can no more create anything at will than the geographer can: he too can only discover what is there, and give it a name'. But we cannot tell simply from the picture what the philosophical doctrine is: we have to enquire how the picture is used.

One application of the platonist picture of a mathematical reality external to us is as a means of expressing the conviction that mathematical statements are determined as objectively either true or false, independently of our means of proving or disproving them, just as are statements about the physical universe, on a realist interpretation of those statements. Clearly such a thesis can only be applied to the statements of a theory for which it is thought that there is (up to isomorphism) only one mathematical structure constituting an intended model of the theory. It would not, for example, be inconsistent with a general platonistic outlook to hold that this is not the case in set theory: that we do not have a specific enough intuitive notion of sets for there to be a unique mathematical structure which we may take our set theory as intended to describe, and hence that there are set-theoretic statements—for instance, the continuum hypothesis—which are neither absolutely true nor absolutely false, but about which the whole truth is that they are true in some models and false in others. But, once it is agreed that some intuitive notion, for example, that of 'natural number', has a determinate extension, and that this constitutes the structure which we are aiming to describe by means of some mathematical theory, in this case number theory, then, on this view, statements of that theory are determinately either true or false irrespective of whether we can or ever shall be able to prove or refute them.

Certain very radical forms of constructivism would deny that any intuitive mathematical notion had a determinate extension unless its extension was straightforwardly finite. Thus, according to the strict finitism (ultra-intuitionism) advocated by Essenin-Volpin, it is wrong to suppose that any two intuitive models of the natural numbers are isomorphic: by the 'natural numbers' is meant such a totality as that consisting of those numbers for which it is in practice possible to write down a numeral in some specified notation, and, according to the notation selected, one such structure may be more extensive than another. A related view is that expressed by Wittgenstein in *Remarks on the Foundations of Mathematics*: the sense of an arithmetical predicate, e.g. 'is prime', is given, not by a method that may 'in principle' be used to decide its application, but by the criterion we accept in practice. Since, for any predicate, there exist numbers too large for the practical application of any criterion we possess at any given time, no arithmetical predicate has, at any time, any determinate sense over the whole range of natural numbers. It is a plain consequence of radical views of this kind that we have no right to assume, of an arbitrary arithmetical statement, that it is determinately either true or false.

For any milder form of constructivism, such as intuitionism, however, the objection to assuming the law of bivalence for arithmetical statements is not of this kind. Although, from an intuitionist point of view, natural numbers are mental constructions, and the totality of natural numbers therefore, like any other infinite totality, a potential totality only, since we cannot at any time have carried out infinitely many constructions, it is nevertheless a fully determinate totality: we have a completely specific procedure for generating natural numbers, and it is therefore determined in advance what is and is not to be recognized as being a natural number. In this sense, the intuitive notion of natural number has, intuitionistically as well as platonistically, a fully determinate extension. Likewise, the sense of an arithmetical predicate is, from an intuitionistic standpoint, given by a method which can in principle be used to decide its application, if such a method exists at all: any other criterion which we employ in practice is accepted as a criterion for the application of that predicate only because it has been recognized as yielding an effective method for determining the result of the original decision procedure, in terms of which the sense of the predicate was given.

The reason for the intuitionistic rejection of the conception of determinate truth-values for arithmetical statements lies, rather, in the adoption of a verificationist account of meaning, at least for the language of mathematics. The question turns, therefore, not on the interpretation of numerical terms nor of primitive (decidable) arithmetical predicates, but on the modes of sentence-formation, in the first place quantification. Since quantification over the totality of natural numbers is not an operation on sentences which preserves the property of decidability, a grasp of the senses of the sentences so formed cannot be taken as consisting in a knowledge of the conditions under which they are true or false, but must, rather, be taken to lie in a capacity for recognizing proofs and disproofs of them, since precisely that is what we learn when we learn to use quantified arithmetical statements.

Now it is evident that the status of natural numbers as objects plays, or at least need play, no role in the opposition between these two views. Someone might be convinced that natural numbers were abstract objects, existing eternally and independently of our knowledge of them, and still hold that quantification over them could not be understood as an operation yielding in each case a statement determinately true or false, but only in terms of our capacity for recognizing such a statement as true or as false. Conversely, someone might hold that natural numbers are mental constructions, the product of human thought-processes, and yet accept the interpretation of quantification in terms of infinite logical sum and product, and thus as yielding sentences true or false irrespective of whether we are able to prove them or not. What is in question here is the correct model of meaning, of what we learn when we learn to use the sentences of our language; and, while one model may more naturally go with a picture of the objects in the domain of quantification as existing externally, and the other with a picture of them as mental entities, neither model of meaning either forces on us or is forced on us by the one picture or the other.

A platonistic interpretation of mathematical statements, in so far as this consists merely in the conception that such statements are given meaning by a specification of their truth-conditions, and that we possess a notion of truth for such statements under which each statement (of a sufficiently specific mathematical theory) is determinately either true or false, thus makes no use of the realistic picture of mathematical terms. As Kreisel has remarked, what is important is not the existence of mathematical objects, but the objectivity of mathematical statements. In so far, therefore, as Frege's mathematical platonism amounts to no more than this, his 'context' doctrine of meaning may be accepted as an explanation and defence of the use of abstract terms, but reference may be ascribed to them only as a façon de parler. Their sense may be thought of as a criterion for recognizing certain identity-statements as true, and the analogy between this and the sense of a genuine proper name allowed as explanatory of the formal resemblance between them and proper names. But their meaning cannot be construed after a realistic model, as determined by a relation of reference between them and external objects; for at no point in the explanation of the truth-conditions of sentences in which they occur is there any need to invoke such objects.

To this it might be replied that we require the notion of an abstract object in order to construe the notion of an abstract term, so that the attempt to explain abstract objects as mere reflections of the use of abstract terms achieves nothing. For example, we are proposing to interpret a statement about a natural number, not in Frege's realistic manner, as involving reference to a certain abstract object, over which the arithmetical predicate is defined, but by means of a direct stipulation of the truth-value of sentences resulting from inserting a numeral in the argument-place of the predicate, so that the abstract object is cancelled out. We seemed to be forced into such an interpretation, since we could find nothing to take as constituting identification of a specific number as the bearer of a numerical term save finding the numeral for that number in some preferred system of notation. But, in order to interpret quantification over the totality of natural numbers, we must consider the totality of all numerals in the given system. Numerals, however, cannot be identified with actual written marks, on pain of making the existence of a natural number a contingent matter, and of ensuring that there are only finitely many of them at any time. They have, instead, to be taken as finite sequences of signs, e.g. of digits: and finite sequences are as much abstract objects as natural numbers themselves.

As a demonstration that it is futile to expect to be able to dispense with abstract objects, this argument can appear very powerful, and rightly so: nominalism is indeed crippling to our powers of expression, and only by the most bizarre contortions can a nominalist take even the smallest fragment of mathematics seriously. But, in the present context, the argument overlooks the distinction between abstract objects in general and pure abstract objects, such as Frege took the natural numbers to be. Finite sequences are certainly abstract objects, when we regard them as guaranteed an existence so long as their terms exist; but they are not pure abstract objects if their terms are not. (Here we must construe the notion of a finite sequence as primitive, or possibly as defined by an extension of the standard set-theoretical definition of an ordered pair; not as defined as a function with an initial segment of the natural numbers as domain. We may consider it as a particular primitive method of introducing a kind of abstract object that, given any n objects, not necessarily distinct, in a particular order, we think of them as determining a single object which is the sequence having those objects as terms.) Singular terms of various kinds present a gradation according to the extent to which their use involves a mastery of a fragment of the language. Names of the concrete objects we encounter in everyday life stand at one end of the scale, terms for pure abstract objects at the other. While the use of any name requires the mastery of some linguistic technique, so that a grasp of the sense of a name never consists in the bare association of the name with an object presented to us as a separable constituent of reality in advance of all use of language, we may regard the position on the scale as indicating the relative contribution of linguistic and non-linguistic capacities to our having the conception of objects of the kind for which the name stands. In the case of abstract terms of any kind, the fragment of language which has to be mastered in order to learn their use is relatively large, and so the contribution made by the acquisition of linguistic capacities to forming the conception of the objects which they stand for is

T•

correspondingly great. But, when the terms are not terms for pure abstract objects, but for, say, shapes of physical bodies or sequences of concrete objects, the use of these terms is still clearly related to processes of observation of the external world and identification of constituents of it. For that reason, therefore, it is still possible to apply to such terms the notion of reference, construed realistically as a relation to something external; although, indeed, the further we travel along the scale, the more stretched becomes the analogy with the prototypical case. It is only when we reach terms for pure abstract objects, however, that the thread snaps completely, and we are concerned with the use of terms which have no external reference at all.

It may be objected, from the other side, that this criticism is unfair to Frege. From a pure mathematician's point of view, natural numbers, considered as the objects of which number theory treats, need have no relation to the external world: but Frege defines the natural numbers in such a way as to display very explicitly their application to empirical reality (as well as to non-empirical reality), their use, namely, to supply answers to empirical questions of the form 'How many . . . ?'. It is therefore entirely unjust to say that, for Frege, natural numbers are pure abstract objects which have no connection with external reality: for Zermelo or von Neumann, no doubt, but not for Frege.

Gg I 40   For Frege (in *Grundgesetze*) a number is a class of classes of the same cardinality. If we admitted, as members of such a class of classes, only classes of concrete objects, then we should get what we might call 'actual numbers'. Actual numbers would be neither pure classes nor pure abstract objects: their status would be similar to that of shapes of physical bodies. Frege's cardinal numbers are neither actual numbers nor pure sets, since (apart from o) all contain classes comprising both abstract and concrete objects among their members. But the notion of a pure abstract object was not meant to be construed by a quite literal analogy with that of a pure set: rather, an abstract object, specified by a certain description, is pure if its existence, under that description, is independent of what concrete objects there are (though its composition may not be). Since Frege wishes to be able to assert the infinity of the number-series independently of the size of the concrete universe, his natural numbers must be understood as pure abstract objects in this sense: they are guaranteed a reference only if to some abstract terms a reference is guaranteed no matter what concrete objects there are.

Sometimes, however, the platonistic picture is put to another use than this. It is held by some platonists that we possess an intuitive apprehension of certain mathematical structures, which guides our formulation of the axioms of the theories which describe them, but may not be, at any given time, fully embodied in those axioms. Such a conception is, for example, invoked to explain the incompleteness of first-order axiomatizations of number theory, in face of our overwhelming inclination to say that we have in mind a unique structure which we are aiming to describe. It is also invoked to suggest that there may be a sense in which set-theoretic statements such as the continuum hypothesis are absolutely true or false, namely relative to an as yet inchoate notion of the kind of model we intend for set theory, a notion which we may later succeed in embodying in new axioms. (The case of set theory of course differs in that the non-categoricity of the axioms cannot be attributed solely to the use of a first- rather than second-order language.)

This is not the place to discuss this contention: we have already made too great an excursion into the philosophy of mathematics. It is plain that other explanations may be possible for the facts which this conception seeks to explain; it is also plain that some acknowledgement must be made of the role of intuitive notions in mathematics. It should be noted that, on this point, the platonist and the constructivist need not be opposed: they merely give different descriptions of the same thing. For the intuitionist, the notion of a mental construction which is the fundamental idea of all mathematics is not one which can be identified with, or even fully represented by, external operations with symbols; the notion of an intuitive proof cannot be expected to coincide with that of a proof in a formal system, and Gödel's incompleteness theorem is thus unsurprising from an intuitionist point of view. What is of importance for us is that platonism of this kind seeks to construe mathematical intuition as playing, with respect to abstract structures, a role analogous to that of perception with respect to physical objects. If such a thesis can be sustained, then indeed the analogy between abstract objects and concrete ones becomes a great deal closer. It ceases to be true that abstract objects are not observable and cannot be involved in causal interaction, since such intuitive apprehension of them may be regarded as just such an interaction. If this analogy can be made out, then all that we have said about pure abstract objects falls to the ground: such objects are possible objects of encounter, and there may be such a thing as identification of such an object which could rightly be compared with the identification of a concrete object. But it is precisely on this possibility of finding some analogue of observation for abstract objects that the tenability of Frege's use of the name/bearer model for abstract terms depends.

CHAPTER 15

Quantification

FREGE'S LOGICAL SYMBOLISM contains only one quantifier, the universal quantifier, since, Frege's logic being classical, the existential quantifier is expressible in terms of the universal one together with negation. The universal quantifier is the simplest instance of an expression for a concept of second level, an expression, namely, containing one argument-place, that argument-place to be filled by any first-level predicate, and the result of filling it being a sentence which in every case is either true or false. The truth-value of the resulting sentence is thought of by Frege as an infinite product of the truth-values of the results of applying the first-level predicate to each of the objects in the domain of the individual variable bound by the quantifier, which, since this domain is always taken to be that consisting of all objects whatsoever, amounts simply to: applying the predicate to each object that there is. If the result of applying the predicate to any one or more objects is false, the universal quantification is false; if the result of applying it is always true, the universal quantification is true. In this way the universally quantified statement will always have a determinate truth-value, though we may not know what it is.

Gg I 8; Bs
11; FB 23

If we had a language relative to which it was adequate to employ a notion of 'object' such that the language could be taken as containing a (simple or complex) name of every object, then this would amount to construing a universally quantified statement as an infinite conjunction of sentences of the language, i.e. all sentences resulting from filling the argument-place of the first-level predicate to which the quantifier was attached by the name of an object. What, in such a case, would be required for an understanding of the universal quantifier would then be two things. First, we should have to have some conception of that totality of objects which an understanding of the language required, and a grasp of the idea of an infinitary function from truth-values to truth-values—a function whose values we could never determine directly, because it took infinitely many arguments. Secondly, in any particular case, we should have to be able to understand how the truth-value of the result of applying the given first-level predicate to an arbitrary object would be determined. On Frege's way of looking at the matter, a complex predicate is to be thought of as formed from a sentence by omission of one or more occurrences of some name. For example, we might arrive at the predicate 'If ξ is a man, then, for some α, ξ loves α' by omitting two occurrences of the name 'Henry' from the sentence 'If Henry is a man, then, for some α, α loves Henry': the complex predicate is not to be thought of as formed by connecting by means of 'if' the two predicates 'ξ is a man' and 'for some α, α loves ξ'. In order to be able to understand the universally quantified sentence 'For every *w*, if *w* is a man, then, for some α, α loves *w*', it is necessary that we should have a general understanding of the predicate 'If ξ is a man, then, for some α, α loves ξ', that we should, as one might express it, know what concept it is that that predicate stands for; we must, that is, have an understanding adequate, not merely for a grasp of the sense of the particular sentence, 'If Henry is a man, then, for some α, α loves Henry', from which the predicate was formed in the first place, but for any sentence which would result from the insertion of any name in the argument-place of the predicate. Frege's tacit supposition is that we do have such a general understanding: that our understanding of the sentence, 'If Henry is a man, then, for some α, α loves Henry', involves an understanding of the name 'Henry', the primitive predicate 'ξ is a man' and the primitive relational expression 'ξ loves ζ', together with a grasp of the sentence-forming operators 'if' and 'for some α, Φ(α)', and the way in which the sentence has been constructed by their means; and that such an understanding is intrinsically sufficient for us to be able to envisage the truth-conditions of any other sentence similarly formed save that some other name, whose sense we knew, was used in place of 'Henry'.

Gg I 30

NS 273 (253)

The conception of an infinitary truth-function is open to grave objection. It is in fact the point at which the gulf first opens between a verificationist account of sense and one, like Frege's, based on truth-conditions. So long as we are considering only a language, or a fragment of language, within which every sentence is at least in principle decidable, there is no effective distinction between these two kinds of account. A sentence is, in this sense, decidable if there always exists some effective means which would in principle lead us to a situation in which we could determine the truth-value of the sentence. For a language containing only such sentences, it would be entirely consonant with Frege's views on sense to construe a grasp of the sense of each constituent expression as consisting of an understanding of the contribution made by that expression to fixing the procedure required for determining the truth-value of a sentence in which it occurred. For instance, the predicates and relational expressions might be decidable, their sense consisting in a procedure for determining, for any given object or pair of objects, whether or not the predicate or relational expression applied. Likewise, it might be the case that, for any name, there existed an effective search procedure for finding the object which was the referent of the name. Such a language could contain quantification provided that the domain of quantification could always be taken as a finite and surveyable totality, that is, one such that there existed a procedure for discovering every member of the totality and a criterion for determining that every member of the totality had been inspected: the truth-value of a quantified statement could then, at least in principle, always be determined as that of a finite conjunction or disjunction. It is arguable that the first uses of expressions of generality that we acquire in learning language are of just this kind—in sentences such as 'Every saucer in the cupboard is chipped', the truth or falsity of which can be determined by inspecting every member of a small and surveyable totality.

If, however, the language contains undecidable sentences in the sense, not of sentences whose truth-value we can never determine, but merely of ones for which we lack an effective means guaranteed even in principle to lead to a determination of truth-value, then we are faced with a choice. On a verificationist account, an understanding of such a sentence, a grasp of its sense, consists merely in the capacity to recognize whatever would decide conclusively in favour of the truth or of the falsity of the sentence; and our notions of truth and falsity, as applied to such a sentence, consist merely in the conception of a situation's occurring which would thus conclusively determine its truth-value. From such a viewpoint, there would be no justification in saying, of such an undecidable sentence, that it must be either true or false, in advance of anything's occurring to enable us to recognize it as one or the other, or at least of information's becoming available which would provide us with what we previously lacked, an effective means of bringing about such a determining situation.

This is not at all Frege's way of looking at the matter. For him, our grasp of the sense of a sentence consists in our understanding of what has to be the case for it to be true, and, if the sentence is not a decidable one, this merely means that that in virtue of which it is true, if it is true, is not something we can effectively recognize as obtaining whenever it obtains. Thus we can grasp what it is for a universally quantified statement to be true, even when the domain of quantification is an unsurveyable or infinite totality, so that we are able, if at all, to determine its truth only indirectly or inconclusively. Although, in such a case, we do not have an effective means for determining the truth of the statement, either because we cannot inspect every member of the domain of quantification, being infinite, or because we cannot tell when we have inspected every member of it, since it is, though finite, unsurveyable, that does not impair our understanding of the sense of the sentence: for we have a perfectly clear grasp of what has to be the case for the sentence to be true, of what it is for it to be true. And, since our grasp of the senses of such sentences is related to an understanding of truth-conditions which we do not pretend to be, in general, effectively recognizable by us, we are fully entitled to maintain that, whenever definite truth-conditions have been laid down, the sentence must be determinately either true or false, quite independently of whether we know the truth-value or have any means of ever discovering it.

The issue between these two conceptions of sense is a very deep one, and it is not proposed to explore it further here. It is evident that the verificationist is in a very strong position, and that he can challenge the Fregean to explain how we come by such a grasp of truth-conditions the direct determination of which lies beyond our powers. We all feel disposed to believe that such a challenge must be able to be met, and we saw in Chapter 13 to what a reply might appeal; but it is obvious that it is no small task   pp. 468–9 to meet the verificationist challenge.

It is plausible to suppose that the learning of language begins with a fragment in relation to which the divergence between the two accounts is not significant, that is, with a fragment within which only decidable sentences can be framed. Later, certain forms of expression and sentence-forming operations are acquired which permit the formation of undecidable sentences (in the present sense of 'undecidable'), and so the dispute between the two accounts must involve a close scrutiny of those ingredients of language which first introduced undecidability into the language. Doubtless, there are many different such ingredients of natural language: for instance, the past tense and the non-truth-functional conditional. But the only one which occurs in Frege's symbolic language is quantification over infinite domains. That language would, of course, allow for the presence of primitive predicates whose application was not effectively decidable, but determinate in some other way: but the only linguistic operation expressly incorporated into the language which necessarily has the effect of generating undecidable sentences is quantification.

Frege takes it for granted that, once the domain of quantification is determinate, in the sense, e.g., that we are able to recognize, of any given thing, whether or not it belongs to the domain, then we understand the truth-conditions of a sentence formed by means of quantification over that domain. He does not argue for such a thesis, because he simply does not envisage any contradiction of it. Stated in this highly general manner, the thesis is certainly false, since, when the domain is too large, for instance, when it is the totality of all sets, in the intuitive sense of 'set', or when it is what Frege thought it could always be regarded as being, the totality of all objects whatsoever, it is, as already remarked, the prime lesson of the discovery of the set-theoretical paradoxes that quantification over that domain cannot be regarded as yielding, in all cases, a sentence with a determinate truth-value. The question whether it is possible to find a circumscription of the kind of totality which may constitute a domain of quantification within the framework of classical two-valued logic (i.e. such that classical logic is applicable to sentences involving quantification over such a domain), the question, that is, how to characterize 'legitimate' totalities, was the immediate problem raised by the discovery of the paradoxes, and the preoccupation of those who worked in the shadow of that discovery: but Frege himself contributed nothing to that enquiry, since his effective work in mathematical logic ended precisely with Russell's discovery of the paradox. A deeper enquiry concerns whether classical logic is ever correct for sentences involving quantification over any but a finite and surveyable domain, the enquiry namely whether a verificationist theory of sense is not to be preferred to a Fregean theory of sense in terms of truth-conditions: but to that also Frege contributed nothing, because he did not so much as conceive of the possibility of a verificationist account.

When the domain of the individual variables is not denumerable, or when for some other reason the language cannot be supposed to contain a name for every object in the domain, a universally quantified statement cannot be construed as an infinite conjunction of sentences of the language, that is, of its instances. We can give no coherent answer to the question of what cardinality Frege took the totality of all objects to be, since the supposition that it contains, for every concept defined over it, a corresponding class as the extension of that concept, is a self-contradictory one, requiring the totality of all objects to be impossibly large: but, in view of this supposition and of the fact that Frege expected to be able to develop classical analysis within his logical theory, there is every reason for saying that he would have taken the domain of his individual variables to be non-denumerable.

The truth-value of a universally quantified statement is, in this case, still determined as a kind of infinite conjunction, in the sense of being the value of an infinitary truth-function: but the arguments of this function—the constituents of the infinite conjunction—are not given as the truth-values of actual sentences of the language. Rather, they are given as the truth-values that result from the application of the predicate to each of the objects constituting the domain. This involves that, given that we understand a sentence from which a predicate has been formed by omission of certain occurrences of a name, we are capable of recognizing what concept that predicate stands for in the sense of knowing what it is for it to be true of or false of any arbitrary object, whether or not the language contains a name for that object. Provided that we do have the required understanding of the totality of objects which forms the domain of quantification, this seems reasonable: for the determination of the truth-value of a particular instance of the quantified sentence, formed by inserting a name in the argument-place of the predicate, proceeds via the identification of an object as the referent of that name; the sense of the name contributes to the determination of the truth-value of the sentence only by providing a criterion for making such an identification. So, if we suppose an object given otherwise than as the referent of a name belonging to the language, the procedure of determining whether the predicate is true or false of it would be exactly the same as that for determining the truth-value of an actual sentence constituting an instance of the quantified statement, once the first step had been taken of identifying that object as the referent of the name which filled the argument-place.

In fact, the ascription to Frege of an interpretation of universal quantification as infinite conjunction needs qualification at exactly this point. Frege expressly rejects this interpretation, taken in a full sense: he mocks the idea that, when I assert, 'All men are mortal', it is any constituent of the thought I express to ascribe mortality to some African chief of whom I have never heard. That is, even if the language contains a name for every object in the domain of quantification, the sense of the universally quantified statement is not that of an infinite conjunction of all its instances, so that the senses of all these instances would be ingredients of the sense of the quantified statement. Such an interpretation of quantification would force the senses of the names occurring in the various instances to be constituents of the sense of the quantified statement: whereas in fact the senses of these names are totally irrelevant to an understanding of the universal quantification. We understand the universally quantified statement because we have, as it were, a *general* grasp of the totality which constitutes the domain of quantification —we, as it were, survey it in thought as a whole—and because we know what it is for the predicate to which the quantifier is attached to be true or false of any one arbitrary element of this domain. We may therefore form the conception of the set of all the truth-values of the results of applying the predicate to each of the objects in the domain, without, so to speak, arriving at this conception via the totality of senses of names of objects in the domain. The respect in which it is right to say of Frege that he understood universal quantification as infinite conjunction is that in which we are viewing conjunction, not as an operation for forming a sentence which expresses a sense out of other sentences which express senses, but as a truth-function mapping truth-values on to a truth-value. That is, given that we are supposed to be able to form the conception of the set of truth-values resulting from application of any given predicate to each member of a given totality of objects, Frege takes it as quite unproblematic that this can then be regarded as a set which either objectively contains only the value *true* or else contains the value *false*, and that we can therefore take the universally quantified statement as being determinately either true or false according to which of these two objective possibilities obtains.

We require, then, for an understanding of first-level quantification, only a general conception of the domain over which the individual variables are to be taken to range. We do not need, in any sense, to know what objects there are which belong to that domain: we need only to have a determinate conception of what it is to belong to the domain, so that it is objectively determined, for each object, whether it is in that domain or not. Once we have such a conception, we have successfully conferred upon the universal quantifier a sense under which there will be associated, with every sentence formed by means of it, a determinate truth-value, true or false, provided of course that the rest of the sentence has been supplied with a definite sense, independently of whether we know of any means to discover what that truth-value may be. Much may remain for us to do if we want to find out what the truth-value of the sentence is; but, once we have specified the domain of quantification by means of a condition of membership of that domain, no more work remains for us to do, in order to guarantee that the sentence *has* a definite truth-value: all the rest is, as it were, accomplished independently of us by objective reality itself. Given a criterion for membership of the domain of quantification, reality determines, for each object that there is, whether or not it belongs to the domain; given a definite sense expressed by the predicate to which the quantifier is attached, reality determines, for each object, whether the predicate applies to it or not; and, given both of these things, the truth-value of the quantified sentence is determined by the infinitary truth-function for which the universal quantifier stands. Hence we are entitled to assume that every sentence involving first-level quantification has a determinate value, true or false, and thus that classical logic is applicable to such sentences.

We shall not probe these assumptions, questionable as they are, because, since Frege did not see them as even capable of being questioned, to do so would take us into an area which he left quite unexplored. We shall instead turn to consider, in the light of Frege's doctrines, a contrast which has much exercised Quine and his followers, that between the classical or 'ontic' account of quantification and the so-called 'substitutional' account.

OR 104–8

Quine has always been careful to distinguish that use of letters, in logical and mathematical symbolism, in which they may be bound by a quantifier from that use in which they may not, reserving the term 'variable' exclusively for the former use and calling those which cannot occur bound by a quantifier 'schematic letters': this contrasts with the usage of many mathematicians and even logicians, who call both kinds of letter 'variables' indiscriminately. (There are, of course, also letters which are used straightforwardly as constants, like 'e', 'i', 'π' and 'ω'; but we are thinking only of letters used to express generality in some way or other.) Thus, within ordinary sentential logic, the sentence-letters 'p', 'q', 'r', . . . (or 'A', 'B', 'C', . . .) do not occur as bound by quantifiers, and hence are to be classified on Quinean principles as schematic letters and not as variables; and the same applies to the predicate-letters 'F', 'G', 'H', . . . of first-order predicate logic, and likewise to so-called individual constants 'a', 'b', 'c', . . . , and to function-symbols 'f', 'g', 'h', . . . in first-order logic. The individual variables 'x', 'y', 'z', . . . of first-order logic are, on the other hand, variables in the strict sense, precisely because they are used as attached to and bound by quantifiers. Obviously, in order to determine whether a letter of a given kind is a schematic letter or a variable, we need to know more than its syntactic category: we need to know whether the formation rules permit letters of that kind to be bound by quantifiers. This will evidently be relative to the language we are considering: within first-order logic, predicate-letters are schematic letters, but within second-order logic they occur as bound by second-level quantifiers, and hence, in that context, are variables in the strict sense (unless, indeed, the particular symbolism maintains a distinction between predicate-letters which may and those which may not be bound by quantifiers, parallel to the distinction between individual constants and individual variables in first-order logic); likewise, in the logical theories known as 'protothetic', sentence-letters can occur bound by quantifiers, and so are variables proper within that theory, whereas in normal sentential logic they are only schematic letters. Similarly, the distinction between schematic letters and constants properly so called is relative to whether we are considering a language under any one intended interpretation or not: the formulas of first-order arithmetic, for example, contain an individual constant 'o' and function-symbols "'", '+' and '.', which, relative to the intended interpretation, are constants in the strict sense, but, when we are wanting to consider non-standard models of arithmetic, are treated merely as schematic letters whose interpretation is not to be considered fixed in advance.

Schematic letters are used merely to indicate the structure of a sentence, or of all possible sentences of some circumscribed language: they show how the sentence, or any specific sentence of the given language, is composed out of constituent expressions, of which all that is displayed is the logical category to which the constituents belong, and the identity or difference of expressions of the same category occurring in different parts of the sentence; only the so-called logical constants within the sentence are shown as carrying a specific meaning. (If we are considering a whole language, say for some formalized theory, the schematic letters are normally thought of as constituting, with the logical constants, the primitive symbols of the language; but, when we are considering a single formula, or some individual deduction within, e.g., predicate logic, there is no such presumption, but the representation of the sentences by the formulas is taken merely as displaying enough of the structure of those sentences for the purpose in hand.)

Quine sees a sharp distinction as obtaining between schematic letters and variables in some such way as this. In order to understand the role of schematic letters within formulas, we need merely to be able to specify the logical category of each schematic letter and to consider it as standing in for any arbitrary expression of that category: we need, that is, to grasp the range of permissible linguistic substitutions for the schematic letters in a formula which would transform that formula into a sentence of the kind whose structure it is intended to display. With variables, however, the matter stands differently: it is the distinguishing characteristic of variables, as opposed to schematic letters, that they may occur bound by quantifiers; and quantification has to be explained by reference to the totality of entities over which the variable ranges. Thus the use of a schematic letter is to be explained in terms of a set merely of linguistic expressions which may be substituted for it, without our having to consider those expressions as standing for any non-linguistic entities; but quantification compels us to interpret it as being over a set of non-linguistic entities, those entities, namely, for which the expressions stand which may be substituted for the variables when those variables occur free.

It is for this reason that, on Quine's view, if we have a language which admits only first-order quantification, we need to ascribe reference to the

names which occur in this language, but we do not need to ascribe reference
to the predicates or other incomplete expressions which occur in it: for the
referents of the names are required to compose the domain over which the
individual variables vary, whereas, there being no predicate-variables,
there is no need to consider predicates as standing for anything. (It is
true that Quine thinks that names can also be eliminated, by treating them as
definite descriptions in the Russellian manner, and, if this were done, there
would be no names to ascribe reference to; it remains the case that, so
long as the language is one which is taken as containing names, we are
bound to consider these names as standing for objects over which the
individual variables range.) Likewise, if, contrary to Quine's own taste,
we were to employ a language involving second-order quantification, we
should be bound to consider the predicates and relational expressions of
this language as standing for entities of a suitable kind, because it would be
only in this way that we could explain what the ranges of the second-order
variables were supposed to be: indeed, it is precisely because of the alleged
difficulty of providing such an explanation that Quine looks askance at
higher-order quantification.

It is thus highly disagreeable to Quine's outlook that some have attempted
an account of at least certain kinds of quantification which does not involve
assigning to the variables a set of non-linguistic entities as their range,
but only a set of linguistic expressions substitutable for them: for such an
account blurs, for him, the radical distinction between schematic letters and
variables. This is what is known as 'substitutional' quantification, which has
been proposed by some (for instance, Geach in *Reference and Generality*) as   RG 94
a means of avoiding the difficulties which can arise in specifying the domain
of quantification on the standard, 'ontic', account. On a substitutional
account, a universally quantified statement is to be regarded as equivalent,
quite literally, to an infinite conjunction of all its instances, and an existentially quantified one to an infinite disjunction of its instances: the universal
quantification is to be explained as true just in case every result of inserting
an expression of the language, of a permissible kind, into the argument-
place of the incomplete expression to which the quantifier is attached is
true, and false if any such instance is false, and the existential quantification
likewise. By this means, we avoid the necessity of saying for what kind of
entities the expressions which may fill the argument-place stand. Thus,
if we have a sentence whose main operator is a universal quantifier governing
a sentence-letter, we do not need to enquire whether sentences stand for
anything, and, if so, whether for truth-values, propositions, or what: we
merely specify that the quantified sentence is true just in case each result of

removing the quantifier and replacing each occurrence of the sentence-variable which it formerly bound by the same arbitrary sentence of the language is true. Likewise, the difficulties over quantification into opaque contexts are supposed to disappear under this treatment: we need no longer worry about what sort of entity we are quantifying over when we say, e.g., 'There is someone here whom I did not expect'; all that is necessary is to specify what expressions constitute permissible means of filling both gaps in '. . . is here and I did not expect that . . . would be here' (a proper name is almost certainly permissible, a description such as 'the host's oldest friend' may not be).

The initial presentation, in this chapter, of Frege's account of quantification, as infinitary conjunction, made it appear more or less a substitutional account: only later did we qualify this, not merely for the case of a non-denumerable domain or other domain for which there did not exist in the language a name for every element, but for the general case, by observing that the senses of the names were irrelevant to an understanding of the quantifier, but that all that was needed was a conception of the totality of their referents, and, at that, only a general conception of this totality, not a precise knowledge of what in fact belonged to it. This qualification is, indeed, necessary, and we can construe Frege's remark about the African chief as a repudiation of a substitutional account of first-level quantification: but the fact is that any very sharp distinction between substitutional and ontic quantification is itself a misconstrual of the situation, as also is the sharp distinction drawn by Quine between variables and schematic letters.

It is only when all that is desired is a very rough explanation of the intended significance of schematic letters that it is true to say that we need allude only to the range of actual expressions which could be substituted for them and not to the references of those expressions. If we are to give any precise account of the matter, that is, a semantic treatment of a formula's being true under an interpretation (true in a structure), it becomes necessary to explain the semantic role of expressions of the category to which each schematic letter belongs: if the schematic letters are sentence-letters, we must explain that a constituent sentence contributes to determining the truth-value of the complex sentence of which it is part in virtue of its truth-value; if the schematic letter is a one-place predicate-letter, that a one-place predicate so contributes in virtue of the set of objects to which it applies; and so on. The association with each schematic letter of an entity of the appropriate kind (truth-value, subset of the domain, etc.) will then serve as specifying, up to semantic equivalence, an interpretation of that schematic letter. (By the phrase 'up to semantic equivalence', it is meant that any more precise specification would be semantically irrelevant.) In so far as reference is to be identified with semantic role, such an interpretation may be said to specify a reference, but not a sense, for the schematic letter.

We argued earlier that there is a tension in Frege's theory of reference between the construal of the reference of an expression as consisting simply in its semantic role, and the use of the name/bearer relation as the prototype of the relation of reference in all logical categories. When reference is construed as semantic role, the contentious character of the ascription of reference to expressions other than singular terms is avoided; on the other hand, the realistic flavour of the doctrine of reference is also eliminated. Frege wants to have a licence to speak of the referents of incomplete expressions, that is, of concepts, relations and functions, as things which are as much constituents of reality as are the bearers of names: and his right to do this is in no way guaranteed by the aseptic characterization of reference as semantic role. If we assume no more about reference than that it constitutes the semantic role of an expression, then we have as yet no entitlement to assume, as we did above, that the semantic role of each expression can be specified by the association to it of an *entity* of one kind or another. (The word 'entity' is un-Fregean, in that it trespasses over the bounds dividing one level from another: but, then, so does the word 'reference' itself. On a strict Fregean interpretation, any sentence containing such a word as 'entity' or as 'reference', when the latter is simultaneously applied to expressions of different levels, cannot meaningfully be taken as a determinate statement at all: but perhaps it can be viewed as something like a typically ambiguous formula within the theory of types, lacking subscripts for type but true whenever any legitimate assignment of them is made.)

It is certainly by taking the name/bearer relation as the prototype of reference, rather than viewing reference as semantic role, that Quine came to think that reference need be ascribed only to expressions of a category to which there also belong variables capable of being bound by quantifiers. The sequence of thought goes something as follows. 'First-order quantification requires, for its explanation, the specification of a domain for the individual variables, a domain which consists of the referents of the names which are capable of replacing free individual variables, or at least of those things which could be the referents of such names. Hence quantification which binds, say, sentential variables or predicate variables must require the specification of a domain consisting of entities which stand to sentences or to predicates as their bearers stand to proper names. It is dubious whether there are any such things: but, even if there are, the assumption of their existence is not needed to explain the mere use of sentences occurring as constituents of a complex sentence or that of predicates, and hence is not needed, either, for the explanation of letters schematic either for constituent sentences or for predicates.'

We maintained that the conception of reference as semantic role was to be taken as the primary explanation of the notion of reference: that, if the appeal to the name/bearer prototype is instead taken as giving the basic meaning of the notion, it becomes obscure how we are to apply this prototype to expressions other than names, or whether there is any such application at all, and that the purpose of employing the notion of reference at all was lost sight of. But we also maintained that we only falsify Frege's doctrines if we try to expel the use of the name/bearer prototype altogether, and that this should be interpreted as a further thesis about the semantic roles of expressions of our language, namely that this always is to be explained by the association with each expression of some entity of a suitable kind, an extra-linguistic correlate constituent of reality.

If reference is construed merely as semantic role, then of course all inclination vanishes to think it problematic, for expressions of any category whatever, that they have reference: schematic letters, accordingly, no longer appear as differentiated from variables in involving no commitment to the referentiality of the expressions to whose category they belong. But the same holds good if we invoke the further Fregean thesis, that which justifies the use of the name/bearer relation as the prototype of reference, that the explanation of the semantic role of any expression will always consist in, or at least validate, the association of some appropriate entity with it. If this further thesis is admitted, we are still in the position that a full explanation of the role of schematic letters will involve a semantic account of the expressions for which they stand proxy, and hence of the kind of referents for which such expressions stand.

Hence, if we are to make sense of Quine's view that only expressions of a category to which also belong bound variables of quantification need to be ascribed a reference, we must attribute to him a denial of Frege's thesis that the semantic role of our expressions always consists in a relation analogous to that of name to bearer. Put like this, the attribution is obviously correct: this is exactly what Quine does deny. How much we are to make of this denial depends, however, on how strong the requirement that the relation between expression and referent be analogous to that of name to bearer is taken to be. We have ourselves seen that, in the case of incomplete expressions, the analogy halts at a critical point, viz. that the sense of the expression does not seem to involve anything that can be described as the identification of something as its referent. Perhaps it is as a result of too literal an interpretation of the analogy that Quine is impelled to make his denial: for certainly it is in no way apparent that he has any alternative type of semantic account to offer, one that does not involve associating with a one-place predicate a concept or set, with a two-place one a relation, with a functional constant a function or with a sentential operator a truth-function. If the semantic account of the language still involves the setting up of such associations between expressions and entities, it matters little whether or not an objection is felt to viewing such associations as analogous to that of bearer with name: even if the analogy is denied, the entities have still been 'countenanced' or admitted to the ontology.

We should note parenthetically that the distinction between variables and schematic letters is not one that can be made in relation to Frege's formal language, at least not as that language is explained by him. It is true that he employs different styles of letter for those which, within a given formula, overtly occur as bound by a quantifier, and those which do not—German letters for the former, italic letters for the latter—and a different style again (Greek vowels) for those overtly bound by some other operator, such as the class-abstraction operator. But the italic letters are not explained by him as schematic letters, but as bound by a tacit initial universal quantifier. Gg I 17 The point of the distinction lies in the possibility of a smoother formulation of the rules of inference: e.g., where modus ponens is formulated as allowing us to infer '———B' from '———A' and '——┬—B' ('If A, then B'),
                                                                    └—A
the sentences 'A' and 'B' may contain any number of italic letters, so that an application of this rule need not, strictly speaking, consist of the inference of the consequent of a conditional from the conditional together with its antecedent, but may consist of the inference of the universal closure of the consequent of an open conditional from the universal closure of the conditional together with the universal closure of its antecedent. Hence Frege does not make any distinction corresponding to that of Quine between variables and schematic letters, but calls his italic, German and Greek variables all alike simply 'letters'. (He disliked the term 'variable', as leading to the misunderstanding that, e.g., a numerical constant stands for a constant number, one whose magnitude never changes, while a numerical variable stands for a variable number, one whose magnitude varies: he therefore used the non-functional term 'letter', taking care that he never employed any letter as a constant, a typographical convention that necessitated the invention of much symbolism unfamiliar to the printer.) It would, of course, be possible to reinterpret Frege's italic letters as schematic letters: but, in relation to Frege's logical system taken

as a whole, there would be no schematic letters belonging to any category to which variables did not also belong.

There remains, indeed, this difference between schematic letters and variables, that variables always require us to specify the totality over which they range, whereas, when we are considering any specific interpretation of a schematic letter, we need only to understand the particular reference that is being ascribed to it, and do not have to envisage that as an element of any precise totality. To say this is merely to say that, in order to understand any individual constituent sentence or any particular predicate, we have merely to know how to determine its reference, without considering the totality of all possible referents of expressions of that kind. But, whenever we want to talk about all possible interpretations of a formula, or of all interpretations under which it comes out true (all models of it), as we frequently do, then we have to invoke a conception of the totality of all semantically distinct interpretations of its constituent schematic letters: this is precisely the notion that we need in investigating questions of logic, when we are concerned with the validity of an inference or the satisfiability of a set of axioms.

But, by the same token, substitutional quantification is not a genuine alternative to 'ontic' quantification, let alone one which provides an escape from otherwise troublesome problems. If it so happens that there is, for the intended range of the quantified variable, an expression in the language corresponding to every element of the range, then of course it must be the case that the universally quantified statement is true if and only if every permissible instance of it is true: here the qualification of 'instance' by 'permissible' is necessitated by the fact that there may be expressions such that the result of inserting them in the argument-place of the incomplete expression to which the quantifier is attached is a meaningful sentence, but one whose falsity would not, under its intended meaning, falsify the universally quantified statement. But this in no way relieves us of the responsibility for assigning a reference to the expressions the insertion of which in the argument-place of the incomplete expression yields the instances of the quantified statement, if we are to provide an adequate semantics for the language: for we need to do this in order to state the truth-conditions of those instances. For example, on the basis of classical logic, the following statement of protothetic is true:

$$\forall p \; \exists q \; \forall r \{ (q \lor p) \; \& \; [(r \lor p) \rightarrow (q \rightarrow r)] \}.$$

On the 'ontic' interpretation of the quantifiers, the sentential variables 'p', 'q' and 'r' range over the two truth-values, true (T) and false (F), and the truth of the sentence is established by observing that if, in the quantifier-free part of the sentence, 'p' takes the value T, then, when 'q' is assigned the value F, the sentence comes out true under either assignment to 'r', while, if 'p' takes the value F, then, when 'q' is given the value T, the same result holds. On the substitutional interpretation of the quantifiers, we do not need to specify the range of possible non-linguistic values of the sentential variables: we need only specify that we are considering all possible replacements of them by actual sentences. But, in order to establish the sentence as true, we have to explain that we are assuming each sentence to have one and only one of the truth-values, true and false, and to give the truth-tables for the sentential connectives: we then again demonstrate the truth of the sentence of protothetic by remarking that we obtain a true sentence by replacing, in the quantifier-free part, 'p' by a true sentence, 'q' by a false one, and 'r' by any sentence, or 'p' by a false sentence, 'q' by a true one, and 'r' by any sentence. The appeal to truth-values has been transferred from the explanation of the quantifiers to the account of the semantic role of the constituent sentences in a complex one: but it was needed for this latter task in any case, so that nothing whatever has been achieved by replacing the 'ontic' account of quantification by a substitutional one. It is futile to object that the 'ontic' account, by requiring the sentential variables to range over the truth-values, forces on us a conception of the truth-values as objects for which sentences stand, whereas, on the substitutional account, we can be content with the assumption of two truth-predicates—'. . . is true' and '. . . is false'—exactly one of which applies to every well-formed sentence. It is only by fastening too insistently upon the name/bearer relation as the prototype of reference that any such illusion can arise. Since sentences are not names or singular terms, there is no warrant for taking their referents to be objects of any kind: there is no substance to any supposed contrast between saying that sentences 'stand for' truth-values and that they 'have' truth-values; there is nothing which the 'ontic' account of quantification requires us to assume that must not also be assumed within a semantics which employs the substitutional account.

In this case we have a finite domain of quantification, and hence, in a formalized semantics for classical protothetic we do not need to quantify over truth-values because we can list them. If the semantics follows the model of the 'ontic' account, then we shall take an open sentence (one containing free sentential variables) as being satisfied by a sequence of truth-values, whereas, if it follows the substitutional account, an open sentence will be taken as satisfied by a sequence of sentences, each one of which either does or does not satisfy the predicate 'x is true': but there is, of course, no metaphysical assumption embodied in the former of these two presentations—the truth-values may, according to choice, be taken to be the numbers o and 1, or a pair of constant sentences which are true and false respectively, or whatever we choose. The interest of classical protothetic does not lie in any ontological consequence concerning the status of truth-values as entities, but in the fact which justifies the inference, for any sentence 'A', of '... A ...' from '$\forall p \ldots p \ldots$', that we are taking a constituent sentence as contributing to the truth-value of the complex sentence only via its own truth-value.

Quine supposes that only quantification over a range of entities requires us to ascribe to the corresponding constant expressions reference to those entities, or commits us to including those entities in our ontology: substitutional quantification thus appears to him as a threat, a device for employing quantification without ontological commitment. The advocates of substitutional quantification share with Quine the assumption that ontological commitment is required only by 'ontic' quantification, and therefore regard substitutional quantification as a means of achieving liberation from ontological commitment. Both are wrong, because it is not quantification which in the first place requires the ascription of reference: reference must be ascribed to any expressions which function as significant units of sentences of a language, if we are to be able to frame a semantic account of that language. To say that a sentence such as 'There is someone here whom I did not expect' is true just in case, for some suitable term 'X', some sentence of the form 'X is here and I did not expect that X would be here' does not, by itself, give a complete account of the semantics of sentences involving quantification into opaque contexts, even if the range of terms 'X' which we should admit has been successfully circumscribed: for we still await an account of the semantics of sentences such as 'Henry is here and I did not expect that Henry would be here'. The existence of the quantified sentence does, indeed, restrict the kind of account we can give of the unquantified one —we cannot, for example, regard the two occurrences of 'Henry' as logically unrelated: but whatever is adequate to explain the semantic role of 'Henry' in the unquantified sentence would equally well provide the basis for an 'ontic' account of the quantified one.

This example helps to illustrate a fact we have already noted, that the kinds of quantification that exist within a language help to determine what has to be counted as a significant unit within a sentence, and thus to which expressions we need to ascribe a reference. If we had a language without first-order quantification, then we should not need to recognize complex predicates as constituents of sentences, and hence should not need to regard them as having a reference; we should need to take account only of the simple predicates out of which atomic sentences were formed. But this is a different point from Quine's: it is the existence of *first*-order quantifiers, not of second-order ones, that compels us to employ the notion of a complex predicate in the analysis of sentence-structure.

What, then, is Frege's idea of the way in which we are able to form the required conception of the domain over which individual variables range? When these individual variables are those of Frege's symbolic language, then, as we have seen, their domain is to be taken simply as the totality of all objects: there is no criterion which an object has to satisfy to be in this domain, for every object automatically belongs to the domain. The notion of 'object' has no substance in application to things: it is true of everything to which it can be meaningfully ascribed. The notion gains its substance from the distinction that can be made between expressions, those that stand for objects as opposed to those which do not. The criterion we need to formulate is not that which a thing must satisfy if it is to be an object, but that which an expression must satisfy if it is to be said to stand for an object, that is, if it is both to be classified as a proper name (singular term) and to be said to have a reference. Hence the notion of an object can only be explained as correlative to that of a 'proper name': an object is the kind of thing which a proper name stands for (when it stands for anything). Since, however, we cannot assume that the language contains a proper name for every object, or even, since there are non-denumerably many objects, that it would be logically possible for it to do so, an object, in general, cannot be required to be the referent of a proper name, but only to be the *kind* of thing which could be such a referent. In forming the conception of the totality of all objects, we must include all those things of each one of which separately it is true that an expression standing for that thing could be added to the language, and would then function as a proper name, even though it is impossible that names of all those things could simultaneously be added to the language.

We have already remarked that the totality of all objects is, par excellence, an illegitimate totality in Russell's sense, a totality which cannot be taken as as a domain of quantification. To call some totality illegitimate is not to say that **every** sentence which purports to involve quantification over that totality is unintelligible: there may be many such sentences which have an evident truth-value, true or false. Even if the variables are taken as ranging over the domain of all objects, the following sentences are all manifestly true:

PM I 37

$$\forall x \; \exists y \; x = y$$
$$\exists x \; \exists y \; x \neq y$$
$$\forall x \; (x \text{ is a man} \to x \text{ is a mammal})$$
$$\exists x \; x \text{ is a natural satellite of the Earth.}$$

What is meant is merely that we cannot take quantification over the totality of all objects as a sentence-forming operation which will always generate a sentence with a determinate truth-value; we cannot, in other words, interpret it classically as infinitary conjunction or disjunction. If we attempt to do so, we shall be led into contradiction.

Simply to say that the totality of all objects is an illegitimate totality appears mystifying if no explanation is given of the obstacle to taking it as a domain of quantification. The reason is that it is an *impredicative* totality, one the specification of which offends against Russell's 'vicious-circle principle'. Objects are the correlates of proper names—as we have seen, the notion of an object has to be explained via the notion of a proper name; and, since the totality of objects includes abstract objects (we know, indeed, of no illegitimate totality containing only concrete objects, at least of none that involves contradiction, and hence, so far as we know, it is possible consistently to quantify over all concrete objects), we cannot restrict the objects we are considering to those indicated by some form of ostension, but have to consider the referents of terms whose use involves no extra-linguistic supplementation. Frege was perfectly ready to include in the totality of objects the referents of proper names of all kinds, including those whose construction itself involves first-order quantification, or, more exactly, bound individual variables. Among term-forming operators of this kind, operators, that is, which form a 'proper name' when attached to a predicate, are the description operator ('the x such that $\Phi(x)$'), the abstraction operator ('the class of x's such that $\Phi(x)$') and the numerical operator ('the number of x's such that $\Phi(x)$'). From the present point of view, the description operator is harmless, but the other two are not. If there is some determinate totality over which the variable 'x' ranges, and if '$F(\xi)$' is any specific predicate which is well defined over that totality, then of course there will be some definite subset of objects of the totality which satisfy the predicate '$F(\xi)$'; and it is perfectly in order to assume that we can form the terms 'the class of x's such that $F(x)$' and 'the number of x's such that $F(x)$', and regard these as standing for specific abstract objects, a class and a cardinal number respectively. What there is no warrant for is the assumption that the objects so denoted must belong to the totality with which we started. It is of no use to say that we assumed that that totality comprised all objects

PM I 37-8
Gg I 11
Gg I 9
Gl 62

whatever, because we have no ground for supposing that there is any totality closed under the operations of mapping arbitrary predicates defined over it on to classes or cardinal numbers: in fact, in the case of classes, Russell's paradox shows that there can be no such totality. If we have first succeeded in specifying a totality, then the use of individual variables ranging over that totality has a perfectly clear content, and we may employ it to form expressions for abstract objects: but we have no right to suppose that those objects must fall within the totality we originally specified. If, however, we attempt to characterize the totality by reference to the kind of expression which can stand for an element of the totality—as, in effect, Frege does—then, for our characterization of the totality to succeed, it must be supposed that the reference of each expression of that kind has been fixed independently of the specification of the totality. If such expressions include ones involving the use of variables ranging over that totality, then their reference is not independent of the specification of the totality, and we have indeed fallen into vicious circularity of the kind which Russell's principle prohibits.

Russell's vicious-circle principle has been thought dubious on various grounds. Part of this is due to Russell's method of formulating it, for instance by saying that a totality cannot contain a member which can be defined only by quantification over that totality. Ramsey questioned this thesis as simply not being evident, and Gödel has held that whether or not we take it as holding of any range of abstract objects must depend upon whether we think of those abstract objects as existing independently of us or as creations of our own thought: if they exist independently, then the vicious-circle principle has no plausibility, but if we construct them by our mental activity, then its validity must be conceded. It is characteristic that Ramsey, in discussing the matter, cites, as instances of characterizations of objects by quantification over a totality to which they belong, ones effected by means of the description operator, which is simply irrelevant in this context. Russell was not concerned, in the first place, with means of characterizing particular members of totalities, but, rather, with the means of characterizing totalities themselves, when they were meant to be taken as domains of quantification. What he was determined to avoid was a vicious circle within such a characterization. What is indisputable is that, if we seek to specify a domain over which a certain kind of variable is to range, and, in so doing, we employ quantification over that very domain, we have committed a vicious circularity: it makes not the slightest difference what metaphysical view we are adopting about the status of the elements of the domain—whether they are objects existing independently of human thought or creations of human thought; if we have committed such a vicious circle in the course of trying to say

FM 41
RML 136

what the domain is to be taken to be, then we simply have not succeeded in specifying any determinate domain. From this it does not follow, of course, that we cannot, for example, find some means of specifying a totality of sub-classes of a given class which satisfies the classical comprehension principle, that is, a totality of which we can be sure that, for any predicate we can define over the given class, even one involving quantification over our totality of sub-classes, there is in the totality a sub-class of those elements of the given class which satisfy that predicate. All that is required by the vicious-circle principle is that, in such a case, we have some *prior* means of specifying the totality of sub-classes: that is, a means which does not consist in explaining the notion of a sub-class belonging to the totality in terms of a specification of that sub-class by means of a predicate which picks out its members. If, on the other hand, we want to take this latter route to an explanation of the notion of a sub-class, and of the totality of sub-classes over which we want to quantify, namely by characterizing sub-classes as the referents of class-terms formed by applying the abstraction operator to predicates defined over the given class, then the vicious-circle principle rightly requires us to restrict the predicates considered to those that are well defined in advance of the characterization of the totality of sub-classes, that is, those that do not involve quantification over it. Frege's notion of an object offends in just the way that the vicious circle principle rules out. As we have seen, Frege recognizes that there is no other route to the general notion of an object save via that of a proper name, i.e. the kind of expression which stands for an object, and, at the same time, assumes that the totality of objects includes those denoted by 'proper names' the reference of which depends upon an understanding of quantification over objects.

We may perhaps regret that, at the time of Russell's discovery of the paradox, Frege was too little in sympathy with Russell's attempts at resolving it to see through Russell's sometimes hazy formulations to the essential insight embodied in the vicious-circle principle. At the very end of his life, Frege became convinced that the introduction of the whole notion of class had been a fundamental error. In one way, that was too radical a diagnosis; but, in any case, Frege never seems to have arrived at any true understanding of where the root of the trouble lay.

BW 226–51 (143–70); NS 288–9 (269–70)

The notion of 'object', like the notions of 'set', 'cardinal number', 'ordinal', etc., in their full intuitive meaning, has to be regarded as an indefinitely extensible one. If we have succeeded in forming some definite conception of a totality of objects, then we are able to introduce into the language quantification over this totality. But, by means of such quantification, together with certain term-forming operators which yield expressions for abstract objects, we are able to form new terms for objects which do not lie within the original totality. Just because the term 'object' is a mere correlate of 'proper name', and the logical behaviour of these new terms is that of proper names in Frege's general sense, the word 'object', as so understood, will still apply to the referents of the new terms. We are thus enabled to form a more extensive conception of a wider totality of objects, and introduce quantification over it, a step which will in turn enable us to form yet further new terms; and the process can continue as long as we please. It is for this reason that there can be no such thing as the domain of all objects.

The foregoing interpretation of the vicious-circle principle is the weakest possible: we have indeed so weakened it as to put its validity beyond question. On this interpretation, we do not prejudge the issue whether or not we have some non-circular means of specifying an impredicative totality, i.e. a totality containing members which we can characterize only by quantification over the totality: we merely preclude any means of specifying the totality which itself involves such quantification. It is a debatable point whether Russell himself intended the vicious-circle principle to be so understood as to prejudge the question of alternative means of specifying impredicative totalities. On the one hand, his initial formulations of the vicious-circle principle strongly suggest that he does intend this: on the other, the content of the celebrated—perhaps one should say 'notorious' —axiom of reducibility is precisely to the effect that the totality of first-order 'propositional functions' (which correspond, according to the number of their arguments, with Frege's concepts and relations), although specified without circularity, is in fact impredicative in the sense of containing elements which we can characterize only as extensionally equivalent with functions described by quantification over this totality.* Whatever the correct interpretation of Russell himself, most proponents of the vicious-circle

---

* This remark is itself questionable. The totality of first-order functions of individuals is characterized in the first place as consisting of those which are expressed by predicates formed within some unspecified language only by means of the sentential operators and quantification over individuals. The axiom of reducibility says that any predicate of individuals whose expression involves quantification over nth-order functions is extensionally equivalent to one which expresses a first-order function. Given a predicate, therefore, which involves quantification over first-order functions, we cannot say that we cannot characterize predicatively the first-order function corresponding to it: but we cannot necessarily, by means of a predicative characterization, identify that function as the one corresponding to the given second-order predicate. To any second-order predicate of individuals which we can frame, there is an extensionally equivalent first-order predicate of our language; but we have no means, in general, to find the first-order predicate, given the second-order one.

U

principle, Weyl for example, have advanced it as prejudging unfavourably the existence of impredicative totalities. So taken, the principle is open to Ramsey's objection that there is no theoretical ground why some totality should not contain elements the only unique characterization of which available to us involves quantification over the totality, and to Gödel's opinion that Ramsey's objection can be sustained so long as we conceive of the elements of the totality as existing in advance of and independently of our descriptions of them. But, understood as we have understood it here, merely as ruling out any circular specification of a totality, the principle becomes indisputable, and independent of any metaphysical views about the ontological character of the elements of the totality: it does not prejudge the existence of impredicative totalities, but merely presents a challenge to those who believe in their existence to find a non-circular means of saying of what they consist. Unfortunately, even when taken in this weakest sense, the vicious-circle principle is easily seen to be violated by Frege's conception of the totality of all objects as a domain for the individual variables of his symbolic language.

The impredicativity of Frege's totality of all objects arises from the assumption that it is closed under certain operations mapping concepts defined over the totality on to objects. The description operator, which stands for such an operation (second-level function), gives no trouble: it merely maps every concept under which there falls exactly one object on to that object, and every totality is closed under such an operation. The abstraction operator and the numerical operator, on the other hand, are governed by assumptions about the conditions for identity and distinctness of the results of the corresponding operations: the second-level function 'the number of x's such that $\Phi(x)$' yields distinct values when applied to concepts not equivalent in cardinality, while the function 'the class of x's such that $\Phi(x)$' has distinct values when applied to concepts not extensionally equivalent. No totality is closed under the latter operation, and only infinite totalities are closed under the former. The inconsistency of the assumption that the totality of objects is closed under the application of the operation of class-abstraction to concepts defined over it is sufficient to show that there can be no general presumption of the legitimacy of assuming that a totality is closed under arbitrary operations of this kind (operations effected by a second-level function over the concepts defined on the totality), let alone that a totality can be characterized in the first place by reference to such operations. The presumption of closure under particular such operations, such as that expressed by the numerical operator, is of course much weaker, and would be allowable if the totality could first be shown to be sufficiently large.

Unfortunately, Frege's only method of showing the totality of objects to be infinite is by reference to the abstract objects, in particular, precisely the cardinal numbers, it contains, and therefore involves a vicious circularity: the circularity could be avoided only by showing that there were infinitely many objects even when the notion of 'object' was explained without reference to the formation of numerical terms by means of the numerical operator.

Gl 82-3
Gg I 114-19

It might be thought that similar objections would already apply at a lower level, or, alternatively, that these objections could be met by reference to lower-level operations. We have located the impredicativity in Frege's conception of the totality of all objects in his tacit appeal, in explaining the notion of 'object', to the use of second-level operators, that is, ones which take a predicate in their argument-place. (The appeal is merely tacit because Frege's insistence that terms formed by means of such operators —e.g. class-terms or numerical terms—have to be considered as proper names like any other is never immediately juxtaposed with his characterization of objects as, in general, the kind of thing which can be the referent of a proper name.) But it might be argued that the assumption that the totality of objects is closed under the kinds of first-level functions which yield abstract objects itself involved a kind of impredicativity: the assumption, namely, that if the totality of objects contains all material objects, then it also contains the colours of all those objects, their shapes, volumes, masses, and so on—the results of applying first-level functions such as 'the colour of ξ', 'the shape of ξ', etc. Put generally, the assumption amounts to saying that the totality of objects is closed under the formation of equivalence classes under any equivalence relation defined over the totality: for the functions are just those which, relative to some equivalence relation defined over their arguments, yield the same value only for equivalent arguments. Alternatively, it might be argued that, if the assumption of closure under the formation of equivalence classes is justified, then the totality of objects must already be infinite, so that the assumption of closure under at least some second-level operations is not circular after all.

It is true enough that, if we start with some given set M, and form the set of all subsets of M which could be equivalence classes under some arbitrary equivalence relation defined over M, what we thus obtain will simply be the restricted power set of M (i.e. the set of all non-empty subsets of M), which is of course of greater cardinality than M provided that M has more than one member. If we now form the union of M with its restricted power set, and then again form the restricted power set of this union, we shall obtain a yet larger set, so that, if we start with a finite non-empty set

M, and reiterate this operation denumerably many times, and finally take the union of all these sets, we shall end with a denumerable set. We could, of course, reiterate the operation further: but we could never arrive at a set which was closed under this operation, since the operation always increases the cardinality.

To view the matter in this way is, however, to make the assumption that the equivalence classes under some partition of M are always to be distinguished from the elements of M. This amounts to saying that, if we start with some totality M of objects, and then introduce new (abstract) objects which can be regarded as equivalence classes of objects in M, these new objects are always to be distinguished from the members of M with which we started. Abstract objects which can be viewed as equivalence classes of other objects are also ones which can be taken as forming the range of values of some function such as 'the shape of ξ' or 'the mass of ξ', a function which, as we have seen, is introduced in connection with some already known equivalence relation which supplies the criterion for the function to have identical values for different arguments: it was Frege's suggestion, in Gl 68 *Grundlagen*, that we may always identify the value of such a function with the equivalence class to which the argument belongs. But the possibility of proposing such an identification of the abstract objects which form the range of the function with equivalence classes, and the fact that we speak of the introduction of (an expression for) the function as the introduction of (means of referring to) new abstract objects, rest upon our indifference to whether the values of the function are to be identified with or distinguished from objects referred to by any different means, or, indeed, to whether such a question is so much as raised. Frege thinks, it is true, that when we aim to give a comprehensive semantics for our language, or, rather, when we so reconstruct our language so as to be able to provide a comprehensive semantics for it, we have to make a decision on this point: since such a reconstructed language is not to be a many-sorted one, with distinct types of individual variable each with its own associated domain, but one with only a single kind of individual variable ranging over one single domain of objects, it is necessary for us to provide specific stipulations determining which pairs of terms of the language have the same referents. But he is perfectly well aware that it is at many points arbitrary how this is done. Part of the need for a reconstruction of natural language stems, on his view, from an actual incoherence latent in the language: in assessing the truth and falsity of sentences of our language, we follow various rules which are potentially inconsistent, that is, which simply cannot be generalized without producing contradictions; among such features are those which lead us to assess certain terms as devoid of reference, and hence certain sentences as devoid of truth-value; also, possibly, the use in complex contexts of the signs of generality employed in natural language. (To this charge of incoherence which Frege levels against natural language we should compare Tarski's similar charge on the basis of the use within natural language of semantic expressions such as 'true' and 'false'.) But another part of the need for a reconstruction of natural language, if a systematic semantics is to be attained, arises from a less serious defect: the existence of gaps which there is no obstacle to filling, but for which the intuitive meanings of the expressions of natural language fail to provide any guidance about the way in which they should be filled. That is, certain sentences can be formed for which we have no direct use, and for which our intuitive understanding of the expressions they contain fails to supply any basis for the determination of any truth-value for those sentences, even though the construction of a systematic semantics must result in a determination of those sentences as true or false: examples of such sentences would be 'Masses are equivalence classes of material objects', 'Directions are classes of parallel lines' and 'Cardinal numbers are classes of concepts'. As a result, when we reconstruct the language, we are free to devise our semantics so as to yield for such sentences either truth-value, according to our convenience. Such a reconstruction will therefore be, to that extent, arbitrary: there will be no right or wrong about the identification or distinction of objects where our employment of natural language supplies no guidance as to whether they are to be identified or not, since, within it, that question is never raised.

Thus, for instance, in *Grundgesetze der Arithmetik*, Frege raises the question under what conditions a class-term—one formed by means of the abstraction operator—is to be counted as having the same referent as a term of some other kind, and proposes the solution later employed by Quine and others, that an object denoted by a term other than a class-term shall be regarded as identical with its own unit class. (The fact that the only terms other than class-terms which occur within the language of *Grundgesetze* are terms for truth-values is here irrelevant: if there were yet other terms, presumably the same device would seem to Frege equally applicable to them.)   Gg I 10

There is thus no principle held by Frege which would require that all abstract objects should be distinguished from all concrete ones, or, for that matter, from abstract objects of other kinds (i.e. referred to by terms of different kinds). Thus, if we start with a set M of concrete objects, say physical bodies, and want to include in our universe also the masses of those bodies, there is no reason why we should not suppose that masses are themselves material bodies. For instance, if the set M can be regarded as well-ordered in some specific way, then we might choose to identify the mass of any body a belonging to M as the first element of M, under the well-ordering, which is equal in mass to a. Likewise, the shapes of elements of M could again be regarded as members of M, the shape of a being the first element of M similar to a. Of course, if Frege's general suggestion is followed, and all abstract objects such as masses and shapes are identified with equivalence classes over M, then, provided that M has more than one element to begin with, not every abstract object can be identified with an element of M, since, by considering all possible equivalence relations, we obtain all non-empty subsets of M as equivalence classes, and there are more of these than elements of M. But this suggestion only makes sense against the background of the general theory of classes: if we had already accepted the totality of objects as closed under the formation of classes, or at least as containing all classes of concrete objects, then it would be a worthwhile economy to identify all abstract objects given as the values of first-level functions defined over concrete objects with equivalence classes of concrete objects. But, in the present context, we are taking a more restricted view. Having agreed that Frege's totality of all objects is in the highest degree impredicative, and having located as the chief source of this impredicativity his assumption of its closure under such second-level operations as class-abstraction and numerical abstraction, we are considering whether his taking the totality of objects to be closed under the first-level operations which generate abstract objects may also be regarded as already a source of the impredicativity. Such operations do not need to be interpreted in terms of equivalence classes; and, in a context where the second-level operations were not admitted, they would not be so interpreted, because we should not have the notion of 'class' at hand to supply such an interpretation.

The answer is, then, that no impredicativity need arise from the application of the first-level functions which yield abstract objects. Each such function may be taken, if we choose, as simply mapping the totality of objects into itself: relative to each single equivalence relation, taken separately, such a mapping is of course always possible, because the worst that can happen is that the set M is partitioned by the equivalence relation into unit classes. From this point of view, abstract objects—at least those which form the values of first-level functions defined over concrete objects—do not need to be regarded as objects of a quite different kind from concrete ones, or even as, so to speak, intrinsically abstract. There is, as we have remarked, nothing to prevent our identifying abstract objects with concrete ones or with abstract objects of other kinds. Our language does not require any such identification; but it does not preclude it either. If we were satisfied, from some other source—perhaps mathematical or logical intuition—that we could specify a totality of objects, perhaps of a highly abstract nature, of sufficient cardinality to contain all the abstract objects like shapes and masses of the kind we are presently concerned with—those given as the values of first-level functions defined over concrete objects—then we should not need to make any such identification of these abstract objects with concrete ones. But we are at liberty to make such an identification if that appears the most solid means of ensuring that we can without circularity envisage a determinate domain for our individual variables which yet contains the abstract objects of this kind which we want to refer to.

So construed, the abstractness of abstract objects of this kind is not, as it were, a feature of the objects themselves but of the means we employ for referring to them. When we speak of the masses or of the shapes of physical bodies, there is no problem as to what sorts of things these masses or shapes are, since we can, if we like, take them to be certain actual physical bodies. The abstract character attaches, rather, to the terms we use to refer to them, terms of the form 'the mass of a' or 'the shape of a', or more complex terms explained ultimately by means of the functional expressions 'the mass of ξ' or 'the shape of ξ'. It is a feature of natural language that such terms are used within it without any governing assumption as to the identity or distinctness of their reference with that of terms of other kinds. It is a feature essential to the use we make of them that the criterion of identity associated with them is given by means of an equivalence relation— e.g. equality of mass or similarity—defined over objects of the kind for which the argument-term 'a' stands. The former feature does not carry over into a reconstructed language, while the latter does: but many alternative schemes of identification of the referents of such terms with those of terms of other kinds are equally consistent with the criterion of identity which is imposed.

Frege was no more conscious of the circularity implicit in his assumptions about the domains over which higher-level variables range than of that implicit in his conception of the totality of objects. Frege takes it for granted that the domain of first-level concepts includes a referent of any first-level predicate which can be constructed in the language, including those which involve quantification over first- or higher-level concepts. Such a supposition cannot be dismissed out of hand, if a claim is made to have a non-circular characterization of the totality of first-level concepts for which a comprehension principle of this kind holds. But Frege makes no such claim, and it is not apparent how he could. The general notion of 'concept' (or, rather, of 'function') is indefinable, and we can only give hints; but these hints relate to the corresponding type of linguistic expression: there seems no route to the general notion of concepts save by taking them as things of the kind for which one-place first-level predicates stand. To grasp *what* concept a given predicate stands for is to be aware of the conditions under which the predicate is true of an arbitrary object. These we evidently cannot know, in the case of a predicate which involves quantification over concepts, until we know what is the totality of concepts which constitutes the domain of such quantification: and so the vicious circle is as overt as it could be. Frege's platonistic understanding of higher-level quantification (displayed more in practice by the kinds of inference he allows and the rules of inference in his formal system than by any explicit general statement) is flatly irreconcilable with his belief that it is via an understanding of the workings of language that we come by a conception of the totality comprised by any one logical type (such as first-level concepts, first-level relations, relations between first-level concepts, etc.). This is not to assert that anyone who claims to have such a platonistic conception of, e.g., the totality of first-level functions must postulate that we have a notion of 'function' antecedently to our grasp of the notion of 'functional expression'. He may well allow that it is an essential preliminary to our acquiring the notion of 'function' that we should learn to employ particular functional expressions, and, later, form the general idea of a functional expression as a linguistic unit. At this stage, the platonist may hold, an initial conception of 'function' may be formed, namely that of the referent of a functional expression of this kind: such a notion is still a predicative one, since the functional expressions considered will not themselves involve quantification over functions (at least if the notion thus formed is not to be circular). But the platonist must grant that, in order to progress from this stage to a conception of the full platonist domain of *all* first-level functions (defined over some given totality of objects), there has to be a leap: at this point the link has to be severed between the notion of 'function' and that of 'functional expression', even if a grasp of the latter notion was a psychologically necessary first step to the attainment of the former. Frege never acknowledged the necessity for any such leap; at the same time, he adhered firmly to a platonist understanding of higher-level quantification.

This is one instance of Frege's blindness to various difficulties which beset a platonistic philosophical outlook and of which we have since become very sharply conscious; and it is at just these points that we encounter matters of contemporary philosophical concern about which we feel that

Frege has nothing to teach us. (The term 'platonism' is, of course, here used to signify a realist attitude to abstract objects and to entities of higher level, in the way made familiar in the philosophy of mathematics by Bernays and by Quine, with little connection with the views of Plato himself. The very sharpness of Frege's distinction between objects and concepts makes it impossible to compare his doctrines at all fruitfully with those actually advanced by Plato.) We cannot criticize Frege for this, since his realism was maintained in a philosophical climate in which the prevalent forms of idealism to which he opposed it bore little resemblance to anything which we should now recognize as a viable alternative to realism. All that we can regret is that Russell's discovery of the set-theoretical paradoxes had so shattering an impact on Frege as effectively to bring his creative work to an end (although his last publication took place two decades later), so that he did not participate in the confused, long drawn out, but immensely fruitful reappraisal of the philosophical foundations of logic and mathematics which was initiated by Russell's discovery. *SPM* 275 *FLPV* 14

That Frege can give no consistent justification for interpreting second-level quantification as ranging over the full impredicative totalities of first-level concepts, relations and functions is, of course, no ground for denying him the right to employ second-level quantifiers at all. Exactly what strength is required in the second-order logic for the derivation of those principles which are essential to Frege's foundations for mathematics is, naturally, a question for the philosophy of mathematics. The only general ontological thesis in Frege's philosophy to which second-level quantification is relevant is, however, the ascription of reference to incomplete expressions, which, as we saw, requires second-level quantification for its proper formulation. Plainly, we shall need to assume, for this purpose, the possibility of quantifying over the full impredicative totality only if we wish to ascribe reference to predicates which themselves involve such quantification, and we shall want to admit such predicates into the language only if we need such quantification for other purposes: so the theory of reference cannot, of itself, provide any temptation to violate the vicious–circle principle. Expressions for second-level generality are deeply embedded in natural language, but are there always interpretable as ranging over a predicative totality; assertion of the existence of a property is taken as needing justification by production of an instance. Second-level quantification is immune to question so long as it remains predicative; there can be no warrant for casting doubt on it even in this restricted case.

CHAPTER 16

*Identity**

Bs 8

Gg I 20

LF 54; Huss 320

IT WAS FREGE who first made identity a logical notion. The sign of identity differs from the other logical constants in not being a sentence-forming operator in the sense of one used to construct complex sentences from simpler ones, but a relational expression used to form atomic sentences. Since a natural criterion for regarding an expression as a logical constant would be that it requires to be represented by an operator of the former type, one which is introduced in the step-by-step formation of complex sentences from atomic ones, it may seem obscure why the sign of identity should be regarded as a logical constant at all, rather than a non-logical relational expression which is useful in all contexts: but it would be capricious to regard the quantifier 'There is at least one . . .' as a logical constant, but not the quantifier 'There is at most one . . .', for whose expression, when not taken as primitive, we require the sign of identity. At any rate, the '$=$' sign was a primitive symbol of Frege's original formulation in *Begriffsschrift* of quantificational logic, and has ever since remained a logical constant. Since Frege's logical system was a higher-order one, and since he accepted Leibniz's law, according to which '$a = b$' is equivalent to 'For every $\mathscr{f}$, $\mathscr{f}(a)$ if and only if $\mathscr{f}(b)$', it may be asked why he needed to take '$=$' as primitive, instead of defining it by means of this equivalence. But, according to Frege, identity is indefinable, since it is required for the formulation of any definition: a definition, at least an explicit definition, must always take the form of a stipulation of the truth of an identity-statement; and, in his

---

* Save for the last paragraph and the first seven, this chapter was written before the publication of David Wiggins's *Identity and Spatio-Temporal Continuity*, concerned with the problem that looms large here. So far as I can see, my conclusions agree substantially with his. Uncertain whether to suppress the chapter, or to recast it so as to provide a commentary on Wiggins's book, I eventually decided to let it stand as originally written, in the hope that the difference of approach may yield something of interest.

writings after *Grundlagen*, Frege recognized the legitimacy of no other
kind of definition than an explicit one. It is true that, in *Grundlagen*, Frege   Gl 65
speaks of Leibniz's law as a 'definition' of identity, and says that he will
adopt it as his own: in both formal systems, however, that of *Begriffsschrift*
and that of *Grundgesetze*, identity is primitive; the argument that it is indefinable because needed in order to frame any definition is advanced in his re-   Huss 320
view of Husserl. The ground is not very convincing. It is only possible for
Frege to say this because he takes the sign of identity to do duty also for the
biconditional, which is in turn possible only because he assimilates sentences
to names, viz. of truth-values; and in any case it seems more natural to take a
definition as a stipulation of the interchangeability of two expressions,
rather than of the truth of a sentence connecting them. But the thesis of the
indefinability of identity does not seem to play any important role in Frege's
philosophy.

Leibniz's law is a biconditional: a is identical with b if and only if a and b
have exactly the same properties (fall under the same concepts). From left
to right, the biconditional is evident. If the result of removing one or more
occurrences of a name 'a' from a sentence is genuinely a predicate applying
to the referent of 'a', i.e. an expression standing for a property which
that object is being said to have (a concept under which the object is being
said to fall), then whether or not the predicate is true of the object must be
independent of the way in which the object is referred to, and hence the
sentence must retain the same truth-value if 'a' is replaced by any name
'b' which has the same referent. Whenever such a replacement involves, or
risks, a change of truth-value, then the incomplete expression resulting
from removing 'a' from the sentence cannot stand for a property being
ascribed to the referent of 'a'. From right to left, the biconditional expresses
the principle of the identity of indiscernibles, which has been considered
contentious. Plainly, if the predicate-variable '$\mathcal{f}$' is allowed to range over
the property of being identical with a, then, if a is distinct from b, there is
one property which a has and b lacks, namely that of being identical with a.
So construed, the principle is trivial. But the principle has been questioned
when the range of the predicate-variable is restricted in some way, for
instance to properties which can be expressed without reference to the
objects a and b. Thus it has been held to be logically conceivable that the
universe should consist solely of two distinct but indistinguishable spheres.
It is, however, evident that, whether or not we are obliged to accept the   NS 40 (36)
identity of indiscernibles, nothing can impugn it as a regulative principle.
If it is really the case that we can find no predicate, not itself involving
reference to either an object a or an object b, which is true of a but not of b,

then nothing can possibly form an obstacle to our regarding *a* as identical with *b*. If, for example, we suppose a completely symmetrical universe, consisting of two spheres and an observer (himself always symmetrical about the plane of points equidistant from the two centres), nothing can stand in the way of a redescription of this universe as consisting of a single sphere and an observer (that is, so to speak, half an observer).

Bs 8   In *Begriffsschrift* Frege held that identity was a relation between names and not between things. His motive for this view was to give an explanation of the informativeness of a true identity-statement: but it makes nonsense of the use of bound variables on either side of the sign of identity. Later, he replaced this view by the more satisfactory explanation in terms of the distinction between sense and reference: identity could now be regarded as a relation between objects—that relation, namely, which any object has to itself and to nothing else—without rendering the informativeness of identity-statements unintelligible. The information conveyed by a relational statement depends both on the senses of the names and on that of the relational expression. Very often the identification of the bearers of the names is unproblematic, and we regard the information conveyed as consisting solely in the fact that the relation in question obtains between those objects. Given that a particular object is the bearer of two names, no information is acquired by learning that that object has to itself a relation which every object has to itself: but the truth-conditions of an identity-statement determine that it can be true only when the same object is the bearer of both names. The informativeness of an identity-statement thus turns entirely on the senses of the two names: but what makes this to be so is precisely the fact that identity is just that relation between objects which it is, viz. the minimal reflexive relation.

Whether or not Leibniz's law can be made to serve as an actual definition of identity, it cannot be used as a criterion for deciding the truth of identity-statements. It can, indeed, provide a ground for concluding to the falsity of an identity-statement, for it may be possible to find a predicate which can be recognized as true of the bearer of one name and false of the bearer of another in advance of a decision whether the names have the same bearer. But the truth of an identity-statement cannot be established by an appeal to Leibniz's law, since, apart from the impossibility of running through the totality of first-level concepts, there will often be no other way of ascertaining that a particular predicate which is true of the bearer of one name is also true of the bearer of the other except by establishing that the two names have the same bearer. There is, for instance, no way of showing that the predicate 'is visible shortly before sunrise', which is plainly true of the Morning Star, is also true of the Evening Star, which does not depend upon showing that the Morning Star and the Evening Star are one and the same celestial body.

It is therefore necessary, if we are to be capable of recognizing any non-trivial identity-statement as true, to have a criterion for its truth. It was one of Frege's fundamental discoveries that, although the expression 'the same' has a univocal and determinate sense, there is no one criterion for the truth of identity-statements, but a variety of different criteria according to the names which occur in them. Not only this, but a determination of this criterion is part of what is involved in providing a sense for any name: any verbal specification of its sense must therefore include a stipulation of the criterion of identity for the object which is the referent of the name. The expression 'criterion of identity', which has figured prominently in later philosophical writing, particularly that of Wittgenstein, was introduced by Frege; and the conception which it expresses is the more important of the two ingredients which compose Frege's doctrine that proper names have a sense and are not, as Mill thought, mere labels attached to objects. Merely to know that a name has as its referent an object with which we are con-fronted, or which is presented to us in some way, at a particular time is not yet to know what object the name stands for: we do not know this until we know, in Frege's terminology, 'how to recognize the object as the same again', that is, how to determine, when we are later confronted with an object or one is presented to us, whether or not it should be taken to be the same object. How this is to be done is not uniform for all objects: it depends precisely on the kind of thing which the name is intended to stand for, and thus on the sense of the name; with different names different criteria of identity will be associated. Very often, a proper name will have associated with it the same criterion of identity as we have already learned to associate with other names, and in this case we are inclined to overlook how much we had to learn in order to grasp this criterion; but whenever it becomes necessary to explain the sense of a whole range of proper names, that is, of names with which is associated a criterion of identity different from that associated with other names, the need to specify the criterion of identity becomes prominent. Thus in *Grundlagen* Frege considers the introduction of numerical terms, which he takes as capable of being cast in the form 'the number of F's' ('the number of α's such that $F(\alpha)$'), where '$F(\xi)$' is some predicate. In order to supply a reference to such names, it will be necessary to stipulate the criterion of identity for numbers, which means the criterion for the truth of a statement of the form 'The number of F's is the same as the number of G's'.

Gl 62

Gl 62

Frege does not add explicitly that the association of a criterion of identity is part of the specification of the sense, not only of proper names, but also of a large number of substantival general terms, such as 'man', 'river', 'city', etc. In order to grasp the sense of such a general term, we have to know, not only what is the criterion for its application, that is, when it is right to say of something that it is a man, a river or a city, but also the criterion of identity associated with it, that is, the correct use of '. . . is the same man (river, city) as . . .'. That this is an additional requirement, beyond the specification of the criterion of application, and not determined by it, and that it is genuinely part of knowing the sense of the general term, is displayed most clearly when there is an ambiguity relating only to the criterion of identity, as happens with the word 'book', in the way we noted in Chapter 4.

p. 74

Since a criterion of identity is associated with a general term of this kind, that to be associated with a proper name can often be specified by stipulating that the name is used as the name of an object to which such a general term applies: if we are told that a proper name is the name of a man, then the criterion of identity associated with the proper name is to be the criterion for 'same man'. Among general terms, there will often be several with which the same criterion of identity is associated, and whose sense thus differs solely in respect of their criteria of application. It will normally be the case, however, that, for any criterion of identity, there will be a substantival term of maximum generality with which that criterion of identity is associated, one applying to all the objects for which that criterion of identity is used. We agreed in Chapter 4 to call such a term a 'categorial predicate', and to speak of the class of objects of which it is true as a 'category'.

p. 76

For Frege, the necessity of stipulating the criterion of identity to be associated with a name, or with all names of a certain range, does not call in question the univocity of the sign of identity. In discussing numerical terms, Frege considers, and rejects, precisely this suggestion, namely that, by laying down a criterion of identity for numbers, he is giving the sign of identity a special sense in the context of numerical terms. No, he replies, he is not giving it a special sense: rather, by taking as given a fixed sense for the sign of identity, that, namely, conferred on it by Leibniz's law, and then stipulating the condition for the truth of a statement of identity between numbers, he is fixing the sense of the numerical terms occurring in such a statement.

Gl 63

In § 54 of *Grundlagen* there occurs the following passage:

A concept, which is that to which a number is assigned, in general delimits in a determinate manner that which falls under it. The concept 'letter in the word *four*' marks off the *f* from the *o*, the *o* from the *u*, and so on. The concept 'syllable in the word *four*' picks out the word as a whole and as indivisible in the sense that no part of it again falls under the concept 'syllable in the word *four*'. Not all concepts are so constituted. We can, e.g., divide up what falls under the concept 'red' in a variety of ways, without the parts thereby ceasing to fall under that concept. To a concept of this kind no finite number belongs. The proposition that units are isolated and indivisible can, accordingly, be formulated as follows: Only a concept which marks off what falls under it in a determinate manner, and which does not permit arbitrary division of it into parts, can be a unit with respect to a finite number.

(The last two sentences are explained by the fact that the passage occurs in the context of a discussion of the notion of a 'unit', and Frege is proposing to identify as the 'unit' the *concept* to which the number is assigned.)

Geach has repeatedly accused Frege of being cagey in what he says about the concept *red* (*Reference and Generality*, pp. 38, 153). For, he says, the difference between the concept *red* and the concept *letter in the word 'four'* is not merely that there are infinitely many red things and only finitely many letters in the word 'four': the difference between the two concepts is much more acute than that. Even if we consider the more circumscribed concept *red things in Geach's study at midnight, 1st January, 1964*, the trouble is not that we cannot make an end of counting the objects falling under it, but that we do not know how to begin: it simply makes no sense to speak of the number of red things, even within a circumscribed region of space-time. Frege was right in holding that the answer '0' to a question 'How many?' is not a rejection of the question in that sense in Huss 327
which the answer 'No one' is a rejection of the question 'Who?' But there are some questions 'How many?' which can only be rejected, not answered: to the question, 'What is the number of red things there have been in this room today?', we can only answer, 'There is no such number'.

Geach's reason for holding this view is that he regards general terms—what Frege called 'concept-words'—as divisible into two classes: those, like 'man', part of whose sense consists in an associated criterion of identity; and those, like 'red', with which is associated no criterion of identity, but whose whole sense resides in what we may call the criterion of application associated with them. To grasp the sense of either kind of general term, we have to learn the associated criterion of application—under what conditions it is true to say of an object that it is a man, or that it is red.

But with general terms of the former kind, we have also learnt something else—the associated criterion of identity—which is not, or at least not completely, determined by the criterion of application: we have, e.g., to learn what '. . . is the same man as . . .' means. With general terms of the second kind, however, there is nothing more to learn: the expression '. . . is the same red thing as . . .' has no univocal sense, and can be supplied with one only by giving the word 'thing' some specific content. The distinction between the two classes of general term corresponds roughly, Geach holds, to the grammatical distinction between (common) nouns and adjectives.

If this is correct, then indeed Geach's conclusion follows, that there can be no determinate answer to the question how many objects there are to which a general term of the second kind applies. As Geach remarks, it is essential to the procedure of counting that we should count each of the objects (falling under the given concept), and count each one only once. If we really lack, in a given case, any criterion for saying whether we are counting the same object as before or not, then we can never say whether or not we have counted any object twice, and hence we cannot say whether we are carrying out the procedure of counting correctly. As Geach observes, it makes no difference if it is pleaded that there are infinitely many objects falling under the concept, since the same objection will apply to any attempt to explain what it means to assign any determinate infinite cardinal number to that concept: any such explanation will employ the notion of one-to-one correlation, which involves that we must assure ourselves that we have correlated *each* object falling under the concept only *once* to some member of a standard totality.

Geach calls general terms of the first class 'substantival', and those of the second class 'adjectival'. His criterion for a general term 'X' to be substantival is that there should be a determinate sense for the phrase 'the same X', and that knowing this sense is a part of knowing the sense of the general term 'X'. This is, for him, only a necessary, not a sufficient, condition for the general term 'X' to be what he calls 'countable', i.e. for it always to have a determinate sense to ask 'How many X's?' (there is, of course, no connection with the use of the word 'countable' to mean 'at most denumerable'). For instance, it is part of the sense of what Quine calls a 'mass term', such as 'gold', that there is a criterion of identity associated with it—we know what it means to say 'the same gold': but for all that it makes no sense to ask, 'How many golds?'. 'Gold' is thus a substantival, but not a countable, general term. Geach does not explain, however, what else has to belong, besides a criterion of identity, to the sense of a general term to render it countable: what other feature of its use has to be specified to confer countability on it. Quine, who, as we shall see, does not accept either of Geach's distinctions, suggests, following Frege's remarks in the passage quoted above, that the valid distinction which Geach is incorrectly formulating is that between a concept under which falls any part of anything that falls under it, and one for which this is not so: thus—for everyday purposes, at least—any part of a red surface is red, and any fragment of a piece of gold is itself gold. As we see from the second example, this must correspond with Geach's distinction between uncountable and countable concepts, not with his distinction between adjectival and substantival ones— if it corresponds with either. In any case, it is clear that Frege overstates the principle of distinction when he suggests, at the beginning of the above-quoted passage, that for count- able concepts, *no* part of anything falling under the concept can also fall under it. The concept *rectangle*, for instance, is evidently countable, and there is a determinate answer to the question how many rectangles there 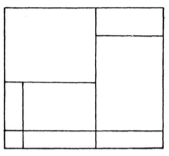 are in the accompanying figure: yet some of the rectangles have other rectangles as parts. The last sentence of the quotation hits the mark better: a countable concept may not permit *arbitrary* division into parts.

If Geach is right, therefore, there is a certain lack of precision in Frege's answer to the question 'What are we saying something about when we make a statement of number?', the answer, namely, 'A concept'. On Geach's account, this answer is excessively general: the proper answer would be 'A countable concept'. But it is clear that Geach is accusing Frege of more than misleading phraseology: he is accusing him of philosophical error. On Geach's view, although in the passage quoted Frege showed that he had glimpsed the distinction between substantival and adjectival concepts, he shut his eyes to it: his 'cagey' pretence that there are infinitely many red things resulted from his determination to take all genuine concepts as being countable. This is clear enough, after all, from what Frege says about classes. A class differs from a mere aggregate in marking off its members each from the others: it is always determinate what constitutes a single member of any given class. And it is precisely on the strength of this that Frege argues that a class cannot be understood save as the extension of a concept: it is via the concept whose extension the class is that the marking off from each other of the objects belonging to the class (i.e. falling under the concept) is accomplished. Frege can only argue in this way if he assumes that every concept—every genuine concept—marks off the objects falling

Gl 46

Schr 434, 442; NS 198–9 (182–3)

under it in the manner in which it is half-conceded in the *Grundlagen* passage quoted that the concept *red* does not. Against this charge of Geach's, it is useless to attempt to defend Frege by terminological legislation, by saying, that is, that, while Frege recognized Geach's distinction, he tacitly intended his expression 'concept-word' to be taken as applying only to substantival (or to countable) general terms, and hence his word 'concept' only to substantival (or countable) concepts. For, to whatever extent Frege recognized the distinction, his formal language, considered as having the semantics with which Frege endowed it, leaves no room for that distinction. We can formally prove, in Frege's system, that, for every predicate, there is a determinate number of objects of which that predicate is true. All that is being assumed, in such a proof, is that it is determinate, for each object, whether the predicate is true of it or not: there seems no need, nor indeed any possibility, of reinforcing the criterion for the application of the predicate with a criterion of identity.

Gl 63   Geach endorses the doctrine, ascribed above to Frege, that, while 'the same' has a univocal and determinate sense, this does not relieve us of the necessity to stipulate, for any name, the criterion of identity for the object which is its referent. In concurring with this doctrine, Geach puts a quite special gloss on the subordinate thesis that 'the same' has a univocal sense; but he does not ascribe the doctrine to Frege, but, rather, upbraids Frege for not having understood it. (Presumably he would ascribe the doctrine to Wittgenstein; it dominates the early sections of the *Investigations*.) Moreover, Geach goes on to draw from the doctrine various consequences very damaging to Frege. Geach's gloss on the univocity of 'the same' is that, while not equivocal or ambiguous, it is a fragmentary expression, having no significance unless we say or mean 'the same X', where 'X' represents some (substantival) general term (*Mental Acts*, p. 69). In this it is to be compared with 'real' or 'good' or with number-adjectives; and Geach rebukes Frege for seeing 'clearly that "one" cannot significantly stand as a predicate of objects unless it is (at least understood as) attached to a general term', and yet failing to see that the same holds true of 'the same' (*Reference and Generality*, p. 39). Neither 'real' nor 'good' stands, by itself, for a property of objects; out of context, it is neither true nor false, but just devoid of meaning, to say of an object that it is real or good. For all that, 'real' and 'good' are not equivocal, taking on different meanings in different contexts. Rather, they represent a kind of operator which forms, from a given general term, another general term whose sense is uniformly related to that of the original general term. It makes no sense to say that something is 'real' or 'good' unless you say or mean 'a real X' or 'a good X', for some suitable general term 'X': but 'good' and 'real' have a single, univocal sense because it is true of both these adjectives that inserting it before any general term which will receive it makes the same modification in the sense of that general term. Geach holds that the same goes for 'the same'. There is no such relation as the relation of identity: '. . . is the same as . . .' does not, taken out of context, stand for any relation at all. If 'X' and 'Y' are substantival general terms, then '. . . is the same X as . . .' and '. . . is the same Y as . . .' will indeed stand for determinate relations; but they will, in general, stand for different relations. Nevertheless, 'the same' is not for this reason equivocal; for any two general terms 'X' and 'Y', the relational expression 'the same X' stands in exactly the same relation to 'X' as does the (non-synonymous) relational expression 'the same Y' to 'Y'.

Here, Geach would hold, the analogy with 'real' and 'good' halts slightly. We do not have, in stipulating the sense of a general term 'X', expressly to stipulate the meaning of 'a real X' or 'a good X': rather, if the sense of 'X' is given, then we can determine the sense of 'a real X' or of 'a good X' —if the latter has a sense, which it will not always have—according to a general principle which constitutes the sense of the modifiers 'real' and 'good'. With 'the same' it is different: it is part of what has expressly to be done in stipulating the sense of a general term 'X' that we should lay down what 'the same X' is to mean; so the sense of 'the same X' is not determined *from* the sense of 'X', but is given with it and is in part constitutive of it. The reason why it is still correct to say that 'the same' has a univocal sense is that there is a formal or logical similarity between the uses of any two expressions of the forms 'the same X' and 'the same Y': the permissible transformations and rules of inference governing sentences containing either expression are the same.

From this doctrine Geach draws various consequences inimical to Frege. First, any of Frege's conceptual analyses, such as that of 'just as many . . . as . . .' in terms of one-one correlation, which employ the notion of the single absolute relation of identity, will require emendation: I will for the moment postpone an account of what Geach conceives that this emendation should consist in.

Secondly, if it is necessary, in stipulating the sense of a substantival general term 'X', expressly to stipulate the sense of 'the same X', without its being possible to derive the sense of this phrase from the other constituent features of the sense of 'X'—i.e. if, in our terminology, the criterion of identity is not determined by the criterion of application, but has to be laid down separately: then the possibility is open that there should be 'adjectival' general terms for which we have not made this additional stipulation, but whose sense consists wholly in their criterion of application, without there being any associated criterion of identity; and we have seen that Geach holds that this is not a mere theoretical possibility, but that our language actually abounds in such adjectival general terms.

Thirdly, Geach uses his doctrine about identity to call Frege's treatment of quantifiers in question. He notes that there are two quite separate features of the quantifier-variable notation whose introduction by Frege liberated logic. One is the feature which was stressed in the earlier part of this book, that the sign of generality does not, as it does in natural language, occupy the argument-place of the predicate, but is placed in front of the predicate attached to a bound variable which also occupies the argument-place. The other, quite distinct, feature is that all quantifiers are unrestricted in range (save, of course, that each bound variable is restricted to a single *type* such as objects, first-level functions of one argument, etc.). Every individual variable ranges, for Frege, over all objects simultaneously, every function variable over all functions of the given type. That the two features are separable is evident: we should achieve the first without the second by replacing each sentence of natural language of the form '. . . some tiger . . .' (where 'some' is the principal operator) by a sentence of the form 'For some tiger x, . . . x . . .' (and '. . . every tiger . . .' by 'For every tiger x, . . . x . . .'); whereas Frege's method is of course to represent '. . . some tiger . . .' as 'For some x, x is a tiger and . . . x . . .' (and '. . . every tiger . . .' as 'For every x, if x is a tiger, then . . . x . . .'). The arguments advanced by Geach do not actually require such a close approximation to natural language (or such a radical departure from contemporary logic) as 'For some tiger x, . . . x . . .'); they would be met if we were to represent '. . . some tiger . . .' as (say) 'For some animal x, x is a tiger and . . . x . . .' (and '. . . every tiger . . .' as 'For every animal x, if x is a tiger, then . . . x . . .'). In general, for any substantival general term 'X', we can find a unique corresponding category term 'A': 'A' will be that substantival general term which has the widest application of all those with which is associated the same criterion of identity as is associated with 'X'. (In the example, I assumed that 'animal' is the category term corresponding to 'tiger': it should be noted that Geach's own use of the word 'category' is quite different.) If 'X' is a substantival general term, and 'A' the corresponding category term, then 'y is the same X as z' means 'y is an X and y is the same A as z'; e.g. 'y is the same tiger as z' means 'y is a tiger and y is the same animal as z'. (Geach does not say this, or speak about category terms at all; in introducing them I am imposing a modification on his doctrine; but he would surely have to allow this as an admissible amplification.) On this account, then, what Geach regards as

Frege's mistake was to carry the above analysis too far, and suppose that '*y* is the same *X* as *z*' meant '*y* is an *X* and *y* is the same (absolutely) as *z*' —e.g., that '*y* is the same tiger as *z*' meant '*y* is a tiger and *y* is the same as *z*'; whereas in fact the unqualified '*y* is the same as *z*' is, for Geach, simply meaningless. For this reason, a restricted quantifier like 'for some tiger *w*' is not to be explained in terms of a totally unrestricted one, 'for some *w*', taken as ranging simultaneously over all objects whatever.

The intended meaning of a phrase like 'for some tiger *w*' or 'for some animal *w*' is evident: but a notation such as 'for some *A w*' is liable to be misconstrued, as Geach realizes, by taking '*A*' to be a variable bound by the quantifier. To avoid this awkwardness, I shall adopt the form 'for some *w* in *A*' (intended as a reading of the existing notation '∃*w*⌐*A*'): this of course does not yield tolerable English if we replace '*A*' by any particular category or substantival term, so in this case I shall revert to the original form 'for some animal *w*'. (In this chapter German letters are always used for bound variables, except in direct quotations from Geach, who uses italic letters for variables, both free and bound.)

How does Geach pass from his doctrine about identity and about substantival general terms to his view about quantification? The argument he gives, though at first sight cogent, proves on examination to rest upon an irrelevant premiss. He employs, for his argument, the ancient paradox of Heraclitus. If, he says, we follow Frege in rendering signs of generality by means of unrestricted quantifiers, then we shall represent the statement:

(1) Heraclitus bathed in some river yesterday, and bathed in the same river today

as:

(3) For some *w*, *w* is a river, and Heraclitus bathed in *w* yesterday, and Heraclitus bathed in *w* today.

Likewise we shall render the statement:

(4) Heraclitus bathed in some water yesterday and bathed in the same water today

as:

(6) For some *w*, *w* is water, and Heraclitus bathed in *w* yesterday, and Heraclitus bathed in *w* today.

Further, the statement:

(i) Whatever is a river is water

will be represented as:

(ii) For any *w*, if *w* is a river, *w* is water.

But this is enough to show that these renderings are wrong: for (6) follows from (3) and (ii), although notoriously (4) does not follow from (1) and (i).

This paradox is announced (*Reference and Generality*, p. 150) as a refutation of what Geach calls the 'orthodox' view that restricted quantification is to be interpreted in terms of unrestricted quantification (that 'for some *w* in *A*, ... *w* ...' is to be explained as meaning 'for some *w*, *w* is an *A* and ... *w* ...'); but, after the paradox has been presented, the conclusion expressly drawn is merely that 'being the same water' cannot be analysed as 'being the same (something-or-other) and being water' (ibid., p. 151). Geach is thus simultaneously arguing for his thesis about identity and his thesis about quantification. We, on the other hand, have already considered the grounds for this thesis about identity, and are wishing to discover how Geach passes from that thesis to the one about quantification. Looked at from this point of view, the Heraclitean paradox is less than compelling. Geach concedes that (6) does tell us that Heraclitus bathed in the same something-or-other on two successive days and that this something-or-other 'is' water (Geach's quotation marks), and that this does follow from (3) and (ii), or from (1) and (i); but, he says, it is a much weaker proposition than (4). If he is right, then the rendering of (4) as (6) is indeed incorrect. But the incorrectness of this rendering is already a consequence of his thesis that '*x* is the same water as *y*' does not mean '*x* is water and *x* is the same as *y*': it proves nothing in addition as to the incorrectness of unrestricted quantification.

It is tempting to ascribe to Geach the reply that the classical semantics of first-order predicate calculus even without identity presupposes the spurious notion of the single absolute relation of identity. It is true that he nowhere expressly comes out with this view; but, if we do not ascribe it to him, there just does not seem to be any connection between his rejection of the one absolute identity-relation in favour of many relativized ones and his opposition to the 'orthodox' conception of unrestricted quantification as underlying the restricted kind. On such a view, there need be no tacit appeal to an absolute relation of identity in the understanding of very simple formulas, like 'For some x, $F(x)$'; but such an appeal would in general be being made whenever we are concerned with formulas containing more than one occurrence of a variable bound by any one quantifier. On this view, in order to determine the truth, under a given interpretation of the predicate-letters 'F' and 'G', of the formula 'For some x, $F(x)$ and $G(x)$', we need to know whether or not we can find some *one* object of which both the predicate-letters '*F*' and '*G*' are true, under this interpretation; and this will require us to determine the answer to such questions as whether some given object of which '*F*' is true is or is not the same as some object of which '*G*' has been found to be true. Geach's marked preference for avoiding bound variables, and using instead either phrases of the form 'that same *A*' or pronouns, glossed as having the meaning 'that same *A*', might well be taken to be intended as subliminal propaganda for such a view. (The view would, mutatis mutandis, apply just as much to restricted quantification as to classically interpreted unrestricted quantification: i.e. a formula of the form 'For some *ν* in *A*, *F*(*ν*) and *G*(*ν*)' would contain a tacit appeal to the specific identity-relation denoted by '. . . is the same *A* as . . .', in just the same way that 'For some *α*, *F*(*α*) and *G*(*α*)' contained a tacit appeal to the general relation of identity.) An example of Geach's replacement of bound variables by phrases like 'the same *A*' is found in formula (7) of p. 154: instead of writing:

> For some *ν* in *A*, *ν* is water, and Heraclitus bathed in *ν* yesterday, and Heraclitus bathed in *ν* today.

Geach writes:

> Some *A* is water, and Heraclitus bathed in that (same) *A* yesterday, and Heraclitus bathed in the same *A* today.

We cannot, however, attribute this view to Geach, for at the very end of his book he expressly repudiates it. Distinguishing the 'predicative' use of 'the same *A*' in the expression 'is the same *A* as' from 'subject-uses', he says (p. 190), 'Subject-uses of "the same *A*" signify only that a number of predicates are supposed to be true all together of a certain individual for which the common name "*A*" stands': it is part of his doctrine that substantival general terms are, in some occurrences, genuine names of individual objects. He goes on, 'Our understanding of "true all together" depends not on the difficult notion of a criterion of identity, but on the much clearer notion of a predicable's being formed out of predicables by a truth-functional connective (viz. by "and")'.

Given this, it is difficult to see just what Geach's ground for his rejection of the 'orthodox' doctrine of unrestricted quantification is supposed to be. He could, it is true, pose this question: If we cannot render (4) as (6), how are we, using unrestricted quantification, to render it? Whether he would ask it or not, this question gives us the first hint that something is awry with Geach's doctrine. Geach says (ibid., p. 151) that the interpretations of (4) to mean (6) and of (1) to mean (3) 'stand or fall together'; and, in view of the argument that he is using against the former of these interpretations, this is the least convincing of his comments on the Heraclitean paradox. It is clear enough how (6) can be true while (4) is false: namely, when Heraclitus bathes in the same river on two successive days, and that river is (or 'is') all the time water, and yet the water in which he bathed yesterday has flowed down to the sea by today. But it is not at all so clear how (3) could be true while (1) was false (perhaps if Heraclitus bathed in the Missouri yesterday and the Mississippi today, and the Mississippi at his bathing-time today was composed of, and only of, the water which had composed the Missouri at his bathing-time yesterday?); while it is obvious that (1) could not be true and (3) false. This observation does not merely exploit accidental features of the example: we ought to consider seriously whether Geach's ignoring, in this context, of the evident differences between the two substantival general terms 'river' and 'water' does not lead him astray in his argument. The difference is that 'water' is what Quine calls a 'mass term' and 'river' is not; or, in Geach's own terminology, that 'river' is a countable general term and 'water', though substantival, is uncountable. It sounds very plausible to say that 'x is the same water as y' does not mean 'x is water and x is the same as y'—at least, if we are allowed to say such things as 'Whatever is a river is water'; but it is much more difficult to make it out that 'x is the same river as y' is not equivalent to 'x is a river and x is the same as y'.

Before we attempt a serious critique, however, we must complete the exposition of his view, which has the enormous merit, as against similar observations by others before him, of having been worked out in detail. First, let us see how Geach proposes to emend those definitions of Frege's which employ the absolute identity-relation. Geach will no longer allow the general notion of a relation's being many-one: for 'R is many-one' is defined as meaning, 'For any $\wp$, x and w, if $\wp$ is R to x and $\wp$ is R to w, then x is the same as w', and this employs the prohibited absolute relation of identity. Instead, the notion is replaced by the relativized one 'R is many-one between A's and B's', where 'A' and 'B' are to be replaced by any substantival terms: 'R is many-one between A's and B's' means 'For any $\wp$ in A, for any x in B and for any w in B, if $\wp$ is R to x and $\wp$ is R to w, then x is the same B as w'. (I have made some verbal alterations here to which no exception could be taken.) 'There are just as many F's and G's' will then be defined to mean 'For some relation $\mathscr{R}$, $\mathscr{R}$ correlates the F's with the G's, and $\mathscr{R}$ is one-one between F's and G's'. The result of this modification will be to restrict admissible interpretations of the predicate-letters 'F' and 'G' to substantival terms, which is of course very nearly

Gl 72

the advantage Geach was seeking. Not quite, however. The relativization of the notion of a relation's being one-one to a pair of general terms imposes on those general terms only the restriction that they be substantival (since they must appear in the contexts 'the same A' and 'the same B'): so it ought to come out that it makes sense to say, 'There are just as many F's as G's', whenever 'F' and 'G' are substantival terms. This, though, was not the doctrine Geach originally enunciated, which was that being substantival was a necessary but not a sufficient condition for being countable. We are still left completely in the dark as to how it comes about that a general term may be substantival and yet not countable; and when we recall that the only example given of a general term that was substantival but not countable was a mass term, our suspicions expressed in the preceding paragraph are reinforced. Mass terms form the only case for which the non-equivalence of 'x is the same A as y' and 'x is A and x is the same as y' has been made plausible; and it is just for this case that the proposed emendation of the definition of 'just as many as' fails to produce the desired effect.

It would be a mistake to suppose that Geach rejects unrestricted quantification as altogether meaningless; he rejects it only in so far as it is explained in the classical fashion. He is not opposed to unrestricted quantification as such, but only to taking it as fundamental and explaining restricted quantification in terms of it. For him the direction of explanation should be the reverse: unrestricted quantifiers are to be explained in terms of restricted ones. Thus, the statement (6), which involves unrestricted quantification, is to be explained as meaning:

(8) For some α, and for some w in α, w is water, and Heraclitus bathed in w yesterday and Heraclitus bathed in w today.

Here the bound variable 'α' ranges over categories, or alternatively over kinds (where kinds are the extensions of substantival terms). The German letter 'α' is of course a bound variable, being used differently from the schematic letter 'A' occurring in earlier examples, and, in particular, quite differently from the restricted quantifier 'for some w in A'. Geach does not use individual variables in his formulation of (8), preferring as we noted, to employ the phrases 'that (same) A' and 'the same A'; but it is hardly to be imagined that he would have any objection to their use.

Thus, on Geach's view, unrestricted quantification is to be understood in terms of restricted quantification (over the objects within a category or kind) combined with a species of higher-level quantification over categories or kinds. How is this higher-level quantification—the quantifier 'for some α'—to be explained?

For such quantifiers Geach adopts a substitutional interpretation. A statement of the form 'For some α, ... α ...' is true just in case there is some substantival general term 'X' such that the result of dropping the quantifier and replacing all other occurrences of the bound variable 'α' by 'X' is a true statement (it would here be possible to restrict 'X' to be a category term); presumably the universal quantifier 'for every α' is to be understood analogously. Thus this kind of quantification is not to be thought of as quantification over a domain of entities—categories or kinds—but as understood in terms of a range of verbal substitutions. We have already seen, in our earlier discussion of the substitutional interpretation of quantifiers, that this contrast is in part spurious: Geach reduces the contrast almost to vanishing point by going on to explain that he does not demand, for the truth of an existentially quantified statement, that there should actually be in the language a substantival general term with which to make the substitution, but only that such a substitution could be made from among any of the substantival general terms each of which could coherently be added to the language.

Having introduced quantifiers like 'for some α' with this substitutional interpretation, Geach proceeds to advocate the use of quantifiers with a similar interpretation but with different ranges. In fact, he allows the introduction of such quantifiers for each *sort* of expression in the language (Geach uses the word 'category' here instead of 'sort', but I have used it already for a different purpose): he defines a 'sort' as a class of all those expressions which can be substituted for a given expression in a statement without loss of meaningfulness. This is surely the wrong explanation to yield, as Geach wishes, that all substantival general terms should form one sort, and all proper names another: for it can hardly be expected that every sentence containing, say, the phrase 'same river' should remain meaningful when 'tiger' is substituted for 'river', or that the proper name of a tiger can always replace the name of a river without loss of significance. This, however, does not matter, save in formulating the general principle, which need not concern us. Now, by using the substitutional interpretation of quantifiers with respect to the sort of expressions which constitute proper names, the use of unrestricted quantification over 'objects can be explained directly, without invoking quantification over kinds or categories. If 'for some ξ' is such an unrestricted quantifier, then 'For some ξ ... ξ ...' is true just in case there is in the language—or could be coherently added to the language—a proper name 'a' such that '... a ...' forms a true statement. Geach insists, however, that this direct explanation of unrestricted quantification is in no way simpler or more economical than the explanation in terms of quantification over kinds or categories: in fact, properly considered, it is virtually equivalent to it. To be able to recognize an expression as a proper name, we must understand the kind of sense a proper name possesses: and it is at least part of this sense that there be associated with the proper name a criterion of identity. This criterion of identity will fix the object which forms the bearer of the proper name as belonging to some category, that consisting of all objects for which this is the correct criterion of identity, and for this category there will be a category term. Hence, properly understood, to say that there exists a proper name '*a*' such that the statement '. . . *a* . . .' is true is to say no more and no less than that there is a substantival (category) term '*A*' such that the statement 'For some *ν* in *A*, . . . *ν* . . .' is true.

Geach pauses to claim it as an advantage of the substitutional interpretation of quantifiers that it can handle quantification into oblique contexts. Thus, if we suppose a situation in which it is true to say:

(11) Jenkins is a man, and Johnson does not believe that de Vere is a shopkeeper and does believe that Jenkins is a shopkeeper, and Jenkins is the same man as de Vere,

we may validly infer, if we interpret 'for some *γ*' substitutionally:

(10) For some *γ*, *γ* is a man, and Johnson does not believe that de Vere is a shopkeeper, and does believe that *γ* is a shopkeeper, and *γ* is the same man as de Vere;

but notoriously this inference is invalid, and (10) in fact meaningless, if we try to interpret 'for some *γ*' classically, as a quantification over the domain of objects (or even of men or animals); for, as Geach underlines, we obtain nonsense if we try to explain (10) as being true just in case the predicate '*ξ* is a man, and Johnson does not believe that de Vere is a shopkeeper and does believe that *ξ* is a shopkeeper, and *ξ* is the same man as de Vere' is true of some object, since we cannot coherently explain under what conditions this predicate should be held to be true of a given object. By the same token, evidently, we cannot explain (10) as meaning:

For some man *ν*, Johnson does not believe that de Vere is a shopkeeper and does believe that *ν* is a shopkeeper, and *ν* is the same man as de Vere.

This example has, of course, nothing to do with unrestricted quantification as such; it is, as we have seen, an instance in which the advantage claimed for the substitutional interpretation of quantifiers is quite specious; and it is a case in which the equivalence claimed by Geach between 'for some *γ*' and 'for some *α* and some *ν* in *α*' does not hold.

Setting aside contexts such as these, Geach now makes the surprising observation that for what he calls 'Shakespearean' predicates, the classical and substitutional interpretations of the result of attaching a quantifier to them coincide. By a 'Shakespearean' predicate Geach means one that does not constitute an oblique context, i.e. a predicate '$F(\xi)$' which is such that, whenever 'a' and 'b' are proper names with the same reference, '$F(a)$' and '$F(b)$' are equivalent in truth-value. Geach does not express this observation in this terminology; what he says (p. 165) is that, if 'ξ is F' is a Shakespearean predicate, then 'For some $\mathbf{\gamma}$, $\mathbf{\gamma}$ is F' is true if and only if the predicate 'ξ is F' is true of something or other, i.e. of some object (nameable by a proper name). I call this observation 'surprising' not because I think it false: it could indeed be called in question by reference to the contrast between a predicative and an impredicative specification of the range of the variables, but that is not what I want to fasten attention on here. Rather, it is surprising because this admission appears to undercut Geach's whole position on unrestricted quantification. First, it seemed that, although Geach did not want to reject unrestricted quantification altogether, he wanted to explain it in terms of restricted quantification, rather than the other way round. Next, it appeared that a direct explanation of unrestricted quantification could after all be given, though one which Geach claimed as being, on analysis, essentially equivalent to the explanation in terms of restricted quantification; so the emphasis now was on a substitutional explanation of the quantifier in contrast to the classical explanation. But now, finally, it turns out that, apart from the irrelevant case of non-Shakespearean predicates, the substitutional and the classical explanations of unrestricted quantification coincide: after all, if we may legitimately consider the totality of proper names which either belong to the language or could coherently be added to it, we may equally legitimately consider the totality of objects (which are or could be named). Thus Geach's polemic against the 'orthodox' (i.e. wrong) conception of unrestricted first-level quantification appears to end by completely evaporating.

In later writings, Geach has given a sharper explanation of the difference between restricted and unrestricted quantification: 'Some A is F' will be true only when, for some proper name 'a' with which is associated a criterion of identity expressed by 'the same A', 'a is F' is true: but 'b is an A' may be true even though a different criterion of identity is associated with 'b', and hence 'For some x, x is an A and x is F' may be true when 'Some A is F' is not. This in effect involves accepting the view Geach formerly rejected (see p. 555).

These views of Geach's were sharply criticized by Quine in his review of Geach's book (*Philosophical Review*, January 1964). Quine is vehemently opposed to Geach's rejection of the one absolute relation of identity in favour of a multitude of relativized ones, on which he comments, 'This doctrine is antithetical to the very notion of quantification, the mainspring of modern logic. Quantification depends on there being values of variables, same or different absolutely; grant quantification and there remains no choice about identity, not for variables. For a language with quantification in it there is but one legitimate version of "$x = y$" (not counting equivalent versions).' This, of course, is an argumentum ad alios homines, as Quine later acknowledges; it is just on the strength of the doctrine Quine is criticizing that Geach advocates a revision of the theory of quantifiers. At any rate it is clear that Quine can see clearly what we have so far been unable to discover, what is the connection between Geach's views on identity and his views on quantification. Quine can find no plausible example of a case in which x is the same F as y and yet a different G from y: he is unconvinced by Geach's saying that 'different official personages may be one and the same man'. Quine agrees that belief in an absolute relation of identity entails that 'x is the same A as y' is to be analysed as 'x is an A and x is the same as y', and also that, for any general term 'A'—at least for one that can occur in the construction 'x is an A'—'the same A' makes sense; but he finds these consequences unobjectionable. He disagrees with Geach's use of Frege's example of the number of red things, and comments, 'This . . . is a consideration gone awry. Because of the conceptual divisibility of red things into red things, there is indeed no counting the red things; but this is not to say there is no telling whether d is the same red thing as e'—as Geach had said there was not. That is, for Quine the general term 'red' *is* uncountable; but there is all the same a criterion of identity for red things (as for everything else). Quine considers the meaning of 'same water' less evident than that of 'same red thing'. On Geach's use of the Heraclitean paradox, he remarks, 'This crisis is overdrawn. A mass term like "water" or "sugar" does not primarily admit "same" nor "an". When it is subjected to such particles, some special individuating standard is understood from the circumstances. Typically, "same sugar" might allude to sameness of shipment. Now in the sense in which one resists saying that Heraclitus bathed in the same water twice, a water is an aggregate only of molecules that were near a man when he once bathed. But a river is not such a water.'

It is now our task to discover both how much truth there is in Geach's views, and how much of those views are to be ascribed to Frege, and how much, on the contrary, is in opposition to his doctrines. Let us start by renewing our attack on the question whether Geach's thesis about identity necessitates abandonment of the classical theory of the quantifiers. We have seen that it is difficult to trace any formal connection between the two views: nevertheless, there is a compelling feeling of incompatibility between the picture that we are accustomed to form of the classical interpretation of the quantifiers and the picture evoked by Geach's doctrine on identity. The picture associated with the classical treatment of (first-level) quantifiers is, as Quine says, that of a domain of objects each of which is definitely distinguished from others. It is true that, in the explanation of what it is for a formula (of first-order predicate calculus *without* identity) to come out true under a given interpretation, no appeal is made to our capacity to determine whether or not two assignments of elements of the domain to the free variables assign the *same* element to any one given free variable; all that is necessary is that we should be able to tell when we have made such an assignment, and, in some way, to survey the totality of such assignments. It is just for this reason that there is no formal entailment between Geach's rejection of absolute identity and his opposition to the classical treatment of the quantifiers. But the *picture* we have of what constitutes a domain of objects which can serve as the range of the individual variables is such that it is impossible to see how there could be any objection to supposing an absolute relation of identity to be defined on it: the elements of the domain are thought of as being, in Quine's words, the same or different absolutely. The picture which Geach's doctrine of identity seems to demand is in conflict with this; though, indeed, it seems difficult to decide just what picture is required. We may start by imagining a determinate domain of objects, between which various relativized identity-relations hold: these 'identity' relations are equivalence relations such that, for certain purposes, we do not need to distinguish between the different members of any one equivalence class. (For instance, we might imagine a domain of material objects, on which is defined the equivalence relation of matching in colour: then to take this relation as an 'identity'-relation would be, in effect, to explain what it meant to use names of colours—colour-words as singular terms—by saying that, in speaking of the colour red, we are treating all the red objects as being, for the present purpose, a single object.) This picture, although it agrees with the way in which, in certain contexts, mathematicians are sometimes disposed to talk, is not yet radical enough: for, underlying the various relativized identity-relations, would be the one absolute identity-relation. Perhaps, indeed, this really is all that Geach has in mind: in this case, his proposal amounts to one whereby we can avoid Frege's device of introducing new objects as equivalence classes of a given totality under equivalence relations defined on it by taking certain expressions of the form '. . . is the same *F* as . . .' as denoting what is not, properly speaking, a relation of identity at all, but an equivalence relation; the corresponding singular terms (terms for *F*'s) would then have to be construed in some equally offbeat way, as not, strictly speaking, being used to stand for determinate individual objects. But it seems unlikely that this is all there is to Geach's thesis: if it were, there would be no reason whatever to see this thesis as involving any serious modification of the standard treatment of quantifiers.

Rather, it seems that Geach means us to picture that over which the variables range as an amorphous lump of reality, in itself not articulated into distinct objects. Such an articulation may be accomplished in any one of many different ways: we slice up reality into distinct individual objects by selecting a particular criterion of identity. Such a criterion of identity will be associated with some substantival general term (in particular, with a category term): this is why quantification over objects has always to be relativized to some substantival term.

Now such a picture does indeed give a just representation of certain features of language: but it is difficult to make it fit what Geach says. He says, let us recall, that 'it makes no sense to judge whether *x* and *y* are "the same" ... unless we add or understand some general term—"the same *F*"'; that 'there is no telling whether *d* is or is not the same red thing as *e*, there being no criterion of identity'; that Frege was wrong to assume that '*x* is the same *A* as *y*' splits up into '*x* is an *A*' and '*x* is the same as *y*'. How are we to understand the letters '*x*', '*y*', '*d*', '*e*', in these remarks? Their familiar use—and certainly the use intended by Frege, who is being directly criticized in two of these passages—is as individual variables: so we know no way of reading these sentences save as saying such things as that there is no telling whether an object *d* is or is not the same red thing as an object *e*; if Geach intended any other way of understanding them, he has not told us what it is (and, if he did, then his remarks do not *directly* contradict Frege). But if we interpret these remarks in this way, they make no clear sense. Granted the conception of an amorphous lump of reality which can be sliced up into individual objects in various different ways according to the direction of cut, it remains that, as soon as we start saying of *an object* that it is or is not the same as *an object*, we are already invoking some way of slicing up reality into objects—at least two particular conceptual acts of carving an object off the lump: and once we assume that, it must be determinate whether or not the same object has been carved off each time. It would do Geach no good to appeal here to his substitutional interpretation of individual variables, which he supposes to dispense with the necessity for assuming entities for the variables to range over (*Reference and Generality*,

p. 157): for, on his own doctrine, every proper name has associated with it a particular criterion of identity, so that, immediately we imagine '*x*' and '*y*', or '*d*' and '*e*', to be supplanted by proper names, a criterion of identity is imposed in accordance with which there is a determinate answer to the question whether the statement of identity is true. It is probably a partial awareness of these difficulties which prompts Geach to avoid expressing his view in the terms I have used in describing it, viz. by saying that there is no absolute relation of identity, but only a variety of relativized identity-relations; for this would provoke the natural question, 'Between what is it that these identity-relations are supposed to hold?'—a question impossible to answer in terms of the amorphous-lump picture, or indeed at all without making the rejection of the absolute relation of identity quite capricious. It is probably in order to suppress this kind of question that Geach always phrases his point with the help of individual variables; but this device does not really enable him to evade it.

A doubt arises whether the amorphous-lump picture is compatible with a correct account of the distinction between the criterion of application and the criterion of identity associated with general terms. In one clear sense, these are independent of one another: not only does the criterion of application not determine the criterion of identity, but it is not determined by it either. Thus 'dog' and 'collie' have the same criterion of identity associated with them, but not the same criterion of application. In the very last paragraph of his book, and in later writings, Geach indeed suggests the opposite, namely that, for a substantival general term '*A*', the predicative use 'is an *A*' can be analysed in terms of the identity-use 'is the same *A* as', by interpreting '*y* is an *A*' to mean 'for some *w* in *A*, *y* is the same *A* as *w*': thus '*y* is a dog' would be rendered 'for some dog *w*, *y* is the same dog as *w*', '*y* is a collie' as 'for some collie *w*, *y* is the same collie as *w*'. But the plausibility of this, if any, as a piece of conceptual *analysis*—i.e. as uncovering the sense-mechanism of the words—depends wholly upon disregarding the difference between substantival terms in general and the special kind of substantival terms we have called 'category terms'. Obviously, what someone who knows what 'dog' means has to learn, in order to know the meaning of 'is the same collie as', is a matter not of any special procedure for *identifying* collies, but of knowing when it is true to say of a dog that it is a collie. If we allow that '*x* is the same dog as *y*' and '*x* is the same collie as *y*' are to be analysed, respectively, as '*x* is a dog and *x* is the same animal as *y*' and as '*x* is a collie and *x* is the same animal as *y*', then the suggested elimination of the predicative expressions 'is a dog' and 'is a collie' is no longer possible, and the difference in sense between 'dog' and 'collie' comes out precisely as a difference in criterion of application and not in criterion of identity.

On Geach's account, there exist general terms, namely adjectival ones, with which is associated a criterion of application but no criterion of identity. Since he does not envisage the reverse possibility, there is a sense, even on his view, in which the criterion of application is prior to the criterion of identity. A general term 'A' with which was associated a criterion of identity but not any criterion of application would be one for which 'is the same A as' made sense, but 'is an A' did not; and it seems implausible to suggest that there are any such general terms. The nearest we can come is a category term like 'animal', which, if not true of everything, is at least true of as much as it is possible for a substantival general term to be true of. Nevertheless, it certainly cannot be maintained that 'is an animal' is senseless, or even useless. While, indeed, it could be eliminated by the device discussed above, viz. by interpreting 'y is an animal' to mean 'for some animal x, y is the same animal as x', and the objection made above to the use of this device for non-category terms would not apply, this would at best mean that we could in this case explain the criterion of application in terms of the criterion of identity, not that we had shown it to be non-existent. Thus, on Geach's account, it seems that with all general terms is associated a criterion of application, and that with some there is also associated a criterion of identity, with others not. The objection would now be that this account of general terms cannot be interpreted by means of the amorphous-lump picture. It would seem that, on this picture, we must first select some determinate way of splitting up reality into discrete objects— one of the many alternative such ways—before we can conceive of some general term as being true of some objects, false of others; so that a criterion of identity would have to be given before any criterion of application could be introduced. We cannot, in terms of the amorphous-lump picture, make any sense of the conception of a predicate's having merely a criterion of application: for we have no way of conceiving of what sort of thing it is supposed to be that such a predicate would be true of or false of, if we do not think of reality as already broken up in some way or other into individual objects. Here, again, we may suspect that Geach's method of expressing himself, by saying that 'is an A' or 'is A' may have a sense while 'is the same A as' does not, rather than by saying that with 'A' is associated a criterion of application but not a criterion of identity, is intended to divert attention from this point; but this phraseology cannot liberate him from the necessity of explaining to what sort of thing it is that the adjective 'red' either applies or fails to apply, given that there is no criterion for what constitutes one red thing.

v

To this objection, however, it would be possible to reply. Geach might agree that it is impossible to apply a predicate, in particular, an adjectival general term, except to an object, and hence in a context in which some criterion of identity is expressly or tacitly invoked; but hold that the criterion of application for such a general term as 'red' is given in such a way as not to determine uniquely the relevant criterion of identity. 'Red' applies, or can significantly be said not to apply, to the results of splitting off objects from the lump in any one of several different ways.

Though it seems reasonable in itself, this reply leaves us unsatisfied. If 'red' can be predicated only of an *object*, then every such predication presupposes some manner of singling out that object, and this involves appeal to a specific criterion of identity: so surely Quine must be right in saying that any one thing which can significantly be said to be red must —absolutely—either be the same as or be distinct from any other (i.e. possibly other) thing which can also significantly be said to be red. If both objects result from the same method of splitting up reality into objects, then we have a specific criterion of identity whereby to judge whether they are the same or different; if they result from different methods of splitting objects off from the parent lump, so that two different specific criteria of identity are associated with them, then surely there is an obvious absolute sense, not relating to what we have been calling a criterion of identity, in which they can correctly be said to be distinct objects. After all, the point at which our metaphor of the amorphous lump breaks down is this: that while a lump of material cannot be simultaneously be sliced up in two different ways, without the result constituting yet a third way of slicing it up, we can consider simultaneously the results of two different methods of conceptually dividing reality into individual objects. If there are several different ways of discriminating individual objects out of the sum total of reality so as to obtain objects which can meaningfully be said to be red, there seems to be no reason why we should not consider as a single totality all the objects resulting from making these several different kinds of discrimination, so as to form the domain of all those objects over which the predicate 'red' is defined: it makes no difference that this domain will comprise sub-totalities each of which has been carved out of the same basic raw material. Since this domain consists of discrete objects, we may consider it as having a single absolute relation of identity defined on it: and so there will after all be some determinate number—even if an infinite and perhaps non-denumerable number—of objects in this domain of which the predicate 'red' is true.

The only reply that could be given to this new objection would be to say that there is no determinate, and certainly no finite, number of ways of splitting reality up into individual objects to which the general term 'red' could significantly be applied in accordance with the principle which constitutes its criterion of application. It may be that, relative to a given language at a given stage of development, we can distinguish some finite number of substantival general terms, simple or complex, associated with distinct criteria of identity and applying to objects which can meaningfully be called 'red'; but there are just indefinitely many such substantival terms each of which could be introduced into the language: so we can form no definite conception of the totality of all objects which could be spoken of and of which, if they were spoken of, we should know what it meant to call them 'red'. Such a claim it is not, indeed, open to Geach to make, since it makes nonsense of his substitutionally interpreted quantification over categories or kinds ('for some α'): but, though no proof has been offered of it, it has some intrinsic plausibility; and it seems at present the only remaining refuge for a supporter of Geach's doctrine.

It is unclear whether the present thesis—that we can form no determinate conception of the totality of objects to which the general term 'red' could be meaningfully applied—is true or not: neither a proof nor a refutation of it seems ready to hand. But that we cannot in general hope to resist conclusions of this kind is something which we have already observed: the one lesson of the set-theoretical paradoxes which seems quite certain is that we cannot interpret individual variables in Frege's way, as ranging simultaneously over the totality of all objects which could meaningfully be referred to or quantified over. This is, as we have noted, why modern explanations of the semantics of first-order predicate calculus always require that a domain be *specified* for the individual variables: we cannot, as Frege supposed, rely on a once-for-all explanation that individual variables are always to be thought of as ranging over the totality of all objects.

For this reason, a crucial part of Geach's onslaught on what he calls the 'orthodox' doctrine rests on an ignoratio elenchi. As we saw, he stigmatizes modern formal logicians, of whom he mentions only Quine by name, as committing the error of explaining restricted quantification in terms of unrestricted quantification: whereas the one thing we may confidently say hardly any modern logician believes in is wholly unrestricted quantification. All modern logicians are agreed that, in order to specify an interpretation of any sentence or formula containing bound variables, it is necessary expressly to stipulate what the range of the variables is to be. Of course, given such a stipulation, a sentence of the form '... some A ...', where 'A' does not apply to every object in the given domain, goes over into 'for some x, x

is an A and . . . *w* . . .', and similarly for the universal quantifier; thus, if the domain consists of the real numbers, then, while '. . . some real number . . .' and '. . . every real number . . .' go over simply into 'for some *w*, . . . *w* . . .' and 'for every *w*, . . . *w* . . .', '. . . some transcendental number . . .' and '. . . every transcendental number . . .' go over, respectively, into 'for some *w*, *w* is transcendental and . . . *w* . . .' and 'for every *w*, if *w* is transcendental, then . . . *w* . . .': and it may be that some writers of textbooks have made the heuristic mistake of making this latter point without re-emphasizing, or even before explaining, the necessity of first stipulating the range of the variables, and so deserve rapping over the knuckles. But the suggestion that most modern logicians believe that restricted quantification is to be reduced to unrestricted quantification is preposterous: they do not believe in un-

RG 144-50 restricted quantification at all. Frege did: but Frege is not mentioned as one of the culprits. (Geach allows, on p. 153, that for some applications of predicate calculus it is sufficient 'to read the quantifiers as restricted to a "universe" delimited by some substantival term like "man" or "(natural) number" ': but he seems to assume that this is recognized by modern logicians only as a matter of occasional convenience, whereas it is in fact generally acknowledged as a matter of universal necessity.)

The observation that it is impossible coherently to understand individual variables as ranging over all objects, or even over all sets, all ordinal numbers, p. 530 etc., was glossed in Chapter 15; it may be well here to expand that gloss. If we attempt to take the observation in a very strong sense, as meaning that there are no quantified statements which can be understood, or at least which can be recognized as true, when the variables are thought of as ranging over all objects, or all sets, or all ordinal numbers, it will be seen to be manifestly absurd. Such a statement as 'For every *w*, *w* is identical with *w*' is true for every object whatsoever; 'For every x and y, $x \cup y = y \cup x$' is true when 'x' and 'y' range over all sets whatever; 'Every ordinal has a successor' and 'For any fixed ordinal *m*, the function $m + \xi$ is a normal function' are statements true for all ordinals without restriction. Likewise, since the statements 'For some x, x has infinitely many members' and 'For some ordinal *m*, *m* has no immediate predecessor' are true for some interpretations of the variables as ranging over specific domains, they must be acknowledged as true when the variables are taken as ranging over *all* sets and over *all* ordinals respectively. But it ought to be clear that the observation is not intended in so strong a sense as to contradict these obvious truths. What is meant, rather, is that it is not possible to suppose that, by specifying the range of some style of individual variables as being over 'all objects', or 'all sets', or 'all ordinals', we have thereby conferred a determinate

truth-value on all statements containing quantifiers binding such variables (even given that the other symbols occurring in these statements have been assigned a determinate sense). Any attempt to stipulate senses for the predicates, relational expressions and functional operators that we shall want to use relative to such a domain will either lead to contradiction or will prompt us to concede that we are not, after all, using the bound variables to range over absolutely everything that we could intuitively acknowledge as being an object, a set, or an ordinal number.

It is true that 'modern logicians' tend to have a preference for a notation which employs—within a single context—only one style of bound individual variables; for example, they would tend to prefer a single domain containing both points and lines to two separate domains. It is also true that this representation distorts the actual pattern of our concept-formation: we do not first form the conception of a totality which includes both points and lines on the plane, and then learn how to tell, of a geometrical object, whether it is a point or a line. Nevertheless, it is evident that, once we have acquired the conception of two distinct totalities with respect to each of which it is possible to quantify, we commit no error by adopting a representation which requires us to form the union of these two totalities and quantify over it; and, since the employment of a single sort of individual variable is thought of only as a convenience and not as any matter of principle, it is plain that we cannot find in this practice any ground for Geach's strictures.

We cannot leave the matter here: for it is evident that there is a genuine insight underlying Geach's doctrine, even though the doctrine as a whole is unacceptable. That Geach is right in holding that the criterion of application for a general term does not determine the criterion of identity associated with it we have already seen from the example of the term 'book'. The question, 'Is that the same book as the one you brought yesterday?', may demand different answers according as 'same book' means 'copy of the same original composition' or 'same copy'. Geach is certainly right in holding that this represents a variation in the sense of 'book', not of 'the same'; and yet, as we saw, it appears that this ambiguity in the sense of the word 'book' affects only the employment of the expression 'same book', and of related expressions like 'five books' and 'how many books?', and not that of the predicate 'is a book', so that it appears natural to say, with Geach, that the criterion of application remains constant while the criterion of identity alters. Geach is also, surely, right in holding that there are adjectival general terms with which is associated no criterion of identity. Now much of Geach's doctrine appears reconcilable with the orthodox account of quantifiers, when this is correctly stated: for instance, that a criterion of identity is always associated with proper names (since, on the orthodox view, a singular term is assigned a reference only within a previously specified domain); or that there are general terms whose sense resides not only in a criterion of application but also in a criterion of identity. But it does seem that other, equally plausible, parts of Geach's doctrine cannot be made to fit this orthodox view, the view namely that we need, for each context, to stipulate what is to be the domain for our individual variables, and then to assign to all the singular terms, predicates and relational and functional expressions within that context interpretations relative to that domain. Such a view leaves no place for purely adjectival general terms; nor for pairs of substantival general terms which have a criterion of application in common but differ in the criterion of identity associated with them. Each domain for the individual variables will constitute the extension of some substantival general term (or at least the union of the extensions of a number of such substantival terms), to (each of) which corresponds a criterion of identity. If the interpretation of a predicate is always relative to such a domain, each predicate must be associated with some one criterion of identity (that corresponding to the domain over which it is defined): we are quite unprovided with any way of recognizing the interpretation of one predicate over a given domain as being 'the same interpretation' as that of another predicate over some distinct domain. This, however, is just what we should need in order to make sense of the conception of a general term's possessing a criterion of application although it is not associated with any criterion of identity, or of two general terms' sharing a criterion of application although differing as to criterion of identity.

The truth of the matter is that Geach's point, in so far as it is valid, relates to the use of general terms in sentences of a kind for which Frege's formal language, and the modern logical formalisms which are its descendants, provide no place: sentences involving demonstratives. The sort of sentence for which it is correct to say, with Geach, that 'the same' is a fragmentary expression, making a definite sense only when it is used or understood in a context of the form 'the same X', where 'X' is a substantival general term, is a question of one of the forms, 'Is this the same (X) as that?' and 'Is that the same (X) as one which . . . ?', or a sentence which can serve as the answer to such a question. Here one might really have occasion to say, 'It's the same man as the one we saw yesterday, but not the same official personage' (or the other way about). Where Geach goes wrong is in concluding from this that there may be (two) objects which *are* different official personages, but at the same time *are* the same man. Demonstratives, 'this' and 'that', do not, by themselves, serve to pick out any *object* at all, even when used in a determinate context and supplemented by a pointing gesture. A demonstrative picks out an object only when the context supplies some specific criterion of identity; and it is not essential, for the successful employment of a demonstrative, that such a criterion of identity should always be supplied. The only sense in which it may be truly said that 'the same things' may be said to be different official personages and yet the same man is that in which we take it, as a criterion for saying that 'the same things' were being spoken of on the two occasions, that demonstratives were used in contexts which were, in relevant respects, the same (the criteria of identity supplied by the expressions 'official personage' and 'man' not being counted as part of the context, but only the direction of pointing and so on). But in this case 'the same things' does not mean 'the same objects'. As Geach himself repeatedly insists, in order to pick out or refer to an object, it is necessary to provide a specific criterion of identity: given such a criterion of identity, there is no question of the object's standing either to itself or to some other object in some relativized identity-relation which corresponds to a different criterion of identity. Thus, given Geach's understanding of the general term 'official personage', it makes no sense to attempt to identify an official personage with a man, since the criterion of identity for men is quite different. Of course, an official personage will have, at any given time, a particular relation to some one man, a relation for which we have no word in ordinary discourse (because we don't actually, in ordinary discourse, use the term 'official personage' quite as Geach does): let us say, then, that, at any time, an official personage is 'realized' by some man (e.g. that in 1961 the President of the U.S.A. was realized by John F. Kennedy). Then it will often be that, at the same or different times, two different official personages are realized by the same man, and that, at different times, the same official personage is realized by two different men: but it will make no sense, on this way of talking, to say that, at any time, some official personage *is* some man, or that two official personages *are* the same man as each other. It is not a question of supplanting an absolute relation of identity by a number of relativized ones: the relation of an official personage either to the man who realizes him (it?) or to a different official personage realized by the same man is not any kind of identity. I have stuck to Geach's lame example because, although we do not in fact talk about official personages in the way he supposes, it is clear that we perfectly well might, and that we do in fact talk in just this way in a multitude of other cases. How many animals are there in the London Zoo? This is like the 'book' example: the answer depends on whether 'animal' is taken to mean 'individual beast' or 'species'; and, apart from the fact that a beast cannot change its species, 'beast' and 'species' would have served as well as 'man' and 'official personage', and so with a host of other examples.

It is essential to the use of a countable general term 'X' that it can be employed, not only in a predicative way in the context 'is an X', but also to form definite descriptions 'the X which . . .'. In order to serve this purpose, it must have associated with it a criterion of identity. Now the predicative use occurs in two rather different kinds of context, namely when the predicate is attached to a proper name or other singular term, and when it is attached to a demonstrative: in the former case, the predication is being made about a determinate object, but, in the latter case, this is not so. Of course, the countable general term 'X' itself supplies a criterion of identity: but it does not follow that this criterion of identity may be used to determine an object as having been referred to by means of the demonstrative. We cannot, e.g., conclude from the fact that I say, 'That is a horse', that I am using the word 'that' to refer to a horse, or even to an animal: for I may be wrong, and there may not even be an animal there, yet there may be something of which I am mistakenly saying that it is a horse. It is also instructive to consider the case in which I say, pointing to a corpse, 'That was a horse', or, 'That was Blue Peter'. Since the corpse of a horse is not a horse, I cannot be meaning, by the use of the demonstrative, to refer to any horse, or to Blue Peter in particular. Moreover, we want to maintain that there is a respect in which the criterion of application is prior to the criterion of identity. This cannot be seen in sentences in which the general term is predicated of an object denoted by a proper name, for then the criterion of identity is supplied by the proper name: so it must relate to sentences of the form 'That is an X', which can be understood before the criterion of identity associated with 'X' is known.

The use of a demonstrative pronoun may be regarded as relating either to a piece of matter, or to a sensory appearance. (The use of demonstratives to mean 'what has just been mentioned', and the like, is not here under discussion.) The first, most primitive, use of general terms is their predicative use in sentences whose subject is a demonstrative pronoun: and we may regard that part of their sense which determines the truth-conditions of such sentences as constituting their 'criterion of application'. It is only certain general terms—those which are the most fundamental in our language—which have such a use at all. For a general term to have such a use, it is necessary that we should be able to understand a predication of it which does not relate to a determinate object, conceived as picked out by the use of a specific criterion of identity. Both 'smooth' and 'man' have such a use: 'narrow-minded' does not. We can understand what it is to predicate narrow-mindedness only when we are capable of grasping that it is to be predicated only of men, and therefore of knowing what it is to identify a man. Countable general terms, in order to be able to be used to form definite descriptions, have first to be assigned a further use, namely in statements of identification (where this is understood to mean sentences of the form 'This is the same X as that', and the like). This involves learning when it is right to point in two different directions on the same occasion, and say, 'This is the same X as that'; and when it is right to say things like, 'That is the same X as the one which we saw on such-and-such a previous occasion'. That feature of the sense of the countable general term 'X' which determines the truth-conditions for such sentences may be called the criterion of identity associated with 'X': the training by which we acquire it consists also in learning the use of proper names of X's, in the first place in such recognition statements as, 'That is a' (where 'a' is the proper name of an X).

Since an ostension effected by using a demonstrative pronoun does not serve to pick out any determinate *object*, and since the criterion of application is prior to the criterion of identity, it is plain how there can be adjectival general terms, like the adjectives 'red' and 'smooth', with which no criterion of identity is associated. Such adjectival general terms quite naturally come to be used to make predications about *objects*, along with other general terms, like 'narrow-minded', which are introduced solely for that purpose: but it is not in view of their use to make predications about objects that we say of them that they have a criterion of application but no associated criterion of identity, but because they are used in the more primitive form of sentence 'That is Y', without occurring in statements of identification of the form 'This is the same Y (thing) as that'. Likewise, it is with respect to sentences whose subject is a demonstrative pronoun that we can speak of two countable general terms as sharing a criterion of application while differing in criterion of identity. I can understand when it is right to say, 'That is a book', before knowing any criterion for the identity of books, or, when I know them, without enquiring which of the two criteria is intended: but there is no one object which can rightly be said to be a book in both senses of 'book'.

We have seen that Geach recognizes the distinction between countable general terms and mass terms like 'water', but that, classifying them both as substantival terms, he is in some embarrassment to explain how it is that we cannot count waters. The difference between the two is this: that the criterion of identity associated with a mass term (ignoring atypical uses like Quine's sameness of shipment) is a criterion of identity over time only. If with one finger I point towards a human leg and with another finger to a

v·

human hand, we know how to determine whether or not I am pointing to the same man with both fingers. Though the part of the criterion of identity for men which it is difficult to learn is the criterion for the identity of a man over a period of time, it remains an essential part of the sense of the word 'man' that we can say what constitutes one and the same man at any given time. For mass terms like 'water' and 'sugar', this is not so: there is no sense provided for the question whether or not this water over here is the same as that water over there. 'Same water' relates only to a circumscribed quantity of water—a quantity circumscribed both now and on the previous occasion. (By contrast, where 'X' is a countable general term, all that is demanded, for me to ask, 'Is that the same X as before?', is that I should be pointing at an X—that the line of my finger, when produced, should intersect an X. I do not have to circumscribe the material object and indicate its boundaries: if I *am* pointing at an X, that is done for me by the criterion of identity associated with the word 'X'. I am here meaning to include such words as 'colour' among countable general terms. True, we do not usually think of a colour as having boundaries: but of course it is part of the sense of the word 'colour' that we have a criterion for the truth of statements of the form 'This is the same colour as that', accompanied by pointing gestures in different directions.) The criterion of identity associated with a mass term is always the criterion for the identity of a piece of *matter*: we may indeed say that 'is the same water as' means 'is water and is the same matter as'.

How, then, is the Heraclitean paradox to be resolved? No objection can be brought against the rendering of:

(1) Heraclitus bathed in some river yesterday, and bathed in the same river today

as:

(3) For some w, w is a river, and Heraclitus bathed in w yesterday, and Heraclitus bathed in w today.

The context demands that the domain of the bound variable in (3) shall include rivers; there is no ambiguity, since, so long as all the rivers there are are included in the domain, it does not matter what else, if anything, is included in it: there is no object which, with any plausibility, can be said to be a river, and yet not to have been the same river yesterday and today. The statement:

(4) Heraclitus bathed in some water yesterday and bathed in the same water today

ought to be rendered:

(6') For some (piece of matter) $\wp$, $\wp$ was water yesterday and Heraclitus bathed in $\wp$ yesterday, and $\wp$ is water today and Heraclitus bathed in $\wp$ today.

Here it is essential, as indicated by the parentheses, that the bound variable be understood as ranging over pieces of matter. Now does it create ambiguity if we allow the domain of the bound variable in (6') to include other things besides pieces of matter, for example rivers? Could we say that, relative to such a domain, the statement (6') might come out true even though the statement (4) was false? Possibly: all depends on how we interpret the crucial phrase '. . . is water'. If we understand a mass term as something that can (at a particular time) be predicated univocally both of a piece of matter and of a material object the criterion for whose identity does not require the constancy of the matter composing it, then the correctness of (6') as a rendering of (4) will depend on stipulating the range of '$\wp$' to be restricted to pieces of matter. If, as seems more natural, we regard '. . . is water' as predicable only of pieces of matter, and distinguish it from the predicate '. . . is made of water', which can be applied to material objects, then (6') is unambiguous as it stands: but then, of course, we shall have to say, 'Whatever is a river is made of water', rather than 'Whatever is a river is water', and the paradox will not even appear to arise. This account agrees almost exactly with Quine's more pithy analysis, save for his irrelevant remarks about shipments.

There is one other kind of general term which Geach mentions, and which he assimilates rather awkwardly to adjectival general terms: such a general term as 'sea'. He says, quite rightly, that 'the term "sea" does not determine any division of the water area in the world into seas in the way that the term "letter" (in the typographical sense) does determine a division of the printed matter in the world into letters' (p. 38); and on this ground classifies it as an adjectival term. The awkwardness of this is that there *are* proper names of seas: this observation is not at all like saying that some red things have proper names, for one could not give any answer to the question what sort of thing it was of which 'the Mediterranean' was a proper name other than 'a sea'. It is clear that, although the common noun 'sea' is, as Geach says, not connected with any principle of division of the sea into individual seas, it is connected with a principle in accordance with which, given any particular demarcation of an individual sea made at any time, we can thenceforward determine what is to constitute the individual sea so demarcated (given no catastrophic changes in the disposition of the Earth's land masses): the criterion for the identity of a sea is, obviously, a topographical one. So we ought to note here a fourth (probably not at all extensive) class of general term: one for which there is no criterion of identity in the sense of a criterion for the truth of such statements as 'This is the same sea as that', made in advance of the assignment of proper names, and therefore no general principle for marking off individual objects to which the general term applies; but for which not only is there a criterion of identity over time, but a principle governing in what kind of way any one individual such object can be specially marked off and given a name.

The view which is both correct and generally accepted, so far from reducing all quantifications to unrestricted quantification, as Geach supposes, outlaws unrestricted quantification altogether: so we still have to account for the kind of sentence which leads Geach to think it necessary to explain unrestricted quantification somehow or other. Such sentences are those in which there is a sign of generality qualified only by an adjectival, not by a countable, general term: for instance, 'There is something sticky on the table-cloth', 'I saw something red up there', 'I stumbled over something spiky'. Geach discusses the problem of unrestricted generality in the void, without giving any examples of the kind of sentence he thinks essentially involves it. When we consider such examples as those just cited, we see how implausible Geach's own explanation is. It appears probable that the first two sentences could frequently be true when there was not even a theoretical possibility of introducing into the language proper names 'a' and 'b' such as to make the statements 'a is on the table-cloth and a is sticky' and 'b is red and I saw b up there' true. If, say, the table-cloth is in one region coated with a mixture of jam, cough-syrup and hairs from a tweed jacket, it appears most unlikely that anything in the least resembling the kind of proper name we employ, duly associated with a definite criterion of identity, could be introduced which would have that sticky coating as its referent. The possibility would, in the second case, be even more dubious if, say, the flash of red which I saw were due to the short-lived refraction of a beam of light through a prism. But then, we do not know—and have not been told by Geach—what limits can be set on the possible introduction of proper names. What is quite clear is that Geach's explanation is false to the epistemological order: it explains a fairly primitive part of language in terms of a much less primitive part. We could learn to understand such sentences as those cited above without being able to apply any criteria of identity or, therefore, to employ any proper names; let alone to form the conception of an arbitrary proper name, associated with an arbitrary criterion of identity.

It does not seem that this kind of unrestricted generality raises problems of so far-reaching a kind as Geach supposes, nor in particular, that it needs to be represented by means of any type of quantifier; for a sign of un-restricted generality such as this cannot meaningfully be attached to more than a very narrow class of predicates formed out of adjectival general terms. For instance, it would not make sense to say, 'There is something on the plate that is not sticky', except where a restricted range for the generalization is tacitly understood (such as: articles of food). Sentences like those cited represent one step away from sentences of the primitive form, 'That is X' (where 'X' is an adjectival term). In these more sophisti-cated sentences, there is no demonstrative: a place and a time, which need not be here and now, are indicated by other verbal devices in the sentence. But that which the adjectival term applies to must be an object of sense, even if, as in the first and the third of our sentences, it is not directly des-cribed as being so. The use of such sentences therefore constitutes an advance, from the description of what is immediately present, to the des-cription, in the same terms, of what is past or elsewhere. This use of the word 'something' has no logical significance: like the 'it' in 'it is raining', it merely fills a place where a grammatical substantive or pronoun is required. It is precisely because sentences containing such occurrences of the word 'something' cannot always, and never need, be thought of as the result of applying a logical operation to a sentence containing a proper name or other singular term, that it is possible to treat them adequately in the fairly casual fashion here indicated.

The picture of reality as an amorphous lump, not yet articulated into discrete objects, thus proves to be a correct one, so long as we make the right use of it. It serves to emphasize that, in learning the use both of countable general terms and of proper names, we have to learn the criterion of identity associated with them, where this means primarily learning the sense of statements of identification of the form, 'This is the same X as that', and of recognition statements of the form, 'That is a'—thus of sentences involving demonstratives. Such a picture corrects the naïve conception, found for example, in Mill, that the meaning of a general term consists just in its connotation (the principle whereby we determine which objects it is true of), and that of a proper name just in its denotation (i.e. which object it is the name of): for this conception presupposes that the world presents itself to us as already dissected into discrete objects, which we know how to recognize when we encounter them again, in advance of our acquiring any grasp of language at all. It is precisely this misconception, with the con-comitant error of regarding proper names as uniquely simple constituents of our language, endowed with an unequivocal meaning by the uniquely simple method of ostensive definition, against which Wittgenstein wages war in the early part of *Philosophical Investigations*. Geach's mistake consists in his transferring this picture, which is the appropriate one to represent our learning to use the most primitive part of our language, to the explanation of a much more sophisticated part, that, namely, of whose structure the formalism of predicate calculus constitutes a model. Frege's logical formalism was undoubtedly adequate for his chief purpose, the representation of mathematical statements and mathematical proofs. He, was aware, as his fragmentary researches into the logic of sentences involving oblique contexts show, that it was not adequate for the representation of all sentences in our language. Where he can be criticized is in not realizing the fundamentally different character of sentences involving demonstratives from that of sentences containing only proper names and other singular terms: where, as he does only very rarely, he mentions demonstatives or such words as 'I' at all, he assimilates them to singular terms, differing only in that something non-linguistic is involved in the determination of their reference. But Geach mistakes what he is about: he misapplies a doctrine which is indeed essential to the account of sentences involving demonstratives in order to obtain an (ultimately incoherent) criticism of the treatment by Frege and by modern logicians of sentences of a quite different sort.

How far is it right to credit Frege with advancing the Wittgensteinian doctrine that the sense of countable general terms and of proper names consists, in part, in their being associated with a criterion of identity? We opened this chapter by ascribing just such a doctrine to Frege, at least for proper names: but we have now arrived at a much more exact understanding of the sense in which this doctrine has to be taken.

In § 62 of *Grundlagen*, Frege proposes to treat a stipulation of the truth-conditions for sentences of the form 'The number of F's is the same as the number of G's' as a (contextual) definition of terms of the form 'the number of F's'; similarly, in § 65, a contextual definition of 'the direction of the line a' might take the form of stipulating that 'the direction of $a =$ the direction of b' is true if and only if 'a is parallel to b' is true. If Frege had ended by endorsing these proposals, then undoubtedly this section of *Grundlagen* would have presented a doctrine closely allied to (though not identical with) that of Wittgenstein; and it may well in fact have formed the inspiration for Wittgenstein's development of his doctrine in the *Investigations*. In §§ 56 and 62 of *Grundlagen* it is emphasized, as a prime characteristic of a 'self-subsistent object', that we are capable of recognizing it as the same again: since 'object' is correlative with 'proper name', we may take it that Frege regards it as a prime characteristic of the sense of a proper name that it supplies us with a standard for re-identifying an object as the referent of that name. This, however, is so far only a hint. The substantial point is the view advanced in § 62, and defended in §§ 63–65, that it is up to us to stipulate what he expressly calls a 'criterion for the identity of numbers', and that, in doing so, we are not violating the principle that 'the same' has a single, univocal sense: and this is presented, not as something special to numerical terms, but as a general type of procedure, applicable in a wide range of cases.

The fact that, in the end, Frege rejects the proposal to treat the stipulation of the criterion of identity for numbers, or for directions, as a contextual definition, or even that he later banned contextual definitions entirely,   Gg II 66 should not by itself deter us from ascribing to Frege an anticipation of Wittgenstein's doctrine about criteria of identity. Frege eventually opts for that kind of explicit definition which has been ineptly called 'definition by abstraction', viz. a definition of numbers, directions, etc., as equivalence classes. If we take the notion of an equivalence class, or, more generally, that of a class, as already known and requiring no further explanation, then, of course, such a definition is an explicit definition in the ordinary sense, explaining the defined term by means of something already understood. But, if we do not take the notion of a class as given in advance, then definition by abstraction has to be looked at simply as a representation of the general form of such contextual definitions as Frege had originally proposed: and, if it were so regarded, the decision to display the definitions of 'the number of F's' and 'the direction of a' by means of this general representation would in no way tell against crediting Frege with Wittgenstein's doctrine. What does tell against this is that Frege did not look on definition by abstraction in this light. We therefore cannot definitely say that Frege taught the doctrine, even in *Grundlagen*; in the later works only the faintest traces of the doctrine remain. He certainly enunciated it in the section of *Grundlagen* we have been considering: but, in the end, we are, in effect, left only with a piece of heuristic advice, that, in seeking a definition of names of a certain form, we do well to ask ourselves what is the condition for the truth of an identity-statement connecting two such names, and then frame our definition so as to yield this condition. This is a weak replacement for the doctrine that, in specifying the sense of a name, we have to stipulate the criterion of identity associated with it; and so we cannot claim that Frege actually endorsed the doctrine which he enunciated.

The doctrine which Frege enunciated is not precisely the same as that advocated by Wittgenstein in the *Investigations*, but only closely related to it: for the case with which Frege is concerned is different from that which principally interested Wittgenstein. As we have seen, an important distinction exists between those names whose referents can also be indicated by the use of demonstratives, and those standing for objects which cannot be so indicated; contrary to what Wittgenstein says at *Investigations* I-28, names of numbers and directions are of the second kind. In *Grundlagen*, Frege is treating of names of the second kind, whereas Wittgenstein is principally concerned with those of the first kind—hence his interest in ostension. A characteristic method of forming names of the second kind is by means of a functional operator such as those considered in *Grundlagen* §§ 62–69: the simplest case is that in which such names are of the form '$f(a)$', where '$f(\xi)$' is an operator and 'a' a name for an object of another kind. Hence the criterion of identity for objects denoted by names formed with the operator '$f(\xi)$' will be the criterion for the truth of statements of the form '$f(a) = f(b)$', and can be stated as a relation between the objects a and b. In this context, Frege's neglect of demonstratives is irrelevant, and in no way impairs his account. We should note that Frege does not explain the univocity of the phrase 'the same', in the face of the necessity to stipulate particular criteria of identity, in Geach's way: he does not hold 'the same' to be a fragmentary expression. We do not need to qualify 'the same' in a sentence like 'The direction of a is the same as the direction of b' by saying, or understanding, 'The direction of a is the same *direction* as the direction of b': the direction of a is either, absolutely, the same as the direction of b, or else absolutely distinct from it. We could, indeed, say, if we wished, 'The line a is the same in direction as the line b'; but then the expression 'the same in direction' would either have to be taken as licensing the transition to 'The direction of a is the same absolutely as the direction of b', or else to be regarded as a unitary expression, not standing for any kind of relation of identity, but merely a paraphrasis for 'parallel'. It is only as it occurs in statements of identity involving demonstratives, i.e. of such forms as 'This is the same (X) as that', that 'the same' is rightly said to be a fragmentary expression; precisely because the demonstratives do not determine what kind of object is being talked about.

Frege would have been incapable of enunciating the Wittgensteinian doctrine of criteria of identity as it applies to proper names and general terms of the first of our two kinds, with the modifications that this case requires, without remedying his failure to distinguish sharply between demonstratives and proper names, and hence between sentences of the forms 'This is the same (X) as that' and 'a is the same as b'. For this case, the notion of a criterion of identity can be explained only as the criterion for the truth of a statement of identification involving demonstratives. The criterion for the identity of directions is that a certain relation should obtain between two lines which have those directions, and the criterion for the identity of numbers is that a certain second-level relation should obtain between two concepts to which those numbers belong: but the criterion of identity for a man, city, planet or river is at least not naturally regarded as the condition that some relation should obtain between any two entities (objects or concepts) whatever, but as the condition for saying, 'This is the same man (city, etc.)'. As we saw, Frege's view of definition 'by abstraction' as a definition in terms of a notion (that of a class) already clearly understood caused the conception of such a definition as the stipulation of a criterion of identity to fade from his mind; and his erroneous belief—not shared by modern logicians—in quite unrestricted quantification over objects further blurred his apprehension of the idea of criteria of identity. Thus it came about that the Wittgensteinian doctrine, quite clearly stated in *Grundlagen* for one of the two types of case to which it applies, disappeared from Frege's philosophy of language.

Frege's failure to formulate the doctrine for the case of objects which can be indicated by means of demonstratives, together with his belief in unrestricted quantification over objects, explains his embarrassment in handling adjectival general terms: his presuppositions did not leave any place where they could be fitted in. What, then, ought Frege to have said about the number of red things? It is clear enough that, if we have stipulated some definite domain to be the range for our individual variables, then, relative to this domain, there will be a determinate answer to the question what is the number of red objects: at least, if there is not, this will have to be ascribed to the fact that the predicate 'red' is vague in its application—for some objects in the domain, there will be no definite answer to the question whether the adjective 'red' applies to them or not. But is there any way of answering the question how many red things there are in a particular place at a particular time without presupposing that a range for the individual variables has been assigned in advance of the asking of the question? (We can answer the question how many men there are in a room at a given time, without presupposing that a domain has been specified in advance, because the countable general term 'man' itself indicates the relevant domain.)

We have already acknowledged as possibilities two things that would make us agree with Geach that there is no such number as the number of red things in a given room at a given time. First, it may well be the case that the statement, 'There is something red in the room', may be capable of being true even though there is nothing in the room which we could recognize as an object—which could be an element in a domain for bound individual variables—to which the predicate 'red' applied: if, for instance, the surface of some liquid displayed a red gleam when looked at from certain angles. Secondly, we must allow it as a possibility that there may be no definite method of surveying the totality of all conceivable ways in which we might slice up the contents of the room into discrete objects. But against this the following objection might be made. We have agreed with Geach that, at least for the standard manner of understanding bound variables, it is necessary to regard them as having, in any given context, some restricted range; but the reasons we have offered for this have been quite different from, and much weaker than, those given by Geach. *Our* reasons all relate to the impossibility of quantifying simultaneously over all abstract objects—over all sets, or all cardinal or ordinal numbers. Hence there is no reason why we should not accept the possibility, which Geach would deny, of quantifying over all concrete objects; or, in particular—to avoid the difficulty that there may be something red although there is nothing red which could be considered as an *object*—over all material objects. Thus, setting aside purely visual objects, such as beams of light, reflections, glints, etc., we have still to answer the question whether there is any such number as the number of red material objects in a room at a particular time; if we wished to avoid further difficulties, we could even confine ourselves to opaque solid objects.

Presumably this question cannot be definitely answered without a firm grasp of the constitution of matter. If 'at a given time' is taken to mean 'at a given instant', and matter is thought of as composed of discrete and identifiable particles, then we could view the quantification as being made over the large but finite totality of sets of particles in the room: of course, we should then need to stipulate precisely the condition under which an arbitrary such set of particles could be said to be red. (The same would apply if we took 'at a given time' to mean 'over a given interval', and considered time as discrete, so that there are only a finite number of empirically distinct instants in a given interval: we should then need the variables to range over sets of particle-instants.) Alternatively, if we regarded matter as continuous, we could take the quantification as being over all continuous surfaces; again, we should need to specify just when an arbitrary continuous surface is to be considered as being red. We have, however, good reason to reject both these pictures as incorrect. The point of such a picture in this context is that it gives us some method of surveying the totality of possible ways in which (a chunk of) the amorphous lump can be dissected into discrete objects. In the absence of any definitive method of surveying this totality, we are forced to agree with Geach's answer: that, unless some method of determining what is to count as *one* material object has been specified in advance, there is simply no way of saying what is the number of red material objects in a given region of space-time.

The use of crude predications, 'This is (an) X', and the fact, remarked above, that the demonstrative pronouns which form their subjects relate either to a piece of matter or to a sensory appearance, furnish the clue to the otherwise puzzling fact that a categorial predicate of concrete objects does not express a merely formal concept in the sense of the *Tractatus*. The first-level predicate 'ξ is a cardinal number' cannot, in general, be informatively applied to an object: for, with trivial exceptions ('what I have in mind', 'what "hachi" stands for in Japanese'), a term for a cardinal number must display the fact that its referent is a cardinal number; one would not know what one was speaking of unless one knew whether or not it was a number. (This ceases to be so if some non-mandatory identification is made, of cardinal numbers with certain sets or with initial ordinals; but in such a case 'cardinal number' ceases to be a categorial predicate.) But a category term like 'animal' (or 'organism') has a genuine criterion of application, in that the crude predication, 'That is an animal', may be informative, although a sentence of the form 'a is an animal' cannot be, where 'a' is a proper name, since, to be understood, the name must already be recognized as the name of an animal. This is because the demonstrative need not refer to an object, but only to some identifiable piece of matter; and there are straightforwardly empirical tests to determine whether or not a material body constitutes an animal or organism. The category term retains its non-formal character in other sentences in which the subject is more complex, but still refers to a piece of matter, e.g. 'What is on this leaf is an animal'. In other cases the .demonstrative cannnot even be taken as referring to a piece of matter, but only to something as presented to the senses in a certain way. If I ask, 'Is that an animal?', you may, on occasion, sensibly reply, 'No, it's only an arrangement of shadows'. This use of general terms may, again, be extended to cases in which the subject is not a demonstrative, as in 'That speck on the horizon is a church spire'. Predication cannot be understood if we try always to construe it after the model of saying something about an object.

CHAPTER 17

*Original Sinn**

Ged 65 (11)   IN *Der Gedanke*, Frege considers an imaginary case in which Leo Peter understands by the name 'Dr. Gustav Lauben' the doctor who lives as the only doctor in a house known to him, while Herbert Garner knows that Dr. Gustav Lauben was born on 13 September 1875 in N.N. and that this is not true of anyone else, but does not know where Dr. Lauben now lives nor anything else about him. In such a case, Frege says, as far as the proper name 'Dr. Gustav Lauben' is concerned, Herbert Garner and Leo Peter do not speak the same language, since, although they do in fact refer to the same man by means of this name, they do not know that they do so. The senses which they attach to the name are different.

     Similar considerations arise with definitions. Frege was often concerned with finding the definitions of mathematical expressions, and he allows, in setting out that kind of demonstration of the truth of a sentence which renders that sentence analytic, appeal to the definitions of the words con-

Iuss 320; Bs 7   tained in the sentence. But he was very well aware that it is frequently possible to define an expression in different ways, in ways which, even if they are analytically equivalent, cannot be regarded as conferring the same sense on the expression unless we are prepared to grant, as Frege is not, that any two analytically equivalent expressions have the same sense. Since a definition of a word provides one way of determining its sense, we should have, in this case too, to say that two individuals who adopt different

Ged 65 (12)   definitions for the same word speak different languages.

     The notion of sense was introduced as something objective and common to all speakers of a language, in contrast to mere subjective associations that may differ from speaker to speaker. Hence the admission that different senses may be attached to the same word by speakers of what would ordinarily

---

* I owe the pun which forms the title of this chapter to Professor Paul Benacerraf of Princeton University.

be said to be one language threatens the whole notion of sense. When sense was said to be something common to all speakers of a language, the word 'language' was intended in its ordinary application, according to which we distinguish French, Japanese, Tamil, etc., as languages: but now it appears that the exigencies of the word 'sense' will force us to discriminate much more finely between languages, so that, for example, two people will speak different languages if their vocabularies, including the proper names with which they are familiar, are different, or if they would give different explanations of the words in those vocabularies. On this account, it is hardly likely that there are any two people who speak the same language. In face of this, it is unclear what becomes of the supposed objectivity of sense, which was characterized in the first place as something in common to all whose language is the same.

Evidently, the notion of sense can be maintained only if it is possible to hold that differences in the sense attached by different individuals to the same word are in principle objectively detectable and resoluble. It is possible to continue to regard the notion of sense as having any serious significance only if, further, there is sometimes an important practical point in so detecting and resolving differences of sense. We have already looked cursorily at this issue. But, since an influential school in the philosophy of language is founded on the repudiation of Frege's notion of sense, a closer examination is in order. Phenomena of the kind we noted at the outset of this chapter obviously blur the application of Frege's theory of meaning to actual language. This would not worry Frege very much, since he started from the assumption that natural language is a defective instrument, and that what the logician needs is not a theory of the working of natural language but a theory of the working of an improved language which could ideally replace it, and, for the most rigorous scientific purposes, may actually do so. This assumption was instilled in him by his first triumph, the solution of the problem of multiple generality, a solution found not by analysing the means of expressing generality available in natural language, but by replacing it with a better form of expression. But we are not as ready as Frege to accept such solutions lightly. We need first to be convinced that what is presented as an ideal really is an ideal, that the deviation of natural language from it really does impede a systematic account of the way in which natural language functions. The extent to which it must be conceded even by Frege that the expressions of natural language fail to have a unique, determinate, objective sense represents a gap which an adherent of Frege's theory of meaning has to fill with excuses, reasons why it is nevertheless profitable to think in terms of the situation Frege presents as an ideal. Even if such excuses can be provided, we have first to ask whether the whole exercise is worth while: whether, by jettisoning the notion of sense altogether, we cannot give a perfectly satisfactory account of the way in which language functions. That is why it is of value to look at attempts to give such an account which dispense with any notion corresponding to that of sense.

FLPV 20-46   In 'Two Dogmas of Empiricism', Quine first sketched an account of such a kind. Quine starts by attacking certain verificationist assumptions which have very little to do with the philosophy of Frege. Verificationism, as represented by the logical positivist school, differs as a theory of meaning from that advanced by Frege in two distinct ways. First, the sense of a sentence is thought of as being fixed by determining, not the conditions under which it is to be true, as Frege thought, but the conditions under which we are able to recognize it as true. The conditions under which a statement is true are conditions which either obtain or fail to obtain quite independently of our ability to recognize them as obtaining or not obtaining; we may in some cases succeed in giving to our sentences a sense such that we may never be able to determine directly, or even with certainty, whether they are true or false. The conditions under which a sentence is recognized as true or as false, on the other hand, are conditions of quite another kind: they have, by the nature of the case, to be conditions which we can recognize as obtaining when they obtain. Only in the very simplest of cases, perhaps such a statement as 'I have toothache', does it hold even for one individual that either that condition in which the sentence is recognized as true obtains, or that condition obtains in which it is recognized as false. The most that we can normally hope for is that we have some effective method of bringing about a situation in which, relative to a given sentence, one or other of these two conditions must obtain: when such an effective method exists, the sentence is effectively decidable. For many sentences, however, no such effective method of deciding their truth-value exists, even in principle. We can search for a deciding situation, i.e. one in which either the condition in which the sentence is recognized as true, or that in which it is recognized as false, obtains, without having any guarantee that our search will terminate in success. Such an account repudiates the idea of a determinate truth-value, considered as attaching to the sentences of our language independently of our capacity for recognizing it, and substitutes, in the theory of meaning, the notions of verification and falsification for those of truth and falsity. It is somewhat obscure whether the account thus given does tally with the intentions of the logical positivists, since a natural consequence of such a view would be a rejection of the law of excluded middle for sentences not in principle effectively decidable, and this was a step which the positivists never appear to have taken; indeed, their writing sometimes suggests that they would deny a complete sense to any sentence not in principle effectively decidable. However, it is at least clear that this was one direction in which positivism had moved away from Frege: meaning was to be tied closely to our means of knowing the truth-value of statements, rather than to that in virtue of which they are true or false, considered as fixed irrespective of our capacity to become aware of it.

With this aspect of verificationism Quine is very little concerned in 'Two Dogmas of Empiricism'. His attention is concentrated upon a second feature of it, also diverging from Frege's theory. This is that the positivists considered the meaning of a statement, taken as determined by the conditions constituting verification or falsification of it, to be given in terms of these conditions characterized in purely sensory terms. This is the empiricist ingredient of positivism. The idea is that all our information comes to us via the stimulation of our senses. If we are able to recognize some condition as obtaining, a condition which constitutes the verification of some sentence, then we do so, ultimately, by recognizing some pattern of sensory stimulation as occurring. In consequence, we can view the meaning of any sentence as given in the following way: among every possible sequence of sense-experiences to which we may be subjected, some are selected as constituting verifications of that sentence and others as constituting falsifications of it; we attach a meaning to it by associating with it two such sets of verifying and falsifying sequences of sense-experiences.

It is evidently possible to accept the first verificationist thesis without the second: to hold that the sense of a sentence is to be thought of as determined by the association with it of conditions for its verification and falsification, rather than conditions for its truth and falsity, without interpreting these verifying or falsifying conditions merely as sets of sense-experiences. But, since the second thesis has been expressed in the context of the first, that is, as a thesis about the kind of condition which constitutes a verifying or falsifying one, or, at least, about the way in which such a condition is to be characterized, it is not at once obvious that we can contrast this thesis with Frege's view independently of the first thesis: since Frege did not think that sense was given in terms of conditions of verification and falsification, for him the question could not arise what constituted such conditions or how they were to be characterized. Since the conditions under which a sentence is true were not, in general, for Frege, conditions that we are necessarily capable of recognizing, it would be absurd to suppose that they consisted in the occurrence of certain sense-experiences.

Nevertheless, such a contrast can be drawn. It is, in fact, necessary to draw it if we are to understand Frege. On the positivist view, logically necessary statements do not have an ordinary sense at all: for no sense-experience could falsify them, and hence no sense-experience is needed in order to verify them; if they are to be conceded a sense, this must be a sense of an entirely different kind from that possessed by empirical statements, a sense *not* to be explained in the same way, in terms of the notions of verification and falsification.

Such a conclusion, though here expressed in terms of the verificationist theory of meaning, is independent of the contrast between such a theory of meaning and one, such as Frege's, stated in terms of truth-conditions. In the positivist case, the second thesis was derived from the first by construing the notion of verification exclusively in terms of what we might call the raw material for the verification of a sentence, prescinding from anything we might have to do in order to recognize that a verification had occurred. In just the same way, it would be possible, within a theory of meaning based on truth-conditions, to interpret the notion of a truth-condition as consisting merely in a particular constitution of the world independently of any particular path to recognizing that the world was so constituted: for instance, one might use as a model of a truth-condition the membership by the actual world in some set of possible worlds. From such an interpretation, just the same consequence could be drawn: a logically necessary statement has no genuine truth-condition, since the world does not have to be constituted in one particular way rather than another for it to be true, and hence such statements cannot have a sense of the same kind as that possessed by empirical statements. Such a consequence is quite repugnant to Frege's manner of thinking. For him, the very same notion of sense applies to analytic and to synthetic statements: we might perfectly well know the sense of a sentence without knowing whether it was analytic or synthetic, something we could not possibly do if the word 'sense' was equivocal as applied to statements of the two kinds. For a positivist, the analytic equivalence of two sentences or two predicates was a guarantee of their possession of the same sense; for Frege, it was a necessary, but by no means a sufficient, condition.

Suppose, then, that we have two sentences which are analytically equivalent, but have different senses. Since they have different senses, they must, on a view of Frege's kind, have different truth-conditions. Since they are analytically equivalent, the world cannot be so constituted that one is true and the other false: the set of possible worlds in which the one is true is the very same set as that of those in which the other is true. How can there be room for Frege to distinguish the truth-conditions of the one from those of the other? In particular, how, in a realistic theory, such as Frege's, can it be legitimate to invoke any notion of the path to recognizing the truth-conditions of either to obtain, when sense is supposed to be given independently of our capacity to recognize truth?

It has been repeatedly stressed, in this account of Frege's philosophy, that the notion of sense, as Frege understood it, relates to our recognition of reference: in particular, then, the sense of a sentence is related to our capacity to recognize that sentence as true or as false. The realistic part of Frege's theory has to do with the doctrine of reference: it is quite wrong to think of Frege's theory of meaning as one in which meaning is quite divorced from knowledge. Why, then, is Frege's theory not a verificationist one? The answer lies in the fact that, on Frege's understanding of the matter, we are capable of conferring on certain of our expressions a sense which relates to a means of recognition which we are not ourselves capable of carrying out. Frege does not, indeed, put the matter in just this way: but this seems to be the only possible way of interpreting him. As already noted, an example of this is quantification over infinite domains. It is not exactly that such quantification is totally unrelated to any means of recognizing the quantified sentence as true or false: it is, rather, that it is a means that we cannot ourselves apply, since we are unable to accomplish infinitely many tasks in a finite time. (This explains why Russell found it necessary to disparage this LE 143–4 impossibility as a 'mere medical' one.) If the question were raised how we ever arrive at such a conception—a question Frege does not raise, let alone answer—the reply would presumably have to be that we arrive at it by analogy with the finite case: having understood quantification over a finite domain in terms of a procedure of determining truth-value that we actually can accomplish, we are able to extend this conception to a procedure which we cannot accomplish. This extension enables us to grasp that a determinate truth-value must attach to the sentence, and to recognize certain indirect means of establishing what that truth-value is, though not, indeed, in general to find any universally applicable method for deciding the sentence as true or as false.

Frege's theory of meaning is a *strongly* realistic theory, but it is not a *purely* realistic theory. A theory of meaning intended for a language in which all sentences are decidable can be both realistic and verificationist: explanation of sense in terms of truth-conditions and in terms of conditions of verification coincide for such a language. (The positivists can, as already noted, be interpreted as holding that the only meaningful sentences are those that are decidable, and hence as advancing a theory of meaning that was realistic and verificationist at the same time: this would explain their failure to repudiate classical logic on verificationist grounds.) If sentences

for which no effective decision method exists are admitted as meaningful
sentences of the language, then, if such sentences are to be regarded as
having determinate truth-values independently of our knowledge, their
senses cannot be explained in terms only of our capacity to recognize their
truth-values. Frege goes as little beyond this as it is possible for a realist
to go: he does not sever the connection between sense and knowledge,
between sense and the recognition of truth; but he allows that it may
consist in a grasp of ideal procedures for the determination of truth-value
which we cannot in practice, or even in principle, carry out.

In a purely realistic theory of meaning the relation between sense and the
recognition of truth will be ignored altogether. As a result, we are then
forced to conceive of truth-conditions, considered as determining sense,
not in terms of any procedure, even ideal, for coming to recognize truth-
value, but as relating solely to the way the world is, independently of our
apprehension of it. The most refined distinction between the senses of two
sentences which it then becomes possible to make is according to the
different possible worlds in which they would be true: hence, as in the
second positivist thesis, analytically equivalent sentences have the same
sense, and analytically true sentences have no ordinary sense at all. This is
exactly what happened in the theory of meaning presented in Wittgenstein's
Tractatus.

But a verificationist theory of meaning did not prevent the positivists
from falling into the same error. Although they regarded sense as determined
by the conditions for the verification of a sentence, they insisted on viewing
these conditions as consisting solely in the bare impact of the external
world upon us, as transmitted through the senses, in abstraction from any
activity of ours which enables us to recognize the sentence as having been
verified. The result is a notion of verification which bears little resemblance
to any procedure we actually employ when we determine the truth-value of a
sentence. In a purely realistic theory, such as that of the *Tractatus*, there
is no room for any notion of sense which plays the same role as the notion
of sense employed by Frege, namely that of explaining our grasp on the
references, and so the uses, of words. The notion of meaning within a
verificationist theory would be expected to play precisely that role: but,
when verification is construed in the bizarre fashion in which the positivists
construed it, it is unable to do so, and thus loses its point altogether. It is
totally implausible to think of the speakers of a language as associating with
each sentence some set of verifying sense-experiences, a verifying situation
characterized in purely sensory terms: the sense of such a sentence as 'the
Earth revolves around the Sun' is fully determinate long in advance of

anyone's having thought out what observations would establish or disprove it. If a verificationist theory of meaning is to be accepted at all, then the notion of verification which it employs ought to be modelled on our actual practice in coming to recognize statements as true.

When we look at this practice, we realize at once that it is only for a very restricted class of sentences that it is remotely plausible to say that their verification or falsification consists in the occurrence of certain sensations. Quite apart from the gap between the supposed sense-datum language and the language of material objects and physical properties, the establishment of an empirical statement rests not merely on observation but proceeds via the mediation of other statements connected with it through deductive or inductive inference. To take one of Quine's examples, the verification even of such an everyday statement as 'Herbert and Anthony are brothers' does not consist *WO* 56 merely in the visual sense-impressions attendant on a reading of two birth certificates: it depends on everything that leads us to believe that human beings reproduce themselves sexually, and, if the birth certificates are relevant at all, then on all that determines the meaning of a certain fragment of the English language, the reliability of registrars, etc.; and the statements here tacitly involved in establishing the truth of the statement of kinship are statements whose sense is such that they could not be grounded on direct observation, but only upon the justification of a whole theory (in an admittedly modest sense of 'theory'), that is, as a result of an inferential process. It characterizes the kind of sense which many sentences of our language possess that we learn to use them precisely in connection with the manipulation of other parts of language, that is to say, as capable of being established only via deductive or inductive inferences. Once this is admitted, there is no obstacle to recognizing that there are certain statements whose sense is such that observation plays no role in establishing them at all, that their verification consists purely in the exhibition of a deductive sequence: these are mathematical statements, which can thus be seen as lying at the extreme end of a scale the other end of which is occupied by purely observational statements, the majority of statements lying somewhere in between. There thus ceases to be any need to invoke some quite different type of sense for mathematical statements to possess, while empirical statements possess the ordinary kind. The senses of all statements are to be explained in terms of the conditions for their verification, where this means the actual situation in which anyone who understands the statement must concede that it has been verified. Verification will, in general, consist in a mixture of observation and inference: in some limiting cases it will consist only in the one, in others only of the other.

This picture of language as an articulated network, some sentences of which lie at a greater depth than others from direct contact or confrontation with experience is, of course, precisely that for which Quine argued at the end of 'Two Dogmas'; and the atomistic character of the positivist theory of meaning, whereby the sense of each sentence consisted in the direct association with it of some set of sequences of sense-experiences as its verification was precisely the target of his attack in that essay; as already remarked, it is not the verificationist nature of the positivist account that he finds objectionable.

So far, then, all seems to be in agreement with Frege's views, modulo the question whether we need a verificationist or a realist theory of meaning. Quine's theory, as presented at the end of 'Two Dogmas', is verificationist, since it has entirely to do with the effect which experience has on what we hold to be true, as opposed to the truth of what we say independently of whether we have reason for it; but we have stressed that Frege's theory, while it is a realist one, is not on the other hand totally anti-verificationist. Where, then, does Quine diverge from Frege?

The image which Quine presents is one of language as an articulated structure which makes contact with reality, or with our experience of reality, only at the periphery. Such an image is designed to express the fact that the sentences of our language are linked by various inferential connections (not necessarily all strictly deductive in character), and that our grasp of the sense of a sentence involves our apprehension of such connections. The peripheral sentences are observation-sentences, and a grasp of their sense consists primarily in a knowledge of how they are verified or falsified by experience. A sentence lying in the interior, on the other hand, can be established only as the result of inference, via the links it has with other sentences in the structure; for it, verification and falsification are not effected by direct confrontation with experience.

In 'Two Dogmas', Quine advances two further theses. First, the contact between experience and the periphery is never so tight that any experience compels us to make a determinate assignment of truth-value to any one particular peripheral sentence: it will always be possible, under the impact of whatever experience, to make adjustments in the interior which will save that sentence from refutation or deprive it of acceptance. Quine says that we tend, but does not suggest that we are constrained, to seek the most economical overall revision to our assignments of truth-values to our sentences; but it is clear that such internal adjustments may sometimes achieve such economy. The peripheral sentences are not sense-datum statements, but statements about the external world of the kind that can serve as reports of observation; and what Quine is appealing to is the idea that we can always dismiss any recalcitrant experience as illusory. Quine moreover generalizes the thesis to sentences at any depth from the interior, though what he is appealing to here is not so evident. The consequence is that, when an experience occurs which is recalcitrant in the sense that it compels us to make some overall revision to our truth-value assignments to sentences, there is never any one such overall revision which it forces upon us: an experience may make *some* revision necessary, but there will always be a number of alternative possible revisions any one of which would be a legitimate response to the given recalcitrant experience.

Secondly, there are no sentences which are so deeply embedded as to be immune from revision. Any sentence whatever, even a logical law (Quine cites the Law of Excluded Middle), may, on occasion, be rejected as false in the course of some adjustment made in response to the impact of experience. Sentences deeper in the interior of the structure have connections with a greater range of other sentences, and their rejection may therefore in itself lead to a more extensive overall revision than that of sentences closer to the periphery: but, if a great deal of strain builds up in other parts of the system, it may be simpler to reject some highly general sentence near the centre, rather than make all the other adjustments necessary to save it.

Unfortunately, Quine's conclusions from these two theses lead to the destruction of the image of language which he presented. From the first thesis, he concludes that we have to go beyond Frege. Frege made an advance by taking the primary vehicle of meaning as the sentence, not the term; but we have to say, rather, that the unit of empirical significance is not even the sentence, but 'the whole of science'. 'Science' is here used as covering every statement which we hold to be true. The response to a recalcitrant experience will be some overall revision of what we may call our 'total theory', namely the partial assignment of truth-values which at any one time we are disposed to make to the sentences of our language. Since any finite sub-theory of the total theory is compatible with any experience whatever, it follows that no one sentence has significance by itself: only a total theory has.

The consequence of this is to subvert the metaphor of periphery and interior. If alternative revisions are always possible, and, in particular, ones which leave the periphery intact, there is no content to saying that the total theory makes contact with experience only at the periphery. Rather, the total theory confronts experience *as a whole*: as a whole, revision is or is not required in it by the occurrence of an experience; but there is not any one point or region in the total theory where the impact is made. The periphery was defined as the set of sentences on which experience directly impinges, the interior as the set of sentences which can receive an impulse from without only when it is transmitted from the periphery via the sentences lying en route. If the system confronts experience only as a whole, then there is no periphery and no interior.

Quine makes some attempt to justify the periphery/interior metaphor by saying that closeness to the periphery is a matter of 'relative likelihood, in practice, of our choosing one statement rather than another for revision in the event of recalcitrant experience'. But we are entitled to ask whether these varying probabilities are derivable from the significance attributed to the theory as a whole, or whether they have to be considered a primitive part of any systematic account of that significance, i.e. of a theory of meaning for a Quinean language. Knowing the empirical significance of a total theory presumably consists in knowing which experiences would be recalcitrant with respect to it, and which overall revisions would be responsive to any given recalcitrant experience. For any particular recalcitrant experience, different overall revisions will be possible, some of which will leave a given sentence intact, and others of which involve the assignment of a new truth-value to it. Now, is it that we can calculate the probability that that sentence will be revised in the face of that recalcitrant experience because we can assign certain probabilities to the various alternative overall revisions, say on the basis of the respective degrees of disturbance they create? Or is it, rather, that we can assign a probability to the revision of the given sentence in the face of that experience in advance of considering the overall revision which would ensue, and that, for any other sentence, we can then assign a probability, conditional upon the revision of the given one, to its revision, and so on?

In the latter case, we should need—as is reasonable—to see each overall revision as proceeding by successive stages. There would be, associated with each sentence and each recalcitrant experience, a certain probability that that sentence would be revised as an initial reaction to the experience. The inferential connections between sentences would then consist in conditional probabilities that, given a revision of a sentence A, a revision of sentence B would immediately ensue. An overall revision would thus be transmitted through the total theory by an impulse spreading out, in accordance with probabilistic laws, from some initial point of disturbance generated by the impact of recalcitrant experience. It is unlikely, however, that this is the model Quine had in mind, since it would contradict his thesis that only the total theory has empirical significance. On this model, each sentence in the theory has significance: not, indeed, a determinate significance in the sense of one provided by criteria for its conclusive verification or falsification by experience; but a significance of a probabilistic kind. The fact that a given sentence might be accepted as true or rejected as false in consequence, not of direct confrontation with experience, but of the acceptance or rejection of other sentences, would no more rob each sentence of its individual significance in the case that the connections between sentences are only probabilistic than in the case that they are rigid.

If, however, the probability of revision of a given sentence in face of a given experience is to be derived from the probability of each overall revision involving it, then the former probabilities—which determine the distance of the sentence from the periphery—are not a primitive part of a theory of meaning for a Quinean language. The basic features of an account of the working of such a language are those which determine the recalcitrance of each experience to a total theory, the overall revisions which may be made in response to it, and, perhaps, the relative probabilities of such revisions. (It is unclear whether we need implicitly to *know* these probabilities in order to understand the language, or whether they are a mere fact of nature of which we may remain unaware.) In this case, while it is still possible to defend the periphery/interior metaphor as having some content, it is irrelevant to our understanding of the language: it makes no difference to our ability to employ a sentence of the theory whether we know how near the periphery it is located or not.

There is indeed a clear sense in which we can say that, for Frege, the sentence is the primary vehicle of meaning: the sense of a word can be explained only by reference to its occurrence in sentences. But Frege's theory does not involve that we attach a sense directly to each sentence as if the sentence were a logically simple expression. On the contrary, Frege holds that we apprehend the sense of the sentence as a complex constructed out of the senses of its component words; and Frege's semantics, his theory of the references of expressions of the various logical types, is an attempt to provide at least the beginning of an account of the way in which we determine the sense of a sentence from the senses of its component parts. Quine's contention that it is the total theory which is the unit (better: the primary vehicle) of significance might be taken in the same way. On such an interpretation, the sense of a sentence could be explained only by reference to its being a constituent in a total theory; but we should derive the significance of the total theory only from the senses of the sentences of which it was composed. This would mean that we should determine whether or not an experience was recalcitrant to a given total theory, and what overall

NS 262 (243)

revisions were possible in response to it, from the senses of the constituent sentences of the theory. These senses would therefore have to consist in a direct relation between a sentence and experience, and in the interconnections between sentences, whether these were deterministic or probabilistic; even though these relations with experience and interconnections could be stated only as something contributing in some manner to the empirical significance of the total theory, i.e. when it was conformable to experience, and how, when not, it was to be revised.

An interpretation of this kind seems to be ruled out, however, by Quine's insistence that nothing is immune to revision. In order to give substance to such an interpretation, we have in particular to have some way of understanding in what the inferential connections between sentences consist. Quine's thesis involves, however, that the principles governing deductive connections themselves form part of the total theory which, as a whole, confronts experience. Presumably, in order to avoid Achilles and the Tortoise troubles of the Lewis Carroll type, we must recognize the total theory as comprising rules of inference as well as logical laws in the form of valid schemata or their instances: but there is no reason to suppose that Quine draws a distinction between the status of such rules as against laws like Excluded Middle; they too must be equally liable to rejection under a heavy enough impact from without. But, in that case, there is nothing for the inferential links between sentences to consist in. They cannot be replaced by superinferential links, compelling us, if we accept certain logical principles, to accept also the consequences under those principles of other sentences we accept: for any such superlogical laws could in turn be formulated and considered as sentences no more immune to revision than any other. More generally, the same is liable to happen to any attempt to explain the significance of a total theory: if a man attempts to state what experiences he would regard as demanding revision of his theory, and what revisions would meet the case, what he says must become just another sentence in his theory, which cannot convey anything unless we already know the significance of the theory as a whole. Meaning thus becomes for Quine something essentially ineffable. We cannot say what meaning our language, or any part of it, has, since any attempt to do so would only yield a further constituent of that to which meaning is to be assigned.

It is quite wrong to view Quine's theory of language, as presented in 'Two Dogmas', as jettisoning the notion of meaning altogether. On the contrary, significance is to be attributed to each total theory, which possesses what significance it does in virtue of whatever principles govern the recognition of an experience as conformable with or recalcitrant to it, and of which overall revisions are admissible when revision is called for. Even though at no stage does a forced move occur, the game has some rules. But the effect of the two theses, that no experience compels the rejection of any sentence, and that no sentence is immune from revision, is to transform Quine's original model of language into a theory quite rightly characterized as holism. As a result of the first thesis, the distinction between periphery and interior disappears, and a total theory must be viewed as confronting experience as a single undifferentiated block. As a result of the second thesis, the internal structure of the theory, consisting in the interconnections of sentences with one another, is totally dissolved, and the theory becomes a mere featureless collection of sentences standing in no special relations to each other.

The imagist theory of meaning may, as Quine remarks, be construed as an attempt to construct an atomistic account of the senses of words: to each word is correlated an idea, and to a complex expression, including a sentence, a complex idea compounded out of the ideas correlated with the constituent words. What Quine describes as Frege's discovery that the sentence, not the word, is the primary vehicle of meaning was his perception that an atomistic theory of the senses of words will not work: we can give an account of the senses of words only in terms of their relation to sentences of which they form part. This does not involve declaring that words do not have senses, or ignoring the composition of sentences out of words. Likewise, Quine is correct in objecting, against the positivists, to an atomistic theory of the senses of sentences, under which each sentence is, in isolation, associated with certain sense-experiences as potential verifications or falsifications of it: an adequate theory of the senses of sentences must take account of the relation of a sentence to other sentences; of the fact, that is, that our understanding of language involves that, for most sentences, the establishment of a truth-value for them will be effected via other sentences with which they are linked, rather than by direct confrontation with experience. Quine deserves great credit for his perception of this necessity, a necessity which, while not to be found expressly formulated by Frege, nevertheless corresponds, as we have seen, with the natural way of interpreting his notion of sense. But the remedy for the errors of the atomistic model is not to deny sense to sentences and ascribe it only to total theories, ignoring their structure as a complex of sentences: it is to provide a better account of the senses of sentences, involving their relations with other sentences as well as to experience. A viable theory of meaning must be required to explain, not to throw overboard, the attribution of sense both to sentences and to words.

A thoroughgoing holism, while it may provide an abstractly intelligible

w

model of language, fails to give a credible account either of how we use language as an instrument of communication, or of how we acquire a mastery of language. A mastery of a holistic language would have to be taken as a grasp of a relation defined over all possible total theories (within the language as syntactically determined) and all experiences: when the relation holds, we may say that the experience is *conformable* to the theory, otherwise that it is *recalcitrant* to it. When a recalcitrant experience occurs, a revision in the theory is called for: and the admissible revisions will be just those that yield a theory to which that recalcitrant experience and all other previous experiences are conformable. Holism demands that this conformability relation should not be derivable from any meaning properties of the constituent sentences of the theory, but be defined directly for total theories taken as units.

Total holism, such as appears to be advocated in 'Two Dogmas', is necessarily solipsistic. Until the very last sentence of the essay, where Quine speaks of 'each man' as warping his scientific heritage under the promptings of his sensory stimulation, Quine speaks continually of 'our' making revisions in 'our' total theory. But, if this is to be a model of language in general, and not just of scientific language in the ordinary, restricted sense of 'scientific', it must give an account of the adoption of beliefs by any one individual which may not be shared by others. We have thus to think of a total theory as representing the totality of beliefs held at any one time by some one individual: others may speak the same language as he, not merely in the syntactic sense, but in the sense of operating with the same conformability relation between total theories and experiences; but each man's theory is his own.

There are two difficulties to making out how a language which functioned in accordance with this model could be used in practice for communication. One derives from the fact that, while it is only the total theory which has empirical significance, all that we know of another's total theory is some fairly small finite subset of the sentences he considers true. We can ascribe a definite content to these sentences only if we make assumptions about the rest of his total theory, assumptions which may well be false. It may be said that this is exactly the situation which we are in: we take a disagreement over the truth-value of a sentence at its face value, as representing a genuine rather than a mere verbal disagreement, until it is proved otherwise. But this, while true, is not the same thing: in fact, we might say that the more that I learn of another person's beliefs, when these prove to be very different from my own, the more likely it becomes that the disagreement was to be taken at face value, Where this breaks down is with those embedded truths that have been described as analytic: if I know of a man that he rejects the law permitting the inference to 'A and B' from 'A' and 'B', then I shall be sceptical whether any genuine disagreement is involved by his unwillingness to accept the statement that France is in Europe and India in Asia, although I shall have as yet no idea what he does mean. But for Quine this law has the same status as any other sentence: on his account of the matter, a man might hold a total theory which was equivalent to mine in the sense that we should recognize just the same experiences as recalcitrant, even though we accorded quite different truth-values to particular sentences and yet recognized just the same conformability relation for total theories. This would be a case of a purely verbal disagreement, although no information about our assignments of truth-values to only finitely many sentences could possibly determine that this was so. I cannot, therefore, know anything that a man believes until I know (or guess) everything that he believes. And so it becomes incomprehensible how anyone can tell another anything.

It is for this reason that we cannot restore a communal character to language by allowing a total theory to be revised by the acceptance of testimony or expert opinion as well as under the impact of experience. For even if I believe that someone else's total theory is, as a whole, correct, that gives no reason why my accepting any one sentence true in it should improve my own total theory; a theory can be judged correct or incorrect only as a whole. The 'Two Dogmas' model can give no account of the communicative function of language; for it was devised in the first place without attention to that function. It may be urged that communication is in fact in constant danger of breaking down; but the holistic picture of language makes it impossible to see how it could even begin.

The other difficulty concerns the language—in the semantic sense— in which a total theory is expressed. Even if I know a man's total theory, I do not know its significance unless I know the relevant conformability relation, at least as defined between that theory and all possible experiences. I have no right to assume that another man recognizes exactly the same conformability relation as myself: but there appears to be an insuperable obstacle to my determining whether this is so. As already observed, I cannot do so by asking him how he would revise his theory in the face of hypothetical future experiences, for all I shall obtain is another sentence of his theory, which, on the present assumption, I already know. The situation is essentially similar to that of a language all of whose sentences consist of single words, i.e. have no internal semantic structure: if these sentences are thought of as having sense in a positivistic fashion, that is, as agreeing or disagreeing with sense-experiences, it becomes unintelligible how the speakers of the language could ever have come to associate these senses with their unitary sentences, let alone to achieve the same association among different individual speakers; or how any one individual could discover the sense attached by another to a sentence, or decide whether it was or was not the same as that which he attached to it. In the same way, if a total theory is represented as indecomposable into significant parts, then we cannot derive its significance from its internal structure, since it has none; and we have nothing else from which we may derive it.

Quine's image of language as an articulated network is an apt one. Quine presses his two additional theses in such a way as utterly to deform this image into something no longer recognizable as a possible instrument of communication. This is not to say that Quine's two theses are incorrect: only that he adopts the wrong means of accommodating them. The first of the two theses is much the less important, and is fairly easily accommodated without destroying the rationale of the periphery/interior distinction. Quine makes it difficult to see how we may continue to maintain that the periphery is where experience impinges in the first place, by omitting to acknowledge the obvious fact that an experience, even if dismissed as illusory, does not go unrecorded. If the observation statement whose acceptance would be the standard response to that experience is rejected, it is still used, qualified by 'It appeared that . . .' or one of its kindred, to describe the experience. The observation statement may be rejected only if there is internal resistance to its acceptance from some other statement incompatible with it. Quine makes it appear that we have a free choice whether to accept the observation statement or not, guided only by the maxim of greatest economy in overall revision. We are, on the contrary, bound to conform our judgment to the balance of probabilities, which cannot be summarized by this maxim (otherwise it would never be rational to allow a well-grounded hypothesis to be overthrown by a single crucial observation): the probability of illusion or observational error of the relevant kind in the given circumstances, versus the probability, in view of the evidence for it, that the incompatible statement is false. Admittedly, owing to the imprecision of assessments of probability, the choice will often be a matter of intuitive estimation, and hence not mandatory. This is of small importance, since such decisions can be subsequently rectified in the light of accumulating evidence: the observation statement reinstated if originally rejected, or repudiated even though originally accepted. What never happens—although, on Quine's account, it perfectly well might—is that the results of different overall revisions are equivalent in the sense, already explained, of being conformable to just the same subsequent experiences; if this could occur, it would make no difference to our future expectations whether we dismissed a given experience as illusory or not.

Quine's second thesis, which is the basis for his rejection of analyticity, is a more serious and more difficult matter. Frege held that analytic statements have sense in the same sense of 'sense' as synthetic ones. Wittgenstein held that they are devoid of sense; and the positivists that they have meaning as well as contingent statements only under an equivocation over the word 'meaning'. Seeking to explain the role of analytic statements in language, the positivists fastened upon their use as elucidatory sentences, serving to convey some feature of the senses of words contained in them. This would ordinarily be thought of as applicable only to those analytic statements which would not normally be regarded as requiring proof: the prototype would be such a sentence as 'January has thirty-one days'. Quine agrees with Frege to this extent, that allegedly analytic and allegedly synthetic statements play similar roles in language—so similar, indeed, that the distinction between them cannot be discerned: neither kind of statement possesses a meaning for itself; both figure only as recipients of truth-values within a total theory.

There is some justice in the positivist account of the role which analytic statements are made to play, at least for some uses of some analytic statements; and certainly Quine's rejection of analyticity is tightly connected with his denial that elucidation is a linguistic operation distinguishable from that of assertion. It is common for philosophers to remark that assertion is the primary function of language—that, e.g., we can imagine a language without questions or commands, but not one without assertions. Quine's 'Two Dogmas' model of language is, however, one in which assertion is the only possible form of linguistic act. There is no place for the enunciation or explanation of the sense which is being attached to some expression: all must be conceived in terms of assignments of truth-values to sentences. And that is the fundamental source of its inadequacy.

Quine holds that every sentence is subject to revision. In a sense, this is obviously true. A child may doubt whether he is right in supposing 'January has thirty-one days' to be the generally accepted sentence; he may also, familiar perhaps with such changes as that from the Fahrenheit to the Centigrade scale, easily perceive how it might cease to command general acceptance. There is no difficulty, at any rate, about the revisability of those analytic statements whose acceptance depends on proof, e.g. mathematical theorems: the discovery of a mistake in the proof remains, save in the simplest cases, an open possibility, and, in face of a purported counter-example, we know how to set about comparing it with the proof to find out whether the proof is erroneous or the counter-example spurious. In the case of analytic statements not requiring proof, the traditional account is that their rejection must depend upon a change of meaning. When the enunciation of the statement can be regarded as a direct stipulation of meaning, as with 'January has thirty-one days', the nature of this change of meaning is unproblematic, at least when a definite replacement for the rejected sentence is proposed. In other cases, a rejection of the statement demands an elucidation of the new meaning to be attached to one or more expressions in it. This means that the rejection of a statement of this kind, while not impermissible, does not have a significance which is provided for in advance: it has to be supplied with it by the explanation of the change of meaning which underlies it.

The property which a sentence has if it cannot be rejected without some change of meaning is one of which it would be a mistake to think that it was incapable of being characterized in Quine's terms. In those terms, it would consist in the fact that no revision involving the rejection of the sentence could be admissible without a change in the conformability relation defined between total theories and experiences. What prevents Quine from acknowledging the existence of statements having this property is not that he has no notion of meaning adequate to expressing it: his notion of the empirical significance of a total theory is sufficient for the purpose. It is, rather, that he cannot admit explanation of meaning as a possible linguistic activity. A man can communicate to another that he has revised his total theory in regard to certain sentences: he has no means by which he can convey that he has modified in this or that respect the language in which his theory is expressed, where a language is taken as defined semantically as well as syntactically (the semantics of a Quinean language being determined by the conformability relation associated with it). Hence, within the context of Quine's model of language, there is no place for sentences which are not unassailable, but whose rejection must be supplemented by an explanation of a change of meaning.

Some of Quine's supporters, notably Gilbert Harman, have thought that Quine's view that there are no unassailable sentences (and hence no analytic ones) can be adequately demonstrated by pointing to circumstances in which someone might withdraw or withhold assent from reputedly analytic *QME* 133-4 sentences. Thus, for instance, Harman draws attention to what he rightly calls the 'familiar point' that someone may reject a word because he rejects the meaning customarily attached to it (either as confused or as resting upon assumptions he would repudiate): he will thereby also withdraw assent from any otherwise undeniable sentence that involves the word. In this way, Harman says, a man might reject the Law of Identity, because he rejected the concept of identity (say because he held a view like that of Geach that there is no relation of unqualified identity). Given that we may thus conceive of someone's rejecting the Law of Identity, Harman does not see why we may not say that it is simply a fact about the world that everything in it is found to be identical with itself.

This is, however, to attribute a naïve view to the believers in analyticity; especially since the 'familiar point' is familiar from the writings of many of them. No one has ever supposed that there are any sentences which, considered as identified merely syntactically, are intrinsically unassailable: the most that has ever been claimed is that there are sentences which cannot be rejected without a change of meaning. If there are really any sentences which could be rejected only as a result of rejecting some word in them altogether, these would possess a very high degree of analyticity indeed. (We may consider destruction of meaning an extreme case of change of meaning.)

Putnam, in 'Is Logic Empirical?', adopts a more sophisticated approach than that of Harman. He proclaims himself agnostic about whether, when a supposedly analytic statement is rejected, there is a change of meaning: but he is anxious to emphasize that, in many cases, it will at any rate not be a *mere* change of meaning. By a 'mere' change of meaning he understands the replacement of one meaning by another, where the old meaning remains straightforwardly expressible by some other phrase. For instance, if 'bachelor' was formerly used to mean 'unmarried man' and now comes to be used to mean 'unmarried person', this would be a mere change of meaning, since the old meaning can now perfectly well be expressed by 'male bachelor'. For an example of something which is not a mere change of meaning, Putnam instances the replacement of Euclidean by Riemannian geometry as applied to physical space (or space-time). It may, he thinks, be right to say that, as a result of this replacement, the meaning of 'straight line', etc., is altered: but not in such a way as to enable us to express what we formerly meant by 'straight line' in some other way. On the contrary, we can now no longer mean by any expression what we previously meant by 'straight line' as applied to lines in physical space.

The distinction thus drawn by Putnam, between what we may agree to call a *mere* change of meaning and what we might call a *substantive* change of meaning, is valid and of great importance. But, in the substantive cases, Putnam's professed neutrality over the issue whether a change of meaning really occurs at all becomes a neutrality distinctly friendly to the side favouring a negative answer. The whole thrust of his argument is that such changes, which involve the abandonment of allegedly analytic statements ('The sum of the interior angles of a triangle is two right angles') and the instatement of others ('The sum of the interior angles of a triangle varies with its area'), occur in response to empirical discoveries; and his conclusion is that the supposedly analytic statements might as well be classified as empirical ones. The conclusion of course follows only if there is no serious ground for asserting that a change of meaning has taken place.

The example to which he applies this thesis is the replacement, for statements of quantum mechanics, of classical logic by a logic in which the distributive law does not hold, as proposed by von Neumann and Birkhoff. The considerations which in the first place prompt this proposal are easily grasped. It is, according to quantum theory, impossible to ascribe simultaneously to a subatomic particle both a determinate position and a determinate momentum. Hence it is proposed that, if 'P' is a statement ascribing a determinate position to a particle at a given instant, and 'M' is a statement ascribing a determinate momentum to it at that instant, the conjunction 'P & M' shall be regarded as false, in fact as contradictory. Hence, if 'M_1', 'M_2', ..., 'M_n' are statements ascribing distinct determinate momenta to that particle at a given instant, the disjunction '$(P \& M_1)$ v $(P \& M_2)$ v ... v $(P \& M_n)$' being a disjunction of contradictory statements, is to be regarded as itself contradictory. On the other hand, we may be in a position to be able to assert both 'P' and the disjunction 'M_1 v M_2 v ... v M_n', and therefore the conjunction 'P & $(M_1$ v M_2 v ... v $M_n)$'. Hence the distributive law fails.*

Putnam's attitude is that we ought to accept the failure of the distributive law as simply an empirical consequence of observed phenomena: in terms of Quine's image, an adjustment at a level deep in the interior—the level at which statements of theoretical physics lie—has led to a further adjustment at the very centre, where the laws of logic are situated. Hence logical laws, though perhaps further from the periphery than any other sentences, do not differ from other sentences in principle; they may be regarded as empirical in that they may be the subject of revision under the impact of experience.

If someone announces that he does not accept the Law of Identity, we can, as yet, do nothing with his utterance: we cannot accept it, as coming from a trustworthy person, nor would we attempt to convince him that the Law was true; we can only ask him what he means. If he replies that he rejects the concept of identity, we know the form of his objection to the

* The example is harmlessly simplified in the same way as is done by Putnam.

Law; but we have no definite idea of its content until he gives us his grounds for rejecting the concept.

Likewise, if someone declares that, in view of quantum theory, he rejects the distributive law, we are, initially, in the position of the schoolboy who hears for the first time of a number whose square is -1. Putnam's attitude, that we have here a mere consequence, for logic, of empirical observations, would be paralleled by the attempt to persuade the schoolboy that he had better accept the existence of imaginary numbers because it has important applications in, e.g., the theory of electricity: he has a proof that every number has a non-negative square, and so he cannot see how a self-contradictory statement *can* have applications, important or otherwise. Similarly, we cannot see how the distributive law can be false, or how it could be refuted by empirical discoveries, however penetrating. And, in reacting thus, we should be quite right. The significance which we attach to a scientific theory, and our evaluation of it, both depend on our knowing the principles whereby observational consequences may be derived from it. If, now, when an antinomy appears to be derivable from some theory, it is to be licit to treat this as casting doubt, not on the theory, but on the principles under which consequences are derived, we can no longer feel that we know what significance any scientific theory has, or what accepting it as correct amounts to.

The schoolboy's bewilderment vanishes as soon as it is explained to him that it is only in a different sense of 'number' from that with which he is familiar that it can be said that there are numbers whose square is negative. In order that he should attach a clear sense to the assertion, it will be necessary to explain to him what this extended sense of 'number' is. This, of course, we can readily do, thanks precisely to the labours of those who thought, with Frege, that it was of value to introduce clarity into the foundations of mathematics. If the attitude had prevailed that mathematics is simply a proper part of our overall scientific theory, and must therefore be tailored to fit the required empirical applications, then the efforts of Frege and others to provide coherent foundations for mathematics would have been set aside as pointless, and mathematics would have remained in the confused condition which Frege stigmatized as scandalous. This is not to prejudge ZS iii the question whether the *ultimate* significance of mathematics may not lie in its empirical applications: it is merely to resist the idea that the only justification needed for any theory, mathematical or physical, is that it should 'work', and that, if it does, no analysis of how or why it works is called for.

Similarly, when someone proposes to reject the distributive law, our initial bafflement is dispelled as soon as he explains that he is advocating

w*

the use of 'and' and 'or' in different senses from those they usually bear; but we still do not know what exactly it is that he is proposing until he explains what these new senses are. Those who profess doctrines like those of Putnam and Quine, which leave no place for the elucidation of meaning, and who regard all linguistic activity as representable in terms of the assignment of truth-values to sentences, are naturally disposed to view logical and mathematical theories in a purely formalistic manner, that is, as consisting in the axiomatic stipulation of certain sentences as true or certain schemas as valid, together with the laying down of rules of inference for deriving further true sentences or valid schemas. It is thus highly characteristic that, in the entire course of his discussion of the revision of classical logic, Putnam should construe the latter as defined solely by its de-rivability-relation, and should make not one overt mention of the explanations of its sentential operators by truth-tables. He does, however, towards the end of his article, and with many protestations of distaste, offer an account of the semantics of the sentential operators of quantum logic, namely an 'operationalist' definition of them. Each atomic statement is supposed to be correlated with a test which, when applied, determines the statement as true or as false. The set of such tests is then asserted to be extendable to a complemented non-distributive lattice, under the relation $S \leqslant T$ which holds when anything which passes test S also passes test T. The o of the lattice is the impossible test, which nothing is counted as passing, and the i of the lattice the empty test, which everything is counted as passing. Then negation is taken as corresponding to complementation, disjunction to join (least upper bound) and conjunction to meet (greatest lower bound); the conditional is not used.

This explanation gives us for the first time in Putnam's essay an account of what the new meanings of 'and' and 'or' are supposed to be, under which the distributive law will fail; and so for the first time we gain an under-standing of the content of the proposed rejection of the distributive law. Putnam makes some attempt to pretend that no change of meaning is involved, on the ground that the very same operationalist definition would serve for the 'and' and 'or' of classical logic. This would be true, however, only in a case in which conjunction and disjunction are applied only to decidable statements; as soon as they are applied to statements for which no effective method of deciding their truth-value exists, then, from a classical standpoint, the meanings of the constituent statements, and hence of the sentential connectives, is not to be given by reference to tests at all. Granted that there is a change of meaning, the question legitimately arises whether it is a mere change or a substantive one. It is a mere change provided that the old, classical meanings of the logical constants can continue to coexist alongside the new operational meanings (obviously with different symbols used for the two kinds of constant); that is, provided that the classical or realist interpretation of meaning in terms of truth-conditions may still be legitimately applied to quantum-mechanical statements. This will be the case provided that a realistic interpretation of the tests associated with the atomic statements is possible. Such an interpretation rests on two assumptions: (*a*) that each test, when applied, reveals the existence of a state of affairs obtaining independently of the test, i.e. one that would have obtained even if the test had not been carried out; and (*b*) that, for each test, even if it is not or even cannot be carried out, there exists an objective answer to the question what the result of the test would have been if the test had been carried out (an answer which may be unknown to us). If these two assumptions are made, then we can suppose each atomic statement to have an objective truth-value, independent of our knowledge; it is this truth-value which determines the result of any test, when it is applied, and, when the test is not or cannot be applied, the answer to the question what the result of the test would have been, if it had applied. The way is now clear for a definition of the sentential operators by means of truth-tables; for certain complex statements constructed by such truth-functional operators, there will be no corresponding test.

It is no part of our present purpose to argue whether quantum mechanics admits a realistic interpretation or not. If it does not, then the replacement of classical logic by quantum logic is a substantive change of meaning: no logical constants can, in this context, be used with the meanings that 'and' and 'or' were formerly taken as possessing. Putnam asserts strongly that a realistic interpretation is possible: but his remarks on the subject appear confused, and hard to reconcile with other things he says; for instance, with his claim that the adoption of quantum logic is not a mere change of meaning. In fact, he advances the absurd contention that it is only in virtue of our giving up the distributive law that we may maintain a realistic interpretation of quantum mechanics; whereas, of course, since truth, as realistically conceived, is distributive over disjunction, as classically interpreted, realism must legitimate a use of 'and' and 'or' for which the distributive law is valid, without thereby precluding an additional, non-truth-functional, use for which it fails.

The failure of Putnam's example demonstrates with great clarity that, while there may be no sentences which can be declared immune to revision, there are certain sentences whose rejection always requires explanation if it is to convey anything definite. Such sentences are ones whose truth is ordinarily taken as constitutive of the senses of the words occurring in them: dissent from them depends, therefore, upon rejection or modification of the sense of some constituent word, and accordingly demands amplification by giving the grounds of rejection of the sense or an elucidation of the modified sense. Quine's image of language as an articulated network is therefore acceptable only when interpreted, not holistically, by denying a sense to individual sentences, but in the natural way, recognizing the existence of definite inferential links between sentences, the sense of a non-peripheral sentence consisting precisely in its links with other sentences. If we regard rules of inference as establishing direct deductive connections between sentences, then further indirect connections will sometimes be induced by the conventional assignment of truth to certain controlling sentences; conversely, the effect of the network of direct connections will sometimes be to confer truth on certain embedded sentences independently of the truth-value assignments made in response to experience. The senses both of peripheral and non-peripheral sentences may undergo gradual unnoticed deformation. The existence of the links between sentences, and the force exerted by experience upon peripheral sentences, are both matters of shared linguistic habit; and the habits of a community may suffer slow modification without anyone's being aware of the process. But an alteration of sense may also occur by way of deliberate decision, and it is this which makes possible the repudiation of previously embedded sentences. An account of this process demands a recognition of the existence of elucidation, i.e. the enunciation of a proposed change of sense, as a linguistic activity different in kind from the ascription of truth-value to sentences taken as having a sense already understood.

Because there can be no room in a holistic account for any such activity as elucidation, Quine is unable to recognize the extent to which natural language incorporates its own semantics. No doubt there is an objection in principle to supposing that a single language could express the whole of its own semantics: but there is no reason why English, for instance, should not be taken to be a language in which the semantics of a very considerable fragment of it may be expressed. Not only a professional student of linguistics or philosophy, but, to a greater or lesser degree, every language-user, strives to attain an understanding of the workings of his own language. It is for this reason that expressions like 'true', 'false', 'mean', 'call', 'correct to say . . .', etc., are part of our language, and serve as instruments both for teaching it and for modifying its employment. When language is regarded not as a seamless garment, but as something decomposable into significant parts, it ceases to be unintelligible that there should be within it different levels, so that the senses of expressions at one level can be conveyed by sentences belonging to a deeper level.

Advocacy of a holistic conception of language has often been backed by an abuse of the word 'theory'. Duhem's model of a scientific theory is, of course, the prototype of Quine's model for language as a whole. The word 'theory' is often used, as in 'set theory', merely to signify a connected body of doctrine. Sometimes it connotes the result of creative thought, undertaken to explain known facts which, together, are too fragmentary to compel any conclusion by ordinary deductive and inductive processes, as, for instance, in historical speculation; an example from science is the Darwinian theory, as originally propounded. Either of these two notions of a 'theory' is much wider than that of a theory for which Duhem's model is apt, that is, one containing theoretical terms. A theoretical term may be taken as one which is deliberately introduced without the provision for it of a complete semantics. The theory in which it is embedded stands or falls as a whole, according as it agrees with observation or not, but no single constituent sentence of the theory can be established or refuted in isolation: the theory thus forms, as it were, a coagulated mass within the total linguistic structure, which behaves more or less as if it were a single sentence.

To say that the sense of a non-observational sentence requires it to be established or refuted via its inferential connections with other sentences is not at all the same as to say that it is a theoretical statement in a Duhemian sense; and advocates of a holistic view of language have been prone to blur this difference. What distinguishes a theoretical statement, in the strict sense, is that there exists no path to its establishment or refutation on its own; for an ordinary non-peripheral sentence, there will normally be such a path, even though it leads via the establishment of other intermediate sentences. In particular, Quine is repeatedly guilty of confusing abstract terms with theoretical ones: he refers, as a matter of course, to statements of logic or of arithmetic as 'highly theoretical'. But, whether we take the *FLPV* 44 applications of natural numbers, as finite cardinals or ordinals, to be intrinsic or extrinsic to the notion of 'natural number', this notion is an abstract but not a theoretical one. If, for example, I make a model of human behaviour which involves ascribing to each individual the assignment of a utility, represented by a real number in the interval $[-1,1]$, to every possible event, this notion of utility remains a theoretical one so long as I do not propose any conclusive means of establishing that a given person assigns a specific utility to some particular event. By contrast, an extra-arithmetical statement involving natural numbers has, on its own, determinate truth-conditions: we are not in the position of having to say that arithmetic, as a theory, must be judged according to whether statements derivable from it, but not involving reference to natural numbers, agree with observation. A sloppy use of the word 'theory' encourages the belief that there are grounds for extending Duhem's model to the whole of language, when such an extension is quite unwarranted.

In subsequent writings, for instance 'Carnap and Logical Truth', Quine has been prepared to concede the occurrence of stipulation—what he calls legislative postulation—as something distinct from the ascription of truth to a sentence the usage of whose constituents is already given: but he regards this as a trait of the linguistic act whereby truth is first assigned to the sentence, not as an enduring characteristic of the sentence. That there are sentences to which this trait seems nevertheless to adhere more than fleetingly—'January has thirty-one days' is one—we have already noted: but the more important fact is that Quine is unable to conceive of sentences as being constitutive of the meanings of the words occurring in them by any other way than that of direct stipulation. He is now prepared to grant that someone cannot reject a law of elementary classical logic, or disagree with another about a sentence of set theory, without thereby displaying a divergent usage of the logical constants or of '$\in$'—given, that is, that the disagreement is irresoluble by deductive argument; but for this very reason the linguistic doctrine of logical truth is empty of content, since there is no independent criterion for difference of usage other than divergence over the truth of sentences. Even if this were so, it would not prove the linguistic doctrine of logical truth vacuous, since, for most sentences, divergence over their truth-value would not be a sufficient condition for difference of usage; if a proof were given—Quine's remarks do not amount to a proof—that there could be no further requirement for recognizing a difference of usage in the case of sentences of logic or set theory, this would be no contentless observation. The fact is, however, that a serious divergence over logic or set theory does not take the form of a confrontation between rival stipulations of postulates or laws. In set theory, Quine says, 'we find ourselves making deliberate choices and setting them forth unaccompanied by any attempt at justification other than in terms of elegance and convenience'. This is, indeed, a fair description of Quine's introduction of his own axiomatic set theory in 'New Foundations': but, as a description of the usual attitude to the subject, it is quite wide of the mark. The standard systems of set theory, Zermelo-Fraenkel and Bernays-Gödel, rest upon a definite type of intuitive model of the kind of structure to be described, the cumulative hierarchy of sets; and further additions to the axioms are likely to be based on the idea that we want to maximize the model relative to its height (i.e., the transition from one rank to the next should be as inclusive as possible). An alternative set theory, like Quine's New Foundations, for which we have no such intuitive model, is simply not a competitor to standard set theory; nor is any additional axiom likely to be adopted unless it has an evidently maximizing character.

The same description, quoted above, of our procedure in set theory, is also applied by Quine to the proposals of 'dissident logicians . . . at the elementary level', and here it is even less apt. An intuitionist or other serious proponent of a non-classical logic is not just engaged in perverse counter-stipulation: he rejects the classical model for the meanings of the logical constants, and offers an alternative model based on a different theory of meaning. A mere announcement by someone that he proposes to disallow the Law of Excluded Middle, or the distributive law, is, so far, un-intelligible: he needs to tell us what model he is using for the meanings of the sentential operators, in place of the truth-table model which is not a mere computational device but regulates our understanding of classical logic and supplies a justification of its laws.*

The account of language given in *Word and Object* differs from that of 'Two Dogmas' in two ways. First, the account is no longer solipsistic, but has been socialized, language now being recognized as an instrument of social communication. In 'Two Dogmas' everything that a man holds to be true stands on the same level, and so all is to be indiscriminately lumped together as comprising the total theory to which he subscribes. In *Word and Object* a speaker's mastery of a language is viewed as consisting in a set of linguistic dispositions construed as dispositions to assent to and dissent from sentences: but not all bits of information or misinformation which he may have are any longer regarded as contributing in an indistinguishable manner to these dispositions; by observing the dispositions of other speakers, we can prise

---

* In *Philosophy of Logic* Quine says, of intuitionist logic, 'A kind of intuitive meaning is intended for its sentence connectives, and explained with help of words and phrases like "refute" and "follow from"; but these explanations go dim when one tries to respect the distinction between saying a sentence and talking about it. One does as well to bypass these explanations and go straight to Heyting's axiomatization of intuitionist logic.' Here Quine, while for once admitting the possibility of giving an explanation otherwise than by the stipulation of formal rules, shows clearly his low estimation of the procedure. Since it can only be on the basis of a rigorous formulation of such intuitive explanations that a sound-ness or completeness theorem can even be stated, Quine thus likewise shows the low value he puts on proofs of soundness or of completeness. In fact, confusion between use and mention is quite inessential to explanations of the intuitionist logical constants—one could as well say that the same confusion was involved when the classical constants are explained in terms of 'true' and 'false'; and it is dubious whether anyone could make a close guess at the intended meanings of the constants of intuitionist logic by studying only its formalization. Certainly he could never grasp the intuitionist objection to classical logic.

PL 87

off those bits of information peculiar to one speaker or to a small class of speakers.

Secondly, the two theses so heavily stressed in 'Two Dogmas' have virtually disappeared. Peripheral sentences appear as observation sentences, and their intuitive meaning is held to be closely approximated by their stimulus-meaning (i.e. our propensity to assent to and dissent from them under certain patterns of sensory stimulation). Analyticity is admitted in the form of stimulus-analyticity, and its function, in simple cases, is conceded to be just what the empiricists had contended that it was, to induce connections between sentences, to anchor one term to another. Thus Quine says that the expressions 'bachelor' and 'unmarried man' are stimulus-synonymous and the sentence 'All bachelors are unmarried men and vice versa' is stimulus-analytic, and explains the usefulness of having, among our linguistic dispositions, one which constitutes this sentence as stimulus-analytic by the fact that it effects a connection between the two expressions, what he calls an 'anchoring' of the one by the other: 'one looks to "unmarried man" as semantically anchoring "bachelor"; . . . sever its tie with "unmarried man" and you leave it no evident social determination, hence no utility in communication'. Further, he says, 'brother', in its synonymy with 'male sibling', is essentially like 'bachelor' in its synonymy with 'unmarried man'. 'We learn "brother" (in its accurate adult use) only by verbal connections with sentences about childbirth, and "sibling" by verbal connections with "brother" and "sister". The occasion sentences "Brother" and "Sibling" are non-observational: their stimulus meanings vary over society in as random a fashion as that of "Bachelor", and it is only the few verbal links that give the terms the fixity needed in communication'. New social determination is, of course, but old meaning writ large. The very example used in 'Two Dogmas' as a case in which empirical discoveries might induce us to revise our logical laws—the abandonment of the Law of Excluded Middle to accommodate quantum mechanics—is expressly repudiated in *PL 86* *Philosophy of Logic*, where Quine appeals to the maxim of minimum mutilation as a deterring consideration, *whatever* the technical merits of the case for revision.

In 'Two Dogmas', no distinction of kind was made between any two sentences which some one individual held to be true. In *Word and Object* two new dimensions are added—the temporal and the social. We can distinguish between those sentences to which an individual assents only under a suitable sensory stimulation, and those to which he assents independently of stimulation; and we can also distinguish between those assented to by one individual and those commanding the assent of all members of the linguistic community. But we can go no further: this is why the notion of being stimulus-analytic—assented to by all speakers under all stimulations—is the closest approach that can be made to that of analyticity. For

WO 38–9

> suppose it said that a particular class Σ comprises just those stimulations each of which suffices to prompt assent to a sentence S outright, without benefit of collateral information. Suppose it said that the stimulations comprised in a further class Σ′, likewise sufficient to prompt assent to S, owe their efficacy rather to certain widely disseminated collateral information, C. Now couldn't we just as well have said, instead, that on acquiring C, men have found it convenient implicitly to change the very 'meaning' of S, so that the members of Σ′ now suffice outright like members of Σ? I suggest we may say either ... The distinction is illusory ... in fact an unreal question. What we objectively have is just an evolving adjustment to nature, reflected in an evolving set of dispositions to be prompted by stimulations to assent to or dissent from sentences. These dispositions may be conceded to be impure in the sense of including worldly knowledge, but they contain it in a solution which there is no precipitating.

Each speaker has, at any time, a set of linguistic dispositions. Assent to or dissent from any one sentence modifies those dispositions by inducing indirect inferential connections between sentences. The best we can do towards approximating the intuitive notion of meaning is to isolate those dispositions which are permanent and shared by all speakers of the language. Hence there can be no principle whereby sentences permanently accepted as true by the whole society can be distinguished from one another in respect of their status: we cannot separate, from a chemically pure precipitate of meaning, the contributions made to determining their common linguistic dispositions to assent and dissent by beliefs, true or false, common to all speakers.

The thesis that it is impossible thus to disentangle the twin factors, experience and convention, which determine linguistic dispositions could be taken in either of two ways: as meaning that there is an impossibility in principle, for any conceivable language; or as meaning merely that, as human beings generally use language, the two factors become inextricably intertwined. Consider the situation schematically described in the above quotation. If we ask a speaker of the language for his grounds for asserting or assenting to S, under a stimulation in Σ′, he will surely cite the collateral information C. (If not, the suggested description of the situation can be dismissed out of hand.) This, of course, does not yet establish the status of C as merely collateral information: we cannot rule it out that C is taken as analytically true. We have, therefore, now to enquire after the justification for believing C. Just this was, indeed, the basis advanced by Frege for distinguishing analytic from synthetic statements: an analytic statement is one of which a certain kind of justification can be given, a synthetic statement one that needs a justification of another kind. If we pursue the matter far enough, we ought, then, to be able to determine whether C is treated by the speakers of this language as analytic or not, according to the kind of justification for it which they offer.

Gl 3

It is scarcely to be denied that it is an integral part of what we learn when we learn to use language that we should acquire the practices of giving reasons for our own assertions, asking after the grounds of another's assertion, and the like. Quine is attempting to characterize the working of language entirely in terms of speakers' dispositions to assent to and dissent from sentences under certain sensory stimulations: or, rather, he is trying to describe the work of a translator whose data are merely the manifestations of such dispositions. It may be that there really is an obstacle in principle to distinguishing, in respect of status, between different stimulus-analytic statements on the basis of evidence of this kind. But that hardly implies that such distinctions are spurious: for there is a great deal more to the use of language than merely the registering of assent and dissent in response to appropriate sensory stimuli; in particular, language is characteristically employed in discourse, much more than in isolated affirmations and denials. Granted, Frege's definition of analyticity is far from being the only candidate: but it is hardly reasonable to deny objective application to the notion when appeal is refused to the very feature which Frege maintained as the ground of distinction between analytic and synthetic. Such reasoning contains the fallacy stigmatized in the old text-books as ignoratio elenchi.

Part of the trouble arises from the restricted framework within which Quine conducts his enquiry, namely in terms of the task of someone who has to devise a scheme of translation for a foreign language among whose speakers he finds himself, without the aid either of an established tradition of translation between a chain of languages starting with his own and ending with the radically foreign language, or of a bilingual interpreter or chain of interpreters. The advantage of such a hypothetical situation is that it prevents appeal to any but observable facts about the linguistic behaviour of the speakers of the language. It is, however, unclear what justification Quine has for placing such severe restraints upon his translator. If we are interested in a theoretical account of what it is to have a mastery of a language, we are not concerned with such practical difficulties as might confront an anthropologist: it would be quite in order to allow him to assume a cloak of invisibility and observe situations which an actual anthropologist would never get to see. But in *Word and Object* the translator's experience of the use of the language appears as limited to observing people muttering things like 'Gavagai' to themselves, and their responses when he has uttered 'Gavagai' in what he hopes will be understood as a questioning tone of voice. In one passage, however, Quine refers to another possibility: *WO* 47

> Section 10 left the linguist unable to guess the trend of the stimulus meaning of a non-observational occasion sentence from sample cases. We now see a way, though costly, in which he can still accomplish radical translation of such sentences. He can settle down and learn the native language directly as an infant might. Having thus become bilingual, he can translate the non-observational occasion sentences by introspected stimulus synonymy.
>
> This step has the notable effect of initiating clear recognition of native falsehoods. As long as the linguist does no more than correlate the native's observation sentences with his own by stimulus meaning, he cannot discount any of the native's verdicts as false—unless ad hoc, most restrainedly, to simplify his correlations. But once he becomes bilingual and so transcends the observation sentences, he can bicker with the native as a brother.

The natural comment here is that, if such a possibility may be envisaged, a great many irrelevant difficulties might have been avoided if, instead of considering the situation of a man initially quite ignorant of the language to be translated, we had taken the case of someone who already knows two languages between which there is no accepted tradition of translation, and enquired what the criteria should be for a good translation or scheme of translation from one to the other. Of course, we should not here allow the criterion to be framed in terms of the notion of meaning, for instance by saying that a translation of a sentence is a good one if the two sentences appear to the bilingual translator to mean the same: but the bilingual individual would have a great deal of information about the linguistic dispositions of the speakers of the two languages, the difficulties in obtaining which are not truly germane to an enquiry into the theoretical character of translation. In particular, he would have at his disposal a much richer store of still purely behavioural data relating to the process whereby he was instructed in the language, if he kept a record of this: all that, in the process of instruction, he was taught to do and say, what was said to him, what he was corrected for. Quine does, briefly, glance at this alternative approach, and says, in effect, that it would be in practice difficult to keep the record of the foreigner's linguistic behaviour untainted by translator's interpretation: he seems to have forgotten for the moment that he is not producing a practical manual for anthropologists, but a theoretical analysis.

It may be replied that, ultimately, the criteria for a good translation would have to be framed in terms of stimulus-meaning. This is a quite unwarranted assumption, not to be confused with the harmless contention that the criteria must ultimately relate to what speakers actually say in particular situations, including ones involving previous utterances by other speakers. Utterances have many functions besides that of registering the speaker's assent to or dissent from a sentence. For instance, if we are enquiring into the kind of justification offered for an assertion, we need to be able to discriminate between what is said as adducing a reason, and what is said by way of changing the subject or the like. It is true, but unhelpful, to say that ultimately our data are of the form that such-and-such an utterance was made in such-and-such external circumstances: we need more elaborate distinctions between modes of utterance before we can get very far. The picking out of certain utterances as registering assent and dissent is itself already a step in this direction: there is no ground for supposing it to be the only such step that has to be taken. Of course, when we are faced with a language of which we are initially quite ignorant, it will take us some time before we can identify the various modes of utterance (the various kinds of force attached to utterances). They will be identified by their 'role in the language-game'; but it is tendentious to maintain that this role can always be characterized in terms of stimulus-meaning, in the particular technical sense Quine gives to that expression. A request for justification, for instance, is to be identified by the kind of response it calls for; a bet by its consequences in terms of payment of money, goods or services: it would be absurd to suppose that one could make any progress towards identifying either mode of utterance by the pattern of sensory stimulation which prompted it.

To this Quine has an answer. He will readily agree that his translator can make only a very little headway on the basis of stimulus-meaning alone. (It can indeed be argued that, by the deployment of more elaborate criteria relating to stimulus-meaning, he can make rather more headway than Quine allows: but we shall pass over this point here.) Once the translator has exhausted the direct resources of stimulus-meaning, he must resort to what Quine calls 'analytical hypotheses', assigning expressions of the language to syntactic categories and extending the as yet very fragmentary scheme of translation. These analytical hypotheses must satisfy certain conditions framed in terms of stimulus-meaning, which are, however, far from determining them: many different choices of analytical hypotheses would do equally well; and from this follows Quine's thesis of the indeterminacy of radical translation.

This is not the place to conduct an examination of this celebrated thesis, which is only obliquely relevant to our present topic. In *Word and Object* the sole argument given for the indeterminacy of radical translation is that relating to the various choices said to be possible in translating 'gavagai' as a term ('rabbit', 'rabbit-stage', etc.). In a much-needed clarification of the thesis, however, 'On the Reasons for Indeterminacy of Translation', Quine refines his terminology, drawing a sharp distinction between the 'gavagai' phenomenon, which he calls the inscrutability of terms, and indeterminacy of translation proper: for there might be irresoluble uncertainty how to translate a term, and yet it be determinate, at least to within obvious equivalence, how to translate sentences containing that term. In asserting indeterminacy of translation, however, Quine is concerned to assert it of whole sentences, not just of constituent terms. Even if the indeterminacy thesis holds in this stronger sense, it is not very plausible that there will be indeterminacy over what is to be identified as the provision of grounds for an assertion: so the thesis of indeterminacy does nothing to discredit the idea that we may distinguish, among stimulus-analytic sentences, different types according to the kind of justification considered appropriate to them. If, on the other hand, translation is determinate with respect to sentences, then, if such distinctions can be drawn for English, they can also be drawn for the foreign language, and will be invariant under change of analytical hypotheses.*

Word and Object retains a great deal of the 'Two Dogmas' picture of language as an articulated network: great stress is laid on the interconnections between sentences both of English and of the radically foreign language. It is precisely because of these interconnections that stimulus-meaning is, in general, a poor surrogate for intuitive meaning; stimulus-meaning is, after all, simply meaning as the positivists construed it. The indeterminacy

WO 51-7, 71-2

---

* Quine's argument for indeterminacy in the stronger sense is based on the claim, over which, he says, he expects wide agreement, that there can be empirically equivalent but logically incompatible physical theories. Even if this claim is granted, the argument is not compelling, since the theories might diverge irreconcilably in internal structure: but the claim is absurd, because there could be nothing to prevent our attributing the apparent incompatibility to equivocation. Indeed, if we can establish the empirical equivalence of the two theories, we must be able to find translations from each to the other.

thesis, however, amounts to the contention that there is no unique way to unravel the network. Stimulus-meaning, inadequate as it is, is the only tool which the poor translator has to work with. There is therefore no way to come close to an adequate account of meaning for non-observational sentences, that is, of their connections with other sentences, except by invoking a general scheme of translation; such a scheme cannot be justified point by point, but must be judged as a whole, in the knowledge that variant schemes might serve equally well.

What makes Quine's mature philosophy of language so peculiarly difficult to grapple with is the continual oscillation between the insistence on the interconnectedness of language and the claim that stimulus-meaning exhausts the behavioural data, at least the data describable without resort to theory-laden terms. One would like to ask: Are there really inter-connections between sentences or not? If there are, must these not be manifested in actual linguistic behaviour? And, if they are so manifested, are they not in principle discoverable, however complex the necessary investigation? The reply seems to be that, while there are such interconnec-tions, they are continually being modified: as soon as some sentence comes to command general assent, it establishes indirect inferential links between sentences, which cannot be distinguished from any others. But now we may ask whether there are not any general principles which underlie this process, that is, which determine what links will be recognized as holding when a sentence is admitted as expressing a shared belief of the community. The natural picture is that indirect links are established as the result of generally admitted rules of inference: a sentence generally accepted as true effects connections by being always available as premiss in an argument. Now, if, for a given language, that is really all that can be said, why, then, that is how that language is. Such a language would have the characteristic that there would be, at any time, a stock of sentences representing shared beliefs of the community, sentences which could figure in the justification by any individual speaker of some assertion of his, but beyond which there was no appeal: once the sentence had attained this privileged status, it would need no justification and would not be open to question. The linguistic dispositions of the speakers of this language would evolve by addition to this stock of sentences 'in the archives'.* If this is an accurate report of how a certain language is used, then a complete account can be given of the language

LFM 104–7

---

* It is worth noting the similarity between Quine's account of language in general and Wittgenstein's account of mathematics. For Wittgenstein, the acceptance of a proof changes our criteria for certain expressions, and hence their meanings; theorems have, in this regard, no different status from axioms.

by describing four things: the stimulus-meanings of the observation sentences; the direct inferential links that are recognized; the existing stock of generally accepted sentences; and the process whereby a new sentence acquires the status of general acceptance.

It should be noted that indeterminacy of *translation* plays no role here. We are concerned with a direct description of the way a language is used, a description which may be framed in English but does not take the form of a translation into English. Quine's example of the Chinese and Japanese 'classifiers' is an excellent one for his thesis of the inscrutability of terms: but, OR 35-8 while a translation-scheme has to opt between equally workable alternatives, this imports no indeterminacy into the description of how the expressions to be translated are in fact used.

How can we determine what direct inferential links are recognized? We are concerned, if one likes to put it so, with intersubjective conditional dispositions to assent to sentences of certain forms given assent to sentences of related forms, and particularly following immediately upon the enunciation of those latter sentences. Such dispositions, however, will tend to reveal also indirect links, corresponding to enthymematic inferences. So we have to look to what is said when a justification is called for or an attempt is made to persuade another, that is, when one speaker attempts to exploit the conditional dispositions of his hearer in order to secure his assent to some assertion. It could happen, imaginably, that the adoption of a new shared belief invariably led to the establishment of a new, direct, link, in the sense that the sentence expressing that belief was never overtly cited in justification or argument. This is a situation which can also be discovered by observation, and described clearly enough so long as we can determine the direct links presently recognized.

But, now, such a picture of language is pretty remote from language as we use it. We are prepared to cite unstated premises for a conclusion, and are ready, in general, to give the grounds for those premises in turn, even when they represent generally acknowledged truths. Of course, any one individual may have to fall back on appeal to expert opinion; but at least he does so in the presumption that the experts can produce justification of an appropriate kind. It is a basic feature of the sense we attach to a sentence, of the use we learn for it, that, as the case may be, we do or do not treat it as a stopping point in the search for justification: reports of observation, or of memory on the part of a witness, are one kind of stopping point; another are sentences which we take as constitutive of meaning.

The notion of a statement's being constitutive of meaning is not intended as a sharp one. To some statements, like 'January has 31 days', it has a sharp and evident application, which we should have no difficulty in conveying to anyone who questioned them: the suggestion that we might all be mistaken in thinking that January always had 31 days embodies an error comparable to that of Littlewood's schoolboy ('Suppose *x* is the number of cows in the field'—'But, sir, suppose *x* is *not* the number of cows in the field'). Other cases lack this transparency. We are here concerned with statements having the following characteristics: (1) we should not normally expect them to be challenged, and most people would be at a loss to provide a justification if asked to do so; (2) we should not take them to be accepted by common consent as true and as requiring no justification, in order to fix meanings, in the straightforward way that 'January has 31 days' is; (3) we nevertheless cannot attach a clear content to their denial, having no grasp of what the consequences of such a denial are supposed to be. For most people, basic logical laws would be in this category, as well as many problematic propositions of the kind discussed by philosophers.

MM 41

For Quine and his sympathizers the obscurity of these cases is evidence that analyticity is an irremediably vague concept; and for Quine himself, at least, that it can be replaced by nothing closer than 'generally accepted as true'. The essential feature of such statements is (3): it is this which distinguishes them from statements which a person might always have unreflectively assumed to be true, but, when challenged, will perhaps admit he could be wrong about and will at least acknowledge the necessity for justifying. The case we are concerned with is that in which a rejection of the statement is not understood as a possible move in the language-game: not merely that we cannot conceive of possible reasons for rejecting it, but that we do not know what would be involved in rejecting it; we do not know what would be supposed to follow from such a rejection, and, further, we feel that, if such a rejection is possible, then we are no longer sure that we understand the grounds or consequences of other sentences containing the crucial words which figure in the rejected statement. The two things hang together: if a denial of a statement has a clear content, then it is in order to ask for a justification of the statement, and conversely.

In the Quinean language, described above, the feature which distinguished the stimulus-analytic sentences from others was that no request for a justification of such a statement, once granted the status of a generally accepted truth, was entertained. (This is not, of course, Quine's definition of 'stimulus-analytic': it is the feature such sentences must have in a language of which it is really true that no finer distinction is possible.) The problematic sentences of our language with which we are now concerned are ones which we do not recognize as needing justification. What makes them problematic is that we do not have sufficient insight into the connections between our sentences to regard them in the same light as ones like 'January has 31 days' which we can immediately classify as conventional in character. But this fact is not an argument for a Quinean dismissal of our reluctance to permit denial of such statements as indicating only a difference in the degree of their distance from the periphery, rather than a difference of kind. It is, on the contrary, an argument for the application of a Fregean model of language; or, rather, for saying that we strive to approximate our language to such a model.

In the Quinean language, a stimulus-analytic sentence was simply treated as not requiring justification. By being so treated, it had the effect which any conventionally accepted sentence does, of inducing various links between other sentences. The difference between the speakers of such a language and ourselves is that the former simply do not care if they cannot command a clear view of the connections between their sentences; and we struggle always to attain such a view. Anyone can see how the conventional acceptance of 'January has 31 days' induces links between various sentences about dates. Replace 'January has 31 days and April 30' by 'January has 30 days and April 31', and the 31st to 120th days of a year (121st of a leap year) get re-labelled. But it is not so clear with, say, 'No effect precedes its cause'. If you drop this, do events become describable as causes of other events which were formerly not so describable? Are there events A and B related exactly as cause to effect save that B precedes A? What exactly are the connections between sentences containing 'cause' and those containing 'bring it about that . . .' or 'in order that . . .', and how would these connections be affected by abandoning 'No effect precedes its cause'?

A sentence like 'No effect precedes its cause' has a problematic status just because we are not content to treat it as the object of a conventional stipulation until we can command a clear view of the interconnections between various related sentences. We are constantly engaged in the endeavour to attain such a view: and this means pursuing questions of justification until they terminate in something which can be regarded as straightforward stipulation. This is often a matter of technical investigation. For most people, as remarked, basic logical laws would be problematic in the way we have been considering; but logicians have attempted, with great success, to lay bare the interrelation of logical laws and provide a semantic analysis of logical validity. Scientists, mathematicians and philosophers all strive, in different areas, to uncover structure at fundamental levels where we are not fully aware of it; and, of course, in doing so, they often make structure definite where before it was vague. Only prejudice can lead one to commend some of these activities as contributing to the advancement of science, and deride others as the pursuit of a will o' the wisp of meaning.

One task of systematization, in philosophy, logic, mathematics or science, is the pursuit of questions of justification beyond the point where most people would be able to go. But to do this is merely to extend a procedure which is integral to our use of language. Learning language involves learning what justifications are required for sentences of different kinds. In its initial stages, it requires the child to respond to the assertions of others; but, later, also to question what may be asserted, even as a matter of common agreement. Language-learning, on Quine's model, could only be indoctrination, the mere instilling of a propensity to recognize certain sentences as true. If a child, who is still learning his language simultaneously with learning what the world is like, were not to be given an indication of the separate roles of convention and of empirical fact in determining what we say, then he would have to learn all commonly accepted truths involving any given word as part of an extended explanation of the meaning of the word, and could not take any part of this teaching as the communication of information. He could then never be started on the process of learning to question and criticize the things presented to him for acceptance, for he would have no way of knowing what revisions would be possible, or what significance any revision would have. In this process, some areas are left obscure; conceptual problems would never arise if this were not so. In particular, there are sentences which we are taught to accept without its being made clear what justification, if any, could be provided for them. It remains an integral part of our practice in the use of language that we enquire after justification, assess arguments for their validity, accept certain sentences as determinative of meaning and require backing for those which play any other role.

Earlier, we raised the question whether Quine's claim that no finer distinction is possible than that between stimulus-analytic and stimulus-synthetic sentences was intended as holding in principle for any possible language, or merely in practice for the language we in fact speak. It may certainly be allowed as correct in principle if the condition is imposed that any distinction must be definable in terms of stimulus-meaning: but to submit to this condition is to let Quine set the rules of the game as well as playing in it; and there is no particular interest in those rules. If we take into account the established practice governing the justification of statements of some given language, there is then no obstacle in principle to distinguishing, among generally accepted statements, between those which are treated as requiring no further justification and those a request for the justification of which is acknowledged as legitimate. The inextricability of fact and convention as determinants of linguistic dispositions thus cannot be a theoretical impossibility, but at most a practical one.

The distinction becomes impossible to apply to a language whose speakers treat all generally accepted statements alike as needing no justification. It becomes uncertain of application in proportion as the practice varies from speaker to speaker and in proportion to the number of problematic cases. The question now comes down to this: do we do better, in application to the kind of language which we in fact speak, with a model of the type Quine advocates, or with one of the type proposed by Frege? Quine's model ascribes to a language the following features: intersubjective stimulus-meaning for observation sentences; and intersubjective connections between sentences, determined in part by direct inferential links and in part by the common acceptance of a stock of stimulus-analytic sentences. The network of interconnections is an evolving one, owing to additions to the stock of stimulus-analytic sentences, which may take place by legislative postulation or by the ordinary mechanism determining assent: but once a sentence has achieved that status, it is treated like any other such sentence; accepting it as true becomes part of learning the language.

The model I have here described appears to be the model Quine is offering, difficult as it is to discern through all the discussion of translation, with which we are not here concerned. It might be thought to be a caricature: I am making Quine treat every stimulus-analytic sentence as determinative of meaning, whereas what he says is that it is all one whether you take it so or as a statement of fact. But I am not concerned with the application of the label 'statement of fact'. What is important is whether, in our model of language, there is for a given sentence any mechanism which determines the conditions of assent to and dissent from that sentence. If stimulus-analytic sentences are indistinguishable from one another, there is no such mechanism. Before the sentence became stimulus-analytic, if it did not do so by stipulation, then assent to it or dissent from it was determined by its connections with other sentences, and, ultimately, with observation sentences: but Quine is explicit that, once it has achieved that status, the ground of its original acceptance becomes of historical interest only. It is true that Quine has sometimes subsequently reverted to speaking of 'revisions' which involve once more discarding such sentences: but we have no model whereby to understand this, save the old unworkable holistic one.

Frege's model is similar in general structure, if we allow for the difference between a verificationist and a realist theory. The difference with which we are presently concerned is that the central core of controlling sentences is much smaller, being occupied only (not indeed by all analytic or a priori statements, but) by those fundamental laws which, Frege says, neither need nor admit of proof. There is no provision in this model for addition to or subtraction from this central core: any alteration in it would be a modification of the language. (It is no objection that a language, in the sociological sense, does undergo such modification.) The reason for the difference is, of course, that the criterion, for Quine, for belonging to the central core is simply commanding general assent under all stimulations, while, for Frege, it is being accepted not only as true but as requiring no justification.

A language to which Frege's model was completely apt would be a rigid and fully regimented language; and natural language is neither rigid nor fully regimented, as Frege constantly complained. If, for example, the truth of an identity-statement, the terms in which originally had distinct senses, becomes common knowledge, then, when one or both of the terms are proper names (in the ordinary sense), the distinction of sense tends to disappear. Proper names of objects which we encounter in different ways are introduced to us in no standard manner, but on first encounter; we cease to recall the circumstances in which we first acquired the use of the name, and, as we become more familiar with the object, or learn more about it, this knowledge goes to influence our malleable propensity to recognize an object as the bearer of the name: nor, in such cases, do we suppose that our propensity for such recognition is exactly the same as anyone else's, or care that it is not. What goes for proper names of objects also goes for words for natural kinds—animal species and chemical substances—and, at least inasmuch as we cease to be disposed to appeal to any one standard sample, for words for sensory qualities identifiable originally only by ostension, e.g. for colour-words. Our linguistic dispositions change not only as a conscious response to a deliberate change of meaning, involving the dislodgement or replacement of a core sentence, but often as a largely unconscious effect of the continued maintenance of a well-established sentence: in the process, statements originally straightforwardly empirical sometimes sink down and become to greater or lesser degree embedded in the central core. There are alternative, equally legitimate, routes to the explanation of a given word, and some of us will have learned it in one way, some in another. The senses of most words are both over-determined and under-determined: over-determined in that different criteria are used, which may later fall apart; under-determined in that there are situations, which we do not expect or have not even envisaged, in which the application of the word has simply not been provided for.

Observations of this kind were commonplace long before Quine developed his philosophy of language: they are the data from which we set out in this chapter, and those which prompted Quine to develop an alternative model of language. Such data force us to concede that natural language only approximates to Frege's model. Nevertheless, Frege's model does justice to important features of our use of language of which no account can be given on Quine's model. Not every commonly known fact about the bearer of a proper name is related in the same way to the identification of an object as the bearer: for instance, most people who know the name 'Alpha Centauri' also know that Alpha Centauri is the nearest visible star to us; yet no one supposes that, if the parallax measurements were found to be in error, and another star turned out to be closer, the name would be transferred to that star (nor would this be so if the nearest star had a genuine proper name like 'Aldebaran'). The fact that we cannot now say what we should do with the name 'Homer' if it were established that the *Iliad* and the *Odyssey* had different authors shows that proper names, like other words, often lack a precise sense, that Frege's model is a sharpened version of what happens in practice; but the fact that we can and do sometimes distinguish criteria of application from well-known properties of the object shows that Quine's model is inadequate, for in it there is no room for any such distinction.

That the Fregean notion of sense really is an ideal—a goal we strive towards—is shown by the fact that, while we often leave sense blurred when it does not matter, we also strive to sharpen it whenever it does matter, for example, as Frege never tired of pointing out, in the case of proper names when questions either of identity or of existence become serious. Such a need to sharpen and make explicit the senses of our words is particularly acute whenever questions of justification arise. Quine's account of postulation in 'Carnap and Logical Truth' makes a valid distinction between legislative and discursive postulation, the former instituting truth by convention, the latter merely selecting axioms as a basis for a deductive development of a theory: but the distinction is too coarse. One out of several motives for axiomatization is to investigate the ultimate justification of a body of truths. (Quine says vaguely that the purpose of discursive postulation is enquiry into logical relationships.) It often happens indeed that we are aware of and indifferent between alternative axiomatic bases for a theory; but, while Quine is right that postulation does not in itself carry any claim that the postulates are true by convention, we are often concerned to discern, among a set of postulates, those which carry substantial assumptions requiring justification, and those able to be construed as conventionally stipulated. In number theory, for example, the recursion equations for

Gg II 56

additional and multiplication may be regarded as stipulating the meanings of these function-symbols; but the third and fourth Peano axioms cannot be viewed as merely part of a stipulation of the meaning of 'natural number', since they require the prior assumption of the existence of an infinite totality. Likewise, in sentential logic, given the rule of modus ponens, the axiom schemas '(A & B)$\rightarrow$A', '(A & B)$\rightarrow$B' and 'A$\rightarrow$(B$\rightarrow$(A & B))' may count as together stipulating the meaning of '&', since they determine the inferential connections of any conjunctive sentence; but Peirce's law, '((A$\rightarrow$B)$\rightarrow$A)$\rightarrow$A' could hardly rank as a partial stipulation of the meaning of '$\rightarrow$'. What Quine calls discursive postulation is often an essential part of the process of regimenting sense.

Systematization or regimentation is not a process apart from our ordinary use of language, but wholly in line with it, differing only in thoroughness or in the technicality of the subject-matter from what happens constantly in ordinary discourse. The procedure of assigning a conventional status to connections between expressions is not only an indispensable part of the process of teaching and learning language, but remains with us as a feature of our regular use of language. Quine is right that we do not acknowledge any great responsibility to the historical circumstances under which a term was first introduced or a sentence first gained acceptance: in natural language, the original *Sinn* conferred on a term has no enduring rights; we are not, as in an axiomatized theory, able to refer back to the original definitions as fixing sense once for all. Linguistic habits alter, and our responsibility is to present habits rather than to ancient custom. But, in our constant endeavour to make explicit to ourselves the workings of our language, we seek also to sharpen meaning, to propose firmer connections or even new ones. We know that, with the passage of time, some of these connections will loosen, and new ones will begin to form: we do not seek to legislate for all future time, only to introduce enough rigidity at critical points to serve our present purposes in evaluating, revising, or simply conferring clarity on what we say.

Frege's model of language is both rigid and static, and therefore fails to be a naturalistic portrait of ordinary language. It represents an ideal, however, just because its interconnections are minimal: there are just as many as are needed to confer on our sentences the use to which we want to put them—what Quine calls utility in social communication—and no more. In consequence, the more nearly a language approximates to this model, the clearer a view we can command of its interconnections and therefore of the content of its sentences. Quine's model, on the other hand, welcomes overdetermination as a virtue: it allows for a change only at the cost of making the principles which govern change undecipherable. At the worst, it is irremediably conservative, because there can be no base from which to criticize whatever is generally accepted: we do not really know any of the language until we know all of the language; and we do not know the language until we accept as true everything that is so accepted by its speakers, since, until we do, we cannot have the same linguistic dispositions as they. At the best, it is simply defeatist: it renders in principle inscrutable the laws which govern the common acceptance of a statement as true or its later demotion. In either case it is, in effect though not in intention, anti-intellectual; for it stigmatizes as misguided any attempt either to discover or to impose such laws.

CHAPTER 18

The Evolution of Frege's Thought

The man who never alters his opinion is like standing water, & breeds reptiles of the mind—William Blake.

MORE THAN THAT of most philosophical writers, Frege's work can be treated as a unity. It would be impossible, for instance, to write about Russell's philosophy as if it formed a single block of doctrine: Russell changed his views too often, and on so many fundamental matters, in the course of his career. With Frege, however, it is possible. There is development in Frege's thought, but seldom retractation, and, when that does occur, it is usually in the nature of an emendation requiring little adjustment in the remainder of the system.

This almost linear character of the development of Frege's philosophy justifies the method that has been adopted in this book, of considering Frege's philosophy as a whole, rather than as it existed at any particular stage. Nevertheless, there were some changes in his views, or at least in his approach, neglect of which can lead to misunderstanding. It is easy, for example, to read back into *Grundlagen* some of the doctrines that were developed later. As far as the distinction between sense and reference is concerned, this has only an elucidatory effect: although Frege had not made this BW 96 (63) distinction explicit when he wrote *Grundlagen*, it is needed for the proper explanation of the notions of object, concept and relation which are there used. If, on the other hand, we read back into *Grundlagen* the general objection to contextual definitions which is so prominent in his later writings, we shall be bound to misunderstand the crucial passage (paragraphs 62–8) in which Frege discusses the definition of the numerical operator 'the number of Φ's', and ends by taking the fatal step of introducing the notion of class into his system. Conversely, the plausibility of Frege's theory of meaning, as expounded in his later writings, is enhanced because we tend to read

628

into it what is not actually there, what is in fact expressly denied—the acknowledgement so strongly emphasized in *Grundlagen* of the quite special role that sentences play within a language. It is a correct instinct which leads us to do this, because the apprehension of the central role of sentences for the theory of meaning was one of Frege's deepest and most fruitful insights, one of those insights, indeed, which seem, once they have become a familiar part of our vision, to be so obvious that we can scarcely grasp how things looked before. Nevertheless, it was an insight which Frege let slip, one which cannot consistently be reconciled with the views which he later held; if we do not hold this fact in mind in reading the post-*Grundlagen* writings, we shall ascribe to the system a tension to which it is not really subject.

In this chapter, I shall attempt to sketch the principal characteristics of the different phases of Frege's development. In doing so, I will single out a few points for discussion which have not been systematically treated elsewhere in the book.

We may divide Frege's career into six periods. The first is that which gave birth to *Begriffsschrift* in 1879, and lasted until 1883: Frege's writings, during the part of this period which followed the publication of *Begriffsschrift*, are principally concerned with explaining the logical system expounded in *Begriffsschrift* and demonstrating its superiority to the work of his predecessors. *Begriffsschrift*, of course, communicates that discovery of Frege's which was the foundation of all his subsequent work and for which alone he would be celebrated, the invention of the notation of quantifiers and variables which marks the beginning of modern mathematical logic and liberated logic from the sterility from which it had suffered for so long. It contains his axiomatization of sentential and predicate logic, the system being a higher-order predicate logic without classes, of which the first-order fragment is complete. It also contains Frege's famous device for converting, by means of higher-level quantification, an inductive definition [Bs 26] into an explicit one. The informal commentary contains the germ of Frege's later doctrine of assertion, here spoken of in terms of the interior act of judging rather than the exterior one of making an assertion. Frege distinguishes between meaningful expressions according as they do or do not present a 'judgeable' content, that is. one which could be the content of a [Bs 2] judgment, and further distinguishes (as earlier writers, such as Kant, had not) between the judgeable content and the act of judgment itself: along with quantifiers, the assertion sign makes its first appearence. There is not yet, of course, the distinction between sense and reference, and, notoriously, the account of identity given in *Begriffsschrift* is not in accord with Frege's

x

mature views, identity being said to be a relation between expressions: but at least the problem which Frege later took as the starting-point for the sense/reference distinction, how true identity-statements can be informative, had been posed.

In the articles expounding the logical system of *Begriffsschrift* Frege stressed not only the greater range of inferences that could be handled in his system than in one like Boole's, but also the fact that his could be used as a language in which actual theories, e.g. mathematical ones, could be expressed. The use of Boole's logical calculus in order to render any proof or argument which it was capable of analysing depended upon a preliminary coding of the relevant predicates or sentences by letters. By contrast, Frege's symbolism depended on no such convention: the notation of quantifiers and variables could be applied directly to any selection of primitive predicates, relational expressions, names and function-symbols.

The next period we may take as extending from the publication of *Grundlagen der Arithmetik* in 1884 to the year 1890. Frege had been bitterly disappointed with the failure of mathematicians and philosophers to appreciate the merits of the system presented in *Begriffsschrift*, and hoped that the publication of a book eschewing symbolism altogether would secure for him that attention from the learned world which he was fully conscious that the originality and fruitfulness of his ideas warranted. In this, he was once more grievously disappointed. Almost the only attention that the book evoked was from the mathematician whose pioneering work was closest to that of Frege, Georg Cantor, a man who had himself been subjected to merciless critical attack by fellow-mathematicians, and one whose work Frege greatly respected: and Cantor's response to *Grundlagen* was to publish a scathing review of it (one of only three the book received), a review which revealed that Cantor had not taken the trouble to read Frege's book with sufficient care to understand it.

The second period of Frege's career was that during which he was at the height of his powers: none of his writing ever again quite equalled the brilliance of *Grundlagen*. In *Grundlagen* he introduced most of his major themes: the irrelevance of mental images to sense; more generally, the objective character of sense and of logic as against the subjective character of psychological processes, and the necessity of preventing reference to the latter from intruding into accounts of the former; and the sharp distinction between objects on the one hand and concepts, relations and functions on the other. Moreover, the emphasis on the central role of sentences in language is very much to the fore in *Grundlagen*, being enshrined in the dictum, four times repeated, that it is only in the context of a sentence that a word

CN 88, 93-7, 204-8; NS 13-14 (12-13)

Gl x, 60, 62, 106

has meaning. Frege was very well aware of the fundamental methodological role played by these principles: indeed, in the Preface to the book he lists as the three basic principles that he has followed: Gl x

always to separate sharply the psychological from the logical, the subjective from the objective;

to ask after the meaning of words only in the context of sentences, not in isolation; and

to keep in view the distinction between concept and object.

These principles belong to the theory of meaning, and, if accepted, must determine a pattern of enquiry in all areas of philosophy: that is why this essay in the philosophy of mathematics has been of such fundamental importance in philosophy generally. Further basic contributions to general philosophy made in *Grundlagen* are the defence of abstract objects and   Gl 58–68
the new explanations of the notions of the analytic and the a priori. In   Gl 3
the philosophy of mathematics, we have Frege's statement and detailed exposition of the logicist thesis that arithmetical statements are analytic and can be explained in purely logical terms and derived from purely logical principles; we also have the first clear formulation of the doctrine of platonism,   Gl 96
set in the context of the attack on formalism. There also occurs the first introduction into Frege's logical theory of the notion of classes, which was   Gl 68–9
to have such disastrous results for the execution of his logicist programme. The one major ingredient of Frege's philosophy that does not yet make its appearance in *Grundlagen* is the distinction between sense and reference.

Analyticity has been a prime preoccupation of twentieth-century analytical philosophy, until the attack launched upon the notion by Quine and his school. Kant had made a priori truth a major philosophical question, but for him the problematic notion was that of the synthetic a priori; on his account analytic truths are themselves trivial, and their existence trivially accounted for. Frege retained Kant's threefold categorization of true statements as analytic, synthetic a priori and a posteriori, but, by redefining 'analytic' so that analytic truths were not, in general, trivial, and by claiming to elucidate the character of a great deal of mathematical truth by demonstrating it to be analytic, he focused attention on the analytic as the important category. Subsequent philosophers repudiated the synthetic a priori altogether, but made the analytic/synthetic distinction a primary tool of their philosophical method.

Because the notion of analyticity figures in Frege's philosophy chiefly in application to mathematics, and plays little role in his general theory of meaning, an examination of his treatment of it will be reserved for the

volume on Frege's philosophy of mathematics: but this very fact—that
for Frege the notion is not central to the theory of meaning—reveals a
respect in which Frege's approach was superior to those of subsequent
philosophers. We have stressed that, for Frege, sense is a cognitive notion:
the distinction between sense and reference is introduced precisely in
order to explain how certain sentences can have a cognitive value (can be
informative), and we can find no place for the notion of sense, as distinct
from that of reference, save as embodying the manner common to speakers
of a language in which they apprehend the semantic roles of the expressions
of the language. Analyticity and apriority are, for Frege, cognitive notions
also: the status of a sentence, as analytic, synthetic a priori or a posteriori,
relates to the means that exist whereby the sentence may be known to be
true (though not to the means whereby we happen, in practice, to know
that it is true, if we know this at all). To this extent, the sense of a sentence
determines its status, independently of the way the world is: a sentence,
if analytically true, or true a priori, is so of necessity, in virtue of its sense
alone. Nevertheless, the connection between the sense of a sentence and its
status is not made by Frege to be anything like as close as was made out by
later analytic philosophers. Sense is so conceived by Frege that synonymy
must be an effectively decidable relation: if the senses of two expressions
are the same, and someone knows the sense of each expression, then he
must know that they have the same sense. An identity-statement is true if and
only if the references of the two names are the same, and informative just in
case their senses are different. Hence, an identity-statement in which the
sign of identity connects two names with the same sense will be true but
trivially true, i.e. uninformative: anyone who understands the sentence,
i.e. knows the senses of its constituents, will be able to recognize it as true
immediately; a failure to acknowledge it as true will be a criterion for
failure to understand it. This condition of triviality emphatically does not
apply, however, to all analytically true identity-statements, on Frege's
view of the matter: if it did, it would be impossible to hold, as Frege does,
that all true arithmetical equations are analytic (where under 'arithmetic'
Frege includes the theory of real and complex numbers, and, in number
theory, 'equations' include ones with symbols for non-computable functions).
An analytically true statement is not necessarily one which is trivial in the
above sense, one which can be recognized as true by anyone who understands
it: it is one for which a certain kind of proof is possible, but such a proof
may be hard to find or may never be found at all. Thus the condition that a
statement of identity connecting two proper names be analytic is much
weaker than the condition that those names have the same sense.

Subsequent philosophers, particularly the Wittgenstein of the *Tractatus* and the logical positivists, almost unanimously identified synonymy (sameness of sense) with analytic equivalence. This represented a divergence, not from Frege's notion of analyticity, but from his notion of sense: while 'analytic' often came to be explained differently from the way Frege had adopted, and, in particular, in a manner which related, not to the means whereby an analytic statement could be known to be true, but to the kind of truth it had, i.e. to the sort of thing that made it true, it was still supposed to have as wide an extension as Frege gave to it, or even wider, for instance to apply to all truths of mathematics. If the identification had been faithful to Frege's conception of sense, it would have narrowed the extension of 'analytic'; analyticity would have shrunk to coincide with triviality, in the sense explained. Rather, sense had now to be taken to be something not effectively recognizable: that is, someone could grasp the senses of two expressions without perceiving that those senses were the same. Or, if this consequence was to be denied, then the ordinary notion of understanding, as exemplified by an ability to employ the expression in everyday discourse, had to be divorced from that of grasping the sense of the expression: the sense would then become something hidden, uncoverable only by analysis. Not, indeed, that these consequences were ever very explicitly drawn: but one or other is inescapable.

All this arose from too tight a connection between the notions of sense and of logical consequence: the sense of a sentence was identified with the set of sentences entailed by it, or, expressed in semantic terms, by the set of models in which it is true. 'Model' is here not quite the right term, because, as ordinarily understood, it allows for varying interpretations of the non-logical constants (predicates, individual constants, etc.); it is more in accordance with the conceptions of these philosophers (for instance, the author of the *Tractatus*) to say: the set of possible worlds in which the sentence is true. Here, as between one possible world and another, the meaning of the non-logical constants is assumed to be in some way kept fixed. An analytic sentence is, then, one which is true in every model, or, more properly, every possible world, and thus its sense in effect vanishes.

The notion of sense, as thus understood, comes to occupy a curious no man's land between the cognitive and the purely extensional: between what we actually apprehend, in grasping the uses of the expressions of our language, and their reference. We can recognize immediately certain entailments, but by no means all entailments; we are far from being able always to recognize that two sentences are analytically equivalent, i.e. true in just the same possible worlds, or that two predicates are analytically co-extensive. The notion of sense thus ceases to be able to play any role in explaining how we operate with language: it is cut off from its correlation with the notion of understanding. On the other hand, it is unclear what role it does play any more. It is supposed to be a richer notion than that of reference, because, to determine sense, we need to relate an expression or sentence to every possible world, whereas the reference of an expression is a relation which it has to the real world only: but, in so far as our language is extensional, we have no need of any notion richer than that of reference in order to explain the semantic roles of expressions of our language, except in so far as we are trying to relate these to our own ability to employ those expressions. The most obvious claimants for the part of intensional contexts that need to be taken seriously are those involving mental attitudes, such as belief and intention: but it is just here that, if we are going to adopt an intensional treatment, we shall need to appeal to that notion of sense which is directly correlative with our own understanding.

Frege's notion of sense is indeed related to the determination of truth-value: if it were not, sense could not be conceived as a mode by which reference is apprehended. When we know the sense of a sentence, we thereby know the most direct means by which that sentence could be determined as true or as false. But there are two caveats which must be entered, when this is said. First, as we have noted, in Chapter 15 and elsewhere, that means of determining the sentence as true or as false which is directly given by the sense of the sentence need not be a means actually available to us. If, for instance, the sentence is a universally quantified number-theoretic statement, then my grasp of the sense of the universal quantifier consists in my understanding of the sentence as being determined as true if each of its denumerably many instances is true, and false otherwise: that method of determining its truth-value which is thus connected with its sense would consist in running through the natural numbers to discover, of each one, whether the predicate applied to it. This procedure is obviously one which we are unable, in general, to carry out: if the sentence happens to be a true one, we could never discover its truth by these means. If such a sentence is true, then, if we are ever to discover its truth, we must do so by some indirect means, that is, by some means not directly given by our understanding of the sense of the sentence: by a proof, for example. This is the second caveat: there is, in general, more than one route to the discovery of the truth-value of a sentence. The sense of the sentence, as determined by the senses of its constituent expressions, yields immediately only one of these, which we called

in Chapter 7 the 'direct' means of establishing its truth-value: but this direct means of determining a sentence as true or as false may not be available to us, and, even if it is, it may not be at all the simplest way. As we saw in Chapter 7, for example, that means of verifying an instance of the Law of Excluded Middle, say 'The Pole Star is visible or it is not visible', which is directly given by its sense will involve determining, by the appropriate means, the truth-value of the constituent sentence, in this case 'The Pole Star is visible', without adverting to the fact that the complex sentence is a tautology. This fact indeed provides a simpler way to recognize the sentence as true, without the necessity for looking up at the sky; and the existence of this simpler way is what constitutes the sentence as analytic. But this simpler method of recognizing the sentence as true is not the direct method, in the above sense: it is not the method which we are immediately given by a grasp of the sense of the sentence; and so it is in principle possible for someone to grasp the sense of the sentence without realizing that this simpler method is available. Of course, in this trivial case, it is unthinkable that it would not occur to anyone that he did not need to look at the sky in order to find out whether or not it was the case that the Pole Star either was or was not visible. But, if we had a complicated tautology, someone might very well determine its truth by observation, without noticing that it was a tautology: all the more is the analogous case possible when we are dealing with an instance of a valid formula of first-order predicate logic, for which we lack any effective decision method.

Of course, our capacity to recognize some indirect means of establishing a sentence as true or as false must depend upon our grasp of the sense of that sentence; and, if this indirect means involves the employment of a chain of deductive inference, then upon our grasp of the senses of other sentences as well. Nevertheless, such indirect means are not immediately given by the senses of the sentences as we understand them: from the point of view of our understanding of those sentences, they represent a roundabout route (even though, on occasion, one which it is much easier or much quicker to travel). No doubt it is philosophically perplexing that deductive inference should be possible, and we may complain that Frege devoted no effort to removing this perplexity. But his conception of sense at least leaves room for an explanation: that adopted by his successors does not. For them, the sense of a sentence is already contained in the sense of one by which it is entailed: a deductive inference will consist only in a gradual evacuation of sense, and its upshot could not merit the name of discovery.

In the writings of his successors, the sense of a sentence is connected only with the constitution of any possible world which would enable the sentence to be true in that world. Thus the notion of sense employed by them, if interpreted as connected with our recognition of the sentence as true or as false, goes with a picture of our comparing the sentence with reality, taken in, as it were, in one glance: we look at our world to see whether it is that kind of world in which the sentence would be true. Such a conception of course obliterates all the fine detail in an account of the process of recognizing truth-values: in particular, it cannot take account of the way in which the recognition of one sentence as true may be mediated by the recognition of others as true, that is, of the role of inference in the recognition of truth; each sentence is directly measured up against reality on its own. It is thus not in the least surprising that it was this conception of sense which was adopted by the logical positivists. Admirers of Wittgenstein have complained that the positivists misinterpreted the *Tractatus* as a positivist manifesto, and it may well be true that there is very little positivism actually in the *Tractatus*: but the complaint is unjustified all the same, because the book directly lends itself to this use. For the positivists, the sense of a sentence consists in the method of its verification, and verification is conceived of as direct confrontation with sense-data: verification, on this view, is pure observation, into which linguistic operations (save the comparison with the actual sentence to be verified) do not enter.

Frege's notion of sense, on the other hand, can only be understood in a quite different way. In relation to his notion of sense, there is no need to idealize the process of recognizing truth, to pretend that we make a direct comparison of the sentence with the world. The sense of the sentence will always be complex, and the direct method of determining it as true or as false will therefore always consist of a complex procedure, whose steps correspond in a natural way to the complexity of the sentence. There is no reason, in general, why linguistic operations, including that of carrying out a chain of deductive inferences, should not, in appropriate cases, form part of such a procedure. (It might, as against this, be suggested that to arrive at the truth of a sentence as the conclusion of a deductive inference always constituted an *indirect* means of establishing that sentence as true: it would take us too far afield to enquire into this thesis here.) It is, for that reason, nothing to be surprised at, on Frege's way of looking at things, that two sentences should differ in sense, in that the direct procedures for determining them as true should be quite unlike one another, and yet be analytically equivalent, because these different procedures must always yield the same result. Nor is there, from Frege's point of view, any tension between the informative character of a sentence and its analyticity. It is analytic if the procedure for determining it as true is such that it can only yield the one result: it is informative if the result is not immediately recognizable. We may understand the sentence without recognizing it as true; we may recognize it as true without grasping that it is analytic; or we may discover that it is analytic: and there is no problem posed by the fact that all three possibilities are, in different cases, realized.

It was, of course, precisely against the monolithic notion of verification employed by the positivists that Quine reacted in 'Two Dogmas of Empiricism', in which the thesis was propounded that it is only for a small minority of 'peripheral' sentences of the language that we can speak of direct confrontation with experience, and that, for most sentences, our recognition of their truth-value is mediated by our assignments of truth-values to other sentences. (We might envisage the determination of the truth-value of a non-peripheral sentence as direct if it is mediated by assignments to sentences all lying closer to the periphery than the sentence in question, and indirect if it involves sentences of equal or greater depth.) In that article, Quine makes one, inaccurate, contrast between his views and those of Frege: but the conceptions he is criticizing do not belong to Frege, and, as we have seen, this part of Quine's thesis tallies much more naturally with Frege's conception of sense than does the monolithic positivist conception.

Frege did, occasionally, in some of his unpublished writings, toy with the ideas that have here been contrasted with his: for example, in one of his unpublished works he advances the suggestion that the senses of two *con-* BW 105-6
tingent sentences should be regarded as coinciding when it is analytic (70-1)
that they have the same truth-value. This suggestion runs counter to his general views, however: it would necessitate a divergent account of sense for contingent and for analytic sentences, whereas it is precisely a virtue of Frege's theory that it permits a uniform account. I am not suggesting that the consequences here drawn from Frege's notion of sense and his account of analyticity were explicitly drawn by Frege: he is, on the contrary, far from explicit about the connection between sense and the determination of truth-value, and the distinction I have made between a direct and an indirect means of determining truth is one I have imposed on his doctrines, not one to be found there. Nevertheless, I think it can be claimed that the account here given is one which follows in a natural, and, indeed, irresistible manner from what Frege actually says, the connections he makes and, more particularly, the connections he does *not* make, between sense, cognitive value and analyticity.

Perhaps the most important of all the contributions made by *Grundlagen* to general philosophy is the attack on the imagist or associationist theory of meaning. This is another of those ideas which, once fully digested, appear completely obvious: yet Frege was the first to make a clean break

x*

with the tradition which had flourished among the British empiricists and had its roots as far back as Aristotle. The attack that was launched by Frege on the theory that the meaning of a word or expression consists in its capacity to call up in the mind of the hearer an associated mental image was rounded off by Wittgenstein in the early part of the *Investigations*, and it is scarcely necessary to rehearse the arguments in detail, the imagist theory now being dead without a hope of revival. Frege's attack is made to appear even stronger than it actually is because of his fallacious insistence on the subjective and ultimately incommunicable character of inner experience in general and of mental imagery in particular. As an example he imagines two rational beings who are able to perceive only projective geometrical properties and relations. He infers that, in view of the well-known duality of projective geometry, it would be impossible to tell whether the visual presentation which one associated with a point was not the same as that which the other associated with a plane, and conversely. Nevertheless, he says, they would be able to communicate with one another, using words like 'point', 'line' and 'plane', and so these words would have for them a common, objective meaning: and this meaning would be independent of the visual presentations or visual images which each associated with the words, since one would associate with the word 'point' what the other associated with the word 'plane', and vice versa. This shows that meaning, considered as something objective and common to all the speakers of a language, has nothing to do with mental imagery or sensory experience.

GI 26

An argument of this kind appears to us as a version, seen in a distorting mirror, of Wittgenstein's argument against the possibility of a private language or of a private ostensive definition. The example is merely a sophisticated variant of the well-known supposition of colour-reversal: I can never tell whether the spectrum, as you experience it, is not the reversal of the spectrum as I experience it, that the colour which we both call 'red' is not perceived by you as the colour which we both call 'violet' is perceived by me, and conversely. Frege supposes that there really are two distinct alternatives: either the two hypothetical beings associate the same visual presentation with the word 'point', and the same one with the word 'plane', or one associates with the word 'point' what the other associates with the word 'plane', and the other way round. What he insists on is, first, that it is undiscoverable which alternative holds; secondly, that nevertheless they can, in either case, communicate equally well by means of the words 'point' and 'plane'; and, hence, that the meanings of these two words, on which the possibility of using them in communication rests, can have nothing to do with the sense-experiences or mental images associated with

Ged 67 (14)

them. Wittgenstein, starting with the same type of hypothetical case, concludes that, since it is in principle undiscoverable which of the two alternatives holds, the supposed distinction between them is spurious: there are not really two distinct alternatives. To suppose that the visual experience which A associates with the word 'point' may be the same as that which B associates with the word 'plane' is to suppose that some application exists for the expression 'the same experience' which is independent of the way in which the experience is described: described, that is, in the language that is common to A and to B. And this is to suppose that the desired application for the phrase 'the same experience' can be correlated with the description of the experience that is given in a language which is private to one of the two: that A can give to the word 'point', alongside the meaning that is common to the two speakers, a special meaning in his own private language; so that, when 'point$_A$' and 'plane$_A$' express these private meanings which A gives to these words, A can ask himself, 'When B sees a point, does he see a point$_A$ or a plane$_A$?'. But the idea that A can confer such private meanings on these words is an illusion. There is no criterion for his correct application of them, and it is, indeed, inconceivable that he could apply them wrongly; but the reason that it is inconceivable is that there is nothing for him to be wrong about, and hence nothing for him to be right about when he applies them 'rightly'. It is not that he cannot help recognizing a point$_A$ when he sees one: it is that no sense has been given to his recognizing something as a point$_A$ other than his calling it a point$_A$, and hence no substance to his calling it that.

The attack on private meanings is not, in itself, an attack on incorrigibility. Wittgenstein recognizes, of several forms of expression, that they are so employed that the notion of a mistake in their application is ruled out: the criterion for their correct application is the criterion for the sincerity of the speaker. The criterion for A's truly saying, 'What I saw looked to me like a plane', is that he really was disposed to say, 'I saw a plane', whether or not it would have been true to say that and whether or not he believes that it would have been true; and hence A cannot be mistaken in supposing that what he saw looked to him like a plane. But the use of the criterion of sincerity has a background: not only is it explained in terms of A's disposition to say, 'I saw a plane', where 'plane' is a word of the language common to A and B; but it is dependent upon A's grasp of the use of that word. If A betrays that he never acquired, or has lost, a mastery of the use of the word 'plane' as a word of the common language, a word whose application has agreed criteria, then his sincerity in saying, 'I saw a plane' or 'I saw something that looked to me like a plane', will no longer provide a criterion for saying that what he saw looked to him like a plane. 'What . . . saw looked to him like a plane' is also an expression of the language common to A and to B, and so its application to B must depend on the same criterion as its application to A, that is, on B's being sincerely disposed to say, 'I saw a plane'. A cannot, by such means, contrive to confer on the word 'plane' a meaning independent of its use in the common language. In particular, he cannot give to the expression 'B sees a plane$_A$' a meaning independent of B's use of the common word 'plane', e.g. by saying that B sees a plane$_A$ when he sees the same thing as A sees when A sees a plane: for no content has been given to the notion of 'seeing the same thing' as it is here being used.

Frege's conclusion and Wittgenstein's are the same, that the meaning of a word is exhaustively explained in terms of the agreed use to which it is put in the language, shared by many, of which it forms part, and that this cannot be accounted for in terms of the association which each individual makes between that word and some mental image or sense-experience. At first sight, Frege's argument appears the more powerful, because he is able to contrast the private, subjective, ultimately incommunicable character of private experience and imagery with the public, objective and essentially communicable character of meaning, whereas Wittgenstein holds that personal experience, sensation and imagery are in principle as capable of being communicated as anything else. In fact, however, Wittgenstein's position is the stronger. Given Frege's position, it is open to an opponent to argue that, while public meaning is independent of particular associations of words to images or sensations, still private meaning is possible and is determined by such associations, and, further, that public meaning rests on private meaning: that the reason why A and B are able to give a common public meaning to the word 'point' is that each attaches to it a private meaning, 'point$_A$' and 'point$_B$', by means of an association of the word with certain private visual sensations, and that the sensations so associated with it, whether the same or different, happen to be correlated so that a common public application for the word becomes possible. To this Frege could only reply that it was the public meaning that he was interested in, not the private psychological mechanism by which each speaker contrived to attach this public meaning to the words of the language: he would have no ground to deny that such a private mental mechanism operated or was required.

This is not to say that the whole of Frege's argument against the imagist theory of meaning turns on the subjectivity and alleged incommunicability of images: even prescinding from these features of images, we can see that they cannot embody meaning. We might (although Frege does not) emphasize this point by replacing the psychological mechanism by a physical one: instead of an inner association whereby the hearing of the word causes the appropriate image to come before the mind, we can imagine a meaning-machine which, as each word is spoken, displays a picture of an appropriate kind (or, in relevant cases, emits a sound, smell, etc.). Wittgenstein in effect takes the same step by imagining actual pictures as replacing visual images. There can be no gainsaying the utility of mnemonic devices: if a man has a very bad memory for personal names, he might keep a set of captioned photographs of his acquaintances; if he found he could never remember the names of colours, he could keep a colour-chart; if a man understood the process of counting, but could never remember the sequence of the number-words, he could refer to a printed table. But the use of such devices depends upon our knowing in each case the use of the kind of word involved—personal proper names, colour-words, number-words, etc.—on knowing all but that part of the senses of the words which distinguished them from other words of the same general kind: it is impossible that a picture could display this generic ingredient of the sense. To borrow an expression from the *Tractatus*, in order to be able to derive the meaning of the word from the picture displayed by the meaning-machine, we must know the method of representation, the way in which the picture is meant to be used; and, as the kind of meaning which the word has varies, so the method of representation varies also. The picture displays the meaning in accordance with the method of representation adopted: it cannot also depict its own method of representation. The bulk of Frege's attack on the imagist theory of meaning consists in pointing out the width of the gap, to be bridged by conventions of application, between the mental image and the employment of the word whose meaning the image is supposed to embody; a grasp of the meaning of the word depends upon an understanding of these conventions, and, once we have seen this, then we are no longer inclined to take the image as playing any essential role, because the conventions governing the employment of the word can be grasped directly rather than as conventions for the application of the image. Among the empiricists, Berkeley, by his distinction between notions and ideas, was the first to admit that the meanings of some words (namely ones not directly applying to or standing for objects observable by the senses) could not be accounted for in terms of their associations with mental images; and he also stressed the necessity for supplying conventions of representation for the mental images associated with those words for whose meanings he still thought we could so account. It was left to Frege to take the final step of denying that the mental image ever played an essential role at all.

It seems to us now next to incredible that so palpably inadequate a

conception of meaning could have retained its grip on the minds of philosophers for so long; especially that it should have continued to do so after
Berkeley had taken the crucial first steps to loosen that grip. In particular,
the ambiguity in the word 'idea', as applying to mental images and to the
meanings of expressions, which played so large a role in lending plausibility
to the imagist theory, now appears to us wholly transparent. This is a
paradigm case of what Wittgenstein meant by saying that the misunder-
standings of our own language of which philosophy attempts to rid us
PI 194   resemble a primitive's misunderstanding of the discourse of civilised men.
Nevertheless, it was not until Frege's attack on it that the imagist theory was
finally exorcized. The refutation of this theory was the condition for the
recognition of the central role of sentences in the theory of meaning; or,
conversely, the recognition of the central role of sentences compels the
abandonment of the imagist theory of meaning. If the meaning of expressions
consists in the association with them of mental images, then a sentence is just
a complex expression of a particular grammatical form, with which is
associated a complex mental image such as is associated with any other
complex expression: the distinction between sentences and phrases can be
regarded only as a grammatical difference, of no basic logical significance
(like, for example, the distinction between active and passive). Conversely,
sentences can play a central role only in a theory of meaning in which the
sense of an expression resides in its capacity to determine the truth-conditions
of that form of linguistic complex which is the bearer of truth-conditions; in
which, therefore, sense must be construed quite otherwise than on the model
of a mental image. Frege was very well aware of the connection between
his rejection of the imagist theory and his allotment of a central role to
sentences: the resort to mental images in an account of the meaning of a
word springs, he says in the Preface to *Grundlagen*, precisely from the mistake
of asking after the meaning of the word in isolation, rather than in the
context of the sentences in which it occurs. When we take the word in
isolation, and try to explain its meaning, we naturally have recourse to
introspection, and think we have given an explanation by reporting the
mental images which concentration upon the word summons up: whereas
what we ought to be doing is examining the truth-conditions of the sentences
in which the word occurs, and discerning the way in which the occurrence of
the word in such sentences helps to determine those truth-conditions.

The third period of Frege's career may be regarded as running from
1891, when the lecture on *Function und Begriff* was delivered and published,
until 1906, when the second of Frege's two series of articles concerning
the foundations of geometry was published. It includes the publication

of the two volumes of *Grundgesetze der Arithmetik*, in 1893 and 1903 respectively. This period, while it saw the birth of one idea, the distinction between sense and reference, of absolutely prime importance, was basically a period of consolidation. Frege worked at two things. One was the systematic development of his philosophy of logic, which he expounded in several articles in the philosophical journals, above all the celebrated essays 'Über Sinn und Bedeutung' and 'Über Begriff und Gegenstand', both in 1892. Frege attempted repeatedly to compose a book devoted entirely to the philosophy of logic: the earliest such attempt dated from the first period of his career, some time after the composition of *Begriffsschrift*; another in 1897, between the publication of the two volumes of *Grundgesetze*; a third in 1906; and the final attempt from 1918 to 1923, of which the first three chapters were published as separate essays, as 'Der Gedanke', 'Die Verneinung' and 'Gedankengefüge'. He never succeeded, however, in completing such a project: but, though he never managed to devote a single book to the subject, he certainly created a system. The second major preoccupation of his third period was the composition of what was to be his chef d'œuvre, *Grundgesetze*, which should accomplish rigorously and in detail, by the use of his logical symbolism, the programme which *Grundlagen* had set out in outline.

This third period was not merely the most productive phase of Frege's career, in terms of pages published, but a highly creative one, in terms of ideas. Much that had been only sketched in *Grundlagen* was developed in detail, while the sense/reference distinction was not only one of the most striking contributions made in modern times to the theory of meaning, but an indispensable tool for the elucidation of the ideas Frege had already put forward. Nevertheless, compared with Frege's style of philosophizing as exemplified in *Grundlagen*, a certain hardening has appeared: Frege is now consciously trying to construct a system, and his approach in consequence sometimes gives evidence of a kind of scholasticism. In *Grundlagen*, nothing is asserted, nothing is argued for, that does not stand on its own feet: one may need to read elsewhere in order to gain a clear understanding of what is being said, but one never needs to do so in order to perceive Frege's reasons for saying it; each point is freshly argued. In the later work, this is no longer so: doctrines are presented, not as having any intrinsic plausibility, but merely as following inexorably from the other laws of the system.

The two principal developments of the doctrine, from the second to the third period, are the distinction between sense and reference and the assimilation of sentences to complex names. Of these, the first is entirely consonant with the doctrines of *Grundlagen*, and supplies a necessary complementation of them. The second appears to have been an almost unmitigated disaster, and is largely responsible for the implausible theses which Frege is now sometimes found to be advancing and for the note of scholasticism in his writing. We have seen that it was both natural and correct for Frege, in extending the distinction between sense and reference from names to expressions of other kinds, to take truth-values to be the referents of sentences. But we have also seen that to do so in no way obliged him to treat sentences as being a special kind of complex proper name, or to declare truth-values to be objects on a par with any others. Of course, the assimilation of sentences to proper names permitted a great economy in Frege's classification of the denizens of his ontological universe: concepts now appeared as merely a special case of unary functions, and relations as a special case of binary ones; a concept is just a function whose value, for any argument, is always a truth-value. This effects a certain streamlining in the formal system of *Grundgesetze* as compared with that of *Begriffsschrift*, and enabled Frege to replace the operator of class abstraction by a more general one which could be applied to any functional expression, yielding a term for the extension of a function, or what Frege called a 'value-range'. (For Frege, value-range is to function what class is to concept: in standard terminology, sets or classes are contrasted with properties or attributes, but the term 'function' is ambiguous as between Frege's 'value-range' and his 'function'.) Classes then become the value-ranges of those functions which happen to be concepts.

Apart from the trivial gain represented by this economy in ontology and in symbolism, however, the only thing which could be claimed as a positive effect of the assimilation of sentences to names is the possibility of taking the incompleteness of functions as the pattern of all incompleteness. It is apparent that the notion of incompleteness is easier to understand for functions than it is for concepts, and it is some help to Frege's later discussions of incompleteness that he is able to say that the incompleteness of concepts is really just a special case of the incompleteness of functions. The advantage is not very great, however, precisely because it leaves a residual feeling that there is, after all, a difference between the two. If truth-values had been admitted as the referents of sentences, but *not* as themselves being objects, it would still have been possible to use the analogy of functions to explain the incompleteness of concepts: but it would have been recognized as only an analogy, precisely because sentences do not really function in any way like proper names.

The most disastrous effect of the new doctrine was the abandonment of one of Frege's most important insights, that of the central role of sentences in the theory of meaning. If sentences are only a special kind of proper name, then the senses of other expressions cannot consist in the contribution which they make to determining the senses of sentences, in particular, in which they may occur: the most we can say is that the sense of an expression is directed towards the determination of the sense of a complex name in which it may occur. It is for this reason that the dictum of *Grundlagen*, that it is only in the context of a sentence that a word has meaning, makes no further appearance in Frege's works. Instead, we find, in the discussion of the reference of class-terms (or rather, terms for value-ranges) that occurs at the beginning of *Grundgesetze*, a thesis to the effect that we can   Gg I 10 fix the reference of a term by fixing the reference of more complex terms of which it forms part: and we are left to wonder why, if the references of certain terms can be stipulated directly, it may be necessary to fix the references of other terms in this indirect way, and what the principle of distinction is as between those terms whose reference may be given directly and those which can be given only indirectly. The text offers us no guidance: and the fact of the matter is that, in the context of his assimilation of sentences to names, there was no reasonable such principle to be found.

Not directly entailed by the assimilation of sentences to names, but strongly connected with it in Frege's mind, are two other ideas of which there is little or no trace in *Grundlagen*, but which become very prominent in the writings of Frege's third period. These are the doctrine of complete definition, and the rejection of contextual definitions.

By the 'doctrine of complete definition' I mean the thesis that every predicate, relational expression or functional expression ought to be defined   FB 20 for every object. Obviously, most predicates of natural language can be meaningfully applied only to objects of certain categories: only a man or something made or done by a man may be said to be ambitious, only an organism or part of an organism may be said to be female, only a triangle may be said to be scalene. If the application of a predicate to an object for which it is not defined is thus said to be meaningless, however, this failure of meaning does not arise from the only source recognized by Frege, namely a violation of the distinctions of level, of the kind which simply cannot occur in a correct notation. Frege regards it as a failure of reference rather than of sense: it is a second source of the possibility of generating, in natural language, sentences which lack a truth-value, and therefore has to be eliminated from a properly constructed language. Indeed, it is not really to be distinguished from the other source of sentences without truth-value, the use of names lacking a referent: for this latter phenomenon occurs as the result of using functional expressions not defined for every object, or of using the description operator (an expression for a function of second level) as yielding terms which have a referent only when it is attached to a predicate applying to just one object. The remedy is, therefore, to secure that, in a properly constructed language, every predicate and every functional expression is defined for every possible argument, that is, for every object, and not just those to which we are interested in applying it. This may be done in any way that seems convenient: if we are dealing with the predicate 'ξ is ambitious', we may lay down its application to stars or to natural numbers in any way that we please; we may, as the whim takes us, determine any object whatever as the value of the function 'the father of ξ' for the Moon as argument. But, if we are to have a language for which a coherent semantics is possible, that is, a systematic provision of truth-conditions for every sentence, then such stipulations will have to be made.

Gg II 56, 64 Partially defined concepts and functions are not really concepts and functions at all, and it is one of the defects of natural language that it uses expressions which stand for such things, or, rather, could only stand for such things if there were any such things to stand for, and, since there are not, must be denied a reference at all.

Obviously, there is an alternative: to employ a many-sorted logic, distinguishing different kinds of individual variables and terms, specifying a distinct domain for each sort of variable to range over, and taking each predicate or functional expression as defined over only one such domain. The most vehement parts of Frege's tirades against partially defined concepts and functions are simply out of place: a concept or function which is well-defined over some specific domain is a perfectly respectable entity, and, indeed, since we have learned that there is no domain of all objects, every sharply defined concept and function must be taken as, in this sense, a partial one. Frege disliked the idea of a many-sorted logic, because he wrongly thought that he had discovered that it was possible in all contexts to take the domain of the individual variables as the same all-embracing totality of all objects. There are certain obvious advantages to using, in any formal theory, a one-sorted language, to achieve which it may be necessary to define certain predicates and functional expressions over a wider domain than, intuitively, they are ordinarily taken to be defined over. But the arguments which Frege employs to suggest that there is actually something improper in using a many-sorted language, and thus restricting the domains of definition of the predicates and functional expressions of the language, are simply fallacious.

Frege is, in particular, guilty of confusing two distinct things—vagueness and the incomplete definition of a predicate or functional expression. He expresses his demand that every predicate and functional expression be everywhere defined by saying that it must be determinate, for every concept, whether, for any given object, that object falls under it or not, and, for every function, what the value of the function is for any given object as argument, and speaks of concepts with fuzzy boundaries as not really being concepts at all. The suggestion is thus made that the phenomenon we are concerned with is that of vagueness: for a vague concept, there may indeed be no answer to the question whether a given object falls under it or not. But this is quite different from the case of a concept with a restricted domain of definition. The boundaries of such a concept are sharp enough: it is merely that, in the case of an object outside its domain of definition there is no question whether or not that object falls under the concept; whereas, in the case of a vague concept, the question arises all right, even in cases in which there is no answer. FB 20

NS 168 (155)

I shall not enquire, in this book, whether Frege was right in believing vagueness to be itself a defect of natural language, another of those features of natural language which form an insurmountable obstacle to our giving a systematic account of the semantics of natural language, just as it is, and require us first to remove this defect before we have a language for which a coherent semantics can be given. The topic of vagueness is a very difficult one, and, although Frege's opinion about it is clearly enough expressed, his consideration of the topic is too cursory to justify the long excursus which an adequate treatment of it would involve. It is, at any rate, evident that we have an intuitive sympathy with Frege's view that a vague expression is one which is, to that extent, defective in sense: any account of vagueness which failed at least to explain this intuitive feeling would be inadequate. At the same time, we have also a contrary intuition, that vagueness is an indispensable feature of our language, that we could not operate with language as we do unless many of its expressions displayed this feature: and it is equally a requirement on any satisfactory account of vagueness that it should at least explain our having this intuition also. Wittgenstein gave powerful expression to this latter intuition in some passages in the *Investigations*, in which he ridicules Frege for believing that vagueness is always a defect our only response to which must be to seek to eliminate it: but Wittgenstein can hardly be claimed to have offered any explanation or analysis of the indispensability of vagueness, let alone a rebuttal of Frege's grounds for thinking that it has to be eliminated. *PI* 71

It is, in any case, clear that the semantics of a language containing vague expressions could not be a straightforward two-valued one, a semantics of the kind which Frege believed to be the only one possible. If we want a language in which we can take every sentence as having a determinate value, true or false, then it must be a language from which every trace of vagueness has been eliminated. To that extent, given that the necessity for a classical two-valued semantics was a part of Frege's credo, he was right in objecting to the admission of vague expressions. Whether it is in fact possible to construct a semantics for a language containing vague expressions, and what this would be like; whether it is necessary, in order to explain the workings of our language, to construct such a semantics, or whether it is enough to regard natural language as merely approximating, sufficiently for practical purposes, to a language for which a two-valued semantics would be correct; and whether the presence of vague expressions in a language represents merely a convenient saving of trouble, or whether they are indispensable in some deeper sense: all these are questions which we shall here set aside.

All this has, however, nothing whatever to do with the admission of incompletely defined predicates and functional expressions: these constitute an entirely different phenomenon from vague expressions, not at all to be conflated in the way Frege attempts to do. Frege tries to pretend that the admission of incompletely defined predicates, etc., will inevitably give rise to the formation of sentences devoid of truth-value: but, under suitable conditions, this need not be so at all. If certain conditions are fulfilled, it will be possible to lay down restrictions in the formation-rules of the language so that the sentences which would lack a truth-value will simply not belong to the language. The conditions are as follows. First, the domain of definition of the given predicate or functional expression must itself be sharply, and, indeed, effectively, defined. Secondly, we must be able to arrange our notation so that we are able to decide, for any term, whether it stands for an object in the domain of definition. Finally, the language must not contain, together with the given expression, any expression for a function some of whose values lie within the domain of definition of the given expression and others of which do not. If the first condition is violated, then we have a species of vagueness: given that an object is in the domain of definition of the predicate, it may be that the predicate then either definitely applies to the object or definitely fails to apply to it; but there are borderline cases of objects for which it is not determined whether the predicate is to be considered as defined for that object or not. The second and third conditions may both be illustrated by the case of an arithmetical predicate left undefined for the number 0: in such a case, the third condition will be violated, and the second one may be. The first condition is satisfied, since the set of numbers other than 0 is an effectively decidable set. If we are able, for any constant numerical term, to determine the number for which it stands, then the second condition is satisfied also; but, if the language allows the formation of numerical terms by means of a description operator or least-number operator, then there may be terms of which we are unable effectively to determine whether they stand for 0 or not, and we shall then be unable to exclude, by means of effective formation rules, sentences which have no truth-value. In any case, the third condition will be violated: if the predicate is '$A(\xi)$', and '$f(\xi)$' is an expression for a function whose value is sometimes 0 and sometimes positive, we shall be in a quandary how to interpret the sentence 'For all x $A(f(x))$': for it will include among its instances some sentences which have a truth-value and others without one.

It was, indeed, cases of this kind to which Frege frequently found occasion to object in the writings of his mathematical contemporaries: and we may sympathize with his objection to them, since in such cases there is no way to avoid, by effective formation-rules, the construction of sentences devoid of truth-value, or of quantified sentences which resist the straightforward classical explanation of the quantifier. Frege had, however, no ground to generalize his objection to incompletely defined predicates: for there are plenty of cases in which the conditions listed above are fulfilled, and it is precisely in these cases that Frege's insistence on each predicate and functional expression being everywhere defined appears most bizarre and doctrinaire.

The idea that every predicate must be defined for every object is absent from *Grundlagen*. There he remarks, apropos of a proposed method for introducing numerical terms, that, so far, such terms have been introduced only as occurring in statements of identity, and that, when we wished later to make provision for their occurrence in other contexts, we should have to take care that certain conditions were fulfilled: it is thus evident that he was not at this stage assuming that a term, once introduced, would be able to stand in the argument-place of any predicate. (He does, however, assume that it is always permissible, for any pair of terms, to form the identity-statement connecting them, and that we must therefore stipulate truth-conditions for all such identity-statements.) The proposed method for introducing numerical terms is a contextual definition: and, though in the end Frege rejects it, on the ground that it will not enable us to lay down truth-conditions for identity-statements in which a numerical term stands on one side and a term of some other kind on the other, and replaces it by an explicit definition, he was evidently not, at the time of writing *Grundlagen*, opposed to contextual definitions in principle. On the contrary, he defends the proposed contextual definition of numerical terms against a general

Gl 63–5 objection to contextual definitions, and invokes his thesis that 'it is only in the context of a sentence that a name stands for anything' as a general justification of the procedure of contextual definition, citing the Gl 60 standard definition of the notation 'dx/dy' for differentiation as an instance.

In his third period, however, Frege became extremely hostile to contextual definition, as also to piecemeal definition (definition by cases) and conditional definition, in fact to definitions of every kind that deviated from straightforward explicit definition. In the case of conditional definition, this is of course directly related to his requirement that every incomplete expression be everywhere defined, since conditional definition is precisely a device for restricting the domain of definition of a predicate or functional expression. Frege's argument on this score rests on a deliberate misconstrual of the intention of a conditional definition: to a definition of the form, 'If R is a congruence relation on the algebra α, then $\alpha/_R$ is the quotient Gg II 65 algebra under R', Frege applies modus tollens to obtain the ludicrous result, 'If $\alpha/_R$ is not the quotient algebra under R, then R is not a congruence relation on α'. Plainly, a conditional definition is not intended as a stipulation of the truth of a conditional statement, but a stipulation, conditional upon the truth of the antecedent, of the truth of the consequent.

Frege's objection to contextual definition does not follow from his repudiation of incompletely defined predicates; but it belongs to the same circle of ideas. Frege compares a contextual definition to an equation which has to be Gg II 66 solved, whereas, he says, a definition ought to give the solution. If one is allowed to present merely the equation as requiring solution, then we shall not in general know whether there is any solution at all, or whether, if there is, it is unique. Frege is here basing his objection upon his idea that a definition ought always to be free of all presupposition: it ought, that is, to be given in such a way that no demonstration is antecedently required that that definition is legitimate, i.e. that it really does succeed in defining something. But, even if this principle be accepted, Frege misses an opportunity to contribute to the resolution of a problem of great importance, and one which arises very naturally in the context of his theory of meaning. He does so because he fails to discern an ambiguity in his notion of a 'solution'. If, in comparing a contextual definition to an equation requiring solution, Frege is taking such a solution to consist of an explicit definition, a rule for the uniform replacement of the defined expression by some already understood expression of the language, then, indeed, there may well be no solution in this sense; but it is not in the least apparent why we have any right to demand that there should be one, let alone a unique one. On the other hand, it is a legitimate requirement that there be a unique solution in a more general sense, that is, that the contextual definition should determine a unique reference for the defined expression.

We may take it as characteristic for a *definition*, as opposed to any other means of introducing an expression, that it provides an effective means of replacing any sentence containing the defined expression by a sentence which does not contain it. An explicit definition does this by providing a single replacement for the defined expression in any occurrence, a contextual definition by giving a rule of a more complex kind for transforming any sentence containing the defined expression. This requirement is independent of the requirement that a unique reference should be determined for the expression being introduced. This latter requirement may be satisfied by stipulations that do not amount to definitions in the above sense, that is, do not provide a rule for the elimination of the new expression: the most familiar case is that of a set of recursion equations for an arithmetical function. There is one and only one arithmetical function which can satisfy the recursion equations: but the equations do not provide a means for eliminating the symbol for that function from all contexts (specifically, not in those in which a variable or term containing a variable occupies the argument-place on which the recursion is being performed).

A contextual definition is required where the resources of the language do not permit an explicit definition to be given. An example would be a formalization of set theory within a first-order language without a description operator. Here we might define the intersection operator contextually by stipulating the equivalence of '$x \in y \cap z$' with '$x \in y \ \& \ x \in z$'. We cannot transform this into an explicit definition of '$y \cap z$' because the language contains no mechanism for the formation of complex terms: nevertheless, given the Axiom of Extensionality and, say, the Axiom of Separation, a unique reference is guaranteed for the operator '$\cap$'. In such cases, there can be no valid objection in principle to the use of contextual definitions. In other cases, however, a contextual definition may be required because the expression introduced is being made to play a syntactic role different from its semantic one. One example is the description operator under Russell's Theory of Descriptions. The notation used suggests that definite descriptions are a kind of complex singular term: but the definition given does not assign to the description operator the role of a genuine term-forming operator; the contextual definition could be transformed into an explicit one only if the notation were adapted to the definition given, i.e., if, instead of a description operator, there were defined what Frege would call an expression for a relation of second level, viz. a quantifier with two argument-places, both to be filled by predicates. Another example is that of Quine's 'virtual classes'.

If in set theory we introduce the expression 'V', defined contextually by setting '$x \in V$' equivalent to '$x = x$', the expression 'V' appears as if it were a constant standing for a set or class; but, if we are operating within ordinary Zermelo-Fraenkel set theory, there are no proper classes and there is, of course, no set satisfying the condition imposed. The procedure is harmless, so long as we know what we are doing, and so long, in particular, as we do not allow 'V' to precede '$\in$' or permit the deduction from a statement '$A(V)$' of the existential generalization '$\exists x\, A(x)$' (whereas, by contrast, the deduction of '$\forall y \,\forall z\, \exists x\, A(x,y,z)$' from '$\forall y \,\forall z\, A(y \cap z,y,z)$' is perfectly legitimate). But the fact remains that what necessitates the use of contextual definition in such a case is the choice of an inappropriate syntactic form for what is being defined: if, instead of a virtual class-term (i.e. a pseudo-term), we had introduced a predicate by means of the same definiens, the definition would have been an explicit one.

There are thus two types of contextual definition: those which succeed in determining a reference for the defined expression, and those which do not. In the former case, our need to employ a contextual rather than an explicit definition arises from the restriction of our linguistic resources; in the latter case, from our employment of an inappropriate symbolism. We may accept Frege's objection to contextual definitions, when they are of the latter kind (except when we have special purposes in view concerning the comparison of theories, as Quine does with virtual classes). But what happens in cases of the former kind, if, with Frege, we rule out contextual definitions of this kind also? There are then only two things we can do, if a contextual definition is proposed: either we can enrich our language, to permit the definition to be transformed into an explicit one; or we take the expression, not as defined, but as primitive, and treat the stipulated equivalence, not as a definition, but as an axiom or postulate. But we are now left entirely in the dark as to the status of such an axiom. The status of a definition is clear: it constitutes the stipulation of the sense of a newly introduced expression. But the question cries out for an answer, under what conditions and in what cases we may accord a similar status to the axioms governing the primitive expressions of a theory.

Ver 150 (42) Frege is never tired of pointing out that it is impossible that all the expressions of a language should be defined. But since we need to learn the senses of all the expressions of the language, including those that are not introduced to us by means of definitions, and since Frege's theory of meaning requires that the sense of an expression be something objective, grasped by all the speakers of the language, the notion of sense, and the whole theory of meaning in which it is embedded, would be much illuminated by an account of the other means that exist, besides definition, for conveying to someone what the sense of an expression is, means other than definition for introducing expressions into the language. Frege's rigorist attitude to definitions, whereby only those which pass the exacting standards required for an explicit definition are conceded the status of definition at all, serves only to exacerbate the problem. At any rate, he failed almost completely to recognize that he owed an account of this matter.

NS 224-5
(207-8)

The problem may be formulated thus: When have we the right to *stipulate* that a certain sentence, or all the sentences of a certain form, shall be taken to be true? Clearly, such a stipulation is in order when, and only when, it can be regarded as a means of laying down the sense of some expression occurring in the sentence or sentences. (What it overtly determines is the reference of the expression, and, by determining it in that particular way, shows what its sense is.) It seems reasonable to require, of any such stipulation, that it should determine a reference for the expression in question: that is, in terms of Frege's metaphor, that there should be at least one solution to the equation, and possibly that there should be a unique such solution. (We might, however, relax the requirement of a unique solution in cases in which different solutions would still yield the same truth-value for each sentence in which the expression was going to occur.) If the stipulation then satisfies the further condition of permitting the actual elimination of the defined expression, it constitutes a definition in the strict sense, whether this be an explicit one or only a contextual one, and, in this case, may be acknowledged as a permissible means of introducing an expression. If it does not satisfy this further condition, then of course it does not rank as a definition; and the question now arises whether the fact of determining a unique reference for the expression is a sufficient condition for such a stipulation to count as a permissible non-definitional means of introducing an expression, or whether some further condition should be required.

I shall not attempt to investigate this question further here, but shall be content with having raised it. Within formalized theories, we are not at present accustomed to recognize more than two kinds of status for expressions of the language—defined expressions and primitive ones: defined expressions are introduced by definitions (explicit ones only or also contextual ones, according to how generously we frame our canons of definition), and are therefore in principle eliminable; primitive expressions are governed by axioms and are, so to speak, in the language from the start. But it is apparent that we have a vague intuitive feeling that the epistemological status of the different axioms of a theory may vary considerably: some can be regarded as the mere results of stipulation, while others appear to embody substantial assumptions in need of justification. (Contrast, for example, the Axiom of Extensionality with the axioms of set-existence; or, in first-order arithmetic, the recursion equations for addition and multiplication with the induction axiom.) Both for epistemological purposes, and for the theory of meaning, we stand badly in need of an account of postulation; that is, of what assumptions we may regard as being simply laid down as a means of fixing the senses of certain expressions, and what assumptions cannot be GG1   taken as the result of mere stipulation. Frege, when he attacked Hilbert for claiming that the axioms of geometry could be taken, en bloc, as an 'implicit definition' of the geometrical primitives, scored some notable hits; and, of course, Hilbert's short way with the problem was simplistic and inadequate. Nevertheless, Frege ought to have realized that the intuition to which Hilbert was appealing was in part sound, and that the problem which Hilbert had raised was one which faced Frege also.

This question bears on the notion of analyticity, on which we have already touched. Despite the very minor role which this notion played in Frege's general philosophy of language, it was important for him, since it was in terms of it that he framed one of his principal theses in the philosophy of mathematics, namely that true arithmetical statements are analytic. Frege defines an analytic statement as one which can be justified in a certain way: and he specifically permits, in the kind of justification whose existence, Gl 3   for a given statement, renders that statement analytic, appeal to definitions of the words occurring in the statement. If we ask why Frege allows appeal to definitions, the only possible answer seems to be that Frege has so framed his definition of 'analytic' as to accord with the intuitive conception whereby an analytic statement is one whose truth can be recognized by appeal only to those principles which govern the senses of the expressions contained in it (a 'statement which is true in virtue of its meaning alone', in the familiar, and inaccurate, formulation). Frege does not put this conception into words: but it seems to be the only rationale for his defining 'analytic' in the way that he did—the only way in which we can explain why the notion of analyticity, defined as Frege defines it, should be an interesting or significant one.

The only feature of definitions which is relevant to the notion of analyticity is that they constitute a means by which the senses of expressions can be laid down. On Frege's own admission, there must be other means of laying down the senses of expressions than by definitions; indeed, this is obvious in any case. It is entirely possible—in fact, overwhelmingly probable—that, among such non-definitional means of laying down the senses of expressions, there are some which consist in or involve the stipulation of the truth of certain sentences. If so, an appeal, in the course of demonstrating the truth of some statement, to the truth of such sentences would have the same interest as an appeal to a definition: the fact that the definition would, and a non-definitional stipulation would not, permit the elimination of the expression whose sense was explained by means of it, is beside the point in this connection. It follows that, even if we accept Frege's ideas about analyticity in general, Frege's actual definition of 'analytic' is only a provisional one. Once we have found a means to characterize those sentences whose stipulation as true may constitute a legitimate means of introducing an expression into the language and fixing its sense, the definition of 'analytic' ought to be widened so as to permit appeal to the truth of such sentences in the course of that kind of demonstration of the truth of a statement which will establish the statement as analytic.

The distinction, among contextual definitions, between those which do and those which do not serve to determine a reference for the defined expression, as so far drawn, permits intermediate cases. The axioms of set theory already provide for the existence of the intersection of any two sets, and rule out the existence of a universe set. A contextual definition introducing a term-forming operator under conditions for which the axioms of the theory neither demand nor forbid the existence of objects to be the referents of the new terms would be an intermediate case. We could judge it as falling on one side of the line or the other according as existential generalization was or was not allowed with respect to a sentence containing a term formed with the new operator. If it was allowed, then, in any model of the whole theory, as now constituted, there must be objects to be the referents of the new terms: but the introduction of the contextual definition has swollen the existential claim made by the theory. Evidently, the legitimacy of a proposed means of introducing an expression, and the status of axioms as the expression of assumption-free postulation, must to a large extent turn on whether they carry any existential consequences. But, with that observation, we shall leave the topic.

It is because the more positive features of Frege's work during his third period have been treated in detail in the body of this book that I have, in this chapter, concentrated on certain negative aspects of it. It would, however, be quite misleading to represent this third period as one in which Frege did little but damage his previous work by introducing doctrinaire and implausible additions to it. The period, which covers nearly twenty years, saw the working out and enrichment of much that was only sketched in *Grundlagen*: if Frege had died after writing *Grundlagen*, we should know of many of his ideas only in embryonic form, and the most celebrated of all his philosophical doctrines, the distinction between sense and reference, we should not know of at all.

In a footnote to the Preface to Volume I of *Grundgesetze*, Frege complains of the neglect of his work even by writers whose work is in neighbouring areas, and mentions specifically Dedekind, Stolz, Helmholtz and Kronecker as being apparently unaware of it; ironically, the second edition of Dedekind's *Was sind und was sollen die Zahlen?*, in which Dedekind paid tribute to the work of Frege, was published only a month after the first volume of *Grundgesetze*. But Frege's complaint was justified: practically no attention was being paid to the work which inaugurated the modern period in the philosophy of mathematics, and which arguably initiated a whole epoch in the history of philosophy in general. But irony marked each phase of Frege's career. In 1902, as Volume II of *Grundgesetze* was in the press, Frege received a deferential letter from an admirer, perhaps the first man to appreciate the full value of Frege's work, and certainly the first to express it to Frege. The admirer was Bertrand Russell: but the letter contained a report, modestly expressed, of Russell's discovery of his famous contradiction in naïve set theory, and, specifically, in the theory of classes (more properly, of value-ranges) embodied in the formal system of *Grundgesetze*. Frege replied, expressing 'consternation', as well he might. The correspondence was continued at length, and it is remarkable how quickly Frege rallied: in later letters, before he had hit on any solution of the paradox, he is still confidently shooting down various suggestions of Russell; even though he does not yet know what is wrong, he remains confident enough to reject a number of proposals Russell makes. In the middle of the correspondence, Frege reports to Russell the modification of his Axiom V, governing the class-abstraction operator, which he believed would restore consistency and which is set out in the Appendix which he added to the second volume of *Grundgesetze*. Russell replied that Frege was probably right: but by that time Russell had become engrossed in the ideas which led to his own method of resolving the contradictions, the ramified theory of types, and there ceases to be any further real communication between the two men.

After Frege's death, Leśniewski gave a proof that, even under Frege's proposed weakening of Axiom V, a contradiction could still be generated, though not, indeed, Russell's contradiction. This fact is not, indeed, immediately obvious, and there is no evidence to indicate that Frege ever became aware of it. But (as noted in the Introduction) there is one step which any mathematician will automatically take if he has been forced to modify or weaken one of his axioms: namely to check whether the proofs of the theorems still go through. Frege received Russell's letter while Volume II of *Grundgesetze* was in the press, and he had to devise a solution to the contradiction, and write an appendix explaining the contradiction and his solution to it,

Marginal notes (left column):

Gg I xin.

BW 211–12 (130–1)

BW 232–3 (150)

BW 233 (151)

Sob

in time for the publication of the book. After this, however, his only possible reaction must have been to check through the proofs in Volume I, and assure himself that they could still be carried through under the weakened axiom. If we assume that he did this, he must very soon have discovered that, in the presence of the weakened axiom, the crucial proof of the infinity of the series of Gg I 114-20 natural numbers failed. This is not something that anyone could overlook: either Frege never checked whether the proofs held up, or he discovered that the proof of this crucial theorem, on which he had rightly laid such stress in *Grundlagen*, collapsed. There survives no direct evidence that Frege made any such check or any such discovery: but inherent plausibility makes it almost certain that he did. Having discovered this, there would have been no natural further modification for Frege to make. In order to restore the proof of the theorem, it would have been necessary to strengthen the revised Axiom V once more: but there is no way to do this without readmitting Russell's contradiction. In the new approach to set theory initiated by Zermelo, cardinal numbers have to be defined in a quite different way from that employed by Frege: not as classes of all those classes having a given cardinality, in Frege's manner, but, for instance, as representative classes having that cardinality; for von Neumann, the cardinal number n is itself a particular n-membered class. To have adopted such an approach would have entailed, for Frege, a far-reaching reconstruction of his theory. Moreover, since class-abstraction is taken by Frege as a primitive operator applicable to any predicate, his Axiom V is not framed as an axiom of class existence, but as one governing the conditions for identity between classes; and this itself would make an approach of Zermelo's kind difficult to hit on.

It thus seems highly probable that Frege came quickly to regard his whole programme of deriving arithmetic from logic as having failed. Such a supposition is not only probable in itself: it is in complete harmony with what we know of his subsequent career. The fourth period of his life may be regarded as running from 1907 to 1913; and it was almost entirely unproductive. He conducted a correspondence between 1908 and 1910 with the logician Leopold Löwenheim about formal arithmetic, which has unfortunately not survived. His only publications during this period were contributions to a controversy with Thomae, initiated by the latter, concerning formalism, and some comments on an article about his work by Jourdain, which were published with the article. In particular, he did not attempt to publish a third volume of *Grundgesetze*. *Grundgesetze*, as we have it, is divided into three parts. Part I is a general exposition of the logical system, with a statement of its axioms and rules of inference, an informal semantics giving its intended interpretation, and some definitions and preliminary derivations. Part II gives the formal construction, within this system, of the theory of cardinal numbers, and of natural numbers in particular: it is divided into fifteen sections, indicated by capital Greek letters, and Volume I breaks off between section Λ and section M. It is as if Frege had just measured out a pile of manuscript which he, or the printer, thought enough for one volume. Volume II completes Part II of the book, down to the final section O, and then begins Part III, which concerns real numbers. Frege aimed in this Part to do for the theory of real numbers what he had done in *Grundlagen* and in Part II of *Grundgesetze* for natural numbers: to show the inadequacy of previous theories, and to derive the whole theory of real numbers from a purely logical basis within his formal system. Part III starts off with a long prose critique of the theories of other writers, intended to refute them as successfully as he had refuted previous theories of natural numbers in the critical sections of *Grundlagen*, and then proceeds to a formal development, which reaches in Volume II only to the end of section Z: the whole plan has been sketched, but, after six sections, the greater part of it still remains to be executed, and the final sub-section of section Z is entitled 'The Next Problem'. It is thus quite evident that Frege intended to issue a third volume, completing the unfinished Part III. The only reason he can have had for thus leaving the task uncompleted was the belief that Russell's discovery entailed a revision of his formal system too extensive for him to have the heart to undertake it.

BW 252 (170)   In 1912 Russell wrote to Frege again to invite him to address a congress of mathematicians in Cambridge. Frege declined the invitation in a letter expressing the deepest depression.

Frege's fifth period may be dated from 1914 to 1918 —the war years. Frege was then retired from his post at Jena, and there was a revival of activity on his part. In the spring of 1914 he wrote, but never published, an

NS 219–70   extended article entitled 'Logik in der Mathematik'; and, as already noted, he
(203–50)   attempted once more to compose a book setting out his whole philosophy of logic. The first three chapters of this latter work were published, the first two in 1918, the third not until 1923, under the general title *Logische*

NS 278–81   *Untersuchungen*. A fourth chapter on generality, intended for publication in
(258–62)   the same journal, has survived in Frege's Nachlass, published in 1969.

These essays have a remarkable freshness of style, and contain several observations not made elsewhere in his published writings. A comparison of them with earlier unpublished writings, however, and particularly with the attempt at a book on logic dating from 1906, shows that they do not contain any doctrines which Frege had not arrived at some years before. Perhaps the most interesting in this regard is the second essay, 'Die Verneinung',

Ver 145 (34)   in which Frege states expressly his view that the sense of a sentential question is a thought, the same as that of the corresponding assertoric sentence; in 'Der Gedanke', he states that the sense of an imperative or an optative sentence is not a thought, that is, not anything to which the predicates 'true' and 'false' can be applied. In 'Die Verneinung' Frege also gives his view that it is impossible to distinguish, among sentences of natural language, between affirmative and negative ones, as well as his argument that, since the sign of negation must be regarded as contributing to the sense of a sentence, because it can occur within a subordinate clause of a complex sentence, there is no need to recognize denial as a kind of force co-ordinate with assertion: the denial of a thought is the assertion of its negation. Ged 62 (6)

The first essay, 'Der Gedanke', contains the most explicit formulation of Frege's argument for the undefinability of truth, and his criticism of the correspondence theory; he is at pains to contrast the truth of a thought or sentence with that of a picture. In 'Der Gedanke' there also occurs Frege's repudiation of facts as entities belonging to the realm of reference: facts are merely true thoughts, and thus belong to the realm of sense. (Frege does not use the expressions 'the realm of reference' and 'the realm of sense' in 'Der Gedanke', which does not introduce the notions of sense and reference; but he does distinguish the realm of thoughts as a 'third realm' besides the realm of ideas and 'the outer world'.) The essay also contains, what is rare in Frege's writings, a more than glancing treatment of token-reflexive expressions, with an insistence that a sentence in which such expressions occur essentially does not of itself determine a thought, but does so only in conjunction with the circumstances surrounding any particular occasion of its utterance; further, Frege discusses expressly the possibility that two users of a proper name may attach different senses to it. In 'Der Gedanke', Frege launches a renewed assault on psychologism, i.e. the intrusion of appeal to mental processes in the analysis of sense, and, in doing so, produces his most uncharacteristic piece of writing: for, in the process, he for once essays a criticism of the idealist thesis that we are aware only of our own ideas, and hence have no ground for believing in the existence of a world external to us. In all his other writing, Frege merely bypasses this notorious philosophical quagmire without a sideways glance: here he deliberately leads his reader into the midst of it, and attempts to provide him with a path out again. An idea, Frege says, can be recognized as something which requires a bearer;* therefore, when I suppose that everything is an idea, I thereby assume a bearer for these ideas. This bearer is I myself: but I cannot be identified with one of my own ideas, that is, the bearer of my ideas cannot itself be one Ged 58–60 (3–4) Ged 69 (17) Ged 67 (15)

* In the sense, obviously, of something or someone whose idea it is, not in that in which a name has a bearer.

of them. Hence, there exists at least one object of my awareness which is not a content of my consciousness, namely myself: I indeed have an idea of myself, but I am not that idea. Even one counter-example is enough to refute the thesis that everything of which I can be aware, every object of my understanding, is an idea, a content of my consciousness; and, once I have recognized the possibility that there exist independent entities, things whose existence does not depend upon my awareness of them, it becomes overwhelmingly probable that most of the things I take as having such independent existence, in particular other people as themselves bearers of ideas, genuinely are so; although, indeed, once we leave the inner world for the outer, we are bereft of the certainty we there possessed, and have to make do with probabilities. In any case, reflection on the character of thoughts themselves reveals to us that they are not ideas, not contents of our consciousness: though they belong to a special realm, they are of their nature things which do not depend upon our thinking.

Although part of 'Der Gedanke' is thus so unlike anything else that Frege ever wrote, it is remarkable how little Frege's fundamental ideas about logic, as set out in the *Logische Untersuchungen*, had changed in the long interval since his previous publications. Indeed, the two sketches for a book on logic dating from 1906 display almost exactly the same plan as is followed in the *Logische Untersuchungen*. The four chapters of the latter concern: thoughts; negation; complex sentences; and generality. The sections of one of the 1906 sketches are: thoughts; the separation of assertoric force from the predicate; negation; complex sentences; and generality. Those of the other are: the separation of assertoric force from the predicate; conditional sentences; generality; and sense and reference. One might be struck, on reading the *Logische Untersuchungen*, by the fact that everything in them, including the explanation of the notion of incompleteness, as applied to predicates and relational and functional expressions, is expressed in terms of sense: not only does Frege not invoke the distinction between sense and reference, but, although he makes general mention of 'things of the outer world', he does not speak of any of the types of entity (objects, concepts, relations, functions, truth-values) which belong to the 'realm of reference': all is in terms of linguistic expressions and their senses. (He speaks in 'Der Gedanke' of the predicate ' . . . is true', but not of truth-values as entities.) The suspicion might thus arise that this omission represented a change of view on Frege's part about the sense/reference distinction: and, indeed, if the notion of reference were to be dropped altogether, this would be the most radical conceivable revision of Frege's doctrines. It is plain, however, that the omission is only a strategic one: Frege is leaving the notion of reference for

NS 201-18
(185-202)

later introduction, as in the 1906 sketch. The distinction between sense and reference is invoked in 'Logik in der Mathematik' in 1914, and also in a short exposition addressed to Ludwig Darmstaedter in 1919. NS 250 (232)
NS 275 (255)

Perhaps more remarkable than the continuity of his views is the total obliviousness which he displays to the work of others. By 1918, the subject of mathematical logic, invented by Frege, had received many profound contributions, from Russell and Whitehead, Hilbert, Zermelo, Löwenheim and others. It is true that, apart from Löwenheim's, these contributions related more to the foundations of mathematics than to elementary logic, about which Frege was concerned in these articles: but, although Frege had an extensive correspondence with Löwenheim, now unfortunately lost, there is not a trace in his published or unpublished writing of any notice on his part of the work that was going on in the field he had opened up; he writes, in the *Logische Untersuchungen*, as if no one had ever thought about these subjects before—just as he had written at the beginning of his career, when they really had not. But perhaps the fact is that Frege was too original a man ever to have been able to work in co-operation with others. Deeply conservative, indeed reactionary, in his outlook on political and social matters, his ideas in philosophy and mathematics are amazingly independent of stimulation from those of others. Few ideas are so new that one cannot trace their origin: one can see them as extensions of older ideas, or as new combinations of older ones, or at least as arising in reaction to previous conceptions or in response to some question that had come to be posed. The well-known difficulty of tracing when an idea first originated is evidence enough of this: most often one can say of the reputed inventor of an idea that he was not the first to think of it, but the first to see its importance. But Frege's ideas appear to have no ancestry. He applied himself to formal logic, and invented a totally new approach; he applied himself to philosophy, and wrote as if the world was young and the subject had only just been invented. It is true that his works are full of diatribes against the mistakes of others: but he never seems to have learned from anybody else, not even by reaction; other authors appear in his writings only as object-lessons in how not to handle the subject. And so, perhaps, it is vain to wish that he had paid more attention to the work of his successors in logic and the foundations of mathematics: perhaps he was incapable of sailing any sea on which other ships were in sight.

Frege had one encounter during this fifth period which may have had some influence upon him, namely his meeting with a young and even more profound admirer than Russell had been, Ludwig Wittgenstein. Wittgenstein wrote to Frege in October 1913, and visited him probably early in the

Y

New Year of 1914: unfortunately, what remained of the correspondence between them was destroyed by American bombing during the Second World War. In letters to Frege before their meeting, Wittgenstein raised objections to Frege's theory of truth, and, in particular, it appears, to his method of stipulating the reference of a functional expression: Frege thought Wittgenstein's views of sufficient interest to compose replies to them, both before and after the meeting. During the war, Wittgenstein sent some field post-cards to Frege, and Wittgenstein's sister gave Frege news of him while he was a prisoner of war. After the war there was some renewed contact between them: Frege sent Wittgenstein a copy of 'Der Gedanke' (to which Wittgenstein is reputed to have objected that Frege was misguided in attacking a theory with which he had no sympathy), and Wittgenstein sent Frege the *Tractatus*.

BW 266

BW 266-7

BW 268

Since the correspondence was destroyed, we have no way of knowing what Frege thought of the *Tractatus*: it is natural to wonder whether the contrast Frege draws in 'Der Gedanke' between the truth of a thought and that of a picture represents a hostile reaction to Wittgenstein's picture theory of meaning, or whether the remark in the same essay that a fact is only a true thought is directed against the second sentence of the *Tractatus* ('The world is the totality of facts, not things'). In any case, it is probably due to Wittgenstein that Frege is read by philosophers today. The *Tractatus* pays profound homage to Frege, homage that is pointedly more intense than that paid to Russell, and is crammed with reference to his doctrines: indeed, the book is virtually unintelligible without an understanding of its Fregean background. If it had not been for the influence of this celebrated book, and of Wittgenstein's other teaching and writing, it is possible that the writings of Frege might have been utterly forgotten.

Frege's final period consisted of the few years that remained of his life, from 1919 to 1925. During this period he published nothing: but he started to write again about mathematics, fragmentary works which have survived in the Nachlass. In these writings, Frege faces squarely the failure of his logicist programme. He locates the source of the mistake in the very introduction of the notion of class, which he now rejects as altogether spurious. This may seem excessive: but Frege was never interested in set theory as a branch of mathematics; for him the notion of class was a logical notion, or it was nothing. So, in this period, he concludes that it is nothing: we are misled by a mere idiom of language into thinking there are any such things as classes. We allow ourselves to express the fact that just the same objects fall under the concept F as under the concept G by saying 'The concepts F and G have the same extension' or 'The extension of the concept F coincides

NS 288 (269)

with that of the concept *G*', and then fall into the illusion that there is some
object which we have succeeded in referring to by means of the phrase 'the
extension of the concept *F*', whereas all that is in question is a manner of
expressing that the second-level relation of co-extensiveness obtains between
the concepts *F* and *G*.

NS 289 (269–70)

Indeed, Frege generalizes the point. The fundamental problem of the
philosophy of mathematics is, he says, the source of the notion of infinity.
In order to ground even the simplest of mathematical theories, the theory of
numbers, we have to be assured of the existence of infinitely many objects; in
saying this, Frege reveals that he has not abandoned another belief vigorously
propounded in *Grundlagen*, that numbers are objects and that the truth
of arithmetical statements depends upon their actual existence. There
are three distinct sources of knowledge: sense-perception; logical intuition;
and geometrical and temporal intuition. (Frege only once uses the word
'intuition', speaking mainly of the logical source of knowledge and the
geometrical source of knowledge: but he evidently means to refer to some
faculty by which we are assured of certain truths, and so the use of the word
'intuition' seems appropriate.) By means of sense-perception we can never
be assured of the existence of infinitely many things, since we can only ever
perceive finitely many. It is an illusion to suppose that logic can provide a
foundation for the existence of infinitely many objects. Indeed, no objects can
be given to us through logic alone. The phrase is reminiscent of the sentence
of the *Tractatus*, 'There are no logical objects', and may indicate the influence
of Wittgenstein on Frege at this late period. Wittgenstein's phrase would be
an apt expression of Frege's repudiation of his earlier views, for 'logical
objects' signifies exactly what classes and, more generally, value-ranges had
been for Frege. If numbers are objects, and arithmetic is reducible to
logic, then there must be logical objects: it was in this way that Frege's
logicism provided the substance of his platonism.

NS 284–5 (265)

NS 298 (278)

NS 299 (279)

TLP 4.441

Gg II 74, 147

Since mathematics must be grounded on the assurance of an infinite
totality, and, since neither logic nor sense-perception can supply this assurance, it must derive from the third source, spatial and temporal intuition.
Frege had always believed in a non-logical but a priori source of knowledge:
he had always held geometry to be synthetic a priori. Now, in effect, he
reverts to the Kantian belief that arithmetic is synthetic a priori too: but
not, as in Kant, because it derives from a separate kind of intuition—temporal, as opposed to spatial. It is still necessary, Frege holds, to unify mathematics: only now we shall seek to derive all mathematics, number theory
included, from geometry. No longer does he hold number theory to occupy
any fundamental place: on the contrary, rather than define the real numbers

Gl 89; BW 163 (100)

NS 297 (277)

in terms of the natural numbers, we must first define the real numbers
directly, on a geometrical basis, and then isolate the natural numbers, considered as non-negative integral reals, within them. This is of course inevitable, once the whole theory of classes has been rejected: for there is no step
from the natural numbers to the classical continuum without using the
notion either of a class or of an infinite sequence.

The few fragmentary writings of Frege's final period are not of high
quality: they are interesting chiefly as showing that Frege did, at least at the
very end of his life, acknowledge the failure of the logicist programme,
which he had announced so confidently in *Grundlagen*, and had the energy
to begin to construct an alternative whole theory of the foundations of
mathematics to replace it. The discovery of Russell's paradox had been a
shattering blow to a man who had repeatedly had to face the discouragement
of neglect when he knew that his work was of the highest value. It was
particularly ironic in view of the pride he justifiably took in the rigour and
care of his informal reasoning and the manipulation of his formal system.
Writing of the contradiction that appeared in Schröder's class-calculus as a
result of Schröder's failure to distinguish between class-membership and
class-inclusion, and of Schröder's attempts to restore consistency by means of
(in effect) a simple theory of types, Frege had said, 'This contradiction comes
like a thunderbolt from a clear sky. How could we be prepared for anything
like this in exact logic? Who can go surety for it that we shall not again
suddenly encounter a contradiction as we go on? The possibility of such a
thing points to a mistake in the original design. . . . This expedient [the
theory of types], as it were, belatedly gets the ship off the sandbank; but if
she had been properly steered, she could have kept off it altogether'. Seven
years later, a thunderbolt descended on Frege from a clear sky. What is
surprising is not that it silenced him for fifteen years, but that he ever started
to write again.

CHAPTER 19

Frege's Place in the History of Philosophy

IF FREGE HAD died in 1880, his place in the history of philosophy, as the founder of modern mathematical logic, would still be secure. As it is, his importance is far greater than that. In part, this can be accounted for by the fact that he initiated the modern era in the philosophy of mathematics, an offspring of the main subject which has often had much to teach its parent. But this explains Frege's significance only in small part. In *Grundlagen*, Frege's discussions of general points in the philosophy of logic or in the theory of meaning appear as subservient to an investigation in the philosophy of mathematics; but no one can read the later essays on non-mathematical topics and suppose that Frege continued to regard these only as a preliminary to a defence of philosophical views about mathematics: they had come to interest him for their own sake. And the same has been true of later discussion of them by others: they have been discussed for their intrinsic interest, and not merely as a basis for certain theses in the philosophy of mathematics.

It is in no way surprising that Frege's contributions to the philosophy of logic should be rated highly by those who work within this field, any more than it is surprising that his contributions to the philosophy of mathematics should be. What needs explanation is the widespread assessment of Frege as a philosopher of the highest importance, not merely in the particular branches of philosophy within which he worked, but to philosophy as a whole. Why should someone whose philosophical output was entirely restricted to two quite specialized areas, who never gave us his views on God, free-will or immortality, on knowledge, goodness or the mind-body problem, be thought of as a philosopher comparable in importance to Aristotle or to Kant?

The answer is that, in concentrating so single-mindedly on the area in which he worked, Frege also gave to it a central place in philosophy; and, in doing this, he achieved a revolution as overwhelming as that

665

of Descartes. The philosophy of mathematics has, indeed, to be regarded as a specialized branch of philosophy. That it often has much to teach the rest of philosophy is due to the fact that problems arise in it which are analogues of problems that arise in other fields, and often in a form which makes the issues stand out sharper; the problems remain exceedingly difficult to resolve, and yet are more tractable than their analogues in other fields, just because attention is restricted to an area within which certain phenomena do not occur; we are, as it were, studying a part of the galaxy not obscured by dust-clouds. Indeed, the progress of analytical philosophy in this century would have been a great deal faster if more attention had been paid to what was going on in the philosophy of mathematics: for instance, the dispute between phenomenalism and realism about the external world would have been much better conducted if both sides had conformed it more to the model of the dispute between intuitionism and platonism in the philosophy of mathematics.

For all this, it is not Frege's work in the philosophy of mathematics which confers on him the status of a figure of the first importance in the history of philosophy in general, but that in the philosophy of logic. And Frege's primary significance consists precisely in the fact that he made this area of philosophy not a specialized branch, but the starting-point for the whole subject.

There is, between the various areas of philosophy, a certain hierarchical ordering. Wittgenstein said that no problem in philosophy can be solved until every philosophical problem has been solved; yet we can discern a certain natural and asymmetric dependence of certain questions on others. A clear example, originally given by Miss Anscombe, is the dependence of ethics on philosophy of mind: questions about free will, about the nature of intention or of action, are clearly crucial for ethics, yet can be considered quite independently of properly moral concepts. Likewise, questions in the philosophy of religion can hardly be discussed until a large number of prior questions, metaphysical, epistemological, ethical, have been resolved: natural theology is as much a species of *applied* philosophy as is political philosophy or philosophy of science.

The question naturally arises, therefore, whether there is any part of philosophy that is in this way prior to every other: whether, as we might express it, philosophy has a foundation. Before Descartes, it can hardly be said that any one part of philosophy was recognized as being thus fundamental to all the rest: the Cartesian revolution consisted in giving this role to the theory of knowledge. Descartes made the question, 'What do we know, and what justifies our claim to this knowledge?' the starting-point of all philosophy: and, despite the conflicting views of the various schools, it was accepted as the starting-point for more than two centuries.

Frege's basic achievement lay in the fact that he totally ignored the Cartesian tradition, and was able, posthumously, to impose his different perspective on other philosophers of the analytic tradition. This is not to say that Frege was uninterested in questions of justification: he was, for example, extremely concerned about the justification of basic mathematical principles, and, therewith, of the axioms of mathematical theories; but he did not make such questions the starting-point, something that must be settled before anything else can be said.

For Frege the first task, in any philosophical enquiry, is the analysis of meanings. He does not, as some later linguistic philosophers did, make this into the whole object of philosophy—philosophy viewed as 'conceptual analysis': once we have achieved a successful analysis of the meanings of the expressions with which we are concerned, then questions of justification may arise, which it may be more or less difficult to settle. But, until we have first achieved a satisfactory analysis of the meanings of the relevant expressions, we cannot so much as raise questions of justification and of truth, since we remain unclear about what we are attempting to justify or what it is about whose truth we are enquiring. It would, of course, be absurd to pretend that previous philosophers had not often concerned themselves with the analysis of meanings: but Frege was the first—at least, since Plato—to make a sharp separation between this task and the later one of establishing what is true and what our grounds are for accepting it; and perhaps the first also to indicate clearly the difficulty of achieving a satisfactory analysis of meaning. Someone who accepted Descartes's perspective according to which epistemology is the starting-point of all philosophy might impatiently concede that it was advisable, before undertaking any discussion, first to agree about the meanings of any possible ambiguous terms, but regard this as a mere preliminary to a philosophical enquiry rather than as part of one. Only when it is clearly grasped how hard it can be to attain an adequate analysis of the meaning of an expression having the kind of generality or depth that makes it of interest to philosophers, can the analysis of meaning be seen as a primary task of philosophy.

Even if the analysis of meanings is an important task of philosophy, and one which must, within any enquiry, occupy our attention before we can proceed to anything more substantial, this by itself would not contradict the Cartesian thesis that epistemology is the foundation of philosophy: it would merely be a methodological maxim about the way in which philosophical enquiries, including epistemological ones, were to be conducted.

It would be a crude caricature of Frege to represent him as merely propounding an improvement in methodology. When, in everyday life, we enquire after the meaning of a term, we should be justifiably irritated if the person whom we asked replied, 'First tell me what you mean by "meaning".' To some extent the same is true in philosophy: but, the deeper our enquiry goes, the more justice there is in such a retort. The more fundamental the notion which a word expresses, the less we are ordinarily accustomed to convey its sense by means of a verbal explanation: and, the less we are accustomed to do this, the less obvious it is what is and what is not to be accepted as an adequate account of its meaning. For this reason, philosophers, attempting to analyse notions like space, probability or pleasure, have not merely differed in the analyses they have given: they have differed over the kind of thing that is to count as an analysis. Our understanding of language is, obviously, built up stage by stage. In the later stages, our increased mastery consists almost entirely in the extension of our vocabulary by words of which verbal explanations or actual definitions can be given, though of course this is not wholly so. Philosophical analysis is, in a sense, an attempt to reverse the process, and, in doing so, to make explicit what had been only implicit in the learning process. The deeper it goes, the more it is concerned with levels of language at which verbal explanation plays a minimal part in the introduction of expressions; at which we acquired an understanding of expressions by learning in practice to employ them, rather than by being told how to use them.

In consequence, the deeper a search for the analysis of the meaning of a word takes us, the more we shall depend upon having a correct model of the way in which language functions. In order to say what the meaning of an expression is, we shall have to have the right conception of what it is to know the meaning of such an expression. This means the right conception of what it is to have grasped the manner of employing sentences in which the expression occurs; and, moreover, the right model for the way in which we derive the use of such sentences from their composition out of that expression together with others.

When we are concerned with the meaning of a term such that its meaning can be given in the simplest of all ways, namely by a definition, i.e. by citing an equivalent expression, we do not need in the least to be able to give an account of what it is to know the meaning of a term: whatever meaning may be, the meaning of this term is the same as the meaning of that expression. But this goes only when we are within an area in which we are accustomed to give definitions of such terms: once outside such an area, we cannot be sure that we can recognize a correct definition even if one is possible and we are presented with one. When we are concerned to analyse terms which we are not accustomed to define, or which are incapable of definition because their use is presupposed by any expressions by means of which a definition might be given, then we require, in order to know the form which an analysis must take, to appeal to some general model of meaning. A very plain example of this is the sentential operators. A doubt about the classical analysis of these is not a doubt about whether the right truth-tables have been given for the various operators, but about whether a truth-table is the right way of laying down the meaning of such an operator at all, or whether, if so, it should be a two-valued one. Opposed to an explanation in terms of truth-tables are 'operationalist' explanations, or ones like those given by intuitionists, in terms of verification or proof. In such cases, it is not the particular analysis offered for an individual operator that is in question, but the whole mode of analysis: in order to decide between them, we have to decide what, in general, it is to know the meaning of a sentential operator.

It is because of this that the theory of meaning is the fundamental part of philosophy which underlies all others. Because philosophy has, as its first if not its only task, the analysis of meanings, and because, the deeper such analysis goes, the more it is dependent upon a correct general account of meaning, a model for what the understanding of an expression consists in, the theory of meaning, which is the search for such a model, is the foundation of all philosophy, and not epistemology as Descartes misled us into believing. Frege's greatness consists, in the first place, in his having perceived this. He does not start from meaning only in the sense that, e.g., an investigation of the meaning of the expression 'natural number' precedes an enquiry into the basis of the laws concerning natural numbers: he starts from meaning by taking the theory of meaning as the only part of philosophy whose results do not depend upon those of any other part, but which underlies all the rest. By doing this, he effected a revolution in philosophy as great as the similar revolution previously effected by Descartes; and he was able to do this even though there was only one other part of philosophy to which Frege applied the results he obtained in the theory of meaning. We can, therefore, date a whole epoch in philosophy as beginning with the work of Frege, just as we can do with Descartes.

A shift in perspective, such as Frege's approach to philosophy involves, naturally brings with it, not merely an alteration in the hierarchical ordering of the various parts of philosophy, but also a change in the way the subject is divided into parts. The part of philosophy which I have here been calling 'the theory of meaning' was called by Frege simply 'logic'. Frege was wont to characterize logic as the theory whose object of study is truth. We

NS 139 (128)

might, therefore, name it the 'theory of truth': the name 'logic' itself seems best reserved for what it has been traditionally applied to—the study of deductive inference. What I am here calling the 'theory of meaning' is often called 'philosophical logic': but this term is quite misleading, suggesting as it does that there are two sorts of logic, mathematical and philosophical. If logic is taken as the study of deductive inference, then, while, as a result of the discoveries originally made by Frege, it has proved amenable to the use of mathematical techniques, often highly sophisticated ones, the use of these techniques, rather than those of a more properly philosophical character, does not involve any shift in motivation or in the object of study: if a subject is defined by its subject-matter, then logic is a unitary subject, whether the techniques used be mathematical or otherwise. There is, indeed, a great deal of overlap between logic and the theory of meaning: Frege's formal logic is an integral part of his theory of meaning. But, while logic may pursue in detail consequences which the theory of meaning does not need to run after, it can, conversely, leave unanalysed certain notions which it is the business of the theory of meaning to elucidate. In particular, in the context of the semantic analysis of the relation of logical consequence, it is quite in order to leave the notion of truth to be explained solely by the truth-definition which specifies the truth-values, in a given model, of the sentences of the language; for what we are interested in is the characterization of valid inferences, and we know in advance that we shall accept as valid any inference which preserves truth. The logician therefore does not need to ask what connects the notion of truth as applied to different languages, or what is the significance of assigning truth-values to the sentences of a language. But, in the theory of meaning, as we saw in Chapter 13, the notion of truth cannot be accepted as defined merely by an inductive stipulation of truth-conditions: we need to know what relation such a stipulation has to the procedure of using the language. A semantics that subserves logic needs to know only under what conditions each sentence is true; a theory of meaning requires the notion of truth as an integral part of a general account of meaning, that is, as playing a role within a model for that knowledge of meaning which constitutes the ability to use a sentence of the language. For these reasons, the term 'theory of meaning' is to be preferred to 'theory of truth'; while logic is to be conceived as a proper part of the theory of meaning (admittedly with extensions that lie somewhat outside it).

Likewise, the term 'philosophy of logic' is even less apt: it suggests that logic is some independent theory, like physics or experimental psychology, about which philosophical questions can be raised. It may, indeed, be said that there is no philosophically neutral theory: that theories within physics, mathematics or psychology are themselves responsive to philosophical criticism. It remains, however, that logic is embedded in the theory of meaning in a way in which the other disciplines are not embedded in the corresponding parts of philosophy. Classical logic is, for example, adapted to a realist theory of meaning as intuitionist logic is adapted to a constructivist theory of meaning: the interest and applicability of classical logic depends upon the acceptance as correct, or as approximating to a correct theory, of the type of semantics which Frege first devised. The formulation, even the significance, of a physical theory may be subject to philosophical criticism: but no one, so far as I know, would maintain that its interest or applicability depended upon the truth of some thesis in the philosophy of science.

Much with which Frege was concerned would today be called by many 'philosophy of language'; and, indeed, this term might be taken as a near-synonym of 'theory of meaning'. Frege would repudiate it, because he was disposed to use the word 'language' as meaning only 'natural language', NS 74-5 (67) and, as already remarked, he had a poor opinion of natural language, and thought it as much of a hindrance as a help to correct logical analysis; still, he often found himself compelled to admit that, misleading as it is, he was forced to give explanations in terms of natural language. It was, after all, with the workings of language that he was concerned: even when he found it possible to sidestep questions about some mode of expression belonging to natural language by inventing some different linguistic device, it is still the workings of language, if not of the actual language which we have, of which he was striving for an account.

Much that traditionally belonged to metaphysics becomes part of the theory of meaning as practised by Frege: in particular, ontological questions. The question about the status of abstract objects, for instance, becomes one about the transferability to abstract singular terms of a model for the meanings of proper names in the more usual sense. Above all, the fundamental question of metaphysics, namely the resolution of the dispute between realism and idealism, comes to be seen as a dispute over the general form which a theory of meaning should take: a dispute between a theory in which the notions of truth and falsity play the central roles, as in Frege's theory, and one in which those roles are taken by the quite different notions of verification and falsification. Those parts of traditional metaphysics which plainly do not belong to the theory of meaning, as for example the philosophy of space and time, can be more properly assigned to the philosophy of physics. There are, indeed, philosophical questions about space and time which can be discussed without any overt reference to physical theory; but then there are questions in the philosophy of mathematics which can be discussed without overt reference to results in the foundations of mathematics: but it can hardly be maintained that there are two separable philosophical topics—space and time as understood by the non-scientist, and space and time as they appear in physical theory.

To say that the theory of meaning is the foundation of philosophy is not to say that nothing else can be done until the main problems in the theory of meaning are resolved. On the contrary, progress can be made on problems that arise in other areas in advance of our having a satisfactory theory of meaning, even when these are problems in the context of which the notion of meaning seems to be naturally invoked. If we had an agreed theory of meaning, then that theory could be appealed to in order to find a resolution of these problems: without one, we are forced to bracket the notion of meaning, that is, to reformulate the problem without express appeal to it. I will cite two examples of this methodological principle of bracketing the notion of meaning, both from the philosophy of mathematics. Consider, first, a dispute, between someone of a platonist turn of mind and someone of constructivist tendencies, concerning an arithmetical statement of the form '$\forall x A(x)$', where '$A(\xi)$' is a decidable number-theoretic predicate; it might be, for example, 'Every natural number is the sum of four squares'. For the constructivist, knowing the meaning of any mathematical statement consists in being able to recognize a proof of it when presented with one; hence to understand a statement of this form, involving universal quantification over the natural numbers, one must be able to recognize a proof—for instance, a proof by induction—of a statement about all natural numbers. (I do not want to assume that our constructivist is a fully-fledged intuitionist, which will commit him to a different standard for the validity of proofs from that recognized by the platonist: the question whether or not to accept the classical criteria for the validity of proofs may be one which he has not yet raised.) For a platonist such as Frege, on the other hand, the understanding of a statement of this kind has nothing to do with capacity to recognize proofs: it is enough to understand the predicate, to have a general grasp of the operation of the quantifier, and to know which objects are in the domain of quantification—in this case, the natural numbers. Once a child has passed the stage of asking what is the largest number, and has grasped the infinity of the series of natural numbers, he knows what is the domain of quantification; and thus, provided that he knows what it means to say of any one number that it is the sum of four squares, and provided that he knows how to interpret the universal quantifier in other contexts, he can, on this account, grasp what it means to say that every number is the sum of four squares. Such a child may have no conception of proof in this area: he may never have seen a number-theoretic proof, as opposed to a computation, or perhaps any other kind of mathematical proof. The platonist might urge that we should not deny, on this score, that such a child understood the statement: after all, he might not only be told it, but believe it.

Faced with such a question, we feel baffled. We know perfectly well exactly what it is that the child can do, and what he cannot do (he can, for instance, apply the rule of universal instantiation to the statement): but we do not know how to set about resolving the dispute over whether his ability to handle the number-theoretic statement in certain ways does or does not amount to his 'understanding' it or 'knowing the meaning' of it. We do not know how to resolve this dispute because we have no agreed theory of meaning; moreover, we feel it to be incredible that any serious philosophical issue can hang on our inclination to come down on one side or other of the dispute. And in this we are quite right: what is at issue is not at all whether knowing what the child knows should be *called* 'understanding the statement'. In order to resolve the issue between the two disputants, we have first to express their disagreement without invoking the contentious notion of 'meaning'. In order to do this, we have to find some other feature of number-theoretic statements about which both disputants will agree that it depends upon their meanings: in the present case, the most likely such feature is the determination of what are to be recognized as valid methods of proof in number theory. Both disputants will, let us suppose, agree that, once the meanings of number-theoretic statements have been fixed, it is thereby determined, for any given proof, whether or not it is valid. We can now express the opposition between them in terms of the validity of number-theoretic proof, without mentioning meaning. The platonist holds that the kind of understanding which the child has of an arithmetical statement—an understanding which he regards as complete, while the constructivist regards it as partial, but for which they can find a neutral characterization, by saying what exactly it is that the child does know—is sufficient for the determination of what is to be accepted as a valid proof. The constructivist denies this: he thinks that, over and above the kind of understanding which the child possesses, there is room for *stipulation* of what is to count as a valid proof (stipulation which is not, of course, free from restrictions). For the platonist, however, the child's understanding involves a grasp of what it is for a universally quantified arithmetical statement to be *true*: hence, even if the child himself has as yet no conception of proofs in number theory, still there is no room for further stipulation;

given a precise notion of truth for arithmetical statements, the notion of validity for inferences involving such statements is thereby already fixed, and requires only to be recognized as obtaining in particular cases.

This is not to say that the issue between the two disputants, as now formulated, is easy to resolve: a great deal of further enquiry about valid inference and the criteria by which it is to be recognized will now take place. The only point being made here is that it is a condition of advance in the dispute that the notion of meaning be bracketed. We start with two disputants who differ on what linguistic abilities are to be regarded as constituting a grasp of the meaning of a statement. In order to prevent the dispute from becoming a purely verbal one about the correct application of 'knowing the meaning', we have to find something to which they will both agree that meaning is firmly tied: we can then reformulate the dispute in terms of this third feature, and ask how the linguistic abilities in question are related to that, leaving out appeal to the notion of meaning altogether.

The second example is similar, and we need not pursue it so far. Wittgenstein's doctrine about the role of proof in mathematics is often expressed by saying that the discovery of a proof changes the meaning of the proposition proved, or of the words involved in its expression. As a reason for this view, it is claimed that the theorem provides a new, or additional, criterion for the application of some of the terms involved. Thus we may say that when we first learn the theorem that a cylinder intersects a plane in an ellipse we acquire an additional criterion for describing a plane figure as an 'ellipse'. Now, of course, in one sense this is incontestable: mathematical proofs would have no point at all if it were not possible to use them, in particular cases, to support the application of descriptions that would otherwise only be reached by more tedious methods. If, then, 'criterion' is so used—as Wittgenstein insists that it should be used—as to refer to any procedure which we actually employ in practice to determine the application of an expression, it is not a thesis of any substance, but a mere truism, that a proof may supply us with a new or additional criterion for the application of some term. But does this constitute a demonstration that, as a result of the proof, the term in question has changed its meaning? In default of an adequate theory of meaning, we are not in a position to say: we do not know what precisely is the connection between the criterion of application ('criterion' being understood as what is used in practice) and the meaning of a term. If a supporter of Wittgenstein insists that the connection must be regarded as rigid, so that any change in the criterion of application must reflect a change in meaning, then he has still done nothing to give substance to Wittgenstein's thesis: it can still be trivialized by the response, 'If by "meaning" you are laying down that you understand "criterion of application actually used in practice", then naturally the discovery of a proof may change the meaning of a term *in this sense of "meaning".*" The thesis has substance only if there is held to be something other than the criterion of application which is connected with the meaning of the term with equal rigidity; if, that is, because of the change of meaning, recognized by the change of criterion, something else must also have changed, some other feature of our use of the term. But, if this is so, then it must be possible to discuss directly whether the change in criterion effected by the proof of the theorem also carries with it a change in this other feature of the use of the term, without bringing in the notion of meaning at all. We need not here pursue the question what, in this case, such another feature might be: we have taken the matter far enough to illustrate the principle that, in disputes of this kind, the notion of meaning must be bracketed before any progress can be made. At least one other example could probably be given from disputes which have arisen within the general philosophy of science.

It might be objected that if, when disputes apparently involving the notion of meaning arise in other branches of philosophy, the correct procedure is to bracket that notion, then the theory of meaning cannot be fundamental to other branches of philosophy, but, on the contrary, quite irrelevant to them. Such an objection would be highly superficial. The theory of meaning is not just an enquiry into a single unitary notion, that of meaning: it is a search for a general account of how language works, for a framework within which we can describe every feature of the use of sentences, and of how we are able to grasp, from the structure of any sentence, what the various features of its use are. When a genuine dispute arises, of a kind in the course of which we are tempted to invoke the notion of meaning, it arises because we are unclear about how to describe two or more different features of the use of sentences of some particular class, or about the connection that exists between them. To resolve such a dispute would be to make a substantial contribution to the theory of meaning. A fully worked out theory of meaning would probably not deploy the notion of meaning as a theoretical term at all, any more than the rules of chess deploy the word 'chess' or an axiomatized geometry deploys the word 'geometry': the theory as a whole gives an account of what meaning is, without the term's being defined within it.

It is no objection to the fundamental character of the theory of meaning that sometimes, as in the cases cited, an advance in resolving a question that arises within some other particular branch of philosophy may be made before the corresponding general question in the theory of meaning has been settled, and may, indeed, be a substantial contribution towards settling that question. It is in general the case that a theory which is logically prior to another is in part tested, and corrected, by observing its consequences in the dependent theory. We do not have to approach questions only in the order of logical priority: but that is no reason for denying that there is such an order. If we had a generally agreed theory of meaning, then there would be no need to bracket the notion of meaning in treating problems such as those cited: we should be able to apply our theory of meaning to such particular localized questions. It may be that philosophical problems are so interwoven that we shall never be in this happy state: even so, in our attempts to solve them, we need to recognize in what direction the theoretical dependence that may obtain between them runs.

Descartes had made the theory of knowledge the foundation of philosophy because he had conceived the task of philosophy as being that of introducing rigour into science (where 'science' is taken in a very general sense, as referring to the whole body of things we conceive ourselves to know). Descartes, like other rationalists after him, thought that it was necessary for all knowledge to achieve the condition that Euclid was thought to have conferred upon geometrical knowledge—to make it completely sharp and absolutely certain. If, in the process, certain things that had passed for knowledge were exposed as not truly so, so much the better. Thus, for Descartes, the question, 'What do we know?', was not only the starting-point of philosophical enquiry, but the central question of all philosophy. For the empiricists, however, the priority of epistemology rested on a different basis. They no longer conceived of philosophy as being essentially a quest for certainty—largely because the goal no longer seemed attainable. For them, rather, epistemology was prior to other branches of philosophy because it indicated the only possible route to the analysis of ideas; and it did this because it represented the only possible route to their acquisition. Since it was only through abstraction, applied to experience, that we could come by our ideas, it could only be by a scrutiny of this process that we could achieve an adequate account of those ideas. The central question was thus changed from 'What do we know?' to 'How do we know?'.

It was Frege who first perceived both the irrelevance of genetic questions and the inadequacy of the empiricist conception of ideas. Doubtless we should not be capable of grasping the thoughts which we now grasp if our experience had been entirely different; and doubtless, also, we should be incapable of grasping them if we were differently constituted. It may well be of interest to enquire into this in more detail, to try and discover what features of our experience, or of our constitution, are essential to our coming to grasp the concepts that we do: but this question, so far from being our only means to an analysis of our concepts, must wait upon such an analysis. (Here 'concept' is being used in an unFregean manner, as corresponding rather to his 'sense'.) If it were impossible to say in what the possession of a certain concept consisted, then there could hardly be a start to the enquiry by what means it was acquired, since we could not say what it was that was being acquired, i.e. what constituted a term to the process of acquisition. Conversely, if it is possible to say in what the possession of the concept consists, then it must be possible to describe this independently of the route taken to possession of the concept. It is as irrelevant to my possession of, for example, the concept of 'magnitude' that I was once a baby as it is that I shall grow old and die.

The empiricist thesis concerning the acquisition of concepts through experience cannot be accepted as an a priori necessity, but must be a thesis about the nature of human beings, since there is nothing contradictory about the legend of men springing up from dragons' teeth. In order to be taken as itself a conceptual truth, it must be restricted, not to any possible means of acquiring concepts, but to that process of acquisition to which we allow the title of 'learning'. It certainly appears to be true that, for a process of acquiring a capability to be called 'learning', there has to be some inner connection between the process and the capability so acquired: but it is exceedingly hard to say just what this connection has to be. Moreover, it still remains that, if we could frame such a criterion, we should, in order to be able to apply it to any particular case, already have to have an analysis of the capability in question; hence an account of the process of learning cannot be essential in order to arrive at such an analysis.

There is, indeed, in Frege an ambivalence of attitude towards the learning process, which has persisted in later philosophers of the analytic tradition, in Wittgenstein in particular. On the one hand, for the reasons just given, a study of it cannot be required for an analysis of sense. On the other, such a study may often guide us to such an analysis. This may be defended by pointing out that, by reflecting on what we take as showing that someone has completed the process of learning something, say the sense or use of a certain expression, we may become clear about what knowing it consists in. But, for Frege at any rate, the significance of the learning process appears to go deeper than this: he assumes the existence of an intimate connection between the way in which an expression is, or can be, introduced into the language and the sense of that expression; for its introduction involves conveying its sense, and the manner of its introduction determines its

z

sense. This can, likewise, be defended on heuristic grounds, since, when we concentrate on the sense of an expression considered as already known, we are apt to overlook, because we take for granted, some general feature of the use of expressions of that kind which had to be mastered when they were originally introduced. It may, nevertheless, be validly objected that to attach such importance to the manner in which an expression is introduced is to make a false assumption that its sense remains static. The introduction of an expression to an individual speaker does not play the role that a definition of a term does in a formal or axiomatic theory, an immutable standard by which the application of the term is to be judged, and to which reference back is repeatedly required. If it did, then indeed each individual would speak a different language: but in fact the sense which a speaker attaches to a word is continually modified by his linguistic experience in using it, so that he no longer either can or needs to say by means of what definition, or by ostensive reference to what instances, it was originally introduced to him. Frege might, perhaps, take such an objection equably: it relates, after all, to the senses of the words of natural language, and Frege never claimed to be giving an accurate account of natural language.

There is another respect in which Frege attached importance to the introduction of expressions. Although there is some latitude for choice when formal definitions are given, since the senses of expressions of natural language lack complete sharpness, the order of definition must correspond to a possible order in which we could acquire an understanding of the terms defined. There would be nothing formally incorrect in defining 'parallel' by stipulating that two lines are parallel with one another if they have the same direction; but, Frege says in *Grundlagen*, such a definition Gl 65 would violate the priority which the word 'parallel' has over the word 'direction', a priority which resides in the fact that we could not acquire a grasp of the sense of the word 'direction' unless we first grasped that of the word 'parallel'.

For all the significance which Frege was inclined to attach to the procedure of introducing a word into the language, it remains true that he was interested in this procedure only as a means of laying down the employment that the word shall have; he repudiated any supposedly essential connection between the sense of the word and the psychological processes which may accompany or precede its acquisition, and which may, within the realm of psychological law, be a necessary condition of that acquisition. We know that, subjected to the same training, a baby chimpanzee will not learn to talk, while a human baby will: so there may be some discoverable difference in the neurological or at least psychological constitution of the two which will account for this different outcome. But that has nothing to do with what it is to master the use of language. Reverting for the moment to using the word 'concept' to correspond with Frege's 'Sinn' rather than with his 'Begriff', we are thus entitled to say that Frege diverted attention from the process of acquiring concepts to the manifestation of possessing them. For human beings at least, the possession of a concept is manifested primarily in the employment of language. The analysis of concepts thus becomes an account of the workings of language. Viewed in this way, the empiricist style of account of our ideas is, at best, not an elucidation of what constitutes possession of the concepts, but a theory of the mechanism of understanding, a mechanism which is supposed to operate by the calling up of mental images: that is, even if the theory were right, it would not explain what it was for a word to have a certain sense, but merely provide a psychological mechanism to account for our ability to associate a sense with a word. Frege of course held that the imagist theory was not merely irrelevant, but simply wrong; and, from his point of view, it is not evident that any theory is needed to fill its place, or that, if it is, it is the business of philosophy, rather than empirical psychology, to supply such a theory. Philosophy is concerned, not with how it comes about that we understand words and sentences, but with what that understanding consists in.

Frege's new perspective was not wholly shared by Russell, who was in many ways so close to Frege in philosophical outlook. Russell was to a considerable extent still under the influence of the ancient tradition, in which epistemological considerations are primary. The first philosopher fully to adopt Frege's perspective was Wittgenstein: the difference between him and Russell is brought out sharply if we compare the *Tractatus* with *The Philosophy of Logical Atomism*; many of the same doctrines are argued for in the two books, but in Russell's work they take on an epistemological guise which is wholly lacking from the *Tractatus*. The *Tractatus* is a pure essay in the theory of meaning, from which every trace of epistemological or psychological consideration has been purged as thoroughly as the house is purged of leaven before the Passover.

Indeed, the purge was excessive. It has been repeatedly stressed in this book that Frege's notion of sense was a cognitive one, in that it relates to our grasp of the semantic role of a word or expression; it is correlative to understanding. If this is not realized, it becomes unintelligible why any notion of sense is needed, beside the notion of reference. In the *Tractatus* Wittgenstein is uninterested in the notion of understanding: for him this is something psychological, which must therefore, on the principles he believes himself to have inherited from Frege, be extruded from logic. The sense of a sentence is for him something that must be uncovered by analysis: such analysis is not merely making explicit what was formerly implicit, but revealing something that may not have been grasped at all, even implicitly; for Wittgenstein's notion of the sense of a sentence, as presented in the *Tractatus*, is in no very close connection with understanding. If two sentences are tautologically equivalent, then they have the same sense: this alone is enough to show that sense is not here being taken as correlative to understanding, since one may, in the ordinary meaning of 'understand', understand two sentences without realizing that they are equivalent. Wittgenstein notoriously used 'Sinn' ('sense') and 'Bedeutung' ('reference') in the *Tractatus* quite differently from Frege: for Wittgenstein, a proper name has Bedeutung, but not Sinn, while a sentence has Sinn, but not Bedeutung. This difference was inevitable, since Wittgenstein does not want any notion to play the role which sense played in Frege's theory of meaning, that role being, on Wittgenstein's puritanical view, psychological rather than logical. Even assertion is dismissed as psychological, and, with it, all differentiations between sentences that serve only to express the force with which they are uttered.

Frege had striven to recognize three realms: the external world, the realm of reference, about which we speak (where, of course, the other two realms are both themselves parts of the realm of reference); the realm of the purely mental; and the realm of sense. Sense, for Frege, is not psychological, in the sense in which the psychological is irrelevant to logic. My act of grasping a sense, e.g. a thought, may be an inner, mental, act: but that which I grasp, the thought, is objective, not the mere content of my consciousness. Only I can have my pain, and there cannot be a pain which no one has; but the thought which I grasp and, perhaps, judge to be true, may be the very same thought which you also grasp, and, perhaps, judge to be false: communication depends upon this possibility. Moreover, a thought does not depend, for its existence, upon anyone's grasping it, as a pain depends upon someone's having it: in this sense, we do not *have* thoughts; in grasping a thought, we stand in a relation to something outside ourselves, even though it is something immutable and imperceptible by the senses.

We have seen that the objectivity of sense is sufficiently guaranteed by its being expressed within the common language: it was not necessary for Frege, in order to safeguard that objectivity, to view it as having an existence independent even of the means of expressing it. Part of his reason for doing so lies in an attempt to overcome the embarrassment he evidently feels in answering the question, 'Is sense something psychological?', an embarrassment which becomes even more acute when he tries to argue that judgment

—the advance from the thought to the truth-value—is not purely psychological either. Having declared that logic has no concern with the psychological, he must place sense, and force as well, essentially outside the psychological realm in order to justify his taking any notice of them in his capacity as a logician.

To assign a reference to an expression is to establish an association between it and its referent. The particular association we establish is the sense of the expression. Frege was quite right to insist upon the sharpest differentiation between sense, as so understood, and inner mental processes: what is remarkable is that he should have seen and held on to the necessity for this differentiation, while lacking a clear account of the principle underlying it. A model of sense is not a description of some hypothesized psychological mechanism: and the reason why we are not here concerned with inner psychological processes is that the notion of sense subserves an account of our operations with language. A model for the sense of a word of some particular kind does not seek to explain *how* we are able to use the word as we do: it simply forms part of an extended description of what that use consists in. Since the word is used only in sentences, the model has to be connected with the models of the senses of other words which could occur in such a sentence in order to obtain anything which could be judged correct or incorrect: the test of correctness is then agreement with our actual linguistic practice. This need not mean the ability to predict our linguistic behaviour with any precision. The theory of meaning need not be conceived after the prototype of a wholly or partially deterministic scientific theory of observed natural phenomena. It is a theory of one large aspect of our behaviour as intelligent, rational beings; and, while it must not, in its completed form, make use of notions specifically related to the use of language (for instance, the notion of assertion or that of communication) which it leaves unexplained, it cannot be required to provide more than the kind of sense which any account of a pattern of rational behaviour is required to have. Suppose that an anthropologist observes people of an alien culture engaging in some complicated co-operative activity. Its nature eludes him: is it a game? a religious ritual? a decision-making process? Perhaps it is none of these: perhaps it does not fall squarely into any category with which we are familiar. He will strive to make sense of it, to render it intelligible to himself as a rational activity: to discover what exactly would count as engaging in that activity correctly; what subsequent consequences it has, if any; what role it plays in the life of the community. If it is classifiable as an activity of some familiar type, then he will so describe it: but, even if it is not, once he has learned to understand it, he will be able to describe

it so as to make it intelligible to us, and hence he does not need to rely upon
a term such as 'game' or 'ritual' already tailored to tell us the kind of point
it has. Such a description, which renders the activity intelligible to us, and
tells us what taking part in it would consist of, and what one would be doing
by taking part in it, need not enable one to predict exactly what the par-
ticipants will do at every stage: my knowing the rules of football does not
enable me to predict the course of any match.

A model for the sense of a word may or may not take the form of an
ability to use that word in some restricted class of sentences; for instance,
the simple model we considered for the senses of proper names of concrete
objects related to the use of recognition statements. A model of sense for a
particular word need not take this form: it may be given in terms that
cannot be directly correlated with any specific linguistic behaviour involving
that word. In this case, the model will not enable us to say, determinately,
for a particular speaker, that he does or does not grasp the sense of that
word. But the theory of meaning for the language, taken as a whole, must
be correlated with the practice of speaking the language; if the model of
sense for particular words which forms part of that theory of meaning is not
directly correlated with the use of restricted forms of sentence, then there
will be cases in which the theory will allow us to say, of a particular speaker,
that he has not grasped the senses of all the words in some sentence, without
our having a definite criterion for picking out which of the words it is
that he misunderstands.

It is because a theory of meaning is thus a theory of the practice of
using a language that the notion of sense—and that of force also—is not a
psychological one. A grasp of the sense of a word is manifested by the
employment of sentences containing the word. It is this conception, which
is part (but only part) of what the later Wittgenstein intended by his slogan
'Meaning is use', to which Frege came so close but never actually formulated:
and it is an inchoate perception of this which compelled Frege to hang
on to his conviction that sense, and force too, are not psychological in
that sense in which psychology has to be expelled from logic, and to hang
on to it despite his inability to find an adequate ground for denying their
psychological character. In this sense, Frege knew in advance what it took
Wittgenstein and other philosophers some decades to discover. Given a
lack of any adequate basis for denying force, or sense, as conceived by
Frege, to be psychological in nature, it was inevitable that Wittgenstein
should have modified Frege's theory as he did in the *Tractatus*; inevitable,
too, that Russell, considering that the advance from the thought to the
truth-value which constitutes judgment is an act of the mind, should have

concluded that the only purely logical analogue of assertion could be the possession of truth.

Frege can thus be considered the father of 'linguistic philosophy', where this phrase is to be taken, not as referring to that temporary deviation known as the 'philosophy of ordinary language', but as denoting all philosophy which sees the key to the analysis of concepts as consisting in the study of the means of their expression. ('Concept' here again means 'Sinn' rather than 'Begriff'.) The 'philosophy of ordinary language' was indeed a species of linguistic philosophy, but one which was contrary to the spirit of Frege in two fundamental ways, namely in its dogmatic denial of the possibility of system, and in its treatment of natural language as immune from criticism. It was to a large extent through Wittgenstein that the Fregean revolution was transmitted; and it is to Wittgenstein that we owe the formulation of the thesis that 'all philosophy is critique of language'. Frege never formulated a programme for philosophy as a whole, nor claimed to be more than a logician and a philosopher of mathematics: we owe the change in perspective which he accomplished in part to the example of his practice, as followed by Wittgenstein; in part to his destruction of the basis of empiricism; and in part to his unparalleled success in constructing the outlines of a workable theory of meaning.

In the early years of the present century, it would have been impossible to see Frege's significance in the way it has here been described, because the impact of the change of perspective had not yet been realized. Rather, it would have been natural to lay emphasis upon Frege's realism, seeing him as belonging to the group of realist philosophers that included Brentano and Meinong. His realism can now be recognised as signally more sophisticated than that of Meinong, and yet more than that of the early writings of Russell and G. E. Moore, who raised the flag of revolt against the Hegelian idealism then dominant in England. The overthrow of idealism, in all its forms, was probably a precondition of advance in philosophy. Frege persistently attacked psychologism, and more than once pointed out that it leads inevitably to idealism; but, with this exception, he seldom attacked idealism directly, but simply passed it by. He undoubtedly would himself have viewed his realism as one of the essential features of his philosophical system; his work indeed represents a classic statement both of a realistic theory of meaning and of the realistic interpretation of mathematics that goes under the name of 'platonism'. For Frege to have achieved the revolutionary change of perspective that has been described, however, it was not logically necessary for him to have been a realist; but it was probably historically necessary. A systematic theory of meaning does not have to assume a realist form. It does not, that is, have to take truth and falsity as the central notions for the theory of meaning; to assume that every sentence with a determinate sense is rendered either true or false by the reality of which it speaks; to take meaning as determined by truth-conditions. Instead, it may, on the model of the intuitionist account of the meaning of mathematical statements, take its central notions as being those of verification and falsification, where the conditions under which a sentence is taken as being verified or falsified are ones which we are capable of effectively recognizing; it may take meaning as determined by conditions for verification or falsification; it may reject the idea that each sentence possesses a definite truth-value, as determined by a reality independent of us, and independent of our capacity to recognize a statement as true or as false. Indeed, we may say that it is a virtue of the Fregean conception of a systematic theory of meaning that it enables us to formulate the antithesis between realism and idealism in this way, as an opposition between two accounts of what, in general, an understanding of our language consists in. But, in order to arrive at the conception of a systematic theory of meaning, it was necessary first to defeat psychologism, to expel psychology from logic and the philosophy of language. Idealism is by its very nature more prone to slip into psychologism, although the possibility of a viable idealistic theory of meaning depends precisely upon the possibility of resisting this temptation. But in any case, in Frege's day the kind of idealism that was everywhere prevalent in the philosophical schools was infected with psychologism through and through: it was not until it had been decisively overthrown that it became possible to envisage a non-psychologistic version of idealism. (Indeed, it is not even yet certain that such a version is possible. Brouwer's writings are steeped in psychologism: the faith that intuitionism is a tenable philosophy of mathematics involves the faith that it is possible to purge it of its psychologistic form. But, at least, thanks to Frege's onslaught on psychologism, we are able to formulate what is required.) Hence it was almost certainly a historical necessity that the revolution which made the theory of meaning the foundation of philosophy should be accomplished by someone like Frege who had for idealism not an iota of sympathy.

Bibliography

The following abbreviations are used for names of journals:

AM—Annals of Mathematics
An.—Analysis
BPdI—Beiträge zur Philosophie des deutschen Idealismus
DL—Deutsche Literaturzeitung
JDMV—Jahresbericht der Deutschen Mathematiker-Vereinigung
JP—The Journal of Philosophy
JSL—The Journal of Symbolic Logic
JZN—Jenaische Zeitschrift für Naturwissenschaft
PR—The Philosophical Review
QJPAM—The Quarterly Journal of Pure and Applied Mathematics
RM—The Review of Metaphysics
ZPpK—Zeitschrift für Philosophie und philosophische Kritik.

The following abbreviations are used for collections of essays:

EF—E. D. Klemke (ed.): *Essays on Frege*, Urbana, 1968.
FLPV—W. V. O. Quine: *From a Logical Point of View*, Cambridge, Mass., 1953.
FM—F. P. Ramsey: *The Foundations of Mathematics and other logical essays*, ed. R. B. Braithwaite, London, 1931.
LK—B. Russell: *Logic and Knowledge, Essays 1901–1950*, ed. R. C. Marsh, London, 1956.
LS—G. H. von Wright: *Logical Studies*, London, 1957.
PL—P. F. Strawson (ed.): *Philosophical Logic*, Oxford, 1967.
PM—P. Benacerraf and H. Putnam (eds.): *Philosophy of Mathematics, Selected Readings*, Englewood Cliffs, N. J., 1964.
SLP—George Boole: *Studies in Logic and Probability*, ed. R. Rhees, London, 1952.

A: Original editions of works by Frege

Only those writings of Frege cited in the book or relevant to it are here listed.

1) *Begriffsschrift, eine der arithmetischen nachgebildete Formelsprache des reinen Denkens*, Halle a. S., 1879.
2) 'Anwendungen der Begriffsschrift' in *JZN*, XIII (1879), Supplement II, pp. 29–33.
3) 'Über die wissenschaftliche Berechtigung einer Begriffsschrift' in *ZPpK*, LXXXI (1882), pp. 48–56.
4) 'Über den Zweck der Begriffsschrift' in *JZN*, XVI (1883), Supplement, pp. 1–10.
5) *Die Grundlagen der Arithmetik: eine logisch-mathematische Untersuchung über den Begriff der Zahl*, Breslau, 1884.

6) 'Erwiderung' in *DL*, VI (1885), no. 28, column 1030. A brief reply to Cantor's review of A (5).

7) *Function und Begriff: Vortrag, gehalten in der Sitzung vom 9. Januar 1891 der Jenaischen Gesellschaft für Medicin und Naturwissenschaft*, Jena, 1891.

8) 'Über das Trägheitsgesetz' in *ZPpK*, XCVIII (1891), pp. 145–61.

9) 'Über Sinn und Bedeutung' in *ZPpK*, C (1892), pp. 25–50.

10) 'Über Begriff und Gegenstand' in *Vierteljahrsschrift für wissenschaftliche Philosophie*, XVI (1892), pp. 192–205.

11) *Grundgesetze der Arithmetik, begriffsschriftlich abgeleitet*, vol. I, Jena, 1893.

12) Review of E. G. Husserl, *Philosophie der Arithmetik*, vol. I, in *ZPpK*, CIII (1894), pp. 313–32.

13) 'Kritische Beleuchtung einiger Punkte in E. Schröders *Vorlesungen über die Algebra der Logik*' in *Archiv für systematische Philosophie*, I (1895), pp. 433–56.

14) Letter to the Editor, *Rivista di Matematica*, VI (1896–9), pp. 53–9.

15) 'Über die Begriffsschrift des Herrn Peano und meine eigene' in *Berichte über die Verhandlungen der Königlich Sächsischen Gesellschaften der Wissenschaften zu Leipzig*, Mathematisch-physische Classe, XLVIII (1897), pp. 361–78.

16) *Grundgesetze der Arithmetik, begriffsschriftlich abgeleitet*, vol. II, Jena, 1903.

17) 'Über die Grundlagen der Geometrie' in *JDMV*, XII (1903), Part I pp. 319–24, Part II pp. 368–75.

18) 'Was ist eine Funktion?' in *Festschrift Ludwig Boltzmann gewidmet zum sechzigsten Geburtstage, 20. Februar 1904*, ed. S. Meyer, Leipzig, 1904, pp. 656–66.

19) 'Über die Grundlagen der Geometrie' in *JDMV*, XV (1906), Part I pp. 293–309, Part II pp. 377–403, Part III pp. 423–30.

20) Notes to P. E. B. Jourdain, 'The Development of the Theories of Mathematical Logic and the Principles of Mathematics: Gottlob Frege' in *QJPAM*, XLIII (1912) pp. 237–69.

21) 'Der Gedanke. Eine logische Untersuchung' in *BPdI*, I (1918), pp. 58–77.

22) 'Die Verneinung. Eine logische Untersuchung' in *BPdI*, I (1918), pp. 143–57.

23) 'Logische Untersuchungen. Dritter Teil: Gedankengefüge' in *BPdI*, III (1923), pp. 36–51.

B: Reprints of Frege's works

1) *Begriffsschrift und andere Aufsätze*, ed. Ignacio Angelelli, Darmstadt and Hildesheim, second edn. 1964.
   Contains A (1)–(4).

2) *Kleine Schriften*, ed. Ignacio Angelelli, Darmstadt and Hildesheim, 1967.
   Contains, inter alia, A (2)–(4), (6)–(10), (12)–(15), (17)–(23).

3) *Funktion, Begriff, Bedeutung. Fünf logische Studien*, ed. Günther Patzig, Göttingen, second edn. 1966.
   Contains A (3), (7), (9), (10) and (18).

4) *The Foundations of Arithmetic. A logico-mathematical enquiry into the concept of number*, ed. and trans. by J. L. Austin, Oxford and New York, second revised edn. 1953.
   Contains text and English translation of A (5) on facing pages.

5) *Die Grundlagen der Arithmetik*, Breslau, 1934, Darmstadt and Hildesheim, 1961.
   Reprints of A (5).

6) *Grundgesetze der Arithmetik*, Darmstadt and Hildesheim, 1962.
   A reprint of A (11) and (16).

7) *Logische Untersuchungen*, ed. Günther Patzig, Göttingen, 1966.
   Contains reprints of A (13) and (21)–(23).

C: English translations of Frege's works

1) *The Foundations of Arithmetic*, trans. by J. L. Austin, New York, 1950
   A translation of A (5). See also B (4).

2) *Translations from the Philosophical Writings of Gottlob Frege*, ed. and trans. by P. Geach and M. Black, Oxford and New York, second revised edn. 1960.
   Contains translations of A (7), (9), (10), (13), (18) and (22), and of parts of A (1), (11), (12) and (16).

3) *The Basic Laws of Arithmetic*, ed. and trans. by M. Furth, Berkeley and Los Angeles, 1964.
   Contains a translation of part of A (11) and of the Appendix to A (16).

4) 'The Thought: A Logical Enquiry', trans. by A. and M. Quinton, in *Mind*, LXV (1956), pp. 289–311; reprinted in *PL*, pp. 17–38, and in *EF*, pp. 507–35.
   A translation of A (21).

5) 'Compound Thoughts', trans. by R. H. Stoothoff, in *Mind*, LXXII (1963), pp. 1–17; reprinted in *EF*, pp. 537–58.
   A translation of A (23).

6) *The Foundations of Geometry*, trans. by M. E. Szabo, in *PR*, LXIX (1960), pp. 3–17; reprinted in *EF*, pp. 559–75.
   A translation of A (17).

7) 'About the Law of Inertia', trans. by R. Rand, in *Synthese*, XII (1961), pp. 350–63.
   A translation of A (8).

8) 'On the Scientific Justification of a Concept-script', trans. by J. M. Bartlett, in *Mind*, LXXIII (1964), pp. 155–60.
   A translation of A (3).

9) 'Begriffsschrift, a formula language, modelled upon that of arithmetic, for pure thought', trans. by S. Bauer-Mengelberg, in J. van Heijenoort (ed.), *From Frege to Gödel, a source book in mathematical logic, 1879–1931*, Cambridge, Mass., 1967, pp. 1–82.
   A translation of A (1).

10) 'On the Purpose of the Begriffsschrift', trans. by V. H. Dudman, in *The Australasian Journal of Philosophy*, XLVI (1968), pp. 89–97.
    A translation of A (4).

11) *Conceptual Notation and related articles*, trans. and ed. by Terrell Ward Bynum, Oxford, 1972.
    Contains translations of A (1)–(4) and of some contemporary reviews of A (1).

12) *On Foundations of Geometry and Formal Theories of Arithmetic*, trans. E.-H. W. Kluge, New Haven and London, 1971.
    Contains, inter alia, translations of A (17) and (19).

D: Frege's posthumous writings

1) G. Frege: *Nachgelassene Schriften*, ed. H. Hermes, F. Kambartel and F. Kaulbach, Hamburg, 1969.
   This contains all those of Frege's unpublished writings which survived the bombing of Münster during the Second World War, with the exception of a diary and the correspondence. An English translation is in preparation. A further volume is planned, to contain all surviving letters to and from Frege.

2) G. Frege: *Schriften zur Logik und Sprachphilosophie. Aus dem Nachlass*, ed. G. Gabriel, Hamburg, 1971.
   Contains a selection from D (1).

E: Frege bibliographies

D (1) contains a bibliography of works by Frege, including translations. *EF*, C (11) and D (2) all contain bibliographies of works both by and about Frege.

F: Works by other authors

This section of the bibliography is intended primarily to enable any reader to find a work referred to in the text. Since I have cited from classical authors—Aristotle, Aquinas, Berkeley, Hume, Kant, Mill, etc.—only well-known views, it has not seemed worth while to include them in the bibliography. On the other hand, every other work mentioned even only in passing has been listed here. Thus this bibliography is not meant to serve as a guide to what has been written about Frege: such guides will be found listed in section (E). Nor is it meant as a guide to the best that has been written about the topics discussed in the book as arising out of consideration of Frege's views: to attempt such a guide would have involved greatly expanding the bibliography, and might also have led to my listing works which I had not read at the time the various chapters were written. On the other hand, I have included a very few works which are not explicitly mentioned in the text, but contain valuable discussions of questions dealt with in it.

G. E. M. Anscombe:
Intention, Oxford, 1957.
'Modern Moral Philosophy' in *Philosophy*, XXXIII (1958), pp. 1–19.
An Introduction to Wittgenstein's Tractatus, London, 1959.
G. E. M. Anscombe and P. T. Geach:
Three Philosophers, Oxford, 1961.
J. L. Austin:
How to Do Things with Words, Oxford, 1962.
A. J. Ayer:
Language, Truth and Logic, London, 1936.
The Problem of Knowledge, Harmondsworth, 1956, and London, 1965.
Philosophical Essays, London, 1959.
N. D. Belnap:
'Tonk, Plonk and Plink' in *An.*, XXII (1962), pp. 130–34; reprinted in *PL*, pp. 132–7.
P. Bernays:
'Sur le Platonisme dans les mathématiques' in *L'Enseignement mathématique*, XXXIV (1935), pp. 52–69; English translation by D. Parsons, 'On Platonism in Mathematics' in *PM*, pp. 274–86.
G. Birkhoff and J. von Neumann:
'The Logic of Quantum Mechanics' in *AM*, XXXVII (1936), pp. 823–43.
George Boole:
The Mathematical Analysis of Logic, being an essay towards a Calculus of Deductive Reasoning, Cambridge, 1847; reprinted in *SLP*, pp. 45–124.
'The Calculus of Logic' in *The Cambridge and Dublin Mathematical Journal*, III (1848), pp. 183–98; reprinted in *SLP*, pp. 125–40.
An Investigation of the Laws of Thought, on which are founded the mathematical theories of Logic and Probabilities, London, 1854; reprinted by Dover Publications, New York, n.d.
G. Cantor:
Review of Frege, *Die Grundlagen der Arithmetik*, in *DL*, VI (1885), no. 20, columns 728–9; reprinted in G. Cantor, *Gesammelte Abhandlungen mathematischen und philosophischen Inhalts*, ed. E. Zermelo, Berlin, 1932, pp. 440–1.

Lewis Carroll:
'What the Tortoise Said to Achilles' in *Mind*, IV (1895), pp. 278-80.
N. Chomsky:
Syntactic Structures, 's-Gravenhage, 1957.
A. Church:
'A Formulation of the Simple Theory of Types' in *JSL*, V (1940), pp. 56-68.
'On Carnap's Analysis of Statements of Assertion and Belief' in *An.*, X (1950), pp. 97-9.
'A Formulation of the Logic of Sense and Denotation' in *Structure, Method and Meaning, essays in honor of H. M. Sheffer*, ed. P. Henle, H. M. Kallen and S. K. Langer, New York, 1951, pp. 3-24.
D. Davidson:
'Truth and Meaning' in *Synthese*, XVII (1967), pp. 304-23.
'True to the Facts' in *JP*, LXVI (1969), pp. 748-64.
R. Dedekind:
Was sind und was sollen die Zahlen?, second edn., Braunschweig, 1893; English translation by W. W. Beman in *Essays on the Theory of Numbers*, Chicago, 1901.
P. Duhem:
La Théorie physique, son objet et sa structure (vol. II of *Bibliothèque de philosophie expérimentale*), Paris, 1906; English translation by P. P. Wiener, *The aim and structure of physical theory*, Princeton, 1954.
M. Dummett:
'Frege on Functions: A Reply' in *PR*, LXIV (1955), pp. 96-107; reprinted in *EF*, pp. 268-83.
'Note: Frege on Functions' in *PR*, LXV (1956), pp. 229-30; reprinted in *EF*, pp. 295-7.
'Nominalism' in *PR*, LXV (1956), pp. 491-505; reprinted in *EF*, pp. 321-36.
'Truth' in *Proceedings of the Aristotelian Society*, LIX (1958-1959), pp. 141-62; reprinted in *Truth* (in series *Contemporary Perspectives in Philosophy*), ed. G. Pitcher, Englewood Cliffs, N. J., 1964, pp. 93-111; also in *PL*, pp. 49-68.
'Frege' in *The Concise Encyclopedia of Western Philosophy and Philosophers*, ed. J. O. Urmson, New York, 1960, pp. 147-50.
'Frege, Gottlob' in *Encyclopedia of Philosophy*, ed. P. Edwards, New York, 1967, vol. III, pp. 225-37.
M. and A. Dummett:
'The Role of Government in Britain's Racial Crisis' in *Justice First*, ed. L. Donnelly, London, 1969, pp. 25-78.
A. S. Essenin-Volpin:
'Le Programme ultra-intuitionniste des fondements des mathématiques' in *Infinitistic Methods* (*Proceedings of the Symposium on Foundations of Mathematics, Warsaw, 2-9 September 1959*), Warsaw and Oxford, 1961, pp. 201-23.
'The ultra-intuitionistic criticism and the antitraditional program for foundations of mathematics' in *Intuitionism and Proof Theory* (*Proceedings of the Summer Conference at Buffalo, N.Y., 1968*), ed. A Kino, J. Myhill and R. E. Vesley, Amsterdam, 1970, pp. 3-45.
P. T. Geach:
Review of *The Foundations of Arithmetic*, trans. by J. L. Austin, in *PR*, LX (1951), pp. 535-44; reprinted in *EF*, pp. 467-78.
'Quine on Classes and Properties' in *PR*, LXII (1953), pp. 409-12; reprinted in *EF*, pp. 479-84.
'Class and Concept' in *PR*, LXIV (1955), pp. 561-70; reprinted in *EF*, pp. 284-94.
'On Frege's Way Out' in *Mind*, LXV (1956), pp. 408-9; reprinted in *EF*, pp. 502-4.
Mental Acts, London, 1957.
'Ascriptivism' in *PR*, LXIX (1960), pp. 221-5.

Reference and Generality, an examination of some medieval and modern theories, Ithaca, N.Y., 1962.
See also: G. E. M. Anscombe and P. T. Geach.
Kurt Gödel:
'Russell's Mathematical Logic' in *The Philosophy of Bertrand Russell*, ed. P. A. Schilpp (*Library of Living Philosophers*), New York, 1944, pp. 125–53; reprinted in *PM*, pp. 211–32.
Nelson Goodman:
The Structure of Appearance, Cambridge, Mass., 1951.
'A World of Individuals' in *The Problem of Universals*, Notre Dame, 1956; reprinted in *PM*, pp. 197–209.
'On Relations that Generate' in *Philosophical Studies*, IX (1958), pp. 65–6; reprinted in *PM*, pp. 209–10.
Nelson Goodman and W. V. O. Quine:
'Steps Towards a Constructive Nominalism' in *JSL*, XII (1947), pp. 105–22.
H. P. Grice:
'Meaning' in *PR*, LXVI (1957), pp. 377–88; reprinted in *PL*, pp. 39–48.
H. P. Grice and P. F. Strawson:
'In Defense of a Dogma' in *PR*, LXV (1956), pp. 141–58.
R. Grossmann:
'Frege's Ontology' in *PR*, LXX (1961), pp. 23–40; reprinted in *EF*, pp. 79–98.
G. Harman:
'Quine on Meaning and Existence' in *RM*, XXI (1967–8), pp. 124–51, 343–67.
R. Harrop:
'On the Existence of Finite Models and Decision Procedures for Propositional Calculi' in *Proceedings of the Cambridge Philosophical Society*, LIV (1958), pp. 1–13.
L. S. Hay:
'Axiomatization of the Infinite-valued Predicate Calculus' in *JSL*, XXVIII (1963), pp. 77–86.
D. Hilbert:
Die Grundlagen der Geometrie, Leipzig, 1899.
'Axiomatisches Denken' in *Mathematische Annalen*, LXXVIII (1918), pp. 405–15; reprinted in *Gesammelte Abhandlungen*, ed. E. Zermelo, Berlin, 1935, vol. III, pp. 146–56.
D. Hilbert and W. Ackermann:
Grundzüge der theoretischen Logik, Berlin, 1928.
E. G. Husserl:
Philosophie der Arithmetik: psychologische und logische Untersuchung, vol. I, Leipzig, 1891.
Logische Untersuchungen, two vols., Halle a. S., 1900–1.
S. Jaśkowski:
'Recherches sur le système de la logique intuitionniste' in *Actes du Congrès International de Philosophie Scientifique*, sec. VI, *Philosophie des mathématiques*, Paris, 1936, pp. 58–61.
P. E. B. Jourdain:
'The Development of the Theories of Mathematical Logic and the Principles of Mathematics: Gottlob Frege' in *QJPAM*, XLIII (1912), pp. 237–69.
G. Kreisel:
'Wittgenstein's Remarks on the Foundations of Mathematics' in *The British Journal for the Philosophy of Science*, IX (1958–9), pp. 135–58.
S. Kripke:
'Naming and Necessity' in *The Semantics of Natural Language*, ed. G. Harman and D. Davidson, Dordrecht, 1972, pp. 253–355.

J. E. Littlewood:
A Mathematician's Miscellany, London, 1953.
J. C. C. McKinsey and A. Tarski:
'The Algebra of Topology' in *AM*, XLV (1944), pp. 141–91.
'On Closed elements in Closure Algebras' in *AM*, XLVII (1946), pp. 122–62.
'Some Theorems about the Sentential Calculi of Lewis and Heyting' in *JSL*, XIII (1948), pp. 1–15.
W. Marshall:
'Frege's Theory of Functions and Objects' in *PR*, LXII (1953), pp. 374–90; reprinted in *EF*, pp. 249–67.
'Sense and Reference: A Reply' in *PR*, LXV (1956), pp. 342–61; reprinted in *EF*, pp. 298–320.
A. Meinong:
Über Annahmen, published as Supplementary Vol. II of *Zeitschrift für Psychologie und Physiologie der Sinnesorgane*, Leipzig, 1902.
Untersuchungen zur Gegenstandstheorie und Psychologie, Leipzig, 1904.
A. Prior:
Time and Modality, Oxford, 1957.
'The Runabout Inference Ticket' in *An.*, XXI (1960–1), pp. 38–9; reprinted in *PL*, pp. 129–31.
Past, Present and Future, Oxford, 1967.
Papers on Time and Tense, Oxford, 1968.
H. Putnam:
'Is Logic Empirical?' in *Boston Studies in the Philosophy of Science* (Proceedings of the Boston Colloquium for the Philosophy of Science), V (1969), ed. R. S. Cohen and M. Wartofsky, pp. 216–41.
W. V. O. Quine:
'New Foundations for Mathematical Logic' in *American Mathematical Monthly*, XLIV (1937), pp. 70–80; reprinted in *FLPV*, pp. 80–94.
'On What There is' in *RM*, V, no. 5 (Sept. 1948), pp. 21–38; reprinted in *FLPV*, pp. 1–19, and in *PM*, pp. 183–96.
'Identity, Ostension and Hypostasis' in *JP*, XLVII (1950), pp. 621–33; reprinted in *FLPV*, pp. 65–79.
'Two Dogmas of Empiricism' in *PR*, LX (1951), pp. 20–43; reprinted in *FLPV*, pp. 20–46.
'Reference and Modality' in *FLPV*, pp. 139–59.
'On Frege's Way Out' in *Mind*, LXIV (1955), pp. 145–59; reprinted in *Selected Logic Papers*, New York, 1966, pp. 146–58, and in *EF*, pp. 485–501.
Review of P. T. Geach, *Reference and Generality*, in *PR*, LXIII (1964), pp. 100–4.
Word and Object, Cambridge, Mass., 1960.
'Carnap and Logical Truth' in *Synthese*, XII (1962), pp. 350–74, and in *Logic and Language: Studies dedicated to Professor Rudolf Carnap on the occasion of his 70th birthday*, ed. B. H. Kasemin and D. Vuysje, Dordrecht, 1962, pp. 39–63; reprinted in *Ways of Paradox and Other Essays*, New York, 1966, pp. 100–25.
'Ontological Relativity' in *JP*, LXV (1968), pp. 185–212; reprinted in *Ontological Relativity and other essays*, New York, 1969, pp. 26–68.
Set Theory and its Logic, Cambridge, Mass., second edn. 1969.
'On the Reasons for Indeterminacy of Translation' in *JP*, LXVII (1970), pp. 178–83.
Philosophy of Logic, Englewood Cliffs, N. J., 1970.
See also: Nelson Goodman and W. V. O. Quine.
F. P. Ramsey:
'Universals' in *Mind*, XXXIV (1925), pp. 401–17; reprinted in *FM*, pp. 112–34.

'The Foundations of Mathematics' in *Proceedings of the London Mathematical Society*, Ser. 2, xxv, Part 5 (1925), pp. 338–84; reprinted in *FM*, pp. 1–61.

'Mathematical Logic' in *The Mathematical Gazette*, XIII (1926), pp. 185–94; reprinted in *FM*, pp. 62–81.

'Facts and Propositions' in *Proceedings of the Aristotelian Society*, Supplementary Vol. VII (1927), pp. 153–70; reprinted in *FM*, pp. 138–55.

H. Rasiowa and R. Sikorski:

The Mathematics of Metamathematics, Warsaw, 1963.

B. Russell:

The Principles of Mathematics, London, 1903.

'On Denoting' in *Mind*, XIV (1905), pp. 479–93; reprinted in *LK*, pp. 41–56.

'The Philosophy of Logical Atomism' in *The Monist*, XXVIII (1918), pp. 495–527, and XXIX (1919), pp. 32–63, 190–222 and 345–80; reprinted in *LK*, pp. 177–281.

Introduction to Mathematical Philosophy, London, 1919.

B. Russell and A. N. Whitehead:

Principia Mathematica, three vols., Cambridge, 1910, 1912, 1913.

D. J. Shoesmith and T. J. Smiley:

'Deducibility and Many-valuedness' in *JSL*, XXXVI (1971), pp. 610–22.

B. Sobociński:

'L'Analyse de l'antinomie russellienne par Leśniewski. IV: La correction de Frege' in *Methodos*, 1 (1949), pp. 220–8.

E. Stenius:

Wittgenstein's Tractatus, a critical exposition of its main lines of thought, Oxford, 1960.

P. F. Strawson:

'Truth' in *An.*, IX (1949), pp. 83–97.

'On Referring' in *Mind*, LIX (1950), pp. 320–44; reprinted in *Essays in Conceptual Analysis*, ed. A. Flew, London, 1956, pp. 21–52.

Individuals, London, 1959.

See also: H. P. Grice and P. F. Strawson.

A. Tarski:

'Der Wahrheitsbegriff in den formalisierten Sprachen' in *Studia philosophica*, 1 (1935), pp. 261–405; trans. as 'The Concept of Truth in Formalised Languages' in *Logic, Semantics, Metamathematics*, ed. and trans. by J. H. Woodger, Oxford, 1956, pp. 152–278.

'The Semantic Conception of Truth and the Foundations of Semantics' in *Philosophy and Phenomenological Research*, IV (1943–4), pp. 341–75; reprinted in *Readings in Philosophical Analysis*, ed. H. Feigl and W. Sellars, New York, 1949, pp. 52–84, and in *Semantics and the Philosophy of Language*, ed. L. Linsky, Urbana, 1952, pp. 13–47.

See also: J. C. C. McKinsey and A. Tarski.

E. Tugendhat:

'The Meaning of "Bedeutung" in Frege' in *An.*, XXX (1970), pp. 177–89.

G. H. von Wright:

'Deontic Logic' in *Mind*, LX (1951), pp. 1–15; reprinted in *LS*, pp. 58–74.

'On Conditionals' in *LS*, pp. 127–65.

F. Waismann:

Einführung in das mathematische Denken, Vienna, 1936; trans. by T. J. Benac as *Introduction to Mathematical Thinking*, New York, 1959.

D. Wiggins:

Identity and Spatio-Temporal Continuity, Oxford, 1967.

L. Wittgenstein:

Tractatus Logico-Philosophicus, with new English translation by D. Pears and B. McGuinness on facing pages, London, 1961.

Philosophical Investigations, ed. by G. E. M. Anscombe, G. H. von Wright and R. Rhees, with English translation by G. E. M. Anscombe on facing pages, Oxford, 1953, second edn. 1958.

Remarks on the Foundations of Mathematics, ed. by G. E. M. Anscombe, G. H. von Wright and R. Rhees, with English translation by G. E. M. Anscombe on facing pages, Oxford, 1956.

Notebooks, 1914–1916, ed. G. H. von Wright and G. E. M. Anscombe, with English translation by G. E. M. Anscombe on facing pages, Oxford, 1961.

Index

ability to use a language, 92

'about', 61, 187, 196–203, 464

absolute identity-relation, *see* identity, absolute relation of

absolute space and time, argument against, 378

abstract noun, 70–80, 176, 472, 508, 609

abstract objects: xxxviii, 58, 70–7, 175–6, 179, 240, 258, 373, 402–3, 407–8, 471–511, 530–9, 582, 631, 671; analogy between reference of names of concrete objects and names of, 499; causal interaction and, 491–3, 511; concrete objects versus, 240, 258–9, 402, 407, 471, 480–91, 537–8; criterion for the existence of, 257–63, 481–9, 501–4; impredicative totalities and, 530–7; no confrontation with, 494, 498; pure, 503, 509–11; reference and the distinction between concrete objects and, 494, 497, 510; senses of names of, 494, 498–9, 501, 505; simultaneous quantification over concrete objects and, 582; whether subject to change, 492

abstract terms, confusion between theoretical terms and, 609

abstraction, xlii, 158, 676

abstraction operator, 479, 501, 530, 532, 534, 537–8, 644, 656–7

accidental property, 124–5, 130, 146; *see also* essential property

Ackermann, W., xxxv, xxxvi

acting, 310–11

actual linguistic practice, 105–7, 142–3, 148–9, 240, 380–1, 396–8, 413, 417, 463, 468–70, 522–7, 569, 585, 590–1, 598–600, 616, 618, 625–7, 681

adjectival general terms, 547–9, 551–5, 576–7, 581

admissible truth-value assignments to pseudo-atomic sentences, 282

advance from a thought to a truth-value, 240

Afla and Ateb, xvii, 47–8, 270, 314

alternative analyses of a given sentence, 28–30, 62–6

ambiguity: 21, 45, 51–2, 65, 67, 113–16, 268, 331, 332, 380, 417, 523, 546; as to criterion of identity, 546; in modal contexts, 113–16

amorphous lump, *see* reality as an amorphous lump

analogy: 5, 6, 119, 173, 184, 186, 191, 207, 209–10, 213, 216, 220–1, 230, 241–4, 246, 296–7, 307, 404, 407–8, 411–13, 428, 465–6, 499, 505, 511, 524–5, 589, 644; between concepts and functions, 184, 186, 644; between decidable and undecidable statements, 119, 465–6, 589; between identity of objects and co-extensiveness of concepts, 173, 207, 209; between quantification over finite and infinite totalities, 119, 465–6, 589; between truth and winning, 296–7, 307; between truth-functions and functions proper, 249; invoked to extend the notion of reference, 181, 186, 191, 210, 241–4, 246, 405, 407–8, 411–13, 428, 499, 524–5; with ostension, 499, 505; with perception, 511

analysis (of language, sentences, thoughts, etc.): 21, 36, 62, 64–6, 248, 322, 374, 376–8, 381, 453, 474, 476–8, 479–80, 564, 667–9, 680, 683; two kinds of, 28–30, 62–6

analytical hypotheses (Quine), 374, 381, 616–17

analyticity: ix, xxxvii, 117–20, 222, 228, 262, 289–91, 433, 502–3, 505, 584, 588, 590, 593, 596, 599, 601–4, 612–14, 620, 624, 631–7, 654–5; ontic, 119; stimulus-, 612–14, 619–23

Anscombe, G. E. M.: xii, 666; on Annahmen, 326; on assertion, 304, 312, 314; on context principle, 193; on formal concepts, 221; on operations and functions, 324; on the reference of incomplete expressions, 205; on truth-tables, 323

Anselm, St., 278

anti-intellectualism, 627

anti-realism, 468–70

695

hypostatization of meanings, 92, 155-7
hypothetical observer, 119-20, 465-8

ideal language, 142, 585, 624-6
idealism: 117, 197-8, 470, 541, 659, 671, 683-4; Hegelian, 683
ideas, 4, 85, 154, 597, 638, 680
identity: 542-83; absolute relation of, 551, 553-64, 566, 571, 580, 603; analogue of, for concepts and functions, 173, 209; as logical constant, 22n, 542; as relation between names, 279, 544, 630; functions, 316; indefinable, 542-3; law of, 71, 542-3, 603-5; of indiscernibles, 543-4; sign of, xxxvi, 22n, 180, 201, 218, 279, 315, 542, 544, 546; sign of, univocal, 546; statement, 94-5, 97, 173, 180, 201, 228, 288, 499-501, 505, 542-5, 579, 624, 632, 649; statement, analytically true, 228, 288-9, 632
illegitimate totality, 529-32
imagist theory of meaning, 85, 157-9, 597, 630, 637-42, 679
imperatives, 3, 303-6, 317, 333
implicit understanding, 35, 65, 236, 668, 680
impredicativity, 530-5, 538, 540-1, 560
impression of meaning, 87-8
inchoate theories of meaning, 107, 458, 462-3, 468
incomplete expressions: 15-16, 21, 28-33, 37-53, 62-4, 169-71, 171-81, 183-4, 188-9, 198-9, 204-63, 291-2, 408, 411-12, 499, 523-4, 540, 644; completion of, 177; formed by omission, 15-16, 23-4, 28-33, 37-43; formed only from complete expressions, 40-44; grounds for recognizing a type of, 48-9; incomplete in absolute sense, 247-8; occurrence in a sentence, 45-8; reference of, *see* reference
incorrigibility, 639
indefinite noun-phrase, 60-1, 67
indeterminacy of future, 393, 398-400
indeterminacy of past, 396, 398-400
indeterminacy of translation, *see* Quine, W. V. O.
indexicals, indexicality, *see* token-reflexive expressions
indirect reference, 186-92, 208, 210, 264-94, 382, 409, 445
indirect sense, xix-xx, 266-9
indirect speech, 186-7, 190-2, 208, 264-9, 272-4, 277-8, 281-3, 285-8, 292, 294, 371-6
inference: 28-9, 591-2, 619, 636; impossible from false premisses, 309, 312-13; rules or principles of, 366, 435-6, 596, 605, 620-1; *see also* logical consequence
inferential links between sentences, 591-2, 596-7, 608-9, 613, 618-19, 621
infinite product/sum (infinite conjunction/disjunction), 164-5, 242, 508, 512-13, 516-18, 521-2, 530

infinity, 663
information content, *see* cognitive value
intensional contexts, *see* opaque contexts
intensional isomorphism, 228-9, 379
intention as determining reference, 139-41, 147-51, 197-8
intention in utterance, 297-302, 319
interior versus exterior acts, 312, 313, 353, 359-360, 362-3
internal structure of sentences, 419-20, 599-600
interrogatives, 306-8, 328, 331, 336-9, 351, 353, 356
introduction rules, 454-5
intuition, xxxv, 56, 58, 82, 156, 511, 610-11, 663
intuitionism, 109, 396, 468, 507, 511, 611n, 666, 671-2, 684
intuitionistic logic, 109, 285, 396, 432, 434-5, 436, 611n, 671
intuitive notions, 83-4, 405-6, 419, 422, 465, 479, 482-3, 506-7, 511, 532, 537, 610-11
'it works' an inadequate justification for a theory, 605

Jaśkowski, S., 432
Johansson, I., 439
Jourdain, P. E. B., 314, 657
judgeable content, 315, 629
judgment, 298-9, 314-16, 362-3, 629, 680
judgment-stroke, 314-16
justification: as bearing on sense, 104-5, 616-625; as determining analyticity, 117, 614, 632; as opposed to consequences, 362, 454-6; as opposed to truth, 450-1, 468; statements not requiring, 620-1

Kant, I.: 665; on analyticity, 502, 631; on existence, 278, 502; on judgment, 629; on objects, xx; on the synthetic a priori, xxxvii, 631, 663
Kaplan, D., xx
knowledge: 285-8; as related to sense, 229-31, 239, 459-62
knowledge-how represented as knowledge-that (theoretical representation of a practical capacity), 462
Kreisel, G., xxxviii-xxxix, 508
Kripke, S. A.: 110-51, 432; advances causal 'theory' of proper names, 147-8; attributes description theory of proper names to Frege, 110; compares mass-terms with proper names, 144-6; compares species-words with proper names, 143-6; compares terms for units of measurement with proper names, 143; criticizes description theory of proper names, 135-43; disclaims possession of theory, 146-7; distinguishes fixing reference from giving meaning, xviii, 111, 127, 132-3; invokes intention to preserve reference,

Harvard University Press is a member of Green Press Initiative (greenpressinitiative.org), a nonprofit organization working to help publishers and printers increase their use of recycled paper and decrease their use of fiber derived from endangered forests. This book was printed on recycled paper containing 30% post-consumer waste and processed chlorine free.